CHARLES W. L. HILL
University of Washington

GARETH R. JONES
Texas A&M University

STRATEGIC MANAGEMENT CASES

10th edition

SOUTH-WESTERN
CENGAGE Learning®

Australia • Brazil • Japan • Korea • Mexico • Singapore • Spain • United Kingdom • United States

SOUTH-WESTERN
CENGAGE Learning·

Strategic Management Cases
Charles W. L. Hill and Gareth R. Jones

Vice President of Editorial, Business:
Jack W. Calhoun

Publisher: Erin Joyner

Sr. Acquisitions Editor: Michele Rhoades

Editorial Assistant: Tammy Grega

Developmental Editor: Suzanna Bainbridge

Marketing Manager: Jonathan Monahan

Marketing Coordinator: Julia Tucker

Marketing Communications Manager:
Jim Overly

Content Project Manager: Jana Lewis

Assoc. Media Editor: Rob Ellington

Manufacturing Planner: Ron Montmongery

Production Service: S4 Carlisle Publishing
Services

Copyeditor: Kelly Lydick

Sr. Art Director: Tippy McIntosh

Internal Designer: Beckmeyer Design, Inc.

Cover Designer: Beckmeyer Design, Inc.

Cover Image: ©Sandra von Stein, iStock

For product information and technology assistance, contact us at
Cengage Learning Customer & Sales Support, 1-800-354-9706
For permission to use material from this text or product,
submit all requests online at **www.cengage.com/permissions**
Further permissions questions can be emailed to
permissionrequest@cengage.com

Library of Congress Control Number: 2012931470

ISBN-13: 978-1-133-48571-1

ISBN-10: 1-133-48571-5

South-Western
5191 Natorp Boulevard
Mason, OH 45040
USA

Cengage Learning products are represented in Canada by Nelson Education, Ltd.

For your course and learning solutions, visit **www.cengage.com**

Purchase any of our products at your local college store or at our preferred online store **www.cengagebrain.com**

Printed in Canada
1 2 3 4 5 6 7 18 17 16 15 14 13 12

Contents

Preface

In the tenth edition of our book, *Strategic Management: An Integrated Approach*, we continue with our mission to provide students the most current and up-to-date account of the changes taking place in the world of business strategy and management. The fast-changing domestic and global environment continues to pressure organizations and their managers to find new and improved ways to respond in order to maintain and increase their performance. In revising our book, we continue to strive to make our text relevant and interesting to students. It encourages students to make the effort necessary to assimilate the text material because they find it useful and relevant. We continue to mirror the changes taking place in strategic management practices by incorporating recent important developments into our text and by providing vivid, current examples of the way managers of well-known companies—large and small—have responded to the dramatic changes in the competitive environment that have been taking place since the turn of the century.

Since the Ninth Edition was published, this book has strengthened its position as a market leader in the Strategic Management market. This tells us that we continue to meet the expectations of existing users and attract many new users to our book. It is clear that most strategy instructors share with us a concern for our currency in the text and its examples to ensure that cutting-edge issues and new developments in strategic management are continually addressed.

Just as in the last edition, our objective in writing the Tenth Edition has been to maintain all that was good about prior editions. As we move steadily into the second decade of the 21st Century, we continue to refine our approach by expanding our discussion of established strategic management issues and adding new material as management trends develop to present a more complete, clear, and current account of strategic management. We believe that the result is a book that is more closely aligned with the needs of today's professors and students and with the realities of competition in the global environment.

Comprehensive and Up-to-Date Coverage

We have updated many of the features throughout the chapters, including all new Opening Cases, Running Cases, and a Focus on Dell feature. In this edition, we have made no changes to the number or sequencing of our chapters. However, we have made many significant changes inside each chapter to refine and update our presentation of strategic management. Continuing real-world changes in strategic management practices such as the increased use of cost reduction strategies like global outsourcing, ethical issues, and lean production, and a continued emphasis on business model as the driver of differentiation and competitive advantage have lead to many changes in our approach.

Throughout the revision process, we have been careful to preserve the *balanced and integrated* nature of our account of strategic management. As we have continued to add new material, we have also shortened or deleted coverage of out-of-date or less important models and concepts to help students identify and focus on the core concepts and issues in the field. We have also paid close attention to retaining the book's readability.

Finally, it is important to emphasize that we have overhauled the case selection. The cases are all either new to this edition, or revised and updated versions of cases that appeared in prior editions. As always, we have used a tight screen to filter out irrelevant cases, and we believe that the selection we offer is the best on the market. We would like to extend our gratitude to the case authors who have contributed to this edition: Isaac Cohen (*San Jose State University*), Alan N. Hoffman (*Bentley College*), Frank Shipper (*Salisbury University*), Charles Manz (*University of Massachusetts*), Karen Manz, Greg Stewart (*University of Iowa*), Oliver Roche (Salisbury University), Anne Lawrence (*San Jose State University*), Vivek Gupta (*Indian School of Business*), Debapratim Purkayastha (*Indian School of Business*), Stephen Adams (*Salisbury University*).

Strategic Management Cases

The thirty-one cases that we have selected for this edition will appeal, we are certain, to students and professors alike, both because these cases are intrinsically interesting and because of the number of strategic management issues they illuminate. The organizations discussed in the cases range from large, well-known companies, for which students can do research to update the information, to small, entrepreneurial business that illustrate the uncertainty and challenge of the strategic management process. In addition, the selections include many international cases, and most of the other cases contain some element of global strategy. Refer to the Contents for a complete listing of the cases with brief descriptions.

To help students learn how to effectively analyze and write a case study, we continue to include a special section on this subject. It has a checklist and an explanation of areas to consider, suggested research tools, and tips on financial analysis.

We feel that our entire selection of cases is unrivaled in breadth and depth, and we are grateful to the other case authors who have contributed to this edition:

Teaching and Learning Aids

Taken together, the teaching and learning features of *Strategic Management* provide a package that is unsurpassed in its coverage and that supports the integrated approach that we have taken throughout the book.

For the Instructor

- **The Instructor's Resource Manual: Theory.** For each chapter, we provide a clearly focused synopsis, a list of teaching objectives, a comprehensive lecture outline, teaching notes for the *Ethical Dilemma* feature, suggested answers to discussion questions, and comments on the end-of-chapter activities. Each Opening Case, Strategy in Action boxed feature, and Closing Case has a synopsis and a corresponding teaching note to help guide class discussion.

- **Case Teaching Notes** include a complete list of case discussion questions as well as a comprehensive teaching note for each case, which gives a complete analysis of case issues.
- **ExamView Test Bank** offers a set of comprehensive true/false, multiple-choice, and essay questions for each chapter in the book. The mix of questions has been adjusted to provide fewer fact-based of simple memorization items and to provide more items that rely on synthesis or application. Also, more items now reflect real or hypothetical situations in organizations. Every question is keyed to the Learning Objectives outlined in the text and includes an answer and text page reference.
- **The Instructor's Resource CD** contains key ancillaries such as Instructor's Resource Manual, PowerPoint® slides, ExamView and Word Test Bank files, and Case Notes and allows instructors the ultimate tool for customizing lectures and presentations.
- **DVD program** highlights a collection of 13 new BBC videos. These new videos are short, compelling, and timely illustrations of today's management world. Topics include Brazil's growing global economy, the aftermath of BP's oil spill, Zappos.com, the Southwest merger with AirTrans, and more. Available on the DVD and Instructor Web site. Detailed case write-ups including questions and suggested answers appear in the Instructor's Resource Manual. Assignable and auto-gradable exercises accompany these videos in CengageNow.
- **CourseMate, text companion website.** This dynamic interactive learning tool includes student and instructor resources. For instructors, you can download electronic versions of the instructor supplements from the password-protected section of the site, including the Instructor's Resource Manual, Test Bank, PowerPoint® presentations, and Case Notes. To access companion resources, please visit www.cengagebrain.com. On the CengageBrain.com homepage, use the search box at the top of the page to search for the ISBN of your title (from the back cover of your book). This will take you to the product page where free companion resources can be found.
- **WebTutor** is a web platform containing premium content such as unique web quizzes, audio summary and quiz files, lecture PowerPoint slides, and crossword puzzles for key terms from the text.
- **CengageNow.** This robust online course management system gives you more control in less time and delivers better student outcomes—NOW. CengageNow™ includes teaching and learning resources organized around lecturing, creating assignments, casework, quizzing, and gradework to track student progress and performance. Multiple types of quizzes, including video quizzes that cover the videos found in the accompanying DVD, are assignable and gradable. We also include assignable and gradable Business & Company Resource Center (BCRC) quizzes that direct students to Gale articles to find expansive, current event coverage for companies featured in the Opening and Closing Cases in the text. Flexible assignments, automatic grading, and a gradebook option provide more control while saving you valuable time. A Personalized Study diagnostic tool empowers students to master concepts, prepare for exams, and become more involved in class.
- **Cengage Learning Write Experience 2.0.** This new technology is the first in higher education to offer students the opportunity to improve their writing and analytical skills without adding to your workload. Offered through an exclusive agreement with Vantage Learning, creator of the software used for GMAT essay

grading, Write Experience evaluates students' answers to a select set of assignments for writing for voice, style, format, and originality.

- **The Business & Company Resource Center (BCRC.)** Put a complete business library at your students' fingertips! This premier online business research tool allows you and your students to search thousands of periodicals, journals, references, financial data, industry reports, and more. This powerful research tool saves time for students—whether they are preparing for a presentation or writing a reaction paper. You can use the BCRC to quickly and easily assign readings or research projects. Visit http://www.cengage.com/bcrc to learn more about this indispensable tool. For this text in particular, BCRC will be especially useful in further researching the featured companies featured.
- **Global Economic Watch.** The current global economic crisis leaves more and more questions unanswered every day and presents "one of the most teachable moments of the century." South-Western delivers the solution. The Global Economic Crisis Resource Center is an online one-stop shopping location that provides educators with current news, journal articles, videos, podcasts, PowerPoint slides, test questions, and much more.

For the Student

- **CourseMate, text companion website** includes chapter summaries, learning objectives, web quizzes, glossary, and flashcards.
- **CengageNow** includes learning resources organized around lecturing, creating assignments, casework, quizzing, and gradework to track student progress and performance. Multiple types of quizzes, including video quizzes that cover the videos found in the accompanying DVD, are assignable and gradable. We also include assignable and gradable Business & Company Resource Center (BCRC) quizzes that direct students to Gale articles to find expansive, current event coverage for companies featured in the Opening and Closing Cases in the text. Flexible assignments, automatic grading, and a gradebook option provide more control while saving you valuable time. A Personalized Study diagnostic tool empowers students to master concepts, prepare for exams, and become more involved in class.
- **The Business & Company Resource Center (BCRC.)** A complete business library at your fingertips! This premier online business research tool allows you to search thousands of periodicals, journals, references, financial data, industry reports, and more. This powerful research tool saves time—whether preparing for a presentation or writing a reaction paper. You can use the BCRC to quickly and easily research projects. Visit http://www.cengage.com/bcrc to learn more about this indispensable tool. For this text in particular, BCRC will be especially useful in further researching the featured companies.

Acknowledgements

This book is the product of far more than two authors. We are grateful to our Acquisitions Editor, Michele Rhoades; our developmental editor, Suzanna Bainbridge; our content production manager, Jana Lewis; and our Marketing Manager, Jon Monahan, for their help in developing and promoting the book and for providing us with timely feedback and information from professors and reviewers, which allowed us to shape the book to meet the needs of its intended market. We are also grateful to Jana Lewis for her adept handling of production. We are also grateful to the case authors for allowing us to use their materials. We also want to thank the departments of management at the University of Washington and Texas A&M University for providing the setting and atmosphere in which the book could be written, and the students of these universities who react to and provide input for many of our ideas. In addition, the following reviewers of this and earlier editions gave us valuable suggestions for improving the manuscript from its original version to its current form:

Andac Arikan, *Florida Atlantic University*

Ken Armstrong, *Anderson University*

Richard Babcock, *University of San Francisco*

Kunal Banerji, *West Virginia University*

Kevin Banning, *Auburn University- Montgomery*

Glenn Bassett, *University of Bridgeport*

Thomas H. Berliner, *The University of Texas at Dallas*

Bonnie Bollinger, *Ivy Technical Community College*

Richard G. Brandenburg, *University of Vermont*

Steven Braund, *University of Hull*

Philip Bromiley, *University of Minnesota*

Geoffrey Brooks, *Western Oregon State College*

Jill Brown, *Lehigh University*

Amanda Budde, *University of Hawaii*

Lowell Busenitz, *University of Houston*

Sam Cappel, *Southeastern Louisiana University*

Charles J. Capps III, *Sam Houston State University*

Don Caruth, *Texas A&M Commerce*

Gene R. Conaster, *Golden State University*

Steven W. Congden, *University of Hartford*

Catherine M. Daily, *Ohio State University*

Robert DeFillippi, *Suffolk University Sawyer School of Management*

Helen Deresky, *SUNY—Plattsburgh*

Fred J. Dorn, *University of Mississippi*

Gerald E. Evans, *The University of Montana*

John Fahy, *Trinity College, Dublin*

Patricia Feltes, *Southwest Missouri State University*

Bruce Fern, *New York University*

Mark Fiegener, *Oregon State University*

Chuck Foley, *Columbus State Community College*

Isaac Fox, *Washington State University*

Craig Galbraith, *University of North Carolina at Wilmington*
Scott R. Gallagher, *Rutgers University*
Eliezer Geisler, *Northeastern Illinois University*
Gretchen Gemeinhardt, *University of Houston*
Lynn Godkin, *Lamar University*
Sanjay Goel, *University of Minnesota—Duluth*
Robert L. Goldberg, *Northeastern University*
James Grinnell, *Merrimack College*
Russ Hagberg, *Northern Illinois University*
Allen Harmon, *University of Minnesota—Duluth*
Ramon Henson, *Rutgers University*
David Hoopes, *California State University—Dominguez Hills*
Todd Hostager, *University of Wisconsin—Eau Claire*
David Hover, *San Jose State University*
Graham L. Hubbard, *University of Minnesota*
Tammy G. Hunt, *University of North Carolina at Wilmington*
James Gaius Ibe, *Morris College*
W. Grahm Irwin, *Miami University*
Homer Johnson, *Loyola University—Chicago*
Jonathan L. Johnson, *University of Arkansas Walton College of Business Administration*
Marios Katsioloudes, *St. Joseph's University*
Robert Keating, *University of North Carolina at Wilmington*
Geoffrey King, *California State University—Fullerton*
Rico Lam, *University of Oregon*
Robert J. Litschert, *Virginia Polytechnic Institute and State University*
Franz T. Lohrke, *Louisiana State University*
Paul Mallette, *Colorado State University*
Daniel Marrone, *SUNY Farmingdale*
Lance A. Masters, *California State University—San Bernardino*
Robert N. McGrath, *Embry-Riddle Aeronautical University*
Charles Mercer, *Drury College*
Van Miller, *University of Dayton*
Tom Morris, *University of San Diego*
Joanna Mulholland, *West Chester University of Pennsylvania*
James Muraski, *Marquette University*
John Nebeck, *Viterbo University*
Jeryl L. Nelson, *Wayne State College*
Louise Nemanich, *Arizona State University*
Francine Newth, *Providence College*

Don Okhomina, *Fayetteville State University*
Phaedon P. Papadopoulos, *Houston Baptist University*
John Pappalardo, *Keen State College*
Paul R. Reed, *Sam Houston State University*
Rhonda K. Reger, *Arizona State University*
Malika Richards, *Indiana University*
Simon Rodan, *San Jose State*
Stuart Rosenberg, *Dowling College*
Douglas Ross, *Towson University*
Ronald Sanchez, *University of Illinois*
Joseph A. Schenk, *University of Dayton*
Brian Shaffer, *University of Kentucky*
Leonard Sholtis, *Eastern Michigan University*
Pradip K. Shukla, *Chapman University*
Mel Sillmon, *University of Michigan—Dearborn*
Dennis L. Smart, *University of Nebraska at Omaha*
Barbara Spencer, *Clemson University*
Lawrence Steenberg, *University of Evansville*
Kim A. Stewart, *University of Denver*
Ted Takamura, *Warner Pacific College*
Scott Taylor, *Florida Metropolitan University*
Thuhang Tran, *Middle Tennessee University*
Bobby Vaught, *Southwest Missouri State*
Robert P. Vichas, *Florida Atlantic University*
John Vitton, *University of North Dakota*
Edward Ward, *St. Cloud State University*
Kenneth Wendeln, *Indiana University*
Daniel L. White, *Drexel University*
Edgar L. Williams, Jr., *Norfolk State University*
Jun Zhao, *Governors State University*

Charles W. L. Hill
Gareth R. Jones

STRATEGIC MANAGEMENT CASES

10th edition

Analyzing a Case Study and Writing a Case Study Analysis

What is Case Study Analysis?

Case study analysis is an integral part of a course in strategic management. The purpose of a case study is to provide students with experience of the strategic management problems that actual organizations face. A case study presents an account of what happened to a business or industry over a number of years. It chronicles the events that managers had to deal with, such as changes in the competitive environment, and charts the managers' response, which usually involved changing the business- or corporate-level strategy. The cases in this book cover a wide range of issues and problems that managers have had to confront. Some cases are about finding the right business-level strategy to compete in changing conditions. Some are about companies that grew by acquisition, with little concern for the rationale behind their growth, and how growth by acquisition affected their future profitability. Each case is different because each organization is different. The underlying thread in all cases, however, is the use of strategic management techniques to solve business problems.

Cases prove valuable in a strategic management course for several reasons. First, cases provide you, the student, with experience of organizational problems that you probably have not had the opportunity to experience firsthand. In a relatively short period of time, you will have the chance to appreciate and analyze the problems faced by many different companies and to understand how managers tried to deal with them.

Second, cases illustrate the theory and content of strategic management. The meaning and implications of this information are made clearer when they are applied to case studies. The theory and concepts help reveal what is going on in the companies studied and allow you to evaluate the solutions that specific companies adopted to deal with their problems. Consequently, when you analyze cases, you will be like a detective who, with a set of conceptual tools, probes what happened and what or who was responsible and then marshals the evidence that provides the solution. Top managers enjoy the thrill of testing their problem-solving abilities in the real world. It is important to remember that no one knows what the right answer is. All that managers can do is to make the best guess. In fact, managers say repeatedly that they are happy if they are right only half the time in solving strategic problems. Strategic management is an uncertain game, and using cases to see how theory can be put into practice is one way of improving your skills of diagnostic investigation.

Third, case studies provide you with the opportunity to participate in class and to gain experience in presenting your ideas to others. Instructors may sometimes call on students as a group to identify what is going on in a case, and through classroom discussion the issues in and solutions to the case problem will reveal themselves. In such a situation, you will have to organize your views and conclusions so that you can present them to the class. Your classmates may have analyzed the issues differently from you, and they will want you to argue your points before they will accept your conclusions, so be prepared for debate. This mode of discussion is an example of the dialectical approach to decision making. This is how decisions are made in the actual business world.

Instructors also may assign an individual, but more commonly a group, to analyze the case before the whole class. The individual or group probably will be responsible for a thirty- to forty-minute presentation of the case to the class. That presentation must cover the issues posed, the problems facing the company, and a series of recommendations for resolving the problems. The discussion then will be thrown open to the class, and you will have to defend your ideas. Through such discussions and presentations, you will experience how to convey your ideas effectively to others. Remember that a great deal of managers' time is spent in these kinds of situations: presenting their ideas and engaging in discussion with other managers who have their own views about what is going on. Thus, you will experience in the classroom the actual process of strategic management, and this will serve you well in your future career.

If you work in groups to analyze case studies, you also will learn about the group process involved in working as a team. When people work in groups, it is often difficult to schedule time and allocate responsibility for the case analysis. There are always group members who shirk their responsibilities and group members who are so sure of their own ideas that they try to dominate the group's analysis. Most of the strategic management takes place in groups, however, and it is best if you learn about these problems now.

Analyzing a Case Study

The purpose of the case study is to let you apply the concepts of strategic management when you analyze the issues facing a specific company. To analyze a case study, therefore, you must examine closely the issues confronting the company. Most often you will need to read the case several times—once to grasp the overall picture of what is happening to the company and then several times more to discover and grasp the specific problems.

Generally, detailed analysis of a case study should include eight areas:

1. The history, development, and growth of the company over time

2. The identification of the company's internal strengths and weaknesses

3. The nature of the external environment surrounding the company

4. A SWOT analysis

5. The kind of corporate-level strategy that the company is pursuing

6. The nature of the company's business-level strategy

7. The company's structure and control systems and how they match its strategy

8. Recommendations

To analyze a case, you need to apply the concepts taught in this course to each of these areas. To help you further, we next offer a summary of the steps you can take to analyze the case material for each of the eight points we just noted:

1. *Analyze the company's history, development, and growth.* A convenient way to investigate how a company's past strategy and structure affect it in the present is to chart the critical incidents in its history—that is, the events that were the most unusual or the most essential for its development into the company it is today. Some of the events have to do with its founding, its initial products, how it makes new-product market decisions, and how it developed and chose functional competencies to pursue. Its entry into new businesses and shifts in its main lines of business are also important milestones to consider.

2. *Identify the company's internal strengths and weaknesses.* Once the historical profile is completed, you can begin the SWOT analysis. Use all the incidents you have charted to develop an account of the company's strengths and weaknesses as they have emerged historically. Examine each of the value creation functions of the company, and identify the functions in which the company is currently strong and currently weak. Some companies might be weak in marketing; some might be strong in research and development. Make lists of these strengths and weaknesses. The SWOT Checklist (Table 1) gives examples of what might go in these lists.

3. *Analyze the external environment.* To identify environmental opportunities and threats, apply all the concepts on industry and macroenvironments to analyze the environment the company is confronting. Of particular importance at the industry level are the Competitive Forces Model, adapted from Porter's Five Forces Model and the stage of the life-cycle model. Which factors in the macroenvironment will appear salient depends on the specific company being analyzed. Use each factor in turn (for instance, demographic factors) to see whether it is relevant for the company in question.

   Having done this analysis, you will have generated both an analysis of the company's environment and a list of opportunities and threats. The SWOT

Table 1 A SWOT Checklist

Potential Internal Strengths	Potential Internal Weaknesses
Many product lines?	Obsolete, narrow product lines?
Broad market coverage?	Rising manufacturing costs?
Manufacturing competence?	Decline in R&D innovations?
Good marketing skills?	Poor marketing plan?
Good materials management systems?	Poor material management systems?
R&D skills and leadership?	Loss of customer good will?
Information system competencies?	Inadequate human resources?
Human resource competencies?	Inadequate information systems?
Brand name reputation?	Loss of brand name capital?
Portfolio management skills?	Growth without direction?
Cost of differentiation advantage?	Bad portfolio management?
New-venture management expertise?	Loss of corporate direction?
Appropriate management style?	Infighting among divisions?
Appropriate organizational structure?	Loss of corporate control?
Appropriate control systems?	Inappropriate organizational
Ability to manage strategic change?	structure and control systems?
Well-developed corporate strategy?	High conflict and politics?
Good financial management?	Poor financial management?
Others?	Others?

Table 1 (*continued*)

Potential Environmental Opportunities	Potential Environmental Threats
Expand core business(es)?	Attacks on core business(es)?
Exploit new market segments?	Increases in domestic competition?
Widen product range?	Increase in foreign competition?
Extend cost or differentiation advantage?	Change in consumer tastes?
Diversify into new growth businesses?	Fall in barriers to entry?
Expand into foreign markets?	Rise in new or substitute products?
Apply R&D skills in new areas?	Increase in industry rivalry?
Enter new related businesses?	New forms of industry competition?
Vertically integrate forward?	Potential for takeover?
Vertically integrate backward?	Existence of corporate raiders?
Enlarge corporate portfolio?	Increase in regional competition?
Overcome barriers to entry?	Changes in demographic factors?
Reduce rivalry among competitors?	Changes in economic factors?
Make profitable new acquisitions?	Downturn in economy?
Apply brand name capital in new areas?	Rising labor costs?
Seek fast market growth?	Slower market growth?
Others?	Others?

Checklist table also lists some common environmental opportunities and threats that you may look for, but the list you generate will be specific to your company.

4. *Evaluate the SWOT analysis.* Having identified the company's external opportunities and threats as well as its internal strengths and weaknesses, consider what your findings mean. You need to balance strengths and weaknesses against opportunities and threats. Is the company in an overall strong competitive position? Can it continue to pursue its current business- or corporate-level strategy profitably? What can the company do to turn weaknesses into strengths and threats into opportunities? Can it develop new functional, business, or corporate strategies to accomplish this change? *Never merely generate the SWOT analysis and then put it aside.* Because it provides a succinct summary of the company's condition, a good SWOT analysis is the key to all the analyses that follow.

5. *Analyze corporate-level strategy.* To analyze corporate-level strategy, you first need to define the company's mission and goals. Sometimes the mission and goals are stated explicitly in the case; at other times, you will have to infer them from available information. The information you need to collect to find out the company's corporate strategy includes such factors as its lines of business and the nature of its subsidiaries and acquisitions. It is important to analyze the relationship among the company's businesses. Do they trade or exchange resources? Are there gains to be achieved from synergy? Alternatively, is the company just running a portfolio of investments? This analysis should enable you to define the corporate strategy that the company is pursuing (for example, related or unrelated diversification, or a combination of both) and to conclude whether the company operates in just one core business. Then, using your SWOT analysis, debate the merits of this strategy. Is it appropriate given the environment the company is in? Could a change in corporate strategy provide the company with new opportunities or transform a weakness into a strength? For example, should the company diversify from its core business into new businesses?

   Other issues should be considered as well. How and why has the company's strategy changed over time? What is the claimed rationale for any changes? Often, it is a good idea to analyze the company's businesses or products to assess its situation and identify which divisions contribute the most to or detract from its competitive advantage. It is also useful to explore how the company has built its portfolio over time. Did it acquire new businesses, or did it internally venture its own? All of these factors provide clues about the company and indicate ways of improving its future performance.

6. *Analyze business-level strategy.* Once you know the company's corporate-level strategy and have done the SWOT analysis, the next step is to identify the company's business-level strategy. If the company is a single-business company, its business-level strategy is identical to its corporate-level strategy. If the company is in many businesses, each business will have its own business-level strategy. You will need to identify the company's generic competitive

strategy—differentiation, low-cost, or focus—and its investment strategy, given its relative competitive position and the stage of the life cycle. The company also may market different products using different business-level strategies. For example, it may offer a low-cost product range and a line of differentiated products. Be sure to give a full account of a company's business-level strategy to show how it competes.

Identifying the functional strategies that a company pursues to build competitive advantage through superior efficiency, quality, innovation, and customer responsiveness and to achieve its business-level strategy is very important. The SWOT analysis will have provided you with information on the company's functional competencies. You should investigate its production, marketing, or research and development strategy further to gain a picture of where the company is going. For example, pursuing a low-cost or a differentiation strategy successfully requires very different sets of competencies. Has the company developed the right ones? If it has, how can it exploit them further? Can it pursue both a low-cost and a differentiation strategy simultaneously?

The SWOT analysis is especially important at this point if the industry analysis, particularly Porter's model, has revealed threats to the company from the environment. Can the company deal with these threats? How should it change its business-level strategy to counter them? To evaluate the potential of a company's business-level strategy, you must first perform a thorough SWOT analysis that captures the essence of its problems.

Once you complete this analysis, you will have a full picture of the way the company is operating and be in a position to evaluate the potential of its strategy. Thus, you will be able to make recommendations concerning the pattern of its future actions. However, first you need to consider strategy implementation, or the way the company tries to achieve its strategy.

7. *Analyze structure and control systems*. The aim of this analysis is to identify what structure and control systems the company is using to implement its strategy and to evaluate whether that structure is the appropriate one for the company. Different corporate and business strategies require different structures. You need to determine the *degree of fit between the company's strategy and structure*. For example, does the company have the right level of vertical differentiation (e.g., does it have the appropriate number of levels in the hierarchy or decentralized control?) or horizontal differentiation (does it use a functional structure when it should be using a product structure?)? Similarly, is the company using the right integration or control systems to manage its operations? Are managers being appropriately rewarded? Are the right rewards in place for encouraging cooperation among divisions? These are all issues to consider.

In some cases, there will be little information on these issues, whereas in others there will be a lot. In analyzing each case, you should gear the analysis toward its most salient issues. For example, organizational conflict, power, and politics will be important issues for some companies. Try to analyze why problems in these areas are occurring. Do they occur because of bad strategy formulation or because of bad strategy implementation?

Organizational change is an issue in many cases because the companies are attempting to alter their strategies or structures to solve strategic problems. Thus, as part of the analysis, you might suggest an action plan that the company in question could use to achieve its goals. For example, you might list in a logical sequence the steps the company would need to follow to alter its business-level strategy from differentiation to focus.

8. *Make recommendations.* The quality of your recommendations is a direct result of the thoroughness with which you prepared the case analysis. Recommendations are directed at solving whatever strategic problem the company is facing and increasing its future profitability. Your recommendations should be in line with your analysis; that is, they should follow logically from the previous discussion. For example, your recommendation generally will center on the specific ways of changing functional, business, and corporate strategies and organizational structure and control to improve business performance. The set of recommendations will be specific to each case, and so it is difficult to discuss these recommendations here. Such recommendations might include an increase in spending on specific research and development projects, the divesting of certain businesses, a change from a strategy of unrelated to related diversification, an increase in the level of integration among divisions by using task forces and teams, or a move to a different kind of structure to implement a new business-level strategy. Make sure your recommendations are mutually consistent and written in the form of an action plan. The plan might contain a timetable that sequences the actions for changing the company's strategy and a description of how changes at the corporate level will necessitate changes at the business level and subsequently at the functional level.

After following all these stages, you will have performed a thorough analysis of the case and will be in a position to join in class discussion or present your ideas to the class, depending on the format used by your professor. Remember that you must tailor your analysis to suit the specific issue discussed in your case. In some cases, you might completely omit one of the steps in the analysis because it is not relevant to the situation you are considering. You must be sensitive to the needs of the case and not apply the framework we have discussed in this section blindly. The framework is meant only as a guide, not as an outline.

Writing a Case Study Analysis

Often, as part of your course requirements, you will need to present a written case analysis. This may be an individual or a group report. Whatever the situation, there are certain guidelines to follow in writing a case analysis that will improve the evaluation your work will receive from your instructor. Before we discuss these guidelines and before you use them, make sure that they do not conflict with any directions your instructor has given you.

The structure of your written report is critical. Generally, if you follow the steps for analysis discussed in the previous section, *you already will have a good structure for your written discussion.* All reports begin with an *introduction* to the case. In it, outline briefly what the company does, how it developed historically, what problems it is experiencing, and how you are going to approach the issues in the case write-up. Do this sequentially by writing, for example, "First, we discuss the environment of Company X. . . . Third, we discuss Company X's business-level strategy. . . . Last, we provide recommendations for turning around Company X's business."

In the second part of the case write-up, the *strategic analysis* section, do the SWOT analysis, analyze and discuss the nature and problems of the company's business-level and corporate strategies, and then analyze its structure and control systems. Make sure you use plenty of headings and subheadings to structure your analysis. For example, have separate sections on any important conceptual tool you use. Thus, you might have a section on the Competitive Forces Model as part of your analysis of the environment. You might offer a separate section on portfolio techniques when analyzing a company's corporate strategy. Tailor the sections and subsections to the specific issues of importance in the case.

In the third part of the case write-up, present your *solutions and recommendations.* Be comprehensive, and make sure they are in line with the previous analysis so that the recommendations fit together and move logically from one to the next. The recommendations section is very revealing because your instructor will have a good idea of how much work you put into the case from the quality of your recommendations.

Following this framework will provide a good structure for most written reports, though it must be shaped to fit the individual case being considered. Some cases are about excellent companies experiencing no problems. In such instances, it is hard to write recommendations. Instead, you can focus on analyzing why the company is doing so well, using that analysis to structure the discussion. Following are some minor suggestions that can help make a good analysis even better:

1. Do not repeat in summary form large pieces of factual information from the case. The instructor has read the case and knows what is going on. Rather, use the information in the case to illustrate your statements, defend your arguments, or make salient points. Beyond the brief introduction to the company, you must avoid being *descriptive*; instead, you must be *analytical*.

2. Make sure the sections and subsections of your discussion flow logically and smoothly from one to the next. That is, try to build on what has gone before so that the analysis of the case study moves toward a climax. This is particularly important for group analysis, because there is a tendency for people in a group to split up the work and say, "I'll do the beginning, you take the middle, and I'll do the end." The result is a choppy, stilted analysis; the parts do not flow from one to the next, and it is obvious to the instructor that no real group work has been done.

3. Avoid grammatical and spelling errors. They make your work look sloppy.

4. In some instances, cases dealing with well-known companies end in 1998 or 1999 because no later information was available when the case was written. If possible, do a search for more information on what has happened to the company in subsequent years.

   Many libraries now have comprehensive Web-based electronic data search facilities that offer such sources as *ABI/Inform, The Wall Street Journal Index,* the *F&S Index,* and the *Nexis-Lexis* databases. These enable you to identify any article that has been written in the business press on the company of your choice within the past few years. A number of nonelectronic data sources are also useful. For example, *F&S Predicasts* publishes an annual list of articles relating to major companies that appeared in the national and international business press. *S&P Industry Surveys* is a great source for basic industry data, and *Value Line Ratings and Reports* can contain good summaries of a firm's financial position and future prospects. You will also want to collect full financial information on the company. Again, this can be accessed from Web-based electronic databases such as the *Edgar* database, which archives all forms that publicly quoted companies have to file with the Securities and Exchange Commission (SEC; e.g., 10-K filings can be accessed from the SEC's *Edgar* database). Most SEC forms for public companies can now be accessed from Internet-based financial sites, such as Yahoo's finance site (http://finance.yahoo.com/).

5. Sometimes instructors hand out questions for each case to help you in your analysis. Use these as a guide for writing the case analysis. They often illuminate the important issues that have to be covered in the discussion.

If you follow the guidelines in this section, you should be able to write a thorough and effective evaluation.

The Role of Financial Analysis in Case Study Analysis

An important aspect of analyzing a case study and writing a case study analysis is the role and use of financial information. A careful analysis of the company's financial condition immensely improves a case write-up. After all, financial data represent the concrete results of the company's strategy and structure. Although analyzing financial statements can be quite complex, a general idea of a company's financial position can be determined through the use of ratio analysis. Financial performance ratios can be calculated from the balance sheet and income statement. These ratios can be classified into five subgroups: profit ratios, liquidity ratios, activity ratios, leverage ratios, and shareholder-return ratios. These ratios should be compared with the industry average or the company's prior years of performance. It should be noted, however, that deviation from the average is not necessarily bad; it simply warrants further investigation. For example, young companies will have purchased assets at a different price and will likely have a different capital structure than older companies do. In addition to ratio analysis, a company's cash flow position is of critical importance and should be assessed. Cash flow shows how much actual cash a company possesses.

Profit Ratios

Profit ratios measure the efficiency with which the company uses its resources. The more efficient the company, the greater is its profitability. It is useful to compare a company's profitability against that of its major competitors in its industry to determine whether the company is operating more or less efficiently than its rivals. In addition, the change in a company's profit ratios over time tells whether its performance is improving or declining.

A number of different profit ratios can be used, and each of them measures a different aspect of a company's performance. Here, we look at the most commonly used profit ratios.

Return on Invested Capital (ROIC)   This ratio measures the profit earned on the capital invested in the company. It is defined as follows:

$$\text{Return on invested capital (ROIC)} = \frac{\text{Net profit}}{\text{Invested capital}}$$

Net profit is calculated by subtracting the total costs of operating the company away from its total revenues (total revenues – total costs). Total costs are the (1) costs of goods sold, (2) sales, general, and administrative expenses, (3) R&D expenses, and (4) other expenses. Net profit can be calculated before or after taxes, although many financial analysts prefer the before-tax figure. Invested capital is the amount that is invested in the operations of a company—that is, in property, plant, equipment, inventories, and other assets. Invested capital comes from two main sources: interest-bearing debt and shareholders' equity. Interest-bearing debt is money the company borrows from banks and from those who purchase its bonds. Shareholders' equity is the money raised from selling shares to the public, *plus* earnings that have been retained by the company in prior years and are available to fund current investments. ROIC measures the effectiveness with which a company is using the capital funds that it has available for investment. As such, it is recognized to be an excellent measure of the value a company is creating.[1] Remember that a company's ROIC can be decomposed into its constituent parts.

Return on Total Assets (ROA)   This ratio measures the profit earned on the employment of assets. It is defined as follows:

$$\text{Return on total assests} = \frac{\text{Net profit}}{\text{Total assets}}$$

Return on Stockholders' Equity (ROE)   This ratio measures the percentage of profit earned on common stockholders' investment in the company. It is defined as follows:

$$\text{Return on stockholders equity} = \frac{\text{Net profit}}{\text{Stockholders equity}}$$

If a company has no debt, this will be the same as ROIC.

Liquidity Ratios

A company's liquidity is a measure of its ability to meet short-term obligations. An asset is deemed liquid if it can be readily converted into cash. Liquid assets are current assets such as cash, marketable securities, accounts receivable, and so on. Two liquidity ratios are commonly used.

Current Ratio   The current ratio measures the extent to which the claims of short-term creditors are covered by assets that can be quickly converted into cash. Most companies should have a ratio of at least 1, because failure to meet these commitments can lead to bankruptcy. The ratio is defined as follows:

$$\text{Current ratio} = \frac{\text{Current assets}}{\text{Current liabilities}}$$

Quick Ratio   The quick ratio measures a company's ability to pay off the claims of short-term creditors without relying on selling its inventories. This is a valuable measure since in practice the sale of inventories is often difficult. It is defined as follows:

$$\text{Quick ratio} = \frac{\text{Current assets} - \text{inventory}}{\text{Current liabilities}}$$

Activity Ratios

Activity ratios indicate how effectively a company is managing its assets. Two ratios are particularly useful.

Inventory Turnover   This measures the number of times inventory is turned over. It is useful in determining whether a firm is carrying excess stock in inventory. It is defined as follows:

$$\text{Inventory turnover} = \frac{\text{Cost of goods sold}}{\text{Inventory}}$$

Cost of goods sold is a better measure of turnover than sales because it is the cost of the inventory items. Inventory is taken at the balance sheet date. Some companies choose to compute an average inventory, beginning inventory, and ending inventory, but for simplicity, use the inventory at the balance sheet date.

Days Sales Outstanding (DSO) or Average Collection Period   This ratio is the average time a company has to wait to receive its cash after making a sale. It measures how effective the company's credit, billing, and collection procedures are. It is defined as follows:

$$\text{DSO} = \frac{\text{Accounts receivable}}{\text{Total sales}/360}$$

Accounts receivable is divided by average daily sales. The use of 360 is the standard number of days for most financial analysis.

Leverage Ratios

A company is said to be highly leveraged if it uses more debt than equity, including stock and retained earnings. The balance between debt and equity is called the *capital structure*. The optimal capital structure is determined by the individual company. Debt has a lower cost because creditors take less risk; they know they will get their interest and principal. However, debt can be risky to the firm because if enough profit is not made to cover the interest and principal payments, bankruptcy can result. Three leverage ratios are commonly used.

Debt-to-Assets Ratio   The debt-to-assets ratio is the most direct measure of the extent to which borrowed funds have been used to finance a company's investments. It is defined as follows:

$$\text{Debt-to-assets ratio} = \frac{\text{Total debt}}{\text{Total assets}}$$

Total debt is the sum of a company's current liabilities and its long-term debt, and total assets are the sum of fixed assets and current assets.

Debt-to-Equity Ratio   The debt-to-equity ratio indicates the balance between debt and equity in a company's capital structure. This is perhaps the most widely used measure of a company's leverage. It is defined as follows:

$$\text{Debt-to-equity ratio} = \frac{\text{Total debt}}{\text{Total equity}}$$

Times-Covered Ratio   The times-covered ratio measures the extent to which a company's gross profit covers its annual interest payments. If this ratio declines to less than 1, the company is unable to meet its interest costs and is technically insolvent. The ratio is defined as follows:

$$\text{Times-covered ratio} = \frac{\text{Profit before interest and tax}}{\text{Total interest charges}}$$

Shareholder-Return Ratios

Shareholder-return ratios measure the return that shareholders earn from holding stock in the company. Given the goal of maximizing stockholders' wealth, providing shareholders with an adequate rate of return is a primary objective of most companies. As with profit ratios, it can be helpful to compare a company's shareholder returns against those of similar companies as a yardstick for determining how well the company is satisfying the demands of this particularly important group of organizational constituents. Four ratios are commonly used.

Total Shareholder Returns   Total shareholder returns measure the returns earned by time $t + 1$ on an investment in a company's stock made at time t. (Time t is the time at which the initial investment is made.) Total shareholder returns include both dividend payments and appreciation in the value of the stock (adjusted for stock splits) and are defined as follows:

$$\text{Total shareholder returns} = \frac{\begin{array}{c} \text{Stock price } (t + 1) - \text{stock price } (t) \\ + \text{ sum of annual dividends per share} \end{array}}{\text{Stock price } (t)}$$

If a shareholder invests \$2 at time t and at time $t + 1$ the share is worth \$3, while the sum of annual dividends for the period t to $t + 1$ has amounted to \$0.20, total shareholder returns are equal to $(3 - 2 + 0.2)/2 = 0.6$, which is a 60 percent return on an initial investment of \$2 made at time t.

Price-Earnings Ratio   The price-earnings ratio measures the amount investors are willing to pay per dollar of profit. It is defined as follows:

$$\text{Price-earnings ratio} = \frac{\text{Market price per share}}{\text{Earnings per share}}$$

Market-to-Book Value   Market-to-book value measures a company's expected future growth prospects. It is defined as follows:

$$\text{Market-to-book value} = \frac{\text{Market price per share}}{\text{Earnings per share}}$$

Dividend Yield   The dividend yield measures the return to shareholders received in the form of dividends. It is defined as follows:

$$\text{Dividend} = \frac{\text{Dividend per share}}{\text{Market price per share}}$$

Market price per share can be calculated for the first of the year, in which case the dividend yield refers to the return on an investment made at the beginning of the year. Alternatively, the average share price over the year may be used. A company must decide how much of its profits to pay to stockholders and how much to reinvest in the company. Companies with strong growth prospects should have a lower dividend payout ratio than mature companies. The rationale is that shareholders can invest the money elsewhere if the company is not growing. The optimal ratio depends on the individual firm, but the key decider is whether the company can produce better returns than the investor can earn elsewhere.

Cash Flow

Cash flow position is cash received minus cash distributed. The net cash flow can be taken from a company's statement of cash flows. Cash flow is important for what it reveals about a company's financing needs. A strong positive cash flow enables a company to fund future investments without having to borrow money from bankers or investors. This is desirable because the company avoids paying out interest or dividends. A weak or negative cash flow means that a company has to turn to external sources to fund future investments. Generally, companies in strong-growth industries often find themselves in a poor cash flow position (because their investment needs are substantial), whereas successful companies based in mature industries generally find themselves in a strong cash flow position.

A company's internally generated cash flow is calculated by adding back its depreciation provision to profits after interest, taxes, and dividend payments. If this figure is insufficient to cover proposed new investments, the company has little choice but to borrow funds to make up the shortfall or to curtail investments. If this figure exceeds proposed new investments, the company can use the excess to build up its liquidity (that is, through investments in financial assets) or repay existing loans ahead of schedule.

Conclusion

When evaluating a case, it is important to be *systematic*. Analyze the case in a logical fashion, beginning with the identification of operating and financial strengths and weaknesses and environmental opportunities and threats. Move on to assess the value of a company's current strategies only when you are fully conversant with the SWOT analysis of the company. Ask yourself whether the company's current strategies make sense given its SWOT analysis. If they do not, what changes need to be made? What are your recommendations? Above all, link any strategic recommendations you may make to the SWOT analysis. State explicitly how the strategies you identify take advantage of the company's strengths to exploit environmental opportunities, how they rectify the company's weaknesses, and how they counter environmental threats. Also, do not forget to outline what needs to be done to implement your recommendations.

Endnote

1 Tom Copeland, Tim Koller, and Jack Murrin, *Valuation: Measuring and Managing the Value of Companies* (New York: Wiley, 1996).

CASE 1

Best Buy Co., Inc.: Sustainable Customer Centricity Model?

Dr. Alan N. Hoffman

Rotterdam School of Management, Erasmus University and Bentley University

Synopsis

Best Buy is the largest consumer electronics retailer in the US, accounting for 19% of the market. Globally, it operates around 4,000 stores in the US, Canada, Mexico, China, and Turkey. Its subsidiaries include Geek Squad, Magnolia Audio Video, Pacific Sales, and Future Shop.

Best Buy distinguishes itself from competitors by deploying a differentiation strategy rather than a low price strategy. In order to become a service-oriented firm, it changed the compensation structure for sales associates and applied a customer-centric operating model to provide end-to-end services. It also heavily invested in the training of sales professionals so they can better understand products and better assist customers. As a result, the company is widely recognized for its superior service.

Best Buy still faces competition, however, from large brick and mortar stores like Wal-Mart, as well as e-commerce stores like Amazon. The economic downturn and technological advances (the frequent introduction of new products) have also put stress on its financial strength and the quality of its customer service. The key challenge for Best Buy is to determine the correct path to improve its differentiation strategy. The main question is: How can Best Buy continue to have innovative products, top-notch employees, and superior customer service while facing increased competition, operational costs, and financial stress?

Best Buy Co., Inc.: Sustainable Customer Centricity Model?

Best Buy, headquartered in Richfield, Minnesota, is a specialty retailer of consumer electronics. It operates over 1,100 stores in the US, accounting for 19% of the market. With approximately 155,000 employees, it also operates over 2,800 stores in Canada, Mexico, China, and Turkey. The company's subsidiaries include Geek Squad, Magnolia Audio Video, Pacific Sales, and in Canada, it operates under both the Best Buy and Future Shop labels.

Best Buy's mission is to make technology deliver on its promises to customers. To accomplish this, it helps customers realize the benefits of technology and technological changes so they can enrich their lives in a variety of ways through connectivity: "To make life fun and easy,"[1] as Best Buy puts it. This is what drives the company to continually increase the tools to support customers in the hope of providing end-to-end technology solutions.

As a public company, Best Buy's top objectives are sustained growth and earnings. This is accomplished in part by constantly reviewing its business model to ensure that it is satisfying customer needs and desires as effectively and completely as possible. The company strives to have not only extensive product offerings but also highly trained employees with extensive product knowledge. The company encourages its employees to go out of their way to

The author would like to thank Kevin Clark, Leonard D'Andrea, Amanda Genesky, Geoff Merritt, Chris Mudarri, and Dan Fowler for their research. Please address all correspondence to Dr. Alan N. Hoffman, MBA Program Director, LaCava 295, Bentley University, 175 Forest Street, Waltham, MA 02452; ahoffman@bentley.edu.

RSM Case Development Centre prepared this case to provide material for class discussion rather than to illustrate either effective or ineffective handling of a management situation.

help customers understand what these products can do and how customers can get the most out of the products they purchase. Employees must recognize that each customer is unique and thus determine the best method to help that customer achieve maximum enjoyment from the product(s) purchased.

From a strategic standpoint, Best Buy moved from being a discount retailer (a low price strategy) to a service-oriented firm that relies on a differentiation strategy. In 1989, it changed the compensation structure for sales associates from commission based to noncommissioned based, which resulted in consumers having more control over the purchasing process and in cost savings for the company (the number of sales associates was reduced). In 2005, Best Buy took customer service a step further by moving from peddling gadgets, to a customer-centric operating model. It is now gearing up for another change to focus on store design and providing products and services in line with customers' desire for constant connectivity.

Company History[2]

From Sound of Music to Best Buy

Best Buy was originally known as Sound of Music. Incorporated in 1966, the company started as a retailer of audio components and expanded to retailing video products in the early 1980s with the introduction of the videocassette recorder to its product line. In 1983, the company changed its name to Best Buy Co, Inc. (Best Buy). Shortly thereafter, it began operating its existing stores under a "superstore" concept by expanding product offerings and using mass marketing techniques to promote those products.

Best Buy dramatically altered the function of its sales staff in 1989. Previously, the sales staff worked on a commission basis and was more proactive in assisting customers coming into the stores as a result. Since 1989, however, the commission structure was terminated and sales associates developed into educators that assist customers in learning about the products offered in the stores. The customer, to a large extent, took charge of the purchasing process. The sales staff's mission was to answer customer questions so that the customer could decide which product(s) fit their needs. This differed greatly from their former mission of simply generating sales.

In 2000, the company launched its online retail store: BestBuy.com. This allowed customers a choice between visiting a physical store and purchasing products online, thus expanding Best Buy's reach among consumers.

Expansion through acquisitions

Since 2000, Best Buy has begun a series of acquisitions to expand their offerings and enter international markets:

2000—Best Buy acquired Magnolia Hi-Fi, Inc., a high-end retailer of audio and video products and services, which became Magnolia Audio Video in 2004. This acquisition allowed Best Buy access to a set of upscale customers.

2001—Best Buy entered the international market with the acquisition of Future Shop Ltd, a leading consumer electronics retailer in Canada. This helped Best Buy increase revenues, gain market share and leverage operational expertise. The same year, it also opened its first Canadian store. In the same year, the company purchased Musicland, a mall-centered music retailer throughout the US (divested in 2003).

2002—Best Buy acquired Geek Squad, a computer repair service provider, to help develop a technological support system for customers. The retailer began by incorporating in-store Geek Squad centers in its 28 Minnesota stores and expanding nationally and then internationally in subsequent years.

2005—Best Buy opened the first Magnolia Home Theater "store-within-a-store" (located within the Best Buy complex).

2006—Best Buy acquired Pacific Sales Kitchen and Bath Centers Inc. to develop a new customer base: builders and remodelers. The same year, it also acquired a 75% stake in Jiangsu Five Star Appliance Co., Ltd, a China-based appliance and consumer electronics retailer. This enabled the company to access the Chinese retail market and led to the opening of the first Best Buy China store on January 26, 2007.

2007—Best Buy acquired Speakeasy, Inc., a provider of broadband, voice, data and information technology services, to further its offering of technological solutions for customers.

2008—Through a strategic alliance with the Carphone Warehouse Group, a UK-based provider of mobile phones, accessories and related services, Best Buy Mobile was developed. After acquiring a 50% share in Best Buy Europe (with 2414 stores) from the Carphone Warehouse, Best Buy intends to open small-store formats across Europe in 2011.[3] Best Buy also acquired Napster, a digital downloads provider, through a merger, to counter the falling sales of compact discs.

The first Best Buy Mexico store was opened.

2009—Best Buy acquired the remaining 25% of Jiangsu Five Star. Best Buy Mobile moved into Canada.

Industry Environment

Industry overview

Despite the negative impact the financial crisis has had on economies worldwide, in 2008 the consumer electronics industry managed to grow to a record high of $694 billion in sales—a nearly 14% increase over 2007. In years immediately prior, the growth rate was similar: 14% in 2007 and 17% in 2006. This momentum, however, did not last. Sales dropped 2% in 2009, the first decline in 20 years for the electronics giant.

A few product segments, including televisions, gaming, mobile phone and blue-ray players, drive sales for the company. Television sales, specifically LCD units, which account for 77% of total television sales, were the main driver for Best Buy, as this segment alone accounts for 15% of total industry revenues. The gaming segment continues to be a bright spot for the industry as well, as sales are expected to have tremendous room for growth. Smartphones are another electronics industry segment predicted to have a high growth impact on the entire industry.

The consumer electronics industry has significant potential for expansion into the global marketplace. There are many untapped markets, especially newly developing countries. These markets are experiencing the fastest economic growth while having the lowest ownership rate for gadgets.[4] Despite the recent economic downturn, the future for this industry is optimistic. A consumer electronics analyst for the European Market Research Institute predicts that the largest growth will be seen in China (22%), the Middle East (20%), Russia (20%), and South America (17%).[5]

Barriers to Entry

As globalization spreads and use of the Internet grows, barriers to entering the consumer electronics industry are diminished. When the industry was dominated by brick and mortar companies, obtaining the large capital resources needed for entry into the market was a barrier for those looking to gain any significant market share. Expanding a business meant purchasing or leasing large stores that incurred high initial and overhead costs. However, the Internet has significantly reduced the capital requirements needed to enter the industry. Companies like Amazon.com and Dell have utilized the Internet to their advantage and gained valuable market share.

The shift towards Internet purchasing has also negated another once strong barrier to entry—customer loyalty. The trend today is that consumers will research products online to determine which one they intend to purchase and then shop around on the Internet for the lowest possible price.

Even though overall barriers are diminished, there are still a few left, which a company like Best Buy can use to their advantage. The first, and most significant, is economies of scale. With over 1,000 locations, Best Buy can use their scale to obtain cost advantages from suppliers due to high quantity of orders. Another advantage is in advertising. Large firms have the ability to increase advertising budgets to deter new entrants into the market. Smaller companies generally do not have the marketing budgets for massive television campaigns, which are still one of the most effective marketing strategies available to retailers. Although Internet sales are growing, the industry is still dominated by brick and mortar stores. Most consumers looking for electronics—especially major electronics—feel a need to actually see their prospective purchases in person. Having the ability to spend heavily on advertising will help increase foot traffic to these stores.

Internal Environment

Finance

While Best Buy's increase in revenue is encouraging (see **Exhibit 1**), recent growth has been fueled largely by acquisition, especially Best Buy's 2009 revenue growth. At the same time, net income and operating margins have been declining (see **Exhibit 2** and **Exhibit 3**). Although this could be a function of increased costs, it is more likely due to pricing pressure. Given the current adverse economic conditions, prices of many consumer electronic products have been forced down by economic and competitive pressures. These lower prices have caused margins to decline, negatively affecting net income and operating margins.

Best Buy's long-term debt increased substantially from 2008 to 2009 (see **Exhibit** 4), which is primarily due to the acquisition of Napster and Best Buy Europe. The trend in available cash has been a mirror image of long-term debt. Available cash increased from 2005 to 2008 and then was substantially lower in 2009 for the same reason.

While the change in available cash and long-term debt are not desirable, the bright side is that this situation is due to the acquisition of assets, which has led to a significant increase in revenue for the company. Ultimately, the decreased availability of cash would seem to be temporary due to the circumstances. The more troubling concern is the decline in net income and operating margins, which Best Buy needs to find a way to turn around. If the problems with net income and operating margins are fixed, the trends in cash and long-term debt will also begin to turn around.

At first blush, the increase in accounts receivable and inventory is not necessarily alarming since revenues are increasing during this same time period (see **Exhibit 5**). However, closer inspection reveals a 1% increase in inventory from 2008 to 2009 and a 12.5% increase in revenue accompanied by a 240% increase in accounts receivable. This creates a potential risk for losses due to bad debts.

Marketing

Best Buy's marketing objectives are fourfold: (a) to market various products based on the customer centricity operating model, (b) to address the needs of customer lifestyle groups, (c) to be at the forefront of technological advances, and (d) to meet customer needs with end-to-end solutions.

Best Buy prides itself on customer centricity that caters to specific customer needs and behaviors. Over the years, the retailer has created a portfolio of products and services that complement one another and have added to the success of the business. These products include seven distinct brands domestically, as well as other brands and stores internationally:

Best Buy—offers a wide variety of consumer electronics, home office products, entertainment software, appliances, and related services.

Best Buy Mobile—stand-alone stores offer a wide selection of mobile phones, accessories, and related eservices in a small-format stores.

Geek Squad—provides residential and commercial product repair, support, and installation services both in-store and on-site.

Magnolia Audio Video—offers high-end audio and video products and related services.

Napster—an online provider of digital music.

Pacific Sales—offers high-end home improvement products primarily including appliances, consumer electronics and related services.

Speakeasy—provides broadband, voice, data, and information technology services to small businesses.

Starting in 2005, Best Buy initiated a strategic transition to a customer-centric operating model, which was completed in 2007. Prior to 2005, the company focused on customer groups such as affluent professional males, young entertainment enthusiasts, upscale suburban mothers, and technologically advanced families.[6] After the transition, it focused more on customer lifestyle groups such as affluent suburban families, trend-setting urban dwellers, and the closely knit families of Middle America.[7] To target these various segments, Best Buy acquired firms with aligned strategies, which could be used as a competitive advantage against its strongest competition, such as Circuit City and Wal-Mart. The acquisitions of Pacific Sales, Speakeasy, and Napster, along with the development of Best Buy Mobile, created more product offerings, which led to more profits.

To market all these different types of products and services is a difficult task. That is why Best Buy's employees have more training than competitors. This knowledge service is a value-added competitive advantage. Since the sales employees no longer operate on a commission-based pay structure, consumers can obtain knowledge from sales people without being subjected to high-pressure sales techniques. This is generally seen to enhance customer shopping satisfaction.

Operations

Best Buy's operating objectives include increasing revenues by growing its customer base, gaining more market share internationally, successfully implementing marketing and sales strategies in Europe, and having multiple brands for different customer lifestyles through M&A.

Domestic Best Buy store operations are organized into eight territories, with each territory divided into districts. A retail field officer oversees store performance through district managers, who meet with store employees on a regular basis to discuss operations strategies such as loyalty programs, sales promotion, and new product introductions.[8] Along with domestic operations, Best Buy has an international operation segment, originally established in connection with the acquisition of Canada-based Future Shop.[9]

In 2009, Best Buy opened up 285 new stores in addition to the European acquisition of 2,414 Best Buy Europe stores, relocated 34 stores, and closed 67 stores.

Human Resources

The objectives of Best Buy's human resources department are to provide consumers with the right knowledge of products and services, to portray the company's vision and strategy on an everyday basis, and to educate employees on the ins and outs of new products and services.

Best Buy employees are required to be ethical and knowledgeable. This principle starts within the top management structure and filters down from the retail field officer through district managers, and through store managers to the employees on the floor. Every employee must have the company's vision embedded in their service and attitude.

Despite Best Buy's efforts to train an ethical and knowledgeable employee force, there have been some allegations and controversy over Best Buy employees, which has given the company a bad black eye in the public mind. One law suit claimed that Best Buy employees had misrepresented the manufacturer's warranty in order to sell its own product service and replacement plan. It accused Best Buy of "entering into a corporate-wide scheme to institute high-pressure sales techniques involving the extended warranties" and "using artificial barriers to discourage consumers who purchased the 'complete extended warranties' from making legitimate claims."[10]

In a more recent case (March 2009), the US District Court granted Class Action certification to allow plaintiffs to sue Best Buy for violating its "Price Match" policy. According to the ruling, the plaintiffs allege that Best Buy employees would aggressively deny consumers the ability to apply the company's "price match guarantee."[11] The suit also alleges that Best Buy has an undisclosed "Anti-Price Matching Policy," where it tells its employees not to allow price matches and gives financial bonuses to employees who do this.

Competition

Brick and mortar competitors

Wal-Mart Stores Inc., the world's largest retailer with revenues over $405 billion, has operations worldwide and offers a diverse product mix with a focus on being a low-cost provider. In recent years, Wal-Mart has increased its focus on grabbing market share in the consumer electronics industry. In the wake of Circuit City's liquidation,[12] it is stepping up efforts by striking deals with Nintendo and Apple that will allow each company to have their own in-store displays. Wal-Mart has also considered using smart phones and laptop computers to drive growth.[13] It is refreshing 3,500 of its electronics departments and will begin to offer a wider and higher range of electronic products. These efforts will help Wal-Mart appeal to the customer segment looking for high quality at the lowest possible price.[14]

GameStop Corp. is the leading video game retailer with sales of almost $9 billion as of January 2009, in a forecasted $22 billion industry. It operates over 6,000 stores throughout the US, Canada, Australia, and Europe, as a retailer of both new and used video game products including hardware, software and gaming accessories.[15]

The advantage GameStop has over Best Buy is the number of locations: 6,207 GameStop locations compared to 1,023 Best Buy locations. However, Best Buy seems to have what it takes to overcome this advantage—deep pockets. With significantly higher net income, Best Buy can afford to take a hit to their margins and undercut GameStop prices.[16]

RadioShack Corp. is a retailer of consumer electronic goods and services including flat panel televisions, telephones, computers, and consumer electronic accessories. Although the company grosses revenues of over $4 billion from 4,453 locations, RadioShack has consistently lost market share to Best Buy. Consumers have a preference for RadioShack for audio and video components, yet prefer Best Buy for their big box purchases.[17]

Second tier competitors are rapidly increasing. Wholesale shopping units are becoming more popular, and companies such as Costco and BJ's have increased their piece of the consumer electronics pie over the past few years. After Circuit City's bankruptcy, mid-level electronics retailers like HH Gregg and Ultimate Electronics are scrambling to grab Circuit City's lost market share. Ultimate Electronics, owned by Mark Wattles, who was a major investor in Circuit City, has a leg up on his competitors. Wattles was on Circuit City's board of executives and had firsthand access to profitable Circuit City stores. Ultimate Electronics has plans to expand its operations by at least 20 stores in the near future.

Online competitors

Amazon.com, Inc. has, since 1994, grown into the United States' largest online retailer with revenues of over $19 billion in 2008 by providing just about any product imaginable through its popular Website. Begun as an online bookstore, Amazon soon ventured out into various consumer electronic product categories including computers, televisions, software, video games and much more.[18]

Amazon.com gains an advantage over its super center competitors as it is able to maintain a lower cost structure compared to brink and mortar companies such as Best Buy. It is able to push those savings through to their product pricing and selection/diversification. With an increasing trend in the consumer electronic industry to shop online, Amazon.com is positioned perfectly to maintain strong market growth and potentially steal some market share away from Best Buy.

Netflix, Inc. is an online video rental service, offering selections of DVDs and Blue-ray discs. Since its establishment in 1997, it has grown into a $1.4 billion company. With over 100,000 titles in its collection, it ships for free to approximately 10 million subscribers. It has also begun offering streaming downloads through their Website, which eliminates the need to wait for a DVD to arrive.

Netflix is quickly changing the DVD market, which has dramatically impacted brick and mortar stores such as Blockbuster and Hollywood Video and retailers who offer DVDs for sale. In a responsive move, Best Buy has partnered with CinemaNow to enter the digital movie distribution market and counter Netflix and other video rental providers.[19]

Core Competencies

Customer centricity model

Most players in the consumer electronics industry focus on delivering products at the lowest cost (Walmart—brick and mortar, Amazon—Web-based). Best Buy, however, has taken a different approach by providing customers with highly trained sales associates who are available to educate customers regarding product features. This allows customers to make informed buying decisions on big-ticket items. In addition, with the Geek Squad, Best Buy is able to offer and provide installation services, product repair and on-going support. In short, it can provide an end-to-end solution for its customers.

Best Buy has used their customer centricity model, which is built around a significant database of customer information, to construct a diversified portfolio of product offerings. This allows the company to offer different products in different stores in a manner that matches customer needs. This in turn helps keep costs lower by shipping the correct inventory to the correct locations. Since Best Buy's costs are increased by the high level of training needed for sales associates and service professionals, it has been important that the company remain vigilant in keeping costs down wherever they can without sacrificing customer experience.

The tremendous breadth of products and services Best Buy is able to provide allows customers to purchase all components for a particular need within the Best Buy family. For example, if a customer wants to set up a first-rate audio-visual room at home, he or she can go to the Magnolia Home Theater store-within-a-store at any Best Buy location and use the knowledge of the Magnolia or Best Buy associate in the television and audio areas to determine which television and surround sound theater system best fits their needs. The customer can then employ a Geek Squad employee to install and set up the television and home theater system. None of Best Buy's competitors offer this extensive level of service.

Successful acquisitions

Through its series of acquisitions, Best Buy has gained valuable experience in the process of integrating companies under the Best Buy family. The ability to effectively determine where to expand has been and will be key to the company's ability to differentiate itself in the marketplace. Additionally, Best Buy has also been successfully integrating employees from acquired companies. Due to the importance of high-level employees to company strategy and success, retaining this knowledge base is invaluable. Best Buy now has a significant global presence, which is important because of the maturing domestic market. This global presence has provided the company with insights into worldwide trends in the consumer electronics industry and afforded access to newly developing markets. Best Buy uses this insight to test products in different markets in its constant effort to meet and anticipate customer needs.

Retaining talent

Analyzing Circuit City's demise, many experts have concluded one of the major reasons for the company's downfall is that Circuit City let go of their most senior and well-trained sales staff in order to cut costs. Best Buy, on the other hand, has a reputation for retaining their talent and is widely recognized for its superior service. Highly trained sales professionals have become a unique resource in the consumer electronics industry, where technology is changing at an unprecedented rate, and can be a significant source of competitive advantage.

Challenges Ahead

Economic downturn

Electronics retailers like Best Buy sell products that can be described as "discretionary items, rather than necessities."[20] During economic recessions, however, consumers have less disposable income to spend. While there has been recent optimism about a possible economic turn around, if the economy continues to stumble, this presents a real threat to sellers of discretionary products.

In order to increase sales revenues, many retailers, including Best Buy, offer customers low interest financing through their private-label credit cards. These promotions have been tremendously successfully for Best Buy. From 2007 to 2009, these private-label credit card purchases accounted for 16% to 18% of Best Buy's domestic revenue. Due to the current credit crisis, however, the Federal Reserve has issued new regulations that could restrict companies from offering deferred interest financing to customers. If Best Buy and other retailers are unable to extend these credit lines, it could have a tremendous negative impact on future revenues.[21]

Pricing and debt management

The current economic conditions, technological advances, and increased competition have put a tremendous amount of pricing pressure on many consumer electronics products. This is a concern for all companies in this industry. The fact that Best Buy does not compete strictly on price structure alone makes this an even bigger concern. Given the higher costs that Best Buy incurs training employees, any pricing pressure that decreases margins puts stress on Best Buy's financial strength. In addition, the recent acquisition of Napster and the 50% stake in Best Buy Europe have significantly increased Best Buy's debt and reduced available cash. Even in prosperous times, debt management is a key factor in any company's success, and it becomes even more concerning during economic downturn.

Products and service

As technology improves, product life cycles, as well as prices, decrease and as a result, margins therefore decrease. Under Best Buy's service model, shorter product life cycles increase training costs. Employees are forced to learn new products with higher frequency. This is not only costly but also increases the likelihood that employees will make mistakes, thereby tarnishing Best Buy's service record and potentially damaging one of its most important, if not the most important, differentiators. In addition, more resources must be directed at research of new products to make sure Best Buy continues to offer the products consumers desire.

One social threat to the retail industry is the growing popularity of the online marketplace. Internet shoppers can browse sites searching for the best deals on specific products. This technology has allowed consumers to become more educated about their purchases, while creating increased downward price pressure. Ambitious consumers can play the role of a Best Buy associate themselves by doing product comparisons and information gathering without a trip to the store. This emerging trend creates a direct threat to companies like Best Buy, which has 1,023 stores in its domestic market alone. One way Best Buy has tried to continue the demand for brick and mortar locations and counter the threat of Internet-based competition is by providing value-added services in stores. Customer service, repairs, and interactive product displays are just a few examples of these services.[22]

Leadership

The two former CEOs of Best Buy, Richard Shultze and Brad Anderson, were extremely successful at making the correct strategic moves at the appropriate times. With Brad Anderson stepping aside in June 2009, Brian Dunn replaced him as the new CEO. Although Dunn has worked for the company for 24 years and held the key positions of COO and President during his tenure, the position of CEO brings him to a whole new level and presents new challenges, especially during the current economic downturn. He is charged with leading Best Buy into the world of increased connectivity. This requires a revamping of products and store setups to serve customers in realizing their connectivity needs. This is a daunting task for an experienced CEO, let alone a new CEO who has never held the position.

Walmart

Best Buy saw its largest rival, Circuit City, go down for good. A new archrival, Wal-Mart, however, is expanding into consumer electronics and stepping up competition in a price war it hopes to win. Best Buy needs to face the competition not by lowering prices, but by coming up with something really different. It has to determine the correct path to improve its ability to differentiate itself from competitors, which is increasingly difficult given an adverse economic climate and the company's financial stress. How Best Buy can maintain innovative products, top-notch employees, and superior customer service while facing increased competition and operational costs is an open question.

Exhibit 1 Quarterly Sales

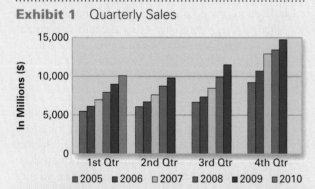

Fiscal Year	1st Qtr ($)	2nd Qtr ($)	3rd Qtr ($)	4th Qtr ($)
2005	5,479	6,080	6,647	9,227
2006	6,118	6,702	7,335	10,693
2007	6,959	7,603	8,473	12,899
2008	7,927	8,750	9,928	13,418
2009	8,990	9,801	11,500	14,724
2010	10,095			

Exhibit 2 Quarterly Net Income

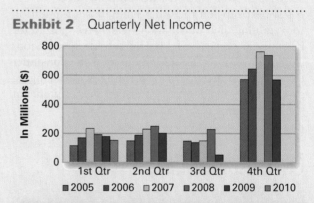

Fiscal Year	1st Qtr ($)	2nd Qtr ($)	3rd Qtr ($)	4th Qtr ($)
2005	114	150	148	572
2006	170	188	138	644
2007	234	230	150	763
2008	192	250	228	737
2009	179	202	52	570
2010	153			

Exhibit 3 Operating Margin

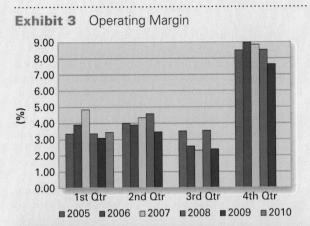

Fiscal Year	1st Qtr (%)	2nd Qtr (%)	3rd Qtr (%)	4th Qtr (%)
2005	3.36	3.98	3.51	8.49
2006	3.91	3.89	2.58	8.97
2007	4.84	4.34	2.31	8.81
2008	3.36	4.58	3.54	8.52
2009	3.08	3.46	2.38	7.63
2010	3.45			

Exhibit 4 Long-Term Debt and Cash

Fiscal Year	2005	2006	2007	2008	2009
Long-Term Debt ($)	528	178	590	627	1,126
Cash ($)	354	748	1,205	1,438	498
LTD/Equity	0.12	0.03	0.10	0.14	0.24
LTD/Total Assets	0.05	0.02	0.04	0.05	0.07

Exhibit 5 Accounts Receivable and Inventory

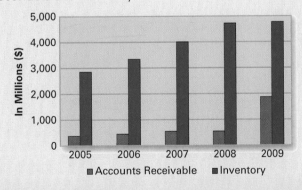

Fiscal Year	2005	2006	2007	2008	2009
Inventory ($)	2,851	3,338	4,028	4,708	4,753
Accounts Receivable ($)	375	449	548	549	1,868

Endnotes

1 Best Buy Co., Inc. (2009, February 28). Form 10-K. Securities and Exchange Commission.

2 Ibid.

3 Ibid.

4 Keller, Greg. (2009, May 18). Threat grows by iPod and laptop. *The Columbus Dispatch*. Retrieved July 10, 2009 from: http://www.dispatch.com/live/content/business/stories/2009/05/18/greener_gadgets.ART_ART_05-18-09_A9_TMDSJR8.html

5 Magid, Larry. (2008, May 2). Consumer electronics: The future looks bright. *CBSNews.com*. Retrieved July 10, 2009 from: http://www.cbsnews.com/stories/2008/05/02/scitech/pcanswer/main4067008.shtml

6 Best Buy Co., Inc. (2009). Form 10-K.

7 Ibid.

8 Ibid.

9 Ibid.

10 Manhattan Institute for Policy Research. (2001). They're making a federal case out of it . . . in state court. *Civil Justice Report 3*. Retrieved from: http://www.manhattan-institute.org/html/cjr_3_part2.htm

11 Best Buy Bombshell. (2009, March 21). HD Guru. Retrieved from: http://hdguru.com/best-buy-bombshell/400/

12 Circuit City Stores, Inc. was an American retailer in brand-name consumer electronics, personal computers, entertainment software, and (until 2000) large appliances. The company opened its first store in 1949 and liquidated its final American retail stores in 2009 following a bankruptcy filing and subsequent failure to find a buyer. At the time of liquidation, Circuit City was the second largest US electronics retailer, after Best Buy.

13 Bissonnette, Z. (2009, May 18). Wal-Mart looks to expand electronics business. *Bloggingstocks.com*. Retrieved from: http://www.bloggingstocks.com/2009/05/18/wal-mart-looks-to-expand-electronics-business/

14 Maestrie, N. (2009, May 19). Wal-Mart steps up consumer electronics push. *Reuters*. Retrieved from: http://www.reuters.com/article/technologyNews/idUSTRE54I4TR20090519

15 Capital IQ. (2009). GameStop Corp. Corporate Tearsheet. *Capital IQ*.

16 Sherman, E. (2009, June 24). GameStop faces pain from Best Buy, downloading. *BNET Technology*. Retrieved from: http://industry.bnet.com/technology/10002329/gamestop-faces-pain-from-best-buy-downloading/

17 Van Riper, T. (2006, February 17). RadioShack Gets Slammed. *Forebes.com*. Retrieved from: http://www.forbes.com/2006/02/17/radioshack-edmondson-retail_cx_tr_0217radioshack.html

18 Capital IQ. (2009). Amazon.com Corporate Tearsheet. *Capital IQ*.

19 Kee, T. (2009, June 5). Netflix beware: Best Buy adds digital downloads with CinemaNow deal. *paidContent.org*. Retrieved from: http://paidcontent.org/article/419-best-buy-adds-digital-movie-downloads-with-cinemanow-deal/

20 Best Buy Co., Inc. (2009). Form 10-K.

21 Ibid.

22 Ibid.

CASE 2

Whole Foods Market: 2010 How to Grow in An Increasingly Competitive Market?

Patricia Harasta and Alan N. Hoffman

Rotterdam School of Management, Erasmus University and Bentley University

Reflecting back over his three decades of experience in the grocery business, John Mackey smiled to himself over his previous successes. His entrepreneurial history began with a single store which he has now grown to the nation's leading natural food chain. Whole Foods is not just a food retailer but instead represents a healthy, socially responsible lifestyle that customers can identify with. The Company has differentiated itself from competitors by focusing on quality as excellence and innovation that allows them to charge a premium price for premium products. This strategy has formed their success over the last 30 years but like any success story there are limits to how far it can go before a new direction is needed so that it remains successful for the next 30 years. While proud of the past, John had concerns about the future direction Whole Foods should head.

Company Background

Whole Foods carries both natural and organic food offering customers a wide variety of products. "Natural" refers to food that is free of growth hormones or antibiotics, where "certificated organic" food conforms to the standards, as defined by the U.S. Department of Agriculture (USDA) in October 2002. Whole Foods Market® is the world's leading retailer of natural and organic foods, with 193 stores in 31 states and Canada and the United Kingdom. John Mackey, current president and cofounder of Whole Foods, opened "Safer Way" natural grocery store in 1978. The store had limited success as it was a small location allowing only for a limited selection, focusing entirely on vegetarian foods. John joined forces with Craig Weller and Mark Skiles, founders of "Clarsville Natural Grocery" (founded in 1979), to create Whole Foods Market. This joint venture took place in Austin, Texas in 1980 resulting in a new company, a single natural food market with a staff of nineteen.

In addition to the supermarkets, Whole Foods owns and operates several subsidiaries. Allegro Coffee Company was formed in 1977 and purchased by Whole Foods Market in 1997 now acting as their coffee roasting and distribution center. Pigeon Cove is Whole Foods seafood processing facility, which was founded in 1985 and known as M & S Seafood until 1990. Whole Foods purchased Pigeon Cove in 1996, located in Gloucester, MA. The Company is now the only supermarket to own and operate a waterfront seafood facility. The last two subsidiaries are Produce Field Inspection Office and Select Fish, which is Whole Foods West Coast seafood processing facility acquired in 2003. In addition to the above, the Company has eight distribution centers, seven regional bake houses and four commissaries.

"Whole Foods Market remains uniquely mission driven: The Company is highly selective about what they sell, dedicated to stringent quality standards, and committed to sustainable agriculture. They believe in a virtuous circle entwining the food chain, human beings and Mother Earth: each is reliant upon the others through a beautiful and delicate symbiosis." The message of preservation and sustainability are followed while providing high quality good to customers and high profits to investors.

The authors would like to thank Will Hoffman, Christopher Ferrari, Robert Marshall, Julie Giles, Jennifer Powers and Gretchen Alper for their research and contributions to this case.

Please address all correspondence to: Dr. Alan N. Hoffman, Department of Management, Bentley University, 175 Forest Street, Waltham, MA 02452-4705, voice (781) 891-2287, ahoffman@bentley.edu, fax (781) 459-0335. Printed by permission of Dr. Alan N. Hoffman, Bentley University.

Whole Foods has grown over the years through mergers, acquisitions and new store openings. The $565 million acquisition of its lead competitor, Wild Oats, in 2007 firmly set Whole Foods as the leader in natural and organic food market and added 70 new stores. The Federal Trade Commission (FTC) focused their attention on the merger on antitrust grounds. The dispute was settled in 2009, with Whole Foods closing 32 Wild Oats stores and agreed to selling the Wild Oats Markets brand.

The organic grocer's stock plunged in 2008 as its sales staggered. Later that year the private equity firm Green Equity Investors invested $425 million in Whole Foods, thereby acquiring about a 17% stake in the chain. For the first time in its 29-year history, Whole Foods reported negative same-store sales in the quarter ended December 2008 as traffic in its stores fell.

Today Whole Foods is listed in the S & P 500 and ranked 284th in the Fortune 500. It is the world's leading natural and organic foods supermarket and is America's first national certified organic grocer. In 2009, it had sales of $8 billion and 289 stores; 273 stores in 38 states of the US and the District of Columbia, 6 stores in Canada, and 5 stores in the UK. The Company has grown from 19 original employees to more than 53,500 team members.[1]

While the majority of Whole Foods locations are in the U.S., European expansion provides enormous potential growth due to the large population and it holds "a more sophisticated organic-foods market than the U.S. in terms of suppliers and acceptance by the public." Whole Foods targets their locations specifically by an area's demographics. The Company targets locations where 40% or more of the residents have a college degree as they are more likely to be aware of nutritional issues.

Whole Foods Market's Philosophy

Their corporate Website defines the company philosophy as follows, "Whole Foods Market's vision of a sustainable future means our children and grandchildren will be living in a world that values human creativity, diversity, and individual choice. Businesses will harness human and material resources without devaluing the integrity of the individual or the planet's ecosystems. Companies, governments, and institutions will be held accountable for their actions.

People will better understand that all actions have repercussions and that planning and foresight coupled with hard work and flexibility can overcome almost any problem encountered. It will be a world that values education and a free exchange of ideas by an informed citizenry; where people are encouraged to discover, nurture, and share their life's passions."

While Whole Foods recognizes it is only a supermarket, they are working toward fulfilling their vision within the context of their industry. In addition to leading by example, they strive to conduct business in a manner consistent with their mission and vision. By offering minimally processed, high quality food, engaging in ethical business practices and providing a motivational, respectful work environment, the Company believes they are on the path to a sustainable future.

Whole Foods incorporate the best practices of each location back into the chain. This can be seen in the Company's store product expansion from dry goods to perishable produce, including meats, fish and prepared foods. The lessons learned at one location are absorbed by all, enabling the chain to maximize effectiveness and efficiency while offering a product line customers love. Whole Foods carries only natural and organic products. The best tasting and most nutritious food available is found in its purest state—unadulterated by artificial additives, sweeteners, colorings, and preservatives.

Whole Foods continually improves customer offerings, catering to its specific locations. Unlike business models for traditional grocery stores, Whole Foods products differ by geographic regions and local farm specialties.

Employee & Customer Relations

Whole Foods encourages a team based environment allowing each store to make independent decisions regarding its operations. Teams consist of up to eleven employees and a team leader. The team leaders typically head up one department or another. Each store employs anywhere from 72 to 391 team members. The manager is referred to as the "store team leader." The "store team leader" is compensated by an Economic Value Added (EVA) bonus and is also eligible to receive stock options.

Whole Foods tries to instill a sense of purpose among its employees and has been named for 13 consecutive years as one of the "100 Best Companies to

Work For" in America by Fortune magazine. In employee surveys, 90% of its team members stated that they always or frequently enjoy their job.

The company strives to take care of their customers, realizing they are the "lifeblood of our business," and the two are "interdependent on each other." Whole Foods' primary objective goes beyond 100% customer satisfaction with the goal to "delight" customers in every interaction.

Competitive Environment

At the time of Whole Foods' inception, there was almost no competition with less than six other natural food stores in the U.S. Today, the organic foods industry is growing and Whole Foods' finds itself competing hard to maintain its elite presence.

In the early- to mid-2000s, its biggest competitor was Wild Oats. In 2007, Whole Foods put a bid on Wild Oats for $670 million[2] and drew an anti-trust investigation from the FTC. The FTC felt that a merger of the two premium natural and organic supermarkets would create a monopoly situation, ultimately harming consumers. It was found that although Whole Foods and Wild Oats were the two key players in the premium natural and organic food market, they are not insulated from competition from conventional grocery store chains. With the decision coming down in favor of Whole Foods and Wild Oats, the transaction was completed. Although this eliminated Whole Foods most direct competitor, they still faces stiff competition in the general grocery market.

Whole Foods competes with all supermarkets. With more U.S. consumers focused on eating healthfully, environmental sustainability, and the green movement, the demand for organic and natural foods has increased. More traditional supermarkets are now introducing "lifestyle" stores and departments to compete directly with Whole Foods. This can be seen in the Wild Harvest section of Shaw's, or the "Lifestyle" stores opened by conventional grocery chain Safeway.

Whole Foods competitors now include big box and discount retailers who have made a foray into the grocery business. Currently, the U.S. largest grocer is Wal-Mart. Not only do they compete in the standard supermarket industry, but they have even begun offering natural and organic products its Supercenter stores. Other discount retailers now competing in the supermarket industry include Target, Sam's Club and Costco. All of these retailers offer grocery products, generally at a lower price than what one would find at Whole Foods.

Another of Whole Foods' key competitors is Los Angeles based Trader Joe's, a premium natural and organic food market. By expanding its presence and product offerings while maintaining high quality at low prices, Trade Joe's has found its competitive niche. It has 215 stores, primarily on the west and east coasts of the U.S., offering upscale grocery fare such as health foods, prepared meals, organic produce and nutritional supplements. A low cost structure allows Trader Joe's to offer competitive prices while still maintaining its margins. Trader Joe's stores have no service department and average just 10,000 square feet in store size.

Additional competition has arisen from grocery stores, such as Stop 'N Shop and Shaw's, which now incorporate natural foods sections in their conventional stores, placing them in direct competition with Whole Foods. Because larger grocery chains have more flexibility in their product offerings, they are more likely to promote products through sales, a strategy Whole Foods rarely practices.

A Different Shopping Experience

The setup of the organic grocery store is a key component to Whole Foods' success. The store's setup and its products are carefully researched to ensure that they are meeting the demands of the local community. Locations are primarily in cities and are chosen for their large space and heavy foot traffic. According to Whole Foods' 10K, "approximately 88% of our existing stores are located in the top 50 statistical metropolitan areas." The Company uses a specific formula to choose their store sites that is based upon several metrics, which include but are not limited to income levels, education, and population density.

Upon entering a Whole Foods supermarket, it becomes clear that the Company attempts to sell the consumer on the entire experience. Team members (employees) are well trained and the stores themselves are immaculate. There are in-store chefs to help with recipes, wine tasting and food sampling. There are "Take Action food centers" where customers can access information on the issues that affect their food such as legislation and environmental factors. Some stores offer extra services such as home delivery, cooking classes, massages and valet parking. Whole Foods goes out of their way to appeal to the above-average income earner.

Whole Foods uses price as a marketing tool in a few select areas, as demonstrated by the 365 Whole Foods brand name products, priced less than similar organic products that are carried within the store. However, the Company does not use price to differentiate itself from competitors. Rather, Whole Foods focuses on quality and service as a means of standing out from the competition.

Whole Foods spends much less than other supermarkets on advertising, approximately 0.4% of total sales in the fiscal year 2009. They rely heavily on word-of-mouth advertising from their customers to help market themselves in the local community. They are also promoted in several health conscious magazines, and each store budgets for in-store advertising each fiscal year.

Whole Foods also gains recognition via their charitable contributions and the awareness that they bring to the treatment of animals. The Company donates 5% of their after tax profits to not-for-profit charities. It is also very active in establishing systems to make sure that the animals used in their products are treated humanly.

The Green Movement

Whole Foods exists in a time where customers equate going green and being environmentally friendly with enthusiasm and respect. In recent years, people began to learn about food and the processes completed by many to produce it. Most of what they have discovered is disturbing. Whole Foods launched a nationwide effort to trigger awareness and action to remedy the problems facing the U.S. food system. It has decided to host 150 screenings of a 12 film series called "Let's Retake Our Plates," hoping to inspire change by encouraging and educating consumers to take charge of their food choices. Jumping on the band wagon of the "go green" movement, Whole Foods is trying to show its customers that it is dedicated to not only all natural foods, but to a green world and healthy people. As more and more people become educated, the Company hopes to capitalize on them as new customers.[3]

Beyond the green movement, Whole Foods has been able to tap into a demographic that appreciates the "trendy" theme of organic foods and all natural products. Since the store is associated with a type of affluence, many customers shop there to show they fit into this category of upscale, educated, new age people.

The Economic Recession

The uncertainty of today's market is a threat to Whole Foods. The expenditure income is low and "all natural foods" are automatically deemed as expensive. Because of people being laid off, having their salaries cut, or simply not being able to find a job, they now have to be more selective when purchasing things. While Whole Foods has been able to maintain profitability, its questionable how long they will last if the recession continues or worsens. The reputation of organic products being costly may be enough to motivate people to not ever enter through the doors of Whole Foods. In California, the chain is frequently dubbed "Whole Paycheck."[4]

However, the Company understood that it must change a few things if it were to survive the decrease in sales felt because customers were not willing to spend their money so easily. They have been working to correct this "pricey" image by expanding offerings of private label products through their "365 Everyday Value" and "365 Organic" product lines. Private label sales accounted for 11% of Whole Foods total sales in 2009, up from 10% in 2008. They have also instituted a policy that their 365 product lines must match prices of similar products at Trader Joe's.[5]

During the economic recession, restaurants had a severe impact. A survey conducted showed that adults were eating out 50% less than they were prior to the economic crash.[6] Whole Foods saw this as opportunity to enter a new area of business, the premade meals sector. They began selling premade dinners and lunches marketing towards those still on the go but interested in eating healthy and saving money. Offering the feed "4 for $15" deal, they were able to recapture some lost sales. In November of 2008, the stock fell to $7 dollars. After the premade meals were created, the stock increased to $28 dollars in September 2009.[7] If Whole Foods continues to come up with innovative ideas to still compete during a recession, there is much opportunity as the economy evolves and climbs up the economic life cycle into recovery, expansion, and boom states.

Organic Foods a Commodity

When Whole Foods first started in the natural foods industry in 1980 it was a relatively new concept and over the first decade Whole Foods enjoyed the benefits of offering a unique value proposition to consumers wanting to purchase high quality natural foods from a trusted retailer. Over the last few years, however, the natural and organic foods industry has attracted the attention of general food retailers that have started to offer foods labeled as natural or organic at reasonable prices.

As of 2007, the global demand for organic and natural foods far exceeded the supply. This is becoming a huge issue for Whole Foods, as more traditional supermarkets with higher purchasing power enter the premium natural and organic foods market. The supply of organic food has been significantly impacted by the entrance of Wal-Mart into the competitive arena. Due to the limited resources within the U.S., Wal-Mart begun importing natural and organic foods from China and Brazil, which led to it coming under scrutiny for passing off non-natural or organic products as the "real thing." Additionally, the quality of natural and organic foods throughout the entire market has been decreased due to constant pressure from Wal-Mart.

The distinction between what is truly organic and natural is difficult for the consumer to decipher as general supermarkets have taken to using terms such as "all natural," "free-range," "hormone free," confusing customers. Truly organic food sold in the U.S. bears the "USDA Organic" label and needs to have at least 95% of the ingredients organic before it can get this distinction.[8]

In May 2003 Whole Foods became America's first Certified Organic grocer by a federally recognized independent third-party certification organization. In July 2009, California Certified Organic Growers (CCOF), one of the oldest and largest USDA-accredited third-party organic certifiers, individually certified each store in the U.S., complying with stricter guidance on federal regulations. This voluntary certification tells customers that Whole Foods have gone the extra mile by not only following the USDA's Organic Rule, but opening their stores up to third-party inspectors and following a strict set of operating procedures designed to ensure that the products sold and labeled as organic are indeed organic–procedures that are not specifically required

by the Organic Rule. This certification verifies the handling of organic goods according to stringent national guidelines, from receipt through repacking to final sale to customers. To receive certification, retailers must agree to adhere to a strict set of standards set forth by the USDA, submit documentation, and open their facilities to on-site inspections—all designed to assure customers that the chain of organic integrity is preserved.

Operations

Whole Foods purchases most of their products from regional and national suppliers. This allows the Company to leverage its size in order to receive deep discounts and favorable terms with their vendors. It still permits store to purchase from local producers to keep the stores aligned with local food trends and is seen as supporting the community. Whole Foods operates ten regional distribution centers to support its stores. It also operates two procurement centers, four seafood-processing and distribution centers, a specialty coffee and tea procurement and brewing operation, five regional kitchens, and eight bake house facilities. Whole Foods largest third-party supplier is United Natural Foods which accounted for 28% of total purchases in 2009, down from 32% in 2008.

Product categories at Whole Foods include, but are not limited to:

- Produce
- Seafood
- Grocery
- Meat and Poultry
- Bakery
- Prepared Foods and Catering
- Specialty (Beer, Wine and Cheese)
- Whole body (nutritional supplements, vitamins, body care and educational products such as books)
- Floral
- Pet Products
- Household Products[i]

While Whole Foods carries all the items that one would expect to find in a grocery store (and plenty that one would not), their ". . . heavy emphasis on perishable foods is designed to appeal to both natural foods and gourmet shoppers." Perishable foods now account for two-thirds of its sales. This is demonstrated by the Company's own statement that, "We believe it is our strength of execution in perishables that has attracted many of our most loyal shoppers."

Whole Foods also provides fully cooked frozen meal option through their private label Whole Kitchen, to satisfy the demands of working families. For example, The Whole Foods Market located Woodland Hills, CA that has redesigned its prepared foods section more than three times in response to a 40% growth in prepared foods sales.

Whole Foods doesn't take just any product and put it on their shelves. In order to make it into the Whole Foods grocery store, products have to undergo a strict test to determine if they are "Whole Foods material." The quality standards that all potential Whole foods products must meet include:

- Foods that is free of preservatives and other additives
- Foods that is fresh, wholesome and safe to eat
- Promote organically grown foods
- Foods and products that promote a healthy life

Meat and poultry products must adhere to a higher standard:

- No antibiotics or added growth hormones
- An affidavit from each producer that outlines the whole process of production and how the animals are treated
- An annual inspection of all producers by Whole Foods Market
- Successful completion of a third-party audit to attest to these findings

Also, due to the lack of available nutritional brands with a national identity, Whole Foods decided to enter into the private label product business. They currently have three private label products with a fourth program called Authentic Food Artisan, which promotes distinctive products that are certified organic. The three private label products: (1) 365 Everyday Value: A well-recognized and trusted brand that meets the standards of Whole Foods and is less expensive then the regular product lines; (2) Whole Kids Organic: Healthy items that are directed at children; and (3) 365 Organic Everyday Value: All the benefits of organic food at reduced prices.

Whole Foods growth strategy is to expand primarily through new store openings. New stores are typically located on premier real estate sites, often in urban, high-population locales. They do not have a standard store design, instead each store's design is customized to fit the size and configuration of the site selected. They have traditionally opened stores in upper-income, more urban neighborhoods that typically have a high percentage of college graduates.[9]

The Company tracks what it calls the "Tender Period" which is the time between when it takes possession of the leased space for construction and other purposes and the time when the store is opened for business. **Exhibit 1** shows the time and cost involved can be significant with preopening expenses running between $2.5 and $3 million dollars and the time required ranging from 8.5 to 12.6 months. If Whole Foods opens 17 stores per year, this will consume $43 to $51 million dollars of its available cash each year.

When opening a new store, Whole Foods stocks it with almost $700,000 worth of initial inventory, which their vendors partially finance. Like most conventional grocery stores, the majority of Whole Foods inventory is turned over fairly quickly; this is especially true of produce. Fresh organic produce is central to Whole Foods existence and turns over on a faster basis than other products.

Financial Operations

Whole Foods Market focuses on earning a profit while providing job security to its workforce to lay the foundation for future growth. The company is determined not to let profits deter the Company from providing excellent service to its customers and quality work environment for its staff. Their mission statement defines their recipe for financial success.

Exhibit 1 Stores—Time & Cost

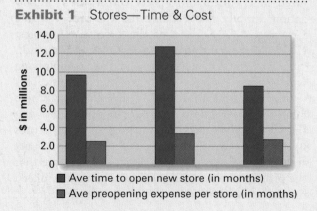

- ■ Ave time to open new store (in months)
- ■ Ave preopening expense per store (in months)

"Whole Foods, Whole People, Whole Planet-emphasizes that our vision reaches far beyond just being a food retailer. Our success in fulfilling our vision is measured by customer satisfaction, Team Member excellence and happiness, return on capital investment, improvement in the state of the environment, and local and larger community support."

Whole Foods also caps the salary of its executives at no more than fourteen times that of the average annual salary of a Whole Foods worker; this includes wages and incentive bonuses as well. The company also donates 5% of their after tax profits to non-profit organizations.

Over a period from September 2005 through January 2010, while total sales of Whole Foods have continued to increase, the operating margin has declined. With the acquisition of the Wild Oats the operating margin decreased significantly from 5.7% in 2006 to 3% in 2008 as Whole Foods struggled to handle the addition of 70+ new stores. The fiscal year 2009 has shown some improvement with the most recent operating margin back up to 3.9% on an annualized basis from the low point of 3.0% for the year ended September 2008. The operating margin has improved due to cost and efficiency improvements[10] (**Exhibit 2**).

Whole Foods strategy of expansion and acquisition has fueled growth in net income since the company's inception. The total number of stores has increased from 175 at September 2005 to 289 in January 2010. They managed to open only a total of ten new stores for the two years ended September 2009. This was a result of their integrating the stores from the Wild Oats acquisition in 2007 and conserving cash in order to pay down some of the debt taken on in that transaction. The Company did open five new stores in the first quarter of 2010 with a projection of an additional ten new stores for the remainder of the year. They forecast to open 17 new stores in each of the following two years (**Exhibit 3**).

Though new stores are being opened, average weekly same store sales have declined from $617,000 for the year ended September 2007 to $549,000 for the year ended September 2009 (**Exhibit 4**). The Company's sales have been impacted by the recession and resultant pullback in consumer spending as well as increased competition as more traditional grocery and discount chains expand their offerings of natural and organic products.[11]

Whole Foods has improved its balance sheet since the acquisition of the Wild Oats chain in 2007.

Long-Term debt has declined from $929 million at September 28, 2008 to $734 million as of January 17, 2010, a reduction of $195 million or 21%. Cash and Short-term Investment balances for the same periods increased from only $31 million to $482 million, an increase of $451 million (**Exhibit 5**). The Company's long- and short-term debt ratios are in line with industry averages and reflect a solid financial condition.[12] These improvements to the balance sheet were primarily the result of a preferred stock offering in late 2008 for approximately $413 million dollars which was subsequently called and converted into common stock. During the fourth quarter of 2008, they suspended the quarterly dividend on common shares for the foreseeable future.

Whole Foods has improved its accounts receivable and inventory levels as compared to sales. In 2005 and 2006, the combined percentage was 5.1%. This jumped dramatically to 8.5% in 2007 with the acquisition of Wild Oats. The Company has now brought this metric back to the historical norm of 5.1% as of January 2010 (**Exhibit 6**).

Whole Foods stock was outperforming the market and its industry based on the Company's growth and earnings prospects (**Exhibit 7**). The Wild Oats acquisition and the economic recession have impacted the stock, but it has subsequently recovered somewhat as Whole Foods has improved its efficiency and resumed its growth strategy through store expansion.

Struggling to Grow in An Increasingly Competitive Market

Whole Foods has historically grown by opening new stores or acquiring stores in affluent neighborhoods targeting the wealthier and more educated consumers. This strategy has worked in the past however the continued focus on growth has been impacting existing store sales. Average weekly sales per store have decreased over the last number of years despite the fact that overall sales have been increasing. It is likely that this trend will continue unless Whole Foods start to focus on growing sales within the stores they have and not just looking to increase overall sales by opening new stores. It is also increasingly difficult to find appropriate locations for new stores that are first are foremost in an area where there is limited competition and also to have the store in a location that is easily accessible by both consumers and the distribution network. Originally Whole Foods had forecast to open 29 new stores in 2010 but this has since been revised downward to 17.

Opening up new stores or the acquisition existing stores is also costly. The average cost to open a new store ranges from $2 to $3 million and it takes on average 8–12 months. A lot of this can be explained by the fact that Whole Foods custom build the stores which reduces the efficiencies that can be gained from the experience of having opened up many new stores previously. Opening new stores requires the company to adapt their distribution network, information management, supply and inventory management and adequately supply the new stores in a timely manner without impacting the supply to the existing stores. As the Company expands this task increases in complexity and magnitude.

The organic and natural foods industry overall has become a more concentrated market with few larger competitors having emerged from a more fragmented market composed of a large number of smaller companies. Future acquisitions will be more difficult for Whole Foods as the FTC will be monitoring the company closely to ensure that they do not violate any

federal antitrust laws through the elimination of any substantial competition within this market.

Over the last number of years there has been an increasing demand by consumers for natural and organic foods. Sales of organic foods increased by 5.1% in 2009 despite the fact that U.S. food sales overall only grew by 1.6%.[13] This increase in demand and high margin availability on premium organic products had led to an increasing number of competitors moving into the organic foods industry. Conventional grocery chains such as Safeway have remodeled stores at a rapid pace and have attempted to narrow the gap with premium grocers like Whole Foods in terms of shopping experience, product quality, and selection of takeout foods. This increase in competition can lead to the introduction of price wars where profits are eroded for both existing competitors and new entrants alike.

Unlike low-price leaders such as Wal-Mart, Whole Foods dominates because of its brand image, which is trickier to manage and less impervious to competitive threats. As competitors start to focus on emphasizing organic and natural foods within their own stores, the power of the Whole Foods brand will gradually decline over time as it becomes more difficult for consumers to differentiate Whole Foods value proposition from that of their competitors.

Exhibit 2   Sales, Net Income and Operating Margin

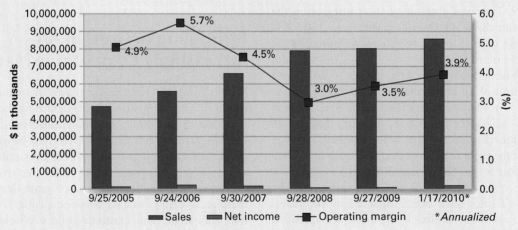

Case 2: Whole Foods Market: 2010 How to Grow in An Increasingly Competitive Market?

C35

Exhibit 3 # Stores

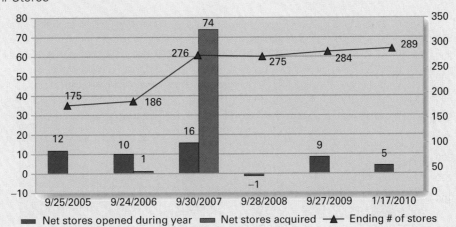

Net stores opened during year ■ ■ Net stores acquired ▲ Ending # of stores

Exhibit 4 Average Weekly Sales per Stores

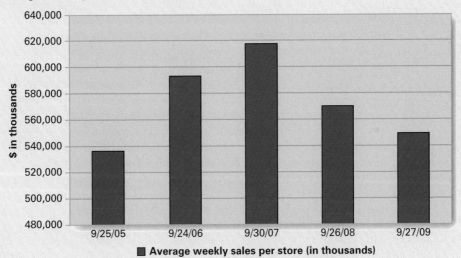

■ Average weekly sales per store (in thousands)

Exhibit 5   Cash & Long-Term Debt

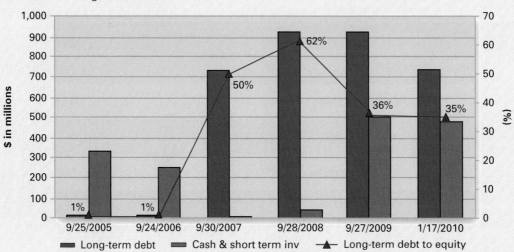

Exhibit 6   A/R & Inventory to Sales

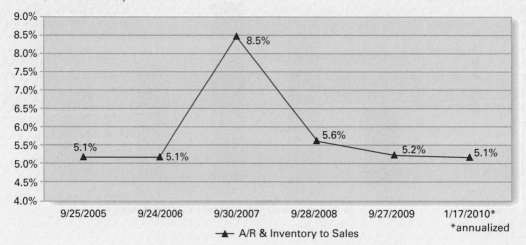

Exhibit 7   WFNI Daily

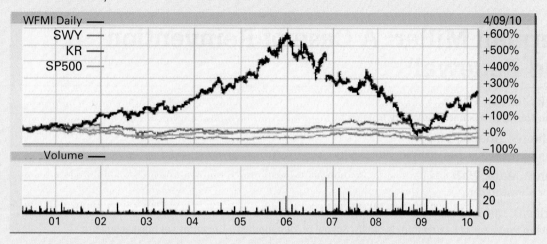

Endnotes

1   Hoover's Company Information, "Thomson Reuters Company in Context Report," Fast Company Magazine, December 2009

2   Lambert, Thomas A. "Four Lessons from the Whole Foods Case: The Antitrust Analysis of Mergers Should Be Reconsidered," Regulation. 31.1 (Spring 2008): 22(8). General Business File ASAP. Gale. Bentley College-Solomon R Baker Lib. 10 April, 2010

3   "Whole Foods Market; Whole Foods Market Challenge: Let's Retake Our Plates!" Food Business Week, 15 April, 2010

4   "Eating Too Fast At Whole Foods," Business Week (2005): Print.

5   "As Sales Slip, Whole Foods Tries Health Push," Katy McLaughlin, 8/15/2009, Wall Street Journal

6   Ziobro, Paul. "Whole Foods Highlights Its Eat-At-Home Values," Wall Street Journal 2009, Web. 10 April, 2010.

7   Ibid.

8   "Whole Foods Markets Organic China California Blend," YouTube, 10 April, 2010. http://www.youtube.com/watch?v=JQ31Ljd9T_Y

9   Whole Foods Market, Inc. SEC filing, Form 10-K dated 27 September, 2009

10   McLaughlin, Katy. "As Sales Slip, Whole Foods Tries Health Push," Wall Street Journal 2009.

11   Steverman, Ben. "Wal-Mart vs. Whole Foods," Business Week, 14 May, 2009

12   Market Edge Research Report, 12 April, 2010

13   Organic Trade Association http://www.organicnewsroom.com/2010/04/us_organic_product_sales_reach_1.html

CASE 3

Herman Miller: A Case of Reinvention and Renewal[1]

Frank Shipper, PhD
Perdue School of Business, Salisbury University

Stephen B. Adams, PhD
Perdue School of Business, Salisbury University

Karen P. Manz, PhD
Author & Researcher

Charles C. Manz, PhD
Nirenberg Professor of Leadership, Isenberg School of Management, University of Massachusetts

At first glance Herman Miller would appear to be only a $1.3 billion dollar manufacturer of office furniture. Herman Miller is, however, a company that is known beyond furniture for its innovation in products and processes since D. J. De Pree became president over 90 years ago.[2] It is one of only four organizations and the only non-high technology one selected to **Fortune's** *100 Best Companies to Work For* and *Most Admired Companies,* and **FastCompany's** *Most Innovative Companies* in both 2008 and 2010. The three high technology organizations selected were Microsoft, Cisco and Google. Not usual company for a firm in a mature industry and definitely not for an office furniture company. Ever since D. J. De Pree became president, Herman Miller has followed a different path from most firms. It is one distinctively marked by reinvention and renewal.

This path has served it well. Early in its history it survived the Great Depression and multiple recessions in the 20th century. In the early part of the 21st century, it recovered from the .com bust. As it enters 2010, Herman Miller once again faces a turbulent economy. Will this path allow it to flourish once again?

Background

Herman Miller's roots go back to 1905 and the Star Furniture Company, a manufacturer of traditional style bedroom suites in Zeeland, Michigan. In 1909, it was renamed Michigan Star Furniture Company and hired Dirk Jan (D. J.) De Pree as a clerk. D. J. De Pree became president in 1919. Four years later D. J. convinced his father-in-law, Herman Miller, to purchase the majority of shares and renamed the company Herman Miller Furniture Company in recognition of his support.[3]

In 1927, D. J. De Pree committed to treating "all workers as individuals with special talents and potential." This occurred after he visited the family of a millwright who had died unexpectedly. At the visit, the widow read some poetry. D. J. De Pree asked the widow who the poet was and was surprised to learn it was the millwright. This led him to wonder whether the millwright was a person who wrote poetry or a poet who was also a millwright. This story is part of the cultural folklore at Herman Miller that continues to generate respect for all employees and fuels the quest to tap the diversity of gifts and skills held by all.

In 1930, the country was in the Great Depression and Herman Miller was in financial trouble. D. J. De Pree was looking for a way to save the company. At the same time, Gilbert Rhode, a designer from New York, approached D. J. De Pree and told him about his design philosophy. He then asked for an opportunity to create a design of a bedroom suite at a fee of $1000. When D. J. De Pree reacted negatively to such a fee, Gilbert Rhode suggested an alternative payment plan, 3% royalty on the furniture sold, to which D. J. agreed figuring that there was nothing to lose.

Sources: Frank Shipper, Salisbury University; Stephen B. Adams, Salisbury University; Karen Manz, Author and Researcher; Charles C. Manz, University of Massachusetts-Amherst. Used by kind permission of the authors.

A few weeks later, D. J. received the first designs from Rhode. Again, he reacted negatively. He "thought that they looked as if they had been done for a manual training school and told him so." Gilbert Rhode explained in a letter his design philosophy—first, "utter simplicity: no surface enrichment, no carvings, no moldings," and second, "furniture should be anonymous. People are important, not furniture. Furniture should be useful." Rhode's designs were antithetical to traditional designs, but D. J. saw merit in them and this set Herman Miller on a course of designing and selling furniture that reflected a way of life.

In 1942, Herman Miller produced its first office furniture—a Gilbert Rhode design referred to as the Executive Office Group. He died two years later and De Pree began a search for a new design leader. Based largely on an article in *Life* magazine, he hired George Nelson as Herman Miller's first design director.

In 1946, Charles and Ray Eames, designers based in Los Angeles, were hired to design furniture. In the same year, Charles Eames designs were featured in the first one-man furniture exhibit at New York's Museum of Modern Art. Some of his designs are now part of the museum's permanent collection.

In 1950, Herman Miller under the guidance of Dr. Carl Frost, Professor at Michigan State University, was the first company in the state of Michigan to implement a Scanlon Plan. Underlying the Scanlon Plan are the "principles of equity and justice for everyone in the company . . ." Two major functional elements of Scanlon Plans are the use of committees for sharing ideas on improvements and a structure for sharing increased profitability. The relationship between Dr. Frost and Herman Miller continued for at least four decades.

During the 1950's, Herman Miller introduced a number of new furniture designs including those by Alexander Girard, Charles and Ray Eames, and George Nelson. Specifically, the first molded fiberglass chairs were introduced and the Eames lounge chair and ottoman were introduced on NBC's *Home Show* with Arlene Francis, a precursor to the *Today Show*. Also in the 1950's, Herman Miller began its first overseas foray selling its products in the European market.

In 1962, D. J. became chairman of the board and his son, Hugh De Pree, became president and chief executive officer. D. J. had served for over 40 years as the president.

During the 1960s, many new designs were introduced both for home and the workplace. The most notable design was the Action Office System, the world's first open-plan modular office arrangement of movable panels and attachments. By the end of the 1960's, Herman Miller had formed a subsidiary in England with sales and marketing responsibility throughout England and the Scandinavian countries. Also, it had established dealers in South and Central America, Australia, Canada, Europe, Africa, the Near East, and Japan.

In 1970, Herman Miller went public and made its first stock offering. The stock certificate was designed by the Eames Office staff. In 1971, it entered the health/science market, and in 1976, the Ergon chair, its first design based on scientific observation and ergonomic principles, was introduced. In 1979, in conjunction with the University of Michigan, it established the Facility Management Institute that established the profession of facility management. Also, in the 70's, Herman Miller continued to expand overseas and introduce new designs.

By 1977, over half of Herman Miller's 2500 employees worked outside of the production area. Thus, the Scanlon plan needed to be overhauled since it had been designed originally for a production workforce. In addition, employees worked at multiple U.S. and overseas locations. Thus, in 1978, an ad hoc committee of 54 people from nearly every segment of the company was elected to examine the need for changes and to make recommendations. By January 1979, the committee had developed a final draft. The plan established a new organization structure based on work teams, caucuses and councils. All employees were given an opportunity to small group settings to discuss it. On January 26, 1979, 96% of the employees voted to accept the new plan.

After 18 years Hugh De Pree stepped down, and Max De Pree, Hugh's younger brother, became chairman and chief executive officer in 1980. In 1981, Herman Miller took a major initiative to become more efficient and environmentally friendly. Its Energy Center generated both electrical and steam power to run its million square foot facility by burning waste.

In 1983, Herman Miller established a plan whereby all employees became shareholders. This initiative occurred approximately 10 years before congressional incentives fueled ESOP (Employee Stock Ownership Plan) growth.

In 1984, the Equa chair, a second chair based on ergonomic principles, was introduced along with many other designs in the 1980's. In 1987, the first nonfamily member, Dick Ruch, became chief executive officer.

By the end of the decade, the Equa chair was recognized as a Design of the Decade by **Time** magazine. Also, in 1989, Herman Miller established its Environmental Quality Action Team. It is to ". . . coordinate environmental programs worldwide and involve as many employees as possible."

In 1990, Herman Miller was a founding member of the Tropical Forest Foundation and was the only furniture manufacturer to belong. That same year, it discontinued using endangered rosewood in its award winning Eames lounge chair and ottoman, and substituted cherry and walnut from sustainable sources. It also became a founding member of the U.S. Green Building Council in 1994. Some of the buildings at Herman Miller have been used to establish Leadership in Energy & Environmental Design (LEED) standards. Because of its environmental efforts, Herman Miller received awards from **Fortune** magazine and the National Wildlife Federation in the 1990's.

In the 90's, Herman Miller again introduced some ground breaking designs. In 1994, it introduced the Aeron chair and almost immediately it was added to the New York Museum of Modern Art's permanent Design Collection. In 1999, it won the Design of the Decade from **Business Week** and the Industrial Designers Society of America.

In 1992, J. Kermit Campbell became Herman Miller's fifth CEO and president. He was the first person from outside the company to hold either position. In 1995, Campbell resigned and Mike Volkema was promoted to CEO. At the time the industry was in a slump and Herman Miller was being restructured. Sales were approximately 1 billion. Mike Volkema had been with Meridian, a company Herman Miller acquired in 1990, for seven years. So with approximately 12 years of experience with either Herman Miller or its subsidiary and at the age of 39 Mike Volkema became CEO.

In 1994, Herman Miller for the Home was launched to focus on the residential market. It reintroduced some of its modern classic designs from the 40's, 50's, and 60's as well as new designs. In 1998, hmhome.com was set up to tap this market.

Additional marketing initiatives were taken to focus on small and midsize businesses. A network of 180 retailers was established to focus on small businesses and a 3-D design computer program was made available to midsize customers. In addition, order entry was digitally linked among Herman Miller, suppliers, distributors and customers to expedite orders and improve their accuracy.

The 2000's

The 2000s started off spectacularly with record profits and sales in 2000 and 2001. An Employee Stock Option Plan (ESOP) was offered in July of 2000 and the Eames molded plywood chair was selected as a "design of the century" by **Time** magazine. Sales had more than doubled in the six years that Mike Volkema had been CEO.

Then the dot.com bubble burst and the events of September 11, 2001 occurred in the U.S. Sales dropped 34% from $2,236,200,000 in 2001 to $1,468,700,000 in 2002. In the same years profits dropped from $144,100,000 to losses of $56,000,000. In an interview for **FastCompany** magazine in 2007, Volkema said, "One night I went to bed a genius and woke up the town idiot."

Although sales continued to drop in 2003, Herman Miller returned to profitability in that year. To do so, Herman Miller had to drop its long-held tradition of life-long employment. Approximately 38% of the work force was laid off. One entire plant in Georgia was closed. Mike Volkema and Brian Walker, then President of Herman Miller North America, met with all the workers to tell them what was happening and why it had to be done. One of the workers being laid off was so moved by their presentation that she told them she felt sorry for them having to personally lay off workers.

To replace the tradition of life-long employment, Mike Volkema, with input from many, developed what is referred to as "the new social contract." He explains it as follows:

> We are a commercial enterprise, and the customer has to be on center stage, so we have to first figure out whether your gifts and talents have a match with the needs and wants of this commercial enterprise. If they don't, then we want to wish you the best, but we do need to tell you that I don't have a job for you right now.

As part of the implementation of the social contract, benefits such as educational reimbursement and 401K plans were redesigned to be more portable. This was done to decrease the cost of changing jobs for employees whose gifts and talents no longer matched customer needs.

Sales and profits began to climb from 2003 to 2008. In 2008, even though sales were not at an all time high, profits were. During this period, Brian Walker became president in 2003 and chief executive officer in 2004. Mike Volkema became chairman of the board in 2004.

Then Herman Miller was hit by the recession of 2009. Sales dropped 19% from $2,012 billion in 2008 to $1,630 billion in 2009. In the same years profits dropped from $152 million to $68 million. In March, Mark Schurman, Director of External Communications at Herman Miller, predicted that the changes made to recover from the 2001–2003 recession would help it better weather the 2007–2009 recession.

Herman Miller Entering 2010

Herman Miller has codified its long practiced organizational values and publishes them on its Website under a page entitled "What We Believe." These beliefs are intended as a basis for uniting all employees, building relationships, and contributing to communities. Those beliefs as stated in 2005 and remaining in effect in 2010 are as follows:

- **Curiosity & Exploration:** These are two of our greatest strengths. They lie behind our heritage of research-driven design. How do we keep our curiosity? By respecting and encouraging risk, and by practicing forgiveness. You can't be curious and infallible. In one sense, if you never make a mistake, you're not exploring new ideas often enough. Everybody makes mistakes: we ought to celebrate honest mistakes, learn from them, and move on.
- **Engagement:** For us, it is about being owners—actively committed to the life of this community called Herman Miller, sharing in its success and risk. Stock ownership is an important ingredient, but it's not enough. The strength and the payoff really come when engaged people own problems, solutions, and behavior. Acknowledge responsibility, choose to step forward and be counted. Care about this community and make a difference in it.

- **Performance:** Performance is required for leadership. We want to be leaders, so we are committed to performing at the highest level possible. Performance isn't a choice. It's up to everybody at Herman Miller to perform at his or her best. Our own high performance—however we measure it—enriches our lives as employees, delights our customers, and creates real value for our shareholders
- **Inclusiveness:** To succeed as a company, we must include all the expressions of human talent and potential that society offers. We value the whole person and everything each of us has to offer, obvious or not so obvious. We believe that every person should have the chance to realize his or her potential regardless of color, gender, age, sexual orientation, educational background, weight, height, family status, skill level—the list goes on and on. When we are truly inclusive, we go beyond toleration to understanding all the qualities that make people who they are, that make us unique, and most important, that unite us.
- **Design:** Design for us is a way of looking at the world and how it works—or doesn't. It is a method for getting something done, for solving a problem. To design a solution, rather than simply devising one, requires research, thought, sometimes starting over, listening, and humility. Sometimes design results in memorable occasions, timeless chairs, or really fun parties. Design isn't just the way something looks; it isn't just the way something works, either.
- **Foundations:** The past can be a tricky thing—an anchor or a sail, a tether or a launching pad. We value and respect our past without being ruled by it. The stories, people, and experiences in Herman Miller's past form a unique foundation. Our past teaches us about design, human compassion, leadership, risk taking, seeking out change, and working together. From that foundation, we can move forward together with a common language, a set of owned beliefs and understandings. We value our rich legacy more for what it shows us we might become than as a picture of what we've been.
- **A Better World:** This is at the heart of Herman Miller and the real reason why many of us come to work every day. We contribute to a better world by pursuing sustainability and environmental wisdom. Environmental advocacy is part of our heritage and a responsibility we gladly bear for

future generations. We reach for a better world by giving time and money to our communities and causes outside the company; through becoming a good corporate citizen worldwide; and even in the (not so) simple act of adding beauty to the world. By participating in the effort, we lift our spirits and the spirits of those around us.

- **Transparency:** Transparency begins with letting people see how decisions are made and owning the decisions we make. So when you make a decision, own it. Confidentiality has a place at Herman Miller, but if you can't tell anybody about a decision you've made, you've probably made a poor choice. Without transparency, it's impossible to have trust and integrity. Without trust and integrity, it's impossible to be transparent

All employees are expected to live these values. In a description of the current processes that follow, numerous examples of these values in action can be found.

Management

Mike Volkema is currently the chairman of the board, and Brian Walker is the president and chief executive officer. Walker's compensation was listed by **Bloomberg Businessweek** as $668,685. Compensation for CEO's at four competitors was listed by **Bloomberg Businessweek** to range from $792,000 to $1,100,000. Walker and four other top executives at Herman Miller took a 10% pay cut in January 2009, and they took another 10% pay cut along with all salaried workers in March 2009. The production workers were placed on a 9 day in two weeks work schedule effectively cutting their pay by 10% as well. That the executives would take a pay cut before all others and twice as much is just one way human compassion is practiced at Herman Miller.

By Securities and Exchange Commission regulations a publicly traded company must have a board of directors. By corporate policy, the majority of the 14 members of the board must be independent. To be judged an independent, the individual as a minimum must meet the NASDAQ National Market requirements for independent directors (NASDAQ Stock Market Rule 4200). In addition, the individual must not have any "other material relationship with the company or its affiliates or with any

executive officer of the company or his or her affiliates." Moreover, any "transaction between the Company and any executive officer or director of the Company (including that person's spouse, children, stepchildren, parents, stepparents, siblings, parents-in-law, children-in-law, siblings-in-law and persons sharing the same residence) must be disclosed to the Board of Directors and is subject to the approval of the Board of Directors or the Nominating and Governance Committee unless the proposed transaction is part of a general program available to all directors or employees equally under an existing policy or is a purchase of Company products consistent with the price and terms of other transactions of similar size with other purchasers." Furthermore, "It is the policy of the Board that all directors, consistent with their responsibilities to the stockholders of the company as a whole, hold an equity interest in the company. Toward this end, the Board requires that each director will have an equity interest after one year on the Board, and within five years the Board encourages the directors to have shares of common stock of the company with a value of at least three times the amount of the annual retainer paid to each director." In other words, board members are held to standards consistent with the corporate beliefs and its ESOP program.

Although Herman Miller has departments, the most frequently referenced work unit is a team. Paul Murray, Director of the Environmental Health and Safety explained their relationship as follows:

> At Herman Miller, team has just been the term that has been used since the Scanlon Plan and the De Prees brought that into Herman Miller. And so I think that's why we use that almost exclusively. The department—as a department, we help facilitate the other teams. And so they aren't just department driven.

Teams are often cross-functional. Membership on a team is based on ability to contribute to that team. As Gabe Wing, Design for the Environment Lead Chemical Engineer described it,

> You grab the appropriate representative who can best help your team achieve its goal. It doesn't seem to be driven based on title. It's based on who has the ability to help us drive our initiatives toward our goal.

Teams are often based on product development. When that product has been developed, the members of that team are redistributed to new projects. New projects can come from any level in the organization. At Herman Miller leadership is shared. One way in which this is done is through Herman Miller's concept of "talking up and down the ladder." Workers at all levels are encouraged to put forth new ideas. As Rudy Bartels, Environmental Specialist said,

> If they try something that they have folks there that will help them and be there for them. And by doing that, either—whether that requires a presence of one of us or an e-mail or just to say, "Yeah, I think that's a great idea." That's how a lot . . . in the organization works.

Because the workers feel empowered, a new manager can run into some behavior that can startle them. As Paul Murray recalled,

> I can remember my first day on the job. I took my safety glasses off . . . and an employee stepped forward and said, "Get your safety glasses back on." At *Company X, Company Y,*[4] there was no way would they have ever talked to a supervisor like that, much less their supervisor's manager. It's been a fun journey when the work force is that empowered.

The beliefs are also reinforced through the Employee Gifts Committee, and Environmental Quality Action Team. True to its practice of shared leadership the Employee Gifts Committee distributes funds and other resources based on employee involvement. As explained by Jay Link, manager of Corporate Giving, the program works as follows:

> . . . our first priority is to honor organizations where our employees are involved. We believe that it's important that we engender kind of a giving spirit in our employees, so if we know they're involved in organizations, which is going to be where we have a manufacturing presence, then our giving kind of comes alongside organizations that they're involved with. So that's our first priority.

In addition, all employees can work 16 paid hours a year with the charitable organization of their choice. Herman Miller sets goals for the number of employee volunteer hours contributed annually to its communities. Progress toward meeting those goals is reported to the CEO.

The Environmental Affairs Team has responsibility for such areas as solid waste recycling and designing products from sustainable resources. It was formed in 1988 with the authorization of Max

De Pree. One success that it has is in the reduction of solid waste taken to the landfill. In 1991, Herman Miller was sending 41 million pounds to the landfill. By 1994 it was down to 24 million pounds and by 2008 it was reduced to 3.6. Such improvements are both environmentally friendly and cost effective.

These beliefs are carried over to the family and community. Gabe Wing related how, "I've got the worst lawn in my neighborhood. That's because I don't spread pesticides on it, and I don't put fertilizer down." He went on to say how his wife and he had to make a difficult decision this the summer of 2009 because Herman Miller has a policy "to avoid PVC (polyvinyl chloride) wherever possible." In restoring their home, they chose fiber cement board over PVC siding even though it was considerably more costly. Gabe went on to say, "Seven years ago, I didn't really think about it."

Rudy Bartels is involved in a youth soccer association. As is typical, it needs to raise money to buy uniforms. Among other fund raisers that it has done is collecting newspapers and aluminum cans. As he tells it, "When I'll speak they'll say, 'Yeah, that's Rudy. He's Herman Miller. You should—you know we're gonna have to do this'."

These beliefs carry over to all functional areas of the business. Some of them are obviously beneficial and some of them are simply the way Herman Miller has chosen to conduct its business.

Marketing

Herman Miller products are sold internationally through wholly-owned subsidiaries in various countries including Canada, France, Germany, Italy, Japan, Mexico, Australia, Singapore, China, India, and the Netherlands. Its products are offered through independent dealerships. The customer base is spread over 100 countries.

Herman Miller uses Green Marketing to sell its products. For example, the Mirra Chair introduced in 2003 with PostureFit Technology was developed from its inception to be environmentally friendly (cradle-to-cradle principles). These chairs are made of 45% recycled materials, and 96% of their materials are recyclable. In addition, they are assembled using 100% renewable energy. Builders that use Herman Miller products in their buildings can earn points toward LEED's (Leadership in Energy & Environmental Design) certification.

In addition, Herman Miller engages in cooperative advertising with strategic partners. For example, at Hilton Garden Inns, some rooms are equipped with Herman Miller's Mirra chairs. On the desk in the room is a card explaining how to adjust the chair for comfort and then lists a Hilton Garden Inn Website where the chair can be purchased.

Production/Operations

Herman Miller is globally positioned in terms of manufacturing operations. In the United States, its manufacturing operations are located in Michigan, Georgia, and Washington. In Europe, it has considerable manufacturing presence in the United Kingdom, its largest market outside of the United States. In Asia, it has manufacturing operations in Ningbo, China.

Herman Miller manufactures products using a system of lean manufacturing techniques collectively referred to as the Herman Miller Performance System (HMPS). It strives to maintain efficiencies and cost savings by minimizing the amount of inventory on hand through a JIT (Just in Time) process. Some suppliers deliver parts to Herman Miller production facilities five or six times per day.

Production is order-driven with direct materials and components purchased as needed to meet demand. The standard lead time for the majority of its products is 10 to 20 days. As a result, the rate of inventory turnover is high. These combined factors could cause inventory levels to appear relatively low in relation to sales volume. A key element of its manufacturing strategy is to limit fixed production costs by out sourcing component parts from strategic suppliers. This strategy has allowed it to increase the variable nature of its cost structure while retaining proprietary control over those production processes that Herman Miller believes provide a competitive advantage. Because of this strategy, manufacturing operations are largely assembly-based.

The success of the Herman Miller Performance System (HMPS) was the result of much hard work. For example, in 1996, the Integrated Metals Technology (IMT) subsidiary was not going well. IMT supplied pedestals to its parent company Herman

Miller. Its prices were high, lead time long, and quality was in the 70% range. The leadership of the subsidiary decided to hire the consulting arm of Toyota, Toyota Supplier Support Center (TSSC) was hired. Significant improvements were made by inquiring, analyzing, and "enlisting help and ideas of everyone." For example, quality defects in parts per million decreased from approximately 9000 in 2000 to 1500 in 2006. Concurrently, on-time shipments improved from 80% to 100% and safety incidents per 100 employees dropped from 10 to 3 per year.

The organizational values mentioned earlier were incorporated into the design of The Greenhouse, Herman Miller's main production facility in Michigan. The building was designed to be environmentally friendly. For example, it takes advantage of natural light and landscaping. Native plants are grown without the use of fertilizers, pesticides, or irrigation. After the facility was opened, aggressive paper wasps found the design to their liking. Employees and guests were stung, frequently. In keeping with Herman Miller beliefs a solution was sought. Through research it was learned that honey bees and paper wasps are incompatible. Therefore, 600,000 honey bees and their 12 hives were colocated on the property. The wasps soon left. Two additional consequences were that due to pollination by the bees the area around the facility blooms with wild flowers and a large amount of honey is produced. Guests to the home office are given a four-ounce bottle of the honey symbolizing its corporate beliefs.

Human Resource Management

Human resource management is considered a strength for Herman Miller. It is routinely listed on **Fortune's 100 Best Companies to Work For** including 2010. It had approximately 278 applicants for every job opening. In the 2009 downturn, Herman Miller cut its workforce by more than 15%, reduced pay of the remaining workforce by at least 10%, and suspended 401 (k) contributions, employees praised management for "handling the downturn with class and doing what is best for the collective whole" according to **Fortune** magazine's February 8, 2010 issue. **Fortune** also estimated voluntary turnover to be less than 2%. On June 1, 2010, the time-and-pay cuts of 10% begun in the spring of

2009 were discontinued due to Herman Miller's quick turnaround.

Herman Miller practices "Business as Unusual" as pointed out many years ago by Hugh De Pree, former president, and it appears to pay off in both good and tough times. Herman Miller shares the gains as well as the pains with its employees especially in regard to compensation.

Pay is geared to firm performance and it takes many forms at Herman Miller. As in other companies all employees receive a base pay. In addition, all employees participate in a profit-sharing program whereby employees receive stock based on the company's annual financial performance. Employees are immediately enrolled in this plan upon joining Herman Miller and immediately vested. Profit sharing is based on corporate performance because as one employee explained:

> The problem we see is you get to situations where project X corporately had a greater opportunity for the entirety of the business, but it was difficult to tell these folks that they needed to sacrifice in order to support the entirety of the business when they were being compensated specifically on their portion of the business. So you would get into some turf situations. So we ended up moving to a broader corporate EVA (Economic Value Added) compensation to prevent those types of turf battles.

The company offers an Employee Stock Purchase Plan (ESPP) through payroll deductions at a 15% discount from the market price. Also, all employees are offered a 401 (k) where they receive a 50% match for the first 6% of their salaries that the employee contributes. Again, employees are immediately eligible to participate in this plan upon joining Herman Miller and immediately vested. The company match was suspended in 2009 due to the recession. Through the profit sharing and the ESPP, the employees own approximately 8% of the outstanding stock.

Furthermore, all employees are offered a retirement income plan whereby the company deposits into an account 4% of compensation on which interest is paid quarterly. Employees are immediately eligible to participate in this plan upon joining Herman Miller, but are required to participate for five years before being vested. Additionally, a length of service bonus is paid after 5 years of employment. Finally, the company pays a universal annual bonus to all employees based on the company's performance

against Economic Value Added (EVA) objectives. EVA is a calculation of the company's net operating profits, after tax, minus a 'charge' for the cost of shareholder capital. This is in addition to the other compensation programs, including profit sharing, with the same calculation used to determine both employee and executive bonus potential.

Thus, pay takes a number of forms at Herman Miller, but most all forms are at least partially, if not wholly, contingent on corporate performance. One employee summed up pay as follows, "You can dip into Herman Miller's pocket several times based on the performance of the company."

Other benefits also take many forms at Herman Miller. Employees are given a range of benefits as they are in many organizations. Some are, however, quite different from those found in other organizations such as a $100 rebate on a bike purchase. It is justified as "part of our comprehensive program designed for a better world around you." Other benefits that Herman Miller provides that are identified by the company as "unique" are,

- 100% tuition reimbursement
- Flexible schedules: job sharing, compressed workweek, and telecommuting options
- Concierge services—from directions, dry cleaning, greeting cards or a meal to take home—these services make it easier for you to balance work and home life
- Employee product purchase discounts
- On-site services including massage therapy, cafeterias, banking, health services, fitness center, fitness classes, and personal trainers

Herman Miller in keeping with its beliefs offers extensive wellness benefits including fitness facilities or subsidized gym memberships, health services, employee assistance programs, wellness programs/classes, and health risk assessments. The other benefits that are offered that most large organization also offer include health insurance, dental insurance, vision care plan, prescription plan, flexible spending accounts, short and long term disability, life insurance, accidental death and disability insurance, and critical illness/personal accident/long-term care. All benefits are available also to domestic partners.

When appropriate, Herman Miller promotes people within the organization. Education and training are seen as key to preparing employees to take on new responsibilities. For example, Rudy Bartels, Environmental Specialist, as well as multiple vice presidents, began their careers at Herman Miller on the production floor.

Three other benefits are unique to Herman Miller. First, every family that has or adopts a child receives a Herman Miller rocking chair. Second, every employee that retires after 25 years with the company and is 55 years or older receives an Eames lounge chair. Third, Herman Miller has no executive retreat, but it does have an employee retreat, The Marigold Lodge, on Lake Michigan. This retreat is available to employees for corporate related events, such as retirement parties and other celebrations, and in some instances includes invited family and guests.

Finance

During normal economic times, financial management at Herman Miller would be considered conservative. Through 2006, its leverage ratio was below the industry average and its times interested earned ratio was over twice the industry average. Due to the drop-off in business the debt to equity ratio rose precipitously from 1.18 in 2006 to 47.66 in 2008. To improve this ratio, over 3 million shares were sold in fiscal year 2009.[5] In the four previous fiscal years, Herman Miller had been repurchasing shares. The debt to equity ratio was reduced to 3.81 by the end of 2009. To improve short-term assets, dividends per share were cut by approximately 70% and capital expenditures were reduced to zero in 2009.

For fiscal year 2008, 15% of Herman Miller's revenues and 10% of its profits were from non-North American countries. In 2007, non-North American countries accounted for 16.5% of revenues and approximately 20% of Herman Miller's profits.

Financially, Herman Miller holds true to its beliefs. Even in downturns, it invests in research and development. In the dot.com downturn it invested tens of millions of dollars in R & D. Inside Herman Miller this investment project was code named "Purple."

In the December 19, 2007 issue of **FastCompany** magazine commenting on this project, Clayton Christensen, Harvard Business School professor and author of **The Innovator's Dilemma** is quoted as saying, "Barely one out of 1000 companies would do what they did. It was a daring bet in terms of increasing spending for the sake of tomorrow while cutting back to survive today."

Accessories Team: An Example of HM's Strategy, Leadership, and Beliefs in Action

The Accessories Team was an outgrowth of project "Purple." One of the goals of this project was to stretch beyond the normal business boundaries. Office accessories is one area in which Herman Miller has not been historically involved even though it is a big part of what the independent dealers sell. Once identified, "Robyn was tapped to put together a team to really explore this as a product segment that we could get more involved with," according to Mark Schurman, Director of External Communications at Herman Miller.

In 2006, Robyn established the team by recruiting Larry Kallio to be the head engineer and Wayne Baxter to lead sales and marketing. Together, they assembled a flexible team to launch a new product in 16 months. They recruited people with different disciplines needed to support that goal. Over the next two years, they remained a group of six. Some people started with the team and then as it got through that piece of work, they went on to different roles within the company. The team during its first eight months met twice a week for half a day. Twenty months out it met only once a week.

The group acts with a fair amount of autonomy, but it does not want complete autonomy because, "We don't want to be out there completely on our own because we have such awesome resources here at Herman Miller," Robyn explained. The group reaches out to other areas in the company when different disciplines are needed for a particular product, and tap people that could allocate some of their time to support it.

Wayne described what happened on the team as follows:

> We all seem to have a very strong voice regarding almost any topic; it's actually quite fun and quite dynamic. We all have kind of our roles on the team, but I think other than maybe true engineering, we've all kind of tapped into other roles and still filled in to help each other as much as we could.

Another member of the accessories team described decision making as follows:

> If we wanted to debate and research and get vary scientific, we would not be sitting here talking about the things that we've done, we'd still researching them. In a sense, we rely upon our gut a lot, which I think is, at the end of the day just fine because we have enough experience. We're not experts, but we're also willing to take risks and we're also willing to evolve,

Thus, leadership and decision making is shared both within the team and across the organization. Ideas and other contributions to the success of the team are accepted from all sources.

Out of this process has grown what is known as the "Thrive Collection." The name was chosen to indicate the focus on the individual and the idea of personal comfort, control and ergonomic health. Products included in the collection are the Ardea® Personal Light, the Leaf® Personal Light, Flo® Monitor Arm, and C2® Climate Control. All of these are designed for improving the individual's working environment. Continuing Herman Miller's tradition of innovative design the Ardea light earned both Gold and Silver honors from the International Design Excellence Awards (IDEA) in June, 2010.

The Industry

Office equipment is an economically volatile industry. The office furniture segment of the industry was hit hard by the recession. Sales were expected to drop by 26.5% from 2008 to 2009. Herman Miller's sales dropped 19%. Herman Miller's stock market value of $1,095,322,000 at the end of 2009 represented 7.3% of the total stock market value of the industry identified by Standard & Poor's Research Insight as Office Services & Supplies. According to Hoover's, Herman Miller's top three competitors are Haworth, Inc., Steelcase, and HNI.

The industry has been impacted by a couple of trends. First, telecommuting has decreased the need of large companies to have office equipment for all employees. Some companies such as Oracle have a substantial percentage of their employees telecommuting. The majority of Jet Blue reservation clerks telecommute. Second, more employees spend more hours in front of computer screens than ever before.

Due to this trend, the need for ergonomically correct office furniture has increased. Such furniture helps to decrease fatigue and injuries such as carpel tunnel syndrome.

As with most industries, the cost of raw materials and competition from overseas has had an impact. These trends tend to impact the low-cost producers more than the high-quality producers.

The Future

In a June 24, 2010, press release Brian Walker, Chief Executive Officer, stated, "One of the hallmarks of our company's history has been the ability to emerge from challenging periods with transformational products and processes. I believe our commitment to new products and market development over the past two years has put us in a position to do this once again. Throughout this period, we remained focused on maintaining near-term profitability while at the same time investing for the future. The award-winning new products we introduced last week at the NeoCon tradeshow are a testament to that focus, and I am incredibly proud of the collective spirit it has taken at Herman Miller to make this happen."

Questions To Address: Will the strategies that have made Herman Miller an outstanding and award winning company continue to provide it with the ability to reinvent and renew itself? Will disruptive global, economic, and competitive forces compel it to change its business model?

Endnotes

1   Many sources were helpful in providing material for this case, most particularly employees at Herman Miller who generously shared their time and viewpoints about the company to help ensure that the case accurately reflected the company's practices and culture. They provided many resources, including internal documents and stories of their personal experiences.

2   Corporate titles such as president and chief executive officer are not capitalized in this case because they are not capitalized in company documents.

3   In Herman Miller people including the D. J. De Pree are referred to by their first or nick names or in combination with their surnames, but hardly ever by their titles or surnames alone.

4   The names of the two Fortune 500 companies were deleted by the authors.

5   Herman Miller's fiscal year ends on May 30 of the following calendar year.

Wells Fargo: The Future of a Community Bank

Alan N. Hoffman

Rotterdam School of Management, Erasmus University and Bentley University

Wells Fargo: The Future of a Community Bank

Wells Fargo, founded in San Francisco during the gold rush as a money delivery express, is now the fourth largest bank in the US and ranks number one in America's deposit market share. It achieved initial success by being a trustworthy custodian of its customers' wealth. By staying true to a customer-centric business model, it aims to fulfill all its customers' needs and help them succeed financially. After establishing itself as one of the best community banks in the US, Wells Fargo has expanded internationally as a global bank. It has also significantly diversified offerings in order to gain market share. Because of a comprehensive range of products, Wells Fargo is exposed to increasing risks and competition. During the global financial crisis, it was negatively impacted due to its large exposure to bad loans through acquisition of Wachovia. Although the combination of advanced online banking technology and its massive physical network makes Wells Fargo stand out from its competitors, it remains challenging for the company to gain or maintain a leading position. If not managed properly, the diversifying strategy may in the end endanger Wells Fargo's overall market share. The 2010 US financial reform legislation may limit growth potential for a large bank like Wells Fargo. How Wells Fargo can succeed in this increasingly regulated yet highly competitive industry is an open question.

Company History

Wells Fargo was founded in San Francisco in 1852 by Henry Wells and William Fargo, two former express messengers. Before launching Wells Fargo, the two, together with several other pioneer expressmen, created the American Express Company. When the directors declined to extend the business westward to California during the gold rush, Wells and Fargo left American Express and created their own company to serve the western frontier.

Wells Fargo quickly expanded throughout the West. The two primary services it offered were banking and express delivery. Following Fargo's vision of a railway system that linked all of America, the company took on the motto of "Ocean to Ocean," connecting the commercial centers of New York and New Jersey through the heartland of America and across to the Pacific Ocean.

Wells Fargo was growing strongly when World War I began and the government nationalized the express network. With its express business gone, all that remained was its banking in San Francisco.[i] Wells Fargo Bank had formally separated from the express business in 1905 and thereafter survived the physical challenges of the San Francisco earthquake and fire, along with the economic hardships brought about by two world wars and the Great Depression.

Wells Fargo, in its current management structure, is primarily the result of an acquisition by Norwest Corporation in 1998.[ii] The new company maintained

The author would like to thank MBA students Andrew Longmire, Stephanie Mancuso, Paul Souppa, and Shanshan Zhou at Bentley University for their research.

RSM Case Development Centre prepared this case to provide material for class discussion rather than to illustrate either effective or ineffective handling of a management situation.

both the San Francisco headquarters and the Wells Fargo name. Its management philosophy allowed it to help grow the West's new agricultural, film, and aerospace businesses. While remaining faithful to its history, Wells Fargo continued to add modern banking features such as automated banking, drive-up tellers, and phone access. It also expanded services to include express lines, credit cards, and online banking.

On 31 December 2008, Wells Fargo acquired Wachovia, one of America's largest financial service providers, after a government-forced sale of Wachovia to avoid a complete failure. Wells Fargo did accept US$25 billion "bailout" money from the US government to cover Wachovia's losses. These losses were due to failing mortgages mostly linked to its 2006 acquisition of Golden West Financial. The Wachovia purchase, at only US$7 a share, was pennies on the dollar even considering the government financial support Wells Fargo took on. After the merger, Wells Fargo became the fourth largest bank in the US by assets, after Bank of America, JP Morgan Chase, and CitiGroup.[iii]

After the acquisition of Wachovia, Wells Fargo now has locations in over 130 countries around the world.[iv] It is represented in 36 European countries and has been increasing its presence in emerging economies, especially the BRIC countries (Brazil, Russia, India, and China). In 2007, it teamed with HSBC to launch cross-border lending in China.[v] In 2006, it set up two offices in India to expand its technology and business processes.[vi] In 2000, it acquired National Bank of Alaska to enter the Russian markets.[vii] In Brazil, Wells Fargo now has four offices open in Sao Paulo, Rio de Janeiro, Sao Bernhard do Campo, and Joinville.[viii]

Industry Environment

The Financial Crisis

The finance industry has been on a rollercoaster ride since 2005; financial institutions have experienced huge earnings and major revenue loss. Since February 2007, the industry has been the focus of ire and blame for the world's economic recession. In 2008 when the credit crisis hit the industry hard, almost all companies in the industry had declined revenue growth. The massive loan loss write-down

as a result of the credit crisis caused the industry to contract overall by 25% between 2007 and 2009. Through US federal bailouts for the "too big to fail" banks and the collapse of over 200 small, middle, and large sized banks in the US alone,[ix] the landscape of the finance industry has changed drastically.

Because of the severity of the financial collapse in the US, the finance industry is seeing more supervision than ever before. In July 2010, the US Congress passed the most sweeping set of changes to the financial regulatory system since the 1930s, ending more than a year-long effort to pass legislation in response to the 2008 financial crisis. The bill aims to strengthen consumer protection, rein in complex financial products and head off more bank bailouts.[x]

As consumer confidence slowly increases and investors have begun purchasing the common stocks of major US banks, the finance industry seems to be on the way to recovery. From 2010 to 2015, industry revenue is expected to increase 6.6% annually, and the market should experience much less volatility with regulation changes.[xi] The big banks are under tighter government control but continue to benefit from government support and try to diversify their products so as to be more competitive. Overall, it will likely take some time for the finance industry to recover and to reestablish clarity on consumer confidence and employment. The surviving banks are in a long transitional period from survival mode to growth mode.

Competition

The finance industry is competitive and increasingly so. Due to mergers and bankruptcies, particularly in 2009, the number of participants in the industry has declined. As a result, the ten largest commercial banks have captured almost 40% of the market share in the US. This figure is expected to further increase with market recovery. The top five financial institutions in the US include Bank of America, J.P. Morgan Chase, CitiGroup, Well Fargo, and PNC Financial Services.

Bank of America, one of the world's largest financial institutions, operates in all 50 states and in over 40 foreign countries. It serves about 59 million consumers and small business. It is also one of the world's largest wealth management companies and employs roughly 20,000 financial advisors with

$2.5 trillion in assets. After the purchase of Merrill Lynch in 2008, Bank of America became one of the largest financial service firms. With all these factors, the company has more cost advantage over other competitors.

Bank of American generates revenues through all different financial sectors. It managed to increase revenue by 33% in 2009 and expects to see an additional 6.7% increase in 2010. Throughout the years, the company has gone through several major mergers and acquisitions to maintain its leading position. The notable ones are ABN, FleetBoston, Countrywide and Merrill Lynch.

Like other financial companies, Bank of America was hit hard by the crisis and received $45 million from the government in bailout money. But it was the second of the big four players to repay its funding, indicating an increased confidence of surviving without help from the government. Despite the financial trouble with Merrill Lynch, Bank of America is starting to regain traction in its recovery. There are plenty of businesses within the bank that could bounce back after the current recession is over.

JP Morgan Chase, one of the largest financial institutions in the world, operates over 5,100 branches, including 2,322 branches added after the acquisition of Washington Mutual. JP Morgan Chase is a diversified bank. Its revenue is divided among several different sectors including investment banking, retail financial services, card services, commercial banking, treasury & security service, and asset management and corporate. The company's comprehensive list of products puts it in a leading spot.

JP Morgan Chase has managed to experience steady revenue increases from 2007 through 2009 despite the recession. It had a total of $38.4 billion revenue in 2009, a 35.7% increase from 2008. Its strong balance sheet enabled it to attract customers and gain the top position in every major investment banking business in 2009. As a result of its strong financial position, JP Morgan Chase was one of the first financial institutions allowed to repay Troubled Asset Relief Program (TARP) funds.

Similar to Bank of America and Wells Fargo, JP Morgan Chase grew through external acquisition during the recession. The two major purchases are Bear Stearns in 2008 and Washington Mutual in 2009. The latter acquisition in particular gave JP Morgan Chase a huge revenue boost.

Even though JP Morgan Chase has its hands full dealing with all the problem assets from Bear Stearns and Washington Mutual, in addition to its own troubled assets, it has a better chance to continue to outperform its competition due to its strong balance sheet.

Citigroup, Inc has the world's largest financial services network, spanning 140 countries with approximately 16,000 offices worldwide. The company employs about 300,000 personnel globally and holds more than 200 million customer accounts. Citigroup operates through four major business groups: consumer banking, global wealth management, global cards and institutional client groups.

Compared to its competitors, Citigroup suffered the most during the financial crisis. Due to huge exposure to toxic mortgages, the company suffered heavy losses and received a massive bailout from the US government. It had negative 2.1% revenue growth in 2008 and negative 5% growth in 2009. In addition to poor financial performance, the acquisitions by Bank of America, Wells Fargo and JP Morgan Chase have severely hurt Citigroup's market share.

PNC Financial Services is the fifth largest bank in the US and the third largest provider of off-premise ATMs in the US. The company manages approximately $290 billion in assets, has over 2,600 branches all over the country and employs about 60,000 workers across the US and abroad. PNC's total earnings increased from $215 million in 2008 to $1.2 billion in 2009, which reflects the acquisition of National City. Provision for credit losses was $1.6 billion in 2009, an increase of $1 billion from 2008. This was mainly driven by real estate, middle market, and the National City acquisition.

PNC's strategy of focusing on risk management has served it well in recent years. It has avoided most of the troubles in subprime mortgages and other high-risk loans. The company maintains a moderate risk profile with a diverse portfolio of commercial, mortgage, home equity, and real estate loans. PNC's latest strategy of cutting expenses and its ability to mark down a large portion of National City's loans has helped the company to save on costs, but its exposure to commercial real estate and business loans will probably continue to create problems in the later stages of the recession and recovery.

A Community Bank

Custom Centricity

Wells Fargo says, "If you find one trusted provider that can satisfy all your financial services needs and save you time and money, why not bring all your business to that trusted provider?"[xii] The company bases its business development on this premise. It tries to satisfy all its customers' financial needs, make it easy for them to arrange financial transactions, and allow them a volume discount.

Wells Fargo has a two-pronged strategy. The first employs its national scope and depth of technology utilization to form a better understanding of its customer investment preferences, which enables it to cross-sell existing products to its current customer base. Furthermore, Wells Fargo expects to grow via the good will it has created and the networking element of loyal customers.

The second strategy is to continuously develop its reputation as a sustainable, trustworthy financial services provider. By maintaining close ties with customers, Wells Fargo is able to keep them on in the face of growing global competition. The company leverages its size and national reach to provide new financial products and better delivery systems. It hopes to maintain the friendly, community bank feeling in an increasingly globalized and impersonal marketplace.

Products

Wells Fargo products include banking, insurance, trust and investments, mortgage banking, investment banking, retail banking brokerage, and consumer finance.[xiii] It offers these products through banking stores, the Internet and other distribution channels in all 50 states of the US. These products cover three different operating segments at Wells Fargo—Community Banking, Wholesale Banking, and Wealth, Brokerage and Retirement.

The company understands that one product does not cater to every customer, so it creates many different vehicles that will meet the needs of every different type of customer at every different stage of his life. Due to the large value of assets under management, as well as the large volume of deposits that it holds, Wells Fargo maintains an economy of scale advantage over small and midsized banks. It is able to offer customers lower rates on loans and higher yields on investments, which further adds to its customer base.

Community Banking is by far the largest source of Wells Fargo's revenues, accounting for 71% of its 2009's total revenue. This segment includes Regional Banking, Diversified Products and the Consumer Deposits groups, as well as Wells Fargo Customer Connection (formerly Wells Fargo Phone Bank and Wachovia Direct Access). Wells Fargo has accounts where the minimum opening deposit is as little as $100 and there are no monthly fees as long as the account is set up with direct deposit or there is a minimum of $1,000 in the account. These accounts are targeted towards the lower net value customers.

Well Fargo's loan services include auto loans, mortgages, home equity loans, and loans for those with less than perfect credit (a service where customers can refinance existing debt that they already have).

The company also offers various insurances such as auto insurance, rental insurance, homeowner insurance, identity and credit theft insurance, life insurance, health insurance, pet insurance, and long-term care insurance for individuals to protect against the downside of bad health. In addition, it offers business owner insurance and workers' compensation.

Wells Fargo's investing services include planning for retirement, children's education and other financial goals. It also takes advantage of America's two major demographic changes—an aging population and a racially more diverse population, and tries to serve the two groups better. Its Elder Services program helps retiring baby boomers with healthcare management, financial management, legal matters, and everyday matters.[ix] The company has won awards and recognition for this program from the American Society on Aging. It has also created Team Networks to better understand the cultures and the market of minorities. These networks include Amigos (Hispanic), Asian Connection, Arab Americans, Employees with Disabilities, Checkpoint (Afro-American), Native Peoples, PRIDE (Gay, Lesbian, Bisexual, and Transgender), and Persian American Connection.

With such a wide range of offerings at hand, Wells Fargo tries to cross sell its products to expand the number of products to which its current customers have access, gain new customers in extended markets, and increase market share with many businesses. With an aim of having an average of eight products per customer, it averaged 5.95 products per customer in 2009, while Wachovia had 4.65 products per customer. Wells Fargo believes there is untapped potential by increasing cross-sale opportunities with the Wachovia retail bank. In the meantime, only one out of every five of Wells Fargo's banking customers has a mortgage with the institution; only one-third of its mortgage customers have a banking relationship. Wells Fargo wants to make each one of its banking customers a mortgage customer, and vice versa.[xiv]

Technology

Wells Fargo sees its technology as one of its strengths and uses it to personalize services. Advanced technology allows the company to keep accurate information about account balances, transaction history, and life events. This helps Wells Fargo predict which products its customers will need at various times so that it can provide better services.[xv]

Wells Fargo offers banking through all electronic channels including Quicken, Money, Prodigy and the Internet. The company launched its mobile banking services in October 2007. At the time, customers could only sign up for the service online and only utilize the service through text messaging. Since February 2010, Wells Fargo has updated its technology to allow customers to sign up for mobile banking through text messaging in order to gain access to customers who have smartphones, but who have yet to take to online banking. Wells Fargo is the first large bank to offer enrollment to mobile banking services through text messaging and is the only one of the five largest US banks to earn a gold rating for the Javelin Mobile Banking scorecard for features, access channels, and marketing through mobile banking services.[xvi] The next step will be to offer alerts such as overdraft alerts or check and deposit clearing alerts.

Social Responsibility

Wells Fargo believes it is important to act ethically and with integrity towards all customers, employees, vendors and stockholders because it reflects upon the company. It has a team member code of ethics and business conduct for all employees to follow. The team member code covers topics such as confidentiality, conflict of interest, insider trading, and sales incentive plans, and this is stated in writing with no gray area.

Wells Fargo also believes that if the communities are doing well, then its business will do well in turn. Its goal is to turn philanthropy into strength and reap the rewards by gaining customers.[xvii] In 2008 alone, it donated $226 million to nonprofit organizations and educational institutions that address community needs. Its philosophy is to listen to local residents because they know what the community needs.

To help Wells Fargo build a strong reputation, management has launched a goodwill program. The company gives an average of $618,000 per day back to the local communities it serves.[xviii] Employees of Wells Fargo give over 1.4 million volunteer hours to charities. This charitable giving and social goodwill encompasses the areas of education, human services, community development, arts and culture, civic services, and environmental issues. Wells Fargo is also environmentally conscious. It eliminated the use of envelopes at ATM machines, which saved more than 30 million envelopes over a two-year period.[xix]

Finance

Wells Fargo aims to maintain a strong balance sheet and have a conservative financial position measured by asset quality, accounting policies, capital levels, and diversity of revenue sources.[xx] Its total revenue grew at 61.25%, from $34,898 million in 2008 to $56,274 million in 2009 (see **Appendix 1**). This mainly is attributed to the acquisition of Wachovia, which was completed at the end of 2008. Community Banking, a growth area for Wells Fargo for many years, is where the company draws the most income. In 2009, 72% of Wells Fargo's revenue came from this segment alone. Wholesale Banking accounts for 21%, while Wealth, Brokerage and Retirement earns about 6% (see **Appendix 2**).[xxi]

The Wachovia acquisition also affected Wells Fargo's net income. The net income for the quarter ending December 2009 was $2,823 million compared to negative $2,734 million for the same quarter in 2008—a greater than 200% increase (see **Appendix 3**). Overall, the net income for 2009 increased to $12,275 million, up from $2,655 million in 2008.

Wells Fargo faces significant credit losses, however. In 2007, its overall credit loss grew over 120% from the 2006, and in 2008 that number went up another 220%, followed by an additional 36% in

2009 (see **Appendix 4**). On a positive note, its elevated profits were able to cover the increasing credit losses by more than two times.

The company's long-term debt fell from $267,158 million in 2008 to $203,861 million in 2009 (see **Appendix 5**). In 2009, Wells Fargo repaid $25 billion to the US Treasury for its TARP funds.

Marketing

Amidst all the financial scandals of recent times, investors are hesitant to trust advisors with their money. Wells Fargo's goal is to help customers become personally accountable for their own financial well-being by assisting them define their goals and then develop a plan that will lead to achieving those goals.[xxii]

Wells Fargo stresses in its promotional campaigns that its products "make everyday life easier." It pushes this slogan within all services, from checking accounts to investing, to mortgages. In June 2008, Wells Fargo began running its first ever national print advertisement campaign in publications like *The Wall Street Journal*, *The Economist*, and *The New York Times*.[xxiii] These campaigns targeted wealthy clients to highlight their relationship with Wells Fargo advisors and to create brand awareness.

In June 2009, it launched a new campaign[i] themed, "With you When," that featured both Wells Fargo and Wachovia brand identities. The idea is to show how Wells Fargo can help customers throughout the course of their lives, such as getting married, retiring, and starting a business.[xxiv]

Challenges after the Financial Crisis

Credit Rating

Wells Fargo has a stellar reputation with investors. Although the company's credit rating was lowered to AA- in light of 2008 financial crisis,[xxv] it was the only US bank to earn Moody's highest credit rating in 2007. The company's strong credit rating has made it attractive to customers (see **Appendix 6**). Its ability to attract low-cost deposits has allowed it to borrow more cheaply than the government during the financial crisis.

Yet, the company's good credit rating is not to be taken for granted. The biggest challenge Wells Fargo faces is that it has to deal with an increasing number of bad commercial and consumer loans. A large majority of these loans came from the 2008 acquisition of Wachovia. These loans were the primary reason why Wells Fargo had to take the $25 billion bailout money from the federal government. Even though it has repaid the federal loan in full, the quarterly write-offs due to these loans have continued. First quarter 2010 results show that nonaccruing loans increased 11% over the last quarter, while other major banks have reported decreasing numbers of non-accruing loans.[xxvi] If the trend continues, Wells Fargo will become less attractive to investors than its competitors, which will result in falling share prices.

Diversified Products

Striving to be the best in community banking, Wells Fargo offers a comprehensive range of products with a strong national backing and global reach. If the company continues on its stated path to "meet all of its customers' financial needs," it may leave itself open to smaller, more focused companies picking off its valued customers.

In the first quarter of 2010, Wells Fargo's net income from Community Banking fell 25% from the previous year. Over the same period, its net income from Wealth, Brokerage, and Retirement also plunged by 60%, despite Wells Fargo stated initiative to be the most respected wealth, brokerage, and retirement service in the US. In addition to its 10,000 stores in North America (see **Appendix 7**), Wells Fargo also has many establishments in other regions it has to oversee. Developing a sound global strategy is compelling if the company wishes to maintain a leading edge over its competition.

In improving its overall business lines by being all things to all customers, Wells Fargo is in the danger of loosing focus. By trying to gain market share through diversified product portfolio, it exposes itself to more risks and competition. Resource allocation and investing in R & D may also be challenging with limited capital. A lack of clear focus would make it more difficult for Wells Fargo to gain or maintain the number one position for its products, especially during a recession. These are serious concerns that Wells Fargo cannot overlook.

Wall Street Reform

In July 2010, the US Congress enacted sweeping financial reform legislation intended to avert another future financial crisis. The US government now has the power to shut down and liquidate any financial institution that could threaten the entire financial system. This legislation would also establish a Consumer Financial Protection Bureau inside the Federal Reserve that could write new rules to protect consumers from unfair or abusive practices in mortgages and credit cards. It creates a new council of regulators, lead by Treasury, that would set new standards for how much cash banks must keep on hand to prevent them from ever triggering a financial crisis. It regulates credit default swaps and derivatives to only being traded over exchanges or clearinghouses to fix the problem of not being able to effectively price these instruments.[xxvii]

Although the regulation changes the playing field in the banking industry, it does so to all companies in the industry. Therefore this could be an opportunity for Wells Fargo to become innovative in its financial products and to use its relatively strong positioning within the industry to grab market share from the other banks. While Wells Fargo did take "bailout" money from the government, the money was mostly to cover the losses of Wachovia.

Wachovia's losses were due to failing mortgages mostly linked to its 2006 acquisition of Golden West Financial.

The threat is that the new legislation may limit growth potential for a large bank like Wells Fargo. Large banks could be forced to sell off or spin off several of their businesses in order to comply with federal regulations. They might lose their economies of scale advantage over small and medium sized banks. How Wells Fargo can succeed in this increasingly regulated yet highly competitive industry is an open question.

Appendix 2   Distribution by Operating Segment

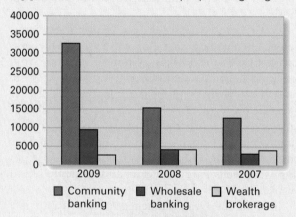

Source: Wells Fargo Annual Report 2009

Appendix 1   Revenues per Quarter

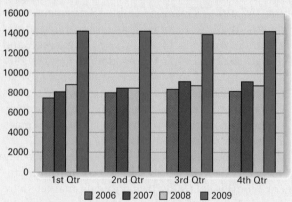

Source: Wells Fargo Annual Report 2009

Appendix 3 Net Income per Quarter

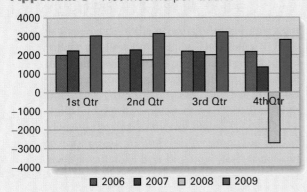

■ 2006   ■ 2007   ☐ 2008   ■ 2009

Source: Wells Fargo Annual Report 2009

Appendix 4 Quarterly Credit Losses

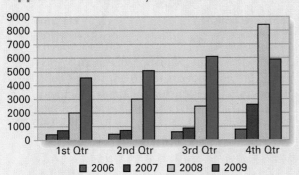

■ 2006   ■ 2007   ☐ 2008   ■ 2009

Source: Wells Fargo Annual Report 2009

Appendix 5 Other Financial Info

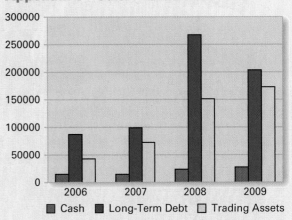

■ Cash   ■ Long-Term Debt   ☐ Trading Assets

Source: Wells Fargo Annual Report 2009

Appendix 6 Five-Year Performance Graph

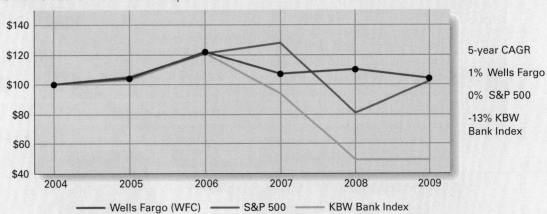

5-year CAGR

1% Wells Fargo

0% S&P 500

-13% KBW Bank Index

——— Wells Fargo (WFC)   ——— S&P 500   ——— KBW Bank Index

Source: Wells Fargo Annual Report 2009

Appendix 7 North America's most extensive network of financial services

Stores
10,000
state by
state (map)

ATMs
12,363

wellsfargo.com
16.7 million
active users

Wells Fargo
Phone Bank
500+ million
customer
contacts
a year

Newfoundland 5

Quebec 23

Ontario 47

Manitoba 5

Saskatchewan 5

Alberta 14

British Columbia 21

Prince Edward Island 2

New Brunswick 6

Nova Scotia 10

Maine 9

Massachusetts 76

Rhode Island 12

Connecticut 114

New Jersey 423

Delaware 34

Maryland 148

D.C. 44

Vt. 8

N.H. 21

New York 234

Pennsylvania 446

Virginia 396

W. Virginia 36

North Carolina 463

South Carolina 198

Georgia 384

Florida 892

Ohio 118

Kentucky 31

Tennessee 77

Alabama 195

Mississippi 38

Michigan 88

Indiana 103

Illinois 173

Wisconsin 122

Minnesota 273

Iowa 115

Missouri 82

Arkansas 33

Louisiana 44

North Dakota 42

South Dakota 67

Nebraska 79

Kansas 41

Oklahoma 38

Texas 1,001

Montana 65

Wyoming 39

Colorado 269

New Mexico 119

Mexico 2

Idaho 118

Utah 171

Arizona 370

Washington 255

Oregon 186

Nevada 166

California 1,615

Hawaii 7

Alaska 68

Puerto Rico 3

Source: Wells Fargo 2009 Annual Report

Endnotes

i https://www.wellsfargo.com/about/history/adventure/since_1852

ii https://www.wellsfargo.com/about/history/adventure/modern_times

iii http://www.ffiec.gov/nicpubweb/nicweb/top50form.aspx

iv https://wfis.wellsfargo.com/ProductServices/A%20to%20Z/WellsFargoGlobalBrokerNetwork/

v https://www.wellsfargo.com/press/20070502_tradebank

vi http://www.naukri.com/gpw/wellsfargo/index.htm

vii http://www.allbusiness.com/marketing-advertising/segmentation-targeting/1061261-1.html

viii https://wfis.wellsfargo.com/ProductServices/A%20to%20Z/WellsFargoGlobalBrokerNetwork/WWNetwork/SouthAmerica/Brazil/Pages/default.aspx

ix http://www.fdic.gov/bank/individual/failed/banklist.html

x http://money.cnn.com/2010/07/15/news/economy/Wall_Street_reform_bill_vote/index.htm

xi http://www.netadvantage.standardpoor.com.ezp.bentley.edu/NASApp/NetAdvantage/index.do

xii https://www.wellsfargo.com/invest_relations/vision_values/3

xiii https://www.wellsfargo.com/downloads/pdf/invest_relations/wf2009annualreport.pdf

xiv https://www.wellsfargo.com/invest_relations/vision_values/9

xv https://www.wellsfargo.com/invest_relations/vision_values/4

xvi http://www.javelinstrategy.com/blog/2010/02/06/wells-fargo%E2%80%99s-mobile-banking-tosses-away-the-crutch-of-online-only-enrollment/

xvii https://www.wellsfargo.com/about/csr/charitable/where

xviii Ibid.

xix http://adobe.americanbanker.com/index.php?option=com_content & view=article & id=19

xx https://www.wellsfargo.com/invest_relations/vision_values/5

xxi Wells Fargo 2009 Annual Report

xxii Ibid.

xxiii http://www.iiwealthmanagement.com/articleFree.aspx?ArticleID=1945459

xiv http://charlotte.bizjournals.com/charlotte/stories/2009/06/01/daily9.html

xv The Standard & Poor's rating scale is as follows, from excellent to poor: AAA, AA+, AA, AA−, A+, A, A−, BBB+, BBB, BBB−, BB+, BB, BB−, B+, B, B−, CCC+, CCC, CCC−, CC, C, D. Anything lower than a BBB− rating is considered a speculative or junk bond.

xvi http://www.washingtonpost.com/wp-dyn/content/article/2010/04/21/AR2010042101634.html

xvii http://money.cnn.com/2010/07/15/news/economy/Wall_Street_reform_bill_vote/index.htm

CASE 5

Staples

Charles W.L. Hill
University of Washington

Introduction

It was 1985, and a 36-year-old retailer called Tom Stemberg was being interviewed by the CEO of the Dutch based warehouse club, Makro, for the top job at Makro's nascent U.S. operation. Stemberg didn't think Makro's concept would work in the United States, but he was struck by one thing as he toured Makro's first U.S. store in Langhorne, Pennsylvania, office supplies were flying off the shelves. "It was obvious that this merchandise was moving very fast," he later recalled, "That aisle (where the office supplies were located) was just devastated."[1] Stemberg began to wonder whether an office supplies supermarket would be a viable concept. He though it might be possible that a supermarket selling just office supplies could do to the office supplies business what Toys"R"Us had done to the fragmented toy retailing industry, consolidate it and create enormous economic value in the process.

Within a year Stemberg had founded Staples, the first office supplies supermarket. Twenty-five years later Staples was a leading retailer in the office supplies business with 1900 stores in the United States and Canada, and another 380 internationally. Its revenues for 2010 were $24.5 billion and net profit was $882 million. Although the company had performed well for most of its history, the 2008–2011 period proved to be challenging as demand fell in the face of a sharp economic pullback following the 2008–2009 global financial crisis. The period was characterized by intense price competition between Staples and its rivals, which depressed profitability. In 2010, Staples' return on invested capital stood at 9.34%. While respectable, it was down significantly from the 17–18% it had earned in 2005–2007. Nevertheless, Staples still had the best operating margins in the industry.[2]

The Founding of Staples

Tom Stemberg

Despite his young age, by 1985 Stemberg had assembled an impressive resume in retailing. Stemberg had been born in Los Angeles but spent much of his teens in Austria, where his parents were originally from. He moved back to the United States to enter Harvard University, ultimately graduating with an MBA from Harvard Business School in 1973. Stemberg was hired out of Harvard by the Jewel Corporation, which put him to work at Star Market, the company's supermarket grocery division in the Boston area.

Henry Nasella, Stemberg's first boss at Jewel, who would later work for Stemberg at Staples, remembers meeting Stemberg on his first day at Jewel: "He came in 15 minutes late, his hair too long, his tie over his shoulder, his shirt hanging out over the back of his pants. I thought, what in the world do I have here?"[3] (Stemberg is still known for his disheveled appearance). What he had was a man who started out on the store floor, bagging groceries, stocking the aisle, and ringing up sales at the checkout counter. Stemberg rose rapidly, however, and by the time he was 28 he had been named Vice President of Sales and Marketing at Star Market, the youngest VP in the history of the Jewel Corporation.

At Jewel, Stemberg became known as an aggressive marketer, competing vigorously on price and introducing generic brands (Stemberg developed and launched the first line of "generic" foods sold in the country).[4] According to Stemberg, "It was a nutso thing we were trying to do, and the fact that it worked out well was a miracle. We opened all these big stores, and we were trying to take market share away from people who were much better financed than we were. They retaliated and lowered prices. . . . I learned to experience the challenges of rapid growth. There was no better experience to have been through. It taught me the necessity of having infrastructure and putting it in place."[5]

One of the supermarkets that Stemberg found himself battling with was Heartland Food Warehouse, the first successful deep discount warehouse supermarket in the country. Heartland was run by Leo Kahn, one of the country's leading supermarket retailers. Kahn had started the Purity Supreme supermarket chain in the late-1940s, making him one of the founding fathers of the supermarket business. Stemberg and Kahn fought relentless marketing battles with each other. In a typical example of their tussles, at one point Kahn ran ads guaranteeing that his customers would get the best price on Thanksgiving turkeys. Stemberg responded with his own ads promising that Star would match the lowest advertised price on turkeys. Technically that made Kahn's claim incorrect, a point that Stemberg made to the Massachusetts Attorney General's office, who told Kahn to pull his ad.

In 1982, Stemberg left Jewel to run the grocery division of another retailer, First National Supermarkets Inc. To build market share, he decided to take the company into the warehouse food business, imitating Leo Kahn's Heartland chain. Stemberg soon came into conflict with the CEO at First National. As we later admitted, "I probably didn't do a very good job, in a corporate political sense, of making sure he understood the risks in what we were trying to do. The situation was very stressful."[6] In January 1985, things came to a head and Stemberg was fired. It was probably the best thing that ever happened to him.

When Kahn heard that Stemberg had been fired, he quickly got in touch with him. Kahn had just sold his own business for $80 million, and he was looking for investment opportunities. He had developed a great respect for his old adversary and wanted to back him in a new retailing venture. As Stemberg paraphrases it, Kahn said "I want to back you in a business kid, what have you got in mind?"[7] Kahn agreed to put up $500,000 in seed money to help Stemberg develop a new venture opportunity. He also took on the role of mentor, evaluating Stemberg's ideas.

Initially Kahn and Stemberg looked at the business they both knew best, supermarket grocery retailing.

But they were put off by the intense competition now raging in the business, and the high price they would have to pay for properties. At this juncture, Bob Nakasone, then president of Toys"R"Us, stepped into the picture. Nakasone had worked at Jewel alongside Stemberg before moving to Toys"R"Us. It was Nakasone who urged Stemberg to "think outside of the food box." Nakasone told Stemberg that there were more similarities than differences across product categories and that profit margins were much better outside of the grocery business.

While mulling over possible entrepreneurial opportunities, Stemberg continued to explore other options, including working for an established retailer. It was this parallel search that took him down to Makro for a job interview, and it was there that he suddenly realized there was a possible opportunity to be had in starting the Toys"R"Us of office supplies.

The Founding of Staples

Hot on the heels of his trip to Makro, Stemberg started to think about his idea. The first thing was to get a handle on the nature of the market. Stemberg started by asking people if they knew how much they spent on office supplies. In his words: "There was this lawyer I knew in Hartford, which is where I lived then. If ever there was a cheap bastard in this world, he was a cheap bastard. And I said, 'Gee, how much do you spend on office supplies?' He said, 'Oh I don't know, I guess about a couple of hundred bucks a person, 40 people in the office, I bet you we spend ten grand'. I said, 'Do me a favor will you? You've got good records. Go through your records and tell me exactly how much you spend.' He calls me up the next day, 'Son of a bitch, I spend $1,000 apiece! But I'm getting a discount, I'm paying 10% of list.' I said, 'Toys"R"Us' is paying 60% of list.' He says, 'Are you kidding me? You mean I could save like half? I could save like twelve grand?' In his mind, this is the payment on his new Jaguar."[8]

Stemberg began to think that this idea had some potential. He reasoned that people want to save money, and in this case, the money they could save might be substantial, but they didn't even know they were paying too much. Small businesses in particular, he thought, might be a viable target market. While working on the idea, the printer ribbon on his printer ran out. It was a weekend. He drove down to the local office supply store in Hartford, and it was closed. He went to another, but that was also closed. He ended up going to BJ's Wholesale Club, a deep discount warehouse club. BJ's was open, and they sold office supplies at low prices, but the selection was limited and they didn't carry the type of ribbon Stemberg wanted. Stemberg immediately saw the opportunity.

Around the same time, Stemberg went to see another mentor of his, Walter Salmon, who taught retailing at Harvard Business School. Over lunch they discussed the supermarket business and Stemberg's quest. Salmon asked Stemberg if he had thought of applying his retailing skills to a product category that was growing faster than the grocery business and was not well served by modern retailers. Stemberg replied that he had been thinking about office supplies. Salmon's response: "Gee, this is a really big idea."

Scoping out the Opportunity

Stemberg ended up hiring a former teaching assistant of Salmon's for $20,000 to do some basic market research on the industry and validate the market. As he tells the story: "I never forget the night I went to her house and we went through the slide deck. I always want to jump ahead. And she puts her hand on my hand and says, 'Wait, we will walk though it.' She's teasing us! Finally she said it was a $45 billion market growing at 15% per year. And it turns out she was lying. That was actually at the manufacturer level. It was actually more than $100 billion already if you looked at retail. She confirmed that the pricing umbrellas were as big as we thought they were and that small businesses were getting raped the way we had said they were. I was pretty damn excited during the long drive home."[9]

The market growth, it turned out, was being driven by some favorable demographic trends. The United States economy was recovering from the recessions of the late-1970s and early-1980s, and underlying economic growth was strong. A wave of new technology was finding its way into American businesses, including personal computers, printers, faxes, and small copiers, and this was driving demand for office supplies including basic equipment along with consumables from paper and printer ink, to diskettes and copy toner.

The wave of downsizing that had swept corporate America in the early-1980s also had a beneficial side effect—unemployed people were starting their own businesses. The rate of new business formation was the highest in years. There were 11 million small businesses in the country, Stemberg's proposed target market, and the vast majority of which had less than 20 employees. This sector was the engine of job growth in the economy—between 1980 and 1986 small enterprises had been responsible for a net increase of 10.5 million jobs. Many of these new jobs were in the service sector, which was a big consumer of office supplies. Each new white collar job meant another $1,000 per year in office supplies.

Stemberg's research started to uncover an industry that was highly fragmented at the retail level, but had some huge participants. Manufacturers were upstream in the value chain. This was a very diverse collection of companies including paper manufacturers such as Boise Cascade, office furniture makers, manufacturers of pencils, pens, and markets such as the BIC Corporation, companies like 3M, which supplied Post it Notes and a whole lot more besides, office equipment companies from Xerox and Canon (manufacturers of copiers and consumables), and manufacturers of personal computers, printers, and faxes such as Apple, Compaq, and Hewlett Packard.

Then there were the wholesales, some of which were very large, such as United Stationers and McKesson. The wholesalers bought in bulk and sold to business clients and smaller retail establishments, either directly or through a network of dealers. The dealers often visited businesses to collect orders and arranged for delivery. The dealers themselves ranged in scale from small one person enterprises to large firms that sold through central warehouses. Some dealers also had a retail presence, while other did not. Manufacturers and wholesalers would also sell directly to large business through catalogs, or a direct sales presence.

The retailers fell into two main categories. There were the local office supply retailers, generally small businesses, and there were the general merchandise discounters, such as BJ's Wholesale and Walmart. The smaller retailers had an intrinsically high cost structure. They were full service retailers who purchased in small lots and delivered in trucks or sold out of the store. The general merchandise discounters purchased from wholesalers, or direct from manufacturers, and their prices were much lower, but they did not carry a wide range of products.

On the consumer side, most large businesses had dedicated personnel for purchasing office supplies. They either bought from dealers, who purchased directly from manufacturers or through wholesalers, or bought direct from the manufacturer. Large firms were able to negotiate on price and received discounts that could be as large as 80% of the list price on some items. Businesses of fewer than 100 people did not generally have someone dedicated to managing office supplies, and they tended to rely primarily on dealers. For these companies, product availability, not price, was viewed as key. In even smaller firms, it was the convenience of being able to get office supplies that seemed to matter more than anything else.

Consistent with his initial insight, Stemberg found that smaller firms were ignored by the big dealers. To verify this he called Boise Cascade, which operated as both a dealer and a manufacturer, to see what service they might offer. First he called on behalf of Ivy Satellite Network, a small company that Stemberg owned that broadcasted events of Ivy League schools to alumni around the world. Boise couldn't even be bothered to send a catalog to this company. Then, he called Boise again, this time representing the 100 person office of a friend of his who was a food broker. This time Boise was happy to send a representative to the food broker. The representative offered the broker deep discounts. A BIC pen from Boise that cost Ivy $3.68 from the local stationary store was offered for just $0.85. More generally, Stemberg found that while an office manager in a company with more than 1,000 employees could often obtain discounts averaging 50% from dealers, small businesses with fewer than 20 employees were lucky to get a 10% discount and often had to pay full price.[10]

Stemberg also found a study produced by researchers at the Wharton School that seemed to confirm his suspicions. "Essentially they first asked dealers. 'What does the customer want?' Ninety percent of the dealers said, 'Better service' and 10% said, 'other'. Then they asked customers, and 90% of the customers said what they really wanted was lower prices. Ha! The dealers were totally out of touch. They were making 40% to 50%, the wholesalers were making 30%, and the manufacturers were making huge margins. Everybody's rich, fat, and happy, and they're all saying: 'What's wrong with this?'"[11]

Creating the Company

Stemberg knew from experience that for Staples to succeed it would have to execute well and do to that, it needed experienced management. Stemberg turned to people he knew, managers who, like him, had quickly risen through the ranks at the Jewel Corporation or other Boston area retailers. From Jewel came Myra Hart, who was to become Staples' Vice President of Growth and Development, Todd Krasnow, who became Vice President of Marketing, Paul Korian, the Staples Vice President of Merchandising, and Henry Nasella, Stemberg's mentor at Star Market, who subsequently became president of Staples. The CFO was Bob Leombruno, who had brought Mammoth Mart, a failed retail operation, out of bankruptcy for a group of investors. Stemberg took on the CEO role, while Kahn became chairman. Most of these people started working full time on January 1, 1986. They gave up secure jobs, high salaries, and annual bonuses, for a salary cut, loss of bonuses, and 14-hour days.

According to Stemberg, the pitch to prospective managers was this: "I'm going to give you a big chunk of stock in this thing. This is your chance. We're all going to work our tails off. We're going to work crazy hours. But here you'll be part of a retailing revolution. If you own 2% of the company and it gets to be worth $100 million, you're going to make $2 million."[12] In the end, each member of the top management team got a 2.5% stake in the company.

By now Stemberg had a name for this nascent company: Staples. Reflecting upon its evolution years later, he noted: "I'm driving between Hartford and Boston. I'm thinking about names. Pencils? Pens? 8½ by 11? Staples? Staples! Staples the Office Superstore. That was it. The bad thing about the name was that when we started out, we had to explain to everybody what it was. Office Depot basically copied Home Depot and put the 'office' in front. It was Home Depot for the office, and it lived off the Home Depot name. Office Club was a Price Club for the office. It lived off the Price Club name. In the early days ours was actually a problem. But those other names aren't a brand. Ours is a brand."[13]

With the management team in place, the next steps were to refine the concept and raise capital. The concept itself was relatively straightforward, implementing it would not be. The plan was to offer a wide selection of merchandise in a warehouse-type setting with prices deeply discounted from those found in mom and pop retailers. Because it would be a supermarket, the idea was to move from full-service to a self-service format. At the same time, the management team recognized that the staff would need to be trained in office supplies so that they could provide advice when asked.

To make the concept viable, a number of issues had to be dealt with. Where would stores be located? How big a population base would be needed to support a store? What kind of selection was required? How many Stock Keeping Units (SKUs) should the store offer? There was also the problem of educating the customer. If potential customers currently didn't know that they were paying excessive prices for office supplies and consistently underestimated how much they spent on the category, what could Staples do to change this?

To get low prices, Staples would need to cut costs to the bone and be managed very efficiently. They would have to get manufacturers or wholesalers to deliver directly to Staples. How could this be done? Wouldn't wholesalers and manufacturers create channel conflict with dealers and established retailers by delivering straight to Staples? How was this to be resolved? Staples also needed to minimize its inventory, thereby reducing its working capital needs. Management knew that if they could turn inventory over 12 times a year, and delay payment to vendors for 30 days, then vendors would essentially finance Staples' inventory. Pulling that off would require state-of-the-art information systems, and state-of-the-art at the time in office supplies did not include bar coding on individual items. How was Staples to deal with this?

There was also the potential competition to worry about. Stemberg was sure that once Staples unveiled its concept, others would follow quickly. To preempt competitors, the plan called for rapid rollout of the concept, with sales ramping up from nothing to $42 million after 3 years. This would require a lot of capital. It also required that the concept be very easy to replicate so that once the first store was opened, others could be opened in quick succession. This meant that the systems that were put in place for the first store had to be the right ones, and able to support rapid expansion. There wasn't much room for error.

As the management team refined the concept, they came to the realization that the information systems

were one of the keys to the entire venture. With the right information systems in place, Staples could closely track sales and inventory at the level of individual items, figure out its gross profit on each item sold, and adjust its merchandising mix accordingly. This would be a departure from existing retailers, the majority of whom lacked the ability to calculate profit on each item sold and could only calculate the average gross profit across a range of items. The right information systems could also be used to collect data on customers at the point of sales, and this would greatly assist in market research and direct marketing to customers.

On the other hand, raising capital proved to be easier than they thought. Stemberg valued Staples, which was still little more than a concept, a management team, and a business plan full of unanswered questions, at $8 million. He went looking for $4 million, which he would exchange for 50% of the company. The venture capitalists were initially reluctant. They seemed to hold back, waiting to see who would commit first. They also valued Staples at $6 million and wanted a 67% stake for the $4 million in first round financing. Stemberg balked at that, and instead focused his efforts on one firm that seemed more willing to break away from the pack. The firm was Bain Venture Capital, whose managing general partner, Mitt Romney, later observed that: "A lot of retailing startups come by, but a lot of them are a twist on an old theme, or a better presentation . . . Stemberg wasn't proposing just a chain of stores, but an entirely new retailing category. That really captures you attention. It slaps you in the face with the idea that this could be big."[14]

To validate the business concept, Romney's firm surveyed 100 small businesses after being urged to do so by Stemberg. Auditing invoices from these companies for office supplies, Romney discovered what Stemberg already knew—the companies were spending about twice what they estimated. Romney then ran the numbers on his own company and found that his firm would save $117,000 a year by purchasing supplies at the discount that Stemberg promised. That was enough for Romney and he committed to investing. Others followed and Staples raised $4.5 million in its first round of financing, which closed on January 23, 1986. This gave the company enough capital to go ahead with the first store. In return for the financing, Staples had to give the VCs a 54% stake in the company. To get the money, however, Staples had to commit to opening its first store on May 1, 1986, and to meet a plan for rolling out additional stores as quickly as possible.

The First Store

With just four months to open their first store, the management team went into overdrive. They would meet every morning at 7 a.m. in a session that could run from 30 minutes to 2 hours. Someone would rush out to get sandwiches for lunch, and they would keep working. The workday came to a close at 9:00 p.m. or 10:00 p.m. There was no template for what they were doing, and they knew they had to put a system in place that would allow them to quickly roll out additional stores.

One of the most difficult tasks fell on the shoulders of Leombruno, the CFO. In addition to setting up an accounting system, he was put in charge of installing the entire information system for Staples. The system had to be able to track customer purchases so that Staples could reorder products. The cash registers, which were to be connected individually to the system, had to be easy to operate so that there would be no congestion at the checkout stands. Stemberg himself was adamant that the register receipts indicate the list price of each item, as well as a much lower Staples price, and an even lower price for customers who became Staples members. He also wanted the system to collect detailed demographics on each customer.

Leombruno insisted that the system be able to do two things: First, calculate the gross profit margin Staples made on each item sold. Most retailers at the time could only calculate the average profit margin across the mix of inventory. Second, Leombruno wanted to make sure that inventory turned over at least 12 times a year, and good information systems were the key to that. With most vendors requiring payment in 30 days, an inventory turnover of greater than 12 would allow Staples to cut its working capital requirements.

As the wish list for the information systems grew, it soon became apparent that it would not be possible to do everything in the allotted time span. No existing software package did what the management team wanted, and they had to hire consultants to customize existing packages. In the end, several proposed features were dropped. However, at Stemberg's insistence, the three way price requirements remained.

To track sales and inventory levels, Staples assigned a six-digit look-up code for each item. While entering the codes was a slower process than scanning items, most manufacturers in the office supplies business were still not marking their products with bar codes, which meant scanning was not feasible.

Another problem was to get suppliers to ship products to the first Staples store. The company was asking suppliers to bypass the existing distribution system, and risk alienating long time customers in the established channel of distribution. To get suppliers on board, Staples used a number of tactics. One was a visionary pitch. The company told suppliers that they were out to revolutionize the retail end of the industry. Staples would be very big, they said, and it was in the best interests of the suppliers to back the startup. Stemberg's punch line was simple: "I'm going to be very loyal to those who stick their necks out for us. But it's going to cost you a lot more to get in later."[15] Connections also helped to get suppliers to deliver to Staples. One of the VC backers of Staples, Bessemer Venture Partners, also owned a paper manufacturer, Ampad. Bessemer told Ampad to start selling to Staples, which they did, despite that existing distributors bitterly complained about the arrangement.

Finding real estate also presented a problem. As an enterprise with no proven track record, Staples found it difficult to rent decent real estate large enough to stock and display the 5,000 SKUs that it was planning for its first store, and to do so at a decent price. Most landlords wanted sky high rent from Staples. In the end, the best that Staples could do was a site in Brighton, Massachusetts that was within site of a housing project and had failed as a site for several different retailers. The one redeeming feature of the site—it was smack in the middle of a high concentration of small businesses.

Despite all of these problems, Staples was able to open its first store on May 1, 1996. The opening day was busy, but only because everybody who worked at Staples had invited everybody they knew. On the second day just 16 people came through the store. On the third day, it was the same number. A few weeks of this, and Staples would have to shut its doors. Desperate, Krasnow decided to bribe customers to get them into the store. The company sent $25 to each of 35 office managers, inviting them to shop in the store and pass along their reactions. According to Krasnow: "A week later we called them back.

They had all taken the money, but none of them had come into the store. I was apoplectic."[16] In the end, 9 of them finally came in, and they gave Staples rave reviews. Slowly the momentum started to build and by August, lines were starting to form at the cash registers at lunch time.

The 1990s: Growth, Competition and Consolidation

Growth

Staples had set of target of $4 million in first year sales from its Brighton store, but within a few months, the numbers were tracking up toward a $6 million annual run rate. The concept was starting to work. The number of customers coming through the door every month was growing, but it was not only customers that were coming. One day Joe Antonini, the CEO of Kmart, was spotted walking around the Staples store. Around the same time, Stemberg heard from contacts that Staples had been mentioned at a Walmart board meeting. He realized that if other discount retailers were noticing Staples when it had just one store, competition could not be far behind.

Within 5 months of the opening of the first Staples store, a clone had appeared in the Southeast; Office Depot. Needing money to quickly fund expansion and lock in Staples territory, Stemberg went back to the venture capitalists. While the initial backers were only willing to value Staples at $15 million, Stemberg held out for and got a valuation of $22 million, raising another $14 million. He pulled off this trick by finding institutional investors who were wiling to invest on a valuation of $22 million. He then went back to the original VCs and told them that the deal was closing fast, which persuaded them to commit.

By May 1987, Staples had 3 stores open and planed to increase the number to 20 by the end of 1988 (it opened 22). Sales were running at anywhere from $300 to $800 per square foot. In contrast, high volume discount stores were lucky to get $300 per square foot. By mid-1989, 3 years after its first store opened, Staples had 27 stores open in the North East and an annual sales run rate of $120 million, way above the original 3-year target of $42 million. The stores now average 15,000 square feet and stock 5,000 items.

Explaining the success, Stemberg noted that "From a value perspective, I think there is no question that we have been a friend to the entrepreneur. If you look at the average small town merchant, we've lowered the costs of his office products—where he was once paying say $4,000 to $5,000 a year, now he's paying $2,000 or $3,000. We've made him more efficient."[17]

Helping to driving sales growth was the development of a direct marketing pitch. Every time Staples opened a store, it purchased a list of small businesses within 15 minutes driving distance. Then a group of telemarketers would go to work, calling up the buyer of office supplies at the businesses. The telemarketers would tell them Staples was opening up a store like Toys"R"Us for office supplies, ask them how much they spent on office supplies every year (often they did not know), cite typical cost savings at small businesses, and send them a coupon for a free item, such as copy paper. Slowly the customers would come in, but momentum would build up as customers realized the scale of the savings they were getting.

Every time a customer redeemed a coupon at a store, they were given a free Staples Card. This "membership" card entitled cardholders to even deeper discounts on select items. The card quickly became the lynchpin of Staples' direct marketing effort. From, the card application, Staples gathered information about the customer—what type of business they were in, how many employees they had, and where they were located. This information was entered into a customer database and every time a card member used that card, the card number and purchases were logged into the database via the cash register. This gave Staples up to date information about what was being purchased and by whom. This information then allowed Staples to target promotions at certain customer groups—for example, card members who were not making purchases. The goal was to get existing customers to spend more at Staples, a goal that was attained over time.

Because Staples started to reach so many of its customers through direct marketing, (about 80% of its sales were made to cardholders) it was able to spend less on media ads—in some areas it dropped media advertising altogether, saving on costs. This was an important source of cost savings in the North East where the media is expensive.

A problem that continued the bedevil Staples as it expanded was the shortage of good real estate locations that could be rented at a reasonable price, particularly in the Northeast. Finding a good site in the early days required flexibility; at various times Staples converted anything and everything from restaurants to massage parlors into Staples stores. As the company grew, its real estate strategy started to take a defensive aspect, with Staples bidding for prime sites in order to preempt competitors.

The high cost of real estate in the Northeast led Staples to establish its first distribution center in 1987 (today it has 30 such centers in North America) This decision was hotly debated within the company and opposed by some of the investors who thought that the capital should be used to build more stores, but Stemberg prevailed. The distribution center was located off an interstate highway in an area of rural Connecticut where land was cheap. The facility cost $6 million to build and tied up a total of $10 million in working capital, almost $0.29 out of every dollar that the company had raised to that point. But Stemberg saw this as a necessary step. The inventory storage capacity at the distribution center enabled the company to operate with smaller stores than many of its rivals, but still offer the same variety of goods. By 1989, the average Staples store was 35% smaller than the Office Depot outlets that were then opening up all over the Southeast, saving on real estate costs. The distribution center also helped save labor costs, since wages were lower in rural areas. Equally important, inventory storage at the distribution centers allowed the stores to remain fully stocked. A Stemberg noted: "In competition with the clones, it will come down to who has the lowest costs and the best in stock position."[18]

The expansion strategy at Staples was very methodical. Stores were clustered together in a region, even to the extent that they cannibalized each other on the margin, so that Staples could become the dominant supplier in that market. The early focus was on major metropolitan areas such as Boston, New York, Philadelphia and Los Angeles. Although high real estate and labor costs in these areas were a disadvantage, strong demand from local businesses helped compensate, as did the distribution centers. In 1990, Staples open its second distribution center in California to support expansion there.

The expansion at Staples was fueled by the proceeds from a 1989 Initial Public Offering, which raised $61.7 million of capital—enough for Staples to accelerate its store openings. By mid-1991, the Staples store count passed 100.

Competition

A rash of imitators to Staples soon appeared on the market. The first of these, Office Depot, focused on the Southeast. By the end of 1988, Office Depot had 26 stores, Office Club had opened 15, Bizmart had established 10, and OfficeMax had around a dozen. More than a dozen other office supplies superstores had also sprung up. Some of these businesses were financed by venture capitalists looking to repeat the success with Staples, and others were financed by established retailers, or even started by them. For example, Ben Franklin stores started Office Station in 1987, but shut it down in 1989 as it failed to gain traction.

Initially, most of the competitors focused in unique regions—Office Depot on the Southeast, Office Club on California, OfficeMax on the Midwest, Bizmart on the Southwest—but as the number of entrants increased, head-to-head competition started to become more frequent. Stemberg's belief had always been that competition was inevitable and that the winners in the competitive race would not necessarily be those that grew the fastest, but those that executed best. It was this philosophy that underpinned Stemberg's insistence that the company should grow by focusing on key urban areas, and achieving a critical mass of stores served by a central distribution system.

Not everyone agreed with this recipe for success. Office Depot did the opposite—the company grew as fast as possible, entering towns quickly to preempt competitors. Office Depot lacked the centralized distribution systems, but made up for that by locating in less expensive areas than Staples, persuading suppliers to ship directly to stores, and keeping more back up inventory on the premises. Although this meant larger stores, the lower rental costs in Office Depot's markets offset this.

What soon became apparent is that the rash of entrants included a number of companies that simply could not execute. Very quickly a handful of competitors emerged in the forefront of the industry—Staples, Office Depot, OfficeMax, and Office Club. As the market leaders grew, they increasingly came into contact with each other. The result was price wars. These first broke out in California. Staples entered the market in 1990 and initially focused on pricing not against Office Club, but against Price Club. Although Price Club was a warehouse store selling food and general merchandise, it still had the largest share of the office supplies market in California. Staples was positioned to have the same low prices as Price Club, but a wider selection of office supplies and no membership fee.

Todd Krasnow, the Executive VP of Marketing at Staples, describes what happened next: "What we failed to realize was that Price Club was very worried about Office Club—and was pricing against Office Club. So when we went and matched Price Club, we were matching Office Club. And Office Club was saying: 'We are not going to let anybody have the same prices as us'."[19] Office Club lowered its prices, causing Price Club to lower prices, and Staples followed. Not willing to be beat, Office Club cut prices again, and so they continued the spiral down. The price war drove profit margins down by as much as 8%.

Ultimately Krasnow noted: "We realized that by engaging in this price war, we were focusing on our competitors, not our customers. Our customers weren't paying attention to this spat. So we raised our prices a little. You feel like you're just doing absolutely the wrong thing, because your whole position is: We have the lowest price."[20] Be that as it may, Office Club and Price Club followed suit, and prices started to rise again. Ultimately, the three companies carved out different price niches, each unwilling to be undercut on about twenty or so top selling items, but in general, they were not the same items.

What happened in California also occurred elsewhere. When OfficeMax entered the Boston market in 1992, for example, a price war broke out again. There was an unanticipated effect this time though, the price cuts apparently broadened the market by making buying from Staples attractive to customers with between 25 and 100 employees, who previously bought directly from mail order and retail stationers.[21]

Ultimately Kransow noted, price wars such as those that started to break out in California and Boston started to moderate. "We finally realized that it's not in any company's self-interest to have a price war because you can get lots of market share without having a price war. And having a price war among low-priced competitors doesn't get you more market share. It doesn't serve any purpose."[22] Other factors that may have contributed toward more rational pricing behavior in the market were the strong economy of the 1990s, and industry consolidation.

Industry Consolidation

At its peak in 1991, there were 25 chains in the office supply industry.[23] Industry consolidation started when some of the clones began to fall by the wayside, filing for bankruptcy. U.S. Office Supply, the result of a merger between two office supplies chains, filed for bankruptcy in 1991, as did Office Stop. Consolidation was also hastened by acquisitions. In 1991, Office Depot acquired Office Club, giving the primary rival of Staples more than twice the number of stores. Staples then acquired HQ Office Supplies Warehouse in 1991, and in 1992, it purchased another smaller chain, Workplace.[24]

As these trends continued, by the mid-1990s it was apparent that three players were rising to dominance in the industry: Office Depot, Staples, and OfficeMax. By mid-1996, Office Depot led the industry with 539 stores, followed by Staples with 517, and OfficeMax with around 500 stores. In terms of revenues, Office Depot had a clear lead with $5.3 billion in 1996, Staples was second with $3.07 billion, and OfficeMax third with $2.6 billion. Staples remained concentrated in the Northeast and California, with a large number of stores in dense urban areas. Office Depot's stores were concentrated in the South, and the company continued to stay clear of congested cities. OfficeMax was still strongest in the Midwest.[25]

The consolidation phase peaked in September 1996, when Staples announced an agreement to purchase its larger rival, Office Depot, for $3.36 billion. The executives of the two companies had apparently been talking about merger possibilities for years, while continuing to pursue their own independent growth strategies. If the merger went through, Tom Stemberg would step into the CEO role. The two companies sold the merger to the investment community on the basis of cost savings. The combined firm would have almost 1,100 stores and revenues of $8.5 billion. The combination, Stemberg argued, would attain terrific economies of scale that would allow it to significantly lower costs, saving an estimated $4.9 billion over 5 years, including $2.2 billion in product cost savings.

In a move to preempt a possible investigation by the Federal Trade Commission (FTC), the companies claimed that since their stores focused on different territories, the combination would not reduce competition. They also noted that Staples still faced intense competition not only from OfficeMax, but also from the likes of Walmart, Circuit City, and mail order outlets. Stemberg claimed that the combined company would still only account for 5% of the total sales of office supplies in the United States.[26]

The FTC didn't buy the arguments, quickly started an investigation, and, in May 1997, sought an injunction to block the deal. The FTC claimed that the deal would stifle competition and raise prices for office supplies, especially in those markets where the two firms competed head-to-head. To buttress its case, the FTC released a report of pricing data which showed that nondurable office supplies such as paper were 10% to 15% higher in markets where Staples faced no direct rivals. Staples claimed that the FTC's pricing surveys were done selectively and were biased.

In July 1997, a federal judge granted the FTC's request for an injunction to halt the merger. Staples realized that it was in a losing fight and pulled its bid for Office Depot. But the failure had a silver lining— not anticipating much interference from the FTC, Office Depot had put most of its expansion plans on hold, opening just 2 stores in 8 months. In comparison, Staples opened 43, allowing the company to close the gap between it and its larger rival.

Staples' Evolving Strategy

Moving into Small Towns

Stemberg has described Staples' initial strategy to deal with the high costs of doing business in the Northeast as follows: "Establish superstores that were smaller than most, save on rent and operating costs, cluster them in densely populated areas to justify paying for expensive advertisements, and stock the stores from a distribution center."[27] The drawback with this strategy, in retrospect, was that Staples ignored a lot of potentially lucrative markets in smaller towns. While Office Depot was barnstorming into towns with populations of just 75,000, Staples could not see how they made it pay. Surely towns of that size were just too small to support an office supplies superstore?

As it turned out, they were not. Staples mistakenly assumed that a store would serve customers within a 10–15 minute drive. But in smaller cities, customers would drive much further to get good prices. The revelation did not hit home until Staples

opened its first store in Portland, Maine. With a population of 200,000, the town was smaller than most areas on which Staples focused, but within a few months the store was doing very well. To test the hypothesis, in 1992 and 1993, Staples opened stores in a number of smaller towns. The results were surprising. Many of the stores actually generated higher sales per square foot that those located in large cities. Sales were helped by the fact that in many of these small towns the only competitors were small "mom and pop" stationers. Many of these small towns also lacked supermarket electronic retailers, such as Circuit City, selling low-priced office equipment, allowing Staples to pick up a much larger share of that business. Moreover, the lower rent, labor costs, advertising costs and shrinkage made these stores significantly more profitable.

From that point on, Staples moved into small towns and suburban locations, where the same economics apply. Stemberg has described not moving into small towns earlier as "one of the dumbest mistakes I made." In 1994, some 10% of Staples stores were in small towns; by 1998 that figure had risen to 28% and some of the most profitable stores in Staples' network were located in small towns.[28]

Selling Direct

Established as a retailer, Staples initially turned its back on customer requests for delivery and mail or telephone order service. The reason for doing this was simple: Staples saw itself as a low cost retailer, and a delivery service would probably raise costs. However, Staples competitors started to offer mail order and delivery service, and customers continued to ask for this service, so in 1988 Staples began to experiment with this.

Initially, the experimentation was halfhearted. Store managers were not enthusiastic about supporting a delivery service that they believed decreased store sales, and Staples discouraged delivery by tacking a 5% delivery charge onto the order price. Moreover, the company questioned whether it could generate the volume to cover the costs of a delivery service and make a decent return on capital.

What changed this was a study undertaken for Staples by a management consulting firm. The study found that the customers who purchased via a catalog and required delivery were not always the same ones who brought directly from the store. While there was a lot of cross-shopping, the mail order customers tended to be bigger and somewhat more interested in service, whereas those buying from the store were often buying for home offices. Staples also could not help but notice that its major rivals were offering a delivery service, and that business seemed to be thriving.

In 1991, Staples set up an independent business unit within the company to handle the mail/telephone order and delivery service, known as Contract and Commercial. The guts of this business unit was a division know as Staples Direct (it is now called Staples Business Delivery). The man put in charge of this business, Ronald Sargent, would ultimately replace Stemberg as CEO of Staples in 2003.

One issue that had to be dealt with was the potential conflict between Staples Direct and the stores. The stores didn't want to push business the way of Staples Direct because they would not get credit for the sale. As Sargent commented later, "We were like the bad guys inside Staples, because the feeling was that if customers got products delivered they wouldn't shop inside our stores."[29] To align incentives, Staples changed the compensation systems so that (a) the store would get credit if a delivery order was placed through the store and (b) the annual bonus of store employees was partly based on how well they met goals for generating delivery sales.

As Staples Direct started to grow, the company also discovered that the delivery infra-structure they put in place could be used to serve clients in addition to the company's established small business customers, which typically had less than 50 employees. Increasingly, medium-sized businesses (with 50–100 employees), and larger businesses with more than 100 employees started to utilize Staples Direct. To support this new business, Staples started to grow by acquisition, purchasing a number of regional stationary companies with established customers and delivery systems. Typically, Staples kept the owners of these businesses on as Staples employees, often because they had long established relationships with key accounts in large organizations such as Xerox, Ford and PepsiCo. Staples, however, established a consistent product line, brand image, and computer and accounting systems across all of the acquisitions.

Between 1991 and 1996, Staples Direct grew from a $30 million business to almost $1 billion. As sales volume ramped up, Staples was able to get greater efficiencies out of its distribution network, which helped to drive down the costs of doing business through

this channel. Staples used a network of regional distribution centers to hold an inventory of some 15,000 SKUs for delivery, compared to 8,000 SKUs in a typical store. In 1998, a Web-based element was added to Staples Direct, Staples.com. Through the Web or catalog, Staples customers could get access to some 130,000 SKUs, many of which were shipped directly from manufacturers with Staples acting as an intermediary and consolidator.

To continue building the direct business, Staples acquired Quill Corporation in 1988 for $685 million in Staples stock. Established in 1956, Quill ran a direct mail catalog business with a targeted approach to servicing the business products needs of around 1 million small- and medium-sized businesses in the United States. Quill differentiated itself through excellent customer service. Staples decided to let Quill keep its own organization, setting it up as a separate division within the Contract and Commercial business unit, but integrated Quill's purchasing with those of the rest of Staples to gain economies of the input side. Quill now operates under two brands—Staples National Advantage, which focuses upon large multiregional businesses, and Staples Advantage, which focuses upon large- and medium-sized regional companies, and has the flexibility to handle smaller accounts (although these are mostly handled via Staples Direct). In justifying the acquisition of Quill, Stemberg noted that the direct business amounted to a $60 billion a year industry, but it was highly fragmented with the top 8 players accounting for less than 20% of the market.[30]

By 2010, the combined delivery business had grown to represent 40% of total sales, with some 2/3 of the Fortune 100 being counted as customers of Staples delivery business.[31]

Going International

Staples' first foray into international markets occurred in the early-1990s when the company was approached by a Canadian retailer, Jack Bingleman, who wanted to start a Staples-type chain North of the border. Bingleman also approached Office Depot and OfficeMax, but had a preference for Staples because of the close geographic proximity. Board members at Staples initially opposed any expansion into Canada, arguing that scarce resources should be dedicated toward growth in the much larger United States, but Stemberg liked Bingleman's vision and pushed the idea. Ultimately, in 1991, Staples agreed to invest $2 million in Bingleman's startup for a 16% equity stake.

Known as Business Depot, the Canadian venture expanded, rapidly modeling itself after Staples. Between 1991 and 1994, the number of Canadian Business Depot stores expanded to 30 stores and the enterprise turned profitable in 1993. In 1994, Staples announced an agreement to purchase Business Depot outright for $32 million.[32] By 2010, there were 325 stores in Canada.

The Canadian venture was soon followed by investments in Europe. Staples entered the UK market in 1992, partnering with Kingfisher PLC, a large UK retailer that operated home improvement and consumer electronics stores among other things. The Canadian venture had taught Staples that a local partner was extremely valuable. As one Staples executive noted later: "You absolutely cannot do it yourself. There are too many cultural impediments for you to know where the booby traps lie. In a retail startup, the most important task is to generate locations. There's no way a U.S. national can go into any country and generate the real estate it needs. That person will be chasing his tail for a long time."[33]

On the heels of entry into the UK, Staples purchased MAXI-Papier, a German company that was attempting to copy what Staples had done in the United States. This was followed by entry into the Netherlands and Portugal. In late 2002, Staples purchased the mail order business of a French company, Guilbert, for nearly $800 million, which boosted delivery sales in Europe from $50 million a year to $450 million a year almost overnight.[34] In 2008, Staples purchased Corporate Express NV, a Dutch office supplies company with a substantial direct delivery business in Europe. By 2010, Staples had stores in 22 countries outside of North America including 139 stores in the UK, 59 in Germany, 47 in the Netherlands, 35 in Portugal and 28 in China. At this point, some 22% of total sales were generated by the international operations, with half of that total coming from direct delivery and the remainder from retail sales.

Changing the Shopping Experience

By the early-2000s, Staples started to realize that its stores looked very similar to those of its two main competitors, Office Depot and OfficeMax. As the number of markets where all three companies competed grew, head-to-head competition increased. Management then started to look for ways to differentiate their stores from those of competitors. What emerged was a new store design, known as "Dover." The core to "Dover" was a customer centric philosophy known as "Easy." Rolled out across the company in 2005, "Easy" is all about making the shopping experience for customers as easy as possible—through store design and layout, through a merchandising strategy that aims to ensure that items are never out of stock, and through superior in-store customer service. The idea is to help to get the customer in and out of the store as expeditiously as possible.

To execute Easy, Staples has had to redesign its store layout, invest in upgrading the knowledge level of its sales associates, and improve its supply chain management processes.[35] Staples started a big push to improve the efficiency of its supply chain management process in 2003, and that is still ongoing today. Elements of this push include better use of information systems to link Staples with its suppliers and extensive use of "cross-docking" techniques at distribution centers, so that merchandise spends less time in distribution centers. As a consequence of this strategy, Staples has increased inventory turnover, reduced inventory holdings, and improved its in-stock experience for customers.

Staples Today

In February 2002, Tom Stemberg announced that he was stepping down as CEO and passing the baton on to Ron Sargent. Stemberg would remain on as Chairman. Upon taking over as CEO, Sargent put the breaks on store expansion, declaring that Staples would open no more than 75 new stores a year, down from over 130 in 2000. He used the slowdown to refocus attention upon internal operating efficiencies. The product line within stores was rationalized, with Staples cutting back on the stocking of low margin items such as personal computers. He also sets up a task force to look for ways to take every excess cent out of the cost structure. As a result, operating margins at Staples stores came in at 5.9% of sales in 2002, the best in the industry, and up from 4.5% in 2000.

By 2003, Sargent was refocusing on attaining profitable growth for the company. Although by this point Staples, or one of its competitors, operated in all major markets in North America, the company's management decided that Staples was in a strong enough position to go head-to-head with major competitors. In 2005, Staples pushed into Chicago, a market previously served only by Office Depot and OfficeMax, where the company opened 25 stores. The Chicago experience proved to be a pivotal one for Staples. In the words of COO, Mike Miles: "What we found in Chicago was we can come into a two-player market and make it a three-player market successfully. There was a little trepidation about that because the model in the first 10–15 years was that office superstores were interchangeable."[36]

As of 2006, there were still a lot of major markets in North America where Staples lacked a presence, including Houston, Miami, Denver, Las Vegas, St. Louis and Minneapolis. Reflecting on this, Sargent is on record as stating that Staples could more than double its North American network to some 4,000 stores. Commenting on this, he notes: "I don't think Walmart spends a lot of time worrying if Kmart is in the market when they decide to open new stores."[37]

Outside of the retail market, Sargent turned his attention to the business where he made its name, the direct delivery business. He points out that although the number of independent office supplies dealers is down to 6,000 from 15,000 a decade ago, the delivery market is still highly fragmented and very large. Ultimately Sargent believes that direct delivery from warehouses can be as big a business as Staples office supplies stores. He also sees huge potential for growth in Europe, which is the second largest office

supplies market in the world, and still years behind the United States in terms of consolidation.

At the same time, Staples continues to face strategic challenges. Additional expansion by Staples in North America is bringing it into head-to-head contact with Office Depot or OfficeMax. Staples also faces continued competition from Sam's Club and Costco, both of which are focusing on small businesses and continue to sell office supplies. In addition, FedEx Office, which has a nationwide network of 1,000 copying and printing stores, is now offering more office supplies in a new store layout.

The 2008–2009 global financial crisis triggered a deep economic recession in the United States and elsewhere. The U.S. Office Supplies industry was hit by price discounting which, resulting in much slower top-line growth for Staples and a decline in net profit. Sargent responded by cutting back on expansion plans and reducing capital spending going forward. Staples however, continued to be the strongest of the big three office supplies retailers (see Exhibit 1).

Exhibit 1   2010 Financial Performance of the Big 3 U.S. Office Supplies Companies

Company	Revenues	Net profit	ROIC
Staples	$24.5 billion	$882 million	9.34%
Office Depot	$11.6 billion	–$37 million	–5.57%
OfficeMax	$7.15 billion	$71 million	2.86%

Source: Company reports.

Endnotes

1 Stephen D. Solomon, "Born to Be Big," Inc., June 1989, 94.
2 J. MacKay, "Staples Achieves Impressive Operating Margins Relative to Peers Due to Scale Advantages." *Morningstar Research Report*, May 19, 2011.
3 Stephen D. Solomon, "Born to be Big," Inc., June 1989, 96.
4 Tom Stemberg, *Staples for Success*, Knowledge Exchange, Santa Monica, California, 1996.
5 Michael Barrier, "Tom Stemberg Calls the Office," *Nation's Business*, July 1990, 42.
6 Michael Barrier, "Tom Stemberg Calls the Office," *Nation's Business*, July 1990, 44.
7 Ibid.
8 Tom Stemberg and David Whiteford, "Putting a Stop to Mom and Pop," *Fortune Small Business,* October 2002, 39.
9 Tom Stemberg and David Whiteford, "Putting a Stop to Mom and Pop," *Fortune Small Business*, October 2002, 40.
10 Tom Stemberg, *Staples for Success*, Knowledge Exchange, Santa Monica, California, 1996.
11 Tom Stemberg and David Whiteford, "Putting a Stop to Mom and Pop," *Fortune Small Business*, October 2002, 40.
12 Tom Stemberg, *Staples for Success*, Knowledge Exchange, Santa Monica, California, 1996, 17.
13 Tom Stemberg and David Whiteford, "Putting a Stop to Mom and Pop," *Fortune Small Business*, October 2002, 41.
14 Stephen D. Solomon, "Born to be Big," Inc., June 1989, 94 and 95.

15 Tom Stemberg, *Staples for Success*, Knowledge Exchange, Santa Monica, California, 1996, 24.

16 Tom Stemberg, *Staples for Success*, Knowledge Exchange, Santa Monica, California, 1996, 27.

17 Tom Stemberg and David Whiteford, "Putting a Stop to Mom and Pop," *Fortune Small Business*, October 2002, 40.

18 Stephen D. Solomon, "Born to Be Big," Inc., June 1989, 100.

19 Tom Stemberg, *Staples for Success*, Knowledge Exchange, Santa Monica, California, 1996, 97.

20 Ibid.

21 Norm Alster, "Penney Wise," *Forbes*, February 1, 1993, 48–51.

22 Tom Stemberg, *Staples for Success*, Knowledge Exchange, Santa Monica, California, 1996, 97.

23 Renee Covion Rouland, "And Then There Were Three," *Discount Merchandiser*, December 1994, 27.

24 Leland Montgomery, "Staples: Buy the Laggard," *Financial World*, November 9, 1993, 22; Anonymous, "The New Plateau in Office Supplies," *Discount Merchandiser*, November 1991, 50–54.

25 James S. Hirsch and Eleena de Lisser, "Staples to Acquire Archrival Office Depot," *Wall Street Journal*, September 5, 1996, A3.

26 Joseph Pereira and John Wilke, "Staples Faces FTC in Antitrust Showdown on Merger," *Wall Street Journal*, May 19, 1997, B4.

27 Tom Stemberg, *Staples for Success*, Knowledge Exchange, Santa Monica, California, 1996, 128.

28 William M. Bulkeley, "Office Supplies Superstores Find Bounty in the Boonies," *Wall Street Journal*, September 1, 1998, B1.

29 William C. Symonds, "Thinking Outside the Big Box," *Business Week*, August 11, 2003, 62.

30 William M. Bulkeley, "Staples, Moving Beyond Wuperstores, Will Buy Quill for $685 Million in Stock," *Wall Street Journal*, April 8, 1998, A1.

31 J. MacKay, "Staples Achieves Impressive Operating Margins Relative to Peers Due to Scale Advantages," *Morningstar Research Report*, May 19, 2011.

32 Steff Gelston, "Staples Goes on Buying Spree to Acquire Business Depot, National Office Supply Company," *The Boston Herald*, January 25, 1994, 24.

33 Tom Stemberg, *Staples for Success*, Knowledge Exchange, Santa Monica, California, 1996, 90.

34 William C. Symonds, "Thinking Outside the Big Box," *Business Week*, August 11, 2003, 62–64.

35 Mike Troy, "Office Supplies: Staples Positioned as the Architect of 'Easy'," *Retailing Today*, August 7, 2006, 30.

36 Anonymous, "Moving in on Major Markets," *DSN Retailing Today*, May 22, 2006, 10.

37 Ibid.

CASE 6

The Apollo Group (University of Phoenix)

Charles W.L. Hill
University of Washington

Introduction

Which is the largest university system in the United States? After some thought, you might be tempted to answer that it is giant the University of California system with its 11 campuses and 208,000 students. You would be wrong. The largest provider of high education in the United States is the University of Phoenix, which has over 400,000 students, and operates around 200 campuses and learning centers in 39 states. The University of Phoenix is the flagship subsidiary of the Apollo Group, which also runs Western International University, the Institute for Professional Development and the College for Financial Planning. In total, the Apollo Group served some 470,000 students in 2010.

The Apollo Group has been a very successful enterprise. Between 1996 and 2010, its revenues expanded from $214 million to $4.9 billion and net profits increased from $21.4 million to $553 million. The University of Phoenix accounts for about 90% of the revenues of the Apollo Group. Apollo's return on invested capital, a key measure of profitability, averaged around 30% over this period, well above its cost of capital, which has been calculated to be around 10%.[1]

The Apollo Group is also a controversial enterprise. Founded by John Sperling, a former economic history professor and one time union organizer at San Jose State University, the University of Phoenix has been depicted by defenders of the educational establishment as a low quality "diploma mill" that has commoditized education and which is willing to sacrifice educational standards for the opportunity to make profits. Scott Rice, a San Jose State University English Professor who has become a vocal critic of for-profit education, summarizes this view when he states that "John Sperling's vision of education is entirely mercenary. It's merely one more opportunity to turn a buck. When education becomes one more product, we obey the unspoken rule of business: to give consumers as little as they will accept in exchange for as much as they will pay. Sperling is a terrible influence on American education."[2]

Sperling, who was still chairman in 2010 despite being 90 years old, certainly does not see things this way. In his view, the University of Phoenix serves a niche that the educational establishment has long ignored, working adults who need a practical education in order to further their careers, and cannot afford the commitment associated with full-time education. Some high powered academics agree. The Nobel Prize winning economist Milton Friedman regard the triumph of the for-profit sector as inevitable, because traditional universities are run "by faculty, and the faculty is interested in its own welfare."[3]

Some analysts suggest that the for-profit sector still has significant growth opportunities ahead of it. The postsecondary education market in the United States is estimated to be worth over $430 billion, with only $20–$25 billion of that currently captured by for-profit enterprises. Looking forward, analysts expect enrollment at for-profit schools to grow as they gain share from traditional higher educational institutions. Supporting this thesis are estimates that 37% of all students (more than 6 million) are older than 24, a large portion of whom are likely to be working and will be attracted to the flexibility that the for-profit sector provides.[4]

On the other hand, the traditional educational establishment is not blind to this opportunity. Many long established public and private not-for-profit universities are now offering part-time degree programs and online degrees aimed at working adults. Some believe that this emerging threat, coupled with the brand advantage enjoyed by big name universities, will limit enrollment growth going forward at the University of Phoenix and similar institutions.

The outlook for the for-profit sector was further clouded in the late-2000s when the sector was attacked in the media, and in Congress, for aggressive recruiting practices and high drop-out rates. More than 80% of the revenue of for-profit institutions comes from government financial aid. Critics claim that companies in this sector targeted low-income students who were most likely to receive student aid, but who may be ill prepared for course work. Those who do graduate often default their loans, leaving the taxpayer to pick up the bill. In June 2011, the Department of Education issued new regulations that were designed to limit such practices.

John Sperling and the Birth of the University of Phoenix

University of Phoenix founder John Sperling was born in rural Missouri in 1921, in a cabin that already housed a family of six.[5] His mother was overbearing, his father habitually beat him. When his father died, Sperling recalled that he could hardly contain his joy. Sperling barely graduated from high school and went off to join the merchant marine—as far away from Missouri as he could get. There he started his real education, reading through the books of his shipmates, many of whom were socialists. Sperling emerged from this experience an unabashed liberal with a penchant for challenging the status quo—something that he still delights in (among other things, Sperling is a regular financial contributor to ballot initiatives aimed at legalizing marijuana).

After two years in the merchant marine, Sperling went to Reed College in Oregon. This was followed by a Master's at Berkeley and a PhD in Economic History at the University of Cambridge. A conventional academic seemed the logical next step for Sperling. By the 1960s, he was a tenured professor of Economic History at San Jose State University. Always the activist, he joined the American Federation of Teachers (AFT) and rose to state and national positions in the union. In his leadership role at the AFT, he persuaded professors at San Jose State to mount a walkout to support striking professors at San Francisco State University. The strike was a failure and almost resulted in the mass firing of 100 professors. Sperling lost his credibility on campus. He was widely reviled and lost his position as head of the United Professors of California, a union that he had built almost single handedly. But Sperling claims that the humiliating defeat taught him an important

lesson: "It didn't make a goddamn but of difference what people thought of me. Without that psychological immunity, it would have been impossible to create and protect the University of Phoenix from hostility, legal assaults, and attempts to legislate us out of existence."[6]

By the early-1970s, Sperling's academic career was going nowhere—but that was all about to change. As part of a federal project to fight juvenile delinquency, San Jose State University arranged a series of courses for the police and school teachers who had to deal with the youngsters. Sperling, who had been experimenting with novel approaches to delivering education, was to run the workshops. He devised a curriculum, divided the classes into small groups, brought in teachers who were expert practitioners in their field to lead each group (none of whom were professors), and challenged each group to complete a project that addressed the problem of juvenile delinquency.

The student feedback was very favorable. More than that, the enthusiastic participants lobbied him to create a degree program. Sperling sketched out a curriculum for working adults in the criminal justice area and pitched the idea to the Academic Vice President at San Jose State. In Sperling's words, the VP was impressed and sympathetic but utterly discouraging. He told Sperling that the University had its hands full with regular students, and saw no need to create part-time programs for working adults. Moreover, to gain approval, such a program would have to navigate its way through the academic bureaucracy at San Jose, a process that could take several years, and at the end of the day what emerged might significantly differ from Sperling's original proposal due to the input of other faculty members.

Unperturbed by the rejection, Sperling started to cast around for other schools who might want to run the program. He contacted the vice president of development at Stanford University, Frank Newman, who told Sperling that educational bureaucracies were inherently inert and would only innovate if they were in financial trouble. Newman advised Sperling to find a school in financial trouble and persuaded them that the program would make a profit.

The former union organizer immediately saw the value in Newman's suggestion. Left wing he might have been, but Sperling was eager to try out his ideas in the marketplace. He formed a private organization, the Institute for Professional Development, with the mission of making higher education available to the working community. Sperling approached the University of San Francisco, a financially troubled Jesuit school. USF agreed to sponsor the IPD program, using its accreditation to validate the degree. The program was an immediate financial success. Before long, Sperling was contracting with other schools for similar programs. The educational establishment, however, reacted with open hostility to Sperling's for-profit venture. For the first time, but not the last, Sperling was accused of devaluing education and producing a diploma mill. Sperling's sin, in his view, was that his model cut the professors out of the educational equation, and they were not about to let that happen.

Although he had been an academic for years, Sperling had up to this point paid little attention to the process of accrediting institutions and degree programs. What he quickly discovered was legitimacy required that the sponsoring institution for a degree program be accredited by recognized accreditation agencies. In the case of USF, this was the Western Association of Schools and Colleges (WASC) which had jurisdiction over California, along with the California State Department of Education. For the first time, but not for the last, Sperling discovered that these regulatory agencies had enormous power and could destroy the legitimacy of his programs by refusing to grant accreditation to the sponsoring institutions. In Sperling's own words:

> "We had no idea the extent to which education is a highly politicized and regulated activity, not the extent to which innovators were to be searched out and destroyed as quickly as possible by the academics who controlled the institutions and by their allies in regulatory agencies."[7]

What followed was a bitter 5-year battle with Sperling trying to get and maintain accreditation for his programs in California, and politicians, professors, and accreditation agencies blocking him every step of the way. Ultimately, Sperling decided that it would be impossible to fully develop his concepts of education for working adults within the confines of an existing institution. He decided to establish a university of his own. Sperling gave up and moved to Phoenix Arizona, where he though regulators would be more open to his ideas. They weren't. The established state institutions were openly hostile to Sperling's venture. It took more campaigning, which

included an all out media campaign's intensive lobbying of the States legislature, and vitriolic debates in the committee rooms of higher education regulators, before Arizona accredited Sperling's venture in 1978, now named the University of Phoenix. Sperling learned the lesson well—today the Apollo Group maintains a staff of 40 or so political lobbyists whose job it is to get and maintain accreditation.

University of Phoenix Business Model[8]

The University of Phoenix (UOP) is designed to cater to the needs of working adults, who make up 95% of its students. The average age is 36, and until recently the minimum age was 23. The emphasis is on practical subjects, such as business, information technology, teaching, criminal justice, and nursing. In addition to undergraduate degrees, UOP offers several graduate degrees, including Master's degrees in business (MBA), counseling, and nursing. Today some 43% of students at the UOP are enrolled in undergraduate courses, 15% are in Master's programs, 42% are taking 2-year Associate degrees and 1.6% are doctoral students.

The UOP views the student as the customer, and the customer is king. Classes are offered at times that fit the busy schedules of the fully employed—often in the evening. The schedule is year round—there are no extended breaks for summer vacation. Steps are taken to make sure that it is as easy as possible for students to get to classes—one of the golden rules is that there should be plenty of parking, and that students should be able to get from their cars to the classroom in 5 minutes.

UOP campuses lack many of the facilities found in traditional universities. There are no dormitories, student unions, athletic facilities, gymnasiums, research laboratories, extensive network of libraries, and the support staff required for all of these facilities. Instead, the typical campus comprises a handful of utilitarian buildings sited close to major roads.

In designing a university for working adults, Sperling introduced several key innovations. The classes are small with 10–15 students each and are run as seminars. Students usually take just one class at a time. Classes generally meet once or twice a week for 5–9 weeks. The faculty is expected to act as discussion leaders and facilitators, rather than lecturers. They are there to help guide students through the curriculum, and to provide feedback and grading. In addition to classes, students are assigned to 3–5 people groups, called "Learning Teams," which work together on group projects and studying.

Since the mid-1990s, UOP has been relying heavily upon online resources to deliver much of the course content. A typical 5-week undergraduate course with a significant online component would go something like this: students would attend class on campus for 4 hours the first week, giving them a chance to meet the instructor and be introduced to their learning teams and coursework. Weeks 2–4 are completed over the Internet, with homework assignments and participation requirements to be fulfilled. Students return to campus in week 5 for presentations.[9]

Sperling hired working professionals who were looking for part-time employment to teach. In 2005, only 400 of the 21,000 faculty at UOP were full-time. Part-time faculty must have a Master's degree or higher and have had 5 years of professional experience in an area related to the subject they teach. New faculty are subject to peer review by other faculty members, are given training in grading and instructing students, and a teaching mentorship with more experienced faculty members. There is no such thing as academic tenure at the UOP and no research requirements for faculty, full-time or part-time.

Third, the UOP established "ownership" over the curriculum taught in classrooms. In traditional universities, it is the faculty that develops and "owns" the curriculum. This can lead to significant variation in the content offered for the same class when taught by different professors in the same university. The decentralized nature of curriculum development in traditional universities makes it very difficult for the central administration to mandate changes to the curriculum. Moreover, in traditional universities significant curriculum change can take a significant amount of time and energy, involving faculty committees, and in the case of new programs, approval from central administration. In contrast, at the UOP content experts, typically the small number of full time faculty, develop the curriculum. Part-time teachers are then expected to deliver this standardized curriculum. This centralization allows UOP to have a uniform curriculum and to rapidly include new material in a curriculum and roll it out system

wide if the need arises. When designing the curriculum, the UOP solicits input from students 2 years after graduation and from employers who hire UOP graduates.

The centralization of curriculum has also enabled UOP to challenge the publishers of traditional textbooks. The UOP contacts authors directly and contracts with them to develop course materials exactly to their specifications, cutting textbook publishers out of the loop. The goal is for all UOP programs to use customized materials that exist entirely in digital form. Today, nearly all UOP students get course materials and resources digitally through the company's resource Internet portal. This eliminates the need for textbooks and is a source of added profit for the UOP. The cost to the student is roughly $60 a course (for undergraduates), while the cost to UOP is about $20.[10]

The contrast between UOP and traditional not-for-profit universities is stark. At the undergraduate level, traditional universities focus on 18–25 year olds who are engaged in full-time education. They have high labor costs due to the employment of full-time faculty, the majority of who have Doctoral degrees. Newly minted professors straight out of a doctoral program often command high starting salaries—as much as $120,000 a year plus benefits in some disciplines such as business. Faculty members are given low teaching loads to allow them to focus on research, which is the currency of the realm in academia. Research output is required for tenure in the "publish or perish" model of academia adopted by traditional universities.

Although the knowledge produced by research faculty can be and often is socially and economically valuable, the research culture of these knowledge factories translates into a high cost of instruction. At the University of Washington, for example, one of the nation's premier research institutions, 3,900 full-time faculty educated 40,000 students in 2005. The average faculty salary was $76,951 for the 9 months of the academic year, which translated into an instructional cost of around $300 million. In contrast, the part-time faculty at the UOP are inexpensive. In 2005, the 21,000 faculty at the Apollo Group were paid $195 million, or roughly $9,200 each—and this to instruct 307,400 students. In addition, student, faculty, and research facilities dramatically increase the capital intensity of traditional universities, while their attendant staff increases the labor costs.

As a consequence of these factors, the total costs of running a traditional university are much higher than at the UOP. At the University of Washington, for example, total operating expenses in 2004–2005 were $2.7 billion, compared to $1.53 billion at the Apollo Group.[11] According to one estimate, the average *cost to the institution* of educating an undergraduate student for 2 semesters at a public university is around 2 1/2 times greater than that at a for-profit institution such as the UOP. At a private institution, it is more than 3 times greater.[12] It is the inherently low cost structure of the UOP that allows the Apollo Group to make its high profits.

Naturally, such comparisons ignore the fact that the mission of many traditional universities such as the University of Washington is fundamentally different from that of the University of Phoenix. The UOP produces zero new knowledge, whereas the nation's research universities have been and will continue to be major producers of the knowledge that underlies technological progress and economic growth.

On the revenue side, estimates suggest that in 2005 it cost around $22,500 to get an Associate degree at UOP, $51,000 for a Bachelor's degree, and $22,932 for a Master's degree (costs vary by program).[13] Students attending the UOP rely heavily upon Federal Assistance Programs to help pay for their college education. Some 85% of students at the UOP in 2010 received financial aid under Title IV programs from the U.S. Department of Education. To be eligible for Title IV funding, a student has to be registered at an institution that is accredited by an agency recognized by the Department of Education and enrolled in a program with at least 30 weeks of instructional time and 24 credit hours.

In addition to Title IV financial aid programs, some 45% of UOP students had some form of tuition assistance from their employer. The IRS code allows an employee to exclude some $5,250 a year in tuition assistance from taxable income.

Accreditation

Accreditation by a respected agency is critical for any university. Accreditation verifies that a proper college education, consistent with the institution's mission, and meeting or exceeding thresholds of approved standards of education quality, is attainable

at an institution.[14] Accreditation is an important element of the brand equity of an institution, is valued by employers who want to know the worth of their degrees earned by their employees, allows students to transfer credits to another institution, and is a pre-request for Title IV financial aid. In addition, most employees will only offer tuition assistance if the student is enrolled at an accredited institution.

The UOP is accredited by the Higher Learning Commission. Accreditation was first granted in 1978, and reaffirmed 5 times since. The next comprehensive review will take place in 2012. The Higher Learning Commission is one of 6 regional institutional accreditation agencies in the United States and is recognized by the Department of Higher Education. Regional accreditation is recognized nationally. In some states it is sufficient authorization to operate a degree granting institution, but in most states, the UOP must also get authorization from state authorities.

In addition to the Higher Learning Commission, the Bachelor and Master of Science programs in nursing are accredited by the Commission on Collegiate Nursing Education, and the Masters' program in Community Counseling is accredited by the Council for Accreditation of Counseling and Related Educational Programs. However, the Bachelors' and Masters' degree programs in business at UOP are not accredited by the Association to Advance Collegiate Schools of Business (AACSB). The AACSB is the largest and most influential accrediting organization for undergraduate, Master's, and Doctoral degree programs in business schools around the world, having granted international accreditation to more than 500 business schools in 30 countries.

Throughout its history, the UOP has found gaining accreditation an uphill battle. For example, the UOP reentered California in 1980. After initially receiving a license to operate based on its accreditation by North Central, a regional accreditation agency recognized by the U.S. Department of Education, the UOP was informed in 1981 that due to a change in California law, North Central accreditation was not sufficient for the UOP to operate in California. Instead, accreditation was required from the Western Association of Schools and Colleges WASC. The WASC was run by an old critic of Sperling, and there was zero chance that it would accredit the UOP, leaving the institution with a stranded investment in California. It took another three years for the UOP to resolve the issue, which it did by extensive political lobbying, ultimately getting a political ally to sponsor a bill in the California legislature that resulted in a change in the law, making WASC accreditation unnecessary for out of state institutions.

The hostility the UOP encountered in California was repeated in many other states, and the UOP was not always successful at countering it. Illinois for example, refused to grant a license to the UOP after existing institutions argued that there were already too many colleges in the state and that the UOP was unnecessary since other institutions already offered similar programs.

In Sperling's views, the persistent hostility to his company reflects the cultural biases of higher education, which are opposed to the idea of a for-profit university. To quote: "The whole regulatory structure of higher education is designed to favor non-profit and public colleges and universities, which it does by placing added regulatory burdens on those institutions organized for profit."[15] One of these burdens is that regulations grant Title IV eligibility to non-profit and public institutions that have achieved candidate for accreditation status, but only grant Title IV eligibility after they have achieved full accreditation.

Apollo's Growth Strategy

The company's strategy has been to grow by opening more campuses and learning centers in new states, by increasing enrollment at existing campuses and learning centers, and by product extensions, including online course offerings and expanding its Associate degree offerings through Axia College.

UOP Expansion

The basic UOP business model has proved to be very scalable. In addition to centrally developed curriculum, UOP has developed customized computer programs that are used for student tracking, marketing, faculty recruitment and training, and academic quality management. These computer programs are intended to provide uniformity among University of Phoenix's campuses and learning centers. In turn, this enhances University of Phoenix's ability to expand rapidly into new markets.

To attract more students, UOP invests heavily in marketing and sales. Selling and promotional costs accounted 22.6% of total revenues in 2010, or $1.12 billion, which is a much higher percentage than at traditional 4-year colleges.

UOP's aggressive marketing has troubled the U.S. Department of Education. In 2004, the Department issued a report that was highly critical of how UOP compensated its enrollment advisors. According to the Department, enrollment advisors at UOP soon found out that UOP based their salaries solely on the number of students they recruit—a practice that is prohibited by Federal Law. One recruiter who started out at $28,000 was bumped up to $85,000 after recruiting 151 students in 6 months. Another who started out at the same level got just a $4,000 raise after signing up 79 students. This report could have ultimately led to UOP being barred from Federal loan programs, which would have been very damaging. Although an Apollo spokesman called the report "very misleading and full of inaccuracies," the company agreed to change its compensation practices and pay $9.8 million fine without admitting guilt.[16]

Online Education

One of the big engines of growth at UOP has been online education. UOP was an early mover in this area. In 1989, Sperling purchased as defunct distance learning company and instructed a team of technicians to come up with a viable, portable electronic education system. By the time the idea of Web-based distance education was discussed among traditional universities, they found that UOP was already there. By 2006, Apollo had more than 160,000 students enrolled in online programs and had become the global leader in online education.[17]

Online classes are conducted in groups of 10–12 students. Prior to the beginning of each class, students pay a fee to access eResource, the online delivery method for course materials. Online there are a series of 8 newsgroups. The main newsgroup is designated for class discussion. There is an assignments newsgroup to which students submit their assignments, a chat newsgroup for students to discuss noncontent related topics, a course materials newsgroup that houses the syllabus and lectures for the class, and 4 newsgroups which function as forums for the Learning Team assignments. Each week, the instructor posts a lecture to the classroom course materials newsgroup. Students log on and read the lecture or print the lecture to read at their convenience. Throughout the week, students participate in class discussions, based on the class content for that week, which is actively facilitated by the instructor. Both the instructor and students are expected to engage in content discussions 5 out of 7 days each class week. In addition to the class participation requirement, students are also expected to complete individual assignments and to work within a small group of 3–5 students on a specific Learning Team assignment.

The online approach appeals to students who work irregular hours, or who struggle to balance the demands of work, family, and education. Flexibility, not cost, is the prime selling point. The cost of an online MBA program at UOP is about $30,000, similar to online education program fees at traditional universities who are moving into this space. The cost of a getting a Bachelors degree online at UOP is about $475 per semester credit hour, which compares to an average of $398 for an online degree at a selection of state institutions, and $446 at private schools.[18]

Axia College

Another major thrust at the Apollo Group has been to expand it 2-year Associate degree offerings. In the last few years, this has been done through Axia College, which initially was part of Apollo's Western International University. Today, Axia is part of the UOP. The demographic strategy at Axia is very different from that at UOP. Axia targets 18–24 year old students with zero to little college education. The revenue per student is lower, but this is balanced by larger class sizes (30–40), fewer dropouts, and lower student acquisition costs, which translates into slightly higher profit margins. The goal is for Axia to become a feeder for the UOP, with students who gain an Associate degree at Axia transferring to UOP to obtain a Bachelor's, either immediately upon graduation or at some time in the future. Due to the rapid growth of Axia, most of which is online, Associate degrees have grown from about 3.9% of Apollo's student base in 2004 to about 42% in 2010. The growth of Axia has hurt Apollo's revenue per student numbers, and the stock price, although many analysts see this as a good long-term strategy.[19]

The Competitive Landscape

The postsecondary education industry in the United States is estimated to be worth around $430 billion, with the for-profit sector capturing about $25 billion of that total in 2010. The industry will continue to grow, fueled by favorable demographics and tuition hikes, which have historically outpaced inflation by a wide margin. The U.S. Department of Education (DOE) expects postsecondary enrollment to grow at 2% per annum. Analysts estimate that the for-profit sector could grow enrollments by 5–6% per annum as it gains share, and increase tuition at 4–5% per annum.[20] To back up these forecasts, they point to DOE figures which suggest that only 26% of Americans 25 and older have a Bachelor's degree or higher.

Although UOP pioneering the for-profit university model, and remains by far the largest institution, it is not alone in the space. Competition has increased and may continue to do so. By 2006, there were around 850 for-profit institutions offering degrees in the United States, up from around 600 in 1996. Most of these institutions, however, are quite small. The largest competitors to the UOP are Corinthian College, with 66,000 students in 2005, ITT Educational Services, with 43,000 students, and Career Education.

Corinthian College focuses primarily on diploma or certificate courses designed for students with little or no college experience who are looking for entry level jobs. As such, it is not a strong direct competitor to UOP. Florida Metropolitan University, the largest school operated by Corinthian College, is currently being investigated for marketing and advertising practices by the Florida Attorney General. ITT Educational Services has traditionally focused on Associate degrees, but has been expanding its offerings of Bachelor's degrees. ITT's niche is technical degrees, although like UOP it also offers business degrees. Career Education is the holding company for a number of for-profit establishments, including Colorado Technical University and American Inter-Continental University. Currently Career Education is mired in legal and accreditation issues that have constrained its ability to expand.

Analysts' estimates suggest that among for-profit universities, UOP has the premium brand, but prices its offerings competitively, which constitutes a compelling value proposition for students (see Exhibit 1).

In addition to other non-profits, UOP faces increased competition from traditional not-for-profit universities. In recent years, both private and public institutions have expanded their part-time and online offerings to adults, particularly in areas like businesses administration. Executive MBA programs have become major revenue generators at many state and private universities. To take one example, at the University of Washington business school the number of students enrolled in part-time evening or executive MBA programs has expanded from around 40 a decade ago to over 300 today. These students pay "market based" fees, and the programs are run as profit centers that contribute earnings to support the operations of the business school. The programs are structured to minimize the demands on working adults (classes are held in the evening or on weekends) and make heavy use of "learning teams" to facilitate the educational process.

Some traditional universities are also getting into the business of online education, although their success has been decidedly mixed so far. One of the leaders, the University of Massachusetts, had 9,200 students taking online courses in 2006. Most were working adults between 25 and 50, and 30% were from out of state. At UMass, online applicants undergo the same admission process as candidates for campus slots. Tuition is slightly higher than that for on-campus students, since Web-based courses are not subsidized by the state. At another state institution, Pennsylvania State University, there are some 6,000 students taking online courses, and demand is growing rapidly. The University of Maryland University College, the open enrollment arm of the state university, had 51,405 online students in 2005, up from 9,696 in 1998. Nearly 40% of these were American military personnel around the world—a market that the UOP also targets.[21]

On the other hand, many top schools have been reluctant to offer online courses, believing that doing so might compromise quality. Underlying this view is a belief that much of the value in education comes from face-to-face interaction with professors, and with other students in a classroom setting. This perspective is backed by empirical and anecdotal evidence. In one recent survey, employers overwhelmingly preferred traditional Bachelor's degrees when hiring over credentials even partially completed online. Two professors asked 270 small- and medium-sized companies in 8 cities about their attitudes toward online credentials. The companies sought entry level employees or managers in engineering, business and information technology. 96 % said they would choose traditional candidates over those with an online degree.[22]

In response to a journalist's question about the value of online degrees, a spokesman at Texas Instruments stated that: "We do not hire people with online degrees. We primarily hire engineers, and we target very well-established engineering degree programs. The chance for someone with an online degree program to get in is not very likely."[23] On the other hand, several employers told the same journalist that an online degree did not limit options so long as it was from an accredited institution. These organizations included Northrop Grumman, United Parcel Service, Boeing and Discovery Communications.

Regulatory Issues: 2006–2011

Between 2006 and 2011 the industry continued to be the target of criticisms and attacks from critics in the media, in traditional higher education, and from Government Agencies. An investigation by the Department of Education in 2010 found practices such as overly aggressive recruiting, in which school representatives barraged potential students with phone calls, gave false information about a college's accreditation, potential, salary and job opportunities after graduation, and doctored federal aid forms. Other investigations found that for-profit recruiters heavily targeted low income and minority students, veterans, and people whose parents have never gone to college.[24]

The same investigations suggest that public investment in educating some students at some for-profit institutions isn't a good deal for taxpayers or for many students. According to the Department of Education, for-profit colleges educated around 1 in 10 students in 2008, but these students took out nearly 1/4 of all federal student financial aid dollars, about $24 billion of taxpayer money. They also accounted for almost 1/2 of all loan defaulters. For many of the larger for-profit schools, such as UOP, federal dollars account for 80–90% of their revenues.

An investigation by the Senate Committee on Health, Education, Labor and Pensions highlighted one of the smaller institutions, Bridgepoint, which enrolled about 8,000 students in Associate degree programs in

2008. By 2010, 85% had withdrawn, and only about 1% had received a degree. The Committee found that dropout rates at most for-profit schools investigated were hovering at around 66%. Compared to 55% at public colleges and 48% at private non-profit schools.[25]

In June 2011, the U.S. Department of Education issued new regulations designed to curb some of the aggressive practices in the for-profit sector.[26] In order to gain access to Federal Funds, schools had to demonstrate that loan repayment rates by students exceeded 45%. In addition, under what is known as the "gainful employment" rules, access to Federal funds required that students' debt payment to income after graduation should not amount to more than 30% of their discretionary income, and annual loan payments must not exceed 12% of their total earnings. The Government will be collecting this data going forward. Although the rules will go into effect in June 2012, the Government gave for-profit colleges until 2015 to comply with them. The new rules join an existing regulation under which schools' lose access to Federal dollars if more than 90% of their revenue comes from such sources.

The Apollo Group was anticipating these changes by the late-2000s and making moves to get ahead of them. In 2010, Apollo changed its compensation system for admissions personnel to eliminate any tie between compensation and enrollment volume. Apollo also introduced a 3-week program called University Orientation for students with limited college experience. The students are not charged fees during this period, but are introduced to curriculum and teaching practices. The idea is to help students determine if enrolling on a program at the UOP is right for them *before* they take on any debt. In 2010, Apollo's revenue from Federal dollars stood at 88% and was approaching the 90% limit. The company recognized that staying below this limit may constrain growth going forward. The UOP was also only 1% over the required 45% loan repayment rate, although the company believed that the University Orientation Program would change this going forward.

Despite the negative publicity, in 2008 and 2009 Apollo registered strong enrollment growth. The major reason for this seems to have been the weak national economy. With unemployment rates pushing over 9%, people were going back to school in larger numbers in order to try and strengthen their position in a tough job market.

Exhibit 1   Graduate Salary and Tuition for Bachelor's Degrees

School	Mean Graduate Salary	Mean Total Tuition
University of Phoenix	$52,597	$51,000
American InterContinental University	$44,363	$43,863
Florida Metropolitan University	$35,019	$50,400
ITT Technical Institute	$39,726	$69,480

Source: Data taken from Paul Bealand, "What's a degree worth?" *Citigroup Equity Research*, February 17, 2006.

Endnotes

1 Standard & Poor's Stock Report, Apollo Group Inc., October 14, 2006.
2 Quoted in B. Breen, "The Hard Life and Restless Mind of America's Educational Billionaire," *Fast Company*, March 2003, 80–86.
3 Quoted in Anonymous, "Survey: Higher Ed Inc," *The Economist*, September 10, 2005, 19–21.
4 Paul Bealand, "What's a Degree Worth?" *Citigroup Equity Research*, February 17, 2006.
5 Sperling describes his life in is autobiography, John Sperling, *Rebel with a Cause*, New York: John Wiley, 2006.
6 Quoted in B. Breen, "The Hard Life and Restless Mind of America's Educational Billionaire," *Fast Company*, March 2003, 80–86.

7 J. Sperling, *Rebel with a Cause*, New York: John Wiley, 2006, 78.

8 Much of the material in this section is drawn from the 2010 10K Reports of the Apollo Group filed with the Securities and Exchange Commission.

9 S. Baltes, "Phoenix Builds Presence Amid Turmoil," *Des Moines Business Record*, September 20, 2004, 14.

10 P. Bealand, "What's a Degree Worth?" *Citigroup Equity Research*, February 17, 2006.

11 University of Washington data is taken from the UW Fact book which can be accessed online at: http://www.washington.edu/admin/factbook/.

12 R.S. Ruch, *Higher Ed Inc: The Rise of the For Profit University*, Baltimore: John Hopkins University Press, 2001.

13 P. Bealand, "What's a Degree Worth?" *Citigroup Equity Research*, February 17, 2006.

14 R.S. Ruch, *Higher Ed Inc: The Rise of the For Profit University*, Baltimore: John Hopkins University Press, 2001.

15 J. Sperling, *Rebel with a Cause*, New York: John Wiley, 2006, 105.

16 W. C. Symonds, "Back to Earth for Apollo Group?" *Business Week*, January 31, 2005, 50.

17 D. Golden, "Degrees@StateU.edu," *Wall Street Journal*, May 9, 2006, B1.

18 P. Bealand, "What's a Degree Worth?" *Citigroup Equity Research*, February 17, 2006.

19 K. Rowland, "Apollo Group A," *Morning Star Research Report*, October 19, 2006.

20 P. Bealand, "What's a Degree Worth?" *Citigroup Equity Research*, February 17, 2006.

21 D. Golden, "Degrees@StateU.edu," *Wall Street Journal*, May 9, 2006, B1.

22 A. Wellen, "Degrees of Acceptance," *Wall Street Journal*, July 30, 2006, A26.

23 Ibid.

24 D. Lipperman and L. Mulvany, "Class Act or Just a Course to Failure?" *Chicago Tribune*, June 21, 2011, 4.

25 Ibid.

26 M. Alva, "Fed's Let For-Profit Colleges off the Regulatory Hook, a Bit," *Investor's Business Daily*, June 21, 2011, A7.

CASE 7

The Evolution of the Small Package Express Delivery Industry, 1973–2010

Charles W.L. Hill
University of Washington

Introduction

The small package express delivery industry is the segment of the broader postal and cargo industries that specializes in rapid (normally 1–3 days) delivery of small packages (small packages are defined as those weighing less than 150 lbs. or having less than 165 inches in combined length and girth). It is generally agreed that the modern express delivery industry in the United States began with Fred Smith's vision for Federal Express Company (now FedEx), which started operations in 1973. FedEx transformed the structure of the existing air cargo industry and paved the way for rapid growth in the overnight package segment of that industry. A further impetus to the industry's development was the 1977 deregulation of the U.S. air cargo industry. This deregulation allowed FedEx (and its emerging competitors) to buy large jets for the first time. The story of the industry during the 1980s was one of rapid growth and new entry. Between 1982 and 1989, small package express cargo shipments by air in the United States grew at an annual average rate of 31%. In contrast, shipments of airfreight and air mail grew at an annual rate of only 2.7%.[1] This rapid growth attracted new entrants such as United Parcel Service (UPS) and Airborne Freight (which operated under the name Airborne Express). The entry of UPS triggered severe price cutting, which ultimately drove some of the weaker competitors out of the market and touched off a wave of consolidation in the industry.

By the mid-1990s, the industry structure had stabilized with four organizations —FedEx, UPS, Airborne Express and the United States Postal Service (USPS)—accounting for the vast majority U.S. express

shipments. During the first half of the 1990s, the small package express industry continued to grow at a healthy rate, with shipments expanding by slightly more than 16% per annum.[2] Despite this growth, the industry was hit by repeated rounds of price cutting as the three big private firms battled to capture major accounts. In addition to price cutting, the big three also competed vigorously on the basis of technology, service offerings, and the global reach of their operations. By the late-1990s and early-2000s, the intensity of price competition in the industry had moderated, with a degree of pricing discipline being maintained, despite the fact that the growth rate for the industry slowed down. Between 1995 and 2000, the industry had grown at 9.8% per year. In 2001, the volume of express parcels shipped by air fell by 5.9%, partly due to an economic slowdown, and partly due to the aftereffects of the September 11 terrorist attack on the United States.[3] Growth picked up again in 2002. Estimates suggest that the global market for small package express delivery should continue to grow by a little over 6% per annum between 2005 and 2025. Most of that growth, however, is forecasted to take place outside of the now mature North American market. Within the United States, the annual growth rate is predicted to match the growth in United States GDP.[4]

In North America, the biggest change to take place in the 2000s was the 2003 entry of DHL with the acquisition of Airborne Express for $1 billion. DHL is owned by Deutsche Post World Net, formally the German post office, which since privatization has been rapidly transforming itself into a global express mail and logistics operation. Prior to 2003, DHL lacked a strong presence in the all-important

United States market. The acquisition of Airborne gave DHL a foothold in the United States. DHL subsequently spent $1.5 billion trying to upgrade Airborne's delivery network in a quest for market share. Despite heavy investments, DHL failed to gain traction and after 5 years of losses, in 2009 it exited the United States market. With the exit of DHL, the United States market looks increasingly like a duopoly. In 2010, FedEx held onto 54% of the $14 billion overnight express market, UPS accounted for 41% and the USPS held 6% (although they actually contracted out its express deliveries to FedEx). UPS dominated the $34 billion ground market in 2010, with a 61% share, followed by FedEx with 22% and the USPS with 16%.[5]

The Industry Before FedEx

In 1973, roughly 1.5 billion tons of freight were shipped in the United States. Most of this freight was carried by surface transport, with airfreight accounting for less than 2% of the total.[6] While shipment by airfreight was often quicker than shipment by surface freight, the high cost of airfreight had kept down demand. The typical users of airfreight at this time were suppliers of time-sensitive, high-priced goods, such as computer parts and medical instruments, which were needed at dispersed locations but which were too expensive for their customers to hold as inventory.

The main cargo carriers in 1973 were major passenger airlines, which operated several all-cargo planes and carried additional cargo in their passenger planes, along with a handful of all-cargo airlines such as Flying Tigers. From 1973 onward, the passenger airlines moved steadily away from all-cargo planes and began to concentrate cargo freight in passenger planes. This change was a response to increases in fuel costs, which made the operation of many older cargo jets uneconomical.

With regard to distribution of cargo to and from airports, in 1973 about 20% of all airfreight was delivered to airports by the shipper and/or picked up by the consignee. The bulk of the remaining 80% was accounted for by three major intermediaries: (1) Air Cargo Incorporated, (2) freight forwarders, and (3) the U.S. Postal Service. Air Cargo Incorporated was a trucking service, wholly owned by 26 airlines, which performed pickup and delivery service for the airlines' direct customers. Freight forwarders were trucking carriers who consolidated cargo going to the airlines. They purchased cargo space from the airlines and retailed this space in small amounts. They dealt primarily with small customers, providing pickup and delivery services in most cities, either in their own trucks or through contract agents. The U.S. Postal Service used air service for transportation of long-distance letter mail and air parcel post.[7]

The Federal Express Concept

Founded by Fred Smith, Jr., Federal Express was incorporated in 1971 and began operations in 1973. At that time, a significant portion of small-package airfreight flew on commercial passenger flights. Smith believed that there were major differences between packages and passengers, and he was convinced that the two had to be treated differently. Most passengers moved between major cities and wanted the convenience of daytime flights. Cargo shippers preferred nighttime service to coincide with late-afternoon pickups and next-day delivery. Because small-package airfreight was subservient to the requirements of passengers' flight schedules, it was often difficult for the major airlines to achieve next-day delivery of airfreight.

Smith's aim was to build a system that could achieve next-day delivery of small-package airfreight (less than 70 lbs.). He set up Federal Express with his $8 million family inheritance and $90 million in venture capital (the company's name was changed to FedEx in 1998). Federal Express established a hub-and-spoke route system, the first airline to do so. The hub of the system was Memphis, chosen for its good weather conditions, central location, and the fact that it was Smith's hometown. The spokes were regular routes between Memphis and shipping facilities at public airports in the cities serviced by Federal Express. Every weeknight, aircraft would leave their home cities with a load of packages and fly down the spokes to Memphis (often with one or two stops on the way). At Memphis, all packages were unloaded, sorted by destination, and reloaded. The aircraft then returned back to their home cities in the early hours of the morning. Packages were ferried to and from airports by Federal Express couriers driving the company's vans and working to a tight schedule. Thus, from door to door, the package was in Federal Express' hands. This system guaranteed that a package picked up from a customer in New York at 5 p.m. would reach its final destination in Los Angeles (or any other major city) by noon the following day. It enabled Federal Express to realize economies in sorting and to utilize its air cargo capacity efficiently. Federal Express also pioneered the use of standard packaging with an upper weight limit of 70 lbs. and a maximum length plus girth of 108 inches. This standard helped Federal Express to gain further efficiencies from mechanized sorting at its Memphis hub. Later entrants into the industry copied Federal Express' package standards and hub-and-spoke operating system.

To accomplish overnight delivery, Federal Express had to operate its own planes. Restrictive regulations enforced by the Civil Aeronautics Board (CAB), however, prohibited the company from buying large jet aircraft. To get around this restriction, Federal Express bought a fleet of twin-engine executive jets, which it converted to mini-freighters. These planes had a cargo capacity of 6,200 lbs., which enabled Federal Express to get a license as an air-taxi operator.

After 1973, Federal Express quickly built up volume. By 1976, it had an average daily volume of 19,000 packages, a fleet of 32 aircraft, 500 delivery vans, and 2,000 employees, and it had initiated service in 75 cities. After 3 years of posting losses, the company turned in a profit of $3.7 million on revenues of $75 million.[8] However, volume had grown so much that Federal Express desperately needed to use larger planes to maintain operating efficiencies. As a result, Smith's voice was added to those calling for Congress to deregulate the airline industry and allow greater competition.

Deregulation And Its Aftermath

In November 1977, Congress relaxed regulations controlling competition in the air cargo industry, one year before passenger services were deregulated. This involved a drastic loosening of standards for entry into the industry. The old CAB authority of naming the carriers that could operate on the various routes was changed to the relatively simple authority of deciding which candidate carriers was fit, willing, and able to operate an all-cargo route. In addition, CAB controls over pricing were significantly reduced. The immediate effect was an increase in rates for shipments, particularly minimum- and high-weight

categories, suggesting that prices had been held artificially low by regulation. As a result, the average yield (revenue per ton-mile) on domestic airfreight increased 10.6% in 1978 and 11.3% in 1979.[9]

Freed from the constraints of regulation, Federal Express immediately began to purchase larger jets and quickly established itself as a major carrier of small-package airfreight. Despite the increase in yields, however, new entry into the air cargo industry was limited, at least initially. This was mainly due to the high capital requirements involved in establishing an all-cargo carrier. Indeed, by the end of 1978, there were only 4 major all-cargo carriers serving the domestic market: Airlift International, Federal Express, Flying Tigers, and Seaboard World Airlines. While all of these all-cargo carriers had increased their route structure following deregulation, only Federal Express specialized in next-day delivery for small packages. Demand for a next-day delivery service continued to boom. Industry estimates suggest that the small-package priority market had grown to about 82 million pieces in 1979, up from 43 million in 1974.[10]

At the same time, in response to increasing competition from the all-cargo carriers, the passenger airlines continued their retreat from the all-cargo business (originally begun in 1973 as a response to high fuel prices). Between 1973 and 1978, there was a 45% decline in the mileage of all-cargo flights by the airlines. This decrease was followed by a 14% decline between 1978 and 1979. Instead of all-cargo flights, the airlines concentrated their attentions on carrying cargo in passenger flights. This practice hurt the freight forwarders badly. The freight forwarders had long relied on the all-cargo flights of major airlines to achieve next-day delivery. Now the freight forwarders were being squeezed out of this segment by a lack of available lift at the time needed to ensure next-day delivery.

This problem led to one of the major post-deregulation developments in the industry: the acquisition and operation by freight forwarders of their own fleets of aircraft. Between 1979 and 1981, 5 of the 6 largest freight forwarders became involved in this activity. The two largest were Emery Worldwide and Airborne Express. Emery operated a fleet of 66 aircraft at the end of 1979, the majority of which were leased from other carriers. In mid-1980, this fleet was providing service to approximately 129 cities, carrying both large-volume shipments and small-package express.

Airborne Express acquired its own fleet of aircraft in April 1980 with the purchase of Midwest Express, an Ohio-based all-cargo airline. In 1981, Airborne opened a new hub in Ohio, which became the center of its small-package express operation. This enabled Airborne to provide next-day delivery for small packages to 125 cities in the United States.[11] Other freight forwarders that moved into the overnight mail market included Purolator Courier and Gelco Courier, and both offered overnight delivery by air on a limited geographic scale.

Industry Evolution, 1980–1986

New Products and Industry Growth

In 1981, Federal Express expanded its role in the overnight market with the introduction of an overnight letter service, with a limit of two ounces. This guaranteed overnight delivery service was set up in direct competition with the USPS's Priority Mail. The demand for such a service was illustrated by its expansion to about 17,000 letters per day within its first 3 months of operation.

More generally, the focus of the air express industry was changing from being predominantly a conduit for goods to being a distributor of information—particularly company documents, letters, contracts, drawings, and the like. As a result of the growth in demand for information distribution, new product offerings such as the overnight letter, and Federal Express' own marketing efforts, the air express industry enjoyed high growth during the early-1980s, averaging more than 30% per year.[12] Indeed, many observers attribute most of the growth in the overnight delivery business at this time to Federal Express' marketing efforts. According to one industry participant, "Federal Express pulled off one of the greatest marketing scams in the industry by making people believe they absolutely, positively, had to have something right away."[13]

Increasing Price Competition

Despite rapid growth in demand, competitive intensity in the industry increased sharply in 1982 following the entry of UPS into the overnight-delivery market. UPS was already by far the largest private package transporter in the United States, with an enormous ground-oriented distribution network and revenues in excess of $4 billion per year. In addition, for a long time, UPS had offered a second-day air service for priority packages, primarily by using the planes of all-cargo and passenger airlines. In 1982, UPS acquired a fleet of 24 used Boeing 727–100s and added four DC-8 freighters from Flying Tigers. These purchases allowed UPS to introduce next-day air service in September 1982—at roughly half the price Federal Express was charging.[14]

Federal Express countered almost immediately by announcing that it would institute 10:30 a.m. priority overnight delivery (at a cost to the company of $18 million). None of the other carriers followed suit, however, reasoning that most of their customers are usually busy or in meetings during the morning hours, so delivery before noon was not really that important. Instead, by March 1983, most of the major carriers in the market (including Federal Express) were offering their high-volume customers contract rates that matched the UPS price structure. Then, three new services introduced by Purolator, Emery, and Gelco Courier pushed prices even lower. A competitive free-for-all followed, with constant price changes and volume discounts being offered by all industry participants. These developments hit the profit margins of the express carriers. Between 1983 and 1984, Federal Express saw its average revenue per package fall nearly 14%, while Emery saw a 15% decline in its yield on small shipments.[15]

Beginning around this time, customers began to group together and negotiate for lower prices. For example, Xerox set up accounts with Purolator and Emery that covered not only Xerox's express packages but also those of 50 other companies, including Mayflower Corp., the moving company, and the Chicago Board of Trade. By negotiating as a group, these companies could achieve prices as much as 60% lower than those they could get on their own.[16]

The main beneficiary of the price war was UPS, which by 1985 had gained the number 2 spot in the industry, with 15% of the market. Federal Express, meanwhile, had seen its market share slip to 37% from about 45% two years earlier. The other 4 major players in the industry at this time were Emery Air Freight (14% of market share), Purolator (10% of market share), Airborne Express (8% of market share), and the U.S. Postal Service (8% of market share).[17] The survival of all four of these carriers in the air express business was in question by 1986. Emery, Purolator, and the U.S. Postal Service were all reporting losses on their air express business, while Airborne had seen its profits slump 66% in the first quarter of 1986 and now had razor-thin margins.

Industry Evolution, 1987–1996

Industry Consolidation

A slowdown in the growth rate of the air express business due to increasing geographic saturation and inroads made by electronic transmission (primarily fax machines) stimulated further price discounting in 1987 and early-1988. Predictably, this discounting created problems for the weakest companies in the industry. The first to go was Purolator Courier, which had lost $65 million during 1985 and 1986. Purolator's problems stemmed from a failure to install an adequate computer system. The company was unable to track shipments, a crucial asset in this industry, and some of Purolator's best corporate customers were billed 120 days late.[18] In 1987, Purolator agreed to be acquired by Emery. Emery was unable to effect a satisfactory integration of Purolator, and it sustained large losses in 1988 and early-1989.

Consolidated Freightways was a major trucking company and parent of CF Air Freight, the third largest heavy shipment specialist in the United States. In April 1989, Consolidated Freightways acquired Emery for $478 million. However, its shipment specialist, CF Air Freight, soon found itself struggling to cope with Emery's problems. In its first 11 months with CF, Emery lost $100 million. One of the main problems was Emery's billing and tracking system, described as a "rat's nest" of conflicting tariff schedules, which caused overbilling of customers and made tracking packages en route a major chore. In addition, CF enraged corporate customers by trying to add a "fuel surcharge" of 4–7% to prices in early-1989. Competitors held the line on prices and picked up business from CF/Emery.[19]

As a result of the decline of the CF/Emery/Purolator combination, the other firms in the industry were able to pick up market share. By 1994, industry estimates suggested that Federal Express accounted for 35% of domestic airfreight and air express industry revenues, UPS had 26%, Airborne Express was third with 9%, and Emery and the U.S.

Postal Service each held onto 4% of the market. The remainder of the market was split among numerous small cargo carriers and several combination carriers, such as Evergreen International and Atlas Air. (Combination carriers specialize mostly in heavy freight, but do carry some express mail.)[20]

The other major acquisition in the industry during this time was the purchase of Flying Tigers by Federal Express for $880 million in December 1988. Although Flying Tigers had some air express operations in the United States, its primary strength was as a heavy cargo carrier with a global route structure. The acquisition was part of Federal Express' goal of becoming a major player in the international air express market. However, the acquisition had its problems. Many of Flying Tigers' biggest customers, including UPS and Airborne Express, were Federal Express' competitors in the domestic market. These companies had long paid Flying Tigers to carry packages to those countries where they had no landing rights. It seemed unlikely that these companies would continue to give international business to their biggest domestic competitor. Additional problems arose in the process of trying to integrate the two operations. These problems included the scheduling of aircraft and pilots, the servicing of Flying Tigers' fleet, and the merging of Federal's nonunionized pilots with Flying Tigers' unionized pilots.[21]

During the late-1980s and early-1990s, there were also hints of further consolidations. TNT Ltd., a large Australian-based air cargo operation with a global network, made an unsuccessful attempt to acquire Airborne Express in 1986. TNT's bid was frustrated by opposition from Airborne and by the difficulties inherent in getting around U.S. law, which limited foreign firms from having more than a 25% stake in U.S. airlines. In addition, DHL Airways, the U.S. subsidiary of DHL International, was reportedly attempting to enlarge its presence in the United States and was on the lookout for an acquisition.[22]

Pricing Trends

In October 1988, UPS offered new discounts to high-volume customers in domestic markets. For the first time since 1983, competitors declined to match the cuts. Then, in January 1989, UPS announced a price increase of 5% for next-day air service, its first price increase in nearly 6 years. Federal Express, Airborne, and Consolidated Freightways all followed suit with moderate increases. UPS announced additional rate increases of 5.9% on next-day air letters in February 1990. Federal Express followed suit in April, and Airborne also implemented selective price hikes on noncontract business of 5%, or $0.50 per package on packages up to 20 lbs.

Just as prices were stabilizing, however, the 1990–1991 recession came along. For the first time in the history of the U.S. air express industry, there was a decline in year-on-year shipments, with express freight falling from 4,455 million ton-miles in 1989 to 4,403 million ton-miles in 1990. This decline triggered another round of competitive price cuts and yields plummeted. Although demand strongly rebounded, repeated attempts to raise prices in 1992, 1993, and 1994 simply did not stick.[23]

Much of the price cutting was focused on large corporate accounts, which by this time accounted for 75% by volume of express mail shipments. For example, as a result of deep price discounting in 1994, UPS was able to lure home shopping programmer QVC and computer mail-order company Gateway 2000 away from Federal Express. At about the same time, however, Federal Express used discounting to capture retailer Williams-Sonoma away from UPS.[24] This prolonged period of price discounting depressed profit margins and contributed to losses at all three major carriers during the early-1990s. Bolstered by a strong economy, prices finally began to stabilize during late-1995, when price increases announced by UPS were followed by similar announcements at Federal Express and Airborne.[25]

Product Trends

Second-Day Delivery Having seen a slowdown in the growth rate of the next-day document delivery business during the early-1990s, the major operators in the air express business began to look for new product opportunities to sustain their growth and margins. One trend was a move into the second-day delivery market, or deferred services, as it is called in the industry. Airborne Express started the move toward second-day delivery in 1991, and that was soon imitated by its major competitors. Second-day delivery commands a substantially lower price point than next-day delivery. In 1994, Federal Express made an average of $9.23 on second-day deliveries, compared to $16.37 on priority overnight service. The express mail operators saw deferred services as a

way to utilize excess capacity at the margin, thereby boosting revenues and profits. Since many second-day packages could be shipped on the ground, the cost of second-day delivery could more than compensate for the lower price.

In some ways, however, the service has been almost too successful. During the mid-1990s, the growth rate for deferred services was significantly higher than for priority overnight mail because many corporations came to the realization that they could live with a second-day service. At Airborne Express, for example, second-day delivery accounted for 42% of total volume in 1996, up from 37% in 1995.[26]

Premium Services Another development was a move toward a premium service. In 1994, UPS introduced its Early AM service, which guaranteed delivery of packages and letters by 8:30 a.m. in select cities. UPS tailored Early AM toward a range of businesses that needed documents or materials before the start of the business day, including hospitals, which expect to use the service to ship critical drugs and medical devices; architects, who need to have their blueprints sent to a construction site; and salespeople. Although demand for the service is predicted to be light, the premium price makes for high profit margins. In 1994, UPS' price for a letter delivered at 10:30 a.m. was $10.75, while it charged $40 for an equivalent Early AM delivery. UPS believed that it could provide the service at little extra cost because most of its planes arrived in their destination cities by 7:30 a.m. Federal Express and Airborne initially declined to follow UPS' lead.[27]

Logistics Services Another development of some note was the move by all major operators into third-party logistics services. Since the latter half of the 1980s, more and more companies have been relying on air express operations as part of their just-in-time inventory control systems. As a result, the content of packages carried by air express operators has been moving away from letters and documents and toward high-value, low-weight products. By 1994, less than 20% of Federal Express' revenues came from documents.[28] To take advantage of this trend, all of the major operators have been moving into logistics services designed to assist business customers in their warehousing, distribution, and assembly operations. The emphasis of this business is on helping their customers reduce the time involved in their production cycles and gain distribution efficiencies.

In the late-1980s, Federal Express set up a Business Logistics Services (BLS) division. The new division evolved from Federal Express' Parts Bank. The Parts Bank stores critical inventory for clients, who are mostly based in the high-tech electronics and medical industries. On request, Federal Express ships this inventory to its client's customers. The service saves clients from having to invest in their own distribution systems. It also allows their clients to achieve economies of scale by making large production runs and then storing the inventory at the Parts Bank.

The BLS division has expanded this service to include some assembly operations and customs brokerage and to assist in achieving just-in-time manufacturing. Thus, for example, one U.S. computer company relies on BLS to deliver electronic subassemblies from the Far East as a key part of its just-in-time system. Federal Express brings the products to the United States on its aircraft, clears them through customs with the help of a broker, and manages truck transportation to the customer's dock.

UPS moved into the logistics business in 1993 when it established UPS Worldwide Logistics, which it positioned as a third-party provider of global supply chain management solutions, including transportation management, warehouse operations, inventory management, documentation for import and export, network optimization, and reverse logistics. UPS based its logistics business at its Louisville, Kentucky, hub. In 1995, the company announced that it would invest $75 million to expand the scope of this facility, bringing total employment in the facility to 2,200 by the end of 1998.[29]

Airborne Express also made a significant push into this business. Several of Airborne's corporate accounts utilized a warehousing service called Stock Exchange. As with Federal Express' Parts Bank, clients warehouse critical inventory at Airborne's hub in Wilmington, Ohio, and then ship those items on request to their customers. In addition, Airborne set up a commerce park on 1,000 acres around its Wilmington hub. The park was geared toward companies that wanted to outsource logistics to Airborne and could gain special advantages by locating at the company's hub. The ability to make shipping decisions as late as 2 a.m. Eastern time was one of these advantages.

Information Systems

Since the late-1980s, the major U.S. air express carriers have devoted more and more attention to competing on the basis of information technology. The ability to track a package as it moves through an operator's delivery network has always been an important aspect of competition in an industry where reliability is so highly valued. Thus, all the major players in the industry have heavily invested in barcode technology, scanners, and computerized tracking systems. UPS, Federal Express, and Airborne have also all invested in Internet-based technology that allows customers to schedule pickups, print shipping labels, and track deliveries online.

Globalization

Perhaps the most important development for the long-run future of the industry has been the increasing globalization of the airfreight industry. The combination of a healthy U.S. economy, strong and expanding East Asian economies, and the move toward closer economic integration in Western Europe all offer opportunities for growth in the international air cargo business. The increasing globalization of companies in a whole range of industries from electronics to autos, and from fast food to clothing, is beginning to dictate that the air express operators follow suit.

Global manufacturers want to keep inventories at a minimum and deliver just-in-time as a way of keeping down costs and fine-tuning production—which requires speedy supply routes. Thus, some electronics companies will manufacture key components in one location, ship them by air to another for final assembly, and then deliver them by air to a third location for sale. This setup is particularly convenient for industries producing small high-value items (for example, electronics, medical equipment, and computer software) that can be economically transported by air and for whom just-in-time inventory systems are crucial for keeping down costs. It is also true in the fashion industry, where timing is crucial. For example, the clothing chain The Limited manufactures clothes in Hong Kong and then ships them by air to the United States to keep from missing out on fashion trends.[30] In addition, an increasing number of wholesalers are beginning to turn to international air express as a way of meeting delivery deadlines.

The emergence of integrated global corporations is also increasing the demand for the global shipment of contracts, confidential papers, computer printouts, and other documents that are too confidential for Internet transmission or that require real signatures. Major U.S. corporations are increasingly demanding the same kind of service that they receive from air express operators within the United States for their far-flung global operations.

As a consequence of these trends, rapid growth is predicted in the global arena. According to forecasts, the market for international air express is expected to grow at approximately 18% annually from 1996 to 2016.[31] Faced with an increasingly mature market at home, the race is on among the major air cargo operators to build global air and ground transportation networks that will enable them to deliver goods and documents between any two points on the globe within 48 hours.

The company with the most extensive international operations by the mid-1990s was DHL. In 1995, DHL enjoyed a 44% share of the worldwide market for international air express services (see Exhibit 1).[32] Started in California in 1969 and now based in Brussels, DHL is smaller than many of its rivals, but it has managed to capture as much as an 80% share in some markets, such as documents leaving Japan, by concentrating solely on international air express. The strength of DHL was enhanced in mid-1992 when Lufthansa, Japan Airlines, and the Japanese trading company Nissho Iwai announced that they intended to invest as much as $500 million for a 57.5% stake in DHL. Although Lufthansa and Japan Airlines are primarily known for their passenger flights, they are also among the top five airfreight haulers in the world, both because they carry cargo in the holds of their passenger flights, and because they each have a fleet of all-cargo aircraft.[33]

TNT Ltd., a $6 billion Australian conglomerate, is another big player in the international air express market, with courier services from 184 countries as well as package express and mail services. In 1995, its share of the international air express market was 12%, down from 18% in 1990.[34]

Among U.S. carriers, Federal Express was first in the race to build a global air express network. Between 1984 and 1989, Federal Express purchased 17 other companies worldwide in an attempt to build its global distribution capabilities, culminating in the $880 million purchase of Flying Tigers. The main asset of Flying Tigers was not so much its aircraft, but its landing rights overseas. The Flying Tigers acquisition gave Federal Express service to 103 countries, a combined fleet of 328 aircraft, and revenues of $5.2 billion in fiscal year 1989.[35]

However, Federal Express has had to suffer through years of losses in its international operations. Start-up costs were heavy, due in part to the enormous capital investments required to build an integrated air and ground network worldwide. Between 1985 and 1992, Federal Express spent $2.5 billion to build an international presence. Faced also with heavy competition, Federal Express found it difficult to generate the international volume required to fly its planes above the break-even point on many international routes. Because the demand for outbound service from the United States is greater than the demand for inbound service, planes that left New York full often returned half empty.

Trade barriers have also proved very damaging to the bottom line. Customs regulations require a great deal of expensive and time-consuming labor, such as checking paperwork and rating package contents for duties. These regulations obviously inhibit the ability of international air cargo carriers to effect express delivery. Federal Express has been particularly irritated by Japanese requirements that each inbound envelope be opened and searched for pornography, a practice that seems designed to slow down the company's growth rate in the Japanese market.

Federal Express has also found it extremely difficult to get landing rights in many markets. For example, it took 3 years to get permission from

Exhibit 1 International Air Express Market Shares, 1995

Company	Market Share
DHL International	44%
Federal Express	21%
UPS	12%
TNT	12%
Others	11%

Source: Standard & Poor's, "Aerospace and Air Transport," *Industry Survey*, February 1996.

Japan to make 4 flights per week from Memphis to Tokyo, a key link in the overseas system. Then, in 1988, just 3 days before the service was due to begin, the Japanese notified Federal Express that no packages weighing more than 70 lbs. could pass through Tokyo. To make matters worse, until 1995 Japan limited Federal Express' ability to fly on from Tokyo and Osaka to other locations in Asia. The Japanese claimed, with some justification, that due to government regulations, the U.S. air traffic market is difficult for foreign carriers to enter, so they see no urgency to help Federal Express build a market presence in Japan and elsewhere in Asia.[36]

After heavy financial losses, Federal Express abruptly shifted its international strategy in 1992, selling off its expensive European ground network to local carriers to concentrate on intercontinental deliveries. Under the strategy, Federal Express relies on a network of local partners to deliver its packages. Also, Federal Express entered into an alliance with TNT to share space on Federal Express' daily trans-Atlantic flights. Under the agreement, TNT flies packages from its hub in Cologne, Germany, to Britain, where they are loaded onto Federal Express' daily New York flight.[37]

UPS has also built up an international presence. In 1988, UPS bought 8 smaller European airfreight companies and Hong Kong's Asian Courier Service, and it announced air service and ground delivery in 175 countries and territories. However, it has not been all smooth sailing for UPS either. UPS had been using Flying Tigers for its Pacific shipments. The acquisition of Flying Tigers by Federal Express left UPS in the difficult situation of shipping its parcels on a competitor's plane. UPS was concerned that its shipments would be pushed to the back of the aircraft. Since there were few alternative carriers, UPS pushed for authority to run an all-cargo route to Tokyo, but approval was slow in coming. "Beyond rights," to carry cargo from Tokyo to further destinations (such as Singapore and Hong Kong), were also difficult to gain.

In March 1996, UPS sidestepped years of frustrations associated with building an Asian hub in Tokyo by announcing that it would invest $400 million in a Taiwan hub, which would henceforth be the central node in its Asian network. The decision to invest in an Asian hub followed closely on the heels of a 1995 decision by UPS to invest $1.1 billion to build a ground network in Europe. In September 1996, UPS went one step further toward building an international air express service when it announced that it would start a pan-European next-day delivery service for small packages. UPS hoped that these moves would push the international operations of the carrier into the black after 8 years of losses.[38]

Industry Evolution, 1997–2010

Pricing Trends

The industry continued to grow at a solid rate through 2000, which helped to establish a stable pricing environment. In 2001, things took a turn for the worse. Recessionary conditions in the United States triggered a 7.6% decline in the number of domestic packages shipped by air. Even though the economy started to rebound in 2002, growth remained sluggish by historic comparison, averaging only 4% per annum.[39] Despite this, pricing discipline remained solid. Unlike the recession in 1990–1991, there was no price war in 2001–2002. In early 2002, UPS pushed through a 3.5% increase in prices, which was quickly followed by the other carriers. The carriers were able to continue to raise prices, at least in line with inflation, through to 2008. They were also successful in tacking on a fuel surcharge to the cost of packages to make up for sharply higher fuel costs.[40] During the 2002–2006, the average revenue per package at both UPS and FedEx increased as more customers opted for expedited shipments and as both carriers shipped a high proportion of heavier packages.[41] The global financial crisis of 2008–2009 and the recession that it ushered in did lead to a slump in volume, a shift to deferred shipping, and more pricing pressures. At FedEx for example, the average revenue per overnight package fell from $18.42 in 2008 to $16.04 in 2010. However, volume and pricing trends improved in 2011 along with the economy, and revenue per package at FedEx rose to $18.08 by the 4th quarter of 2010.[42]

Continuing Growth of Logistics

During 1997–2010 all players continued to build their logistics services. During the 2000s, UPS was much more aggressive in this area than FedEx.

By 2010, UPS' logistics business had revenues of $8.7 billion. UPS was reportedly stealing share from FedEx in this area. FedEx reportedly decided to stay more focused on the small package delivery business (although it continues to have a logistics business). Most analysts expected logistics services to continue to be a growth area. Outside of the North American market, DHL emerged as the world's largest provider of logistics services, particularly following its 2006 acquisition of Britain's Exel, a large global logistics business.

Despite the push of DHL and UPS into the global logistics business, the market remains very fragmented. According to one estimate, DHL, now the world's largest logistics company, has a 5.5% share of the global market in contract logistics, UPS has a 3% share and TNT has a 2.2% share.[43] The total global market for contract logistics was estimated to be worth over $200 billion in 2005. In 2006, TNT sold its logistics business to Apollo Management L.P. for $1.88 billion so that it could focus more on its small package delivery business.

Expanding Ground Network

In the late-1990s and early-2000s all the main carriers supplementing their air networks with extensive ground networks and ground hubs to ship packages overnight. With more customers moving from overnight mail to deferred services, such as second-day delivery, this shift in emphasis has become a necessity. Demand for deferred services help up reasonably well during 2001, even as demand for overnight packages slumped. Prices for deferred and ground services are considerably lower than are prices for air services, but so are the costs.

UPS has been the most aggressive in building ground delivery capabilities (of course, it already had extensive ground capabilities before its move into the air). In 1999, UPS decided to integrate overnight delivery into its huge ground transportation network. The company spent about $700 million to strengthen its ground delivery network by setting up regional ground hubs. By doing so, it found it could ship packages overnight on the ground within a 500-mile radius. Because ground shipments are cheaper than air shipments, the result was a significant cost savings for UPS. The company also deferred delivery of about 123 aircraft that were on

order, reasoning that they would not be needed as quickly because more of UPS' overnight business was moved to the ground.[44]

FedEx entered the ground transportation market in 1998 with its acquisition of Caliber Systems for $500 million. This was followed by further acquisitions in 2001 and 2006 of significant U.S. trucking companies, including the 2006 acquisition of Watkins Motor Lines, a provider of long haul trucking services in the U.S. with sales of around $1 billion. Watkins was re-branded as FedEx National LTL. By 2002, FedEx was able to provide ground service to all U.S. homes, giving it a similar capability to UPS.

In addition, FedEx struck a deal in 2001 with the U.S. Postal Service (USPS), under which FedEx agreed to provide airport-to-airport transportation for 250,000 lbs. of USPS Express Mail packages nightly and about 3 million lbs. of USPS Priority Mail packages. The Priority Mail was to be moved on FedEx planes that normally sit idle during the day. The deal was reportedly worth $7 billion in additional revenues to FedEx over the 7-year term of the agreement. In addition, FedEx reaped cost savings from the better utilization of its lift capacity.[45] As of 2010, FedEx and the USPS still cooperated with each other.

Bundling

Another industry wide trend has moved toward selling various product offerings—including air delivery, ground package offerings, and logistics services—to business customers as a bundle. The basic idea behind bundling is to offer complementary products at a bundled price that is less than if each item had been purchased separately. Yet again, UPS has been the most aggressive in offering bundled services to corporate clients. UPS is clearly aiming to set itself up as a one-stop shop offering a broad array of transportation solutions to customers. FedEx has also made moves in this area. Airborne Express started to bundle its product offerings in mid-2001.[46]

Retail Presence

In 2001, UPS purchased Mail Boxes Etc. for $185 million. Mail Boxes Etc. had 4,300 franchisees, most in the United States, who operated small retail packaging, printing and copying stores. At the time, Mail Boxes Etc. was shipping some 40 million packages per year, around 12 million of which were via UPS. UPS stated that it would continue to allow the Mail Boxes stores to ship packages for other carriers. In 2003, the stores were re-branded as the UPS Store. While some franchisees objected to this move, the vast majority ultimately switched to the new brand.[47] In addition to the franchise stores, UPS has also begun to open wholly owned UPS stores, not just in the United States, but also internationally, and by 2006 had 5,600 outlets. In addition to The UPS Store, the company put UPS Centers in office supplies stores, such as Office Depot, and by 2006 it had some 2,200 of these.

In 2004, FedEx followed UPS by purchasing Kinko's for $2.4 billion. Kinko's, which had 1,200 retail locations, 90% in the United States, focused on providing photocopying, printing and other office services to individuals and small businesses. FedEx has plans to increase the network of Kinko's stores (now called FedEx Office) to 4,000. In addition to providing printing, photocopying, and package services, FedEx is also experimenting using FedEx Office stores as mini warehouses to store high value goods, such as medical equipment, for its supply chain management division.[48]

The Entry and Exit of DHL

In the late-1990s, DHL was acquired by Deutsche Post. Deutsche Post also spent approximately $5 billion to acquire several companies in the logistics business between 1997 and 1999. In November 2000, Deutsche Post went private with an initial public offering that raised $5.5 billion and announced its intention to build an integrated global delivery and logistics network. Many believed it was only a matter of time before the company entered the United States. Thus, few were surprised when in 2003 DHL acquired Airborne Express. Under the terms of their agreement, Airborne Express sold its truck delivery system to DHL for $1.05 billion. Airborne's fleet of planes were moved into an independent company called ABX Air, owned by Airborne's shareholders, and which continues to serve DHL Worldwide Express under a long-term contract. This arrangement overcame the U.S. law that prohibits foreign control of more than 25% of a domestic airline. In the meantime, DHL spun its own fleet of U.S.-based planes into a U.S.-owned company called Astar,

to also escape the charge that its U.S. airline was foreign owned. Between 2003 and 2005 DHL reportedly invested some $1.2 billion to upgrade the capabilities of assets acquired from Airborne.[49]

The DHL acquisition created 3 major competitors in both the U.S. and global delivery markets. By the fall of 2003, DHL had launched an ad campaign aimed at UPS and FedEx customers promoting the service and cost advantages that they would benefit from because of its merger with Airborne. DHL targeted specific zip code areas in its advertising promoting its claim to be the number one in international markets, something important to many companies given the increasing importance of global commerce. In its ads, DHL reported that "current Airborne customers will be connected to DHL's extensive international delivery system in more than 200 countries."[50]

DHL's stated goal was to become a powerhouse in the U.S. delivery market. While its share of the U.S. small package express market remained small after the acquisition at around 10%, many thought that DHL would benefit from ownership by Deutsche Post and from its own extensive ex-U.S. operations. When it first acquired Airborne, Deutsche Post stated that the U.S. operation would be profitable by the end of 2006.

However, the company ran into "integration problems" and suffered from reports of poor customer services and missed delivery deadlines. In 2006, DHL management stated that they now did not see the North American unit turning profitable until 2009. DHL lost some $500 million in the U.S. in 2006.[51] In 2007, they lost close to $1 billion. With corporate customers leaving for rivals, and market share sliding, in late-2008, DHL announced that it would exit the U.S. market. DHL shut down its air and ground hubs, laid off 9,600 employees, and took a charge against earnings of some $3.9 billion. In explaining the exit decision, DHL management stated that they underestimated just how tough it would be to gain share against FedEx and UPS.[52]

Continued Globalization

Between 1997 and 2010, UPS and FedEx continued to build out their global infrastructure. By 2010, UPS delivered to more than 200 countries. Much of the within country delivery is handled by local enterprises. The company has 5 main hubs. In addition to its main U.S. hub in Louisville, Kentucky, it has hubs in Cologne, Taipei, Miami (serving Latin American traffic), and the Philippines. In 2002, UPS launched an intra-Asian express delivery network from its Philippines hub. In 2004, it acquired Menlo World wide Forwarding, a global freight forwarder, to boost its global logistics business. In the same year, it also acquired complete ownership of its Japanese delivery operation (which was formally a joint venture with Yamato Transport Company). In 2005, UPS acquired operators of local ground networks in the UK and Poland, and it is pushing into mainland China, which it sees as a major growth opportunity.

Like UPS, FedEx serves more than 200 countries around the world, although also like UPS, most of the local ground delivery is in the hands of local partners. FedEx has recently been focusing upon building a presence in both China and India. The company has announced the development of a new Asian Pacific hub in Guangzhou China. This will be FedEx's 4th international hub. The others are in Paris (handling intra-European express), the Philippines (handling intra-Asian express), and Alaska (which handles packages flowing between Asia, North America, and Europe). In 2006, FedEx signaled its commitment to the Chinese market by buying out its joint venture partner, Tianjin Datian W. Group, for $400 million. The acquisition gave FedEx control of 90 parcel handling facilities and a 3,000 strong work force in China.[53]

While UPS and FedEx dominate the U.S. market for small package express delivery services, in Europe DHL and TNT lead with 23% and 11% respectively (TNT, formally an Australian enterprise, was acquired by the Royal Netherlands Post Office in 1996). In the intercontinental market, DHL leads with a 36% share, while in intra-Asian traffic Asia Yamato of Japan is the leader with a 20% share followed by Sagawa with 16%. The fragmented nature of the European and intra-Asia Pacific markets suggest that much is still at stake in this increasingly global business.

The U.S. and Global Markets in 2010

With DHL out of the picture in the United States, FedEx and UPS tightened their hold on the market. The USPS held onto a small share of the overnight express market and a somewhat bigger share of the

ground market (see Exhibit 2). Despite challenging economic conditions, UPS and FedEx were both able to push through list rate increases of around 4–5% during the late-2000s, although after negotiations with large corporations, those increases were often reduced to 2–3%. They were also able to add fuel surcharges to prices, which helped given the high price of oil in the late-2000s.

Domestic volume continued to expand at a moderate pace and tended to match the growth in U.S. GDP. Most of the domestic volume growth was in the ground network. International volume growth was correlated to the growth in international trade and was generally higher than domestic growth. The volume of international trade had slumped in 2009, but rebounded strongly in 2010 and 2011. While the volume of document shipments was declining due to electronic transmission, the slack was being picked up by increased shipment of goods purchased online, and growth of low weight high value inventory, such as electronic components. The globalization of supply chains and moves toward just-in-time inventory was helping both companies.[54]

By 2010, UPS was shipping some 15 million packages a day through its network, while FedEx was moving between 6 and 7 million. Peak volumes were hitting 25 million for UPS and 16 million for FedEx.

Both FedEx and UPS were solidly profitable in 2010 (see Exhibit 3). Profit margins in the industry were leveraged to volume; higher volume meant significant margin expansion. Both FedEx and UPS were looking to a strong 2011 as volume expanded. The USPS, however, was deep in the red. In 2010, the

Exhibit 2: U.S. Market Share (%), 2010

	Overnight Express	Deferred Air	Ground
FedEx	54%	48%	22%
UPS	41%	52%	61%
USPS	6%	0%	16%
Market Size	$14 billion	$6 billion	$34 billion

Source: W.J. Greene et al, "Airfreight and Surface Transport: Parcel Industry Primer," *Morgan Stanley*, May 25, 2011.

Exhibit 3: Comparing FedEx and UPS in 2010

	FedEx	UPS
Revenue	$34.7 billion	$49.5 billion
Net Income	$1.12 billion	$3.49 billion
Cash Flow	$3.14 billion	$3.84 billion
Capital Expenditure	$2.82 billion	$1.39 billion
ROIC	7.41%	19.39%

Source: Company Reports

USPS lost $8 billion on total revenues of $67 billion. Traditional mail delivery was now a declining business as ever more mail was sent electronically. Some believed that the privatization of the USPS was inevitable.

Despite its exit from the U.S. market, DHL still was the largest operator globally in 2010 with $71 billion in revenues, and $2 billion in net income, followed by UPS and FedEx. TNT was in 4th place with $15 billion in revenues and $1 billion in net income.

Endnotes

1 Standard & Poor's, "Aerospace and Air Transport," *Industry Surveys,* February 1996.
2 Ibid.
3 Standard & Poor's, "Airlines," *Industry Surveys,* March 2002.
4 John Kartsonas, "United Parcel Service," *Citigroup Global Capital Markets*, November 13, 2006. W.J. Greene et al, "Airfreight and Surface Transport: Parcel Industry Primer," *Morgan Stanley*, May 25, 2011.
5 W.J. Greene et al, "Airfreight and Surface Transport: Parcel Industry Primer," *Morgan Stanley*, May 25, 2011.
6 C.H. Lovelock, "Federal Express (B)," Harvard Business School Case No. 579–040, 1978.
7 Standard & Poor's, "Aerospace and Air Transport," *Industry Surveys,* January 1981.
8 Lovelock, "Federal Express (B)."
9 Standard & Poor's, "Aerospace and Air Transport," *Industry Surveys,* January 1981.
10 Ibid.
11 Ibid.
12 Standard & Poor's, "Aerospace and Air Transport," *Industry Surveys*, January 1984.
13 C. Hall, "High Fliers," *Marketing and Media Decisions*, August 1986, p. 138.
14 Standard & Poor's, "Aerospace and Air Transport," *Industry Surveys,* January 1984.
15 Standard & Poor's, "Aerospace and Air Transport," *Industry Surveys,* December 1984.
16 B. Dumaine, "Turbulence Hits the Air Couriers," *Fortune,* July 21, 1986, pp. 101–106.
17 Ibid.
18 C. Hawkins, "Purolator: Still No Overnight Success," *BusinessWeek*, June 16, 1986, pp. 76–78.
19 J. O'C. Hamilton, "Emery Is One Heavy Load for Consolidated Freightways," *BusinessWeek,* March 26, 1990, pp. 62–64.
20 Standard & Poor's "Aerospace and Air Transport," *Industry Surveys,* February 1996.
21 "Hold That Tiger: FedEx Is Now World Heavyweight," *Purchasing,* September 14, 1989, pp. 41–42.
22 Standard & Poor's, "Aerospace and Air Transport," *Industry Surveys,* April 1988.
23 Standard & Poor's, "Aerospace and Air Transport," *Industry Surveys,* February 1996.
24 D. Greising, "Watch Out for Flying Packages," *BusinessWeek*, November 1994, p. 40.
25 Staff Reporter, "UPS to Raise its Rates for Packages," *Wall Street Journal*, January 9, 1995, p. C22.
26 M. Royce, "Airborne Freight," *Value Line Investment Survey,* September 20, 1996.
27 R. Frank, "UPS Planning Earlier Delivery," *Wall Street Journal,* September 29, 1994, p. A4.
28 Frank, "Federal Express Grapples with Changes in U.S. Market."
29 Company Press Releases (http://www.ups.com/news/).
30 J. M. Feldman, "The Coming of Age of International Air Freight," *Air Transport World,* June 1989, pp. 31–33.
31 Standard & Poor's, "Aerospace and Air Transport," *Industry Surveys,* February 1996.
32 Ibid.
33 P. Greiff, "Lufthansa, JAL, and a Trading Firm Acquire a Majority Stake in DHL," *Wall Street Journal,* August 24, 1992, p. A5.
34 Standard & Poor's, "Aerospace and Air Transport," *Industry Surveys,* February 1996.
35 "Hold That Tiger: FedEx Is Now a World Heavyweight."
36 D. Blackmon, "FedEx Swings from Confidence Abroad to a Tightrope," *Wall Street Journal,* March 15, 1996, p. B4.
37 D. Pearl, "Federal Express Plans to Trim Assets in Europe," *Wall Street Journal,* March 17, 1992, p. A3.
38 Company Press Releases (http://www.ups.com/news/).
39 C. Haddad and M. Arndt, "Saying No Thanks to Overnight Air," *Business Week*, April 1, 2002, p. 74.
40 Salomon Smith Barney Research, Wrap It Up—Bundling and the Air Express Sector, May 3, 2002. J. Kartsonas,

"United Parcel Service," *Citigroup Global Capital Markets*, November 13, 2006.

41 J. Kartsonas, "FedEx Corp," *Citigroup Global Capital Markets*, November 13, 2006.

42 W.J. Greene and A. Longson, "FedEx Corporation" *Morgan Stanley Research*, June 22, 2011.

43 Data from Deutsche Post World Net, 2005 Annual Report.

44 C. Haddad and M. Arndt, "Saying No Thanks to Overnight Air," *Business Week,* April 1, 2002, p. 74.

45 E. Walsh, "Package Deal," *Logistics*, February 2001, pp. 19–20.

46 Salomon Smith Barney Research, Wrap It Up—Bundling and the Air Express Sector, May 3, 2002.

47 R. Gibson, "Package Deal: UPS' Purchase of Mail Boxes Etc. Looked Great on Paper," *Wall Street Journal,* May 8, 2006, p. R13.

48 A. Ward, "Kinko's Plans to Push the Envelope Further," *Financial Times*, August 7, 2006, p. 22.

49 J.D. Schultz, "DHL Crashes the Party," *Logistics*, August 2005, pp. 59–63.

50 P. Needham, "Coming to America," *Journal of Commerce,* April 22, 2002, p. 12.

51 B. Barnard, "Logistics Spurs Deutsche Post," *Journal of Commerce*, November 8, 2006, p. 1.

52 A. Roth and M. Esterl, "DHL Beats a Retreat from the U.S.," *Wall Street Journal*, November 11, 2008, p. B1.

53 A. Ward, "A Dogfight for Courier Service Dominance," *Financial Times*, February 15, 2006, p. 10.

54 W.J. Greene et al, "Airfreight and Surface Transport: Parcel Industry Primer," *Morgan Stanley*, May 25, 2011.

CASE 8

Airborne Express: The Underdog

Charles W.L. Hill
University of Washington

Introduction

Airborne Inc., which operated under the name Airborne Express, was an air-express transportation company, providing express and second-day delivery of small packages (less than 70 lbs.) and documents throughout the United States and to and from many foreign countries. The company owned and operated an airline and a fleet of ground-transportation vehicles to provide complete door-to-door service. It was also an airfreight forwarder, moving shipments of any size worldwide. In 2003, Airborne Express held third place in the U.S. air express industry, with 9% of the market for small package deliveries. Its main domestic competitors were Federal Express, which had 26% of the market; United Parcel Service (UPS), which had 53% of the market. There were several smaller players in the market at the time, including DHL Airways, Consolidated Freightways and the U.S. Postal Service, each of which held under 5% of the market share.[1] DHL however, had a huge presence outside of North America and was in fact the largest small package delivery company in the world. In 2003, after years of struggling to survive in the fiercely competitive small package express delivery industry, Airborne was acquired by DHL, which was owned by Deutsche Post, the large German postal, express package, and logistics company.

The evolution of the air express industry and the current state of competition in the industry were discussed in a companion case to this one, "The Evolution of the Air Express Industry, 1973–2010." The current case focuses on the operating structure, competitive strategy, organizational structure, and cultures of Airborne Express, from its inception until it was acquired by DHL in 2003. It also deals with the aftermath of the DHL acquisition.

History of Airborne Express

Airborne Express was originally known as Pacific Air Freight when it was founded in Seattle at the close of World War II by Holt W. Webster, a former Army Air Corps officer. (See Table 1 for a listing of major milestones in the history of Airborne Express.) The company was merged with Airborne Freight Corporation of California in 1968, taking the name of the California company, but retaining management direction by the former officers of Pacific Air Freight. Airborne was initially an exclusive airfreight forwarder. Freight forwarders such as Airborne arrange for the transportation of air cargo between any two destinations. They purchase cargo space from the airlines and retail this in small amounts. They deal primarily with small customers, providing pickup and delivery services in most cities, either in their own trucks or through contract agents.

Following the 1977 deregulation of the airline industry, Airborne entered the air express industry by leasing the airplanes and pilots of Midwest Charter, a small airline operating out of its own airport in Wilmington, Ohio. However, Airborne quickly became dissatisfied with the limited amount of control they were able to exercise over Midwest,

This case was made possible by the generous assistance of Airborne Express. The information given in this case was provided by Airborne Express. Unless otherwise indicated, Airborne Express and Securities and Exchange Commission's 10–K filings are the sources of all information contained within this case. The case is based on an earlier case, which was prepared with the assistance of Daniel Bodnar, Laurie Martinelli, Brian McMullen, Lisa Mutty, and Stephen Schmidt.

Table 1 Major Milestones at Airborne Express[2]

1946: Airborne Flower Traffic Association of California is founded to fly fresh flowers from Hawaii to the mainland.

1968: Airborne of California and Pacific Air Freight of Seattle merge to form Airborne Freight Corporation. Headquarters are in Seattle, Washington.

1979–81: Airborne Express is born. After purchasing Midwest Air Charter, Airborne buys Clinton County Air Force Base in Wilmington, Ohio, becoming the only carrier to own and operate an airport. The package sort center opens, creating the "hub" for the hub-and-spoke system.

1984–86: Airborne is the first carrier to establish a privately operated Foreign Trade Zone in an air industrial park.

1987: Airborne opens the Airborne Stock Exchange, a third-party inventory management and distribution service. In the same year, service begins to and from more than 8,000 Canadian locations.

1988: Airborne becomes the first air express carrier to provide same-day delivery, through its purchase of Sky Courier.

1990: The International Cargo Forum and Exposition names Airborne the carrier with the most outstanding integrated cargo system over the previous two years.

1991: A trio of accolades: Airborne is the first transportation company to receive Volvo-Flyg Motors' Excellent Performance Award. Computerworld ranks us the "most effective user of information systems in the U.S. transportation industry." In addition, we receive the "Spread the Word!" Electronic Data Interchange (EDI) award for having the largest number of EDI users worldwide in the air express and freight forwarding industry.

1992: Airborne introduces Flight-ReadySM—the first prepaid Express Letters and Packs.

1993: Airborne introduces Airborne Logistics Services (ALS), a new subsidiary providing outsourced warehousing and distribution services. IBM consolidates its international shipping operation with Airborne.

1994: Airborne opens its Ocean Service Division, becoming the first express carrier to introduce ocean shipping services. Airborne Logistics Services (ALS) establishes the first new film distribution program for the movie industry in 50 years. We also become the first company to provide on-line communication to Vietnam.

1995: Airborne Alliance Group, a consortium of transportation, logistics, third-party customer service operations and high-tech companies providing value-added services, is formed. Airborne opens a second runway at its hub, which is now the United States' largest privately owned airport. We also expand our fleet, acquiring Boeing 767–200 aircraft.

1996: Airborne Express celebrates 50 years of providing value-added distribution solutions to business.

1997: Airborne Express has its best year ever, with net earnings increasing three-and-a-half-fold over the previous year. Airborne's stock triples, leading to a two-for-one stock split in February, 1998.

1998: Airborne posts record profits and enters the Fortune 500. The first of 30 Boeing 767s is introduced to our fleet. The Business Consumer Guide rates Airborne as the Best Air Express Carrier for the 4th consecutive year.

1999: Airborne@home, a unique alliance with the United States Postal Service, is introduced. It enables e-tailers, catalog companies and similar businesses to ship quickly and economically to the residential marketplace. Optical Village is created. Part of Airborne Logistics Services, this new division brings together some of the biggest competitors in the optical industry to share many costs and a single location for their assembly, storage, inventory, logistics, and delivery options.

(continued)

Table 1 (*continued*)

2000: Airborne announces several changes in senior management, including a new President and Chief Operating Officer, Carl Donaway. Several new business initiatives are announced, most notably a ground service scheduled to begin April 1, 2001. Airborne also wins the Brand Keys Customer Loyalty Award, edging out our competition for the second consecutive year.
2001: Airborne launches Ground Delivery Service and 10:30 A.M. Service, giving Airborne a comprehensive, full-service industry competitive capability. Airborne.com launches its Small Business Center, as well as a variety of enhancements to help all business customers speed and simplify the shipping process. We also release the Corporate Exchange shipping application, simplifying desktop shipping for customers while giving them greater control. Advanced tracking features are added to airborne.com and Airborne eCourier is released, enabling customers to send confidential, signed documents electronically.
2003: Airborne's ground operations acquired by DHL for $1.1 billion.

© Cengage Learning 2013

which made it very difficult to achieve the kind of tight coordination and control of logistics that was necessary to become a successful air express operator. Instead of continuing to lease Midwest's planes and facility, in 1980 Airborne decided to buy "the entire bucket of slop; company, planes, pilots, airport and all."

Among other things, the Midwest acquisition put Airborne in the position of being the only industry participant to own an airport. Airborne immediately began the job of developing a hub-and-spoke system capable of supporting a nationwide distribution system. An efficient sorting facility was established at the Wilmington hub. Airborne upgraded Midwest's fleet of prop and propjet aircraft, building a modern fleet of DC-8s, DC-9s, and YS-11 aircraft. These planes left major cities every evening, flying down the spokes carrying letters and packages to the central sort facility in Wilmington, Ohio. There the letters and packages were unloaded, sorted according to their final destination, and then reloaded and flown to their final destination for delivery before noon the next day.

During the late-1970s and early-1980s, dramatic growth in the industry attracted many competitors. As a consequence, the high-growth rate price competition became intense, forcing a number of companies to the sidelines by the late-1980s. Between 1984 and 1990 average revenues per domestic shipment at Airborne fell from around $30 to under $15 (in 2003 they were just under $9).

Airborne was able to survive this period by pursuing a number of strategies that increased productivity and drove costs down to the lowest levels in the industry. Airborne's operating costs per shipment fell from $28 in 1984 to around $14 by 1990, and to $9.79 by 2001. As a consequence, by the late-1980s Airborne had pulled away from a pack of struggling competitors to become one of the top three companies in the industry, a position it still held when acquired by DHL in 2003.

Air Express Operations

The Domestic Delivery Network

As of 2002, its last full year as an independent enterprise, Airborne Express had 305 ground stations within the United States. The stations were the ends of the spokes in Airborne's hub-and-spoke system and the distribution of stations allows Airborne to reach all major population centers in the country. In each station there were about 50–55 drivers plus staff. About 80% of Airborne's 115,300 full-time and 7,200 part-time employees were found at this level. The stations were the basic units in Airborne's delivery organization. Their primary task was to ferry packages between clients and the local air terminal. Airborne utilized approximately 14,900 radio-dispatch delivery vans and trucks to transport packages, of which 6,000 were owned by the company. Independent contractors provided the balance of the company's pickup and delivery services.

Airborne's drivers made their last round of major clients at 5 P.M. The drivers either collected packages directly from clients or from one of the company's 15,300 plus drop boxes. The drop boxes were placed at strategic locations, such as in the lobbies of major commercial buildings. To give clients a little more time, in most major cities there were also a few central drop boxes emptied at 6 P.M. If a client needed still more time, so long as the package could be delivered to the airport by 7 P.M., it would make the evening flight.

When a driver picked up a package, he or she read a bar code attached to the package with a hand-held scanner. This information was fed directly into Airborne's proprietary FOCUS (Freight, On-Line Control and Update System) computer system. The FOCUS system, which had global coverage, records shipment status at key points in the life cycle of a shipment. FOCUS allowed a customer direct access to shipment information through the Internet. All a customer needed to do is access Airborne's Website and key the code number assigned to a package, and the FOCUS system would tell the customer where in Airborne's system the package was.

When a driver completed a pickup route, she or he took the truck to Airborne's loading docks at the local airport. (Airborne served all 99 major metropolitan airports in the United States.) There the packages were loaded into C-containers (discussed later in this case study). C-containers were then towed by hand (or by tractor) to a waiting aircraft, where they were loaded onto a conveyor belt and moved through the passenger door of the aircraft. Before long the aircraft was loaded and departed. It would either fly directly to the company's hub at Wilmington, or make one or two stops along the way to pick up more packages.

Sometime between midnight and 2 A.M., most of the aircraft would have landed at Wilmington. An old strategic air command base, Wilmington's location places it within a 600-mile radius (an overnight drive or 1-hour flying time) of 60% of the U.S. population. Wilmington has the advantage of a good-weather record. In all the years that Airborne operated at Wilmington, air operations were "fogged out" on only a handful of days. In 1995, Airborne opened a second runway at Wilmington. Developed at a cost of $60 million, the second runway made Wilmington the largest privately owned airport in the country. The runway expansion was part of a $120 million upgrade of the Wilmington sort facility.

After arrival at Wilmington, the plane taxed down the runway and parked alongside a group of aircraft that were already disgorging their load of C-containers. Within minutes, the C-containers were unloaded from the plane down a conveyor belt and towed to the sort facility by a tractor. The sort facility had the capacity to handle 1.2 million packages per night. At the end of 2001, the facility handled an average of 1 million packages per night. The bar codes on the packages were read, and then the packages were directed through a labyrinth of conveyor belts and sorted according to final destination. The sorting was partly done by hand and partly by automation. At the end of this process, packages were grouped together by final destination and loaded into a C-container. An aircraft bound for the final destination was then loaded with C-containers, and by 5 A.M. most aircraft had departed.

Upon arrival at the final destination, the plane was unloaded and the packages sorted according to their delivery points within the surrounding area. Airborne couriers then took the packages on the final leg of their journey. Packages had a 75% probability of being delivered to clients by 10:30 A.M., and a 98% probability of being delivered by noon.

Regional Trucking Hubs

Although about 71% of packages were transported by air and passed through Wilmington, Airborne also established 10 regional trucking hubs to deal with the remaining 29% of the company's domestic volume. These hubs sorted shipments that originated and had a destination within approximately a 300-mile radius. The first one opened was in Allentown, Pennsylvania, centrally located on the East Coast. This hub handled packages transported between points within the Washington, D.C., and Boston areas. Instead of transporting packages by air, packages to be transported within this area were sorted by the drivers at pickup and delivered from the driver's home station by scheduled truck runs to the Allentown hub. There they were sorted according to destination and taken to the appropriate station on another scheduled truck run for final delivery.

One advantage of ground-based transportation through trucking hubs is that operating costs are much lower than for air transportation. The average cost of a package transported by air is more than 5 times greater than the cost of a package transported on the ground. However, this cost differential is transparent to the customer, who assumes that all packages are flown. Thus, Airborne could charge the same price for ground-transported packages as for air-transported packages, but the former yielded a much higher return. The trucking hubs also had the advantage of taking some of the load of the Wilmington sorting facility, which was operating at about 90% capacity by 2003.

International Operations

In addition to its domestic express operations, Airborne was also an international company providing service to more than 200 countries worldwide. International operations accounted for about 11% of total revenues in 2002. Airborne offered two international products: freight products and express products. Freight products were commercial-sized, larger-unit shipments. This service provides door-to-airport service. Goods were picked up domestically from the customer and then shipped to the destination airport. A consignee or an agent of the consignee got the paperwork and cleared the shipment through customs. Express packages are small packages, documents, and letters. This was a door-to-door service, and all shipments were cleared through customs by Airborne. Most of Airborne's international revenues come from freight products.

Airborne did not fly any of its own aircraft overseas. Rather, it contracted for space on all-cargo airlines or in the cargo holds of passenger airlines. Airborne owned facilities overseas in Japan, Taiwan, Hong Kong, Singapore, Australia, New Zealand, and London. These functioned in a manner similar to Airborne's domestic stations. (That is, they had their own trucks and drivers and were hooked into the FOCUS tracking system.) The majority of foreign distribution, however, was carried out by foreign agents. Foreign agents were large, local, well-established surface delivery companies. Airborne entered into a number of exclusive strategic alliances with large foreign agents. It had alliances in Japan, Thailand, Malaysia, and South Africa. The rationale

for entering strategic alliances, along with Airborne's approach to global expansion, is discussed in greater detail later in this case.

Another aspect of Airborne's international operations was the creation at its Wilmington hub, the only privately certified Foreign Trade Zone (FTZ) in the United States. While in an FTZ, no taxes are to be paid and no customs duty is required until merchandise leaves. Thus, a foreign-based company could store critical inventory in the FTZ and have Airborne deliver it just-in-time to U.S. customers. This allowed the foreign company to hold inventory in the United States without having to pay customs duty on it until necessary.

Aircraft Purchase and Maintenance

As of 2002, Airborne Express owned a fleet of 118 aircraft, including 24 DC-8s, 74 DC-9s, and twenty Boeing 767s. In addition, approximately 70 smaller aircraft were chartered nightly to connect smaller cities with company aircraft that then operate to and from the Wilmington hub. To keep down capital expenditures, Airborne preferred to purchase used planes. Airborne converted the planes to suit its specifications at a maintenance facility in its Wilmington hub. Once it got a plane, Airborne typically gutted the interior and installed state-of-the-art electronics and avionics equipment. The company's philosophy was to get all of the upgrades that it could into an aircraft. Although this can cost a lot up front, there is a payback in terms of increased aircraft reliability and a reduction in service downtime. Airborne also standardized cockpits as much as possible. This made it easier for crews to switch from one aircraft to another if necessary. According to the company, in the early-1990s, the total purchase and modification of a secondhand DC-9 cost about $10 million, compared with an equivalent new plane cost of $40 million. An additional factor reducing operating costs was that Airborne's DC-9 aircraft only required a 2-person cockpit crew, as opposed to the 3-person crews required in most FedEx and UPS aircraft at that time.

After conversion, Airborne strove to keep aircraft maintenance costs down by carrying out virtually all of its own fleet repairs. (It was the only all-cargo carrier to do so.) The Wilmington maintenance facility could handle everything except major engine repairs and had the capability to machine critical aircraft parts, if needed. The company saw this in-house facility as a major source of cost savings. It estimated that maintenance labor costs were 50–60% below the costs of having the same work performed outside.

In December 1995, Airborne announced a deal to purchase 12 used Boeing 767–200 aircraft between the years 1997 and 2000, and it announced plans to purchase a further 10–15 used 767–200s between the years 2000 and 2004. These were the first wide-bodied aircraft in Airborne's fleet. The cost of introducing the first 12 aircraft was about $290 million, and the additional aircraft would cost another $360 million. The shift to wide-bodied aircraft was promoted by an internal study, which concluded that with growing volume, wide-bodied aircraft would lead to greater operating efficiencies.

During 2001, Airborne was using about 66.6% of its lift capacity on a typical business day. This compared with 76.7% capacity utilization in 1997, and 70% utilization in 2000. In late-2001, Airborne reduced its total lift capacity by some 100,000 lbs. to about 4 million lbs. per day. It did this to try and reduce excess capacity of certain routes and better match supply with demand conditions.

C-Containers

C-containers are uniquely shaped 60-cubic-foot containers, developed by Airborne Express in 1985 at a cost of $3.5 million. They are designed to fit through the passenger doors of DC-8 and DC-9 aircraft. They replaced the much larger A-containers widely used in the air cargo business. At 6 times the size of a C-container, A-containers can only be loaded through specially built cargo doors and require specialized loading equipment. The loading equipment required for C-containers is a modified belt loader, similar to that used for loading baggage onto a plane, and about 80% less expensive than the equipment needed to load A-containers. The use of C-containers meant that Airborne did not have to bear the $1 million per plane cost required to install cargo doors that would take A-containers. The C-containers are shaped to allow maximum utilization of the planes' interior loading space. Fifty of the containers fit into a converted DC-9, and about 83 fit into a DC-8-62. Moreover, a C-container filled with packages can be

moved by a single person, making them easy to load and unload. Airborne Express took out a patent on the design of the C-containers.

Information Systems

Airborne utilized three information systems to help it boost productivity and improve customer service. The first of these systems was the LIBRA II system. LIBRA II equipment, which included a metering device and PC computer software, was installed in the mailroom of clients. With minimum data entry, the metering device weighed the package, calculated the shipping charges, generated the shipping labels, and provided a daily shipping report. By 2002, the system was in use at approximately 9,900 domestic customer locations. The use of LIBRA II not only benefited customers, but also lowered Airborne's operating costs since LIBRA II shipment data were transferred into Airborne's FOCUS shipment tracking system automatically, thereby avoiding duplicate data entry.

FOCUS was the second of Airborne's three main information systems. As discussed earlier, the FOCUS system was a worldwide tracking system. The bar codes on each package were read at various points (for example, at pickup, at sorting in Wilmington, at arrival, and so forth) using hand-held scanners, this information was fed into Airborne's computer system. Using FOCUS, Airborne could track the progress of a shipment through its national and international logistics system. The major benefit was increased customer service. Through an Internet link, Airborne's customers could track their own shipment through Airborne's system on a 24-hour basis.

For its highest-volume corporate customers, Airborne developed Customer Linkage, an electronic data interchange (EDI) program and the third information system. The EDI system was designed to eliminate the flow of paperwork between Airborne and its major clients. The EDI system allowed customers to create shipping documentation at the same time they were entering orders for their goods. At the end of each day, shipping activities were transmitted electronically to Airborne's FOCUS system and captured for shipment tracking and billing. Customer Linkage benefited the customer by eliminating repetitive data entry and paperwork. It also lowered the company's operating costs by eliminating manual data entry. (In essence, both LIBRA II and Customer Linkage reallocated a lot of the data-entry work into the hands of customers.) The EDI system also included electronic invoicing and payment remittance processing. Airborne also offered its customers a program known as Quicklink, which significantly reduced the programming time required by customers to take advantage of linkage benefits.

Strategy

Market Positioning

In the early-1980s, Airborne Express tried hard to compete head-to-head with FedEx. This included an attempt to establish broad market coverage, including both frequent and infrequent users. Frequent users are those that generate more than $20,000 of business per month, or more than 1,000 shipments per month. Infrequent users generate less than $20,000 per month, or less than 1,000 shipments per month.

To build broad market coverage, Airborne followed FedEx' lead of funding a television advertising campaign designed to build consumer awareness. However, by the mid-1980s, Airborne decided that this was an expensive way of building market share. The advertising campaign bought recognition but little penetration. One of the principal problems was that it was expensive to serve infrequent users. Infrequent users demanded the same level of service as frequent users, but Airborne would typically only get one shipment per pickup with an infrequent user, compared with 10 or more shipments per pickup with a frequent user, so far more pickups were required to generate the same volume of business. Given the extremely competitive nature of the industry at this time, such an inefficient utilization of capacity was of great concern to Airborne.

Consequently, in the mid-1980s Airborne decided to become a niche player in the industry and focus on serving the needs of high-volume corporate accounts. The company slashed its advertising expenditure, pulling the plug on its TV ad campaign, and invested more resources in building a direct sales force, which grew to be 460 strong. By focusing upon high-volume corporate accounts, Airborne was able to establish scheduled pickup routes and

use its ground capacity more efficiently. This enabled the company to achieve significant reductions in its unit cost structure. Partly due to this factor, Airborne executives reckoned that their cost structure was as much as $3 per shipment less than that of FedEx. Another estimate suggested that Airborne's strategy reduced labor costs by 20% per unit for pickup, and 10% for delivery.

Of course, there was a downside to this strategy. High-volume corporate customers have a great deal more bargaining power than infrequent users, so they can and do demand substantial discounts. For example, in March 1987, Airborne achieved a major coup when it won an exclusive 3-year contract to handle all of IBM's express packages weighing less than 150 lbs. However, to win the IBM account, Airborne had to offer rates up to 84% below FedEx's list prices! Nevertheless, the strategy does seem to have worked. As of 1995 approximately 80% of Airborne's revenues came from corporate accounts, most of them secured through competitive bidding. The concentrated volume that this business represents helped Airborne to drive down costs.

Delivery Time, Reliability, and Flexibility

A further feature of Airborne's strategy was the decision not to try to compete with Federal Express on delivery time. FedEx and UPS have long guaranteed delivery by 10:30 A.M. Airborne guaranteed delivery by midday, although it offered a 10:30 guarantee to some very large corporate customers. Guaranteeing delivery by 10:30 A.M. would mean stretching Airborne's already tight scheduling system to the limit. To meet its 10:30 A.M. deadline, FedEx has to operate with a deadline for previous days' pickups of 6:30 P.M. Airborne could afford to be a little more flexible and arrange pickups at 6:00 P.M. if that suited a corporate client's particular needs. Later pickups clearly benefit the shipper, who is, after all, the paying party.

In addition, Airborne executives felt that a guaranteed 10:30 A.M. delivery was unnecessary. They argued that the extra hour and a half would not make a great deal of difference to most clients, and they are willing to accept the extra time in exchange for lower prices. In addition, Airborne stressed the reliability of its delivery schedules. As one executive put it, "a package delivered consistently at 11:15 A.M.

is as good as delivery at 10:30 A.M." This reliability was enhanced by Airborne's ability to provide shipment tracking through its FOCUS system.

Deferred Services

With a slowdown in the growth rate of the express mail market toward the end of the 1980s, in 1990 Airborne decided to enter the deferred-delivery business with its Select Delivery Service (SDS) product. The SDS service provides for next-afternoon or second-day delivery. Packages weighing 5 lbs. or less are generally delivered on a next-afternoon basis, with packages of more than 5 lbs. being delivered on a second-day basis. SDS shipment comprised approximately 42% of total domestic shipments in 1995. They were priced lower than overnight express products, reflecting the less time-sensitive nature of these deliveries. The company utilized any spare capacity on its express flights to carry SDS shipments. In addition, Airborne used other carriers, such as passenger carriers with spare cargo capacity in the bellies of their planes, to carry less urgent SDS shipments.

Early in 1996 Airborne began to phase in two new services to replace its SDS service. Next Afternoon Service was available for shipments weighing 5 lbs. or less, and Second Day Service was offered for shipments of all weights. By 2001, deferred shipments accounted for 46% of total domestic shipments.

Ground Delivery Service

In April 2001, Airborne launched a Ground Delivery Service (GDS) in response to similar offerings from FedEx and UPS. Airborne came to the conclusion that it was very important to offer this service in order to retain parity with its principle competitors, and to be able to offer bundled services to its principle customers (that is, to offer them air, ground, and logistics services for a single bundled price). Airborne also felt that they could add the service with a relatively minor initial investment, $30 million, since it leveraged existing assets, including trucks, tracking systems, and regional ground hubs and sorting facilities.

The new service had initially been introduced on a limited basis, and targeted large corporate customers. GDS was priced less than deferred services, reflecting the less time sensitive nature of the GDS offering. GDS accounted for 1.5% of domestic shipments in 2001, and 4% in the fourth quarter of 2001.

Logistics Services

Although small-package express mail remained Airborne's main business, through its Advanced Logistics Services Corp. (ALS) subsidiary, the company increasingly promoted a range of third-party logistics services. These services provided customers with the ability to maintain inventories in a 1-million-square-foot "stock exchange" facility located at Airborne's Wilmington hub, or at 60 smaller "stock exchange" facilities located around the country. The inventory could be managed either by the company or by the customer's personnel. Inventory stored at Wilmington could be delivered utilizing either Airborne's airline system or, if required, commercial airlines on a next-flight-out basis. ALS' central print computer program allowed information on inventories to be sent electronically to customers' computers located at Wilmington, where Airborne's personnel monitored printed output and shipped inventories according to customers' instructions.

For example, consider the case of Data Products Corp., a producer of computer printers. Data Products takes advantage of low labor costs to carry out significant assembly operations in Hong Kong. Many of the primary component parts for its printers, however, such as microprocessors, are manufactured in the United States and have to be shipped to Hong Kong. The finished product is then shipped back to the United States for sale. In setting up a global manufacturing system, Data Products had a decision to make: either consolidate the parts from its hundreds of suppliers in-house and then arrange for shipment to Hong Kong, or contract out to a company that could handle the entire logistics process. Data Products decided to contract out, and they picked Airborne Express to consolidate the component parts and arrange for shipments.

Airborne controlled the consolidation and movement of component parts from the component part suppliers through to the Hong Kong assembly operation in such a way as to minimize inventory-holding costs. The key feature of Airborne's service was that all of Data Products' materials were collected at Airborne's facility at Los Angeles International Airport. Data Products' Hong Kong assembly plants could then tell Airborne what parts to ship by air as and when they are needed. Airborne was thus able to provide inventory control for Data Products. In addition, by scheduling deliveries so that year-round traffic between Los Angeles and Hong Kong could be guaranteed, Airborne was able to negotiate a better air rate from Japan Air Lines (JAL) for the transportation of component parts.

International Strategy

One of the major strategic challenges that Airborne faced (along with the other express mail carriers) was how best to establish an international service that is comparable to their domestic service. Many of Airborne's major corporate clients were becoming ever more global in their own strategic orientation. As this occurred, they were increasingly demanding a compatible express mail service. In addition, the rise of companies with globally dispersed manufacturing operations that relied upon just-in-time delivery systems to keep inventory holding costs down created a demand for global air express services that could transport critical inventory between operations located in different areas of the globe (consider the example of Data Products discussed earlier in this case study).

The initial response of FedEx and UPS to this challenge was to undertake massive capital investments to establish international airlift capability and international ground operations based upon the U.S. model. Their rationale was that a wholly owned global delivery network was necessary to establish the tight control, coordination, and scheduling required for a successful air express operation. In the 1990s, however, FedEx pulled out of its European ground operations, while continuing to fly its own aircraft overseas.

Airborne decided upon a quite different strategy. In part born of financial necessity (Airborne lacks the capital necessary to imitate FedEx and UPS), Airborne decided to pursue what they referred to as a *variable cost strategy*. This involved two main elements: (1) the utilization of international airlift on existing air cargo operators and passenger aircraft to get their packages overseas and (2) entry into strategic alliances with foreign companies that already had established ground delivery networks. In these two ways, Airborne hoped to be able to establish

global coverage without having to undertake the kind of capital investments that Federal Express and UPS have borne.

Airborne executives defend their decision to continue to purchase space on international flights rather than fly their own aircraft overseas by making a number of points. First, they pointed out that Airborne's international business was 70% outbound and 30% inbound. If Airborne were to fly its own aircraft overseas, this would mean flying them back half-empty. Second, on many routes Airborne simply didn't have the volume necessary to justify flying its own planes. Third, national air carriers were giving Airborne good prices. If Airborne began to fly directly overseas, the company would be seen as a competitor and may no longer be given price breaks. Fourth, getting international airlift space was not a problem. While space can be limited in the third and fourth quarters of the year, Airborne was such a big customer that it usually had few problems getting lift.

On the other hand, the long-term viability of this strategy was questionable given the rapid evolution in the international air express business. Flying Tigers was once one of Airborne's major providers of international lift. However, following the purchase of Flying Tigers by FedEx, Airborne had reduced its business with Flying Tigers. Airborne worried that its packages would be "pushed to the back of the plane" when Flying Tigers had problems of capacity overload.

With regard to strategic alliances, Airborne had joint venture operations is Japan, Thailand, Malaysia, and South Africa. The alliance with Mitsui was announced in December 1989. Mitsui is one of the world's leading trading companies. Together with Tonami Transportation Co., Mitsui owns Panther Express, one of the top-five express carriers in Japan, and a company with a substantial ground network. The deal called for the establishment of a joint venture between Airborne, Mitsui, and Tonami. To be known as Airborne Express Japan, the joint venture combined Airborne's existing Japanese operations with Panther Express. Airborne handled all of the shipments to and from Japan. The joint venture was 40% owned by Airborne, 40% by Mitsui, and 20% by Tonami. The agreement specified that board decisions had to be made by consensus between the three partners. A majority of two could not outvote the third. In addition, the deal called for Mitsui to invest $40 million in Airborne Express through the purchase of a new issue of nonvoting 6.9% cumulative convertible preferred stock and a commitment to Airborne from Mitsui of up to $100 million for aircraft financing. There is no doubt that Airborne executives saw the Mitsui deal as a major coup, both financially and in terms of market penetration into the Japanese market. Airborne executives claimed that the primary advantage of expanding via strategic alliances is that the company got an established ground-based delivery network overseas without having to make capital investments.

Organization

In 2001, Carl Donaway became CEO, replacing the long time top management team of Robert Cline, the CEO, and Robert Brazier, the president and COO, both of whom had been with the company since the early-1960s. Prior to becoming CEO, Donaway was responsible for the airline operations, included managing the Wilmington hub, the package sorting facility, and all aircraft and flight maintenance operations. The philosophy at Airborne was to keep the organizational structure as flat as possible, to shorten lines of communication and allow for a free flow of ideas within the managerial hierarchy. The top managers generally felt that they were open to ideas suggested by lower-level managers. At the same time, the decision-making process was fairly centralized. The view was that interdependence between functions made centralized decision making necessary. To quote one executive, "Coordination is the essence of this business. We need centralized decision making in order to achieve this."

Control at Airborne Express was geared toward boosting productivity, lowering costs, and maintaining a reliable high-quality service. This was achieved through a combination of budgetary controls, pay-for-performance incentive systems, and a corporate culture that continually stressed key values.

For example, consider the procedure used to control stations (which contained about 80% of all employees). Station operations were reviewed on a quarterly basis using a budgetary process. Control and evaluation of station effectiveness stressed four categories. The first was service, measured by the time between pickup and delivery. The goal was to achieve 95–97% of all deliveries before noon. The second category was productivity, measured by total shipments per employee hour. The third category was controllable cost, and the fourth station profitability. Goals for each of these categories were determined each quarter in a bottom-up procedure that involved station managers in the goal-setting process. These goals are then linked to an incentive pay system whereby station managers can earn up to 10% of their quarterly salary just by meeting their goals with no maximum on the upside if they go over the goals.

The direct sales force also had an incentive pay system. The target pay structure for the sales organization was 70% base pay and a 30% commission. There was, however, no cap on the commissions for salespeople. So in theory, there was no limit to what a salesperson could earn. There were also contests that are designed to boost performance. For example, there was a so-called Top Gun competition for the sales force, in which the top salesperson for each quarter won a $20,000 prize.

Incentive pay systems apart, however, Airborne is not known as a high payer. The company's approach is not to be the compensation leader. Rather, the company tries to set its salary structure to position it in the middle of the labor market. Thus, according to a senior human resource executive, "We target our pay philosophy (total package—compensation plus benefits) to be right at the 50th percentile plus or minus 5%."

A degree of self-control was also achieved by trying to establish a corporate culture that focused employees' attention upon the key values required to maintain a competitive edge in the air express industry. The values continually stressed by top managers at Airborne and communicated throughout the organization by the company's newspaper and a quarterly video, emphasized serving customers' needs, maintaining quality, doing it right the first time around, and excellent service. There was also a companywide emphasis on productivity and cost control. One executive, when describing the company's attitude to expenditures, said, "We challenge everything. . . . We're the toughest sons of bitches on the block." Another noted that "among managers I feel that there is a universal agreement on the need to control costs. This is a very tough business, and our people are aware of that. Airborne has an underdog mentality—a desire to be a survivor."

The DHL Acquisition and its Aftermath

By 2002 Airborne Express faced a number of key strategic opportunities and threats. These included (1) the rapid globalization of the air express industry, (2) the development of logistics services based on rapid air transportation, (3) the growth potential for deferred services and ground-based delivery services, (4) lower margins associated with the new GDS offering, (5) the superior scale and scope of its two main competitors, FedEx and UPS, (6) an economic slowdown in the United States, and (7) persistently high fuel costs (oil prices rose from $18 a barrel in mid-1995 to $25 a barrel in 2002). The company's financial performance, which had always been volatile, was poor during 2001, when the company lost $12 million on revenues of $3.2 billion. In 2002, Airborne earned $58 million on revenues of $3.3 billion, even though average revenue per shipment declined to $8.46 from $8.79 a year earlier. Management attributed the improved performance to strong employee productivity, which improved 9.4% over the prior year. In their guidance for 2003, management stated that they would be able to further improve operating performance—then in March 2003 DHL made its takeover bid for the company. Under the terms of the deal, which was finalized in 2003, DHL acquired the ground assets of Airborne Express, while the airline continued as an independent entity.

In the late-1990s, DHL had been acquired by Deutsche Post, the German postal service. Deutsche Post had been privatized some years earlier. Deutsche Post spent approximately $5 billion to acquire several companies in the logistics business between 1997 and 1999. In November 2000, Deutsche Post went private with an initial public offering that raised $5.5 billion and announced its intention to build an integrated global delivery and logistics network.

DHL's goal with the Airborne acquisition was to expand its presence in the United States, where it had long been a marginal player. In 2004–2005 DHL spent some $1.5 billion upgrading Airborne's network to handle higher volumes. The company also embarked upon an aggressive media advertising campaign, presenting itself as a viable alternative to FedEx and UPS. In doing this, DHL seemed to be departing from Airborne's highly focused niche strategy.

The results were disappointing. The company reportedly ran into significant "integration problems" and suffered from reports of poor customer services and missed delivery deadlines. In 2006, DHL management stated that they did not see the North American unit turning profitable until 2009. DHL lost some $500 million in the U.S. in 2006.[3] In 2007, they lost close to $1 billion. With corporate customers leaving for rivals, and market share sliding, in November 2008, DHL announced that it would exit the U.S. market. DHL shut down its air and ground hubs, laid off 9,600 employees, and took a charge against earnings of some $3.9 billion. In explaining the exit decision, DHL management stated that they underestimated just how tough it would be to gain share against FedEx and UPS.[4]

Endnotes

1 Standard & Poor's Industry Survey, Airlines, March, 2002.
2 Source: www.airborne.com/Company/History.asp?nav=AboutAirborne/CompanyInfo/History
3 B. Barnard, "Logistics Spurs Deutsche Post," *Journal of Commerce*, November 8, 2006, 1.
4 A. Roth and M. Esterl, "DHL Beats a Retreat from the U.S.," *Wall Street Journal*, November 11, 2008, B1.

CASE 9

Internet Search and the Growth of Google

Charles W.L. Hill
University of Washington

Introduction

In the early-2000s, many Internet users started to gravitate toward a new search engine. It was called Google, and it delivered remarkable results. Put in a keyword, and in a blink of an eye the search engine would return a list of links, with the most relevant links appearing at the top of the page. People quickly realized that Google was an amazing tool, enabling users to quickly find almost anything they wanted on the Web—to effortlessly sort through the vast sea of information contained in billions of Web pages and retrieve the precise information they desired. It seemed like magic. Before long, "to Google" became a verb (in June 2006, the verb Google was added to the Oxford English Dictionary). To find out more about a person, you would "Google them." To find out more about a subject, you would "Google it." Enter a key word in Google, and a list of relevant links would be returned in an instant. For many users, Google quickly became the "go to" page every time they wanted information about anything.

What captured the attention of the business community, however, was Google's ability to monetize its search results. Google's core business model was the essence of simplicity. The company auctioned off the keywords used in searches to advertisers. The highest bidders would have links to their sites placed on the right hand side of a page returning search results. The advertisers would then pay Google every time someone clicked on a link and was directed to their site. Thus, when bidding for a keyword, advertisers would bid for the price per click. Interestingly, Google did not necessarily place the advertiser who bid the highest amount per click at the top of the page. Rather, the top spot was determined by the amount per click multiplied by Google's statistical estimate of the likelihood that someone would actually click on the advertisement. This refinement maximized the revenue that Google got from its valuable real estate.

By May 2011, some 65.5% all U.S. Internet searches were conducted through Google sites.[1] Yahoo! (15.9% share), Microsoft (14.1% share), and Ask Network (2.9% share) were Behind Google. Google had been gaining ground; 5 years earlier its share had stood at 45%.[2] In an effort to catch up to Google, Microsoft and Yahoo! had joined forces. Yahoo! had agreed to use Microsoft's Bing search engine (or *decision engine* as Microsoft preferred to call it). In late-2010, Bing powered searching was implemented throughout Yahoo! properties, making Bing's share 30% in May 2011. The belief at Microsoft was that adding Yahoo! search queries to the mix would enable Bing to gain scale economies and boost revenues per search.

As more users gravitated to Google's site, more advertisers were attracted to it, and Google's revenues and profits took off. From a standing start in 2001, by 2010 revenues had grown to $29.3 billion and net income to $8.5 billion. Google had become the gorilla in the online advertising space. In 2001, Google garnered 18.4% of total US search ad spending. By 2005, its share had increased to 48.5% and according to the research firm eMarketer, 75% of all U.S. search-advertising dollars went to Google in 2007.[3] Moreover, the future looks bright. In 2010, Internet advertising spending looked set to exceed $25 billion, up from $16.9 billion in 2006, and accounting for 15.1% of all media spending in the U.S.[4] Google was reportedly accounting for well over 70% of *worldwide* search marketing spending. Forecasts called for Google's revenues to hit $36 billion by 2012, as ever more advertisers moved from traditional media to the Web.[5]

Flushed by this success, Google introduced a wave of new products, including mapping services (Google Maps and Google Earth), an e-mail service (gmail), Google Desktop (which enables users to search files on their own computers), Google Apps, which includes free online word processing and spread sheet programs that have much of the look, feel, and functionality of Microsoft's Word and Excel offerings, its own Web browser, Chrome, and its smartphone operating system, Android. These products fueled speculation that Google's ambitions extended outside search capabilities and that the company was trying to position itself as a platform company supported by an ecosystem that would rival that fostered by Microsoft, the long-dominant player in the software industry.

Search Engines[6]

A search engine connects the keywords that users enter (queries) to a database it has created of Web pages (an index). It then produces a list of links to pages (and summaries of content) that it believes are most relevant to a query.

Search engines consist of four main components—a Web crawler, an index, a runtime index, and a query processor (the interface that connects users to the index). The Web crawler is a piece of software that goes from link to link on the Web, collecting the pages it finds and sending them back to the index. Once in the index, Web pages are analyzed by sophisticated algorithms that look for statistical patterns. Google's page rank algorithm, for example, looks at the links on a page, the text around those links, and the popularity of the pages that link to that page, to determine how relevant a page is to a particular query (in fact, Google's algorithm looks at more than 100 factors to determine a page's relevance to a query term).

Once analyzed, pages are tagged. The tag contains information about the pages, for example, whether it is porn, or spam, written in a certain language, or updated infrequently. Tagged pages are then dumped into a runtime index, which is a database that is ready to serve users. The runtime index forms a bridge between the back end of an engine, the Web crawler and index, and the front end, the query processor and user interface. The query processor takes a keyword inputted by a user, transports it to the runtime index, where an algorithm matches the keyword to pages, ranking them by relevance, and then transports the results back to the user, where they are displayed on the user interface.

The computing and data storage infrastructure required to support a search engine is significant. It must scale with the continued growth of the Web and with demands on the search engine. In 2007, Google had $2.7 billion in information technology assets on its balance sheet, had close to 400,000 computers configured in large scale clusters dedicated to the job of running its search engine, and spent around $600 million on maintaining its system.[7]

The Early Days of Search

Search did not begin with Google. The first Internet search engine was Archie. Created in 1990, before the World Wide Web had burst onto the scene, Archie connected users through queries to the machines on which documents they wanted were stored. The users then had to dig through the public files on those machines to find what they wanted. The next search engine, Veronica, improved upon Archie, as it allowed searchers to connect directly to the document they had queried.

The Web started to take off after 1993, with the number of Websites expanding from 130 to more than 600,000 by 1996. As this expansion occurred, the problem of finding the information you wanted on the Web became more difficult. The first Web-based search engine was the WWW Wanderer, developed by Matthew Gray at MIT. This was soon surpassed by Web Crawler, which was a search engine developed by Brian Pinkerton of the University of Washington. Web Crawler was the first search engine to index the full text of Web pages, rather than just the title. Web Crawler was sold to AOL for $1 million in 1995. This marked the first time anyone had ascribed an economic value to a search engine.

In December 1995, the next search engine appeared on the scene, Alta Vista. Developed by an employee at Digital Equipment Corporation (DEC), Louis Monier, like Web Crawler, Alta Vista indexed the entire text of a Web page. Unlike Web Crawler, however, Alta Vista sent out thousands of Web crawlers, which enabled it to build the most complete index of the Web to date. Avid Web users soon came to value the service, but the search engine was handicapped by two things. First, it was very much a step child within DEC, which was seen as a hardware-driven business and didn't really know what to do with Alta Vista. Second, there was no obvious way for Alta Vista to make much money, which meant that it was difficult for Monier to get the resources required for Alta Vista to keep up with the rapid growth of the Web. Ultimately, DEC was acquired by Compaq. Compaq then sold Alta Vista and related Internet properties to a high-flying Internet firm, CMGI, at the height of the Internet boom in 1999, for $2.3 billion in CMGI stock. CMGI did have plans to spin off Alta Vista in an Initial Public Offering, but it never happened. The NASDAQ stock market collapsed in 2000, taking CMGI's stock down with it, and the market had no appetite for another dot.com IPO.

Around the same time that Alta Vista was gaining traffic, two other companies introduced search engines, Lycos and Excite. Both search engines represented further incremental improvement. Lycos was the first search engine to use algorithms to try and determine the relevance of a Web page for a search query. Excite utilized similar algorithms. However, neither company developed a way of making money directly from search. Instead they saw themselves as portal companies, like Yahoo!, AOL and MSN. Search was just a tool to increase the value of their portal as a destination site, enabling them to capture revenues from banner ads, ecommerce transactions, and the like. Both Lycos and Excite went public and then squandered much of the capital raised on acquiring other Internet properties, before seeing their value implode as the Internet bubble burst in 2000–2001.

Another company that tried to make sense out of the Web for users was Yahoo!, but Yahoo! did not use a search engine. Instead it created a hierarchical directory of Web pages. This helped drive traffic to its site. Other content kept users coming back, enabling Yahoo! to emerge as one of the most popular portals on the Web. In contrast to many of its smaller competitors, Yahoo!'s industry leading scale allowed it to make good money from advertising on its site. Yahoo! did add a search engine to its offering, but until 2003 it always did so through a partner. At one time, Alta Vista powered Yahoo!'s search function, then Inktomi, and ultimately Google. Yahoo!'s managers did consider developing their own search engine, but they saw it as too capital intensive—search required a lot of computing power, storage and bandwidth. Besides, there was no business model for monetizing search. That, however, was all about to change, and it wasn't Google that pioneered the way, it was a serial entrepreneur called Bill Gross.

GoTo.com: A Business Model Emerges[8]

Bill Gross made his first million with Knowledge Adventure, which developed software to help kids learn. After he sold Knowledge Adventure to Cendant for $100 million, Gross created IdeaLab, a business incubator that subsequently generated a number of Internet startups including GoTo.com.

GoTo.com was born of Gross' concern that a growing wave of spam was detracting from the value of search engines such as Alta Vista. Spam arose because publishers of Websites realized that they could drive traffic to their sites by including commonly used search key words such as "used cars" or "airfares" on their sites. Often the words were in the same color as the background of the Website (e.g., black words on a black background) so that they could not be seen by Web users, who would suddenly wonder why their search for used cars had directed them to a porn site.

Gross also wanted a tool that would help drive good traffic to the Websites of a number of Internet businesses being developed by IdeaLab. In Gross' view, much of the traffic arriving at Websites was undifferentiated—people who had come to a site because of spam, bad portal real estate deals, or poor search engine results. Gross established GoTo.com to build a better search engine, one that would defeat spam, produce highly relevant results, and eliminate bad traffic.

Gross concluded that a way to limit spam was to charge for search. He realized that it was unworkable to charge the Internet user, so why not charge the advertiser? This led to his key insight—the keywords that Internet users typed into a search engine were inherently valuable to the owners of Websites. They drove traffic to their sites, and many sites made money from that traffic, so why not charge for the keywords? Moreover, Gross realized that if a search engine directed higher quality traffic to a site, it would be possible to charge more for relevant keywords.

By this time, GoTo.com had decided to license search engine technology from Inktomi and focus its efforts on developing the paid search model. However, GoTo.com faced a classic chicken and egg problem—to launch a service the company needed both audience and advertisers, but it had neither.

To attract advertisers GoTo.com adopted two strategies.[9] First, GoTo.com would only charge advertisers when somebody clicked on a link and was directed to their Website. To Gross' way thinking, for merchants this pay-per-click model would be more efficient than advertising through traditional media, or through banner ads on Web pages. Second, GoTo.com initially priced keywords low—as low as $0.01 a click (although they could, of course, be sold for more).

To capture an audience, a Website alone would not be enough. GoTo.com needed to tap into the traffic already visiting established Websites. One approach was to pay the owners of high-traffic Websites to place banner ads that would direct traffic to GoTo.com's Website. A second approach, which ultimately became the core of GoTo.com's business, was to syndicate its service, allowing affiliates to place a co-branded GoTo.com search box on their site, or to use GoTo.com's search engine and identify the results as "partner results." GoTo.com would then split the revenues from search with them. GoTo.com had to pay an upfront fee to significant affiliates, who viewed their Websites as valuable real estate. For example, in late-2000 GoTo.com paid AOL $50 million to syndicate GoTo.com's listings on its sites, which included AOL, CompuServe, and Netscape.

To finance its expansion, GoTo.com raised some $53 million in venture capital funding—a relatively easy proposition in the heady days of the dot.com boom. In June 1999, GoTo.com raised another $90 million through an initial public offering.[10]

GoTo.com launched its service in June 1998 with just 15 advertisers. Initially GoTo.com was paying more to acquire traffic than it was earning from click-through-ad revenue. According to its initial IPO filing, in its first year of operation, GoTo.com was paying $0.055 a click to acquire traffic from Microsoft's MSN sites and around $0.04 a click to acquire traffic from Netscape. The average yield from this traffic, however, was still less than the cost of acquisition, resulting in red ink—not an unusual situation for a dot.com in the 1990s.

However, the momentum was beginning to shift toward the company. As traffic volumes grew, and as advertisers began to understand the value of keywords, yields improved. By early-1999, the price of popular keywords was starting to rise. The highest bidder for the keyword "software" was $0.59 a click, "books" was $0.38 a click, "vacations" $0.36 a click, and "porn," the source of so much spam, $0.28 a click.[11]

The turning point was the AOL syndication deal signed in September 2000. Prior to signing with AOL,

GoTo.com was reaching 24 million users through its affiliates. After the deal, it was reaching 60 million unique users, or some 75% of the United States Internet audience (AOL itself had 23 million subscribers, CompuServe 3 million, and Netscape—which was owned by AOL—another 31 million registered users).[12] With over 50,000 advertisers now in its network and a large audience pool, both keyword prices and click-through rates increased. GoTo.com turned profitable shortly after the AOL deal was put into effect. In 2001, the company earned net profits of $20.2 million on revenues of $288 million. In 2002, it earned $73.1 million on revenues of $667.7 million, making it one of the few dot.com companies to break into profitability.

In 2001, GoTo.com changed its name to Overture Services. The name change reflected the results of a strategic shift. By 2001, the bulk of revenues were coming from affiliate sites, with the GoTo.com Website only garnering 5% of the company's total traffic.[13] Still, because GoTo.com had its own Website, it was in effect competing with traffic going to affiliates and creating potential channel conflict. Many in the company feared that channel conflict might induce key affiliates, such as AOL, to switch their allegiance. After much internal debate, the company decided to phase out the GoTo.com Website, focusing all of its attention on the syndication network.

Around the same time, Bill Gross apparently talked to the founders of another fast growing search engine, Google, about whether they would be interested in merging the two companies. At the time Google had no business model. Gross was paying attention to the fast growth of traffic going to Google's Website. He saw a merger as an opportunity to join a superior search engine with Overture's advertising and syndication network (the company was still using Inktomi's search engine). The talks stalled, however, reportedly because Google's founders stated that they would never be associated with a company that mixed paid advertising with organic results.[14]

Within months, however, Google had introduced its own advertising service using a pay-for-click model that looked very similar in conception to Overture's. Overture promptly sued Google for patent infringement. To make maters worse, in 2002 AOL declined to renew its deal with Overture, and instead switched to Google for search services.

By 2003, it was clear that although still growing and profitable, Overture was losing traction to

Google (Overture's revenues were on track to hit $1 billion in 2003 and the company had 80,000 advertisers in its network)[15]. Moreover, Overture was invisible to many of its users, who saw the service as a part of the offering of affiliates, many of whom were powerful brands in their own right, including Yahoo! and Microsoft's MSN. Yahoo! and Microsoft were also waking up to the threat posed by Google. Realizing that paid search was becoming a highly profitable market, both began to eye Overture to jump start their own paid search services. While Microsoft apparently decided to build its own search engine and ad service from scratch, Yahoo! decided to bid for Overture. In June 2003, a deal was announced, and Overture was sold to Yahoo! for $1.63 billion in cash. The payday was a bittersweet one for Bill Gross. IdeaLab had done very well out of Overture, but Gross couldn't help but feel that a bigger opportunity had slipped through his fingers and into the palms of Google's founders.

As for the patent case, this settled in 2004 when Google agreed to hand over 2.7 million shares to Yahoo!. This represented about 1% of the outstanding stock, which at the time was valued at $330. Today the value of those shares is closer to $1 billion.[16]

Google Rising

Google started as a research project undertaken by Larry Page while he was a computer science PhD student at Stanford in 1996. Called BackRub, the goal of the project was to document the link structure of the Web. Page had observed that while it was easy to follow links from one page to another, it was much more difficult to discover links *back*. Put differently, just by looking at a page, it was impossible to know who was linking to that page. Page reasoned that this might be very important information. Specifically, one might be able to rank to value of a Web page by discovering which pages were linking to it and if those pages were linked to many other pages.

To rank pages, Page knew that he would have to send out a Web crawler to index pages and archive links. At this point, another PhD student, Sergey Brin became involved in the project. Brin, a gifted mathematician, was able to develop an algorithm that ranked Web pages according not only to the number of links into that site, but also the number of links into each of the linking sites. This methodology had the virtue of discounting links from pages that had few if any links into them.

Brin and Page noticed that the search results generated by this algorithm were superior to those returned by Alta Vista and Excite, both of which often returned irrelevant results, including a fair share of spam. They had stumbled onto the key ingredient for a better search engine—rank search results according to their relevance using a back link methodology. Moreover, they realized that the bigger the Web, the better the results would be.

Brin and Page released the basic details of what was now a search engine on the Stanford Website in August 1996. They christened their new search engine "Google" after googol, the term for the number 1 followed by 100 zeros. Early on Brin and Page talked to several companies about the possibility of licensing Google. Executives at Excite took a look but passed, as did executives at Infoseek and Yahoo!. Many of these companies were embroiled in the portal wars—and portals were all about acquiring traffic, not about sending it away via search. Search just didn't seem central to their mission.

By late-1998, Google was serving some 10,000 queries per day and was rapidly outgrowing the computing resources available at Stanford. Brin and Page realized that to get the resources required to keep scaling Google they needed capital, and that meant starting a company. Here Stanford's deep links into Silicon Valley came in useful. Before long they found themselves sitting together with Andy Bechtolsheim, one of the founders of another Stanford startup, Sun Microsystems. Bechtolsheim watched a demo of Google and wrote a check on the spot for $100,000.

Google was formally incorporated on September 7, 1998 with Page as CEO and Brin as President. From this point on, things began to rapidly accelerate. Traffic was growing by nearly 50 % a month, enough to attract the attention of several angle investors (including Amazon founder Jeff Bezos), who collectively put in another million. That was not enough; search engines have a voracious appetite for computing resources. To run its search engine, Brin and Page had custom designed a low-cost, Linux based server architecture that was modular and could be rapidly scaled. But to keep up with the growth of the Web and return answers to search queries in a fraction of a second, they needed ever more machines (by late-2005, the company was reportedly using over 250,000 Linux servers to handle more than 3,000 searches a second).[17]

To finance growth of their search engine, in early-1999 Brin and Page started to look for venture capital funding. It was the height of the dot.com boom and money was cheap. Never mind that there was no business model, Google's growth was enough to attract considerable interest. By June 1999, the company had closed its first round of venture capital financing, raising $25 million from two of the premier firms in Silicon Valley, Sequoia Capital and Kleiner Perkins Caufield & Byers. Just as importantly perhaps, the legendary John Doerr, one of Silicon Valley's most successful investors and a Kleiner Perkins partner, took a seat on Google's board.

By late-1999, Google had grown to around 40 employees, and it was serving some 3.5 million searches a day. However, the company was burning through $500,000 a month, and there was still no business model. They had some licensing deals with companies that used Google as their search technology, but they were not bringing in enough money to stem the flow of red ink. At this point, Google started to experiment with ads, but they were not yet pay-per-click ads. Rather, Google began selling text-based ads to clients that were interested in certain keywords. The ads would then appear on the page returning search results, but not in the list of relevant sites. For example, if someone typed in "Toyota Corolla," an ad would appear at the top of the page, above the list of links for Toyota Corolla cars. These ads were sold on a "cost per thousand impressions" basis, or CPM (the M being the Roman numeral for thousand). In other words, the cost of an ad was determined by how many people were estimated to have viewed it—not how many clicked on it. It didn't work very well.

The management team also started to ponder placing banner ads on Google's Website as a way of generating additional revenue, but before they made that decision the dot.com boom imploded, the NASDAQ crashed, and the volume of online advertising dropped precipitously. Google clearly needed to figure out a different way to make money.

Google Gets a Business Model

Brin and Page now looked closely at the one search company that seemed to be making good money, GoTo.com. They could see the value of the pay-per-click model, and of auctioning off keywords, but

there were things about GoTo.com that they did not like. GoTo.com would give guarantees that Websites would be included more frequently in Web crawls, making sure they were updated, provided that the owners were prepared to pay more. Moreover, the purity of GoTo.com's search results was biased by the desire to make money from advertisers, with those who paid the most being ranked highest. Brin and Page were ideologically attached to the idea of serving up the best possible search results to users, uncorrupted by commercial considerations. At the same time, they needed to make money.

Although Bill Gross pitched the idea of GoTo.com teaming up with Google, Brin and Page decided to go it alone. They believed they could do as good a job as GoTo.com, so why share revenues with the company?[18]

The approach that Google ultimately settled on combined the innovations of GotTo.com with Google's superior relevance based search engine. Brin and Page had always believed that Google's Web page should be kept as clean and elegant as possible—something that seemed to appeal to users. Moreover, they knew that users valued the fact that Google served up relevant search results that were unbiased by commercial considerations. The last thing they wanted to do was alienate their rapidly growing user base. So they decided to place text-based ads on the right hand side of a page, clearly separated from search results by a thin line.

Like GoTo.com, they decided to adopt a pay-per-click model. Unlike GoTo.com, Brin and Page decided that in addition to the price an advertiser had paid for a keyword, ads should also be ranked according to relevance. Relevance was measured by how frequently users clicked on ads. More popular ads rose to the top of the list, less popular ones fell. In other word's, Google allowed their users to rank ads. This had a nice economic advantage for Google, since an ad that is generating $1.00 a click, but is being clicked on three times as much as an ad generating $1.50 a click would make significantly more money for Google. It also motivated advertisers to make sure that their ads were appealing.

The system that Google used to auction off keywords was also different in detail from that used by GoTo.com. Google used a *Vickery second price auction* methodology. Under this system, the winner pays only $0.01 more than the bidder below them. Thus, if there are bids of $1, $0.50 and $0.25

for a keyword, the winner of the top place pays just $0.51 not $1, the winner of the second place $0.26, and so on. The auction is nonstop, with the price for a keyword rising or falling depending upon bids at each moment in time. Although the minimum bid for a keyword was set at $0.05, most were above that, and the range was wide. One of the most expensive search terms was reputed to be "mesothelioma," a type of cancer caused by exposure to asbestos. Bids were around $30 per click! They came from lawyers vying for a chance to earn lucrative fees by representing clients in suits against asbestos producers.[19]

While developing this service, Google continued to grow like wildfire. In mid-2000, the service was dealing with 18 million search queries per day and the index surpassed one billion documents, making it by far the largest search engine on the Web. By late-2000, when Google introduced the first version of its new service, which it called "AdWords," the company was serving up 60 million search queries a day—giving it a scale that GoTo.com never came close to achieving. In February 2002, Google introduced a new version of AdWords that included for the first time the full set of pay-per-click advertising, keyword auctions, and advertising links ranked by relevance. Sales immediately started to accelerate. Google had hit on the business model that would propel the company into the big league.

In 2003, Google introduced a second product, AdSense. AdSense allowed third party publishers large and small to access Google's massive network of advertisers on a self-service basis. Publishers could sign up for AdSense in a matter of minutes. AdSense would then scan the publisher's site for content and place contextually relevant ads next to that content. As with AdWords, this is a pay-per-click service, but AdSense splits the revenues with the publishers. In addition to large publishers, such as online news sites, AdSense has been particularly appealing to many small publishers, such as Web Bloggers. Small publishers found that by adding a few lines of code to their site, they could suddenly monetize their content. However, many advertisers feel that AdSense is not as effective as AdWords in driving traffic to their sites. Google allowed advertisers to opt out of AdSense in 2004. Despite this, AdSense has also grown into a respectable business, accounting for 15% of Google's revenues in 2005, or close to $1 billion.

Google Grows Up

Between 2001 and 2010, Google changed in a number of ways. First, in mid-2001 the company hired a new CEO to replace Larry Page, Eric Schmidt. Schmidt had been the Chief Technology Officer of Sun Microsystems, and then CEO of Novell. Schmidt was brought on to help manage the company's growth with the explicit blessing of Brin and Page. Both Brin and Page were still in their 20s, and the board felt they needed a "grown up" who had run a large company to help Google transition to the next stage (Google turned a profit the month after Schmidt joined). Brin and Page became the Presidents of Technology and Products, respectively. When Schmidt was hired, Google had over 200 employees and was handling over 100 million searches a day.

According to knowledgeable observers, Schmidt, Brin and Page acted as a triumvirate, with Brin and Page continuing to exercise a very strong influence over strategies and policies at Google. Schmidt may have been CEO, but Google was still very much Brin and Page's company.[20] Working closely together, the three drove the development of a set of values and an organization that would come to define Google's unique way of doing things. In January 2011, Schmidt retired from the CEO position, passing the reins back to Larry Page. Schmidt remained Chairman.

Vision and Values

As Google's growth started to accelerate, there was concern that rapid hiring would quickly dilute the vision, values and principles of the founders. In mid-2001, Brin and Page gathered a core group of early employees and asked them to come up with a policy for ensuring that the company's culture did not fracture as the company added employees. From this group, and subsequent discussions, emerged a vision and list of values that have continued to shape the evolution of the company. These were not new, rather, they represented the formalization of principles to which Brin and Page felt they had always adhered.

The central vision of Google is to *organize the world's information and make it universally acceptable and useful.*[21] The team also articulated a set of 10 core philosophies (values), which are now listed on its Website.[22] Perhaps the most significant and certainly the most discussed of these values is captured by the phrase "*don't be evil.*" The central message underlying this phrase was that Google should never compromise the integrity of its search results. Google would never let commercial considerations bias its rankings. Don't be evil, however, has become more than that at Google; it has become a central organizing principle of the company, albeit one that is far from easy to implement. Google got positive press from libertarians when it refused to share its search data with the U.S. government, which wanted the data to help fight child porn. However, the same constituency reacted with dismay when the company caved into the Chinese government and removed from its Chinese service offending results for search terms such as "human rights" and "democracy"! Brin justified the Chinese decision by saying that "it will be better for Chinese Web users, because ultimately they will get more information, though not quite all of it."[23]

Another core value at Google is "*focus on the user, and all else will follow.*" In many ways, this value captures what Brin and Page initially developed. They focused on giving the user the best possible search experience—highly relevant results, delivered with lightening speed to an uncultured and elegant interface. The value also reflects a belief at Google that it is okay to deliver value to users first and then figure out the business model for monetizing that value. This belief seems to reflect Google's own early experience.

Yet another key principle, although it is not one that is written down anywhere, is captured by the phrase "*launch early and often.*" This seems to underpin Google's approach to product development. Google has introduced a rash of new products over the last few years, not all of which are initially that compelling, but through rapid upgrades, it has subsequently improved the efficacy of those products.

Google also prides itself on being a company where decisions are *data driven*. Opinions are said to count for nothing unless they are backed up by hard data. It is not the loudest voice that wins the day in arguments over strategy, it is the data. In some meetings, people are not allowed to say "I think . . ." but instead "The data suggests. . . ."[24]

Finally, Google devotes considerable resources to making sure that its employees are working in a supportive and stimulating environment. To quote from the company's Website:

Google Inc. puts employees first when it comes to daily life in our Googleplex headquarters. There is an emphasis on team achievements and pride in individual accomplishments that contribute to the company's overall success. Ideas are traded, tested, and put into practice with an alacrity that can be dizzying. Meetings that would take hours elsewhere are frequently little more than a conversation in line for lunch and few walls separate those who write the code from those who write the checks. This highly communicative environment fosters a productivity and camaraderie fueled by the realization that millions of people rely on Google results. Give the proper tools to a group of people who like to make a difference, and they will.[25]

Organization

By all accounts, Google has a flat organization. In November 2005, Google had 1 manager for every 20 line employees. At times, the ratio has been as high as 1:40. For a while—one manager had 180 direct reports.[26] The structure is reportedly based on teams. Big projects are broken down and allocated to small, tightly focused teams. Hundreds of projects may be going on at the same time. Teams often release new software in 6 weeks or less and look at how users respond hours later. Google can try a new user interface, or some other tweak, with just 0.1% of its users and get massive feedback very quickly, letting it decide a project's fate in weeks.[27]

One aspect of Google's organization that has garnered considerable attention is the company's approach toward product development. Employees are expected to spend 20% of their time on something that interests them, away from their main jobs. Seemingly based on 3M's famous 15% rule, Google's 20% rule is designed to encourage creativity. The company has set up forums on its internal network where anyone can post ideas, discuss them, and solicit help from other employees. As a natural part of this process, talent tends to gravitate to those projects that seem most promising, giving those who post the most interesting ideas the ability to select a talented team to take them to the next level.

Like 3M, Google has set up a process by which projects coming out of 20% time can be evaluated, receive feedback from peers, and ultimately garner funding. Marissa Myer, one of Google's early employees, acts as a gatekeeper, helping to decide when projects are ready to be pitched to senior management (and that typically means Brin and Page). Once in front of the founders, advocates have 20 minutes, and no more, to make their pitch.[28] Myer has also articulated a number of other principals that guide product development at Google.[29] These include:

1. Ideas come from everywhere: Set up a system where good ideas rise to the top.
2. Focus on users, not money: Money follows consumers. Advertisers follow consumers. If you amass a lot of consumers you will find ways to monetize your ideas.
3. Innovation, not instant perfection: Put products on the market, learn and iterate.
4. Don't kill projects, morph them: If an idea has managed to make its way out of the door, there is usually some kernel of truth to it. Don't walk away from ideas, think of ways to replace or rejuvenate them.

One of the early products to come out 20% time was Google News, which returns news articles ranked by relevance in response to a key word query. Put the term "oil prices" into Google News, for example, and the search will return news dealing with changes in oil prices, with the most relevant at the top of the list. A sophisticated algorithm determines relevance on a real-time basis by looking at the quality of the news source (e.g., *The New York Times* rates higher than local news papers), publishing date, the number of other people who click on that source, and numerous other factors. Krishna Bharat, a software engineer from India, initiated the project, who, in response to the events of September 11, 2001, had a desire to learn what was being written and said around the world. Two other employees worked with Bharat to construct a demo that was released within Google. Positive reaction soon got Bharat in front of Brin and Page, who were impressed and gave the project a green light; Bharat started to work on the project full time.[30]

Another feature of Google's organization is its hiring strategy. Like Microsoft, Google has made a virtue out of hiring people with a high IQ. The hiring process is very rigorous. Each prospect has to take an "exam" to test their conceptual abilities. This is followed by interviews with 8 or more people, each of who rate the applicant on a 1–4 scale (4 being "I would hire this person"). Applicants also undergo detailed background checks to find out their work-

ing styles. Reportedly, some brilliant prospects don't get hired when background checks find state they are difficult to work with. In essence, all hiring at Google is by committee, and while this can take considerable time, the company insists that the effort yields dividends.

While accounts of Google's organization and culture tend to emphasize their positive aspects, not everyone has such a sanguine view. Brain Reid, who was recruited into senior management at Google in 2002 and fired 2 years later, told author John Battelle "Google is a monarchy with two kings, Larry and Sergey. Eric is a puppet. Larry and Sergey are arbitrary, whimsical people . . . they run the company with an iron hand . . . Nobody at Google from what I could tell had any authority to do anything of consequence except Larry and Sergey."[31] According to Battelle, several other former employees made similar statements.

Other former employees have noted that in practice 20% time turns out to be 120% time, because people still have their regular work load. There are also complaints that the culture is one of long work days and 7-day work weeks, with little consideration for family issues. Several employees have complained that Google's organization is not scaling that well and that with nearly 14,000 employees on the books, the firm's personnel department is "collapsing" and that "absolute chaos reigns." One former employee noted that when she was hired, nobody knew when or where she was supposed to work.[32]

Many of the early employees, who are now financially wealthy, are starting to leave. As a result, employee turnover is increasing. At the same time, there are reports that the company's free wheeling culture has led to a rather anarchic resource allocation process, and extensive duplication, with multiple teams working on the same project.[33]

The IPO

As Google's growth started to accelerate, the question of if and when to undertake an IPO became more pressing. There were two obvious reasons for doing an IPO—gaining access to capital and providing liquidity for early backers and the large number of employees who had equity positions. On the other hand, from 2001 onward, the company was profitable, generating significant cash flows, and could internally fund its expansion. Moreover, management felt that the longer they could keep the details of what was turning out to be an extraordinarily successful business model private, the better. In the end, the company's hand was forced by an obscure SEC regulation that required companies that give stock options to employees to report as if they were public company by as early as April 2004. Realizing that the cat would be out of the bag anyway, Google told its employees in early-2004 that it would go public.

True to form, Google flouted Wall Street tradition in the way it structured its IPO. The company decided to auction off shares directly to the public using an untested and modified version of a Dutch auction, which starts by asking for a high price and then lowers it until someone accepts. Two classes of shares were created, Class A and B; Class B's shares had 10 times the votes of Class A shares. Only Class A shares were auctioned. Brin, Page and Schmidt were holders of Class B shares. Consequently, although they would own 1/3 of the company after the IPO, they would control 80% of the votes. Google also announced that it would not provide regular financial guidance to Wall Street financial analysts. In effect, Google had thumbed its nose at Wall Street.

The controversial nature of the IPO, however, was overshadowed by the first public glimpse of Google's financials, which were contained in the offering document. They were jaw dropping. The company had generated revenues of $1.47 billion in 2003, an increase of 230% over 2002. Google earned net profits of $106 million in 2003, but accountants soon figured out that the number was depressed by certain one time accounting items and that cash flow in 2003 had been over $500 million!

Google went public on August 19, 2004 at $85 a share. The company's first quarterly report showed sales doubling over the prior year, and by November the price was $200.

In September 2005, with the stock close to $300 a share, Google undertook a secondary offering, selling 14 million shares to raise $4.18 billion. With positive cash flow adding to this, by June 2008 Google was sitting on $12.8 billion in cash and short-term investments, prompting speculation as to the company's strategic intentions.

Strategy

Since 2001, Google has endeavored to keep enhancing the efficacy of its search engine, continually im-

proving the search algorithms and investing heavily in computing resources. The company has branched out from a text-based search engine. One strategic thrust has been to extend search to as many digital devices as possible. Google started out on PCs, but can now be accessed through PDAs and cell phones. A second strategy has been to widen the scope of search to include different sorts of information. Google has pushed beyond text into indexing and offering up searches of images, news reports, books, maps, scholarly papers, a blog search, a shopping network (Froogle), and videos. Google Desktop, which searches files on a user's personal computer, also fits in with this schema. However, not all of these new search formats have advertising attached to them (e.g., images and scholarly papers do not include sponsored links, while map and book searching does).

Not all of this has gone smoothly. Book publishers have been angered by Google's book project, which seeks to create the world's largest searchable digital library of books by systematically scanning books from the libraries of major universities (e.g., Stanford). The publishers have argued that Google has no right to do this without first getting permission from the publishers and is violating copyright by doing so. Several publishers have filed a complaint with the U.S. District Court in New York. Google has responded that users will not be able to download entire books and that in any event creating an easy to use index of books is fair use under copyright law and will increase the awareness and sales of books, directly benefiting copyright holders. On another front, the World Association of Newspaper Publishers has formed a task force to examine the exploitation of content by search engines.[34]

Over the last 6 years Google has introduced a rash of product offerings, not all of which have a strong affinity with the company's search mission. Many of these products grew out of the company's new product development process. They have include free e-mail (gmail) and online chat programs, a calendar, a blog site (Blogger), a social networking site (Orkut), a finance site (Google Money), a service for finding, editing and sharing photos (Picasa), and plans to offer citywide free WiFi networks.

Google has introduced several Web-based applications that seem squarely aimed at Microsoft's Office franchise, collectively known as Google Apps. In March of 2006, the company acquired a word processing program, Writely. This was quickly followed by the introduction of a spreadsheet program, Google Spreadsheets. These products have the look and feel of Microsoft Word and Excel, respectively. Both products are designed for online collaboration. They can save files in formats used by Microsoft products, although they lack the full feature set of Microsoft's offerings. Google states that the company is not trying to match the features of office and that "90% of users don't necessarily need 90% of the functions that are in there."[35] For an annual licensing fee of $50, Google provides corporate customers with an Apps service that includes gmail and its Office-like products.

In July 2006, Google introduced a product to compete with PayPal, a Web-based payment system owned by the online auction giant, eBay. Google's product, known as "Checkout," offers secure online payment functionality for both merchants and consumers. For merchants, the fee for using Checkout is being priced below PayPal's. Moreover, Checkout is being integrated into Google's AdWords product, so merchants who participate will be highlighted in Google's search results. In addition, merchants who purchase Google's search advertising will get a discount on processing fees. According to one analysis, a merchant with monthly sales of $100,000 who uses Checkout and AdWords stands to reduce their transaction costs by 28%, or $8,400 a year. If they use just Checkout, they will reduce their transaction costs by 4%, or $1,200 a year.[36] However, with 105 million accounts in mid-2006, PayPal will be difficult to challenge.

In late-2007, Google announced another new product, this time a suite of software for smartphones that include an operating system, Android, and applications that work with it. Android is squarely aimed at Apple's iPhone and Research In Motion's BlackBerry, which are the two runaway successes in the smartphone space. The attraction for Google is that advertising is increasingly being inserted into content viewed on mobile handsets. By one estimate, worldwide spending on mobile advertising will rise to $19 billion in 2012, up from $2.7 billion in 2007.[37] Google gives away Android for free, and aims to make money through mobile search.

By 2011, Android was gaining strong traction, with a number of equipment manufacturers including HTC, Motorola, Samsung, and LG offering Android powered smartphones. In January 2011, Android powered phones led the U.S. smartphone

market with a 31.2% share, followed by RIM with a 30.4% share, and Apple with a 24.7% share.[38] Phones powered by a Microsoft operating system had only an 8% share. Android was gaining share at the expense of all other players except Apple—its share had increased from 13% in May 2010. In October 2010, Google reported that its mobile advertising revenues were growing strongly and had hit an annualized run rate of $1 billion.[39]

Some analysts have questioned the logic behind Google's new product efforts, noting that their track record on new product offerings has been mixed. One noted that: "Google has product ADD. They don't know why they are getting into all of these products. They have fantastic cash flow, but terrible discipline on products."[40] Another has accused Google of having an insular culture and argued that "Neither Froogle or Google's travel efforts has gained any traction, at least partly because of Google's tendency to provide insufficient support to its ecosystem partners and its habit of acting in an independent, secretive manner."[41] However, others argue that Google has been successful in upgrading the quality of its new offerings and that several products that were once laggards, such as Google News, are now the best in breed.[42] Moreover, it is very difficult to argue with the success of Android.

On the acquisition front, Google stuck to purchasing small technology firms until 2006. This changed in October 2006 when Google announced that it would purchase YouTube for $1.64 billion in stock. YouTube is a simple, fun Website to which anybody can upload video clips in order to share them. In October 2006 some 65,000 video clips were being uploaded every day and 100 million were being watched. Like Google in its early days, YouTube had no business model. Google thought it would find ways to sell advertising that is linked to video clips on YouTube.[43]

Over the next 4 years, YouTube continued to grow at a rapid pace. By May 2011, YouTube ranked as the top U.S. online video site with 147 million unique viewers, followed by Vevo, the fast growing music video site, which had 60.4 million unique viewers. Yahoo! sites were next with 55.5 million, followed by Facebook sites with 48.2 million.[44] Although detailed figures are not available, it appears that Google is starting to make significant money from YouTube by selling display ads, and through a service where advertisers pay Google whenever a user clicks on and watches one of their ads.

Another notable Google acquisition was its $3.1 billion purchase of DoubleClick in 2007. DoubleClick is an online display advertising specialist, using formats such as banner ads that are targeted at building brand awareness. Internet publishers pay DoubleClick to insert display ads on their Websites as users visit their Websites. While display advertising has not grown as rapidly as search-based advertising, it is a big business accounting for around 1/4 of all Internet advertising revenue with significant upside potential as companies begin to apply demographic technology to increase the effectiveness of Internet display ads.[45] The DoubleClick deal was criticized by Google's rivals, including Microsoft, on antitrust grounds, but regulators in the United States and the EU approved the deal, which closed in 2008. By the end of 2010, Google was reporting that annualized revenues for display ads were running at around $2.5 billion.

Critics argue that as Google moves into these additional areas, its profit margins will be compressed. Henry Blodget of Cherry Hill Research notes that in its core business, Google makes profit margins of about 60%. In its more recent business of placing advertisements on Web pages belonging to other people, such as bloggers, its profit margins are 10–20%, because it is harder to make the advertisements as relevant to the audience and it must share the resulting revenues. Display advertising also offers lower returns. Google, not surprisingly, does not see things this way. The company argues that since its costs are mostly fixed, and incremental revenue is profit, it makes good sense to push into other markets, even if its average revenue per viewer is only $0.01 (compared with $0.50 for each click on the Web).[46]

The Online Advertising Market in 2010

There is an old adage in advertising that half of all the money spent on advertising is wasted—advertisers just don't know which half. Estimates suggest that around 1/2 of the $500 billion worldwide advertising spent is wasted because the wrong message is sent to the wrong audience.[47] The problem is that traditional media advertising is indiscriminate. Consider a 30 second ad spot on broadcast TV. Advertisers

pay a rate for such a spot called CPM (costs per thousand). The CPM is based on estimates of how many people are watching a show. There are numerous problems with this system. The estimates of audience numbers are only approximations at best. The owners of the TV may have left the room while the commercials are airing. They may channel surf during the commercial break, be napping, or talking on the telephone. The viewer may not be among the intended audience—a Viagra commercial might be wasted on a teenage girl, for example. Or the household might be using a TiVo or a similar digital video recorder that skips commercials.

By contrast, new advertising models based on pay-per-click are more discriminating. Rather than sending out ads to a large audience, only a few of whom will be interested in the products being advertised, consumers select in to search based ads. They do this twice, first, by entering a key word in a search engine, and second, by scanning the search results as well as the sponsored links, and clicking on a link. In effect, potential purchasers pull the ads toward them through the search process. Advertisers only pay when someone clicks on their ad. Consequently, the conversion rate for search-based ads is far higher than the conversion rate for traditional media advertising.

Moreover, traditional advertising is so wasteful that most firms only advertise 5%–10% of their products in the mass media, hoping that other products will benefit from a halo effect. In contrast, the targeted nature of search-based advertising makes it cost effective to advertise products that only sell in small quantities. In effect, search based Internet advertising allows producers to exploit the economics of the long tail. Pay-per-click models also make it economical for small merchants to advertise their wares on the Web.

The Growth Story

Powered by the rapid growth of search based pay-per-click advertising, and the increasing amount of time people spend online, total advertising spending on the Internet is expected to account for 15.1% of all global advertising spending in 2011, up from 13.9% in 2010 and 10.2% in 2008.[48] This structural growth trend is likely to continue for some time, since consumers in many developed nations are now spending over 25% of their media time online.[49] In terms of the mix of advertising online, search-based advertising dominates accounting for 47.2% of U.S. online advertising spending in 2010, followed by display advertising with a 36.1% share (classifieds and lead generation makes up most of the balance).[50]

Google has been the main beneficiary of this trend. In mid-2011 Google was the dominant search engine in America with a 65.5% share of all searches, up from 45% in 2006, followed by Yahoo! (15.9%) and Microsoft (14.1%). Google's share of total U.S. paid search advertising is larger still at around 75%. In the world's second largest market for search advertising, Europe, Google is estimated to command a staggering 97% of advertising spent.[51]

Google's rise is reflected in its increased share of all Internet traffic. In mid-2006 Google's Websites had the fourth largest unique audience on the Web, close behind the longer established portal sites maintained by Microsoft (MSN), Yahoo! and Time Warner (AOL) respectively. By mid-2010 Google's We sites were tied with Yahoo! sites for the number 1 spot, followed by Microsoft, Facebook, and AOL. In no small part, the addition of YouTube has helped to propel Google to the top of the traffic rankings.[52]

Google's Competitors

Google's most significant competitors are Yahoo! and Microsoft. As paid search has grown, all three have increased their investment in search.[53] Both Yahoo! and Microsoft spent several years and hundreds of millions in R&D spending trying to improve their search engine technology and gain market share at the expense of Google. Yahoo! failed, and their share has declined, while Microsoft recorded small market share gains of around 2% after it launched its Bing search engine in 2008. However, Microsoft has never made any money in the online search arena—in fact, it has lost billions. In fiscal 2010, its annualized run rate losses in this business were projected to be around $2.3 billion. Put differently, absent of any financial improvement, if Microsoft closed its search business tomorrow, this would boost the company's earnings per share by about $0.26, which at a price-to-earnings ratio of 15 represents a $3.90 increase in the share price. CEO Steve Ballmer, however, has indicated that search is a key strategic business for the company and exiting the business does not seem to be an option.

In February 2008, Microsoft launched an unsolicited takeover bid for Yahoo!. Microsoft offered $44.6 billion, or $31 a share, for Yahoo!, representing a 62% premium over the closing share price before the takeover announcement. Microsoft's rationalization for the takeover rested on the assumption that the combined entity would be able to realize substantial scale economies, with its expanded Web properties offering a more attractive value proposition to advertisers. In addition, Microsoft argued that it would be able to reduce costs by $1 billion per year by combining some assets, such as data centers.

After several months of difficult negotiations, during which Microsoft raised its bid to $33 a share and also threatened to fight a proxy battle to replace Yahoo!'s board with one favorable to the bid, Microsoft eventually withdrew its offer to acquire Yahoo!. In rationalizing its decision, Microsoft argued that Yahoo!'s continuing market share erosion during the months of negotiations had made the acquisition far less compelling. Yahoo!'s managers continued to argue that Microsoft was not offering enough.

Yahoo!, however, continued to lose market share. After some top management changes at Yahoo!, in June 2009, Microsoft and Yahoo! announced a broad based partnership in the search area. Under the terms of the agreement, Bing will be the exclusive search platform at Yahoo!. Yahoo! will be the exclusive seller to both companies' Premium Search advertisers, while Microsoft's AdCenter will handle self-service advertising. Each company will continue to manage their own display advertising business. Yahoo! also has the option to use Bing on their mobile properties.

The partnership received regulatory approval in mid-2010, and both companies began to implement the agreement in late-2010. To succeed, the partnership must (a) increase search query volume and (b) drive greater revenues per search. In 2009, estimates suggest that Google was generating $36.37 of revenue per thousand search queries, Yahoo! $17.06, and Microsoft $14.31.

Search query volume could increase if the greater traffic improves the relevance of search results generated by Bing and if consumers and advertisers notice this. Revenues per search could increase if advertisers are willing to bid more for keywords on Bing given the greater traffic volume of the search engine.

Another significant strategic partner for Microsoft is Facebook, the leading social network site with over 750 million registered users. Microsoft invested $240 million in Facebook in 2007 for a 1.6% stake. Since then, the two companies have worked together to introduce advertisements on Facebook. In October 2010, the two companies announced an extended deal that will incorporate Facebook data into Bing search results. Bing results will now include a Facebook module offering users the likes, images, comments, and other public data from their network of friends. Thus, when searching for restaurants, you can see if any of your friends liked or recommended a restaurant. There is no question that the evolving partnership between Microsoft and Facebook is in part a response to their common rival, Google.

Looking Forward

With online advertising predicted to grow strongly, Google seems to be in the driver's seat. It has the largest market share in search, the greatest name recognition, and is capturing a proportionately greater share of search based advertising than its rivals.

However, despite market share losses, Microsoft and Yahoo! cannot be dismissed. As their partnership in search progresses, will they be able to leverage their substantial assets and capabilities to gain ground of Google? As for Google, what is its long-term game plan? Recent strategic moves suggest that it is attempting to expand beyond search, but where will this take the company, and what does that mean for other Internet companies?

Endnotes

1 comScore Releases May 2011 Search Engine Rankings, comScore Press Release, June 10, 2011.

2 Nielsen/Net Ratings, "Google Accounts for Half of all U.S. Searches," May 25, 2006.

3 Dadid Hallerman, "Search Marketing: Players and Problems," *eMarketer,* April 2006; "Search Marketing Still Dominates Online Advertising," *eMarketer Press Release,* January 29, 2008.

4 Citigroup Global Markets, "The Microhoo Search Transaction," May 23, 2010.

5 Citigroup Global markets, "Google Inc.," September 26, 2010.

6 This section draws heavily upon the excellent description of search given by John Battelle. See John Battelle, *The Search* (Penguin Portfolio, New York, 2005).

7 Google 10K for 2007.

8 The basic story of GoTo.com is related in John Battelle, *The Search* (Penguin Portfolio, New York, 2005).

9 Karl Greenberg, "Pay-for-placement Search Services Offer Ad Alternatives," *Adweek,* September 25, 2000, 60.

10 M. Gannon, "GoTo.com Inc," *Venture Capital Journal,* August 1, 1999, 1.

11 Tim Jackson, "Cash is the Key to a True Portal," *Financial Times,* February 2, 1999, 16.

12 Karl Greenberg, "Pay-for-placement Search Services Offer Ad Alternatives," *Adweek,* September 25, 2000, 60.

13 Sarah Heim, "GoTo.com Changes to Overture Services, Launches Campaign," *Adweek,* September 10, 2001, 7.

14 This little gem comes from John Battelle, *The Search* (Penguin Portfolio, New York, 2005). There is no independent confirmation of the story.

15 Anonymous, "Yahoo! to Acquire Overture Services for 2.44 Times Revenues," *Weekly Corporate Growth Service,* July 21, 2003, 8.

16 Richard Waters, "Google Settles Yahoo! Case with Shares," *Financial Times,* August 19, 2004, 29.

17 Fred Vogelstein, "Gates vs Google: Search and Destroy," *Fortune,* May 2, 2005, 72–82.

18 This is according to David A. Vise, *The Google Story* (Random House, New York, 2004).

19 David A. Vise, *The Google Story* (Random House, New York, 2004).

20 John Battelle, *The Search* (Penguin Portfolio, New York, 2005). There is no independent confirmation of the story.

21 http://www.google.com/corporate/index.html

22 http://www.google.com/corporate/tenthings.html

23 Andy Kessler, "Sellout.com," *Wall Street Journal,* January 31, 2006, A14.

24 Quentin Hardy, "Google Thinks Small," *Fortune,* November 14, 2005, 198–199.

25 http://www.google.com/corporate/tenthings.html

26 Quentin Hardy, "Google Thinks Small," *Fortune,* November 14, 2005, 198–199.

27 Quentin Hardy, "Google Thinks Small," *Fortune,* November 14, 2005, 198–199.

28 Ben Elgin, "Managing Google's Idea Factory," *Business Week,* October 3, 2005, 88–90.

29 Michael Krauss, "Google's Mayer Tells How Innovation Gets Done," *Marketing News,* April 1, 2007, 7–8.

30 David A. Vise, *The Google Story* (Random House, New York, 2004).

31 John Battelle, *The Search* (Penguin Portfolio, New York, 2005), 233.

32 *The Economist,* "Inside the Googleplex," September 1, 2007, 53–56.

33 B. Lashinsky and Y.W. Yen, "Where does Google go Next?" *Fortune,* May 26, 2008, 104–110.

34 Jacqueline Doherty, "In the Drink," *Barrons*, February 13, 2006, 31–36.

35 K.J. Delaney and R.A. Guth, "Google's Free Web Services Will Vie with Microsoft Office," *Wall Street Journal*, October 11, 2006, B1.

36 Mark Mahany, "Building Out the Option Value of Google," *Citigroup Portfolio Strategist*, July 13, 2006.

37 *eMarketer*, "Mobile Ad Spending to Soar," eMarketer Press Release, August 20, 2008.

38 *comScore*, "comScore Reports January 2011 Mobile Subscriber Market Share," ComScore Press release, March 7, 2011.

39 Citigroup Global Markets, "Google Inc.," October 14, 2010.

40 Ben Elgin, "So Much Fanfare, So Few Hits," *Business Week*, July 10, 2006, 27.

41 David Card, "Understanding Google," *Jupiter Research*, March 10, 2006.

42 Mark Mahany, "Building Out the Option Value of Google," *Citigroup Portfolio Strategist*, July 13, 2006.

43 *The Economist*, "Two Kings Get Together; Google and YouTube," October 14, 2006, 82–83.

44 *comScore*, "May 2011 Online Video Rankings," comScore Press Release, June 17, 2011.

45 R. Hof, "Ad Wars: Google's Green Light," *Business Week*, March 3, 2008, 22.

46 *The Economist*, "Inside the Googleplex," September 1, 2007, 53–56.

47 *The Economist*, "The Ultimate Marketing Machine," July 8, 2006, 61–64; K.J. Delaney, "Google Push to Sell Ads on YouTube Hits Snag," *Wall Street Journal*, July 9, 2008, A1.

48 Emily Fredrix, "Firm Boosts This Year's Advertising Forecasts," *The Canadian Press*, October 18, 2010.

49 *The Economist*, "The Ultimate Marketing Machine," July 8, 2006, 61–64.

50 Citigroup Global Markets, "The Microhoo Search Transaction," May 23, 2010.

51 Citigroup Global Markets, "The Microhoo Search Transaction," May 23, 2010.

52 Nielsen/Net Ratings Press Release, "U.S. Broadband Composition Reaches 72% at Home," June 21, 2006; comScore, "comScore Media Matrix Ranks top 50 US Web Properties for August 2010," comScore Press Release, September 23, 2010.

53 David Hallerman, "Search Marketing, Players and Problems," *eMarketer*, April 2006.

CASE 10

Employee Ownership and the Entrepreneurial Spirit: The Case of HCSS[1]

Prof. Olivier Roche, PhD.
Perdue School of Business, Salisbury University

Prof. Frank Shipper, PhD
Perdue School of Business, Salisbury University

"Never settle for being as good as you currently are"[2]

Introduction

HCSS (Heavy Construction Systems Specialists, Inc.) was founded in 1986. For the first few years, the companys office was in the home of its founder and president, Mike Rydin. Mike had previously worked in the estimating department of a large heavy construction company where he understood, firsthand, the importance of bidding and time crunches.[3] He decided to address this critical issue. Within a few years he hired his first employee, a programmer named Carl, and they created a software package, the DOS version of HeavyBid. This estimating software was made for infrastructure contractors who bid on projects ranging from $50,000 to over one billion dollars. A key feature this young company offered was 24/7 product support; this was unusual at the time. Many times calls for help came in the middle of the night and were responded to by the president himself. Today HCSS still offers 24/7 instant support, now to over 3,500 companies.

In 1989, HCSS moved into its first office building and the company has continued to expand ever since. Starting as a single-product company, HCSS's product lines currently include a half dozen other software programs. HeavyJob, for example, gives foremen the kind of information they need to manage their work responsibly and efficiently. On a daily basis, this job tracking software transforms the information collected from the construction site so that it can be used at headquarters by management. This includes time card entry on both PC and handheld devices, instant production/cost analysis, and billing and forecasting, all of which interface with the contractors accounting software. Another example of successful software developed by the company is Equipment360, an equipment maintenance program that gives a company/customer the ability to track, identify, analyze and resolve equipment maintenance issues before a major problem occurs. This delivers cost savings to the company through less down time and fewer major equipment repairs, as well as lower fuel consumption. [A complete listing of the company's product lines is provided in Appendix 1].

Today the company has 110 employees and sales of almost $18 million [see additional financial data in Appendix 2]. In August 2009, the company moved into its own 45,000-square-foot state-of-the-art facilities in Sugar Land, Texas, near Houston. Mike appreciates that HCSS has come a long way from its humble beginnings, yet he considers that much remains to be accomplished; there is always room for improvement. In the case of HCSS, this company growth has happened at the same time as adjusting to a more challenging economic environment with the downturn of 2008–2009. HCSS has managed to keep its business profitable during this period, and Mike plans to resume the company expansion in 2011. The new facilities are built to accommodate twice as many employees as the company currently has. Mike is confident that HCSS has the financial resources to achieve its target growth, which is to double its activities over the next three years. While adding additional human resources has always been

---

Sources: Olivier Roche, Salisbury University and Frank Shipper, Salisbury University. The research on this company was partially supported by the Foundation for Enterprise Development and the ESOP Association. Used by kind permission of the authors.

An earlier version of this case is in press at the *Journal of Business Case Studies*.

a challenge in this industry, HCSS has so far been very successful in attracting and retaining motivated and highly capable employees while increasing its activities at a double-digit growth rate.

Business Environment and Strategy

HCSS operates in a highly competitive environment. In addition to large companies offering standardized software with an established brand, such as the traditional Microsoft Excel software package, there are also a host of small companies, such as "BID2WIN" or "Hard Dollar," offering customized software. For HCSS, a smooth interaction with its customers is not only critical to increase sales but also to develop new products. Over the years, most of the ideas for new products have come out of discussion with customers. As one of the company's software development managers Minh likes to repeat to the new recruits, "Our software is developed by our customers. The customers tell us what they need and we simply deliver what they want."

While this statement is true, it is deceptively simple. The most important part of the work actually takes place between the phase of listening to what the customers want and that of delivering the right product. The next critical piece is the reliable and personable after-sale support. The company's competitive edge lies in the implementation of this inventive phase where the employees translate a customer's needs into software that meets or exceeds their requirements, at the same time maintaining high standards of work ethics and the motivation to solve customer's problems in an efficient and timely manner. No doubt, the skillful communication and good relationships between the marketing, sales, development and support departments are major factors in this seamless service delivery [see the organization chart in Appendix 3]. To achieve this level of coordination, employees have to be responsive, creative and flexible. They must be able to address customer's needs at the same time they are team players, looking beyond their own department's interests to look at those of the company as a whole. In other words, each employee has to behave like an entrepreneur developing his own business.

Minh [Manager, Software Development]: "I think it [i.e., the employee's ownership mentality] means that I need to do whatever it takes to take care of the issues that come up. Having pride in what you do and deliver. I think a reflection on the entire company is what we're delivering. How we connect with customers. How we talk to customers. Having that ownership of, 'Whatever I do does make an impact'. In my group, in particularly, I really emphasize the importance of team chemistry, teamwork; getting people involved early beyond the scope [of their regular duties]. We endorse creativity and we want that from our employees. It's not, 'Here's your job, go do it' It's, 'Whatever you want to do. Come to me and let me know what your ideas are'. We really foster the idea that you have and help you grow it."

At a more senior level, there is also an understanding that a corporation is a legal structure necessary to run operations and deal with other organizations. However, the company's real business and competitive advantage resides one level below. That is where the relationship between HCSS employees and the customer's employees develops and the problems of the latter are understood and resolved.

Tom [Vice President of Technical Services]: "So from an employer's standpoint, we wanted to make the kind of company that people wanted to stay at and be part of for the long term. And then from a software supplier standpoint, the thing that infuriated more customers than anything was the lack of ability to get somebody to go actually help them. The whole trend in software over the last 15 years has been to outsource your support and outsource your development. So all the parts of the software company got further and further away from their customers. The programmers just became people who wrote code, and the quality assurance personnel just became somebody who didn't really know the product, but they knew how to press the buttons to break the code. Support just became somebody to look through a manual and answer questions over the phone. We wanted to do just the opposite of that. So we 'reverse modeled' as an employer, but we also 'reverse modeled' as a business. We wanted to be the kind of company that our customers and our employees would have relations with and know each other."

This "employee-to-employee relationship approach" focuses on people's needs and not simply on business needs [see Appendix 4 for a description of the company's culture and its branding]. It can be illustrated by two examples of special services provided by HCSS. The first is the "Help-inar," developed by Tom (VP, Technical Services) three years ago. This concept is based on the premise that to develop a genuine relationship with potential customers, the best person to market HCSS services is not always a salesman. Tom, with a background in psychology, believes that rather than being in the business of selling services, the company is there to solve customers' problems. Since most of the actual end users of the software are the client companies' "techies," the best people to interface with them are HCSS "techies," without the interference of the sales department.

> Tom [Vice President of Technical Services]: "And all a 'Help-inar' is, we take our technical people and travel them around the country and put them in a meeting room in a hotel. Customers can come in and ask them questions all day. They just get help. The end result of that is—the customers love it. They're able to come in and get help, but then also hear about some of the other stuff that we're doing and a lot of our new products. So they become sales events, but there's no salesman there. It's only the technical people, which mean that customers hear what you're doing, but they don't hear it with a sales spin. They're hearing from an employee who's technical in nature, which they almost take that differently."

At that stage of interaction, removing the salesman from the equation allows HCSS to establish a different relationship with it's customers. It also allows the company to find ideas for its new products without the filtering of the sales department.

The second service provided by HCSS is instant support. Mike considers this to be fundamental. When clients encounter technical issues with the company's software, they contact the support department; with 24-hour live support, there is no waiting. During conferences and industry fairs, end users talk to each other and share their experiences with various software providers. HCSS's responsiveness to its customer's needs is now well established in the industry and this has contributed to the firm's rapid development to become a leader in the construction and heavy highway market.

> Tom [Vice President of Technical Services]: "It always sounds kind of old and stale to say your people are your competitive advantage, but I think that it's not just the people here, it's the combination of the people without the restrictive rules that keep them from connecting with customers."

Human Resource Practices at HCSS

Hiring the Right Employees: HCSS uses several methods to recruit, like many other organizations in the industry. In addition to advertising on the web and in local media, candidates are recommended by former colleagues. The recruitment process has evolved over time, but it has always been very thorough, to the point where it is sometimes perceived as lengthy to a fault, especially when there is pressure to fill a critical position. Indeed, recently Mike and the senior management team were seeking to hire a marketing director to fill a role that had been open for almost a year. The most recent candidate, after six interviews, was not hired. At the same time, there were eight other more junior positions open. Mike was optimistic that they would be quickly filled with the current high unemployment rate; nevertheless, with so many people involved in the selection process, staffing an empty slot is a time-consuming endeavor. Unlike the recruitment process in many other organizations, Mike and other senior executives are directly involved, not only for senior positions such as marketing director, but also for entry-level positions. At the mid-manager level, future team members participate in the process. Between human resources' criteria and that of the functional departments, Mike is aware that there are slight differences in the traits required for the best candidates, which leads to lengthy discussions. Mike supports this "collective wisdom"; the discussions are ultimately very healthy.

The result of this extensive process is a workforce well appreciated by HCSS clients for both its technical expertise and its diligence in solving problems. In addition, HCSS has a very low annual turnover (usually in the 2–3% range). Mike believes that time invested up front is time saved later in several ways. It avoids a situation where employees who cannot adjust to HCSS corporate culture have to be terminated and replacements hired, and it saves the training that would be required for those replacements.

Over the years, employees have joined the company for various reasons. The remuneration package is attractive, but it is not the principal factor. Indeed, in some cases, particularly at the lower levels, employees only realize how generous it is once they have experienced the profit sharing program, which may be six months to one year after they have joined. Instead, most employees quickly learn to appreciate the "intangible" advantages associated with a position at HCSS. Through the open dialogue in the lengthy interview process, candidates learn about the atmosphere in the company and its casual environment. Both parties learn about the other; in the end, both must feel that there is a good match.

> Sebabi [Organizational Development Manager]: "Before I accepted the position, I asked, 'I'd like to talk to some of the employees just to find out what they really think about the company and the culture . . . Sophie said, 'Sure. You can come this afternoon. You can talk to anybody you want. Just walk around and pull anybody you'd like'. I was going 'What? You're not going to tell me, "Talk to this person or only that person"?' And that impressed me. And that helped me to know that it was the right decision to come here, knowing that I could talk to anybody. And I came and talked to a few people, but just that freedom to talk to any employee stood out to me."

By talking to so many potential colleagues at different levels, both the employer and candidate are able to evaluate if they have work/family values and work ethics in common. If they do, the candidate is hired.

> Melissa [Business Analyst]: "That goes back to the ownership mentality that your peers are the ones you're working with every day. They probably have a really good idea whether you're going to fit into their little group or not, and how you're going to react with the different personalities in their group."

HCSS treats its employees very well but performance is expected. Even after the extremely selective interview process, in some critical and customer oriented departments, such as support, the turnover is substantial during the first 90 days of employment. For a small company operating in this industry, there is very little room for slackers or people who don't share the same work ethics and "can do" attitude.

> Eric [Major Account Manager]: "Some get weeded out in those 90 days. [During the interview] they may say all the right things like, 'Oh, I'm loyal to customers. I have a good attitude. I'll go the extra mile.' Until you get them over there and let those guys [other employees in the support department] determine that, you don't really know. If you ask our customers, 'What's the biggest thing here?' it's the support, your attitude, your attitude towards support. And if someone comes in and they don't have that, they don't come close to making 90 days."

That said, past the 90-day introductory period, the voluntary turnover is only around three percent.

This is very low for a company operating in this industry. In 90 days, both parties will have assessed their compatibility.

In terms of background, HCSS is quite open with regard to the profile of its employees. This reflects the diverse background of the senior management and the belief that during his/her career at HCSS, an employee will assume many responsibilities that were not anticipated when drafting the initial job description. In this way, the "can do" attitude, motivation and aptitude to learn, are as important as a degree or past experience. HCSS hires a person knowing that his/her job functions will continue to be adjusted, either because of changes in the challenges facing the company or to adapt to the person's abilities and willingness to accept responsibilities and grow within the organization.

The recruitment process of Daniel, the receptionist and corporate ambassador, is a good example of the company's philosophy. Even the double title is illustrative. After completing a dual degree in international business and Spanish, Daniel was hired by a large US company. As he was about to finish his training program to become a manager, he decided to leave, unhappy with the corporate culture and the working conditions. Daniel decided to go back to school to get a Master's degree in acupuncture, but at the same time he applied for the HCSS position as a receptionist. He was interviewed by human resources, his future manager and colleagues, and finally by Mike. He was obviously overqualified for the position, but during the interview process his interest in health and wellness was discussed. One thing led to another and his job evolved, based on the qualities he offered.

> Daniel [Corporate Ambassador]: "When I first started, I was asked if I would actually take on more responsibilities to help out some of the other managers [in the wellness area]. And they just thought I'd be a natural fit for it. I really enjoyed it. [After a couple of months] I realized that I needed more feedback from more people in the company, so I helped form a wellness committee, where one person from every single department is represented and they come to the meetings and we figure out where we want to go with the wellness program in the company. . . . I'm the lowest rung of the company and yet I can go and talk to the CEO."

New Employee Orientation / Acculturation Process: At HCSS the support provided to employees during the first few months of their assignment is as important as the initial recruitment process. In a traditional orientation program, companies spend most of their time discussing matters such as benefits, health insurance, how to log into the network systems, and various company policies. These topics are also covered at HCSS, but most of the orientation program is spent discussing the history of the company, the characteristics of the industry, the interpersonal relationships within and outside the company and why these are so important for the success of HCSS.

In addition, the company has developed a mentorship program in which a new employee is paired with an experienced one from another department. The mentor acts as a "confidante" to make sure that the integration process is progressing smoothly. The new employee can feel free to discuss any personal or family issues, as well, which is why it is important that the two work in different departments.

Finally, because of the rapid expansion, senior management decided that there was a need to organize additional opportunities for a direct interface between new employees, their families and the senior management team.

Tom [Vice President of Technical Services]: "It's hard to connect with new employees now because there are usually multiple layers. So between them and myself, there are a couple different levels of supervision. They don't really work with me all the time. Between them and Mike, there's another level of supervision. So we try to do things with new employees where they get some one-on-one time with the executives at the company as a way for us to tell them what HCSS wants to be, and why we want to be that, and we're going to get there. So we have dinners that we do when we hire a new employee. Or we'll take the new employee and the spouse to dinner with the executives, and so that the new employee and the spouse both get the opportunity to meet us. And we get to meet them and just kind of break down the barriers a little bit. And we do some stuff within their orientation where they get the chance to talk to the executives at the company."

Performance Review. Development and Job Promotion: At HCSS, the collective hiring process described earlier is perceived as a logical preliminary step; the annual employee evaluations benefit from a similar 360-degree perspective. It is an anonymous review made up of two components. First, evaluaters fill out a questionnaire in which each employee gets numeric grades (one to ten) for performance and ability to work as a team member, seven being considered the company average. Second, a group of peers is selected,

usually including the colleagues with whom the employee interfaced the most during the preceding year. The members of this group make anonymous qualitative comments regarding the employee's performance. Then the direct supervisor discusses these comments with the employee to assess in which areas improvements are needed, as well as how to assist the employee in achieving his/her objectives. It is also a good opportunity for the employee to discuss any problem or challenges he or she faces in the organization.

At HCSS, formal titles do not mean a lot. Knowledge, people or technical skills and the ability to solve problems are the reasons an employee is sought out by colleagues or customers. To some extent, job titles are a reflection of these recognized abilities. In this fast-paced environment, employees are problem solvers who do not always follow the chain of command. For instance, employee X may report to Y on the organization chart but he/she will not hesitate to talk directly to Y's supervisor or another colleague of Y's in another department, if this person has the information or the ability to solve the problem at hand.

John [Software Developer]: "I do custom programming. I talk with customers about what they want, help work it up and prototype it for them, make sure this is what they want. . . . I also help support when they have a problem, if they can't figure it out. 'Is that a bug in the system?' Or a customer is making a suggestion that needs technical input. 'Is this something that we can look at putting in? We'll work with the product manager. 'What's coming up?' And ways we can do it. It's a pretty flexible position really, and you can make of it what you want here. I mean, we're not structured in that, 'Okay, in this role, you only do this, and in this role you only do that'. It's really, 'How much do you want to do and handle?' And so really, I think the main core ingredient at this company is problem solving."

There are several additional reasons why titles are not so important. First, employees, to some extent, "create their own job." They may have been initially hired for a specific task, but their job definition will change over time without any change in their title. As their skills improve, they may be able to spend more time solving other issues or they may discover some other tasks that they like to do or for which they have a natural talent. Second, the company and its environment change constantly. Some tasks disappear or, with experience and/or new software, take less time to complete; meanwhile, the organization faces new challenges. In this fast-changing environment, employees are task-oriented. That is why adaptability and aptitude to learn technical skills and develop people skills to be able to handle emerging challenges are so important within the organization.

> Melissa [Business Analyst]: "So what I envision [in the near future] is a lot of the things I currently do now, that I've spent a lot of time on, would be made a lot more efficient, a lot more automated. And then I will look for other avenues to use my skills in the company to make another area better. Or to learn more knowledge about the software we sell. That's one of the beautiful things here is if you do a good job and you have an interest in another area, as long as you do a good job, if you want to move that route, you're more than welcome to do that. Because here we concentrate on what your strengths are [and] how can we use them better."

A final reason is efficiency and cost effectiveness. At HCSS, a good employee is an employee who is versatile and who understands the synergies that can be achieved when departments work together; someone willing to pitch in, whenever and wherever it's needed, for the good of the company as a whole. There is very little room for a "silo mentality" where an employee is only interested by the performance of his/her own department.

> Genaro [Regional Manager for Technical Services]: "I've got a few roles. I help manage implementation support for our 1,200 to 1,300 companies in our West Coast region, which includes everything basically west of Texas. Recently, in the last seven or eight months, I've been assigned as the quality assurance manager for our flagship product as well, and took over that department to help Kinda get some things in order. I help out with a lot of sales calls in our region, as well, and from some of the other regions, as well."

HCSS also encourages its employees to explore various interests outside the organization. For instance, expenses for employees attending ownership conferences are paid, as are those related to attending meetings of professional associations that present opportunities for development. For example, Chris (Regional Manager for Technical Services & Training and Implementation Manager) participates at conferences as an active member of the National Utility Contractors Association where some of HCSS's existing and potential customers can be found.

HCSS grooms its own managers and rarely recruits them externally (an exception being the current search for a marketing director). However, while a promotion means facing new challenges, it does not necessarily guarantee an increase in salary or a larger office.

> Chris [Regional Manager for Technical Services & Training and Implementation Manager]: "I went from technical services to training manager to implementation manager, regional manager, product manager. These are the things that I am going after. They'll give you the opportunity, especially if you vouch for one, and you knocked it out. Then you can really move to different areas in the company but none of those [moves] dictates my salary."

HCSS provides tuition assistance for work-related training programs at any University or College. The company also pays for off-premises seminars but primarily relies on peer-training and self-learning. Most employees are self-starters who learn new technologies and other things on their own. The organization has books they recommend, such as *First Break All the Rules*.[4] About half of the staff has read it and participated in book studies. HCSS also offers courses in management and leadership to employees, some of which are taught by company executives. In an example of organizational development through peer interaction, the leadership team, composed of four or five senior managers, meets every month to discuss areas that need improvement. They start with basic information from the "Best Places to Work" surveys and they research what areas the employees would like to see improved in the company.

The attitude of each employee to never settle for what they already know creates a culture where everybody is constantly learning new things to ensure that they are up-to-date with their skills and their abilities to deliver high quality performance for the company. This dynamic self-perpetuates as employees recruit candidates with similar attitudes and abilities. At the same time, the organization supports new initiatives by paying for employees to go to conferences, training programs and certifications. Once these outside programs are completed, employees teach what they have learned to colleagues. HCSS tries to encourage employees to think, "How can I enhance not just my own value but also that of everybody else?"

> Genaro [Regional Manager for Technical Services]: "We like to self-learn. I would say that there is some technical training that we'll go through, and get everybody; but a lot of times, it's other people who took it upon themselves first to learn and then

they're teaching the rest of us. That's how we keep current with a lot of things. Somebody will go—just the interest in it so much that they figure it out, and say 'Hey. We might, as a support department, need to know about this' and then share that information with everybody else. So, it makes it—and we do send people over to do technical training. We've done that in the past, but a lot of our guys are better off just tinkering with stuff."

Overall, through the hiring, integration and promotion processes of its employees, HCSS is continuously defining and refining its corporate culture. The end result is that employees tend to be versatile in terms of their abilities and willingness to complete various tasks. They are also "problem solvers," more interested in meeting new challenges than in getting a new title and a larger office. In addition, they tend to be self-starters willing to learn and share their knowledge with other employees. Finally, as noted earlier, there is very little room for the "silo mentality." Employees are networkers who know how to reach out to other communities /departments within or outside the company.

Fringe Benefits and Wellness: HCSS provides comprehensive health care and retirement benefits. The company does not provide day care, per se, but it is very family oriented. In the case of an unexpected circumstance, employees are allowed to bring their children to the office. Often this benefits the company because employees facing emergencies do not have to call in sick; they can still work. This reduces the stress for the employee and at the same time it is another way to connect the employee's family to the work place.

As for the health and wellness of employees, HCSS does not only "talk the talk"; the organization also "walks the walk." In addition to modern workout facilities, a soccer field and a basketball court, there is also a running track on the company's premises.

> Maria [Controller] ". . . You'll see people running the track throughout the day, taking walks around the track, and take breaks. Maybe sales will go out and walk around. I don't know if they're talking business, but they're walking around the track. It brings people together. It's kind of a team-building issue, too."

In addition, HCSS sponsors and pays registration fees for events such as: 5-K runs, marathons and bike races. Some employees prefer indoor activities. Daniel (Corporate Ambassador),[5] along with his other numerous responsibilities, organizes Pilates sessions, teaches yoga and is valued as a personal trainer. As well, he provides assistance and advice to employees during lunch breaks.

As for refreshments, company refrigerators are stocked with soft drinks, juices and Gatorade. Each week a different department is in charge of kitchen duty, restocking on a daily basis with fresh fruits and vegetables—avocados, apples, oranges, grapes, carrots, strawberries or whatever is in season and healthy.

Work and Family Life: HCSS organizes picnics and Christmas parties and invites the employees' families. Beyond these formal events, many employees continue their social interactions after office hours on and off the company premises. For instance, when some employees organize a movie night, the company picks up the tab for basic food and drinks. Other employees might go to a show with colleagues and their children. Finally, HCSS tolerates "underground" activities, such as on-line video games on company's computers, as long as it is after office hours.

Building Leadership and the Entrepreneurial Spirit

HCSS offers courses and training programs in management. It offers financial incentives to enhance employees' performance, but it does not stop there. Mike believes that perks and training opportunities would not fundamentally change the attitudes of the employees if it was not for the existence of three major characteristics of HCSS corporate culture: access to information, involvement in the decision-making process and tolerance for honest mistakes.

Access to Information: In this fast-changing environment, it is essential for the senior management and decision-makers to keep an "open-door policy," not just in theory but also in practice. An open-door policy does not only mean that any employee can talk to the senior management and the CEO whenever they have ideas or problems. It also means that the senior management will provide them with the information they need to accomplish their objectives without having the manager "breathing down their neck" to make sure that the job is done. Very early in the company's development, Mike realized the limits of the hierarchical structure in which a CEO tells his manager what to do, who in turn tells the employee what to do. As a company grows, the temptation to add layers of management is difficult to resist, but a bureaucratic structure is not particularly cost-effective. Instead, Mike thinks it is better to invest time recruiting the right people, give them the adequate information and let them run their business with little supervision. He decided that a flat structure in which employees assume ownership of their ideas and performance leads to a far more effective organization, particularly when these employees have been selected for their "can do" attitude and their ability to learn on their own.

> Melissa [Business Analyst]: "I think that its important for your employees to feel like they're a part of something bigger. That's a big basis for the ownership culture for me—communicating, open-book policy. It's more like you come here and you work more with family than you do, you don't just clock in and clock out. I mean you take ownership for the things you do, the things your coworkers do."

Chris [Regional Manager for Technical Services & Training and Implementation Manager], like the receptionist Daniel, was overqualified for the position that he initially accepted at HCSS. Although he had managed about 80 franchisees in his former job, Chris started as a support technician. Within one year, his managerial skills were recognized and he was promoted to the position of training manager. As a new technician, he had a firsthand experience of the company's open-door policy.

> Chris [Regional Manager for Technical Services & Training and Implementation Manager]: "As we were working on our annual end-users meeting during which 800 to 1,000 people come to Houston to visit with us, I saw an opportunity to refine our knowledge of HCSS customer base. I said to Mark [his supervisor at that time], 'How many of our top customers show up to user group meeting?' Mark did not know the answer and he asked me to find this info and others. So, I went to our CEO and asked him. It seemed like real internal [confidential] information that you would not give a new employee . . . and he gave it to me . . . Mike always says he wants to give us the tools to do our job. So, it's very rare, very rare that you would ask for information on something that Mike wouldn't share with you. . . . He tells us a lot of stuff that I can promise you you'd never hear in another company if you're not on the executive level. From the biggest deals we're working on to the money we'll make out of these deals. . . . He will share this information with us, to make sure that we're all engaged. . . . Because we're owners, we should know."

Trusting and Involving Employees in the Decision-Making Process: At HCSS, employees are involved in all major decisions, from hiring future colleagues to the deadline for a software release or the choice of the lay-out for their offices in the new building. One of the recent issues discussed with employees was the need to change the company's insurance provider, as well as the level of coverage that was needed. For these important deliberations, large meetings were held and everyone was invited to share their views and to help make the final decision.

> Chris [Regional Manager for Technical Services & Training and Implementation Manager]: "I remember this specifically. It was . . . 'If we spend this much, this is the level of service we would get' And if we wanted to increase that, 'We can spend more to get this higher level, but it's gonna come out of our bottom line'. And at the end of the year, your share of the company's profits—and we all decided to self-insure some risks but to spend more on others because we wanted a higher level of insurance. It wasn't four or five people at the executive level saying 'This is what we're doing'. They let us decide. And that's just one example of a lot of things. So, yes, we do have a tremendous amount of trust with our executives."

Nevertheless, HCSS is a company, not a democracy. At the end of a discussion, Mike or a senior manager will make the final decision, notably when there is a stalemate or when an outcome is uncertain. Interestingly, there is less resistance from employees to implement a decision, even if they disagree with the final choice, when all options have been discussed and understood.

Tolerating Honest Mistakes: When an employee makes an honest error which is not repeated and the company tolerates it, there are benefits on two levels. First, it is very difficult for employees to take initiatives if there is zero tolerance for failure. Self-managed employees at HCSS, like managers in other companies, have to make decisions and take initiatives in a complex and fast-changing environment. A lack of tolerance stifles creativity and the entrepreneurial spirit of employees who fear negative consequences for their decisions. Second, a company's negative attitude towards failure inadvertently encourages employees to hide their mistakes as well as the consequences of their mistakes. Often, it is not the initial mistake that jeopardizes the viability of an organization but the long-term consequences of a cover-up when an employee fears sanctions.

Melissa [Business Analyst]: "I was in a test environment. I did a lot of testing to change some things. I accidentally sent out 2,000 alerts and faxes to customers telling them that they had not paid their maintenance fees. I don't know how accurate they were because we hadn't been using them in a long time. We immediately get these phones ringing off the wall; our in-boxes get filled with these replies to 'What are you talking about?' So the first thing I did was I ran to Mike [CEO] and Tom [Supervisor] and I said, 'Look, I just sent out these emails by accident and dah, dah, dah', and I was upset. Rather than yell at me or whatever, Tom immediately sent out emails to all the same customers saying, 'We were doing some testing. We apologize for the mistake'. . . . At the end of the day, we did collect almost $10,000 from clients who had not actually paid their maintenance fees and we also installed a new password system to avoid repeating the same mistake. Here, we accept mistakes. We expect you to learn from them and try not to make the same mistake again. But mistakes are a good way to grow and realize that something needs to be changed."

Corporate Governance and the Meaning of "Ownership"

Governance Structure: HCSS is an S Corporation and the company does not have to disclose any financial information to anyone. Still, they provide some data to Dun & Bradstreet and to large customers, in order to assure the latter that HCSS is a service provider in good financial health before they sign a long-term contract to design and roll out software. HCSS also provides information on financial performance and ongoing transactions to employees so they can assess the size and likelihood of their next "profit sharing" check. For obvious reasons, the company closely guards certain critical information, such as its ownership structures and margins on certain products and services.

With regard to ownership, a few stock options were provided to employees and outsiders who were associated with the start-up during the early years of operation, as well as to a couple of external investors who financed the venture. Otherwise, the company remains essentially owned and the finances controlled by Mike and his family. Only Mike, his wife, Sophie, and Tom (VP, Technical Services) are members of the board and attend board meetings. ESOP, the Employee Stock Ownership Plan, can vote as an entity for the most important decisions, such as the eventual or hypothetical sale of the company.

Employees, as individuals, do not vote their shares. Therefore, employees' ownership mentality and sense of empowerment are not only derived from share ownership through ESOP. Indeed, the impact of the share ownership program on employees' behavior is leveraged through management practices that give employees access to information and actively involve them in the decision-making process whenever the company faces key issues. Here the practical meaning of ownership is that the employees "do business" the way an owner would, and the proportional sharing of the company's profit is an integral part of that.

Employee Stock Ownership Plans (ESOP): Within the first few years, Mike had already decided to develop the entrepreneurial mentality of the employees and to encourage their involvement in the company's affairs. Nevertheless, the decision to implement an ESOP was not an easy one. There are pros and cons for employee-owned corporations. HCSS set up a trust and made tax-deductible contributions to it. These discretionary cash contributions were initially used to buy shares from selling owners and, subsequently, shares from employees leaving HCSS or selling their shares to diversify their portfolios. The stocks acquired by the trust are allocated to the individual account of each employee based on the level of their remuneration, which also serves as the basis to compute their end of the year share of the company's profits. At HCSS, 25% of the profit sharing program is paid in shares that go to the ESOP account of each individual. All full-time employees with at least six months of service are included. The accounts vest overtime and, at HCSS, employees are fully vested after six years of service.

In addition to the tax breaks for both the owners and the employees, there are a few other advantages attached to ESOPs. First of all, participants are able to build their nest eggs for retirement while developing a sense of ownership in the company. Second, as employees build their stake in HCSS, there is an increased incentive to stay. This is particularly important in industries with high turnover rates such as the software development industry where employees typically stay an average of only 18 to 24 months with the same employer.

There are also a few disadvantages to ESOPs. First of all, employees have fewer options to diversify their portfolio. Indeed, most of the employees living in the Houston area, including HCSS employees, are painfully aware of the Enron bankruptcy. This bankruptcy ended up being particularly costly, especially for employees who had a lifetime commitment to and investment in this corporation; after the bankruptcy proceeding was closed, there was not much left for Enron retirees to live on. Second, as employees build their stake in the company and become majority shareholders, complex decisions can become difficult to make. Every shareholder has a different time frame. When long-term investments such as capital expenditures and research have a negative short-term effect on cash at hand and the profit sharing program, disagreements may emerge and, ultimately, the collective decision may not benefit the long-term interest of the company.

All the above scenarios were carefully considered before setting up the employee's stock ownership plans. Today, Mike still owns 33% of the shares and the employees about 34%. Currently, 19 employees, those who joined the company during its early years, own a majority of the 34%. With the growth of the company, fewer shares were available to newcomers. As a result, over the last few years, these 19 employees were given the option to sell 10% of those shares every year. This allows the more senior employees to diversify their portfolio over time and for the company to have shares available to new employees. The balance, about one-third of the shares, is owned by the few external investors mentioned earlier who either financed the start-up or provided technical advice, such as the accountant, lawyer and programmer who accepted shares in lieu of cash as payment for their services.

Stock Appreciation Rights [SARS]: To complement the ESOPs, it was decided in 2007 to offer additional incentives and to increase the stake that each new employee had in the company. The main objective of SARS was to offer new employees, who had not benefitted from the company's fast growth as a start-up, the opportunity to benefit from future growth. This had to be achieved without offering shares, as they were not available, due to the limitations imposed on an S-Corp capital structure. Any employee who had worked more than 1,000 hours during that year was granted rights on 700 shares on the basis of the stock price at that time. At the end of the fourth year, i.e., 2011, if the stockprice has appreciated, each employee will exercise those rights and pocket the difference between the initial benchmark and the value of the stock. This stock appreciation will be considered and paid out as ordinary income.

End-of-Year Profit Sharing Program: At HCSS, the profit sharing program computation is

straightforward. The first 10% of the company's net profits is booked as retained earnings for the company's use. The profit sharing pool for employees represents 60% of any profits above the 10% (which, in 2007, was $1.6 million and, in 2009, $0.9 million). The profit sharing pool is then shared among employees, calculated on their base salary. The profit sharing program represents the same percentage of every employee's basic salary, from entry-level employees to senior executives. For 2009, which was a difficult year in the industry, the profit sharing program represented about 17% of the employee's base salary. During better years, it has sometimes reached or exceeded 35%. Seventy-five percent of the profit sharing program is paid in cash and 25% in stocks that go to the employee's ESOP account.

Sebabi [Organizational Development Manager]: "And the thing that impresses me the most is that our CEO and our entire executive team do not sit there and make the assumption that, because they're at that level, they should get a disproportionately higher percentage of the profits of the company. It is still based on W-2 wages, of course, whatever your wages are. But everybody gets the same percentage. So if it's 25% for that year, then everybody gets 25% for that year. And I think that really, not only for me, personally, but for every employee, it makes them really buy into the whole concept that we're all in this together as a company, to help it to be more successful."

One advantage of the profit sharing program, particularly when the company has an established track record of treating its employees well and fairly, is that some employees accept a pay cut when they join HCSS. Others, particularly at entry level, accept salaries that would be considered low by industry standards. During the long interview process, nothing is more convincing for a candidate than to hear his/her future colleagues talking about their rewarding experience with such a system. By keeping starting salary at or slightly below industry average, the company is in a better position in the case of an economic downturn. However, the company annual raises are far above industry averages and, over time, with or without profit sharing award, an employee's income rival or exceed industry norms.

Besides motivating employees, another major advantage of the HCSS profit sharing program is that it reduces difficulties in relationships between departments with different objectives. For instance, while the sales and support departments have different priorities, employees in one area know that what is good for the other department is also good for them.

> Eric [Major Account Manager]: "They [the support department] help me on my demos all the time and you'd think maybe there'd be some animosity because they spent all this time on a sale and they're helping the salesman and the salesman is the one that ends up getting the commission. But that support guy knows that it's going to the bottom line. It's going to profit share, too."

In retrospect, Mike reflects that while the initial plan to make employees feel and behave like owners was a good idea, ESOP was probably not the best way to achieve these objectives. Indeed, over the years, ESOP triggered a few unexpected issues in the areas of tax and succession planning. In addition, as ESOP reached a certain threshold, cash payments had to be made to employees selling their shares at times when the company needed the financial resources for its expansion. Finally, ESOP was too complex for most employees to see it as a motivator to join the company and to stay during the first years of their employment.

> Tom [Vice President of Technical Services]: "The ESOP is important, but it doesn't get people in the door. And it doesn't get them excited because a) people don't understand the ESOP, and b) it takes them a number of years to build enough value in the ESOP where the ESOP becomes attention-worthy."

Profit sharing programs are more palatable than other incentive mechanisms for the employees at any level and far easier to manage by the company during every phase of the business cycle. However, to make the profit sharing program even more meaningful to employees, Mike quickly understood that two additional conditions had to be met. First, the profit sharing program must be easy to understand and the allocation process transparent. Second, the amount paid must be significant and fairly allocated among employees. As noted earlier, transparency and fairness are essential to enhance teamwork within and between departments. Over the years, several employees have mentioned to Mike how many opportunities they had in their daily work to help colleagues. Any assistance provided to a colleague is a plus for the company as a whole and each employee knows that the added value generated will be fairly shared at the end of the year.

Each month a member of the senior management team leads the company lunch meeting to discuss financial performance and the ongoing transactions. However, not every employee has a financial background. Therefore, discussions about financials are usually limited to a basic review of the income statement. From the employee's point of view, the main interest is that he/she can estimate in real time the size that the profit sharing pool will attain by the end of the year. In addition, making employees aware of the financial situation by the company directly, as opposed to hearing through the rumor mill, is preferable, especially in a time of financial difficulty. Finally, when efforts such as pay cuts and/or reduced hours are needed during an economic downturn, employees are able to put the request for sacrifice within the current business context. Financial pain is more bearable when it is understood and spread evenly.

> Maria [Controller]: "Every week we meet at the company lunch meetings with employees and we discuss various things going on in the company. It's very open. Everybody knows what's going on, what's going on with our products, what's new, what's different, et cetera. Some people go off, visit customers. They'll come back and tell us how that went, what they did, everything like that. But once a month, we will go over the financials. . . . We look at sales. Sale figures, why they might have gone up or down. They'll ask, 'Why is electricity so high this month?' . . . Pretty much anything. Then we look at our margins and see where they are."

Moving Forward: Expanding While Keeping a Competitive Edge

HCSS is conservatively managed, but well managed. The company has remained profitable even during the economic downturn and, except for the recent acquisition of their new headquarters, the company has managed to finance its activities out of its own cash flow. Therefore, to finance future rapid growth, both internal and external financial resources are available.

One issue Mike has faced since the beginning is the pace of company growth. While subject to market conditions, an unlisted, family-controlled company has no real obligation to grow rapidly. To contrast HCSS with publicly listed companies, at HCSS there is no analyst's meeting at the end of every quarter during which so-called experts, who often do not know much about the industry, pressure for "growth," "upside potential" and "market momentum." Neither are there venture capitalists and institutional investors on the board of the company pushing for a strategy that would deliver a rapid growth in sales and profits in the medium term at the expense of the long-term viability of the company. Mike is not under these pressures. Therefore, one option is to simply maintain the same pace. It took 25 years for Mike to grow the company to its current level and it could take another 25 years to double its size.

But is it so simple? The company has come a long way since its humble beginnings and Mike did not spend half of his life growing HCSS to let it stagnate at its current level. Besides, the company always has new products in its pipeline and in this fast-changing environment, not taking advantage of market opportunities could be very costly in the long term. In this industry, competitors do not sit idle. In fact, HCSS is about to launch a new safety software product with applications not only for companies in the construction industry where most of HCSS's current customers operate, but also for other industries, especially the large manufacturing segment. This new software offers tremendous growth potential and the opportunity to create real value not only to clients but to employees and shareholders, as well. However, introduction of this new software to a larger market requires the company to grow rapidly to get and keep the first mover advantage.

Could the company double in size over the next three years without destroying its culture and its competitive advantage? Mike recalls that even during the downturn, he still had six or seven entry-level positions open and unfilled. Quite a few applications were received but candidates rarely made it from HR to the department interested in hiring additional employees. In addition to the lengthy recruiting process, for more senior positions, there are other issues.

For instance, considering its current corporate and governance structure, would it be possible for HCSS to attract and motivate the outside talent needed to complement the company's pool of internal managers? If so, what kind of incentive package would motivate these new senior executives to make the organization more efficient without destroying its unique corporate culture?

The company is currently headed by three senior managers: Mike with a background in philosophy, Tom with a background in psychology and Steve with an MBA. It is this unusual mix of creativity and pragmatism, coupled with the fact that none of them are fundamentally money-driven, that made the company a success. Would a "hired gun" take the same pride in growing the business?

In recent years, leaders have been selected internally but Mike is aware of the limitations this creates. As the company grows rapidly, HCSS could find itself led by managers and directors who do not have prior leadership experience. And in fact, the grooming process is time consuming. Situations can also arise where the company does not have internal candidates available. Hiring outsiders is always possible, but it is not an easy process, either. If anything, the ongoing search for a marketing director has proven frustrating and time consuming, considering the number of people involved in the process. Yet the collective wisdom attached to the current selection process has been key to hiring high-quality employees who quickly adjust to the company's corporate culture.

In addition to the human resources issues, both at entry and more senior levels, there are also issues related to the communication flows between departments. Being close to the customer and being very responsive to their needs means that the channels of communication have to remain highly effective. In this regard, is the current corporate structure adequate? Mike is aware of areas that need improvement. The support, implementation and programming departments communicate well together, but the marketing, sales and programming interface is not as effective. Can the company double its size while keeping the same structure?

Even at its current size, communication has become an issue, both horizontally and vertically. Often Mike spots disconnects between the outcome of a discussion of the senior team members and the perception and understanding of this decision by the employees at more junior levels; sometimes the message becomes confused. Mike was adamant that the open-door policy was the best way to communicate directly with everyone but he wonders if this strategy will be sustainable with 200 employees when it is already difficult to succeed with 100.

Mike knows that he must deal with these issues rather sooner than later. In a recent meeting with Chris, he noticed that employees in the customer support department were putting in long hours, even during the economic downturn. While there is nothing wrong with long hours over a short period of time, with business picking up, there is a risk that the situation would lead to the burnout of a few key employees. And in a business that relies heavily on employees' creativity and dedication to customers' needs, this situation cannot be left unattended for long without some unpleasant consequences that would be preferable to avoid.

Appendix 1   Product Lines

HEAVYBID: HeavyBid is a powerful construction estimating software for infrastructure contractors bidding projects ranging from $50,000 to over one billion dollars.

HEAVYJOB: Heavyjob is complete job tracking software that transforms job site information into valuable management information on a daily basis. It includes time card entry on both PCs and handheld devices, instant production/cost analysis, billing, forecasting and interfaces to the customer's accounting software,

DISPATCHER: The Dispatcher is a resource management software. It allows a company to track the usage of its equipment, tools, materials and crews and to get the most out of them. It allows a company to plan, analyze, and improve usage of these resources.

EQUIPMENT360: An equipment maintenance program that delivers cost savings to customers through lower down times, less major repairs, lower fuel consumption, and greater availability of its equipment. In essence, Equipment360 gives the customer the ability to track, identify, analyze, and resolve equipment maintenance issues before they become a problem.

BIDHISTORY.COM: This is a collection of historical bid pricing and bid tabs compiled from public DOT sites throughout the United States. The benefits of using Bidhistory.com include tracking and reviewing historical bid pricing tabulations and viewing historical average prices for specific bid items.

SAFETY: A safely management software that helps a company to capture daily activities and incidents in the field, manage data in the office and deliver reportables to the management team.

VECTR GPS: Integration with the Dispatcher brings customers total control over the fleet of vehicles. It allows customers to make better decisions based on real information coming directly from the field. HCSS provides all-inclusive packages that include the GPS hardware units, data service coverage and integration with the Dispatcher.

FUELERPLUS: This is a fuel management software that allows a company to easily track the amount of fuel and other fluids being dispensed into equipment and fuel trucks. It captures all the activities of a fueler, automates the flow of this data to other systems such as other HCSS applications and other accounting systems. It also allows the company to generate reports to help managers realize the true cost of fuel as well as the fueler's activities.

Extracted from HCSS Website

Appendix 2   Financials

[In US$]	2007	2008	2009
Current Assets	9,213,653	6,491,900	7,264,040
Current Liabilities	4,216,079	5,650,387	6,146,784
Sales	17,494,651	19,288,557	17,867,967
Long-Term Liabilities	—	—	6,294,179
Net Profit (Loss)	2,986,656	2,458,502	1,733,857

Note: The long-term debt of $6.3 million was incurred to finance the construction of the new building which can accommodate 230 employees.

Appendix 3 Organization Chart

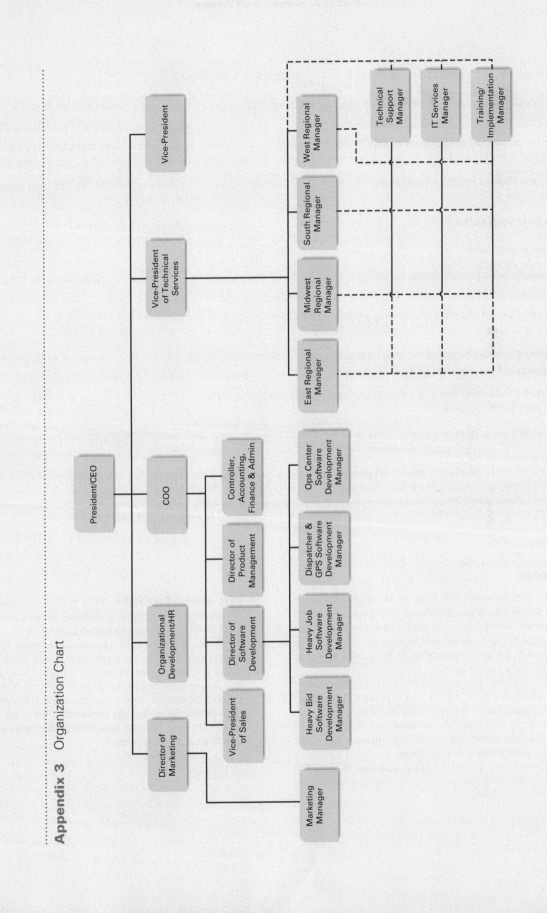

Appendix 4   Lessons Learned about Building an Employment Brand

Don't waste time trying to fabricate an employer brand: You've already got a brand; your company's culture already defines your employer brand.

Use your culture to define your brand: You don't have to be a nationally known billion-dollar company in order to have a good employer brand. Build your brand around your culture and the people you hire will fit, excel, and stay.

Recruiters should become marketers: Recruiters must become expert marketers and champions of the company culture and brand.

Don't hide your culture: The culture of your company is already known to applicants from the moment they walk into your office or interact with the employees that work at your company. An authentic brand will build a better pipeline of applicants.

Hire people who fit your culture: The biggest mistake you can make is to hire someone who does not fit the culture.

Make your brand toxic for the wrong people: Showcase your culture to make it toxic for the wrong people and appealing to the right people. You will inevitably find the right people and the right people will find you.

Use multiple tools to promote your brand: Increase your brand recognition using social media, videos, dedicated Websites and job board branding.

Celebrate those who live the culture: Let your employees live up to their full potential and promote them to others as a great example.

Prove you have a great culture: Compete in "best companies to work for" contests to get feedback and gain credibility and recognition for your culture, which helps enhance your brand.

Executives must genuinely desire employees to have a great life: If the goals of helping employees live up to their full potential is solely driven by revenue/profit goals, your culture and brand will never flourish.

Extract from keynote speech handout: "Your Culture Defines Your Brand" by Sebabi Leballo, Organizational Development Manager

Endnotes

1 The authors would like to thank the employee-owners of HCSS who graciously shared their knowledge, experiences, and perspectives about the company. Their viewpoints were invaluable in ensuring that this case provides a true representation of the culture and practices of the company.

2 This statement was made by Melissa, a business analyst at HCSS. It reflects a value that is pervasive among her colleagues. HCSS employees are confident that they are "doing the job right." At the same time, they never stop looking for better ways to do it or opportunities to use their skills to solve new problems.

3 All employees are referred to in this case by their first name including the president because that is standard practice in HCSS.

4 *First, Break All the Rules: What the World's Greatest Managers Do Differently,* by Markus Buckingham and Curt Coffman. Simon & Schuster, May 1999.

5 At HCSS, the corporate ambassador is more than a receptionist. This person greets visitors and helps them out. It is important for clients and visitors to have a first and lasting good impression of the company. The corporate ambassador knows and remembers the names of the visitors. He is also the person employees speak to when they have logistics issues to resolve, similar to a concierge at a luxury hotel.

KCI Technologies, Inc.
Engineering the Future, One Employee at a Time[*1]

Vera L. Street, PhD
Perdue School of Business, Salisbury University

Christy Weer, PhD
Perdue School of Business, Salisbury University

Frank Shipper, PhD
Perdue School of Business, Salisbury University

To an outsider, KCI Technologies may appear to be a typical, run of the mill engineering firm. However, once introduced, prospective clients soon understand why KCI was recently ranked 83rd on the *Engineering News-Record's* list of the top 500 Engineering Firms in the country, 7th on its list of Top 20 Telecommunications Firms, and 55th out of the Top 100 "Pure" Designers. With a focus on providing the highest quality service through a commitment to innovation and employee development, KCI is clearly positioning itself for the future.

KCI Technologies is currently the largest employee-owned, multidisciplined engineering firm in Maryland. Providing consulting, engineering, and environmental construction management services, KCI had revenues of approximately $131 million in 2009 and serves clients in the Northeast, Southeast and Mid-Atlantic regions of the US. The more than 900 employee owners of KCI operate out of offices in 12 states—Delaware, Florida, Georgia, Indiana, Maryland, New York, North Carolina, Ohio, Pennsylvania, Tennessee, Virginia and West Virginia, as well as the District of Columbia.

KCI has undergone incredible changes over the last several decades. From a basement dream, to a multimillion dollar employee owned organization, KCI is poised to face the future. However, with an uncertain economy and reduced governmental and private-sector spending, will the loyalty and commitment of the employee-owners be enough for KCI to continue building the impressive set of awards and recognition for which the company has become accustomed?

Background

The company now known as KCI was founded in Baltimore County, Maryland in 1955 in the basement of one of its cofounders. In 1977, the company was purchased by industrial products conglomerate Walter Kidde & Company and was subsequently merged with three other architectural and engineering firms into an engineering subsidiary that came to be known as Kidde Consultants Inc., or KCI. In 1987, Kidde was purchased by Hanson Trust PLC, a British manufacturing company with diversified holdings worldwide.

Although Hanson favored some of the Kidde businesses, there was a lack of fit between KCI and its new parent company. In particular, being a service-driven firm, as opposed to a product-oriented manufacturing company, KCI's measures of profitability were not consistent with Hanson's expectations. As an example, Terry Neimeyer, KCI's CEO explained:

> They had a term called, "Return on Capital Employed," . . . and they expected any company that worked for them to have an ROCE of 80 percent. . . . We said, "Well, look, we are an engineering company,

Sources: Vera Street, Salisbury University; Christy Weer, Salisbury University, Frank Shipper, Salisbury University. The research on this company was partially supported by the Foundation for Enterprise Development and the ESOP Association. Used by kind permission of the authors.

Keywords: ESOP, Shared leadership, Intellectual capital, Organizational culture

*An earlier version of this case was published in the Journal of Business Case Studies, 2011, Vol. 7, No. 1, pp. 57–68.

we're lucky to do 5 or 6 percent and we think we're doing well at 5 or 6 percent." And they said, "Look, our number's 80 percent."

Even beyond the inconsistencies with respect to financial expectations, the corporate cultures of Hanson and KCI differed drastically. KCI was used to having autonomy in decision making and authority. Hanson on the other hand, took a much more centralized, top-down approach to management. For example, as Neimeyer remembers, "if you wanted to buy a computer, you would have to go to London and make a presentation."

It was no secret that Hanson's business strategy was to enter the U.S., buy a conglomerate, keep what they viewed to be their profitable assets—assets that would be returning 80 percent—and then divest the unprofitable assets. Thus, aware that Hanson would likely want to sooner rather than later divest of KCI, senior managers had an idea. Driven largely by self-preservation, but also with a touch of optimism, the top management team thought, "Hey, let's see what we can do to buy ourselves." And why not? Who knew what would happen if KCI were to be taken over by another company? Indeed, there was a level of excitement over the potential of being a part of, and perhaps even leading, an employee owned company.

Unfortunately, Hanson was not at all receptive to the idea. As Neimeyer remembers, Hanson's view on selling KCI to its employees was;

> Absolutely not. We do not sell to people. We do not sell to former employees. It's just not what we do. We'd like to sell and rid ourselves of this [company] and it's over . . . and we don't do it [sell to former employees].

However, by this time, the KCI senior management team was actively seeking a strategy to make a buy-out happen. Having determined that alone the senior managers could not come up with enough equity to leverage a deal, they sought the buy-in of the 800 KCI employees. An existing Kidde profit sharing plan, which had accumulated some significant funds, laid the foundation for employee contributions. According to Neimeyer,

> We said, let's look at doing this where we'll ask people [employees] if they'd like to do it. We'll put out perspectives; we'll do a whole pro forma, which we did. And then people [employees] would have the option of contributing whatever they wanted. They could contribute 0 percent, they could contribute

100 percent, they could contribute anywhere in between. So, [based on our calculations as to the value of the company at that time], we basically had the scenario where ballpark figures it was 80 percent employee owned, with 20 percent held by these managers.

However, Hanson refused the offer. They were just not interested in selling the company to former employees.

Disappointed, but ever cognizant of the potential harsh consequences of being purchased by another organization, senior management at KCI went back to the drawing board. They knew the risks of upping the offer, but they also had confidence in their organization and, perhaps even more importantly, in their employees. Ultimately, they presented an increased, leveraged offer Hanson could not refuse. Shortly thereafter, KCI initiated an employee buyout and became a majority employee-owned company on December 15, 1988. On January 1, 1990, KCI established a qualified retirement program for the stock of KCI Technologies, Inc., to be held in trust by an Employee Stock Ownership Plan (ESOP). The ESOP initially owned approximately 82% of KCI stock, however, in June 1998, the company bought all of the management shares (non-ESOP shares) and became 100% employee-owned. Terry Neimeyer is the current Chief Executive Officer and Chairman of the Board of KCI; Nathan Beil is the President.

Operations and Quality Management

Although most people know an engineer or have at least met one, many may not know exactly what engineers do. To help better understand the nature of KCI, Harvey Floyd, a Senior Vice President and Chief Client Services Officer, offered the following as an explanation of KCI's businesses to outsiders:

> You know what architects do, you know what lawyers do, you know what doctors do, but you have no idea what engineers do . . . you know when you get up in the morning and you turn the lights on; How do you think that light comes on? It's from the generators that were built by engineers, the power plants, the transmission lines, everything built by, everything was designed by engineers. [To clarify] Not built, but designed by engineers. Then, you walked over and turned the water on, and out came

water. Well, where do you think the water came from? From the reservoirs, the towers, the pumps, the pumping stations, all designed by engineers. You flush the toilet. Where do you think it all goes? Pipes, the treatments plants, all designed by engineers. You drove across a road to get here. Where do you think the road came from? The bridge you drove over . . . who designed the bridges?

In other words, KCI is in the business of designing and coordinating facility and infrastructure projects and improvements for both the public and private sectors. Much of their work, approximately 80%, involves public sector work from various Departments of Transportation (e.g., MD DOT, Georgia DOT, PennDOT). Examples of work KCI may become involved with in the private sector include projects at research parks and universities for contractors and developers. Figure 1 provides examples of recent projects undertaken by KCI.

The competitive environment facing KCI, as well as the need for precision in the nature of the projects undertaken, drives a quality-focused culture at KCI. In part, there is the recognition that repeat business is critical, and to get that repeat business, projects must be completed to precision. When things do not

go as well as expected, it is not uncommon for KCI employees to get out in the field to figure out what could be improved upon for future projects.

Quality is important on both the business side as well as the technical side of the work done at KCI. On the business side there are quality issues with, for example determining project scope, understanding and negotiating client needs, and understanding regulations. On the technical side, the quality of designs, calculations, and reports and plans must be regulated. Because there are no set products that are being produced, as every project is different, these are challenging tasks.

Obtaining and maintaining ISO certification (verification by the International Organization on Standardization that relevant business standards are met) has been an important quality initiative at KCI. However, obtaining this certification has not been without its challenges. To begin, the standard was initially developed for manufacturing firms. Thus, as a service firm, KCI has had to adopt very broad interpretations of various components of the standard. Additionally, as a requirement, KCI had to explicitly write down their business processes. This proved to be somewhat of a hurdle, because, as Floyd put it, ". . . a lot of these

Figure 1 Example KCI Projects*

Project	Discipline	Location	Description
St. Mary's County Courthouse	Construction	Leonardtown, MD	Construction management over renovation and expansion of historic courthouse.
Clarice Smith Stormwater Management Pond	Environment	College Park, MD	Designed changes to stormwater management pond.
Capitol West Refrigeration Plant Expansion	Land Development	Washington, DC	Survey and layout services for plant expansion.
Gettysburg Interchange	Transportation	Cumberland County, PA	Team lead for highway interchange project.
Bonita Springs Tower	Telecommunications	Bonita Springs, FL	Worked on repair of tower damaged by hurricane.
Verizon	Telecommunications	Varies	On-call to provide engineering services to Verizon.
Suwannee Pedestrian Bridge	Transportation	Suwanee, GA	Engineering services for bridge and Boardwalk.

*Adapted From KCI Website

things are "that's just the way we do it"." Another issue was getting people to exert the extra effort required to obtain the certification. Senior management tried to make this as painless as possible, and they were quick to point out that, although some extra effort was necessary, often times this effort resulted in not only a step toward certification, but also in making business processes easier than they were before.

Logically, they began slowly, just focusing on part of the company. Then as the benefits were seen, it was decided to begin certification for the whole company in order to take the quality of their processes to the next level. The requisite codification of best business and quality control practices has helped to impose a level of discipline in the company's processes that may not have been present prior to the certification. And, although it is not necessarily required by all clients, it is looked upon very favorably and helps to win business. At this time, not all of KCI businesses have been certified however, they are actively seeking how to do so.

Marketing

Given that KCI is an engineering services firm, marketing is different than in a traditional manufacturing company and is even different from many other types of service firms. Marketing is primarily done through the preparation of proposals and statements of qualification for potential clients. Ultimately, work is secured because of the "expertise and experience of the technical staff at KCI." According to Deborah Boyd, Director of Proposal Preparation;

> I would say that 90 percent of our marketing falls within developing project descriptions of work that we've done in the past, employee resumes. Our marketing is very technical in nature, where it revolves around the projects and the staff team qualifications and the qualifications of our sub-consultants.

The process begins by finding potential clients who have jobs that need to be done. This primarily happens in two ways. The first, more conventional route is done by searching for client advertisements. This is usually done by the marketing staff searching online and/or looking in trade publications. A second, perhaps more fruitful route is done by a type of networking. Here, the Business Development staff, as well as other employees working on various projects, keeps in contact with current and past clients to see what other projects they have in the pipeline. Other consultants that KCI has worked with also often prove to be a good source of leads. The marketing staff track these potential projects. Then, a qualified technical lead is brought in to work on the proposal that will be drawn up for the potential client.

The business development staff meets with the potential clients to ascertain information that will help in the proposal writing process. They try to determine what exactly the potential client is looking for, e.g. a probable price range, or any "hot buttons." Whereas general advertisements by these clients can be fairly generic and don't always contain everything the client is looking for, the Business Developers play a critical role in information gathering. The marketing staff then pulls together this information, matches it with the qualifications of KCI and prepares a package to submit to the potential client.

A key to this process is to get shortlisted. This is an area in which KCI may be able to improve. As Boyd put it,

> So either we're not qualified to do the job or we're qualified and we didn't show it very well. And if we're qualified and we didn't show it very well, that's a reflection on me because that means my proposal didn't answer the questions in the RFP.

An important part of the marketing effort is building project descriptions on prior work and maintaining a database of these descriptions. The project descriptions are like a project "resume." They contain information about the project, including the qualifications of the team that worked on it, and qualifications of any subconsultants.

Additionally, there are efforts aimed at increasing potential clients' awareness of KCI. One way that KCI attempts to build awareness is by standardizing their proposals. Consistency in fonts and colors is maintained so that potential clients can recognize a KCI proposal at a glance. Another example of how KCI attempts to increase awareness is through their corporate website. The website is continually updated to highlight successful projects they are currently working on or have completed. Other corporate communications are also available to interested parties. They produce folders of information including descriptions of successful projects they have completed, indications of awards they've won, and lists of where they are operating. Additionally, presentations at conferences and seminars help to promote the employees of KCI as experts in their respective fields.

HR and Intellectual Capital Development

Clearly, in such a technically focused, service oriented organization, employee knowledge and expertise are key elements for success, and this is not taken for granted at KCI. There are many ways in which intellectual capital is developed, starting right from the beginning; every attempt is made to hire the right people!

With a focus on shared leadership, hiring managers have a hand in developing realistic job descriptions. Openings are first posted internally, allowing current employees the opportunity to investigate and pursue available positions. After five days, the openings are posted externally. Often, department managers are involved in the entire hiring process, from creating job descriptions to prescreening applicants, to interviewing and making final hiring decisions. Although talent is hard to come by, Tammy Jones, a Vice President and HR Director, feels that KCI gets high quality applicants due to the company's reputation for doing great work in high profile projects—projects of which employees are proud to be a part.

Once hired, employees have the option to become involved in a year-long formal mentoring program at KCI. This program, launched about three years ago, was established, in large part, in an attempt to keep the intellectual capital developed at KCI from moving to competitor firms. New hires are paired with more senior employees and move through a 12-month formal mentoring regime. Most senior managers mentor two or three new hires each year and the program appears to be paying off. As indicated by Jones;

> When I came to KCI, which has been almost five years ago, previous employee surveys, and as well as our turnover reports indicated that we were losing employees at two to three years. So thus launched the formal mentoring program. Actually, I was reviewing those statistics recently and we're retaining about 33 percent more than we did prior [to the mentoring program].

Beyond the mentoring program, formal training and development programs are a cornerstone of intellectual capital development at KCI. Perhaps most notably is an extensive set of leadership development programs for which employees at various levels of the organization can be nominated. The series includes three programs: Emerging Leaders, Professional Leaders, and The Advanced Leadership Program.

The Emerging Leaders Program typically consists of 40–60 individuals who have been with the company for fewer than five years. Designed by an outside consultant, employees are nominated and accepted into the Emerging Leaders program based on their leadership potential as noted by their immediate manager. Participants meet every other month for 24 months and have a culminating project focusing on the development of a KCI initiative.

According to Beil;

> On the Emerging Leaders, for example, you have the team building piece as well as training on interpersonal skills, basic management, priority management, conflict management or resolution, stress management, positive reinforcement, and motivation. Sometimes it's hard to motivate even yourself, so expressing yourself in the proper way. And, we actually have a graduation program for these folks . . .

The Professional Leaders program is more selective and is typically limited to 20 employees. This program was also designed with the help of an outside consultant and is continuously customized based on survey feedback from KCI middle managers. The program runs for one year—in Spring and Fall "semesters"—and focuses on topics such as motivating others, coaching and developing others, and relationship management. Participants complete a number of self-assessments, which allow them to better understand themselves and their roles within the organization. With a variety of "credits" to choose from, the program culminates in a three-day off site Foundations of Leadership Program offered by the University of Maryland.

The third and final component, the Advanced Leadership Program is facilitated by an outside consultant. This intimate, high-level, high-touch component is composed of only those nominated employees who are deemed as potential Vice Presidents of KCI. The Advanced Leadership component is an intense development program consisting of deep level soft skills training. This program has not been offered at KCI in a while.

Another development program is the Project Management Academy. This is a one day, annual event during which participants become deeply involved in project and quality management issues. There are three levels for the program, all focused on project scope, scheduling, and budgeting, but at the highest level the soft skills of management are also honed. Participants in this program are typically those at the project management level or above.

Other types of development are available or supported as well. For instance, there is support for CAD training, safety training, LEED certification, and various software training. KCI hires and supports interns. Additionally, there is a licensure management system to help everyone stay on top of their licenses. And all of this is not to mention the informal training that occurs at KCI on a daily basis. As one can imagine, KCI earmarks significant resources for these training and development programs. Senior management at KCI feels that these career-development initiatives are a necessity to recruit and retain the high-quality talent for which KCI is known.

KCI also offers generous benefits to its employees. These vary from a 401K with a company match, to a floating holiday. One benefit that employees find particularly beneficial is tuition assistance. KCI pays 100% after an individual has been with the company for more than five years and 80% if not. Many employees feel that it is an excellent program. As one employee who recently completed a graduate program put it,

> Excellent, excellent program. I mean, I wouldn't have been able to pay for it had it not been for KCI. So to me, that's another huge benefit. I feel like I owe them [KCI] something because of the benefit. I mean, it's huge.

Tuition assistance also enriches the firm by increasing KCI's intellectual capital and qualifications needed to successfully bid on additional projects.

Finance

Given the recent economic downturn, most firms have been faced with financial difficulties. KCI is no exception. This is exhibited by a considerable drop in revenue in recent years. In 2007, total revenues were $142 million, in 2008 revenues stayed constant at $142 million; however, in 2009, revenues dropped to $131 million. Despite this decline, Neimeyer is optimistic, "dealing with this economy—this is my fourth recession, you know—this will pass. I know that it will."

Neimeyer has reason to be optimistic. According to a recent Business Week article, one way to help a company overcome an economic downturn is to practice open book management. Open book management is when a company shares its financial and other data with its employees and often times helps these employees to understand how this data relates to their work. And, KCI does just this. The financials for the company are open. Employees can ask to see most anything regarding the financial health of the organization. This is important to employees as a portion of their compensation is based on the financial well-being of the company. KCI makes an ESOP contribution based on a percentage of an employee's salary, currently 6.5%, which vests in five years. Despite its ups and downs, the ESOP share price is impressive. At inception, one share was worth $1,000, now it is valued at almost 10 times that amount. (see Figure 2).

Figure 2 KCI Stock Value

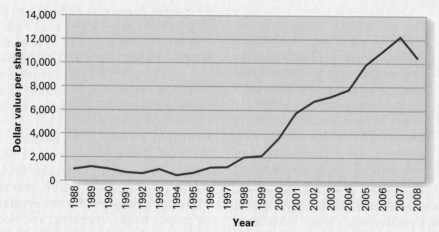

As one employee commented,

It was amazing to see over the years how much the ESOP continued to make money over time. One of my coworkers who has been here 12 years now, he has thousands of dollars in this ESOP that he's never had to put any money aside.

To get continued employee buy-in, ESOP education is constant. The company has several events during the year that promote awareness about the program, such as a contest where employees guess the exact value of the stock. Interestingly, and a good sign, many employees' guesses are not too far from the true value. ESOP bingo is another exciting event where employees—even those out in the field -have a chance to play and learn ESOP definitions and terminology.

Sharing in the ESOP is truly that—equal sharing. The largest stock holder is only so because he has been with the company for the longest length of time. No one receives extra perks to make their percentage of stock ownership particularly high, and unlike cash flow issues that can sometime arise when employees leave an employee-owned company, KCI has not had issue with cashing people out. So they know the money from the ESOP is real and truly is the employees'.

Since in service organizations employee compensation is typically such a huge part of the financial outlay, it is worth noting other forms of compensation here. Aside from the ESOP and regular wages or salaries, top earners at KCI have an "at risk" compensation incentive. A portion, typically 5–30% of their compensation is based on the profitability of the business for which they are involved. Additionally, the top 20 earners have a deferred compensation plan. This plan is designed to make the compensation of top employees a bit more competitive with that at rival partnership firms.

The Competitive Marketplace

Considering such a large portion of KCI's projects are public sector projects, it is important to consider this marketplace. There are opposing forces at work here. On one hand, the aging infrastructure in the US could create great demand for the services of firms like KCI. On the other hand, there are potentially severe budget constraints that could limit the number and profitability of projects requiring those services.

That being said, KCI faces fierce competition. Because they are a multidisciplined (e.g., construction, environmental, transportation) engineering firm, the competitors that they meet for a given project depend upon the business line(s) needed for that project. Some of their competitors are regional, employee-owned firms of about the same size, like JMT. Others are large, international publically traded firms like Michael Baker Corporation. Additionally, there are many partnerships in the mix, like RK&K, LLP. But, it's important to note that in this field, the competition is not always the competition. Often times firms will be competing with each other for one project and be partners on another. That is, when there is considerable overlap in the skills between two firms, they may compete with one another for a project. However, sometimes the firms will have complementary skills needed to best meet the demands of a potential client, so they will partner with one another.

Two keys to successful competition in this arena are having the proper qualifications for a potential client's project and having relationships built with clients and partners. A company must have the talent available to meet the needs of a potential client's project. This means having available employees with the proper education, experience, and certifications. But just having this talent is not quite enough. As previously mentioned, the company must be able to expertly demonstrate the fit between the company's expertise and the client's needs. Proper coordination of talent and being able to show the fit to the project can be challenging.

Having strong relationships with potential clients and partners is critical to get a leg up on the competition. These relationships are used to both learn about new projects and to find out more detail about potential projects. The earlier a company can start working on a proposal for a potential project and the more specific the proposal is, the more likely they are to beat the competition.

An additional significant area of competition is the competition not for clients, but rather for employees. In the US, the engineering population is "graying." That is, there is a great shortage of new talent, so firms have to fight over the talent that's out there. According to Beil, KCI relies on their challenging work environment and open culture to capture great talent. Beil also mentioned that they had hoped that the ESOP would be a great recruitment tool, but this has not turned out to be the case. Today's applicant pool is really looking for a job for a couple of years, rather than a career with an organization. As such, they would not be as likely to see the benefits of the ESOP. But that is not to say it is without its recruitment merits. When one employee was asked what brought her to KCI, she commented, "The things I really liked about KCI, besides the staff—we have a great staff here. They had a really good benefits package. The ESOP was very appealing to me . . ."

At the upper management level, a different scenario plays out. Many of KCI's competitors are partnerships, and partnerships allow the partners to have a higher earning potential than that expected of the top executives in an ESOP. As such, it could be difficult to recruit into these positions. But, at least recently, according to Beil, finding upper managers has not been an issue. He believes this due in part to the nature of financial risk differences in the two types of organizations. The financial risk facing the upper managers in an ESOP firm tends to be less than that which faces partners in a partnership.

Shared Leadership

Leadership is about integrity and credibility. Accordingly, Beil feels that letting people know where things stand is important, and never promising more than you feel you can deliver gets real buy in. It's not at all about 'just barking orders to employees." The KCI leaders see their role as articulating a vision that resonates with employees.

This mentality is largely derived from the culture at KCI, but it is also a result of being employee owned. Employee involvement resonates through the organization, and it is clear that the employees play a large role in the overall direction of the organization. For instance, an employee designee serves on the board of directors. According to Beil,

> So our employees actually have a popular election where they elect a member to the Board of Directors . . . They go out and they have to get ballots and they have to get 35 shareholders sign [the ballot] to say the employee is "OK." And then there's this popular election . . .

Now the true power in any ESOP organization is in its trustees, as trustees control the voting of the stock on all things with the exception of mergers and

acquisitions and major changes to corporate bylaws. Interestingly, two nonmanagement employee members are also on the Board of Trustees at KCI—one elected employee member and one appointed. Having an employee representative involved in governing and approving major decisions for the organization is a true example of shared leadership.

In addition to having formal representation on the Board of Directors and the Board of Trustees, it is clear that there are many avenues for open communication that allow ideas to filter from the lower ranks of the organization to the upper echelons. Niemeyer commented,

> One thing about it, and it may be our management style, is that our people have a tendency to speak up. And when they do speak up, they speak up without fear of repercussion. So it's not as if they're worried about saying something in a meeting or to me or to the president and all of a sudden seeing the Grim Reaper come and fire them.

Others in the organization have echoed the idea that there is open and easy communication up the organizational ladder. Indeed, the leaders at KCI provide many avenues through which employees can bring up issues, comment on processes, and make other suggestions to management. As an example, The Companywide Employee Committee was formed whereby 36 members, representing each department, meet on a regular basis to discuss issues that are raised from members of their respective departments. In essence, this committee, for which membership rotates on a yearly basis, acts as a sounding board for employee concerns.

In addition, anonymous survey boxes are located in the cafeteria, and an annual survey provides an outlet for employees to provide feedback on a wide range of topics including job satisfaction, human resource issues, compensation, supervisors, and coworkers. Moreover, a blog, to which employees may anonymously post, will soon be available as another mechanism for employee feedback. Townhall meetings, though in practice are primarily a top-down information dissemination tool, provide an additional venue where employees could voice their ideas. Moreover, senior management pride themselves on their availability and openness through an open-door policy.

It is not unusual to hear that organizations are "employee friendly" or have "open door communication"; however, sometimes these espoused views are simply not enacted. However, at KCI, what they preach is exactly what they practice. Employee suggestions do not go unheeded. One key example is the creation of one of KCI's business lines, the Geographic Information Systems (GIS) group. According to Neimeyer,

> The GIS group idea really came up through the organization by some computer folks who weren't in the engineering field, but said, "Look, I think there is going be a business line in geographic information systems. And it's something that we can really deal with the engineering or the planning sector even though it's not typical engineering." And, so one gent came and said, "Hey look, let me take this on. I think I can create a business on this and make a business line." And, that's an example of an idea that came up [through the ranks] and spawned a business.

Another initiative generated from the employees is a technology refresh program, where technology updating is based on technological advancements rather than on a fixed time interval. Neimeyer jokes, "It's not like I come up with all these ideas. I've been here 32 years. My new ideas are limited." These examples make apparent the notion that employee ideas get heard and implemented.

The idea of open lines of communication and continuous implementation of employee ideas is not only an upper echelon perception. Employees do indeed feel like their ideas are respected and welcomed. As one employee put it, "the culture is one where everyone, from the leaders at the top to the newest nonmanagement employees, is in it together."

Information Sharing

Communication of information is critical in any organization, however, in an ESOP, employees have more of a vested interest in understanding, retaining, and utilizing information disseminated to them. Neimeyer and Beil have similar views,

> . . . on the ESOP side [as compared to a partnership], communication skills probably have to be a step up. I think your ability to have a vision, and articulate it, then lead the company through it, has to be a step up.

Employees' echo this sentiment. For instance, an employee offered,

> I've worked for a partnership before. I had no idea how I was doing on a project, how much money we were making, how much money the company was making, whether my project was a success or not because the profits all went to the partners. In an ESOP culture, we're all owners. We all know what's going on, and because of that, we push information down to our employees.

Another employee added,

> We try really hard to communicate what's going on. We have town meetings once a month. The managers are very open to talking to employees. I mean, they'll tell you, "I can't tell you; it's not for discussion right now," and they're honest.

KCI has formal approaches to getting important and worthwhile information out to employees. As mentioned above, Townhall meetings play an important role in information sharing. These open meetings are held by the President once per month at headquarters with those in remote locations tele-, video-, or web-conferencing in. The meetings are also recorded and shared on the company intranet. During these meetings the status of the company is shared, company-wide issues are addressed, like changes to benefits or austerity measures, and exciting new projects are announced. Financial results are also shared quarterly.

In addition to Townhall meetings, departmental managers hold monthly meetings with the hope that the information shared will be funneled down through the company ranks. To help facilitate this process, minutes from the meetings are sent out to second tier management.

Beyond these formal approaches, more informal channels of communication exist as well. Even the CEO takes a hands-on approach to information sharing. For example, he attempts to reach out and visit branch offices. On his visit he says his approach is to, "just sit with the people and you ask them how things are going and have a little staff meeting and tell them what's going on." Regarding information sharing in general, he comments,

> And again, we try and continue to do it. It's a never ending cycle. You can never do enough of it. And in our company we get critiqued for not doing enough of it. No matter what we do, we still have to do more.

Growth and Change through Innovation and Initiatives

It is well understood that KCI cannot simply rest on its laurels and continue to do business as it has always done. Innovation is key to continued growth and development and KCI has been involved in some innovation, forward thinking projects. For instance, Floyd recalls one innovation done to mitigate the impact of a bridge on the environment:

> There were just a number of things that were blocking fish passages, so the fish couldn't go back up the river to spawn, they hadn't for years. So as part of the mitigation effort, the State Highway Administration agreed to create these natural fish passages. They didn't want fish ladders. They didn't want pipes. They wanted natural. Well, this is something that we haven't necessarily done on the East coast, but they're doing it in the West. So some of our guys went out to the West and studied what was being done out there by literature searches, talking with people, and going out visiting.
>
> We saw what they were doing, but what they were doing they were doing in a rural area. We had to do this in an urban area, so our environmental scientists and our hydrologic people actually developed the design method to take that technology and apply it in an urban environment. What they did was they built these natural fish passages in the bottom of the streams, so depending on what type of fish you had, it would determine how strong the fish—what current the fish could swim up, how strong the current could be, and how long they could (swim against) it, their endurance. So what they had to do was they had to design these rock ladders, basically, these fish ladders so that the fish could make it up through the current, and then they had to space boulders to form these little resting areas for the fish so they could get up the stream . . . you would never know that it was a manmade thing. It just looks like it's natural, but in actuality, they were purposely built and constructed so the fish could get up over the natural blockages. We won a lot of awards for that because that was very innovative.

Providing environmental-friendly solutions to client problems comes natural to KCI, perhaps because the company and its employee owners are invested in sustainability themselves. KCI's headquarters, one of Maryland's newest green buildings, has recently been awarded the US Green Building Council's (USGBC) Leadership in Energy and Environmental Design (LEED) gold certification. The 120,000 square foot building features a white solar reflective roof, which reflects sunlight in the summertime reducing the air-conditioning requirements, a stormwater management pond, and high-performance climate control plumbing and electrical systems, all designed by KCI engineers and LEED specialists. According to Neimeyer, the facility uses resources more efficiently than traditional office buildings and offers employees a healthier and more comfortable work environment.

Indeed, KCI has a forward-thinking mindset. Not being afraid to take on new initiative is another hallmark of KCI's continued growth. In a typical year, 15–20% of profits are used to fund new corporate initiatives—those that are funded at the corporate level because they tend to be too expensive for an individual division. Usually, an initiative runs upward of $250,000. A prime example is the aforementioned GIS division. This began as a corporate initiative and was funded as such until it reached a critical mass of clients. It now operates on its own with 22 employees. This is not to say that all initiatives work. If an initiative is not on target at year three, funding will be reallocated to other projects, and the initiative will be discontinued. But, one cannot expect rewards without taking some risks.

The Reorganization

KCI is in the process of reorganizing. This is a step they have been considering since the mid-1990s. For the most part, KCI has taken a geographic approach to their structure. Now, they are moving to a discipline-based approach. This includes such disciplines as transportation facilities, site management, telecom, and urban planning and development surveys. The headquarters has been somewhat organized by discipline, but the remainder of company has not. The geographic regions were initially established to help promote geographic expansion, and to aid in succession planning at KCI. Unfortunately, particularly during downtimes in the economy, regions would be very protective of their resources and be out for themselves—not for the good of the whole company. It is expected that the new discipline based approach will be more integrated and less territorial.

The President has vested a great deal of time and effort into trying to facilitate a smooth transition. He has discussed the expectations for the reorganization with individuals, small groups, and large groups. Employee survey data indicate that employees are generally favorably disposed toward the reorganization; however there are employees who feel that they aren't really affected and that it's mostly a management reorganization. Some believe that people will not quite understand what is happening and why until the official reorganization has taken place and until results start coming in. Additionally, there is some sentiment that the reorganization will be quite challenging because, although senior management realizes that role definition will be important, the lines of authority in the organization may not be as clear after the reorganization. It is expected that there will be more shared and collaborative leadership.

Looking Forward

With the current economic uncertainty, KCI faces an all too common challenge among businesses—securing enough business to keep their highly talented and committed employees working. According to Beil,

> We don't hire for a job and then we fire them later. That's really not our efforts. . . . right now, we're just maintaining it [the firm], finding enough work so that we don't have to tell a good person to find work elsewhere is probably what keeps me awake at night the most.

This is not to say that KCI is not constantly looking for good talent. When asked about the future of the organization, Beil, was quick to mention,

> Our challenge will always be finding highly competent people. We're laying people off in a certain sector, but there are other sectors that are strong where we're looking to hire people. And finding talented people is a marathon struggle for us.

References

1. http://www.businessweek.com/small-business/
2. http://www.kci.com
3. http://www.iso.org/iso/support/faqs/faqs conformity assessment and certification.htm
4. http://www.nceo.org/main/article.php/id/28/

Endnotes

1 The authors would like to thank the employee-owners of KCI Technologies who graciously shared their knowledge, experiences, and perspectives about the company. Their viewpoints were invaluable in ensuring that this case provides a true representation of the culture and practices of the company. In addition, the authors would like to thank the Beyster Institute and the Foundation for Enterprise Development for their support of this work.

CASE 12

Developing Global Teams to Meet 21st Century Challenges at W. L. Gore & Associates*

Frank Shipper
Professor of Management, Franklin P. Perdue School of Business, Salisbury University

Charles C. Manz
Nirenberg Professor of Leadership, Isenberg School of Management, University of Massachusetts Amherst

Greg L. Stewart
Professor & Tippie Research Fellow, Tippie College of Business, University of Iowa

In 2008, W. L. Gore & Associates celebrated its 50th year in business. During the first four decades of its existence, Gore became famous for its products and for its use of business teams located in a single facility. To facilitate the development of teams, corporate facilities were kept to 200 associates or fewer. Due to the challenges of a global market place, business teams are no longer in a single facility. They are now often spread over three continents. Products are sold on six continents and used on all seven, as well as under the ocean and in space. The challenge of having a successful global presence requires virtual teams to enable a high degree of coordination in the development, production and marketing of products to customers across the world. As previously, teams are defined primarily by product, but no longer by facility. Team members are now separated by thousands of miles, multiple time zones, and a variety of languages and cultures. Growth and globalization present significant challenges for W. L. Gore as it strives to maintain a family-like, entrepreneurial culture. According to Terri Kelly, the president of Gore and a 25-year associate,[1]

> In the early days, our business was largely conducted at the local level. There were global operations, but most relationships were built regionally, and most decisions were made regionally. That picture has evolved dramatically over the last 20 years, as businesses can no longer be defined by brick and mortar.

Today, most of our teams are spread across regions and continents. Therefore, the decision-making process is much more global and virtual in nature, and there's a growing need to build strong relationships across geographical boundaries. The globalization of our business has been one of the biggest changes I've seen in the last 25 years.

Elements of the culture at Gore are captured in Figure 1. The core belief in the need to take the long-term view in business situations, and to make and keep commitments, drives cooperation among individuals and small teams. This is supported by key practices that replace traditional, hierarchical structure with flexible relationships and a sense that all workers are "in the same boat." The ultimate focus is on empowering talented associates to deliver highly innovative products.

Despite substantial growth, the core values have not changed at Gore. The "objective" of the company, "To make money and have fun," set forth by the founder Wilbert (Bill) Gore is still part of the Gore culture. Associates around the world are asked to follow the company's four guiding principles:

1. Try to be fair.
2. Encourage, help, and allow other associates to grow in knowledge, skill, and scope of activity and responsibility.

---

*Many sources were helpful in providing material for this case, most particularly associates at Gore who generously shared their time and viewpoints about the company to help ensure that the case accurately reflected the company's practices and culture. They provided many resources, including internal documents and stories of their personal experiences. Copyrighted © 2009 by the case authors.

Sources: Frank Shipper, Salisbury University; Charles C. Manz, University of Massachusetts-Ameherst; Greg L. Stewart, University of Iowa. Used by kind permission of the authors.

Figure 1 W. L. Gore & Associates' Culture

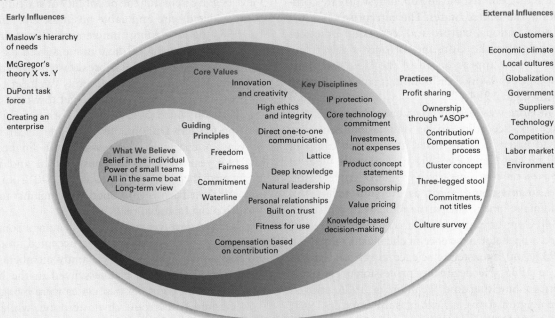

3. Make your own commitments, and keep them.
4. Consult with other associates before taking actions that may be "below the waterline."

The four principles are referred to as *fairness, freedom, commitment,* and *waterline.* The waterline principle is drawn from an analogy to ships. If someone pokes a hole in a boat above the waterline, the boat will be in relatively little real danger. If, however, someone pokes a hole below the waterline, the boat is in immediate danger of sinking. The expectation is that "waterline" issues will be discussed across teams, plants, and continents as appropriate before those decisions are made. This principle is still emphasized even though team members who need to share in the decision making process are now spread across the globe.

Commitment is spoken of frequently at Gore. The commitment principle's primary emphasis is on the freedom associates have to make their own commitments, rather than having others assign them to projects or tasks. But commitment may also be viewed as a mutual commitment between associates and the enterprise. Associates worldwide commit to making contributions to the company's success. In return, the company is committed to providing a challenging, opportunity-rich work environment that is responsive to associate needs and concerns.

Background

Gore was formed by Wilbert L. "Bill" Gore and his wife in 1958. The idea for the business sprang from Bill's personal, technical, and organizational experiences at E. I. du Pont de Nemours & Co. and, particularly, his involvement in the characterization of a chemical compound with unique properties. The compound, called polytetrafluorethylene (PTFE), is now marketed by DuPont under the Teflon brand name. Bill saw a wide variety of potential applications for this unique new material, and when DuPont showed little interest in pursuing most of them directly, he decided to form his own company and start pursuing the concepts himself. Thus, Gore became one of DuPont's first customers for this new material.

Since then, Gore has evolved into a global enterprise, with annual revenues of more than $2.5 billion, supported by more than 8,500 associates worldwide. This placed Gore at No. 180 on *Forbes* magazine's 2008 list of the 500 largest private companies in the United States. The enterprise's unique, and now famous, culture and leadership practices have helped make Gore one of only a select few companies to appear on all of the U.S. "100 Best Companies to Work For" rankings since they were introduced in 1984.

Bill Gore was born in Meridian, Idaho, in 1912. By age six, according to his own account, he was an avid hiker in Utah. Later, at a church camp in 1935, he met Genevieve (Vieve), his future wife. In their eyes, the marriage was a partnership. He would make breakfast and Vieve, as everyone called her, would make lunch. The partnership lasted a lifetime.

Bill Gore attended the University of Utah and earned a bachelor of science in chemical engineering in 1933, and a master of science in physical chemistry in 1935. He began his professional career at American Smelting and Refining in 1936, moved to Remington Arms, a DuPont subsidiary, in 1941, and then to DuPont's headquarters in 1945. He held positions as research supervisor and head of operations research. While at DuPont, he felt a sense of excited commitment, personal fulfillment, and self-direction while working with a task force to develop applications for PTFE.

Having followed the development of the electronics industry, he felt that PTFE had ideal insulating characteristics for use with such equipment. He tried many ways to make a PTFE-coated ribbon cable but with no success until a breakthrough in his home basement laboratory. One night, while Bill was explaining the problem to his 19-year-old son, Bob, the young Gore saw some PTFE sealant tape and asked his father, "Why don't you try this tape?" Bill explained that everyone knew that you could not bond PTFE to itself. After Bob went to bed, however, Bill remained in the basement lab and proceeded to try what conventional wisdom said could not be done. At about 5:00 AM Bill woke up Bob, waving a small piece of cable around and saying excitedly, "It works, it works." The following night father and son returned to the basement lab to make ribbon cable insulated with PTFE. Because the idea came from Bob, the patent for the cable was issued in his name.

After a while, Bill Gore came to realize that DuPont wanted to remain a supplier of raw materials for industrial buyers and not a manufacturer of high-tech products for end-use markets. Bill and Vieve began discussing the possibility of starting their own insulated wire and cable business. On January 1, 1958, their wedding anniversary, they founded Gore. The basement of their home served as their first facility. After finishing breakfast, Vieve turned to her husband of 23 years and said, "Well, let's clear up the dishes, go downstairs, and get to work."

When Bill Gore (a 45-year-old with five children to support) left DuPont, he put aside a career of 17 years and a good, secure salary. To finance the first two years of their new business, he and Vieve mortgaged their house and took $4,000 from savings. All their friends cautioned them against taking on such a big financial risk.

The first few years were challenging. Some of the young company's associates accepted stock in the company in lieu of salary. Family members who came to help with the business lived in the home as well. At one point, 11 associates were living and working under one roof. One afternoon, while sifting PTFE powder, Vieve received a call from the City of Denver's water department. The caller wanted to ask some technical questions about the ribbon cable and asked for the product manager. Vieve explained that he was not in at the moment. (Bill and two other key associates were out of town.) The caller asked next for the sales manager and then for the president. Vieve explained that "they" were also not in. The caller finally shouted, "What kind of company is this anyway?" With a little diplomacy the Gores were eventually able to secure an order from Denver's water department for around $100,000. This order put the company over the start-up hump and onto a profitable footing. Sales began to take off.

During the decades that followed, Gore developed a number of new products derived from PTFE, the best-known of which is GORE-TEX® fabric. The development of GORE-TEX® fabric, one of hundreds of new products that followed a key discovery by Bob Gore, is an example of the power of innovation. In 1969, Gore's Wire and Cable Division was facing increased competition. Bill Gore began to look for a way to expand PTFE: "I figured out that if we could ever unfold those molecules, get them to stretch out straight, we'd have a tremendous new kind of material." The new PTFE material would have more volume per pound of raw material with no adverse effect on performance. Thus, fabricating costs would be reduced and profit margins increased. Bob Gore took on the project; he heated rods of PTFE to various temperatures and then slowly stretched them. Regardless of the temperature or how carefully he stretched them, the rods broke. Working alone late one night after countless failures, Bob in frustration stretched one of the rods violently. To his surprise, it did not break. He tried it again and again with the same results. The next morning, Bill Gore recalled, "Bob wanted to surprise me so he took a rod and stretched it slowly. Naturally, it broke. Then he pretended to get mad. He grabbed another rod and said, 'Oh, the hell with this,' and gave it a pull. It didn't break—he'd done it." The new arrangement of molecules not only changed the Wire and Cable Division, but led to the development of GORE-TEX® fabric and many other products.

In 1986, Bill Gore died while backpacking in the Wind River Mountains of Wyoming. Vieve Gore continued to be involved actively in the company and served on the board of directors until her death at 91 in 2005.

Gore has had only four presidents in its 50-year history. Bill Gore served as the president from the enterprise's founding in 1958 until 1976. At that point, his son Bob became president and CEO. Bob has been an active member of the firm from the time of its founding, most recently as chairman of the board of directors. He served as president until 2000, when Chuck Carroll was selected as the third president. In 2005, Terri Kelly succeeded him. As with all the presidents after Bill Gore, she is a long-time employee. She had been with Gore for 22 years before becoming president.

The Gore family established a unique culture that continues to be an inspiration for associates. For example, Dave Gioconda, a current product specialist, recounted meeting Bob Gore for the first time—an experience that reinforced Gore's egalitarian culture:

> Two weeks after I joined Gore, I traveled to Phoenix for training ... I told the guy next to me on the plane where I worked, and he said, "I work for Gore, too." "No kidding?" I asked. "Where do you work?" He said, "Oh, I work over at the Cherry Hill plant." ...
>
> I spent two and a half hours on this plane having a conversation with this gentleman who described himself as a technologist and shared some of his experiences. As I got out of the plane, I shook his hand and said, "I'm Dave Gioconda, nice to meet you." He replied, "Oh, I'm Bob Gore." That

experience has had a profound influence on the decisions that I make.

Due to the leadership of Bill, Vieve, Bob, and many others, Gore was selected as one of the U.S. "100 Best Companies to Work For" in 2009 by *Fortune* magazine for the twelfth consecutive year. In addition, Gore was included in all three *100 Best Companies to Work For in America* books (1984, 1985, and 1993). It is one of only a select few companies to appear on all 15 lists. Gore has been selected also as one of the best companies to work for in France, Germany, Italy, Spain, Sweden, and the United Kingdom.

As a privately held company, Gore does not make its financial results public. It does share, however, financial results with all associates on a monthly basis. In 2008, *Fortune* magazine reported that Gore sales grew just over 7% in 2006, the latest year for which data were available.

Competitive Strategy at W. L. Gore

For product management, Gore is divided now into four divisions—Electronics, Fabrics, Industrial, and Medical. The Electronic Products Division develops and manufactures high-performance cables and assemblies as well as specialty materials for electronic devices. The Fabrics Division develops and provides fabric to the outdoor clothing industry as well as the military, law enforcement, and fire protection industries. Gore fabrics marketed under the GORE-TEX®, WINDSTOPPER®, CROSSTECH®, and GORE® CHEMPAK® brands provide the wearer protection while remaining comfortable. The Industrial Products Division (IPD) makes filtration, sealant and other products. These products meet diverse contamination and process challenges in many industries. The Gore Medical Products Division (MPD) provides products such as synthetic vascular grafts, interventional devices, endovascular stent-grafts, surgical patches for hernia repair, and sutures for use in vascular, cardiac, general surgery, and oral procedures. Although they are recognized as separate divisions, they frequently work together.

Since it has four divisions that serve different industries, Gore can be viewed as a diversified conglomerate. Bob Winterling, a financial associate, described how the four divisions work together financially as follows:

> The thing I love about Gore is that we have four very diverse divisions. During my time here, I've noticed that when one or two divisions are down, you always have one, two or three that are up. I call them cylinders. Sometimes all four cylinders are working really well; not all the time though. Normally it's two or three, but that's the luxury that we have. When one is down—it's good to know that another is up.

At the end of 2007, all four divisions were performing well. Having four diversified divisions not only protects against swings in any one industry, but it also provides multiple investment opportunities. Entering 2008, Gore was investing in a large number of areas, with the heaviest area of investment in the Medical Products Division. This was a conscious choice, as these opportunities were judged to be the largest intersection between Gore's unique capabilities and some very large, attractive market needs. As Brad Jones, an enterprise leader, said, "All opportunities aren't created equal, and there's an awful lot of opportunity that's screaming for resources in the medical environment." At the same time, the leadership at Gore scrutinizes large investments so those in what Brad Jones refers to as "big burn" projects are not made unless there is a reasonable expectation of a payoff.

Developing Quality Products by Creating and Protecting Core Technology

The competitive objective of Gore is to use core technology derived from PTFE and ePTFE to create highly differentiated and unique products. In every product line the goal is not to produce the lowest cost goods but rather to create the highest quality goods that meet and exceed the needs of customers. Of course, Gore works hard to maintain competitive pricing, but the source of competitive advantage is clearly quality and differentiation. Gore is a company built on technological innovations.

Leaders at Gore often refer to a three-legged stool to explain how they integrate operations. As shown in Figure 2, the three legs of the stool are technology, manufacturing, and sales. For each product, the legs of the stool are tied together by a product specialist. For instance, a product specialist might coordinate efforts to design, make, and sell a vascular graft. Another product specialist would coordinate efforts related to the creation and marketing of fabric for use in winter

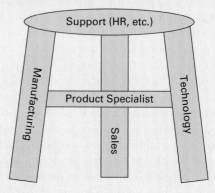

Figure 2   Coordinating Technology, Manufacturing, and Sales at Gore

parkas. Support functions such as human resources (HR), IT, and Finance also help tie together various aspects of technology, manufacturing, and sales.

Gore's Fabrics Division practices cooperative marketing with the users of its fabrics. In most cases, Gore does not make the finished goods from its fabrics; rather, it supplies the fabrics to manufacturers such as North Face, Marmot, L. L. Bean, Salomon, Adidas, and Puma. On each garment is a tag indicating that it is made using GORE-TEX® fabric. According to a former president of Cotton Inc., Gore is a leader in secondary branding. For example, a salesman in a golf pro shop related how he initially tried to explain that he had GORE-TEX® fabric rain suits made by various manufacturers. After realizing that his customers did not care who manufactured it, only that it was made from GORE-TEX® fabric, he gave up, and just led the customers to the GORE-TEX® fabric rain suits.

Because of its commitment to producing superior goods, Gore emphasizes product integrity. For example, only certified and licensed manufacturers are supplied with Gore's fabrics. Gore maintains "rain-rooms" in which to test new garment designs. Shoes with GORE-TEX® fabric in them will be flexed in water approximately 300,000 times to ensure that they are waterproof.

After all the preventive measures, Gore stands behind its products regardless of who the manufacturer is and even if the defect is cosmetic in nature. Susan Bartley, a manufacturing associate, recounted a recent recall:

> A cosmetic flaw, not a fitness for use flaw, was found in finished garments, so we (Gore) bought back the

garments from the manufacturer, because we didn't want those garments out on the market.

Such recalls due to either cosmetic or fitness for use flaws happen infrequently. One associate estimated that the last one happened 10 years before the most recent one. Gore is, however, committed to quality of its products and will stand behind them.

Gore's Fabrics sales and marketing associates believe positive buyer experiences with one GORE-TEX® product (for instance, a ski parka) carry over to purchases of other GORE-TEX® products (gloves, pants, rain suits, boots, and jackets). Also, they believe that positive experiences with their products will be shared among customers and potential customers, leading to more sales.

The sharing and enhancing of knowledge is seen as key to the development of current and future products. Great emphasis is placed on sharing knowledge. According to Terri Kelly,

> There's a real willingness and openness to share knowledge. That's something I experienced 25 years ago, and it's not changed today. This is a healthy thing. We want to make sure folks understand the need to connect more dots in the lattice.

Associates make a conscious effort to share technical knowledge. For example, a core leadership team consisting of eight technical associates gets together every other month, reviews each other's plans and looks for connections among the upcoming products. According to Jack Kramer, an enterprise leader, "We put a lot of effort into trying to make sure that we connect informally and formally across a lot of boundaries." One way associates connect formally to share knowledge is through monthly technical meetings. At the monthly meetings, scientists and engineers from different divisions present information to other associates and colleagues. Attended regularly by most technical associates in the area, these presentations are often described as "passionate" and "exciting."

Even though Gore shares knowledge within the organization, much of its highly technical know-how must be protected for competitive reasons. In a global environment, protection of specialized knowledge is a challenge. Some of the technology is protected by patents. In fact, some of the products are protected by an umbrella of patents. Normally, under U.S. law, patents expire 20 years from the earliest claimed filing date. Thus, the original patents have expired on

GORE-TEX® fabric and some other products. Globally, patent procedures, protection and enforcement vary. Both products and the processes are patentable. To protect its knowledge base, Gore has sought and been granted more than 2,000 patents worldwide in all areas in which it competes, including electronics, medical devices, and polymer processing. However, patents can sometimes be difficult or expensive to enforce, especially globally. Therefore some of the technology is protected internally. Such knowledge is commonly referred to as proprietary.

Within Gore proprietary knowledge is shared on a need to know basis. Associates are encouraged to closely guard such information. This principle can lead to some awkward moments. Terri Kelly was visiting Shenzhen, China and was curious about a new laminate that was being commercialized. The development engineer leader kept dodging her questions. Finally he smiled, and he said, "Now, Terri. Do you have a need to know?"

As Terri retold the incident, "He played back exactly what he was supposed to, which is don't share with someone, even if it's a CEO, something that they have no need to know." She laughed and said, "You're right. I'm just being nosy."

Terri continued, "And everyone's—I could see the look in their eyes—thinking, 'Is he going to get fired?' He had taken a great personal risk, certainly for that local culture. We laughed, and we joked and for the next week, it became the running joke." Through stories like this the culture is shared with others in Gore.

The sharing and enhancing of its technology have brought recognition from many sources. From the United Kingdom, Gore received the Pollution Abatement Technology Award in 1989 and the Prince Philip Award for Polymers in the Service of Mankind in 1985. In addition, Gore received or shared in receiving the prestigious Plunkett Award from DuPont—for innovative uses of DuPont fluoropolymers—nine times between 1988 and 2006. Bill and Vieve Gore, as well as Bob Gore, received numerous honors for both their business and technical leadership.

Continuing Globalization and Deliberate Growth

Ever since the company was founded, Gore has recognized the need for globalization. Gore established its first international venture in 1964, only six years after its founding. By 2008, it had facilities in two dozen countries and manufacturing facilities in six countries distributed across four continents (See Figure 3). One example of Gore's global reach is the fact that it is the dominant supplier of artificial vascular grafts to the global medical community. Gore's Fabrics Division also generates most of its sales overseas.

In addition to globalization, Gore has a strategy of continued growth. Growth is expected to come from two sources. One source will be from Gore associates contributing innovative ideas. The Gore culture is designed to foster such innovation and allow ideas to be energetically pursued, developed and evaluated. These ideas will lead to new products and processes. Within Gore this form of growth is referred to as organic. Gore encourages both new products and extensions of existing products. To encourage innovation all associates are encouraged to ask for and receive raw material to try out their ideas. Through this process multiple products have come from unexpected areas. For example, the idea for dental floss came from the Industrial and not the Medical Division. Two associates who were fabricating space suits took to flossing their teeth with scraps. Thus, Gore's highly successful dental floss,

GLIDE® floss, was born. GORE™ RIDE ON® bike cables came from a couple of passionate mountain bikers in the Medical Division. ELIXIR® guitar strings also came from the Medical Division from an associate who was also a musician. Due to Gore's track record of developing innovative products, *Fast Company* magazine called it "pound for pound, the most innovative company in America."

A second but much less significant source of growth can come from external acquisitions. Gore evaluates opportunities to acquire technologies and even companies based on whether they offer a unique capability that could complement an existing, successful business. The leadership at Gore considers this strategy a way to stack the probability deck in its favor by moving into market spaces its associates already know very well. To facilitate this growth strategy, Gore has a few associates who evaluate acquisition opportunities at the enterprise level. They do not do this in isolation, but in concert with leaders within each division.

By a multibillion dollar corporate standard, the acquisitions made by Gore are small. To date, the largest company acquired employed approximately 100 people. Another attribute of these acquisitions is that no stock swap occurs. Since Gore is a privately

Figure 3   Locations of Gore's Global Facilities

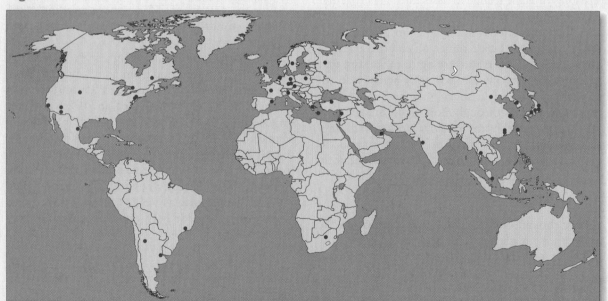

held company, stock swaps are not an option. Acquisitions are made with cash.

A clear issue to any acquisition that Gore considers is cultural compatibility. Gore will consider the leadership style in an acquired company. According to Brad Jones, "If you're acquiring a couple patents and maybe an inventor, that's not a big issue, although if he's a prima donna inventor, it will be an issue." When acquiring a company, the culture that made it successful is closely examined. Issues regarding integrating the acquired company's culture with Gore's, and whether Gore's culture will add value to the acquired company, are just two of many cultural considerations. Gore wants to be able to expand when necessary by buying complementary organizations and their associated technologies, but not at the expense of its culture of 50 years.

Occasionally, Gore must divest itself of a product. One example is GLIDE® dental floss. The product, developed by Gore, was well received by consumers due its smooth texture, shred resistance and ability to slide easily between teeth. To meet demand when the product took off, leaders were processing credit cards; human resource people and accountants were out on the manufacturing floor packaging GLIDE® floss, and everybody else in the facility pitched in to make sure that the product got out the door. One associate observed that by rolling up their sleeves and pitching in, leaders built credibility with other associates.

Not long after its introduction, mint flavor GLIDE® floss became the biggest selling dental floss. That attracted the attention of the traditional dental floss manufacturers. Eventually, Procter & Gamble (P&G) and Gore reached an agreement whereby P&G bought the rights to market GLIDE® floss, while Gore continued to manufacture it.

Gore made this agreement with the understanding that no one would be laid off. The announcement of the agreement was made to all the GLIDE® floss team members on a Thursday. It did come as a shock to some. By Monday, however, the same team was working on a transition plan. Associates that were not needed in the manufacturing or selling of GLIDE® floss were absorbed into other fast-growing Gore businesses. In addition, everybody in the enterprise received a share of the profit from the P&G purchase.

Leadership at Gore

Competitive strategy at Gore is supported by a unique approach to leadership. Many people step-forward and take on a variety of leadership roles, but these roles are not part of a hierarchical structure and traditional authority is not vested in the roles. Leadership is a dynamic and fluid process where leaders are defined by 'followership.' Future leaders emerge because they gain credibility with other associates. Gore refers to this process as "Natural Leadership." Credibility is gained by demonstrating special knowledge, skill, or experience that advances a business objective, a series of successes, and involving others in significant decisions.

Associates step forward to lead when they have the expertise to do so. Within Gore this practice is referred to as *knowledge-based decision-making*. Based on this practice decisions are ". . . made by the most knowledgeable person, not the person in charge," according to Terri Kelly. This form of decision making flows naturally from the four guiding principles established by Bill Gore.

Leadership responsibilities can take many forms at Gore. In an internal memo Bill Gore described the following kinds of leaders and their roles:

1. *The Associate who is recognized by a team as having a special knowledge, or experience* (for example, this could be a chemist, computer expert, machine operator, salesman, engineer, lawyer). This kind of leader gives the team *guidance in a special area.*
2. *The Associate the team looks to for coordination of individual activities in order to achieve the agreed on objectives of the team.* The role of this leader is to persuade team members to *make the commitments* necessary for success (commitment seeker).
3. *The Associate who proposes necessary objectives and activities and seeks agreement and team consensus on objectives.* This leader is perceived by the team membership as having a good grasp of how the objectives of the team fit in with the broader objectives of the enterprise. This kind of leader is often also a "commitment seeking" leader.
4. *The leader who evaluates the relative contribution of team members (in consultation with*

other sponsors) and reports these contribution evaluations to a compensation committee. This leader may also participate in the compensation committee on relative contribution and pay and *reports changes in compensation* to individual Associates. This leader is then also a compensation sponsor.

5. The leader who coordinates the research, manufacturing, and marketing of one product type within a business, interacting with team leaders and individual Associates who have commitments to the product type. These leaders are usually called *product specialists.* They are respected for their knowledge and dedication to their products.

6. *Plant leaders* who help coordinate activities of people within a plant.

7. *Business leaders* who help coordinate activities of people in a business.

8. *Functional leaders* who help coordinate activities of people in a "functional" area.

9. *Corporate leaders* who help coordinate activities of people in different businesses and functions and who try to promote communication and cooperation among all Associates.

10. *Intrapreneuring Associates who organize new teams* for new businesses, new products, new processes, new devices, new marketing efforts,

or new or better methods of all kinds. These leaders invite other Associates to "sign up" for their project.

Developing A Unique and Flexible Leadership Structure

The leadership structure that works at Gore may have the world's shortest organizational pyramid for a company of its size. Gore is a company largely without titles, hierarchical organization charts, or any other conventional structural arrangement typically employed by enterprises with billions of dollars in sales revenues and thousands of employees.

There are few positions at Gore with formal titles presented to the public. Due to laws of incorporation, the company has a president, Terri Kelly, who also functions as CEO. Terri is one of four members of the cross-functional Enterprise Leadership Team, the team responsible for the overall health and growth of the Enterprise.

The real key to the egalitarian culture of Gore is the use of a unique lattice rather than a hierarchical structure (See Figure 4). The features of Gore's lattice structure include the following:

1. Direct lines of communication—person to person—with no intermediary.

Figure 4   Gore's Lattice Structure

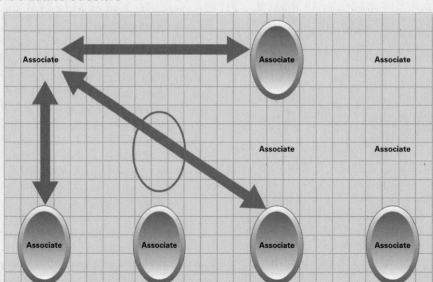

2. No fixed or assigned authority.
3. Sponsors, not bosses.
4. Natural leadership as evidenced by the willingness of others to follow.
5. Objectives set by those who must "make them happen."
6. Tasks and functions organized through commitments.

The lattice structure, as described by the people at Gore, is complex and depends on interpersonal interactions, self-commitment to group-known responsibilities, natural leadership, and group-imposed discipline. According to Bill Gore, "Every successful organization has an underground lattice. It's where the news spreads like lightning, where people can go around the organization to get things done."

One potential disadvantage of such a lattice structure could be a lack of quick response times and decisive action. Gore associates say adamantly that this is not the case, and they distinguish between two types of decisions. First, for time-critical decisions, they maintain that the lattice structure is faster in response than traditional structures because interaction is not hampered by bureaucracy. The leader who has responsibility assembles a knowledge-based team to examine and resolve the issue. The team members can be recruited by the leader from any area of the company if their expertise is needed. Once the issue is resolved the team ceases to exist, and its members return to their respective areas. Associate Bob Winterling asserted, "We have no trouble making crisis decisions, and we do it very swiftly and very quickly."

The other response is for critical issues that will have a significant impact on the enterprise's long-term operations. Associates will admit that such decisions can sometimes take a little longer than they would like. Chrissy Lyness, another financial associate, stated,

> We get the buy-in up front instead of creating and implementing the solution and putting something out there that doesn't work for everybody. That can be frustrating to new associates, because they're used to a few people putting their heads together, saying, "This is what we're going to do. This is a solution." That's not the way it works at Gore.
>
> Here, you spend a lot of time at the beginning of the decision-making process gaining feedback, so that when you come out of that process, you have something that's going to work, and the implementation is actually pretty easy.

The associates at Gore believe that time spent in the beginning, tapping into the best ideas and gaining consensus, pay off in the implementation. They believe that authoritarian decision-making may save time initially, but the quality of the decision will not be as good as one made by consensus. In addition, they believe that authoritarian decisions will take longer to implement than those made by consensus.

The egalitarian culture is supported also informally. For example, all associates are referred to and addressed by their first names. This is true as true for the president as for any other associate.

Gore's leaders believe that its unique organization structure and culture have proven to be significant contributors to associate satisfaction and retention. *Fortune* magazine reports a turnover rate of 5% for Gore. In addition, it reports 19,108 applicants for 276 new jobs in 2008. In other words, it is harder to get a job a Gore than to get accepted at an elite university.

Global Human Resource Practices

The competitive strategy of using cutting-edge technology, empowered teams and collaborative leadership to create high quality goods is supported by a number of innovative human resources (HR) practices, globally. Many HR initiatives are designed to support the concept that all associates are stakeholders in the enterprise and have a shared responsibility for its success. Parking lots have no reserved parking spaces for leaders. Dining areas—only one in each plant—are set up as focal points for associate interaction. As an associate in Arizona explained, "The design is no accident. The lunchroom in Flagstaff has a fireplace in the middle. We want people to like to be here." The location of a plant is also no accident. Sites are selected on the basis of transportation access, nearby universities, beautiful surroundings, and climate appeal. To preserve the natural beauty of the site on which a production facility was built in 1982, Vieve Gore insisted that the large trees be preserved, much to the dismay of the construction crews. The Arizona associate explained the company's emphasis on selecting attractive plant sites, stating, "Expanding is not costly in the long run. Losses are what you make happen by stymieing people and putting them into a box." Such initiatives are practiced at Gore facilities worldwide.

Getting the Right People on Board

Gore receives numerous applicants for every position. Initially, job applicants at Gore are screened by personnel specialists. Then each candidate who passes the initial screening is interviewed by a group of associates from the team in which the person will work. Finally, personnel specialists contact multiple references before issuing a job offer. Recruitment is described by Donna Frey, leader of the global human resources function and one of four members of the Enterprise Leadership Team (ELT), as a two-way process. She explained:

> Our recruiting process is very much about us getting to know the applicants and them getting to know us. We are very open and honest about who we are, the kind of organization we have, the kind of commitments we want and whether or not we think that the applicant's values are aligned with ours. Applicants talk to a number of people that they'll be working directly with if hired. We work very hard in the recruiting process to really build a relationship, get to know people and make sure that we're bringing people in who are going to fit this enterprise.

When someone is hired at Gore, an experienced associate makes a commitment to be the applicant's sponsor. The sponsor's role is to take a personal interest in the new associate's contributions, interests, and goals, acting as both a coach and an advocate. The sponsor tracks the new associate's progress, offers help and encouragement, points out weaknesses and suggests ways to correct them, and concentrates on how the associate can better make use of his or her strengths. Sponsoring is not a short-term commitment. When individuals are hired initially, they are likely to have a sponsor in their immediate work area. As associates' commitments change or grow, it is normal for them to change sponsors, or in some cases add a second sponsor. For instance, if they move to a new job in another area of the company, they may gain a sponsor there and then decide whether to keep their former sponsor or not. Because sponsorship is built on the personal relationship between two people, the relationship most often continues even if the official sponsorship role does not.

New associates are expected to focus on building relationships during the first three to six months of their careers. Donna Frey described the first months for a new associate at Gore as follows:

> When new associates join the enterprise, they participate in an orientation program. Then, each new associate works with a starting sponsor to get acclimated and begin building relationships within Gore. The starting sponsor provides the new hire with a list of key associates he/she should meet with during the next few months.
>
> We encourage the new hire to meet with these associates one-on-one. It's not a phone conversation, but a chance to sit down with them face-to-face and get to know them.
>
> This process helps demonstrate the importance of relationships. When you're hiring really good people, they want to have quick wins and make contributions, and building relationships without a clear goal can be difficult. Often, new associates will say, "I don't feel like I'm contributing. I've spent three months just getting to know people." However, after a year they begin to realize how important this process was.

To ensure that new associates are not overwhelmed by what is probably their first experience in a nonhierarchical organization, Gore has a 2-day orientation program it calls Building on the Best. New associates are brought together with other new associates after two or three months to participate in the program, which addresses many of Gore's key concepts, who Gore is and how the enterprise works. The program includes group activities and interactive presentations given by leaders and other long-time associates.

Helping Associates Build and Maintain Relationships

Gore recognizes the need to maintain initial relationships, continuously develop new ones, and cement on-going relationships. One way this is fostered is through its digital voice exchange called Gorecom. According to Terri Kelly, "Gorecom is the preferred media if you want a quick response." An oral culture is fostered because it encourages direct communication.

To further foster the oral culture, team members and leaders are expected to meet face-to-face regularly. For team members and especially leaders, this can mean lots of travel. As one technical associate joked, "Probably, in the last 12 years, I spent 3 years traveling internationally, a couple weeks at a time."

Another way that Gore facilitates the development of teams and individuals is through training. An associate in Newark noted that Gore "works with associates who want to develop themselves and their talents." Associates are offered a variety of in-house training opportunities, not only in technical and engineering areas but also in leadership development. In addition, the company has established cooperative education programs with universities and other outside providers. will step forward.

In many ways, Gore can feel like an extended family for its associates and the communities in which they live. Based on their own interests and initiatives, associates give back to their communities through schools, sports clubs, universities and other local organizations. Recently, Gore has encouraged their U.S. associates' community outreach activities by providing up to 8 hours of paid time off for such efforts. Through this program associates worked nearly 7,800 hours at nonprofits in Gore's last fiscal year. In reality, Gore associates volunteer much more of their personal time. The associates individually or in teams decide to what to commit their time.

Rewarding Associates for Contributions

Compensation at Gore has both short- and long-term equity sharing components. Its compensation goal is to ensure internal fairness and external competitiveness. To ensure fairness, associates are asked to rank their team members each year in order of contribution to the enterprise. In addition, team members are asked to comment on their rationale behind the ranking, as well as on particular strengths or potential areas of improvement for the associates. To ensure competitiveness, each year Gore benchmarks pay of its associates against a variety of functions and roles with their peers at other companies.

Gore also uses profit sharing as a form of short-term compensation. Profits remaining after business requirements are met are distributed among associates as profit sharing. Profit shares are distributed when established financial goals are reached. Every month the business results are reviewed with associates, and they know whether they are on track to meet forecasts. The first profit sharing occurred in 1960, only two years after the founding of the company.

Beyond short-term equity sharing, Gore has an associates' stock ownership program (ASOP). Each year Gore contributes up to 12% of pay to an account that purchases Gore stock for associates with more than one year of service. Associates have ownership of the account after three years of service, when they become 100% vested. Gore also has a 401(K) Plan. It provides a contribution of up to 3% of pay to each associates' personal investment accounts. Associates are eligible after one month of service. Associates are 100% vested immediately.

A particular area where Gore's practices differ from traditional practices at other organizations is in how the majority of the sales force is compensated. They are paid not on commission, but with salary, stock through ASOP and profit sharing with all the other associates.[2] When a sales associate was asked to explain this practice, he responded as follows:

> The people who are just concerned with making their sales numbers in other companies usually struggle when they come to Gore. We encourage folks to help others. For example, when we hire new sales associates, we ask experienced sales associates to take some time to help get them acclimated to Gore and how we do things. In other companies where I've worked, that would have been seen as something that would detract from your potential to make your number, so you probably wouldn't be asked to do such a thing.

In other words, they see individual sales commissions as detracting from mentoring and sharing what is at the core of the Gore culture.

The entire package of compensation extends beyond direct monetary payments. As with most companies, associates receive a range of benefits, such as medical and dental insurance. Another benefit extended to associates is onsite child care. In addition, in *Fortune* magazine's 2008 story about Gore being one of the "100 Best Companies to Work For," onsite fitness centers and are listed as benefits. Gore does have such benefits, but they are not driven from the top-down. Gore does support multiple wellness programs, but there is not one enterprise-wide program. In keeping with Gore's principles and philosophy, Gore looks for an associate or a group of associates to initiate a program. For example, in the Fabrics Division an associate who is a committed runner will champion a group at lunch time. Gore will then support such activities with fitness centers, softball fields, volleyball courts and running trails. Pockets of associates all over Gore pursue these and other wellness activities.

GORE™ RIDE ON® Bike Cables: An Example of Strategy, Leadership, and HR in Action

A good example of strategy, leadership, and effective talent deployment is illustrated by the development of a product called GORE™ RIDE ON® bike cables. Initially, the cables were derailleur and brake cables for trail bikes. They were developed by some trail bike enthusiasts at the medical facilities in Flagstaff, Arizona in the 1990s. When the trail bike market declined, the product was withdrawn from the market. In 2006, a group of young engineers went to Jack Kramer, a technical leader at Gore, and said that they wanted to learn what it takes to develop a new product by reviving the cables. His response was, "You need someone who has some experience before you go off and try to do that."

One of the young engineers approached Lois Mabon, a product specialist who had about 16 years of experience at Gore and worked in the same facility, and asked her to be the group's coach. Lois went back to Jack and talked to him. He was still not sold on the idea, but he allowed Lois to find out what had happened to the bike cables and explore with the group what it would take to bring a new product to market. Within Gore, associates are encourage to set aside some *dabble* time. Dabble time is when people have the freedom to develop new products and evaluate their viability. After some exploration of what happened to the cables, Lois led a group that made a presentation to Jack and some others in the company, and even though they still were not sure, they said, "All right, keep working on it."

After about nine or ten months of exploring the possibility, a team of excited and passionate associates developed a set of GORE™ RIDE ON® products. In their exploration, the team learned that the road bike market is larger than the trail bike market, and there might potentially be a product for the racing market.

A presentation, referred to within Gore as a "Real-Win-Worth" presentation was prepared and presented to the Industrial Products Division (IPD) leadership team. Real-Win-Worth is a rigorous discipline that Gore uses to help hone in on the most promising new opportunities. The three issues that must be addressed in "Real-Win-Worth" are (1) Is the idea real, (2) Can Gore win in the market, and (3) Is it worth pursuing? After listening and questioning the presenters, the IPD leadership team responded, "You know what? You do have some really good ideas. Let's do a market study on it. Let's see if the market is interested."

Some samples of the new product were made and taken to 200 top bike stores across the U.S. They were handed out to the store owners, and in turn, the store owners were asked to fill out a survey. The survey focused on three questions: (1) Is this a product you would buy? (2) Is it a product you would recommend to your customers? (2) How would you compare this to the other products out in the industry?

An analysis of the surveys showed that 65% to 75 percent of all respondents would either definitely buy the product or were interested in it. Based on these results, the team concluded that people would really want to buy the product.

So with that data in hand, another presentation was made to the IPD leadership team in August 2006. The response was, "Okay, go launch it." The product team had 12 months to improve the mountain bike cables, develop the new road bike cables, redesign the packaging, redesign the logo, set-up production, and do everything else that is associated with a new product introduction.

Every Gore division was involved in producing the cables. The product is overseen by a team in the Industrial Products Division. The GORE BIKE WEAR™ products team in the Fabrics Division serves as the sales team. The Medical Products Division makes a component that goes in it. And the Electronics Products Division coats the cables.

In September 2007, the product was officially launched at two bike shows. The first one was the Euro-Bike on Labor Day and the other was the Inter-bike show held in Las Vegas at the end of September. The top 100 GORE BIKE WEAR™ product customers and shops were invited to these shows.

In fewer than three months Gore had sold approximately 8,000 pairs of cables. In addition, Gore had teamed with one of the top shifter manufacturers to co-market their products. The shift manufacturer uses the Gore cables in its best-selling shifter line, introduced in November 2007.

Facing the Future Together

Associates at Gore believe that their unique organizational culture will allow the company to continue maximizing individual potential while cultivating an environment where creativity can flourish. The unique culture results from an unwavering commitment to the use of cutting-edge technology for developing high quality products. This strategy is carried out through a unique approach to leadership and human resource management. The record of success is demonstrated not only by high financial profitability but also the creation of a highly desirable workplace. Nevertheless, success in the past cannot be seen as

assurance of success in the future. As Brad Jones of the Enterprise Leadership Team said:

Twenty or thirty years ago, markets in different parts of the world were still somewhat distinct and isolated from one another. At that time, we could have pretty much the entire global business team for a particular market niche located in a building. Today, as our markets become more global in nature, we are increasingly seeing the need to support our customers with global virtual teams. How do our paradigms and practices have to change to accommodate those changing realities? Those are active discussions that apply across these many different businesses.

The answer of how Gore will evolve to meet these challenges is not something that will be decided by an isolated CEO or an elite group of executives. Critical decisions, those below the waterline, have never been made that way and there is no expectation that this will change.

Endnotes

1 Throughout this case the word *associate* is used because Gore always uses the word *associate* instead of *employee*. In fact, the case writers were told that the term associates evolved early in the company's history because it expressed the belief that everyone had a stake in the success of the enterprise.

2 Gore's ASOP is similar legally to an employee stock ownership plan. Again, Gore simply has never allowed the word *employee* in any of its documentation. The ASOP and profit sharing will be explained in more detail later.

The Home Video Game Industry, 1968 to 2010

An Industry is Born

In 1968, Nolan Bushell, the 24-year-old son of a Utah cement contractor, graduated from the University of Utah with a degree in engineering.[1] Bushnell then moved to California, where he worked briefly in the computer graphics division of Ampex. At home, Bushnell turned his daughter's bedroom into a laboratory (she was relegated to the couch). There, he created a simpler version of Space War, a computer game that had been invented in 1962 by an MIT graduate student, Steve Russell. Bushnell's version of Russell's game, which he called Computer Space, was made of integrated circuits connected to a 19-inch black-and-white television screen. Unlike a computer, Bushnell's invention could do nothing but play the game, which meant that, unlike a computer, it could be cheaply produced.

Bushnell envisioned video games like his standing next to pinball machines in arcades. With hopes of having his invention put into production, Bushnell left Ampex to work for a small pinball company that manufactured 1,500 copies of his video game. The game never sold, primarily because the player had to read a full page of directions before he or she could play the game—way too complex for an arcade game. Bushnell left the pinball company and with a friend, Ted Dabney, put up $500 to start a company that would develop a simpler video game. They wanted to call the company Syzygy, but the name was already taken, so they settled on Atari, a Japanese word that was the equivalent of "check in the go."

In his home laboratory, Bushnell built the simplest game he could devise. People knew the rules immediately, and it could be played with one hand. The game was modeled on table tennis, and players batted a ball back and forth with paddles that could be moved up and down the sides of a court by twisting knobs. He named the game "Pong" after the sonar-like sound that was emitted every time the ball connected with a paddle.

In the fall of 1972, Bushnell installed his prototype for Pong in Andy Capp's tavern in Sunnyvale, California. The only instructions were "avoid missing the ball for a high score." In the first week, 1,200 quarters were deposited in the casserole dish that served for a coin box in Bushnell's prototype. Bushnell was ecstatic; his simple game had brought in $300 in a week. The pinball machine that stood next to it averaged $35 a week.

Lacking the capital to mass-produce the game, Bushnell approached established amusement game companies, only to be repeatedly shown the door. Down, but hardly out, Bushnell cut his hair, put on a suit, and talked his way into a $50,000 line of credit from a local bank. He set up a production line in an abandoned roller skating rink and he hired people to assemble machines, while Led Zeppelin and The Rolling Stones were played at full volume over the speaker system of the rink. Among his first batch of employees was a skinny 17-year-old named Steve Jobs, who would later found Apple Computer (now Apple) and NeXT. Like others, Jobs had been attracted by a classified ad that read "Have Fun and Make Money."

In no time at all, Bushnell was selling all the machines that his small staff could make—about 10 per day—but to grow, he needed additional capital. While the ambience at the rink, with its mix of rock music and marijuana fumes, put off most potential investors, Don Valentine, one of the country's most astute and credible venture capitalists, was impressed with

---

This case was prepared by Charles W. L. Hill, University of Washington.

This case is intended to be used as a basis for class discussion rather than as an illustration of either effective or ineffective handling of the situation. Reprinted by permission of Charles W. L. Hill.

the growth story. Armed with Valentine's money, Atari began to increase production and expand their range of games. New games included "Tank" and "Breakout"; the latter was designed by Jobs and a friend of his, Steve Wozniak, who had left Hewlett Packard to work at Atari.

By 1974, 100,000 Pong-like games were sold worldwide. Although Atari manufactured only 10% of the games, the company still made $3.2 million that year. With the Pong clones coming on strong, Bushnell decided to make a Pong system for the home. In fact, Magnavox had been marketing a similar game for the home since 1972, although sales had been modest.[2] Bushnell's team managed to compress Atari's coin-operated Pong game down to a few inexpensive circuits that were contained in the game console. Atari's Pong had a sharper picture and more sensitive controllers than Magnavox's machine. It also cost less. Bushnell then went on a road show, demonstrating Pong to toy buyers, but he received an indifferent response and no sales. A dejected Bushnell returned to Atari with no idea of what to do next. Then, the buyer for the sporting goods department at Sears came to see Bushnell, reviewed the machine, and offered to buy every home Pong game Atari could make. With Sears' backing, Bushnell boosted production. Sears ran a major television ad campaign to sell home Pong, and Atari's sales soared, hitting $450 million in 1975. The home video game had arrived.

Boom and Bust

Nothing attracts competitors like success, and by 1976 about 20 different companies were crowding into the home video game market, including National Semiconductor, RCA, Coleco, and Fairchild. Recognizing the limitations of existing home video game designs, Fairchild came out in 1976 with a home video game system capable of playing multiple games. The Fairchild system consisted of three components—a console, controllers, and cartridges. The console was a small computer optimized for graphics processing capabilities. It was designed to receive information from the controllers, process it, and send signals to a television monitor. The controllers were hand-held devices used to direct on-screen action. The cartridges contained chips encoding the instructions for a game.

The cartridges were designed to be inserted into the console.

In 1976, Bushnell sold Atari to Warner Communications for $28 million; Bushnell stayed on to run Atari. Backed by Warner's capital, in 1977 Atari developed and bought its own cartridge-based system, the Atari 2600. The 2600 system was sold for $200, and associated cartridges retailed for $25–$30. Sales surged during the 1977 Christmas season. However, a lack of manufacturing capacity on behalf of market leader Atari, and a very cautious approach to inventory by Fairchild led to shortages and kept sales significantly below what they could have been. Fairchild's cautious approach was the result of prior experience in consumer electronics. A year earlier it had increased demand for its digital watches, only to accumulate a buildup of excess inventory that had caused the company to take a $24.5 million write-off.[3]

After the 1977 Christmas season, Atari claimed to have sold about 400,000 units of the 2600 VCA, about 50% of all cartridge-based systems in American homes. Atari had also earned more than $100 million in sales of game cartridges. By this point, second-place Fairchild sold around 250,000 units of its system. Cartridge sales for the year totaled about 1.2 million units, with an average selling price of around $20. Fresh from this success and fortified by market forecasts predicting sales of 33 million cartridges and an installed base of 16 million machines by 1980, Bushnell committed Atari to manufacturing 1 million units of the 2600 for the 1978 Christmas season. Atari estimated that total demand would reach 2 million units. Bushnell was also encouraged by signals from Fairchild that it would again be limiting production to around 200,000 units. At this point, Atari had a library of 9 games. Fairchild had 17.[4]

Atari was not the only company to be excited by the growth forecasts. In 1978, a host of other companies, including Coleco, National Semiconductor, Magnavox, General Instrument, and a dozen other companies, entered the market with incompatible cartridge-based home systems. The multitude of choices did not seem to entice consumers, however, and the 1978 Christmas season brought unexpectedly low sales. Only Atari and Coleco survived an industry shakeout. Atari lost Bushnell, who was ousted by Warner executives. (Bushnell went on to start Chuck E. Cheese Pizza Time Theater, a restaurant chain that had 278 outlets by 1981.) Bushnell later stated that part of the problem was a disagreement over strategy. Bushnell wanted Atari to price the 2600 at cost and make money on sales of software; Warner wanted to continue making profits on hardware sales.[5]

Several important developments occurred in 1979. First, several game producers and programmers defected from Atari to set up their own firm, Activision, and to make games compatible with the Atari 2600. Their success encouraged others to follow suit. Second, Coleco developed an expansion module that allowed its machine to play Atari games. Atari and Mattel (which entered the market in 1979) did likewise. Third, the year 1979 saw the introduction of three new games to the home market—Space Invaders, Asteroids, and Pac-Man. All three were adapted from popular arcade games and all three helped drive demand for players.

Demand strongly recovered in late-1979 and kept growing for the next 3 years. In 1981, U.S. sales of home video games and cartridges hit $1 billion. In 1982, they surged to $3 billion, with Atari accounting for half of this amount. It seemed as if Atari could do no wrong; the 2600 was everywhere. About 20 million units were sold, and by late-1982, a large number of independent companies, including Activision, Imagic, and Epyx, were now producing hundreds of games for the 2600. Second-place Coleco was also doing well, partly because of a popular arcade game, Donkey Kong, which it had licensed from a Japanese company called Nintendo.

Atari was also in contact with Nintendo. In 1982, the company very nearly licensed the rights to Nintendo's Famicom, a cartridge-based video game system machine that was a big hit in Japan. Atari's successor to the 2600, the 5200, was not selling well, and the Famicom seemed like a good substitute. The negotiations broke down, however, when Atari discovered that Nintendo had extended its Donkey Kong license to Coleco. This allowed Coleco to port a version of the game to its home computer, which was a direct competitor to Atari's 800 home computer.[6]

After a strong 1982 season, the industry hoped for continued growth in 1983. Then, the bottom dropped out of the market. Sales of home video games plunged to $100 million. Atari lost $500 million in the first 9 months of the year, causing the stock of parent company Warner Communications to drop by half. Part of the blame for the collapse was laid at the feet of an enormous inventory overhang of unsold games. About 1–20 million surplus game cartridges were left over from the 1982 Christmas season (in 1981, there were none). On top of this, around 500 new games hit the market in 1993. The average price of a cartridge plunged from $30 in 1979 to $16 in 1982, and then to $4 in 1983. As sales slowed, retailers cut back on the shelf space allocated to video games. It proved difficult for new games to make a splash in a crowded market. Atari had to dispose of 6 million "ET: The Extraterrestrial" games. Meanwhile, big hits from previous years, such as Pac-Man, were bundled with game players and given away free to try to encourage system sales.[7]

Surveying the rubble, commentators claimed that the video game industry was dead. The era of dedicated game machines was over, they claimed. Personal computers were taking their place.[8] It seemed to be true. Mattel sold off its game business, Fairchild moved on to other things, Coleco folded, and Warner decided to break up Atari and sell its constituent pieces—at least, those pieces for which it could find a buyer. No one in America seemed to want to have anything to do with the home video game business; no one, that is, except for Minoru Arakawa, the head of Nintendo's U.S. subsidiary, Nintendo of America (NOA). Picking through the rubble of the industry, Arakawa noticed that there were people who still packed video arcades, bringing in $7 billion a year, more money than the entire movie industry. Perhaps it was not a lack of interest in home video games that had killed the industry. Perhaps it was bad business practice.

The Nintendo Monopoly

Nintendo was a century-old Japanese company that had built up a profitable business making playing cards before diversifying into the video game business. Based in Kyoto and still run by the founding Yamauchi family, the company started to diversify into the video game business in the late-1970s. The first step was to license video game technology from Magnavox. In 1977, Nintendo introduced a home video game system in Japan based on this technology that played a variation of Pong. In 1978, the company began to sell coin-operated video games. It had its first hit with "Donkey Kong," designed by Sigeru Miyamoto.

The Famicom

In the early-1980s, the company's boss, Hiroshi Yamauchi, decided that Nintendo had to develop its own video game machine. He pushed the company's engineers to develop a machine that combined superior graphics-processing capabilities and low cost. Yamauchi wanted a machine that could sell for $75, less than half the price of competing machines at the time. He dubbed the machine the Family Computer, or Famicom. The machine that his engineers designed was based on the controller, console, and plug in the cartridge format pioneered by Fairchild. It contained two custom chips—an 8-bit central processing unit and a graphics-processing unit. Both chips had been scaled down to perform only essential functions. A 16-bit processor was available at the time, but to keep costs down, Yamauchi refused to use it.

Nintendo approached Ricoh, the electronics giant, which had spare semiconductor capacity. Employees at Ricoh said that the chips had to cost no more that 2,000 yen. Ricoh thought that the 2,000-yen price point was absurd. Yamauchi's response was to guarantee Ricoh a 3-million-chip order within 2 years. Because the leading companies in Japan were selling, at most, 30,000 video games per year at the time, many within the company viewed this as an outrageous commitment, but Ricoh went for it.[9]

Another feature of the machine was its memory—2,000 bytes of random access memory (RAM), compared to the 256 bytes of RAM in the Atari machine. The result was a machine with superior graphics-processing capabilities and faster action that could handle far more complex games than Atari games. Nintendo's engineers also built a new set of chips into the game cartridges. In addition to chips that held the game program, Nintendo developed memory map controller (MMC) chips that took over some of the graphics-processing work from the chips in the console and enabled the system to handle more complex games. With the addition of the MMC chips, the potential for more-sophisticated and more complex games had arrived. Over time, Nintendo's engineers developed more powerful MMC chips, enabling the basic 8-bit system to do things that originally seemed out of reach. The engineers also figured out a way to include a battery backup system in cartridges that allowed some games to store information independently—to keep track of where a player had left off or to track high scores.

The Games

Yamauchi recognized that great hardware that would not sell itself. The key to the market, he reasoned, was great games. Yamauchi had instructed the engineers, when they were developing the hardware, to make sure that "it was appreciated by software engineers." Nintendo decided that it would become a haven for game designers. "An ordinary man," Yamauchi said, "cannot develop good games no matter how hard he tries. A handful of people in this world can develop games that everyone wants. Those are the people we want at Nintendo."[10]

Yamauchi had an advantage in the person of Sigeru Miyamoto. Miyamoto had joined Nintendo at the age of 24. Yamauchi had hired Miyamoto, a graduate of Kanazawa Munici College of Industrial Arts, as a favor to his father and an old friend, although he had little idea what he would do with an artist. For 3 years, Miyamoto worked as Nintendo's staff artist. Then, in 1980, Yamauchi called Miyamoto into his office. Nintendo had started selling coin-operated video games, but one of the new games, Radarscope, was a disaster. Could Miyamoto come up with a new game? Miyamoto was delighted. He had always spent a lot of time drawing cartoons, and as a student, he had played video games constantly. Miyamoto believed that video games could be used to bring cartoons to life.[11]

The game Miyamoto developed was nothing short of a revelation. At a time when most coin-operated video games lacked characters or depth, Miyamoto created a game around a story that had both. Most games involved battles with space invaders or heroes shooting lasers at aliens; Miyamoto's game did neither. Based loosely on *Beauty and the Beast* and *King Kong*, Miyamoto's game involved a pet ape who runs off with his master's beautiful girlfriend. His master is an ordinary carpenter called Mario, who has a bulbous nose, a bushy mustache, a pair of large pathetic eyes, and a red cap (which Miyamoto added because he was not good at hairstyles). Mario does not carry a laser gun. The ape runs off with the girlfriend to get back at his master, who was not especially nice to the beast. The man, of course, has to get his girlfriend back by running up ramps, climbing ladders, jumping off elevators, and the like, while the ape throws objects at the hapless carpenter. Since the main character is an ape, Miyamoto called him Kong; because the main character is as stubborn as a donkey, he called the game "Donkey Kong."

Released in 1981, Donkey Kong was a sensation in the world of coin-operated video arcades and a smash hit for Nintendo. In 1984, Yamauchi again summoned Miyamoto to his office. He needed more games, this time for Famicom. Miyamoto was made the head of a new research and development (R&D) group and told to come up with the most imaginative video games ever.

Miyamoto began with Mario from Donkey Kong. A colleague had told him that Mario looked more like a plumber than a carpenter, so a plumber he became. Miyamoto gave Mario a brother, Luigi, who was as tall and thin as Mario was short and fat. They became the Super Mario Brothers. Since plumbers spend their time working on pipes, large green sewer pipes became obstacles and doorways into secret worlds. Mario and Luigi's task was to search for the captive Princess Toadstool. Mario and Luigi are endearing bumblers, unequal to their tasks yet surviving. They shoot, squash, or evade their enemies—a potpourri of inventions that include flying turtles and stinging fish, man-eating flowers and fire-breathing dragons—while they collect gold coins, blow air bubbles, and climb vines into smiling clouds.[12]

"Super Mario Brothers" was introduced in 1985. For Miyamoto, this was just the beginning. Between 1985 and 1991, Miyamoto produced 8 Mario games. About 60–70 million were sold worldwide, making Miyamoto the most successful game designer in the world. After adapting Donkey Kong for Famicom, he also went on to create other top-selling games, including another classic, "The Legend of Zelda." While Miyamoto drew freely from folklore, literature, and pop culture, the main source for his ideas was his own experience. The memory of being lost among a maze of sliding doors in his family's home was re-created in the labyrinths of the Zelda games. The dog that attacked him when he was a child attacks Mario in Super Mario. As a child, Miyamoto had once climbed a tree to catch a view of far-off mountains and had become stuck; Mario gets himself in a similar fix. Once Miyamoto went hiking without a map and was surprised to stumble across a lake. In the Legend of Zelda, part of the adventure is in walking into new places without a map and being confronted by surprises.

Nintendo in Japan

Nintendo introduced Famicom into the Japanese market in May 1983. Famicom was priced at $100, more than Yamauchi wanted, but significantly less than the products of competitors. When he introduced the machine, Yamauchi urged retailers to forgo profits on the hardware because it was just a tool to sell software, and that is where they would make their money. Backed by an extensive advertising campaign, 500,000 units of Famicom were sold in the first 2 months. Within a year, the figure stood at 1 million, and sales were still rapidly expanding. With the hardware quickly finding its way into Japanese homes, Nintendo was besieged with calls from desperate retailers frantically demanding more games.

At this point, Yamauchi told Miyamoto to come up with the most imaginative games ever. However, Yamauchi also realized that Nintendo alone could not satisfy the growing thirst for new games, so he initiated a licensing program. To become a Nintendo licensee, companies had to agree to an unprecedented series of restrictions. Licensees could issue only 5 Nintendo games per year, and they could not write those titles for other platforms. The licensing fee was set at 20% of the wholesale price of each cartridge sold (game cartridges wholesaled for around $30). It typically cost $500,000 to develop a game and took around 6 months. Nintendo insisted that games not contain any excessively violent or sexually suggestive material and that they review every game before allowing it to be produced.[13]

Despite these restrictions, 6 companies (Bandai, Capcom, Konami, Namco, Taito, and Hudson) agreed to become Nintendo licensees, not least because millions of customers were now clamoring for games. Bandai was Japan's largest toy company. The others already made either coin-operated video games or computer software games. Because of these licensing agreements, they saw their sales and earnings surge. For example, Konami's earnings went from $10 million in 1987 to $300 million in 1991.

After the 6 licensees began selling games, reports of defective games began to reach Yamauchi. The original 6 licensees were allowed to manufacture their own game cartridges. Realizing that he had given away the ability to control the quality of the cartridges, Yamauchi decided to change the contract for future licensees. Future licensees were required to submit all manufacturing orders for cartridges to Nintendo. Nintendo charged licensees $14 per cartridge, required that they place a minimum order for 10,000 units (later the minimum order was raised to 30,000), and insisted on cash payment in full when the order was placed. Nintendo outsourced all manufacturing to other companies, using the volume of its orders to get rock bottom prices. The cartridges were estimated to cost Nintendo between $6 and $8 each. The licensees then picked up the cartridges from Nintendo's loading dock and were responsible for distribution. In 1985, there were 17 licensees. By 1987, there were 50. By this point, 90% of the home video game systems sold in Japan were Nintendo systems.

Nintendo in America

In 1980, Nintendo established a subsidiary in America to sell its coin-operated video games. Yamauchi's American-educated son-in-law, Minoru Arakawa, headed the subsidiary. All of the other essential employees were Americans, including Ron Judy and Al Stone. For its first 2 years, Nintendo of America (NOA), originally based in Seattle, struggled to sell second-rate games such as Radarscope. The subsidiary seemed on the brink of closing. NOA could not even make the rent payment on the warehouse. Then they received a large shipment from Japan: 2,000 units of a new coin-operated video game. Opening the box, they discovered Donkey Kong. After playing the game briefly, Judy proclaimed it a disaster. Stone walked out of the building, declaring "it's over."[14] The managers were appalled. They could not imagine a game less likely to sell in video arcades. The only promising sign was that a 20-year employee, Howard Philips, rapidly became enthralled with the machine.

Arakawa, however, knew he had little choice but to try to sell the machine. Judy persuaded the owner of the Spot Tavern near Nintendo's office to take one of the machines on a trial basis. After one night, Judy discovered $30 in the coin box, a phenomenal amount. The next night there was $35, and $36 the night after that. NOA had a hit on its hands.

By the end of 1982, NOA had sold over 60,000 copies of Donkey Kong and had booked sales in excess of $100 million. The subsidiary had outgrown its Seattle location. They moved to a new site in Redmond, a Seattle suburb, where they located next to a small but fast-growing software company run by an old school acquaintance of Howard Philips, Bill Gates.

By 1984, NOA was riding a wave of success in the coin-operated video game market. Arakawa, however, was interested in the possibilities of selling Nintendo's new Famicom system in the United States. Throughout 1984, Arakawa, Judy, and Stone met with numerous toy and department store representatives to discuss the possibilities, only to be repeatedly rebuffed. Still smarting from the 1983 debacle, the representatives wanted nothing to do with the home video game business. They also met with former managers from Atari and Coleco to gain their insights. The most common response they received was that the market collapsed because the last generation of games was awful.

Arakawa and his team decided that if they were going to sell Famicom in the United States, they would have to find a new distribution channel. The obvious choice was consumer electronics stores. Thus, Arakawa asked the R&D team in Kyoto to redesign Famicom for the U.S. market so that it looked less like a toy (Famicom was encased in red and white plastic), and more like a consumer electronics device. The redesigned machine was renamed the Nintendo Entertainment System (NES).

Arakawa's big fear was that illegal, low-quality Taiwanese games would flood the U.S. market if NES was successful. To stop counterfeit games being played on NES, Arakawa asked Nintendo's Japanese engineers to design a security system into the U.S. version of Famicom so that only Nintendo-approved games could be played on NES. The Japanese engineers responded by designing a security chip to be embedded in the game cartridges. NES would not work unless the security chips in the cartridges unlocked, or shook hands with, a chip in NES. Since the code embedded in the security chip was proprietary, the implication of this system was that no one could manufacture games for NES without Nintendo's specific approval.

To overcome the skepticism and reluctance of retailers to stock a home video game system, Arakawa decided in late-1985 to make an extraordinary commitment. Nintendo would stock stores and set up displays and windows. Retailers would not have to pay for anything they stocked for 90 days. After that, retailers could pay Nintendo for what they sold and return the rest. NES was bundled with Nintendo's best-selling game in Japan, Super Mario Brothers. It was essentially a risk-free proposition for retailers, but even with this, most were skeptical. Ultimately, 30 Nintendo personnel descended on the New York area. Referred to as the Nintendo SWAT team, they persuaded some stores to stock NES after an extraordinary blitz that involved 18-hour days. To support the New York product launch, Nintendo also committed itself to a $5 million advertising campaign aimed at the 7- to 14-year-old boys who seemed to be Nintendo's likely core audience.

By December 1985, between 500 and 600 stores in the New York area were stocking Nintendo systems. Sales were moderate, and only about half of the 100,000 NES machines shipped from Japan were sold, but it was enough to justify going forward. The SWAT team then moved first to Los Angeles, then to Chicago, then to Dallas. As in New York, sales started at a moderate pace, but by late-1986 they started to accelerate rapidly, and Nintendo went national with NES.

In 1986, around 1 million NES units were sold in the United States. In 1987, the figure increased to 3 million. In 1988, it jumped to over 7 million. In the same year, 33 million game cartridges were sold. Nintendo mania had arrived in the United States. To expand the supply of games, Nintendo licensed the rights to produce up to 5 games per year to 31 American software companies. Nintendo continued to use a restrictive licensing agreement that gave it exclusive rights to any games, required licensees to place their orders through Nintendo, and insisted on a 30,000-unit minimum order.[15]

By 1990, the home video game market was worth $5 billion worldwide. Nintendo dominated the industry, with a 90% share of the market for game equipment. The parent company was, by some measures, now the most profitable company in Japan. By 1992, it was netting over $1 billion in gross profit annually, or more than $1.5 million for each employee in Japan. The company's stock market value exceeded that of Sony, Japan's premier consumer electronics firm. Indeed, the company's net profit exceeded that of all the American movie studios combined. Nintendo games, it seemed, were bigger than the movies.

As of 1991, there were over 100 licensees for Nintendo, and over 450 titles were available for NES. In the United States, Nintendo products were distributed through toy stores (30% of volume), mass merchandisers (40% of volume), and department stores (10% of volume). Nintendo tightly controlled the number of game titles and games that could be sold, quickly withdrawing titles as soon as interest appeared to decline. In 1988, retailers requested 110 million cartridges from Nintendo. Market surveys suggested that perhaps 45 million could have been sold, but Nintendo allowed only 33 million to be shipped.[16] Nintendo claimed that the shortage of games was, in part, due to a worldwide shortage of semiconductor chips.

Several companies had tried to reverse-engineer the code embedded in Nintendo's security chip, which competitors characterized as a lockout chip. Nintendo successfully sued them. The most notable was Atari Games, one of the successors of the original Atari, which sued Nintendo of America in 1987 for anticompetitive behavior. Atari claimed that the purpose of the security chip was to monopolize the market. At the same time, Atari announced that it had found a way around Nintendo's security chip and would begin to sell unlicensed games.[17] NOA responded with a countersuit. In a March 1991 ruling, Atari was found to have obtained Nintendo's security code illegally and was ordered to stop selling NES-compatible games. However, Nintendo did not always have it all its own way. In 1990, under pressure from Congress, the Department of Justice, and several lawsuits, Nintendo rescinded its exclusivity requirements, freeing up developers to write games for other platforms. However, developers faced a real problem: what platform could they write for?

Sega's Sonic Boom

In 1954, David Rosen, a 20-year-old American, left the U.S. Air Force after a tour of duty in Tokyo.[18] Rosen had noticed that Japanese people needed lots of photographs for ID cards, but that local photo studios were slow and expensive. He formed a company, Rosen Enterprises, and went into the photo-booth business, which was a big success. By 1957, Rosen had established a successful nationwide chain. At this point, the Japanese economy was booming, so Rosen decided it was time to get into another business—entertainment. As his vehicle, he chose arcade games, which were unknown in Japan at the time. He picked up used games on the cheap from America and set up arcades in the same Japanese department stores and theaters that typically housed his photo booths. Within a few years, Rosen had 200 arcades nationwide. His only competition came from another American-owned firm, Service Games (SeGa), whose original business was jukeboxes and fruit machines.

By the early-1960s, the Japanese arcade market had caught up with the U.S. market. The problem was that game makers had run out of exciting new games to offer. Rosen decided that he would have to get into the business of designing and manufacturing games, but to do that he needed manufacturing facilities. SeGa manufactured its own games, so in 1965 Rosen approached the company and suggested a merger. The result was Sega Enterprise, a Japanese company with Rosen as its CEO.

Rosen himself designed Sega's first game, "Periscope," in which the objective was to sink chain-mounted cardboard ships by firing torpedoes, represented by lines of colored lights. Periscope was a big success not only in Japan, but also in the United States and Europe, and it allowed Sega to build up a respectable export business. Over the years, the company continued to invest heavily in game development, always using the latest electronic technology.

Gulf and Western, a U.S. conglomerate, acquired Sega in 1969, and Rosen ran the subsidiary. In 1975, Gulf and Western (G&W) took Sega public in the United States, but left Sega Japan as a G&W subsidiary; Hayao Nakayama, a former Sega distributor, was drafted as president. In the early-1980s, Nakayama pushed G&W to invest more in Sega Japan so that the company could enter the then-booming home video game market. When G&W refused, Nakayama suggested a management buyout. G&W agreed, and in 1984, for the price of just $38 million, Sega became a Japanese company once more. (Sega's Japanese revenues were around $700 million, but by now the company was barely profitable.)

Sega was caught off guard by the huge success of Nintendo's Famicom. Although it released its own 8-bit system in 1986, the machine never commanded more than 5% of the Japanese market. Nakayama, however, was not about to give up. From years in the arcade business, he understood that great games drove sales. Nevertheless, he also understood that more powerful technology gave game developers the tools to develop more appealing games. This philosophy underlay Nakayama's decision to develop a 16-bit game system, Genesis.

Sega took the design of its 16-bit arcade machine and adapted it for Genesis. Compared to Nintendo's 8-bit machine, the 16-bit machine featured an array of superior technological features, including high-definition graphics and animation, a full spectrum of colors, two independent scrolling backgrounds that created an impressive depth of field, and near CD quality sound. The design strategy also made it easy to port Sega's catalog of arcade hits to Genesis.

Genesis was launched in Japan in 1989, and in the United States in 1990. In the United States, the machine was priced at $199. The company hoped that sales would be boosted by the popularity of its arcade games, such as the graphically violent Altered Beast. Sega also licensed other companies to develop games for the Genesis platform. In an effort to recruit licensees, Sega asked for lower royalty rates than Nintendo, and it gave licensees the right to manufacture their own cartridges. Independent game developers were slow to on board, however, and the $200 price tag for the player held back sales.

One of the first independent game developers to sign up with Sega was Electronic Arts. Established by Trip Hawkins, Electronic Arts had focused on designing games for personal computers and consequently had missed the Nintendo 8-bit era. Now Hawkins was determined to get a presence in the home video game market, and aligning his company's wagon with Sega seemed to be the best option. The Nintendo playing field was already crowded, and Sega offered a far less restrictive licensing deal than Nintendo. Electronic Arts subsequently wrote several popular games for Genesis, including John Madden football and several gory combat games.[19]

Nintendo had not been ignoring the potential of the 16-bit system. Nintendo's own 16-bit system, Super NES, was ready for market introduction in 1989—at the same time as Sega's Genesis. Nintendo introduced Super NES in Japan in 1990, where it quickly established a strong market presence and beat Sega's Genesis. In the United States, however, the company decided to hold back longer to reap the full benefits of the dominance it enjoyed with the 8-bit NES system. Yamauchi was also worried about the lack of backward compatibility between Nintendo's 8-bit and 16-bit systems. (The company had tried to make the 16-bit system so that it could play 8-bit games but concluded that the cost of doing so was prohibitive.) These concerns may have led the company to delay market introduction until the 8-bit market was saturated.

Meanwhile, in the United States, the Sega bandwagon was beginning to gain momentum. One development that gave Genesis a push was the introduction of a new Sega game, "Sonic the Hedgehog." Developed by an independent team that was contracted to Sega, the game featured a cute hedgehog that impatiently tapped his paw when the player took too long to act. Impatience was Sonic's central feature—he had places to go, and quickly. He zipped along, collecting brass rings when he could find them, before rolling into a ball and flying down slides with loops and underground tunnels. Sonic was Sega's Mario.

In mid-1991, in an attempt to jump-start slow sales, Tom Kalinske, head of Sega's American subsidiary, decided to bundle Sonic the Hedgehog with the game player. He also reduced the price for the bundled unit to $150, and he relaunched the system with an aggressive advertising campaign aimed at teenagers. The campaign was built around the slogan "Genesis does what Nintendon't." The shift in strategy worked, and sales accelerated sharply.

Sega's success prompted Nintendo to launch its own 16-bit system. Nintendo's Super NES was introduced at $200. However, Sega now had a 2-year head start in games. By the end of 1991, about 125 game titles were available for Genesis, compared to 25 for Super NES. In May 1992, Nintendo reduced the price of Super NES to $150. At this time Sega was claiming a 63% share of the 16-bit market in the United States, and Nintendo claimed a 60% share. By now, Sega was cool. It began to take more chances with mass media–defined morality. When Acclaim Entertainment released its bloody "Mortal Kombat" game in September 1992, the Sega version let players rip off heads and tear out hearts. Reflecting Nintendo's image of their core market, its version was sanitized. The Sega version outsold Nintendo's 2:1.[20] Therefore, the momentum continued to run in Sega's favor. By January 1993, there were 320 titles available for Sega Genesis, and 130 for Super NES. In early-1994, independent estimates suggested that Sega had 60% of the U.S. market and Nintendo had 40%, figures Nintendo disputed.

3DO

Trip Hawkins, whose first big success was Electronic Arts, founded 3DO in 1991.[21] Hawkins' vision for 3DO was to shift the home video game business away from the existing cartridge-based format and toward a CD-ROM-based platform. The original partners in 3DO were Electronic Arts, Matsushita, Time Warner, AT&T, and the venture capital firm Kleiner Perkins. Collectively, they invested over $17 million in 3DO, making it the richest start-up in the history of the home video game industry. 3DO went public in May 1993 at $15 per share. By October of that year, the stock had risen to $48 per share, making 3DO worth $1 billion—not bad for a company that had yet to generate a single dollar in revenues.

The basis for 3DO's $1 billion market cap was patented computer system architecture and a copyrighted operating system that allowed for much richer graphics and audio capabilities. The system was built around a 32-bit RISC microprocessor and proprietary graphics processor chips. Instead of a cartridge, the 3DO system stored games on a CD-ROM that was capable of holding up to 600 megabytes of content, sharply up from the 10 megabytes of content found in the typical game cartridge of the time. The slower access time of a CD-ROM compared to a cartridge was alleviated somewhat by the use of a double-speed CD-ROM drive.[22]

The belief at 3DO—a belief apparently shared by many investors—was that the superior storage and graphics-processing capabilities of the 3DO system would prove very attractive to game developers, allowing them to be far more creative. In turn, better games would attract customers away from Nintendo and Sega. Developing games that used the capabilities of a CD-ROM system altered the economics of game development. Estimates suggested that it would cost approximately $2 million to produce a game for the 3DO system and could take as long as 24 months to develop. However, at $2 per disc, a CD-ROM cost substantially less to produce than a cartridge.

The centerpiece of 3DO's strategy was to license its hardware technology for free. Game developers paid a royalty of $3 per disc for access to the 3DO operating code. Discs typically retailed for $40 each.

Matsushita introduced the first 3DO machine into the U.S. market in October 1993. Priced at $700, the machine was sold through electronic retailers that carried Panasonic high-end electronics products. Sega's Tom Kalinsky noted, "It's a noble effort. Some people will buy 3DO, and they'll have a wonderful experience. It's impressive, but it's a niche. We've done the research. It does not become a large market until you go below $500. At $300, it starts to get interesting. We make no money on hardware. It's a cutthroat business. I hope Matsushita understands that."[23] CD-ROM discs for the 3DO machine retailed for around $75. The machine came bundled with "Crash'n Burn," a high-speed combat racing game. However, only 18 3DO titles were available by the crucial Christmas period, although reports suggested that 150 titles were under development.[24]

Sales of the hardware were slow, reaching only 30,000 by January 1994.[25] In the same month, AT&T and Sanyo both announced that they would begin to manufacture the 3DO machine. In March, faced with continuing sluggish sales, 3DO announced that it would give hardware manufacturers two shares of 3DO stock for every unit sold at or below a certain retail price. Matsushita dropped the price of its machine to $500. About the same time, Toshiba, LG, and Samsung all announced that they would start to produce 3DO machines.

By June 1994, cumulative sales of 3DO machines in the United States stood at 40,000 units. Matsushita announced plans to expand distribution beyond the current 3,500 outlets to include the toy and mass merchandise channels. Hawkins and his partners announced that they would invest another $37 million in 3DO. By July, there were 750 3DO software licensees, but only 40 titles were available for the format. Despite these moves, sales continued at a very sluggish pace and the supply of new software titles started to dry up.[26]

In September 1996, 3DO announced that it would either sell its hardware system business or move it into a joint venture.[27] The company announced that about 150 people, 1/3 of the work force, would probably lose their jobs in the restructuring. According to Trip Hawkins, 3DO would now focus on developing software for online gaming. Hawkins stated that the Internet and Internet entertainment constituted a huge opportunity for 3DO. The stock dropped $1.375 to $6.75.

Sony's Playstation

In the fall of 1995, Sony entered the fray with the introduction of the Sony PlayStation.[28] PlayStation used a 32-bit RISC microprocessor running at 33 MHz and using a double-speed CD-ROM drive. PlayStation cost an estimated $500 million to

develop. The machine had actually been under development since 1991, when Sony decided that the home video game industry was getting too big to ignore. Initially, Sony was in an alliance with Nintendo to develop the machine. Nintendo walked away from the alliance in 1992, however, after a disagreement over who owned the rights to any future CD-ROM games, Sony went alone.[29]

From the start, Sony felt that it could leverage its presence in the film and music business to build a strong position in the home video game industry. A consumer electronics giant with a position in the Hollywood movie business and the music industry (Sony owned Columbia Pictures and the Columbia record label), Sony believed that it had access to significant intellectual property that could form the basis of many popular games.

In 1991, Sony established a division in New York: Sony Electronic Publishing. The division was to serve as an umbrella organization for Sony's multimedia offerings. Headed by Iceland native Olaf Olafsson, then just 28 years old, this organization ultimately took the lead role in both the market launch of PlayStation and in developing game titles.[30] In 1993, as part of this effort, Sony purchased a well-respected British game developer, Psygnosis. By the fall of 1995, this unit had 20 games ready to complement PlayStation: "The Haldeman Diaries," "Mickey Mania" (developed in collaboration with Disney), and "Johnny Mnemonic," based on the William Gibson short story. To entice independent game developers such as Electronic Arts, Namco, and Acclaim Entertainment, Olafsson used the promise of low royalty rates. The standard royalty rate was set at $9 per disc, although developers that signed on early enough were given a lower royalty rate. Sony also provided approximately 4,000 game development tools to licensees in an effort to help them speed games to market.[31]

To distribute PlayStation, Sony set up a retail channel separate from Sony's consumer electronics sales force. It marketed the PlayStation as a hip and powerful alternative to the outdated Nintendo and Sega cartridge-based systems. Sony worked closely with retailers before the launch to find out how it could help them sell the PlayStation. To jump-start demand, Sony set up in-store displays to allow potential consumers to try the equipment. Just before the launch, Sony had lined up an impressive 12,000 retail outlets in the United States.[32]

Sony targeted its advertising for PlayStation at males in the 18- to 35-year age range. The targeting was evident in the content of many of the games. One of the big hits for PlayStation was Tomb Raider, whose central character, Lara Croft, combined sex appeal with savviness and helped to recruit an older generation to PlayStation.[33] PlayStation was initially priced at $299, and games retailed for as much as $60. Sony's Tokyo-based executives had reportedly been insisting on a $350–$400 price for PlayStation, but Olafsson pushed hard for the lower price. Because of the fallout from this internal battle, in January 1996, Olafsson resigned from Sony. By then, however, Sony was following Olafsson's script.[34]

Sony's prelaunch work was rewarded with strong early sales. By January 1996, more than 800,000 PlayStation systems had been sold in the United States, plus another 4 million games. In May 1996, with 1.2 million PlayStations shipped, Sony reduced the price of PlayStation to $199. Sega responded with a similar price cut for its Saturn. The prices on some of Sony's initial games were also reduced to $29.99. The weekend after the price cuts, retailers reported that PlayStation sales were up by between 350% and 1,000% over the prior week.[35] The sales surge continued through 1996. By the end of the year, sales of PlayStation and associated software amounted to $1.3 billion, out of a total for U.S. sales at $2.2 billion for all video game hardware and software. In March 1997, Sony cut the price of PlayStation again, this time to $149. It also reduced its suggested retail price for games by $10 to $49.99. By this point, Sony had sold 3.4 million units of PlayStation in the United States, compared to Saturn's 1.6 million units.[36] Worldwide, PlayStation had outsold Saturn by 13 million to 7.8 million units, and Saturn sales were slowing.[37] The momentum was clearly running in Sony's favor, but the company now had a new challenge to deal with: Nintendo's latest generation game machine, the N64.

Nintendo Strikes Back

In July 1996, Nintendo launched Nintendo 64 (N64) in the Japanese market. This release was followed by a late-fall introduction in the United States. N64 is a 64-bit machine developed in conjunction with Silicon Graphics. Originally targeted for introduction a year earlier, N64 had been under development

since 1993. The machine used a plug-in cartridge format rather than a CD-ROM drive. According to Nintendo, cartridges allow for faster access time and are far more durable than CD-ROMs (an important consideration with children).[38]

The most-striking feature of the N64 machine, however, was its 3D graphics capability. N64 provides fully rounded figures that can turn on their heels and rotate through 180 degrees. Advanced ray tracing techniques, borrowed from military simulators and engineering workstations, added to the sense of realism by providing proper highlighting, reflections, and shadows.

N64 was targeted at children and young teenagers. It was priced at $200 and launched with just 4 games. Despite the lack of games, initial sales were very strong. Indeed, 1997 turned out to be a banner year for both Sony and Nintendo. The overall U.S. market was strong, with sales of hardware and software combined reaching a record $5.5 billion. Estimates suggest that PlayStation accounted for 49% of machines and games by value. N64 captured a 41% share, leaving Sega trailing badly with less than 10% of the market. During the year, the average price for game machines had fallen to $150. By year-end there were 300 titles available for PlayStation, compared to 40 for N64. Games for PlayStation retailed for $40, on average, compared to over $60 for N64.[39]

By late-1998, PlayStation was widening its lead over N64. In the crucial North American market, PlayStation was reported to be outselling N64 by a 2:1 margin, although Nintendo retained a lead in the under-twelve category. At this point, there were 115 games available for N64 versus 431 for PlayStation.[40] Worldwide, Sony had now sold close to 55 million PlayStations. The success of PlayStation had a major impact on Sony's bottom line. In fiscal 1998, PlayStation business generated revenues of $5.5 billion for Sony, 10% of its worldwide revenues, but accounted for $886 million, or 22.5%, of the company's operating income.[41]

The 128-Bit ERA

When Nintendo launched its 64-bit machine in 1996, Sony and Sega didn't follow, preferring instead to focus on the development of even more powerful 128-bit machines.

Sega was the first to market a 128-bit video game console, which it launched in Japan in late-1998 and in the United States in late-1999. The Dreamcast came equipped with a 56-kilobit modem to allow for online gaming over the Internet. By late-2000, Sega had sold around 6 million Dreamcasts worldwide, accounting for about 15% of console sales since its launch. Sega nurtured Dreamcast sales by courting outside software developers who helped develop new games, including Crazy Taxi, Resident Evil, and Quake III Arena. The company had a goal of shipping 10 million units by March 2001, a goal it never reached.[42]

Despite its position as first mover with a 128-bit machine, and despite solid technical reviews, by late-2000 the company was struggling. Sega was handicapped first by product shortages due to constraints on the supply of component parts and then by a lack of demand as consumers waited to see whether Sony's 128 bit offering, the much anticipated PlayStation 2 (PS2), would be a more attractive machine. In September 2000, Sega responded to the impending U.S. launch of Sony's PS2 by cutting the price for its console from $199 to $149. Then in late-October, Sega announced that, due to this price cut, it would probably lose over $200 million for the fiscal year ending March 2001.[43]

Sony's PlayStation 2

PlayStation 2 was launched in Japan in mid-2000 and in the United States at the end of October 2000. Initially priced at $299, PlayStation 2 is a powerful machine. At its core was a 300-megahertz graphics processing chip that was jointly developed with Toshiba and consumed about $1.3 billion in R&D. Referred to as the Emotion Engine processor, the chip allows the machine to display stunning graphic images previously found only on supercomputers. The chip made the PlayStation 2 the most powerful video game machine yet.

The machine was set up to play different CD and DVD formats, as well as proprietary game titles. As is true with the original PlayStation, PlayStation 2 could play audio CDs. The system was also compatible with the original PlayStation: any PlayStation title could be played on the PlayStation 2. To help justify the initial price tag, the unit doubled as a DVD player with picture quality as good as current players. The PlayStation 2 did not come equipped with a modem, but it did have networking capabilities and a modem could be attached using one of two USB ports.[44]

Nintendo GameCube

Nintendo had garnered a solid position in the industry with its N64 machine by focusing on its core demographic, 7- to 12-year-olds. In 1999, Nintendo took 33% of the hardware market and 28% of the game market. Nintendo's next generation video game machine, GameCube, packed a modem and a powerful 400-megahertz, 128-bit processor made by IBM into a compact cube. GameCube marked a shift away from Nintendo's traditional approach of using proprietary cartridges to hold game software. Instead, software for the new player came on 8-cm compact disks, which are smaller than music compact disks. The disks held 1.5 gigabytes of data each, far greater storage capacity than the old game cartridges. Players could control GameCube using wireless controllers.[45]

Nintendo tried to make the GameCube easy for developers to work with rather than focusing on raw peak performance. While developers no doubt appreciated this, by the time GameCube hits store shelves in late-2001, PlayStation 2 had been on the market for eighteen months and boasted a solid library of games. Despite its strong brand and instantly recognized intellectual property which included Donkey Kong, Super Mario Brothers, and the Pokemon characters, Nintendo was playing catch up to Sony. Moreover, another new entrant into the industry launched its 128-bit offering at around the same time; Microsoft.

Microsoft's Xbox

Microsoft was first rumored to be developing a video game console in late-1999. In March 2000, Bill Gates made it official when he announced that Microsoft would enter the home video game market in fall 2001 with a console code named Xbox. In terms of sheer computing power, the 128-bit Xbox had the edge over competitors. Xbox had a 733-megahertz Pentium III processor, a high-powered graphics chip from NVIDIA Corp, a built-in broadband cable modem to allow for online game playing and high-speed Internet browsing, 64 megabytes of memory, CD and DVD drives, and an internal hard disk drive. The operating system was a stripped-down version of its popular Windows system optimized for graphics-processing capabilities. Microsoft claimed that because the Xbox was based on familiar PC technology, it would be much easier for software developers to write games for, and it would be relatively easy to convert games from the PC to run on the Xbox.[46]

Although Microsoft was a new entrant to the video game industry, it was no stranger to games. Microsoft had long participated in the PC gaming industry and was one of the largest publishers of PC games, with hits such as "Microsoft Flight Simulator" and "Age of Empires I" and "II" to its credits. Sales of Microsoft's PC games have increased 5% annually between 1998 and 2001, and the company controlled about 10% of the PC game market in 2001. Microsoft had also offered online gaming for some time, including its popular MSN Gaming Zone site. Started in 1996, by 2001 the Website had become the largest online PC gaming hub on the Internet with nearly 12 million subscribers pay $9.95 a month to play premium games such as Asheron's Call or Fighter Ace. Nor is Microsoft new to hardware; its joysticks and game pads outsell all other brands and it has an important mouse business.

To build the Xbox, Microsoft chose Flextronics, a contract manufacturer that already made computer mice for Microsoft. Realizing that it would probably have to cut Xbox prices over time, Microsoft guaranteed Flextronics a profit margin, effectively agreeing to subsidize Flextronics if selling prices fell below a specified amount. By 2003, Microsoft was thought to be losing $100 on every Xbox sold. To make that back and turn a profit, Microsoft reportedly had to sell between 6 and 9 video games per Xbox.[47]

Analysts speculated that Microsoft's entry into the home video game market was a response to a potential threat from Sony. Microsoft was worried that Internet-ready consoles like PlayStation 2 might take over many Web-browsing functions from the personal computer. Some in the company described Internet-enabled video game terminals as Trojan horses in the living room. In Microsoft's calculation, it made sense to get in the market to try and keep Sony and others in check. With annual revenues in excess of $20 billion worldwide, the home video game market is huge and an important source of potential growth for Microsoft. Still, by moving away from its core market, Microsoft was taking a big risk, particularly given the scale of investments required to develop the Xbox, reported to run as high as $1.5 billion.

Mortal Combat: Microsoft versus Sony

The launch of Xbox and Game Cube helped propel sales of video game hardware and software to a record $9.4 billion in 2001, up from $6.58 billion in 2000. Although both Xbox and Nintendo initially racked up strong sales, the momentum started to slow significantly in 2002. Microsoft in particular, found it very difficult to penetrate the Japanese market. By September 2002, Sony had sold 11.2 million units of PS2 in the United States, versus 2.2 million units of Xbox, and 2.7 million units of Nintendo's game Cube. Unable to hold onto market share in the wake of the new competition, Sega withdrew from the console market, announcing that henceforth, it would focus just on developing games for other platforms.

In June 2002, Sony responded to the new entry by cutting the price for PS2 from $299 to $199. Microsoft quickly followed, cutting the price for Xbox from $299 to $199, while Nintendo cut its price from $299 to $149.[48] A year later, Sony cut prices again, this time to $179 a console. Again, Microsoft followed with a similar price cut, and in March 2004 it took the lead, cutting Xbox prices to $149. Sony followed suit two months later.[49]

Microsoft's strategy, however, involved far more than just cutting prices. In November 2002, Microsoft announced that it would introduce a new service for gamers, Xbox Live. For $50 a year, Xbox Live subscribers with broadband connections would be able to play online enabled versions of Xbox games with other online subscribers. To support Xbox Live, Microsoft invested some $500 million in its own data centers to host online game playing.

Online game playing was clearly a strategic priority from the outset. Unlike the PS2 and Game Cube, Xbox came with a built in broadband capability. The decision to make the Xbox broadband capable was made back in 1999, when less than 5% of U.S. homes were linked to the Internet with a broadband connection. Explaining the decision to build broadband capabilities into the Xbox at a time when rivals lacked them, the head of Xbox, Jay Allard, noted that "my attitude has always been to bet on the future, not against it."[50] While Sony's PS2 can be hooked up to the Internet via a broadband connection, doing so requires purchase of a special network adapter for $40.

By mid-2003 Xbox Live had some 500,000 subscribers, versus 80,000 who had registered to play PlayStation 2 games online. By this point, there were 28 online games for Xbox, and 18 for PS2. By January 2004, the comparative figures stood at 50 for Microsoft and 32 for Sony. By mid-2004, Xbox live reportedly had over one million subscribers, with Sony claiming a similar number of online players.[51] In May 2004, Microsoft struck a deal with Electronic Arts, the world's largest video game publisher, to bring EA games, including its best selling Madden Football, to the Xbox live platform. Until this point, EA had only produced live games for Sony's platform.

In spite of all these strategic moves, by late-2004 Xbox was still a distant second of PS2 in the video game market having sold 14 million consoles against Sony's 70 million (Nintendo had sold 13 million Game Cube consoles by this point). While Sony was making good money from the business, Microsoft was registering significant losses. In fiscal 2004, Microsoft's home & entertainment division, of which Xbox is the major component registered $2.45 billion in revenues, but lost $1.135 billion. By way of contrast, Sony's game division had $7.5 billion of sales in fiscal 2004 and generated operating profits of $640 million.

Microsoft, however, indicated that it was in the business for the long term. In late-2004, the company got a boost from the release of "Halo 2," the sequel to Halo, one of its best selling games. As first day sales for Halo 2 were totaled up, executives at Sony had to be worried. Microsoft announced that Halo 2 had sales of $125 million in its first 24-hours on the market in the United States and Canada, an industry record. These figures represented sales of 2.38 million units, and put Halo 2 firmly on track to be one of the biggest video games ever with a shot at surpassing Nintendo's "Super Mario 64," which had sold $308 million in the U.S. since its September 1996 debut. Moreover, the company was rumored to be ahead of Sony by as much as a year to bring the next generation video game console to market. In late-2004, reports suggest that Xbox 2 would be on the market in time for the 2005 Christmas season, probably a full year ahead of Sony's PlayStation 3. Sony was rumored to be running into technical problems as it tries to develop PlayStation 3.[52]

The Next Generation

As the battle between PS2 and Xbox drew to a close, it was clear that clear that Sony was the big winner. From 2001 through the Fall of 2006, when Play Station 3 (PS3) hit the market, Sony had sold around 110 million PS2 consoles, versus 25 million for Microsoft's Xbox and 21 million for Nintendo's Game Cube.[53] Sony's advantage is installed base translated into a huge lead in number of games sold—some 1.08 billion for PS2 by mid-2006, versus 200 million for the Xbox.[54] With the console companies reportedly making an average royalty on third party software of $8 per game sold, the financial implications of Sony's lead with PS2 are obvious.[55] Indeed, in 2005, Sony's games division contributed to 6.24% of the company's total revenue, but 38% of operating profit. In contrast, Microsoft's home and entertainment division lost $4 billion between the launch of Xbox and mid-2006.

However, by 2006 this was all history. In November 2005, Microsoft introduced its next generation machine, Xbox 360, beating Sony and Nintendo to the market by a solid year. The Xbox 360 represented a big technological advance over the original Xbox. To deliver improved picture quality, the Xbox 360 could execute 500 million polygons/sec—a four-fold increase over the Xbox. The main microprocessor was 13 times faster than the chip in the Xbox. Xbox 360 had 512 megabytes of memory, an 8-fold increase, and a 20 gigabyte hard drive, 2.5 times bigger than that found on the Xbox. Xbox 360 is of course, enabled for a broadband connection to the Internet.

Flextronics and Wistron two contract manufacturers (a third started production after launch) made the machine. Priced at $299, Xbox 360 was sold at a loss. The cost for making Xbox 360 was estimated to be as high as $500 at launch, falling to $350 by late-2006. Microsoft's goal was to ultimately break even on sales of the hardware as manufacturing efficiencies drove down unit costs.

To seed the market with games, Microsoft took a number of steps. Taking a page out of its Windows business, Microsoft provided game developers with tools designed to automate many of the key software programming tasks and reduce development time and costs. The company had also expanded its own in-house game studios, in part by purchasing several independent game developers including Bungie Studios, makers of Halo. This strategy enabled

Microsoft to offer exclusive content for the Xbox 360, something that third party developers were reluctant to do.

With the costs of game development increasing to between $10–15 million for more complex games, and development time stretching out to between 24 and 36 months, Microsoft also had to provide and inducement to get third party developers onboard. Although details of royalty terms are kept private, it is believed that Microsoft offered very low royalty rates, and perhaps even zero royalties, for a specified period of times to game developers who committed early to Xbox 360. One of those to commit early was Electronic Arts, the leading independent game development company, which reportedly budgeted as much as $200 million to develop some 25 versions of its best selling games, such as its sports games, for Xbox 360. Microsoft itself budgeted a similar amount to develop its own games.[56]

In the event, some 18 games were available for the November 2005 launch of Xbox 360, and by the end of 2006, this figure had increased to around 160. "Halo 3," which was expected to be one of the biggest games for Xbox 360, was released in September 2007. Exclusive to the Xbox 360, Halo 3 racked in first day sales of $170 million, which was an industry record. "Grand Theft Auto 4," the most popular franchise on PS2, was also launched simultaneously for both Xbox 360 and PS3 in 2007—a major coup for Microsoft.

The initial launch of Xbox 360 was marred by shortages of key components, which limited the number of machines that Microsoft could bring to market. Had Sony been on time with its launch of PS3, this could have been a serious error, but Sony delayed its launch of PS3, first until Spring of 2006, and then to November 2006. By the time Sony launched PS3 in November 2006, some 6 million Xbox 360 consoles had been sold, and Microsoft was predicting sales of 10 million by the end of 2006.

As with Xbox, Microsoft is pushing Xbox Live with Xbox 360. The company invested as much as $1 billion in Live from its inception. By late-2006, Microsoft was claiming that some 60% of Xbox 360 customers had also signed on for Xbox Live and that the service 4 million subscribers. By early-2008 there were over 10 million subscribers. Xbox Live allows games to play against each other online, and to download digital content from Xbox Live

Marketplace. Looking forward, there is little doubt that Microsoft sees Xbox Live as a critical element of its strategy, enabling Xbox owners to download any digital content—games, film, music—onto their consoles, which could become the hub of a home digital entertainment system.

The business model for Xbox 360 depends upon the number of games sold per console, the percentage of console owners who sign up for Xbox Live, sales of hardware accessories (e.g., controllers, an HD-DVD drive, wireless networking adapter), and the console itself achieving break even production costs. Reports suggest that Microsoft will breakeven if each console owners buys 6–7 games, 2–3 accessories, and if some 10 million sign on to Xbox Live (Microsoft splits Xbox Live revenues with game developers). By the end of 2006, it was estimated that some 33 million games had been sold for Xbox 360.[57]

Sony finally introduced PS3 on November 11 in Japan, and on November 17 in the United States. The delay in the launch of PS3 was due to Sony; decision to bundle a Blu-ray drive with PS3, and problems developing the "cell" processor that sits at the core of the PS3. Blu-ray is Sony's proprietary high definition DVD format. The company is currently locked in a format war with Toshiba, which is pushing its rival HD-DVD format (which can be purchased as an accessory for the Xbox 360). Sony has argued that the combination of its cell processor and Blu-ray DVD drive will give PS3 a substantial performance edge over Xbox 360. While this is true in a technical sense (the Blu-ray discs have 5 times the storage capacity of the DVD discs for Xbox 360), few reviewers have noticed much in the way of difference from a game playing perspective—perhaps because few games were initially available that showed the true power of the PS3.

What is certain is that incorporating Blu-ray drives in the PS3 has significantly raised the costs of the PS3. Sony is selling its stand alone Blu-ray drives for $999, which suggests that the PS3, initially priced at between $500 and $600 depending upon configuration, is in a sense a subsidized Blu-ray player. Shortages of blue diodes, a critical component in high definition DVD drives, also limited supply of the PS3 after its launch. Only 93,000 PS3 players were available for the Japanese launch. At launch, there were some 20 games available for the PS3. Sony also announced its own Live offering to compete with Xbox Live and stated that it would be free to PS3 users.

Nintendo also joined the fray again. In November 2006, it launched its own next generation offering, Wii. When developing the Wii, Nintendo made a number of interesting strategic decisions. First, they decided not to compete with Microsoft and Sony on graphics processing power. Instead of developing a high powered machine crammed full of expensive custom built components, they used off-the-shelf components to assemble a much cheaper machine that could be sold at a much lower price point (the initial price was $250). While this machine did not offer the graphics processing capabilities of Xbox 360 or PS3, the games where cheaper to develop, around $5 million each as opposed to as much as $20 million for the PS3. Second, Nintendo decided to target a new demographic, indifferent people who had no interest in video games, as opposed to the stereotypical game player. Nintendo already had some evidence that this market could be tapped and that it was extremely lucrative. In 2004, Nintendo had introduced a game for its handheld player, the DS, that was aimed not at its core 7- to 12-year old demographic, but at much wider market. The game, "Brain Age," based on a brain training regime developed by a Japanese neuroscientist, was a huge hit in Japan, with sales of more than 12 million units. It made the DS a hit in such unlikely places as nursing homes. Third, rather than processing power, Nintendo decided to focus on developing a motion sensitive wireless controller that could detect arm and hand motions and transfer them to the screen. This enabled the development of interactive games, with players physically controlling the action on screen by moving their arms, whether by swinging an imaginary bat, driving a go kart, or slashing a sword through the air.[58]

By early-2007, it was clear that the Wii was turning into a surprise hit. The combination of low price, innovative design, and a portfolio of recognizable games based on Nintendo's long established franchises, such as Mario Brothers and Pokémon, helped to drive sales forward. Moreover, as planned, the Wii seemed to have appeal to a broad range of age groups and to both genders. Soon articles started to appear explaining how retirement homes were buying the Wii so that residents could play virtual baseball with their visiting grandchildren and sales stated to accelerate.

The Industry in 2010

As 2010 drew to a close, it was clear that the Wii had been the major success story of this generation of gaming consoles. Since their respective launches, the Wii had sold 74.5 million units, compared to 43.8 million for Xbox 360 and 38.7 million of PlayStation 3. Nintendo also had a strong lead in the popular handheld market, with 135 million units sold worldwide, compared to 60.5 million for the PSP, Sony's hand held game player (Microsoft did not have a hand held player).[59] On the other hand, a key to the success of a console is the number of games sold per box, and on this measure Xbox 360 had the best performance. After each console had been on the market for 29 months, Xbox had sold 7.5 games per box, compared to 6.5 for PlayStation and 6.2 for Nintendo. By October 2010, the ratio had risen to around 9.0 games per box for Xbox 360 (these figures are for the U.S. only).[60]

Total industry sales in the United States peaked in 2008 at $22.11 billion, before declining to $20.2 billion as the recession cut into demand (worldwide sales were $54 billion in 2008). Despite the recession, all three players in the market were profitable on an operating basis in 2009 and 2010. Worldwide sales are expected to exceed $60 billion in 2012. Both Microsoft and Sony had shot themselves in the foot with quality problems and component shortages early in the product cycle (Microsoft had to take a $1.05 billion write off in 2007 for replacing poor quality consoles), but were now performing well. Microsoft is predicting that this generation of console will last about 10 years, making it the longest generation ever.

Looking forward, and number of factors may change the industry. In November 2010 Microsoft released its response to Nintendo's motion sensor with a device known as Kinect. Kinect may fundamentally alter the way users interact with digital content. Kinect combines technologies such as body movement detection, facial recognition, and voice recognition, to let gamers use natural motions and voice to control games. The input device is a camera and depth sensor mounted on top of the TV. In essence, Kinect is a potentially revolutionary step forward in human machine interface design that could have implication that go way beyond video games. To start, Microsoft will use Kinect to go after the casual gamers with which Nintendo's Wii has been so successful.

As always with a new game technology, the success of Kinect will hinge crucially upon the quality of the games available. While it will take some time until games utilize the full power of Kinect, the early sales figures bode well for the device. Between launch and the start of March, 2011, Microsoft sold over 10 million Kinect devices, making it the fastest selling consumer electronics device of all time.[61]

Online gaming is also continuing to gain traction. Xbox Live has turned into a big hit for Microsoft and now has some 25 million subscribers who use it for everything from playing multiplayer games to streaming movies from Netflix and browsing Facebook. It is estimated that about 50% of Xbox Live subscribers are paying Gold Member subscribers. In fiscal 2009 (which ended June 30, 2010) Microsoft generated over $1.2 billion in revenues of Xbox Live subscriptions and services. This seems to be a growth engine going forward. Microsoft has announced the Xbox Live will be fully integrated into Windows 8, the next version of its Windows operating system now under development.

Interestingly enough, the largest multiplayer online game, however, has no connection with any of the console platforms. The "World of Warcraft," the massive multiplayer online game with 12 million paying subscribers and annual revenues in excess of $1.2 billion, making it the best-selling game of all time.

Endnotes

1   A good account of the early history of Bushnell and Atari can be found in S. Cohen, *Zap! The Rise and Fall of Atari* (New York: McGraw-Hill, 1984).
2   R. Isaacs, "Video Games Race to Catch a Changing Market," *Business Week,* December 26, 1977, 44B.
3   P. Pagnano, "Atari's Game Plan to Overwhelm Its Competitors," *Business Week,* May 8, 1978, 50F.
4   R. Isaacs, "Video Games Race to Catch a Changing Market," *Business Week,* December 26, 1977, 44B.
5   P. Pagnano, "Atari's Game Plan to Overwhelm Its Competitors," *Business Week,* May 8, 1978; D. Sheff, *Game Over* (New York: Random House, 1993).
6   S. Cohen, *Zap! The Rise and Fall of Atari* (New York: McGraw-Hill, 1984).
7   L. Kehoe, "Atari Seeks Way out of Video Game Woes," *Financial Times,* December 14, 1983, 23.
8   M. Schrage, "The High Tech Dinosaurs: Video Games, Once Ascendant, Are Making Way," *Washington Post,* July 31, 1983, F1.
9   D. Sheff, *Game Over* (New York: Random House, 1993).
10 Ibid.
11 Ibid.
12 D. Golden, "In Search of Princess Toadstool," *Boston Globe,* November 20, 1988, 18.
13 N. Gross and G. Lewis, "Here Come the Super Mario Bros.," *Business Week,* November 9, 1987, 138.
14 D. Sheff, *Game Over* (New York: Random House, 1993).
15 D. Golden, "In Search of Princess Toadstool," *Boston Globe,* November 20, 1988, 18.
16 Staff Reporter, "Marketer of the Year," *Adweek,* November 27, 1989, 15.
17 C. Lazzareschi, "No Mere Child's Play," *Los Angeles Times,* December 16, 1988, 1.
18 For a good summary of the early history of Sega, see J. Battle and B. Johnstone, "The Next Level: Sega's Plans for World Domination," *Wired,* Release 1.06, December 1993.
19 D. Sheff, *Game Over* (New York: Random House, 1993).
20 J. Battle and B. Johnstone, "The Next Level: Sega's Plans for World Domination," *Wired,* Release 1.06, December 1993.
21 For background details, see J. Flower, "3DO: Hip or Hype?" *Wired,* Release 1.02, May/June 1993.
22 R. Brandt, "3DO's New Game Player: Awesome or Another Betamax?" *Business Week,* January 11, 1993, 38.
23 J. Flower, "3DO: Hip or Hype?" *Wired,* Release 1.02, May/June 1993.
24 S. Jacobs, "Third Time's a Charm (They Hope)," *Wired,* Release 2.01, January 1994.
25 A. Dunkin, "Video Games: The Next Generation," *Business Week,* January 31, 1994, 80.
26 J. Greenstein, "No Clear Winners, Though Some Losers; The Video Game Industry in 1995," *Business Week,* December 22, 1995, 42.
27 Staff Reporter, "3DO Says 'I Do' on Major Shift of Its Game Strategy," *Los Angeles Times,* September 17, 1996, 2.
28 S. Taves, "Meet Your New Playmate," *Wired,* Release 3.09, September 1995.
29 I. Kunni, "The Games Sony Plays," *Business Week,* June 15, 1998, 128.
30 C. Platt, "WordNerd," *Wired,* Release 3.10, October 1995.
31 I. Kunni, "The Games Sony Plays," *Business Week,* June 15, 1998, 128.
32 J.A. Trachtenberg, "Race Quits Sony Just Before U.S. Rollout of Its PlayStation Video-Game System," *Wall Street Journal,* August 8, 1995, B3.
33 S. Beenstock, "Market Raider: How Sony Won the Console Game," *Marketing,* September 10, 1998, 26.
34 J.A. Trachtenberg, "Olafsson Calls It Quits as Chairman of Sony's Technology Strategy Group," *Wall Street Journal,* January 23, 1996, B6.
35 J. Greenstein, "Price Cuts Boost Saturn, Playstation Hardware Sales," *Video Business,* May 31, 1996, 1.

36 J. Greenstein, "Sony Cuts Prices of Playstation Hardware," *Video Business*, March 10, 1997, 1.

37 D. Hamilton, "Sega Suddenly Finds Itself Embattled," *Wall Street Journal*, March 31, 1997, A10.

38 Staff Reporter, "Nintendo Wakes Up," *The Economist*, August 3, 1996, 55–56.

39 D. Takahashi, "Game Plan: Video Game Makers See Soaring Sales Now—And Lots of Trouble Ahead," *Wall Street Journal*, June 15, 1998, R10.

40 D. Takahashi, "Sony and Nintendo Battle for Kids Under 13," *Wall Street Journal*, September 24, 1998, B4.

41 I. Kunni, "The Games Sony Plays," *Business Week*, June 15, 1998, 128.

42 R.A. Guth, "Sega Cites Dreamcast Price Cuts for Loss Amid Crucial Time for Survival of Firm," *Wall Street Journal*, October 30, 2000, A22.

43 Ibid.

44 T. Oxford and S. Steinberg, "Ultimate Game Machine Sony's PlayStation 2 Is Due on Shelves Oct. 26. It Brims with Potential—But at This Point Sega's Dreamcast Appears a Tough Competitor," *Atlanta Journal/Atlanta Constitution*, October 1, 2000, P1.

45 R.A. Guth, "New Players from Nintendo Will Link to Web," *Wall Street Journal*, August 25, 2000, B1.

46 D. Takahashi, "Microsoft's X-Box Impresses Game Developers," *Wall Street Journal*, March 13, 2000, B12.

47 K. Powers, "Showdown," *Forbes*, August 11, 2003, 86–87.

48 *The Economist*, "Console Wars," *The Economist*, June 22, 2002, 71.

49 R.A. Guth, "Game Gambit: Microsoft to Cut Xbox Price," *Wall Street Journal*, March 19, 2004, B1.

50 K. Powers, "Showdown," *Forbes*, August 11, 2003, 86–87.

51 E. Taub, "No Longer a Solitary Pursuit: Video Games Move Online," *New York Times*, July 5, 2004, C4.

52 J. Greene and C. Edwards, "Microsoft Plays Video Leapfrog," *Business Week*, May 10, 2004, 44–45.

53 "Playing a Long Game," *The Economist*, November 18, 2006, 63–65.

54 B. Thill, "Micrsoft: Gat Game? Update on Vista, Xbox and the Tender," *Citigroup Capital Markets*, August 30, 2006.

55 Ibid.

56 D. Takahashi, "The Xbox 360 Uncloaked," *Spider Works*, 2006.

57 B. Thill, "Micrsoft: Gat Game? Update on Vista, Xbox and the Tender," *Citigroup Capital Markets*, August 30, 2006.

58 J.M. O'Brian and C. Tkaczyk, "Wii Will Rock You," *Fortune*, June 11, 2007, 82–92.

59 D. Takahashi, "The Video Game Console War Could End in a Three-Way Tie," June 9, 2010, Venturebeat.com.

60 M. Matthews, "Console Tie Rations Reveal Market Dynamics," April 22, 2009, http://www.gamasutra.com

61 S. Kessler, "Microsoft Kinect Sales Top 10 Million," *Mashable*, March 9, 2011.

TomTom: New Competition Everywhere!

Alan N. Hoffman

Bentley University and Rotterdam School of Management, Erasmus University

Synopsis

TomTom, an Amsterdam-based company that provides navigation services and devices, leads the navigation systems market in Europe and is second in the US. Its most popular products include TomTom Go and TomTom One for cars, TomTom Rider for bikes, TomTom Navigator (digital maps), and TomTom for iPhone—its most recent release.

The company attributes its market leadership to its technology, large customer base, distribution power, and prominent brand image. But as the US and European personal navigation device market gets saturated, TomTom's sales growth rate declines. The company also faces increasing competition from other platforms using GPS technology like cell phones and smart phones with a built-in navigation function. Legal and environmental restrictions on the digital navigation industry make TomTom's future even more uncertain. Whether TomTom can keep expanding may well depend on whether it can become the prime mover in creating digital maps and navigational services for developing countries.

TomTom: New Competition Everywhere!

TomTom is one of the largest producers of satellite navigation systems in the world, comprised of both stand alone devices and applications. It leads the navigation systems market in Europe while stands second in the United States. TomTom attributes its position as a market leader to the following factors: the size of its customer and technology base; its distribution power; and its prominent brand image and recognition.[19]

With the acquisition of Tele Atlas, TomTom has become vertically integrated and also controls the map creation process now. This has helped TomTom establish itself as an integrated content, service and technology business. The company is Dutch by origin and has its headquarters based in Amsterdam, Netherlands. In terms of geography, the company's operations span from Europe to Asia Pacific, covering North America, Middle East and Africa.[19]

TomTom is supported by a workforce of 3,300 employees from 40 countries. The diverse workforce enables the company to compete in international markets.[4] The company's revenues have grown from €8 million in 2002 to €1.674 billion in 2008. However, more recently, because of the Tele Atlas acquisition and the current economic downturn the company has become a cause of concern for investors. On 22nd July 2009, TomTom reported a fall of 61% in its net income at the end of 2nd quarter 2009.[3]

TomTom is in the business of navigation based information services and devices. The company has been investing structurally and strategically in Research and Development to bring new and better products and services to its customers. The company's belief in radical innovation has helped it remain at the cutting edge of innovation within the navigation industry.

The vision of TomTom is to improve people's lives by transforming navigation from a 'don't-get-lost solution' into a true travel companion that gets people from one place to another safer, faster, cheaper and better informed. This vision has helped the company to be a market leader in every market place in the satellite navigation information services market.[6]

The author would like to thank Will Hoffman, Mansi Asthana, Aakashi Ganveer, Hing Lin, Che Yii for their research. Please address all correspondence to Professor Alan N. Hoffman, Bentley University, 175 Forest Street, Waltham, MA 02452; ahoffman@bentley.edu. Printed by permission of Dr. Alan N. Hoffman.

The objectives of the company focus around radical advances in three key areas:

Better Maps: This objective is achieved by maintaining TomTom's high quality map data base that is continuously kept up to date by a large community of active users who provide corrections, verifications and updates to TomTom. This is supplemented by inputs from TomTom's extensive fleet of surveying vehicles.[6]

Better Routing: TomTom has the world's largest historical speed profile data base IQ Routes™ facilitated by TomTom HOME, the company's user portal.[6]

Better Traffic Information: TomTom possesses unique real time traffic information service TomTom HD traffic™ which provides users with high quality, real time traffic updates.[6] These three objectives form the base of satellite navigation, working in conjunction to help TomTom achieve its mission.

TomTom's Products

TomTom offers a wide variety of products ranging from portable navigation devices to software navigation applications and digital maps. The unique features in each of these products make them truly "the smart choice in personal navigation."[19] Some of these products are described below:

TomTom Go and TomTom One

These devices come with a LCD screen that makes it easy to use with fingertips while driving. They provide 1,000 Points of Interests (POI) that help in locating petrol stations, restaurants and places of importance. A number of other POIs can also be downloaded. Precise, up to minute traffic information, jam alerts and road condition alerts are provided by both these devices.[3]

TomTom Rider

These are portable models especially for bikers. The equipment consists of an integrated GPS receiver that can be mounted on any bike and a wireless headset inside the helmet. Similar to the car Portable Navigation Devices (PNDs), the TomTom Rider models have a number of POI applications. The interfaces used in TomTom Rider are user friendly and come in a variety of languages.[3]

TomTom Navigator and TomTom Mobile

These applications provide navigation software along with digital maps. Both of these applications are compatible with most mobiles and PDAs, provided by companies like Sony, Nokia, Acer, Dell and HP. These applications come with TomTom HOME which can be used to upgrade to the most recent digital maps and application versions.[3]

TomTom for iPhone

On August 17, 2009, TomTom released TomTom for the iPhone. "With TomTom for iPhone, millions of iPhone users can now benefit from the same easy-to-use and intuitive interface, turn-by-turn spoken navigation and unique routing technology that our 30 million portable navigation device users rely on every day," said Corinne Vigreux, Managing Director of TomTom. "As the world's leading provider of navigation solutions and digital maps, TomTom is the most natural fit for an advanced navigation application on the iPhone."[6]

The TomTom app for iPhone 3G and 3GS users includes a map of the US and Canada from Tele Atlas and is available for $99.99 USD.

The TomTom app for iPhone includes the exclusive IQ Routes™ technology. Instead of using travel time assumptions, IQ Routes bases its routes on the actual experience of millions of TomTom drivers to calculate the fastest route and generate the most accurate arrival times in the industry. TomTom IQ Routes empowers drivers to reach their destination faster up to 35% of the time.

Company Background

Company History

TomTom was founded as 'Palmtop' in 1991 by Peter-Frans Pauwels and Pieter Geelen, two graduates from Amsterdam University, Netherlands. Palmtop started out as a software development company and was involved in producing software for hand held computers, one of the most popular devices of the 90s. In the following few years the company diversified into producing commercial applications including software for personal finance, games, a dictionary and maps. In the year 1996, Corinne Vigreux joined Palmtop as the third partner. In the same year, the company announced the launch of Enroute and RouteFinder, the first navigation software titles. As more and more people using PCs adopted Microsoft's operating system, the company developed applications which were compatible with it. This helped the company increase its market share. The year 2001 marks the turning point in the history of TomTom. It was in this year that Harold Goddijn, the former Chief Executive of Psion joined the company as the fourth partner. Not only did Palmtop get renamed to TomTom, but it also entered the satellite navigation market. TomTom launched TomTom Navigator, the first mobile car satnav system. Since then, as can be seen in Exhibit 1, the company has celebrated the successful launch of at least a product each year.[3]

In 2002, the company generated revenue of €8 million by selling the first GPS-linked car navigator, the TomTom Navigator to PDAs. The upgraded version, Navigator 2 was released in early 2003. Meanwhile, the company made efforts to gain technical and marketing personnel. TomTom took strategic steps to grow its sales. The former CTO of Psion, Mark Gretton, led the hardware team while Alexander Ribbink, a former top marketing official looked after sales of new products introduced by the company.

TomTom Go, an all in one car navigation system, was the next major launch of the company. With its useful and easy-to-use features TomTom Go was included in the list of successful products of 2004. In the same year, the company launched TomTom Mobile, a navigation system which sat on top of smartphones.[3]

TomTom completed its IPO on the Amsterdam Stock Exchange in May 2005. It raised €469 million ($587 million) from this offer. The net worth of the company was nearly €2 billion after the IPO. A majority of the shares were with the four partners.[5] From the years 2006 to 2008, TomTom strengthened itself by making three key strategic acquisitions. Datafactory AG was acquired to power TomTom WORK through WEBfleet technology, while Applied Generics gave its technology for Mobility Solutions Services. However, the most prominent of these three was the acquisition of Tele Atlas.[5]

In July of 2007, TomTom bid for Tele Atlas, a company specializing in digital maps. The original bid price of €2 billion was countered by a €2.3 billion offer from Garmin, TomTom's biggest rival. With TomTom raising the bid price to €2.9 billion, the two companies had initiated a bidding war for Tele Atlas. Although there was speculation that Garmin would further increase its bid price, in the end they decided not to pursue Tele Atlas any further. Rather, Garmin struck a content agreement with Navteq. Finally, TomTom's shareholders approved the takeover in December, 2007.[13]

TomTom's Customers

TomTom is a company that has a wide array of customers each with their own individual needs and desires. TomTom has a variety of products to meet the requirements of a large and varied customer base. As an example, their navigational products range from $100–$500 in the United States, ranging from lower end products with fewer capabilities, to high end products with advanced features.

The first group is the individual consumers who buy stand alone portable navigation devices and services. The second group is automobile manufacturers. TomTom has teamed up with companies such as Renault to develop built-in navigational units to install as an option in cars. A third group of customers is the aviation industry and pilots with personal planes. TomTom produces navigational devices for air travel at affordable prices. Another group of customers is business enterprises. Business enterprises refers to companies such as Wal-Mart, Target, or Home-Depot; huge companies with large mobile-work-forces. To focus on these customers, TomTom formed a strategic partnership with a technology company called 'Advanced integrated solutions' to "optimize business fleet organization and itinerary planning on the TomTom pro series of navigation devices". This new advanced feature on PNDs offers ways for fleet managers and route dispatchers to organize, plan and optimize routes and to provide detailed mapping information about the final destination. "Every day, companies with mobile workforces are challenged to direct all their people to all the places they need to go. Our customers appreciate having a central web repository to hold and manage all their location and address information," says Scott Wyatt, CEO of Advanced Integrated Solutions.[7] TomTom's last group of customers is the coast guards. They are able to use Tom-Tom's marine navigational devices for their everyday responsibilities.

Mergers and Acquisitions

TomTom has made various mergers and acquisitions as well as partnerships that have positioned the company well. In 2008 TomTom acquired a digital mapping company called Tele Atlas. The acquisition has significantly improve TomTom customers' user experience and created other benefits for the customers and partners of both companies, including: more accurate navigation information, improved coverage, and new enhanced features such as map updates and IQ routes which will be discussed in the scarce/unique resource section of the paper. Commenting on the proposed Offer, Alain De Taeye, Co-founder and CEO of Tele Atlas said:

> ". . .the TomTom-Tele Atlas partnership signals a new era in the digital mapping industry. The combination of Tom-Tom's customer feedback tools and Tele Atlas' pioneering map production processes allows Tele Atlas to dramatically change the way digital maps are continuously updated and enhanced. The result will be a completely new level of quality', content and innovation that helps our partners deliver the best navigation products. This transaction is not only very attractive to our shareholders but demonstrates our longstanding commitment towards all of our partners and customers to deliver the best digital map products available."[1]

TomTom also formed a partnership with a company called Advanced Integrated Solutions, adding an itinerary planning and route guidance feature to the pro series of navigation devices to help businesses enterprises with large mobile-workforces. A few years ago they also partnered with Avis, adding their user-friendly navigation system to all Avis rental cars. This partnership began in Europe and recently the devices have made their way into Avis rental cars in North America as well many other countries where Avis operates. Harold Goddijn, chief executive officer of TomTom commented:

> "Any traveler can relate to the stress of arriving in a new and unfamiliar city and getting horribly lost, with the availability of the TomTom GO 700 we're bringing unbeatable, full feature car navigation straight into the hands of Avis customers."[2]

TomTom has acquired several patents for all of their different technologies. By having these patents for each of its ideas, the company has protected itself against its competition and other companies trying to enter into the market.

TomTom prides itself on being the innovator in its industry and always being a step ahead of the competition in terms of its technology. On their Website they say, "TomTom leads the navigation industry with the technological evolution of navigation products from static 'find-your-destination' devices into products and services that provide connected, dynamic 'find-the-optimal-route-to-your-destination', with time-accurate travel information. We are well positioned to maintain that leading position over the long-term because of the size of our customer and technology base, our distribution power, and our prominent brand image and recognition. By being vertically integrated and also control the map creation process TomTom is in a unique position to evolve into an integrated content, service and technology business."[6]

TomTom's has a strong brand name/image. TomTom has positioned itself well throughout the World as the leader in portable navigation devices. It markets its products through its very user-friendly online Website and also through large companies such as Best Buy and Wal-Mart. Recently TomTom teamed up with Locutio Voice Technologies and Twentieth Century Fox Licensing & Merchandising to bring the original voice of Homer Simpson to all TomTom devices via download. "Let Homer Simpson be your TomTom co-pilot" is just one of the many interesting way's TomTom markets its products and its name to its consumers.[9]

TomTom's Resources and Capabilities

The company believes that there are three fundamentals to a navigation system—digital mapping, routing technology and dynamic information. Based on these requirements three key resources can be identified that really distinguished TomTom from its competition.

The first of these resources is their in-house *routing algorithms*. These algorithms enable them to introduce technologies like—IQ Routes, that provides "community based information database." IQ Routes calculate your routes based on the real average speeds measured on roads at that particular time. Their Website says, "The smartest route hour-by-hour, day-by-day, saving you time, money and fuel."[5]

The second unique resource identified was Tele-Atlas and the *digital mapping technology* that the TomTom group specializes in. Having the technology and knowledge in mapping that the company brought to TomTom, has allowed them to introduce many unique features to their customers. Firstly, TomTom recently came out with a map update feature. The company recognizes that roads around the world are constantly changing and because of this they used the technology to come out with four new maps each year, one per business quarter. This allows their customers to always have the latest routes to incorporate into their everyday travel. A second feature they recently introduced is their MapShare program. The idea behind this is that customers of TomTom who notice mistakes in a certain map are able to go in and request a change be made. The change is then verified and checked directly by TomTom and is shared with the rest of their global user community. "One and a half million map corrections have been submitted since the launch of TomTom Map Share™ in the summer of 2007."[5]

The third unique resource identified was *automotive partnerships* with two companies in particular; Renault and Avis. At the end of 2008, TomTom reached a deal with Renault to offer its navigation devices installed in their cars as an option. An article in Auto-week magazine said the following about the deal. "Renault developed its new low-cost system in partnership with Amsterdam-based technology company TomTom, the European leader in portable navigation systems. The system will be an alternative to the existing satellite navigation devices in Renault's upper-end cars."[8] The catch here is the new price of the built in navigation units. The cost of a navigation device installed in Renault's cars before TomTom was €1,500. Now with TomTom system it costs only €500. As talked about earlier in the paper, TomTom also partnered with Avis back in 2005 to offer its navigation devices, specifically the model GO700 in all Avis rental cars, first starting in Europe and expanding into other countries where Avis operates.

Competition Facing TomTom

Traditional Competition

TomTom faces competition from two main companies. The first of these is Garmin which holds 45% of the market share, by far the largest and dou-

ble Tom-Tom's market share (24%). Garmin was founded in 1989 by Gary Burrell and Min H. Kao. The company is known for their on-the-go directions since its introduction into GPS navigation in 1989. At the end of 2008, Garmin reported annual sales of $3493.1 million. Last year Garmin competed head-to-head with TomTom in trying to acquire Tele-Atlas for their mapmaking. Garmin withdrew their bid when it became evident that it was becoming too expense to own Tele-Atlas. Garmin executives made a decision that it was cheaper to work out a long-term deal with its current supplier than to try to buy out a competitor. Garmin's current supplier for map services is Navteq which was also acquired by Nokia in 2008.

The second direct competitor is Magellan, which holds 15% of the market share. Magellan is part of a privately held company under the name of MiTac Digital Corporation. Similar to Garmin, Magellan products use Navteq based maps. Magellan was the creator of Magellan NAV 100 that was the world's first commercial handheld GPS receiver which was created in 1989. The company is also well known for their award-winning RoadMate and Maestro series portable car navigation systems.

Together these three dominant players account for about 85% of the total market. Other competitors in the personal navigation device market are: Navigon, Nextar, and Nokia. Navigon and Nextar compete in the personal navigation devices with TomTom, Magellan, and Garmin who are the top three in the industry. But Navigon competes in the high-end segment which retails for more than any of the competitors but offer a few extra features in their PNDs. Nextar compete in the low-end market and its strategy is low cost. Finally, Nokia is mention as a competitor in this industry because they recently acquired Navteq who is a major supplier of map services in this industry. Along with that, Nokia has a big market share in the cell phone industry and plans on incorporating GPS technology in every phone making them a potential key player to look at for in the GPS navigation industry.

New Competition

Cell Phones Cell phones are a widely used technology by people all around the world. With the 2005 FCC mandate that requires the location of any cell phone used to call 911, phone manufacturers have now included GPS receiver in almost every cell phone.

Due to this mandate, cell phone manufacturers and cellular services are now able to offer a GPS navigation services through the cell phone for a fee.

ATT Navigator GPS Navigation with AT&T Navigator and AT&T Navigator Global Edition feature real-time GPS enabled turn-by-turn navigation on AT&T mobile Smartphones (iPhone and Blackberry) or static navigation and Local Search on a non-GPS AT&T mobile Smartphone.

ATT Navigator features Global GPS turn-by-turn navigation—Mapping and Point of Interest content for three continents, including North America (U.S., Canada, and Mexico), Western Europe, and China where wireless coverage is available from AT&T or its roaming providers. The ATT Navigator is sold as a subscription service and costs $9.99 per month.

Online Navigation Applications Online navigation Websites that are still popular amongst many users for driving directions and maps are MapQuest, Google Maps, and Yahoo Maps. Users are able to use this free site to get detail directions on how to get to their next destination. In today's economic downturn many people are looking for cheap, or if possible free solutions to solve their problems. These online Websites offer the use free mapping and navigation information that will allow them to get what they need at no additional costs. However, there are down-sides to these programs, "such as they are not portable and may have poor visualization designs (such as vague image, or text-based)."[12]

Built-In Car Navigation Devices In car navigation device first came about in more luxury, high-end vehicles. In today's market it has become more mainstream and now being offered in mid to lower tier vehicles. These built-in car navigation devices offer similar features to the personal navigation device but don't have the portability so you won't have to carry multiple devices but come with a hefty cost. Some examples of these are Kenwood, Pioneer, and Eclipse units all installed into your car. These units tend to be expensive and over-priced because of the fact that they are brand name products and require physical installation. For example, the top of the line Pioneer unit is $1,000 for the monitor and then another $500 for the navigation device plus the physical labor. When buying such products, a customer is spending a huge amount of money on a product that is almost identical to a product TomTom offers at significantly lower prices.

Physical Maps Physical maps have been the primary option for navigating for decades until technology came around. Physical maps provide detail road information to help a person get from point A to point B. Although cumbersome to use than some of the modern technology alternatives, it is an alternative for people who are not technically savvy or for whom navigation device is an unnecessary luxury that they do not feel the need to spend money on.

Potential Adverse Legislation and Restrictions

In the legal and political realm, TomTom is facing two issues that are not critical now, but may have significant ramifications to not only TomTom in the future, but also the entire portable navigation device industry. TomTom's reactions to each of these issues will determine whether or not there is an opportunity for gain or a threat of a significant loss will occur.

The most important issue deals with the possible legislative banning of all navigational devices from automobiles. In Australia, there is growing concern over the distraction caused by PNDs and the legislature has taken the steps toward banning these devices entirely from automobiles.[26] There is a similar sentiment in Ontario, Canada where a law that is currently under review would ban all PNDs that were not mounted either to the dashboard or to the windshield itself.[27]

With the increase in legislation adding to the restrictions placed on PND devices, the threat that the PND market in the future will be severely limited cannot be ignored. All of the companies within the PND industry, not just TomTom, must create a coordinated and united effort to stem this tidal wave of restrictions as well as provide reassurance to the public that they are also concerned with the safe use of their products. An example of this opportunity comes from the toy industry where safety regulations are fast and furious at times. Many companies within the toy industry have combined to form the International Council of Toy Industries[23] to be proactive in regards to safety regulations as well as lobby governments on behalf the toy industry against laws that may unfairly threaten the toy industry[23].

The other issue within the legal and political spectrum that TomTom must focus on is the growing use of GPS devices as tracking devices. Currently, law enforcement agents are allowed to use their own GPS devices to track the movements and locations of individuals they deem to be suspicious, but how long will it be before budget cuts reduce the access to these GPS devices and then the simple solution will be to use the PND devices already installed in many automobiles?

This issue also requires the industry as whole to proactively work with the consumers and the government to come to an amicable resolution. The threat of having every consumer's GPS information at the finger tips of either the government or surveillance company will most certainly stunt or even completely halt any growth within the PND industry and that is why the industry must be on the offensive and not become a reactor.

Another alarming trend is the rise in PND thefts around the country[22]. With the prices for PNDs at a relatively high level, thieves are targeting vehicles that have visible docking stations for PNDs either on the dashboard or windshield. The onus will be on TomTom to create new designs that will help not only hide PNDs from would-be thieves but also deter them from ever trying to steal one. Consumers who are scared to purchase PNDs because of this rise in crime will become an issue if this problem is not resolved.

There is also a trend currently that is labeled the GREEN movement,[29] that aims to reduce any activities that will endanger the environment. This movement is a great opportunity for TomTom to tout its technology as the smarter and more environmentally safe tool if driving is an absolute necessity. Not only can individuals tout this improved efficiency, but more importantly on a larger scale, businesses that require large amounts of materials to be transported across long stretches can show activists that they too are working to becoming a green company.

It is ironic that the core technology used in TomTom's navigation system, the GPS system, is proliferating into other electronic devices at such a rapid pace that it is causing serious competition to the PND industry. GPS functionality is virtually a requirement for all new smartphones that enter the market and soon will become a basic functionality

in regular cellular phones. TomTom will be hard pressed to compete with these multifunctional devices unless they can improve upon their designs and transform themselves into just a single focused device.

Another concern not only for TomTom, but for every company that relies heavily on GPS technology, is the aging satellites that support the GPS system. Analysts predict that these satellites will be either replaced or fixed before there are any issues, but this issue is unsettling due to the fact that TomTom has no control over it[24]. TomTom will have to devise contingency plans in case of catastrophic failure of the GPS system much like what happened to Research in Motion when malfunctioning satellites caused disruption in their service.

Currently TomTom is one of the leading companies in the PND markets in both Europe and the United States. Although they are the leader in Europe, that market is showing signs of becoming saturated, and even though the U.S. market is currently growing, TomTom should not wait for the inevitable signs of that market's slowdown as well. TomTom needs to be proactive to the next big market instead of using its large resources to become a *fast follower*.

The two main opportunities for TomTom to expand, creating digital maps for developing countries and creating navigational services can either be piggybacked one on top of each other or can be taken in independent paths. The first-mover advantage for these opportunities will erect a high barrier of entry for any companies that do not have large amounts of resources to invest in the developing country. TomTom is already playing catch-up to Garmin and their already established service in India. Being proactive is an important and valuable opportunity that TomTom should take advantage of.

Globalization of any company's products does not come without a certain set of issues. For TomTom, the main threat brought on by foreign countries is two fold. The first threat which may be an isolated instance, but could also be repeated in many other countries is the restriction of certain capabilities for all of TomTom's products. Due to security and terrorism concerns, GPS devices are not allowed in Egypt since 2003[28]. In these times of global terrorism TomTom must be vigilant of the growing trend for countries to become overly protective of foreign companies and their technologies.

Internal Environment

Finance

TomTom's current financial objectives are to diversify and become a broader revenue based company. The company not only seeks to increase the revenue base in terms of geographical expansion but also wants to diversify its product and service portfolio. Additionally, another important goal the company strives to achieve is to reduce its operating expenses.

Sales Revenue and Net Income In Exhibit 2 it can be observed that from 2005 to 2007 there is a consistent growth in sales revenue and a corresponding increase in net income too. However, year 2008 is an exception to this trend. In this year sales revenue decreased by 3.7% and the net income decreased by 136%. In fact, in the first quarter the net income is actually negative totaling -€37 million. The decrease in sales can be accounted by the downturn in the economy. Actually, according to their 2008 annual report, the sales are in line with their expectations from the market. However, the net income plummeted much more than the decrease in sales. This was actually triggered by its acquisition of a digital mapping company—Tele Atlas, which was funded by both cash assets and debt.

1. **Quarterly sales**—In second quarter of 2009 TomTom received sales revenue of €368 million compared to €213 million in first quarter and €453 million in the same quarter last year. (Exhibit 3) By evaluating quarterly sales for a three year period from 2007 till present, it is apparent that the sales do follow a seasonal trend in TomTom. With highest sales in last quarter and lowest in the first quarter. However, focusing on just the first and second quarter for three years one can infer that the sales revenue as a whole is also going down year after year. To investigate further on the causes of this scenario we will have to delve deeper into its revenue base. TomTom's sources of revenue can be broadly grouped into two categories—market segment and geographic location.

   Revenue per segment: TomTom's per segment revenue stream can be divided into PNDs and others, where others consist of services and content. Evaluating first quarter of 2008 against that of 2009 and last quarter of 2008,

TomTom experienced steep decline of 40% and 68%.(Exhibit 4) This could be a consequence of compounded effect of the following—Firstly, the number of devices (PNDs) decreased by a similar amount both the time periods. And secondly, the average selling price of PNDs has also been decreasing consistently. In a technology company a decrease in average selling price is a part and parcel of doing business in a highly competitive and dynamic market place. Nevertheless, the revenue stream from business units other than PNDs has seen a steady increase in both the scenarios.

   Revenue per region: TomTom's per region revenue stream can be further divided into Europe, North America and the rest of the world. Comparing first quarter of 2009 against 2008 it can be seen that, revenue from both Europe and North America are on decline, with a decrease of 22% and 52% respectively (Exhibit 5). At the same time, revenue from rest of the world has seen a huge increase of 90%. Both of these analyses support TomTom's current objective to increase their revenue base and is aligned with their long-term strategy of being a leader in navigation industry.

2. **Long term debt**—In 2005 TomTom was cash-rich company but the recent acquisition of Tele Atlas which amounted to €2.9 billion and was funded by cash, release of new shares as well as long term debt, which is in this case a borrowing of €1.2 billion. Currently, TomTom's debt is €1,006 million.

3. **Operating Margin**—TomTom saw a consistent increase in operating margin till 2006 (exhibit 7). But since 2007 operating margin has been decreasing for the firm. In fact, by the end of 2008 it came down to 13% compared to 26% in 2006.

Marketing

Traditionally high quality and ease of use of solutions have been of utmost importance to TomTom. In 2006, in an interview, TomTom's Marketing Head Anne Louise Hanstad, could not have emphasized more on the importance of simplicity and ease of use of their devices. (Hanstad) This underlines the TomTom's belief that—"People prefer fit for purpose devices that are developed and designed to do one specific thing very well." At that time both of these were core to the TomTom's strategy as their targeted customers were *early adopters*, but now as navigation industry has moved from embryonic to a growth industry TomTom's current customers are *early majority*, and hence, simplicity and ease alone could no longer provide it with competitive advantage.

Recently, to be in line with its immediate goal of diversifying into different market segment, TomTom is more focused on strengthening its brand name. In December 2008, TomTom's CEO stated—". . .we are constantly striving to increase awareness of our brand and strengthen our reputation for providing smart, easy-to-use, high-quality portable navigation products and services."[19]

Along with Tele Atlas the group has gained the depth and breadth of expertise over the last 30 years, and this makes it a trusted brand. Three out of four people are aware of the brand of the TomTom business across the markets. The Tom-Tom group has always been committed to three fundamentals of navigation—mapping, routing algorithm and dynamic information. Tele Atlas' core competency is the digital mapping database and TomTom's is routing algorithms and guidance services using dynamic information, and the group together create synergies that enable them to introduce products almost every year advancing on one or a combination of these three elements. Acquiring their long time supplier of digital maps, Tele Atlas, in 2008 gives them an edge with in-house digital mapping technology.

TomTom provides a range of PND devices like—TomTom One, TomTom XL and TomTom Go Series. Periodically, it tries to enhance those devices with new features and services, that they build based on the feedback from customers. Examples of services are—IQ routes and LIVE services. While IQ routes provides drivers with the most efficient route planning; accounting for situations as precise as speed bumps and traffic lights, LIVE services forms a range of information services delivered directly to the LIVE devices. The LIVE services bundle includes Map Share and HD Traffic—that is bringing the content collected from vast driving community directly to the end user.

These products and services accentuate effective designs and unique features, and require TomTom to work along with its customers to share precise updates and also get feedback for future improvements. Hence, effective customer interaction becomes essential to its long term goal of innovation. In 2008, J.D. Power associates recognized TomTom for providing outstanding customer service experience.[18] Although, it awarded TomTom for customer service satisfaction, J.D. Power and associates ranked Garmin highest in overall customer satisfaction. Tom-Tom followed Garmin in the ranking, performing well in the routing, speed of system and voice direction factors.[16]

As mentioned previously, when the navigation industry was still in its embryonic stages—Features, ease of use and high quality of its solutions gave TomTom products a competitive edge. Eventually, the competition increased in the navigation industry and even substitutes pose substantial threat to market share now. Currently, TomTom offers PNDs in different price ranges, broadly classified into—high-range and mid-range PNDs, with an average selling price of €99. There are entry-level options that allow a savvy shopper to put navigation in his/her car for just over $100. Higher-end models add advanced features and services previously described.

TomTom sells its PNDs to consumers through retailers and distributors. After acquiring Tele Atlas it is strategically placed to gain the first mover advantage created by its rapid expansion of geographical coverage.[19] This is of key importance when it comes to increasing the global market share.

TomTom directs its marketing expenditure towards B2B advertising that is direct to retailers and distributors. TomTom also invested in an official blog Website as well as search optimization which places it in premium results in online searches. This has enabled TomTom to do effective word-of-mouth promotion while keeping flexible marketing spending, in accordance to changes in the macroeconomic environment or seasonal trends[19]. Although, this approach gives it spending flexibility, it lacks a direct B2C approach. Currently only 21% US adults own PNDs while 65% US adults neither own nor use navigation[14]. By not spending on B2C marketing TomTom is discounting on the opportunity both to attract first-tier noncustomers and glean an insight of needs of second-tier noncustomers.[17]

Operations

The focus of operations has always been on innovation. More recently, TomTom's operational objective is to channel all the resources and core capabilities to create economies of scale so as to be aligned with their long term strategy. TomTom aims to focus and centralize R&D resources to create scale economies to continue to lead the industry in terms of innovation.[19]

Implementation of this strategy is well underway and the changes are visible. By second quarter of 2009 mid-range PNDs were introduced with capabilities from high-range devices, 50% of PNDs were soldwith IQ Routes Technology, first in-dash product was also launched in alliance with Renault and TomTom iPhone application was also announced[19].

After aquiring Tele Atlas, to better support the broader navigation solutions and content and services, the group underwent restructuring. New organization structure consists of four business units, that have clear focus on a specific customer group and are supported by two shared development centers.

TomTom's supply chain and distribution model is outsourced. This increases TomTom's ability to scale up or down the supply chain, while limiting capital expenditure risks. But, at the same time, it depends on a limited number of third parties and in certain instances sole suppliers, for component supply and manufacturing, which increases its dependency on these suppliers.

TomTom's dynamic content sharing model uses high quality digital maps along with the connected services, like HD Traffic, Local Search with Google and weather information, provides our customers with relevant real-time information at the moment they need it, and this is helping them deliver the benefits of innovative technology directly to the end user and that to now at affordable prices. Although, the network externalities previously mentioned are one of the advantages of TomTom's LIVE, it has also increased TomTom's dependency on the network of the connected driving community. Bigger the network will be, the more effective would be the information from the guidance services.

Furthermore, in order to reduce operating expenses and strengthen the balance sheet, undue emphasis has been placed on the cost cutting program. Currently the cost reductions are made up of—Reduction of staff, Restructuring and integration of Tele Atlas, Reduced discretionary spending and Reduction in the number of contractors and Marketing spenditures. However, if not executed wisely it could hamper TomTom's long term objective of being a market leader. For example one of the core capabilities of any technology company is its staff; reducing it can hinder future innovative projects. Likewise, reducing the marketing expenditures in a market which still holds rich prospects of high growth. There are still 65% of US adults who don't own any kind of navigation system either a device, or in-car, or that of phone.[14]

Human Resources

Like any other technology company success of individual employees is very important to TomTom. Additionaly, TomTom has a vision that success for TomTom as a business should also mean success for the individual employee. Therefore, at TomTom, employee competency is taken very seriously and talent development programs are built around it. There is a personal navigation plan that provides employees with a selection of courses based on competencies in their profile. In 2008 TomTom completed its Young Talent Development Program which was aimed at broadening the participants' knowledge, while improving their technical and personal skills.

TOMTOM GROUP	TOMTOM B2C	TELE ATLAS B2B	WORK B2B	AUTOMOTIVE B2B
→	→ Consumers	→ PND → Automotive → Mobile → Internet → GIS	→ Commercial fleets	→ Car industry → Car industry suppliers
	DYNAMIC CONTENT & PUBLISHING			
	SHARED TECHNOLOGIES			

TomTom's motto is to do business efficiently, profitably as well as responsibly. This underlines its corporate social responsibility. TomTom's headquarters is one of the most energy efficient buildings in Amsterdam. As mentioned before, earlier navigation was oriented towards making the drivers arrive their their destintion without getting lost. TomTom was the pioneer in introducing different technology that actually helps drivers to make their journeys safer and more economical. This shows their commitment to their customer base as well as to the community as a whole.

Issues of Concern for TomTom

First, TomTom is facing increasing competition from other platforms using GPS technology. Two main areas that come to mind are cell phones and smartphones. In the cell phone industry, Nokia is leading the charge in combing cell phone technology with GPS technology. They have a plan to put GPS technology in all their phones. Around the same time TomTom acquired Tele Atlas, Nokia also purchased Navteq, a competitor to Tele Atlas. With the acquisition of Navteq, Nokia hopes to shape the cell phone industry by merging cell phone, internet, and GPS technology together.

As we see the Smartphone industry emerging with the IPhone and the Palm Pre, we also see a shift in how people are able to utilize these technologies as a navigation tool. A big trend in smartphones these days are applications. Because of the ease of developing software on platforms for smartphones, more and more competitors are coming to the forefront and developing GPS navigation application.

For TomTom, both of these sectors might signal major change is in the horizon and that there is no longer a need for hardware for GPS navigation devices. And that we're heading towards a culture where consumers want an all-in-one device such as cell phone or Smartphone that will do everything they need including a GPS navigation services. In a recent study done by Charles Golvin for Forrester, he believes that by 2013 phone-based navigation will dominate the industry. And the reason is due to Gen Y and Gen X customers who are increasingly reliant on their mobile phone and who will demand social networking and other connected services integrated into their navigation experience[14].

The other problem TomTom is facing is a mature US & European personal navigation device market. After 3 years of steady growth in the PND market, TomTom has seen decreasing growth rate for PND sales. There could be many factors that are causing this such as the world wide recession but we felt that base on sales figure we're seeing the same trend in the US market as we have seen in the European market for TomTom. Initially entering the European market 12 months before entering the US market, TomTom has seen 21% dip in sales for the European market. Although, TomTom experiences some growth in the US market for 2008, they are noticing the growth rate has not been as good as the prior years.

Exhibit 1   Company history

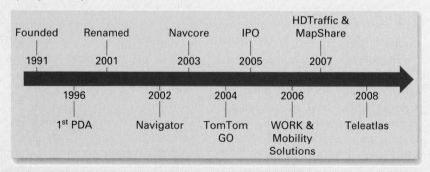

Exhibit 1 (*continued*)

Year	Historical Event
1991	Palmtop founded by Harold Goddijn, Peter-Frans Pauwels and Pieter Geelen.
1994	Corinne Vigreux joined the Company to sell Palmtop applications in Europe.
1996	First navigation software for PDAs, EnRoute and RouteFinder launched.
2001	Palmtop renamed TomTom. Harold Goddijn joins TomTom as CEO. Number of employees 30.
2002	First GPS-linked car navigation product for PDAs, TomTom NAVIGATOR shipped. €8 million revenue.
2003	NavCore Software Architecture developed, on which all TomTom products are still based. Number of employees 90.
2004	First portable navigation device shipped, the TomTom GO. 248,000 PND units sold.
2005	TomTom listed on Euronext Amsterdam. €720 million revenue.
2006	TomTom WORK and TomTom Mobility Solutions launched. Number of employees 818.
2007	TomTom makes offer for Tele Atlas. TomTom HD Traffic and TomTom Map Share launched. 9.6 million PND units sold.
2008	TomTom acquired Tele Atlas.

Source: http://investors.tomtom.com/overview.cfm

Exhibit 2 Sales Revenue and Net Income (€)

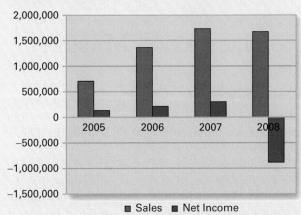

Exhibit 3 Quarterly sales (in millions €)

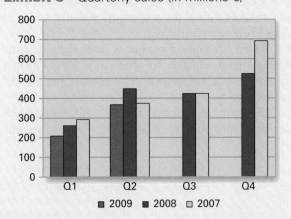

Exhibit 4 Revenue per segment

(in € millions)	Q1'09	Q1'08	y.o.y	Q4'08	q.o.q
Revenue	172	264	−35%	473	−64%
PNDs	141	234	−40%	444	−68%
Others	31	29	5%	29	5%
# of PNDs sold (in thousands)	1,419	1,997	−29%	4,443	−68%
Average selling price (€)	99	117	−15%	100	−1%

Exhibit 5 Revenue per region

(in € millions)	Q1'08	Q1'09	Difference
Europe	178,114	146,549	−22%
North America	84,641	55,558	−52%
Rest of world	1,087	10,976	90%
Total	263,842	213,083	−24%

Exhibit 6 Cash versus Long term debt (in thousand €)

	12/31/2005	12/31/2006	12/31/2007	12/31/2008	6/30/2009
Long Term Debt	301	338	377	4,749	4,811
Cash Assets	178,377	437,801	463,339	321,039	422,530
Borrowings	0	0	0	1,241,900	1,195,715

Exhibit 7 Operating Margin

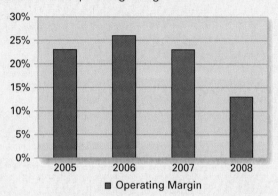

APPENDIX: GOOGLE DRIVES INTO NAVIGATION MARKET
RUETERS
Wed Oct 28, 2009 11:30 am EDT

SAN FRANCISCO (Reuters)—Google Inc. is adding Garmin Ltd and TomTom to its growing list of rivals as the Internet search giant weaves technology for driving directions into new versions of its smartphone software.

Google said its new Google Maps Navigation product will provide real-time, turn-by-turn directions directly within cell phones that are based on the new version of its Android software.

The navigation product, which features speech recognition and a visual display that incorporates Google's online archive of street photographs, marks the latest step by Google to challenge Apple Inc's iPhone and Microsoft Corp's Windows Mobile software with its Android smartphone software.

It also represents a direct competitive threat to companies like Garmin and TomTom which sell specialized hardware navigation devices. TomTom also makes a software navigation app for the iPhone that sells for $99.99 in the U.S.

Google executives told reporters at a press briefing on Tuesday ahead of the announcement that the company decided to offer turn-by-turn driving directions in its four-year-old maps product because it was the most requested feature by users.

CEO Eric Schmidt said that expanding into a new market with new competitors was not a part of Google's motivation.

"Those are tactical problems that occur after the strategic goal which is to offer something which is sort of magical on mobile devices using the cloud," Schmidt said.

The new navigation service will work with Google's forthcoming Android 2.0 software, the next version of the smartphone operating system developed by Google. The company announced development tools for Android 2.0 on Tuesday, but a spokeswoman said specific details about when Android 2.0 will be available should be directed to phone-makers and wireless carriers.

Google said the product, which will initially be limited to driving directions in the U.S., will be free for consumers.

Reporting by Alexei Oreskovic; Editing Bernard Orr
© Thomson Reuters 2009 All rights reserved.

Bibliography

1. TeleAtlas Press Release. <http://www.teleatlas.com/WhyTeleAtlas/Pressroom/PressReleases/TA_CT015133>.
2. TomTom press release. TomTom and Avis Announce the First Pan-European Deal to Provide TomTom GO.
3. Compare GPS Sat Nav Systems. <http://www.satellitenavigation.org.uk/gps-manufacturers/tomtom/>; Daniel, Robert. TomTom Net Fell 61%, Revenue Off 19%. <http://www.foxbusiness.com/story/markets/industries/telecom/tomtom-net-fell—revenue/>.
4. TomTom Challenge. <http://www.tomtomchallenge.nl/resources/AMGATE_400083_1_TICH_R76719135691/>.
5. TomTom NV. <http://www.answers.com/topic/tomtom-n-v>.
6. TomTom. TomTom, portable GPS car navigation systems. <http://investors.tomtom.com/overview.cfm>.
7. Advanced Integrated Solutions. TomTom and Advantage Integrated Solutions Partner to Deliver an Intelligent Fleet Routing Solution for Businesses. March 2009. <http://www.highbeam.com/doc/1G1-196311252.html>.
8. Auto-Week Article. Renault, TomTom promise cheap navigation. <http://www.autoweek.com/article/20080929/free/809299989#ixzz0MQ8bKdYo>.
9. Boston Business Article. <http://www.boston.com/business/ticker/2009/06/let_homer_simps.html)>.
10. Garmin Website. <http://www8.garmin.com/about Garmin/>.
11. Gis Development Article. <http://www.gisdevelopment.net/technology/lbs/techlbs008.htm>.
12. Magellan Website. <http://www.magellangps.com/about/>.
13. Thomson Reuters. TomTom launches 2.9 bln euro bid for Tele Atlas. 19 November 2007. <http://www.reuters.com/article/technology-media-telco-SP/idUSL1839698320071119>.
14. Forrestor Research. "Phone-Based Navigation Will Dominate By 2013." 27 March 2009.
15. Hanstad, L. Anne. TomTom VP of Marketing Fletch. 27 September 2006.
16. J.D. Power and Associates. Garmin Ranks Highest in Customer Satisfaction with Portable Navigation Devices. 23 October 2008. <http://www.jdpower.com/corporate/news/releases/pressrelease.aspx?ID=2008221>.
17. Kim, W. Chan and Mauborgne. Blue Ocean Strategy. Boston: Harvard Business School Press, 2005.
18. Reuters. TomTom Inc. Recognized for Call Center Customer Satisfaction Excellence by J.D. Power. 7 January 2008. <http://www.reuters.com/article/pressRelease/idUS141391+07-Jan-2008+PRN20080107>.
19. TomTom AR-08. "TomTom Annual Report 2008." TomTom Annual Report 2008. December 2008.
20. TomTom Q2 2009. "Investor relations." TomTom Website. <http://investors.tomtom.com/reports.cfm?year=2009>.
21. Foley, Ryan. Chicago Tribune. 7 May 2009. 29 July 2009 <http://archives.chicagotribune.com/2009/may/07/news/chi-ap-wi-gps-police>.
22. GPS Magazine. GPS Magazine. 23 September 2007. 29 July 2009 <http://gpsmagazine.com/2007/09/gps_thefts_rise.php>.
23. ICTI. ICTI. 2009. 29 July 2009 <http://www.toy-icti.org/>.
24. Jones, Nick. Garnter. 5 January 2009. 29 July 2009 <http://www.gartner.com/resources/168400/168438/findings_risks_of_gps_perfor_168438.pdf>.
25. PriceGrabber.com. Price Grabber. April 2007. 29 July 2009 <https://mr.pricegrabber.com/2007_GPS_Pricing_Trends_Report.pdf>.
26. Richards, David. Smarthouse. 17 June 2009. 29 July 2009 <http://www.smarthouse.com.au/Automotive/Navigation/P4P3H9J8>.
27. Talaga, Tanya and Rob Ferguson. TheStar.com. 28 Oct 2008. 29 July 2009 <http://www.thestar.com/News/Ontario/article/525697>.
28. US News. US News. 14 October 2008. 29 July 2009 <http://usnews.rankingsandreviews.com/cars-trucks/daily-news/081014-GPS-Devices-Banned-in-Egypt/>.
29. Webist Media. Web Ecoist. 17 August 2008. 29 July 2009 <http://webecoist.com/2008/08/17/a-brief-history-of-the-modern-green-movement/>.

CASE 15

Alarm Ringing: Nokia in 2010

"[…]Nokia's problems are still fixable but the window is closing. I am not optimistic that they will be fixed in 2010 because there isn't much time left, and if they aren't fixed in 2011, Nokia will be in big trouble."[1]

—Nick Jones, vice president, Gartner, Inc.[2] in 2010.

Market Leader In Trouble

In September 2010, Stephen Elop (Elop) joined Nokia Corporations (Nokia) as the President and CEO. Elop, former head of Microsoft's Business Division[3] (MBD), was brought in to fix the numerous problems faced by the world's leading mobile phone company. His tasks included the onerous job of reversing not only Nokia's eroding market share in the high-end smartphone segment but also its slumping profits. "My role, as the leader of Nokia, is to lead this team through this period of change, take the organization through a period of disruption. My job is to create an environment where those opportunities are properly captured, to ultimately ensure we are meeting the needs of our customers, while delivering superior financial result,"[4] said Elop.

The Finland-based Nokia had a presence in over 160 countries as of 2010. Though it was the world's largest mobile phone maker with a market share of 35% in the first quarter of 2010, Nokia had been losing market share consistently in the high-end mobile phone market. According to analysts, problems began for the company with the increase in the global demand for smartphones, a segment in which Nokia was unable to find its footing compared to rivals like Research In Motion[5] (RIM) and Apple.[6] Nokia was not only slow in launching smartphones with the latest version of its Symbian[7] operating system (OS), but also in catching up with the touch-screen technology, they said. Nokia's major problems were development of new software services, hardware design, and North American distribution. The plunging market share price and dwindling investor confidence ultimately led to Elop replacing Olli-Pekka Kallasvuo (Kallasvuo), who had been CEO since mid-2006. Experts opined that under Kallasvuo, Nokia had struggled to keep up with rivals in the smartphone segment, the most profitable and fastest-growing segment in the global mobile phone market.

Analysts felt that Elop had a tough road ahead as he had to establish the company's presence in the smartphone segment and increase its profits. Moreover, he would have to revitalize the Nokia brand and stand up against the competition. What made the assignment even more challenging for Elop was the deeply-entrenched culture at Nokia. Being a Canadian, who had spent most of his time managing the affairs of US-based companies, he was expected to face resistance from the management team with a strong Finnish cultural bias. Elop's appointment elicited mixed reactions from analysts. However, they were unanimous in their view that the decisions he took would determine whether Nokia would be able to regain its past glory or whether it would capitulate to the fast emerging competition.

About Nokia

As of 2010, Nokia employed about 123,553 employees and operated under three business segments—Devices & Services, NAVTEQ (a leader in comprehensive digital mapping and navigation services), and Nokia Siemens Networks. It operated 15 manufacturing facilities in nine countries and maintained R&D facilities in 12 countries. Nokia had been market leader in the mobile phone market since 1998.

In the new millennium, though the company developed expensive high-end handsets based on 3G technology to capture a substantial share of the high-end phone market, its greatest strength was in the lower end of the market. In countries such as China, Brazil, and India there was a huge demand for low-priced mobile phones. The early-2000s saw a major erosion in the company's brand value. In particular, 2004, saw a huge drop in the company's market share as well as brand value, as younger buyers opted for the trendier mobile phones offered by rivals such as Motorola,[8] Samsung,[9] and Sony Ericsson.[10] In 2004, its market share declined to less than 30% from around 40% in 2003.[11] Analysts felt that the company had also failed to foresee how popular clamshell mobile phones would become. While its rivals were offering such models, it continued to churn out the single-piece design popularly called 'Candy Bar.' Some analysts felt the brand was losing its sheen and that it was counted among the world's top ten brands more because of its size than for its ability to form a meaningful relationship with its customers.

In 2005, Nokia put renewed emphasis on new product development and branding and moving beyond the umbrella branding that it had been zealously following. Analysts felt that the two sub-brands, the Nseries and the Eseries, had helped Nokia in capturing the new market for high-end multimedia mobile phones and business-oriented mobile phones respectively. In addition, Nokia entered the Internet services space with the 'Ovi' brand on August 29, 2007. 'Ovi' was an umbrella brand for a range of Internet services offered by Nokia—such as an online music store, an online navigation service, and an online games store. These initiatives led to some improvements. However, some analysts felt the emerging markets of India and China were largely responsible for Nokia's revival in the mid-2000s and the company could expect more growth in these markets as the consumers upgraded to more expensive models. For instance, for 2006, the Average Selling Price (ASP) of Nokia in the Asia-Pacific region including India, rose by 4.1 percent to €77, while in China it rose by 3.8 percent to €81.[12]

Meanwhile, in June 2006, Jorma Ollila (Ollila), who had been CEO of Nokia since 1991, made way for Kallasvuo, the head of the handset division. Ollila himself became chairman. In the same month, Nokia merged its networks business with the carrier-related operations of Siemens AG[13] to form a new unit called Nokia Siemens Networks which provided equipment, services, and solutions for communications networks globally. On July 10, 2008, Nokia acquired NAVTEQ Corporation.[14]

In 2009, Nokia's net sales decreased by 19% to €40,984 million (€50,710 million in 2008). Net sales of Devices & Services for 2009 decreased by 21% to €27,853 million (€35,099 million). In 2009, Europe accounted for 36% of Nokia's net sales, Asia-Pacific 22%, Greater China 16%, the Middle East & Africa 14%, Latin America 7%, and North America 5% (Refer Exhibits I, II, and III).

Nokia's Problems

Drop in Smartphone Market Share

Though Nokia remained the largest mobile phone maker by units, with a global market share of about 35% (Q1 2010), the company struggled to keep pace with rivals such as Apple, Google,[15] and RIM in the high-end smartphone market[16] (Refer Exhibit IV). It had lost a significant market share in the smartphone segment as it was slow in launching premium handsets and failed to foresee the boom in the smartphone market, analysts felt. In the first quarter of 2010, Nokia's global market share in smartphones fell to 44.3% from 48.8% a year earlier.[17]

According to analysts, since the launch of the iPhone in 2007, Nokia began to lose share in the smartphone market as it was unsuccessful in releasing a compelling touchscreen model that could compete with the iPhone. Nokia's only successful high-end phone was the N95,[18] unveiled in 2006. The N95 smartphone launched in December 2008 failed to make an impact in the market. As a result, consumers' loyalty shifted to the iPhone. It was reported that since 2007, Nokia's share price had fallen by almost two-thirds, thereby eliminating about €60 billion of the company's market capitalization. "The high-end user they've lost to the iPhone has signed up for iTunes and put their information on Apple; Nokia won't get them back or not without an enormous amount of pain,"[19] said Stuart O'Gorman, co-head of UK-based investment management firm, Henderson Global Investors.

Nokia also postponed the launch of its latest flagship smartphone, the touchscreen equipped Nokia

N8. The N8, based on the Symbian 3 OS, was slated for release in April 2010, but the release was postponed to the year-end owing to software problems. According to industry insiders, the delay generated a lot of negative attention for the company and led to a drop in its stock price. In the second quarter of 2010, Nokia's market share in the smartphone market dropped to 38.1% from 40.3% in the corresponding period of the previous year[20] (Refer Exhibit V).

In the smartphone OS market, competitors were quickly catching up with Nokia's Symbian platform. As the Symbian OS was not optimized for touch-screen devices, users were turning to the Android, Blackberry OS, and Apple's iOS. While Nokia's new Linux-based mobile OS MeeGo, developed in association with Intel[21] to power high-end smartphones, was yet to be released, its Symbian began to lose market share to rivals like Android and iOS. Its market share fell to 44.3% in Q1 2010, compared to 48.8% in Q1 2009.[22] Analysts said Symbian's market share was expected to further drop to 34% in 2011.

Besides, Nokia's limited presence and minimum brand recognition in the US smartphone market also led to a drop in its worldwide market share, said analysts. The major problem for Nokia was its inability to break into the US market, considered the fastest growing market for smartphones in the world. In March 2002, Nokia's market share in the US was 35%. This dropped to 10% in 2008. By June 2009, Nokia's share in the US was just 7%.[23] Experts said Nokia had failed to build long-term partnerships with any of the major wireless carriers in the US such as Sprint Nextel, AT&T, Verizon Wireless, and Vodafone Group which sold more than 90% of all mobile phones in the US. As a result, Nokia's smartphones were not offered with subsidies on these carrier networks. While wireless subscribers could get an iPhone for US$199 they had to pay full retail price for a Nokia smartphone. "Despite holding 38 percent market share of the smartphone market, Nokia's failure to compete with the iPhone and high-tier Android devices, combined with its lack of progress in gaining significant traction in the United States, has led to press and investor dissatisfaction,"[24] said Pete Cunningham, an analyst at technology research firm Canalys.

Some analysts said that over the past few years, Nokia had begun developing new services such as Ovi instead of building phones and mobile applications and concentrating on important markets like North America. But these services were not picking up as expected and Nokia had to had shut down certain services.[25] According to analysts, the company's digital mapping service Navteq too was not a big success. Nokia Siemens Networks was also struggling with falling revenues due to reduced operator investments and tough competition. Experts said Nokia's loss of focus had affected its market share significantly, leaving it struggling to catch up with its competitors.

In a brand-ranking study released in May 2010 by Millward Brown Optimor,[26] Nokia ranked 43rd, tumbling 30 places compared to the previous year. As per the study, the company lost 58% of its brand value.[27] According to Allen Nogee (Nogee), principal analyst at In-Stat, "Nokia has a huge market in the low-end part of the market, which in some ways could present a negative image among people who want state-of-the-art smartphones."[28]

Competition

Nokia was facing increasing competition from Apple and Google's Android OS for smartphones which hit the market in 2010. It was reported that the adoption of Android was growing faster as more leading smartphone makers such as Samsung, Motorola, LG, and Sony Ericsson were backing it. Analysts predicted that by end 2010, Android would become the top mobile OS in the US. Talking about Nokia's problems, Tony Cripps (Cripps), principal analyst at UK-based consultancy firm, Ovum, said, "Nokia's well reported problems competing in the high-end handset market against Apple are being further compounded by the inroads smartphones based on Google's Android platform are making far down into the traditional mid-range. Add in the lowering wholesale prices of mass market handsets and even Nokia's massive global shipments of low cost phones are struggling to compensate."[29]

Analysts were of the view that Nokia had been edged out by rivals in the smartphone market, who had launched new, better products. In the third quarter of 2009, Apple emerged as the world's most profitable phone-maker, generating US$1.6 billion in profit on the iPhone in the quarter compared to Nokia's US$ 1.1 billion.[30] Experts said though Nokia had spent almost six times as much as Apple on R&D in 2009, it had failed to develop a device with the same appeal as the iPhone.[31]

In order to hold on to its global market share, Nokia cut the prices of its handsets and shipped more low-priced models, resulting in a drop in profits. The ASP of Nokia handsets was low compared to that of other manufacturers. For instance, in the third quarter of 2009, the ASP for a Nokia handset was €62 compared to €72 in the corresponding quarter of the previous year. For a smartphone, Nokia charged €155 in the first quarter of 2010, down from €190 in the last quarter of 2009. In the second quarter 2010, Nokia's ASP was €143 compared to €181 in the second quarter 2009.[32] Experts felt the reduced ASP per device had brought down Nokia's profits. In 2009, Nokia sold about 40% of the world's cell phones, with strong business in Europe and in India and China. Despite selling several times more devices than its rivals, Nokia made lower profits as most of the devices it sold were lower-priced models with limited profit margins. Nokia's competitors, on the other hand, were shipping fewer handsets but making more profit per handset sold.

Dwindling Sales

In Q2 2010, Nokia's net income dropped by 40% to €227 million, down from €380 million a year earlier.[33] Analysts attributed the drop to the company's falling sales in the smartphone market. Analysts said Nokia's sales increased by only 0.9% to €10 billion in Q2 despite its shipping more than 111 million mobile devices, an increase of 8% compared to the corresponding quarter of the previous year. Devices & Services net sales increased 3% to €6.8 billion, compared with €6.6 billion in the second quarter of 2009 (Refer Exhibit 6). Shipments in North America declined by 19% year-on-year and 4% quarter-on-quarter, to 2.6 million. According to experts, factors such as the competitive environment, shifts in product mix toward lower gross margin products, the depreciation of the Euro, operating expenses, and global pricing strategies negatively impacted Nokia's business in the second quarter. Some analysts predicted that with global shipments and profits set to decline further, Nokia might even lose its market leadership in the future.

Since the company reported its first quarter earnings in March 2010, its share price dropped about 20% in the two weeks, wiping out €8.2 billion (US$10.5 billion) in market value. As of May 2010, Nokia's market capitalization was €34 billion (US$44 billion) compared to Apple's US$230 billion.[34] Nokia announced that in 2010, its volume market share in the mobile device segment would be lower than in 2009.

Management Issues

According to experts, at Nokia, decisions were not based on product vision. Besides, potential ideas were either delayed or ignored by top management. The management was not innovative enough and there were too many silos in the company working independently without any communication with other departments. According to Juhani Risku (Risku), former senior Executive of Nokia, "I would say that the highest abstraction level of the problem is that there are incompetent people managing, ordering, or directing things. When incompetent people are managing the chain, they have the mandate but don't have that courage. Even when we bring something to market, we're always developing versions from 1.0 to 1.2, but not to version 3 or 4."[35]

Analysts said investors were expecting challenging products from the company that had once had the innovative edge in the industry. But that had not happened since Kallasvuo took over as the CEO in 2006. Though Kallasvuo promised to tackle problems and establish the company's presence in North America, he had failed to do so and had only seen the market share decline from 20% in 2006 to 7% as of June 2010.[36] Some experts opined that Nokia's top management had failed to bring innovative products to market, despite a rich R&D base and had also made some wrong strategic decisions.

In 2009, when Nokia reported the first third quarter loss of €559 million (US$ 834 million) since it began reporting quarterly in 1996,[37] the company shuffled its management. In October 2009, Nokia's CFO Rick Simonson was replaced by Timo Ihamuotila, who had been head of global sales. Simonson was put in charge of the low-end mobile-phone unit in the devices division. Later, in the first quarter of 2010, when Nokia again reported lower than expected earnings, the top management was reshuffled again to revive its core business units. In July 2010, marketing chief Anssi Vanjoki was appointed head of the smartphone unit which included the company's smartphones and services operations, while Mary McDowell took over Nokia's key mobile phones unit from Simonson. According to some analysts,

Nokia's multiple reshuffle of the top management did not, however, get the expected results.

In early 2010, Nokia's management was under increasing pressure from analysts and shareholders as the company's share price was consistently falling. The company had 156,000 shareholders at the end of 2009, with 38% of shares owned in the US. Reports showed that between 2007 and 2010, Nokia's share plummeted 67% and the company lost almost €60 billion (US$77 billion) in market value (Refer Exhibit VII). Investors called for management changes and Kallasuvo came in for severe criticism.

Analysts opined that Kallasvuo had failed to understand the company's problems and had not done anything right to fix them. He could have reclaimed the company's share in the smartphone market as it had the opportunity to acquire Palm's WebOS,[38] which would have provided it with not just a good OS to compete with rivals but also a strong presence in the US, they said. During the last three years of Kallasuvo's tenure, Nokia lost 75% of its market capitalization, plunging from US$40 per share in 2007 to less than US$10 in 2010. In April 2010, investors were further disappointed when Kallasvuo announced a delay in the release of the updated Symbian software until later in 2010.

In May 2010, Ollila confirmed that the board was looking at a replacement and that the search for a new CEO had started after a review of the company's strategy. It was rumored that Nokia had auditioned heads of several US-based technology companies but that some of them had rejected the offer because Nokia wanted the new CEO to move to Finland. However, some analysts were not sure that merely changing the CEO would change Nokia's fortunes. "While CEO Olli-Pekka Kalasvuo is the man who must take ultimate responsibility for Nokia's falling profitability, the problem is unlikely to go away simply by replacing him at the helm,"[39] said Cripps.

Elop Joins Nokia

On September 10, 2010, Nokia's Board of Directors replaced Kallasvuo with Elop. Elop had earlier been president of MBD, which makes the Office suite of applications. His tenure at Microsoft was marked by the successful launch of Microsoft's Office 2010 suite. Before joining Microsoft in January 2008,

he had served as CEO of Juniper Networks[40] for a year. Prior to that, in 2005, Elop was CEO of graphics software developer at Macromedia[41] and later became president of worldwide field operations at Adobe Systems[42] after Adobe acquired Macromedia. He also worked as a CIO at Boston Chicken.[43] Elop held a degree in computer engineering and management from McMaster University in Hamilton, Canada, his home country.

Analysts felt the appointment of Elop was an unusual move and a major shift for Nokia as he would be the first non-Finn CEO to run the company in its long history. According to Ollila, Elop was the right candidate to drive both innovation and efficient execution of the company strategy.[44] According to the company, Elop had adequate exposure to the inner workings of Nokia as he had represented Microsoft when the two companies had partnered to develop software for Nokia phones. Industry observers said Elop was as a well-traveled executive with a very broad software experience and deep knowledge of the North American market. However, just after the announcement was made, Vanjoki, who had been considered the prospective candidate for the CEO position, decided to quit the company.

Elop's appointment evoked mixed reactions. Some analysts felt that having worked closely with Microsoft and Macromedia, Elop had adequate software knowledge and experience. Elop's experience of working in the US market and knowledge of the US corporate culture in the highly competitive field of technology would be a big advantage for Nokia as it would help the company regain its share in the North American mobile phone market, they added. "He's worked at the biggest software firm in the world. This is very important for Nokia, which is trying to go from being a Finnish box maker to being a player in the U.S.-centric software and Internet-services business,"[45] said Lee Simpson, an analyst at Jefferies International.[46] Analysts were of the view that Elop would be able to chalk out a strategy wherein the company would be able to take advantage of both the Symbian and MeeGo platforms.[47]

Some analysts said Elop was an aggressive leader. As CEO of Macromedia, he had focused on Flash Internet software instead of bigger product lines and organized the company's US$3.4 billion sale to Adobe Systems in 2005. "Macromedia bore the brunt when the dot-com bubble burst, and Elop was there. He had a lot of challenges he rode through. I tell you, there were lots of CEOs who didn't make it through those tumultuous years. That tells you something about Elop's professionalism, his ability to execute,"[48] said Chris Swenson of NPD Group.[49] At Microsoft, Elop revamped the Office software and was responsible for making MBD profitable. It was reported that MBD was one of Microsoft's biggest and most profitable units. In fiscal year 2009, MBD generated US$18.6 billion in sales—about 30% of the company's total sales.[50]

However, some critics felt Elop was not the right candidate for the job as he did not have the hardcore experience in the mobile phone industry required for the strong strategy overhaul that Nokia would need in the future to be a global smartphone competitor. He was involved more in networking and enterprise software and not mobile phones, they said. "We think Elop ticks most but not all of the right boxes . . . However, it remains to be seen how well he will do on hardware devices,"[51] said Mawston of Strategy Analytics. They said he could be a good manager but not a consumer product visionary, which was what Nokia needed. "He comes from a software background, which is good, but he also comes from a company that's had the same issues as Nokia in terms of adapting to a new world,"[52] said Carolina Milanesi, research director, mobile device and consumer-services practice, Gartner. Moreover, analysts pointed out, barring Microsoft, Elop had never run a business as large as Nokia. According to Jones, "Nokia's board has made a safe choice when they should have made a courageous choice. In the current state of the market when the two main competitors, Google and Apple, are very much headed by recognizable visionaries, you need someone who is charismatic and can explain how you're driving the industry forward in new directions."[53]

Challenges Galore

Elop's biggest challenge would be to manage a quick turnaround of the company and reassert Nokia's place as the largest mobile maker in the world. His other tasks included focusing on the smartphone market, addressing loss in earnings, and establishing the company's business in the US. "Elop faces a daunting task. Nokia has lost its leadership in high-tier phones and has struggled with the rise of Inter-

net-led services,"[54] said Ben Wood, head of research at UK-based telecoms analyst firm CCS Insight.

According to experts, one of the most important tasks for Elop would be to develop a challenger to iPhone as the smartphone market was expected to expand and occupy about 40% of the total device market by 2013. Smartphones accounted for 17.3% of all mobile handset sales in the first quarter of 2010, up from 13.6% in the same period in 2009 (Refer Exhibit VIII). Experts pointed out that Apple and RIM, which had had just about 3% market share in the mobile devices as of 2009, had over 50% share in industry profits which proved the high profitability of the smartphones. Analyst Kevin Restivo from IDC said, "Lower smartphone average selling prices, increased consumer interest, and aggressive expansion plans on the part of key suppliers will keep the device type growing above market growth rate."[55]

Elop would have to steer Nokia in a new and innovative direction and build up the brand image of the company. He had to plan a new strategy for the company and build an efficient OS that lived up to the competition in the smartphone market. Some experts were of the view that Elop needed to drop the Symbian and adopt the Android OS to regain Nokia's footing in the smartphone market. But for Elop, Nokia's transition to the Android would be difficult as the company had already made a huge investment in Symbian and had several Symbian-based devices.

Establishing Nokia's presence in North America was another daunting challenge for Elop who needed to strike major deals with US cell phone carriers and work closely with them. "Hiring Elop is an indication of reinvigorated commitment to the U.S. market at the highest levels in the company. But Elop's background seems more focused on business rather than consumer products where the real need is, and he does not seem to have any prior background working with operators who really control the U.S. market,"[56] noted Satish Menon, senior analyst at Forward Concepts, a US-based market research firm. Moreover, he would have to develop and design an interface that suited the US market as the typefaces, screen layouts, and hardware designs of Nokia phones reflected European sensibility, according to some experts.

Adjusting to Nokia's corporate culture would also be a challenge for Elop, the first non-Finnish CEO of the company. According to Risku, "Nokia is so Finnish. We have so many Americans, they're very good but arrogance and aggression is not the Finnish way of working."[57] They noted that Nokia's product creation right from concept to design was very Finnish, usually characterized by long approval processes and lack of leadership. Moreover, they expected Elop to face problems playing a strong leadership role, as he would be stuck between a very powerful chairman Ollila and a long standing management team with a strong cultural bias. Rod Hall, an analyst at investment management firm JPMorgan, said, "Nokia's business culture tends to be very consensus oriented versus the star system more prevalent within N. American tech companies."[58] Moreover, Nokia's choice of a Canadian CEO did not go down well with the Finnish press.

According to Dan Frommer of *Business Insider,* "Nokia's board just hired another CEO who is a seasoned manager, but not a consumer product visionary. So unless Stephen Elop, Nokia's new boss, has hidden talents, he may represent more of the same for Nokia—which would be a disaster."[59]

Road Ahead

Some analysts were optimistic that Nokia, under Elop, would overcome its problems and retain its position as the largest mobile maker in the world. Though Nokia was not doing well in the smartphone market, it was still strong at the entry-level with a global manufacturing and distribution base. It was also a major player in the emerging markets like China and India that would contribute to Nokia's growth in the future, they said. However, others felt the company would have to invest heavily in its strategy for developed markets as well. They felt transforming Nokia would by no means be an easy task. It would require Elop to bring about a change in its corporate culture. "That Finnish mindset of caution has to be overturned,"[60] said Simpson. Moreover, he would have to change the perception that Nokia was a conservative business with a Finnish mindset. It would be interesting to watch how Elop brought about the change in a big company like Nokia and balanced short-term results with long-term goals for Nokia, analysts said.

However, as rivals continued to grab market share, some analysts were skeptical about whether Elop would be able to solve Nokia's problems and restore it to its past glory. Time was fast running out for Nokia, they said. Jeff Kagan, of *E-Commerce Times,* noted: "Will Stephen Elop, the new Nokia CEO, be able to turn the company around? That is the question. It all depends on what he does—this is a big job. He has to focus on transforming not only the technology, but also the brand. He has to reinvent Nokia's image in the mind of the customer. Will it work? Will Nokia be able to re-energize with new leadership, or is it in the process of passing the torch to the next generation of competitors?"[61]

Exhibit I   Nokia's Consolidated Income Statement

(in € millions except per share data)	2009	2008	2007
Net Sales	40,984	50,710	51,058
Cost of Sales	27,720	33,337	33,781
Gross profit	13,264	17,373	17,277
Research and development expenses	5,909	5,968	5,636
Selling and marketing expenses	3,933	4,380	4,379
Administrative and general expenses	1,145	1,284	1,165
Impairment of goodwill	908	—	—
Other income	338	420	2,312
Other expenses	510	1,195	424

Exhibit I (*continued*)

(in € millions except per share data)	2009	2008	2007
Operating profit	1,197	4,966	7,985
Share of results of associated companies	30	6	44
Financial income and expenses	265	2	239
Profit before tax	962	4,970	8,268
Tax	702	1,081	1,522
Profit	260	3,889	6,746
Profit attributable to equity holders of the parent	891	3,988	7,205
Loss attributable to minority interests	631	99	459
Earnings per share			
Basic	0.24	1.07	1.85
Diluted	0.24	1.05	1.83
Average number of shares (1000's)			
Basic	3,705,116	3,743,622	3,885,408
Diluted	3,721,072	3,780,363	3,932,008

Source: www.nokia.com/about-nokia/financials/key-data/reportable-segments

Exhibit II Nokia's Balance Sheet

(in € millions)	2009	2008
Assets		
Fixed assets and other noncurrent assets		
Intangible assets		
Capitalized development costs	13	21
Intangible rights	46	52
Other intangible assets	418	152
	477	228
Tangible assets		
Investments		
Investments in subsidiaries	12109	12084
Investments in associated companies	30	10
Long-term loan receivables from Group companies	10	8
Other non-current assets		

(*continued*)

Exhibit II (continued)

(in € millions)	2009	2008
Current assets		
Inventories and work in progress		
Raw materials and supplies	45	84
Work in progress	86	100
Finished goods	86	70
Receivables		
Deferred tax assets	1	—
Trade debtors from Group companies	1080	899
Trade debtors from other companies	713	913
Short-term loan receivables from Group companies	3472	12039
Short-term loan receivables from other companies	—	1
Prepaid expenses and accrued income from Group companies	15	65
Prepaid expenses and accrued income from other companies	1858	2179
	7139	16096
Short-term investments	35	2
Bank and cash	70	197
Total	20161	28920
Shareholders' Equity and Liabilities		
Shareholders' equity		
Share capital	246	246
Treasury shares	−685	−1885
Reserve for invested nonrestricted equity	3154	3291
Retained earnings	3788	4489
Net profit for the year	767	1749
Liabilities		
Long-term liabilities		
Long-term finance liabilities to other companies	3255	—

Exhibit II (*continued*)

(in € millions)	2009	2008
Short-term liabilities		
Current finance liabilities from Group companies	3380	13345
Current finance liabilities from other companies	473	2598
Advance payments from other companies	217	182
Trade creditors to Group companies	3280	2377
Trade creditors to other companies	531	695
Accrued expenses and prepaid income to Group companies	73	217
Accrued expenses and prepaid income to other companies	1682	1616
Total liabilities	9636	21030
Total	12891	21030

Source: Nokia_in_2009.pdf

Exhibit III Nokia's Ten Major Markets Based on Net Sales

	(in € millions)	
	2009	2008
China	5 990	5 916
India	2 809	3 719
UK	1 916	2 382
Germany	1 733	2 294
USA	1 731	1 907
Russia	1 528	2 083
Indonesia	1 458	2 046
Spain	1 408	1 497
Brazil	1 333	1 902
Italy	1 252	1 774

Source: www.nokia.com/about-nokia/financials/key-data/markets

Exhibit IV   Worldwide Mobile Phone Sales (Units)

	Q2 2010 (millions)	Share Q2 2010 (%)	Q2 2009 (millions)	Share Q2 2009 (%)
Nokia	111.5	34.2	105.4	36.8
Samsung	65.3	20.1	55.4	19.3
LG	29.4	9.0	30.5	10.7
RIM	11.2	3.4	7.7	2.7
Sony Ericsson	11.0	3.4	13.6	4.7
Motorola	9.1	2.8	15.9	5.6
Apple	8.7	2.7	5.4	1.9
HTC	5.9	1.8	2.5	0.9
ZTE	5.5	1.7	3.7	1.3
GFive	5.2	1.6	—	—
Others	62.6	19.3	46.0	16.1
Total	325.6	100.0	286.1	100.0

Source: www.bloomberg.com

Exhibit V   Worldwide Smartphone Sales by Platform

	Units Q2 2010 (millions)	Share Q2 2010 (%)	Units Q2 2009 (millions)	Units Q2 2009 (%)
Symbian	25.4	41.2	20.9	51.0
RIM	11.2	18.2	7.8	19.0
Android	10.6	17.2	0.8	1.8
iPhone OS	8.7	14.2	5.3	13.0
Windows Mobile	3.1	5.0	3.8	9.3
Linux	1.5	2.4	1.9	4.6
Others	1.1	1.8	0.5	1.2
Total	61.6	100.0	41.0	100.0

Source: www.bloomberg.com

Exhibit VI Nokia: Reported Second Quarter Results

(in € millions)	Q2/2010	Q2/2009	YoY Change	Q1/2010
Net sales	10 003	9 912	1%	9 522
Devices & Services	6 799	6 586	3%	6 663
NAVTEQ	252	147	71%	189
Nokia Siemens Networks	3 039	3 199	−5%	2 718
Operating profit	295	427	−31%	488
Devices & Services	643	763	−16%	831
NAVTEQ	−81	−100		−77
Nokia Siemens Networks	−179	−188		−226
Operating margin	2.9%	4.3%		5.1%
Devices & Services	9.5%	11.6%%		12.5%
NAVTEQ	−32.1%	−68.0%		−40.7%
Nokia Siemens Networks	−5.9%	−5.9%		−8.3%
EPS, EUR Diluted	0.06	0.10	−40%	0.09

Source: www.nokia.com/about-nokia/financials/quarterly-and-annual-information/q2-2010

Exhibit VII Nokia's Three-year Stock Price Chart

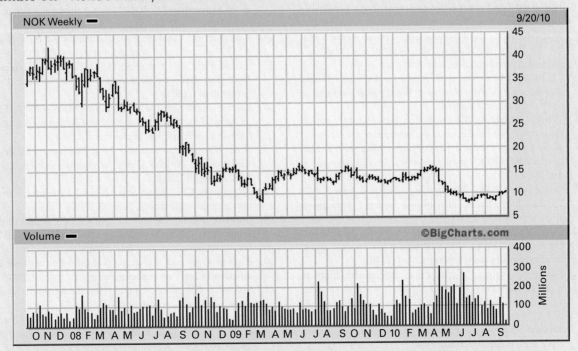

Source: http://bigcharts.marketwatch.com

Exhibit VIII   Global Smartphone Share

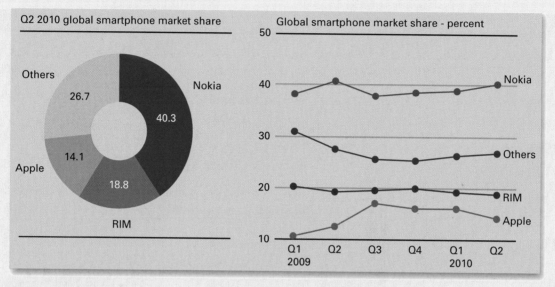

Source: www.reuters.com

References & Suggested Readings:

1. Diana ben-Aaron, "Nokia Investors Left without Buzz, Increasing Pressure on Elop," www.bloomberg.com, September 16, 2010.
2. Jeff Kagan, "The Mountain Elop has to Climb to Keep Nokia on Top," www.ecommercetimes.com, September 16, 2010.
3. Kerri Shannon, "Will Nokia's CEO Change be the Catalyst to Boost Its Share in the Smartphone Market?" www.dailymarkets.com, September 13, 2010.
4. Christopher Lawton and Joann S. Lublin, "Nokia Replaces CEO with Microsoft Boss," http://online.wsj.com, September 11, 2010.
5. "Nokia Turns to Microsoft for New Chief," http://economictimes.indiatimes.com, September 11, 2010.
6. Aude Lagorce, "Nokia Corp. Names Microsoft Executive as New CEO," www.marketwatch.com, September 10, 2010.
7. Ben Popper, "The Wrong Guy: Nokia's New CEO, Stephen Elop, Lacks Smartphone Smarts," www.bnet.com, September 10, 2010.
8. Dan Frommer, "Nokia Makes the Same Mistake Again: Hires a Manager, Not a Product Visionary," www.businessinsider.com, September 10, 2010.
9. Diana ben-Aaron, "Nokia Hires Microsoft's Elop as CEO to Reverse Losses to Apple," www.bloomberg.com, September 10, 2010.
10. Erika Morphy, "Nokia's New CEO May Whip up Savvier Smartphone Strategy," www.ecommercetimes.com, September 10, 2010.
11. "How Microsoft's Elop Could Turn Nokia Around," http://blogs.forbes.com, September 10, 2010.
12. Kevin J. O'Brien, "Nokia Chooses a Microsoft Officer as Its New Chief Executive," www.nytimes.com, September 10, 2010.
13. "Nokia Appoints Stephen Elop to President and CEO as of September 21, 2010," http://investors.nokia.com, September 10, 2010.
14. Rick Meritt, "Analyst: Five Challenges for New Nokia CEO," www.eetimes.com, September 10, 2010.
15. Tarmo Virki and Georgina Prodhan, "Nokia Brings in Microsoft Exec to Replace CEO," www.reuters.com, September 10, 2010.
16. Surojit Chatterjee, "Nokia Appoints Microsoft Top Exec as New CEO, Market Hopeful but Challenges Remain," http://uk.ibtimes.com, September 10, 2010.
17. Rafe Blandford, "Stephen Elop Replaces Olli-Pekka Kallasvuo as Nokia's CEO," www.allaboutmeego.com, September 10, 2010.
18. "Replacing CEO Won't Solve Nokia's Problems," http://about.datamonitor.com, July 30, 2010.
19. "Mobile Phone Demand Expands 14.5% as Market Fragments; Top 5 Pressured by Challengers, Says IDC," www.businesswire.com, July 29, 2010.
20. Andrew Orlowski, "Rescuing Nokia? A Former Exec has a Radical Plan," www.theregister.co.uk, July 22, 2010.
21. "Nokia's Fall from Grace: The Background Story," www.mobileindustryreview.com, July 22, 2010.
22. Diana ben-Aaron, "Nokia Board Faces Call for Change on $77 Billion Lost Value," www.bloomberg.com, July 16, 2010.
23. Mikael Ricknäs, "Nokia on Long Comeback Trail after Smartphone Misses," www.macworld.com, July 2, 2010.

24. Kit Eaton, "Nokia Profit Warning: It's Been Outmaneuvered by Apple," www.fastcompany.com, June 16, 2010.

25. Steve Goldstein and Aude Lagorce, "Nokia Issues Profit Warning at Handset Division," www.marketwatch.com, June 16, 2010.

26. "Nokia Shares Fall on Profit Warning Talk-Traders," http://uk.reuters.com, June 9, 2010.

27. Gabriel Perna, "Nokia's Top Position Erodes," www.ibtimes.com, June 7, 2010.

28. "Gartner: Worldwide Smarphone Sales Grew 49% in Q1 2010," http://smartphone.biz-news.com, May 20, 2010.

29. Chad Berndtson, "Google Android, RIM Lead Big Smartphone Sale Gains in Q1," www.crn.com, May 19, 2010.

30. "Gartner Says Worldwide Mobile Phone Sales Grew 17 Per Cent in First Quarter 2010," www.gartner.com, May 19, 2010.

31. Diana ben-Aaron, "Nokia Investors Lose Patience 3 Years after IPhone (Update2)," www.businessweek.com, May 6, 2010.

32. "Apple Becomes Top Phone Maker by Profits-Research," www.reuters.com, November 10, 2009.

33. Kevin J. O'Brien, "Nokia Tries to Undo Blunders in U.S.," www.nytimes.com, October 18, 2009.

34. Diana ben-Aaron and Marcel van de Hoef, "Nokia CFO Simonson Moved to New Post after Loss (Update4)," www.bloomberg.com, October 16, 2009.

35. Eric Lai, "How will Stephen Elop Fare at Microsoft?" http://blogs.computerworld.com, January 11, 2008.

36. www.nokia.com

37. Nokia Annual Reports

38. http://bigcharts.marketwatch.com

39. www.reuters.com

40. www.bloomberg.com

Endnotes

1 Mikael Ricknäs, "Nokia on Long Comeback Trail after Smartphone Misses," www.macworld.com, July 2, 2010.

2 Gartner, Inc. is an IT research and advisory firm.

3 The Microsoft Business Division develops Microsoft's line of Office software that includes Microsoft Office Applications.

4 Rafe Blandford, "Stephen Elop Replaces Olli-Pekka Kallasvuo as Nokia's CEO," www.allaboutmeego.com, September 10, 2010.

5 Founded in 1984, Research In Motion Limited is a Canadian telecommunication and wireless device company, best known as the developer of the BlackBerry smartphone. The company's revenues for fiscal 2010 second quarter were US$ 4.62 billion.

6 Apple Inc. designs, manufactures, and markets personal computers and related personal computing and mobile communication devices along with a variety of related software and services. In the third quarter ended June 26, 2010, Apple posted revenues of US$15.7 billion and a net quarterly profit of US$3.25 billion.

7 Symbian OS is Nokia's mobile operating system for mobile devices and smartphones.

8 Based in Schaumburg, Illinois, Motorola Inc. is a manufacturer of wireless telephone handsets and network infrastructure equipment such as cellular transmission base stations and signal amplifiers.

9 Samsung Electronics Co. Ltd., headquartered in Seoul, South Korea, is one of the world's largest electronics companies. Its revenues for the fiscal year 2005 were US$78.99 billion.

10 Sony Ericsson Mobile Communications AB is a mobile phone company formed in 2001 as a joint venture between one of the leading consumer electronics companies Sony Corporation (Sony) of Japan and a leading mobile phone company Ericsson AB (Ericsson) of Sweden. It was the world's fourth largest mobile phone company as of July 2007. Its revenues for the fiscal year 2006 were €10,959 million.

11 "Nokia: Nseries Leads Nokia Brand Revival," www.brandrepublic.com, January 25, 2007.

12 Juho Erkheikki, "Nokia Owes Revival to Emerging Markets," www.iht.com, July 17, 2007.

13 Headquartered in Berlin and Munich, Siemens is one of the world's largest electrical engineering and electronics companies. The company offers innovative technologies to customers in over 190 countries.

14 NAVTEQ Corporation developed and delivered digital map, traffic, and location data for navigation and location-based platforms.

15 Google Inc. is a global technology company that provides a Web-based search engine through its Website. The Company offers a wide range of search options, including Web, image, groups, directory, and news searches. In the second quarter ended June 30, 2010, Google's revenues were US$5.1 billion.

16 "Gartner Says Worldwide Mobile Phone Sales Grew 17 Per Cent in First Quarter 2010," www.gartner.com, May 19, 2010.

17 Gabriel Perna, "Nokia's Top Position Erodes," www.ibtimes.com, June 7, 2010.

18 The N95 was Nokia's first handset with GPS navigation. When the N95 was introduced in 2006, it sold more than 10 million units and increased the operating margin in devices to more than 21% that year.

19 Diana ben-Aaron, "Nokia Investors Lose Patience 3 Years after IPhone (Update2)," www.businessweek.com, May 6, 2010.

20 Surojit Chatterjee, "Nokia Appoints Microsoft Top Exec as New CEO, Market Hopeful but Challenges Remain," http://uk.ibtimes.com, September 10, 2010.

21 Intel Corporation is a US-based technology company, and one of the largest semiconductor chip makers in the world.

22 Chad Berndtson, "Google Android, RIM Lead Big Smartphone Sale Gains in Q1," www.crn.com, May 19, 2010.

23 Kevin J. O'Brien, "Nokia Tries to Undo Blunders in U.S.," www.nytimes.com, October 18, 2009.

24 "Nokia Turns to Microsoft for New Chief," http://economictimes.indiatimes.com, September 11, 2010.

25 Nokia was to shut its cloud-based file-sharing service known as Ovi File, from October 1, 2010. It also dropped its "share on Ovi" media-sharing site in 2009. The company also planned to discontinue its N-Gage gaming service later in 2010.

26 Millward Brown Optimor is the brand finance and ROI arm of leading market research and consultancy firm Millward Brown.

27 Diana ben-Aaron, "Nokia Investors Lose Patience 3 Years after IPhone (Update2)," www.businessweek.com, May 6, 2010.

28 Erika Morphy, "Nokia's New CEO May Whip up Savvier Smartphone Strategy," www.ecommercetimes.com, September 10, 2010.

29 "Replacing CEO Won't Solve Nokia's Problems," http://about.datamonitor.com/media/archives/4563, July 30, 2010.

30 "Apple Becomes Top Phone Maker by Profits -Research," www.reuters.com, November 10, 2009.

31 Diana ben-Aaron, "Nokia Investors Lose Patience 3 Years after IPhone (Update2)," www.businessweek.com, May 6, 2010.

32 www.nokia.com/about-nokia/financials/quarterly-and-annual-information/q2-2010.

33 www.nokia.com/about-nokia/financials/quarterly-and-annual-information/q2-2010.

34 Diana ben-Aaron, "Nokia Investors Lose Patience 3 Years after IPhone (Update2)," www.businessweek.com, May 6, 2010.

35 By Andrew Orlowski, "Rescuing Nokia? A Former Exec has a Radical Plan," www.theregister.co.uk, July 22, 2010.

36 Surojit Chatterjee, "Nokia Appoints Microsoft Top Exec as New CEO, Market Hopeful but Challenges Remain," http://uk.ibtimes.com, September 10, 2010.

37 Diana ben-Aaron and Marcel van de Hoef, "Nokia CFO Simonson Moved to New Post after Loss (Update4)," www.bloomberg.com, October 16, 2009.

38 Palm webOS is proprietary mobile operating system of Palm Inc., a smartphone manufacturer based in Sunnyvale, California. According to analysts, Palm's OS failed because of Palm's poor sales and marketing strategy. While Nokia could have solved Palm's sales and distribution problems with its massive global channels, Palm, on its part, could have given Nokia a strong presence in the Silicon Valley and the North American market.

39 "Replacing CEO Won't Solve Nokia's Problems," http://about.datamonitor.com/media/archives/4563, July 30, 2010.

40 Founded in 1996, Juniper Networks, Inc. is an information technology and computer networking products company. It is headquartered in Sunnyvale, California.

41 Macromedia Inc. is a US-based graphics and Web-development software company which developed the Flash video and Dreamweaver software. In December 2005, Macromedia was acquired by Adobe Systems, for US$ 3.4 billion in 2005.

42 Founded in 1982, Adobe Systems Inc. is a leading provider of graphic design, publishing, and imaging software for Web and print production. The company is headquartered in San Jose, California.

43 Boston Market, known as Boston Chicken until 1995, is a chain of American fast casual restaurants.

44 "Nokia Appoints Stephen Elop to President and CEO as of September 21, 2010," http://investors.nokia.com, September 10, 2010.

45 Aude Lagorce, "Nokia Corp. Names Microsoft Executive as New CEO," www.marketwatch.com, September 10, 2010.

46 Based in the UK, Jefferies International Limited offers asset management services including convertible bonds and securities.

47 Erika Morphy, "Nokia's New CEO May Whip up Sawier Smartphone Strategy," www.ecommercetimes.com, September 10, 2010.

48 Eric Lai, "How will Stephen Elop Fare at Microsoft?" http://blogs.computerworld.com, January 11, 2008.

49 NPD group is a global provider of consumer and retail market research information.

50 Tarmo Virki and Georgina Prodhan, "Nokia Replaces CEO Kallasvuo with Microsoft's Elop," http://in.reuters.com, September 10, 2010.

51 Surojit Chatterjee, "Nokia Appoints Microsoft Top Exec as New CEO, Market Hopeful but Challenges Remain," http://uk.ibtimes.com, September 10, 2010.

52 Aude Lagorce, "Nokia Corp. Names Microsoft Executive as New CEO," www.marketwatch.com, September 10, 2010.

53 Diana ben-Aaron "Nokia Hires Microsoft's Elop as CEO to Reverse Losses to Apple," www.bloomberg.com, September 10, 2010.

54 Tarmo Virki and Georgina Prodhan, "Nokia Brings in Microsoft Exec to Replace CEO," www.reuters.com, September 10, 2010.

55 "Mobile Phone Demand Expands 14.5% as Market Fragments; Top 5 Pressured by Challengers, Says IDC," www.businesswire.com, July 29, 2010.

56 RickMeritt, "Analyst: Five Challenges for New Nokia CEO," www.eetimes.com, September 10, 2010.

57 Andrew Orlowski, "Rescuing Nokia? A Former Exec has a Radical Plan," www.theregister.co.uk, July 22, 2010.

58 Diana ben-Aaron "Nokia Hires Microsoft's Elop as CEO to Reverse Losses to Apple," www.bloomberg.com, September 10, 2010.

59 Dan Frommer, "Nokia Makes the Same Mistake Again: Hires a Manager, Not a Product Visionary," www.businessinsider.com, September 10, 2010.

60 Surojit Chatterjee, "Nokia Appoints Microsoft Top Exec as New CEO, Market Hopeful but Challenges Remain," http://uk.ibtimes.com, September 10, 2010.

61 Jeff Kagan, "The Mountain Elop Has to Climb to Keep Nokia on Top," www.ecommercetimes.com, September 16, 2010.

CASE 16

AB Electrolux Challenges Times in the Appliance Industry: Relocating Manufacturing to Low-Cost Countries and Sustainability

Alan N. Hoffman

Rotterdam School of Management, Erasmus University and Bentley University

Axel Wenner-Gren is the founding father of AB Electrolux. In 1908, he passed by a vacuum cleaner in a store window in Vienna and thought to himself that "there should be one of these in every home" despite the fact that this vacuum cleaner cost a small fortune and weighed about 45 pounds. Two years later, this visionary founded the company known today as Electrolux. In 1912, Electrolux produced the first household vacuum cleaner known as the Lux 1. Wenner-Gren had an ability to grasp the basic needs of customers and produce and sell appropriate products and services and in 1925, the company entered the refrigerator market.

As World War II paralyzed many of Electrolux's manufacturing plants, the company reorganized some of its production facilities and made air filters and steel fittings for the Swedish defense forces. Following the end of the war, the company continued on its path to dominating the household appliance industry by introducing the first household washing machine in 1951 and the first household dishwasher in 1959. Acquisitions of other companies played an important role in the growth of Electrolux throughout the past 90 years and it helped the company become a global player in the industry. It has acquired over 300 companies from various countries throughout the world providing Electrolux with better production capabilities and access to large mature markets and established brand names, such as Eureka, Frigidaire and Kelvinator. Following years of acquisitions, in 1997, Eletrolux began a two-year restructuring program in an effort to improve its bottom line. It divested several of its sectors including industrial products, sewing machines and vending machines, the company laid off 11,000 employees and closed 23 plants and 50 warehouses. Following its success in the European markets, Electrolux-branded appliances were introduced in North America in 2004. Hans Stråberg was appointed Electrolux's President & CEO in 2002 and remains in that position today. The company is currently the world's second largest appliance maker, behind Whirlpool. Electrolux has over 50,000 employees in over 50 countries around the world. Its headquarters are in Stockholm.

Product Offerings & Brands

Electrolux sells over 40 million products to customers in over 150 different global markets every year in two product categories: consumer durables and professional products. Its consumer product offerings are broken down into three segments: kitchen products such as fridges and freezers, laundry products such as washers and dryers, and floor-care products such as vacuums. Electrolux also sells spare parts and services associated with its products. In its professional products division, it offers food-service equipment for restaurants and industrial-kitchens as well as laundry equipment for the health-care industry and apartment-buildings. As illustrated in Exhibit 1, consumer durables are a core piece of Electrolux's business, representing 93% of overall sales in 2009. Kitchen products represent a majority of the Electrolux consumer product category with 57% of overall company sales. Electrolux's roots are in the floor-care business and today, those products only contribute 8% of the company's annual sales. The

The author would like to thank MBA students Owen Bacewicz, Chris Iafolla, Marisa Iafolla, and Paul Weber at Bentley University for their research.

Alan Hoffman, RSM Case Development Centre. Printed by permission of Dr. Alan N. Hoffman.

professional products business makes up a smaller portion of its sales at only 7% in 2009. Through its acquisition strategy in the 1980s and 1990s, Electrolux has acquired many different brands in several global markets with various brands offered in different regions of the world. Exhibit 2 illustrates some examples of the brand names under AB Electrolux. Approximately half of the 40 million products Electrolux sold in 2009 were sold under the global Electrolux brand.

Strategic Direction

Electrolux is in the business of developing and marketing premium household and professional appliances. The guiding principle that the company follows is to offer products and services that consumers prefer, that benefit both people and the environment and for which consumers are willing to pay a higher price. The company is truly in the premium market category of household appliances. Electrolux is also a very consumer-driven company. The "Thinking of You" slogan indicates the high importance the company places on understanding customer needs. Whether it's in product development, design, production, marketing, or service, the customer is always at the forefront of Electrolux's mind.

The vision of Electrolux coincides with the vision of its founding father 90 years ago when he believed that there should be a vacuum cleaner in every home. The company's vision is to surpass Whirlpool and become the world's largest manufacturer of household appliances. Their aim is "To be the world leader in making life easier and more enjoyable with the help of powered appliances."[1] This vision is illustrated throughout their marketing campaign in N. America featuring Kelly Ripa with the tag line "be even more amazing." The focus is on the customer and helping to make their day-to-day life simpler with its products.

Industry Environment

Recently, the appliance industry has seen sluggish sales moving through the current recession. There have been several government programs similar to the Cash for Clunkers program but instead implemented for the appliance industry. These programs are intended to rid homes of nonenergy-efficient appliances but also have a second motive, to spur demand. In an attempt to satisfy consumer demand, appliance companies have been developing more and more Energy Star approved efficient products. Further, appliance companies have been producing their products in a more environmentally friendly manner.[2,3]

According to a paper published in 2008, the income elasticity of appliances is less than one, and in the case of washers and dryers, income elasticity was found to be merely 0.26; a figure proving that appliance sales are quite inelastic. This means that if a person's income were to increase or decrease, their expenditures on appliances will, on average, not increase or decrease at a similar rate. This makes sense as many consumer appliances are considered a necessity to which a family cannot live without. It can also be inferred that with such a low income elasticity, the appliance industry could be insulated from a recession.[4] Finally, the appliance industry is mainly dominated by Electrolux and Whirlpool. The industry market capitalization is about $12 billion with an industry profit margin of approximately 8.42%.[5,6]

Competition

Whirlpool Corporation, a company devoted strictly to the appliance market, has a market capitalization of over $6 billion. Whirlpool is currently the largest appliance manufacturer in the world. Prior to 2006, Electrolux held that title, however following Whirlpool's acquisition of Maytag, it surpassed Electrolux as the world's largest appliance maker. Whirlpool produces products under the brand names Kitchenaid, Jenn-Air, and Amana. Whirlpool currently has approximately $20 billion in sales, an operating margin of 5.8%, and a growth rate of 8.8%; quite below the industry average growth rate of over 29%. Whirlpool's current product mix is one of medium cost and quality. Many of the company's products excel beyond their generic counterparts, but fall behind in features that many luxury appliance brands offer. Whirlpool Corporation employs approximately 67,000 people.[7,8]

GE Appliances, a subsidiary division owned by General Electric, currently has a product mix that is most similar to that of Electrolux. GE Appliances produces high-quality ranges, ovens, and refrigerators that have many of the same features as Electrolux products, including an induction cook top. This type of cook top has become quite desirable as it uses electro magnetism to create precise heat in half the time while using much less energy than a classic gas or electric stove. While financial information specific to GE Appliances is not widely available, General Electric, the parent company, currently has a market capitalization of over $167 billion. One benefit to a diversified large company, such as General Electric, is that it can use resources from another division and reallocate the resources to the appliance subsidiary if needed.[9,10]

LG Electronics, a privately owned subsidiary of LG, Lucky Goldstar, offers a lower cost product mix with a few high-end appliances, but does not have certain features other brands offer, including induction cook tops. The financial information specific to the appliance division of LG Electronics is not readily available, but it is estimated that it employs 28,895 people. LG Electronics also has the benefit that it is part of a very large diversified parent company that can transfer resources to the appliances division if needed.[11,12]

Sustainability

For the past six years, Electrolux has been implementing a production restructuring program that involves relocating approximately 60% of its manufacturing to low-cost countries such as Mexico and China. Electrolux also has a goal of reducing its overall energy consumption by 15% of the 2008 levels by 2012 in an effort to achieve more efficient energy consumption in its manufacturing process. The company also has goals specific to its sustainability focused on four issues: climate change, sound business practices, responsible sourcing and restructuring.

Every business sector of Electrolux has launched a "green" range of products in its efforts to increase awareness of the company's energy-efficient and climate-smart products.

Increasingly, sustainability initiatives are creeping into the collective consciousness of governments and the general consumer. There is an awareness level around sustainability that is pervasive and now influences consumers' purchasing behavior. In addition, this movement has become so strong that it is now a major part of nearly every legislative agenda around the world. The American Recovery and Reinvest-

ment Act, passed into law in 2009, has earmarked a whopping $27.2 billion to energy efficiency and renewable energy research and investment.[13] Going "green" is no longer a fad—it's a behavior incentivized by governments. For example, in the near future there will be criteria for lower energy consumption when appliances are in standby mode as well as smart electricity meters that distribute power consumption more evenly throughout day and night. Currently, these types of incentives generally take the form of rebates offered to the consumer for buying brands that have met a standard level of energy conservation requirements. In the future, it is likely that governments will not only provide rebates on the purchase of energy-efficient appliances, but mandate it as well. Industries like home and commercial lighting are already feeling the impact of this type of directive with the law that incandescent bulbs will no longer be available on shelves after 2014. These mandates are a significant opportunity for Electrolux. The company is in a prime position to capitalize on this trend by rapidly rolling out energy efficient products that capitalize on today's consumer awareness and positions it well for tomorrow's mandates.

The 2008–2009 Global Recession

The appliance market is impacted greatly by the fluctuations of the credit market. Clearly, the current state of the global economy has taken its toll on major appliance makers such as Electrolux. Retailers had limited credit to stock appliances and consumers were operating with shoestring budgets. Instead of purchasing new appliances, many were forgoing the purchase altogether and opting to repair an outdated appliance. Of course, the economy is cyclical and by most accounts has already hit bottom. As the recovery moves forward, the credit markets will open and provide a new opportunity for Electrolux. This expanding credit market will inevitably lead to an increased rate of new appliance purchases. The purchase of new appliances is also inextricably linked to home buying. People tend to buy major appliances in the midst of a new home purchase or remodel. As credit becomes available, home buying will surge upward and serve as the tailwind needed to jumpstart appliances.

Like the automotive industry before it, the appliance market is facing stiff competition from Asian companies such as LG, Haier and Samsung. These companies will pose a significant challenge to the success of an established brand like Electrolux. In addition, as Electrolux looks to outsource production to developing nations—it needs to be mindful of the increasing cost of labor in these countries. China, once the epicenter of global outsourcing is already being viewed as a risk when it comes to outsourcing due to the inevitable increase in wages. In July of 2010, 18 provinces in China increased the minimum wage by an average of 20 percent.[14] This increase in wages could offset the cost advantages Electrolux hopes to achieve by moving production. Finally, Electrolux has recently churned out a few encouraging quarters in a row and have trumpeted the fact that its operating margin is slowly creeping upward. Part of this is because commodity prices are cyclically low. This is a natural reaction to a down economy. When the economy suffers, commodity prices tend to fall. Electrolux has benefitted from this reduction in commodity prices as it has helped to reduce the company's costs throughout the supply chain. A manufacturer like Electrolux relies heavily on commodities such as steel for the production of its appliances. As the recovery continues, commodity prices will increase and impact the operating margin and bottom line earnings of the company. Some of this increase should be offset by the ability to charge higher prices but the threat is still present.

The Growing Middle Class in Asia

As the social and demographic trends continue to evolve so do the opportunities afforded to Electrolux. The most significant demographic shift globally is the growing middle class in Asia, which includes families with incomes between $6,000 and $30,000. It is estimated that by 2020 there will be 1 billion more people in the global middle class than there were in 2010.[15] Correlated with rising incomes worldwide, homeownership has also increased at a substantial rate giving rise to increased demand for consumer durables such as refrigerators, washing machines, and dishwashers.[16]

Consumers worldwide are also working longer hours with increased workplace demands and consequently, their "free" time to maintain their domiciles is shrinking.[17] Consumers are expecting more out of their appliances to fit their unique needs including

faster cycle times for washers and dryers and automation of processes. For example, consumers are looking for ovens that automatically determine at what temperature food needs to be cooked, how long it needs to be cooked for, and automatically shut-off when the food is done cooking. For refrigerators, consumers are more focused on the freshness of stored food and they are using this as a guiding principle in appliance comparisons.[18]

Consumers are no longer simply concerned about the usability of their appliances, but from whom the appliance comes from, how the appliance was made, and what happens to the appliance after its use. Corporate social responsibility is a growing factor in differentiating companies for consumers and it has become more and more important for companies to invest in the communities of their target customer. Consumers are also more concerned about the environment, now more than ever, and companies have to be creative in incorporating environmentally friendly practices. Energy consumption, pollution, and recyclability of appliances are all variables that consumers keep in mind when selecting their home appliances.

Aside from practical and environmentally conscious concerns, there are also the continually evolving tastes of consumers. The kitchen has become the favored entertainment space for people, which has led to a more fashionably conscious consumer in picking out kitchen appliances. It's important to recognize new consumer tastes of aesthetics rather than just focusing on the practicability of appliances.

The greatest social and demographic threats to Electrolux are the erroneous perceptions of consumers about appliances in regard to energy consumption and ease of use. Currently, less than half of the households in Europe own dishwashers.[19] A substantial segment of consumers in Europe still believe that dishwashers consume an exorbitant amount of water for each cycle. With the development of energy efficient dishwashers, the average dishwashing cycle consumes only 10–15 liters of water.[20] A comparable load of dishes washed by hand would use nearly 80–90 liters of water.[21]

Technical Advancements

The evolution of technology has allowed companies like Electrolux to meet the ever-changing consumer demands and tastes for appliances. One of the most important factors for consumers in selecting home appliances is the level of energy consumption. Consumers are not only using this as a variable in selecting fuel efficient cars and electricity saving light bulbs, but now also dishwashers, stoves, and refrigerators. The AEG-Electrolux Super-Eco washing machine is a great example of energy efficiency, in that it features a cycle that only uses cold water.[22]

The ability to create appliances like AEG-Electrolux Super-Eco has come from several technical advancements. Refrigerators now have the ability to store food with sustained freshness and frost-free freezers.[23] In line with becoming more environmentally friendly, the Electrolux Lagoon is a system for washing, drying, and finishing using only water and biologically degradable detergents. This system can even wash and dry linens that normally would only allow for dry cleaning.[24] These technological advancements are most significant for cookers, ovens and hobs where technical differentiation is extremely important to customers.[25] As previously mentioned, the Inspiro oven is just one example of Electrolux's aim at incorporating new technologies in its products.

Driven by consumer preferences, there has been a growing demand for lower noise emitting vacuums. With this in mind, Electrolux has focused on developing vacuums that are much less noisy than past models. One of Electrolux's vacuum models focuses on air-flow, enhances the performance of the vacuum and reduces the noise level, resulting in an effectively silent vacuum cleaner.[26]

While the demand to incorporate new technologies into appliances to increase the standard of living persists, the ability to use different recyclable raw materials in developing appliances is also another technological opportunity. Environmentally conscious consumers look for appliances that use as least some recycled material and are taking into consideration the recyclability of their appliances after their use. This presents a unique opportunity for Electrolux to use new technologies to meet these environmentally conscious consumers.

One of the more significant threats for Electrolux is the internet. The internet allows consumers faster and more extensive access to information about products and services, which in turn leads to greater price awareness.[27] Products like refrigerators and dishwashers, which have low profit margins in geographic areas like Europe and are more difficult to differentiate except by price, suffer the most from the use of tools like the internet. Consumers can easily shop online to discover the lowest priced appliance without ever interfacing with a sales person, or traveling to an appliance store.

In general, kitchen appliances like refrigerators, stoves, and dishwashers are heavy and bulky which makes shipping these goods much more expensive.[28] Products like these need to be manufactured and produced near their end-market to reduce the cost of shipping. As mentioned before, many of these appliances already have a low-profit margin so any reduction in cost to produce and ship allows Electrolux the ability to be more competitive based on price. In a push by the appliance industry to produce in low-cost countries, heavy and bulky appliances create a complex problem that companies must overcome in order to remain price competitive.

Global Opportunities and Threats

One of the most important opportunities for any manufacturing company is the ability to manufacture at low costs. There are several regions and countries of the world that allow companies to establish manufacturing plants that reduce the cost of goods sold especially in the production of appliances. For Electrolux, all vacuum cleaners are produced in low-cost countries.[29] As previously mentioned, part of Electrolux's campaign to relocate production facilities to low-cost countries has resulted in Electrolux plants in Poland, Hungary, Mexico, China and Thailand to reach the company's global market.[30] As indicated before, certain bulky appliances must be produced near the end market. For example, the Mexico manufacturing facilities for Electrolux serve its North American market.[31] Manufacturing facilities in Thailand on the other hand, serve the Australian market.[32]

With rising incomes and increasing worldwide homeownership, there are several attractive markets for appliances including Southeast Asia, Latin America, Mexico, Argentina, and Brazil.[33] For dishwashers in particular, the European market has experienced tremendous growth with increased demand for dishwashers of 20% since 2004.[34]

It's important for companies to also identify countries where governments have introduced economic recovery plans that favor appliance corporations. For example, Brazil's government has rolled out a stimulus package that led directly to an increase in demand for consumer durables supported by lower taxes on domestically produced appliances as well as lower interest rates and greater access to credit.[35]

While predicting the next boom of consumer durable demand globally is difficult, there is one variable that helps companies determine when to ramp up production and prepare for increased demand. As previously stated, there is a direct positive correlation between raw-material prices and strong economic periods.[36] As the price of raw-materials increases, Electrolux can use this relationship phenomenon to identify future economic booms.

With the opportunities available for companies that take advantage of the global market, there are certainly threats that make it difficult to maintain a competitive advantage. For Electrolux, operating and manufacturing in dozens of countries across the globe opens the company up to currency risk exposure in fluctuating markets. With such economic uncertainty, as witnessed from this most recent economic recession, it is now more important than ever to hedge currency risks and identify, and respond to, markets that are a detriment to the business.

Raw material prices also fluctuate with great volatility and are difficult to forecast. A complicating factor, supporting price volatility for companies, is the scarcity of natural resources used to manufacture appliances like steel.[37] Companies must balance short fluctuating prices of raw materials and adjust menu prices as needed while keeping in mind what consumers must be willing to accept and pay for the price variations.

Financials

Consumer products make up 93% of Electrolux's sales. **Exhibit 4** breaks down the company's sales and income position by geographic market. North America and Europe are its largest markets in both sales and income. However, sales in Latin America have continued to increase over the past few years as the company gains greater market share in Brazil. As discussed in the global opportunities section, the Asian market is growing at a rapid pace and as such the company has seen an increase in sales and market share in this region as well. The company's income in all regions increased in 2009 primarily due to the lower cost of raw materials and cost-cutting measures taken by the company.

Exhibit 5 illustrates the company's net income and sales over the past 8 years. The company has had a tough time increasing its sales since 2002 and its year-over-year sales growth has been less than 10% in that time period. In 2005, the company's net income loss was mainly due to the higher cost of raw materials, namely steel. Raw material costs make up approximately 20% of the price of an Electrolux appliance so the fluctuation in cost has a significant impact on the company's profitability. During 2005, the company also faced a weakening market in North America and significant competitive challenges in the Chinese market. These factors all contributed to their 2005 loss. Despite the global economic crisis in 2008, the company's sales remained flat year-over-year. Due to the decreasing demand for Electrolux premium appliances in 2008, the company decreased their prices in an effort to keep their sales flat, however this had a negative impact on their bottom line profitability. The company also took cost cutting measures in order to prepare for the uncertain economic climate in 2009 by reducing headcount and transferring production to low-cost countries such as Thailand, China, and Mexico. In 2009, Electrolux was able to slightly increase its sales by 4% and significantly improve its income from SEK 366M to SEK 2.6B. The increase in income was a result of the company's cost savings initiatives and a lower cost for raw materials. Some of the cost cutting methods the company took in 2009 include closing 16 plants, reducing headcount by over 3,000 employees and reducing the number of component variants in its products. Electrolux has moved 60% of its production to low-cost countries and expects that this manufacturing restructure will generate annual savings of approximately SEK 3 billion. The company also cut its plant capacity to respond to the decrease in demand so that Electrolux's capacity utilization is only 60% versus a normal of over 85%. Electrolux's laser focus on maintaining cost efficiency helped it to survive and emerge stronger from the recession. Electrolux needs to maintain a lean cost structure and focus investments on marketing to strengthen its brand.

Operations

Before evaluating the operational objectives of Electrolux and the company's strengths and weaknesses in that area, it is important to first understand how the company is structured. The operational structure of a company provides a glimpse into the overall strategy of the company. In the case of Electrolux, it has four global regions for the sale of major appliances: Europe, North America, Latin America and Asia Pacific. For the remaining product divisions, the company established a single global entity that manages the entire line—in this case floor care and small appliances along with professional products (See Exhibit 11). This operational structure aligns with the strategy of focusing on high-end, premium appliances. More attention has been devoted to the appliance business because it represents the largest growth sector and the highest-margin products for the company.

The primary objective of Electrolux from an operational standpoint is to achieve an operating margin of 6%. For the last few years, the company has been laser-focused on improving its operating margin. This focus developed as the company realized its cost base was significantly higher than the majority of the industry. In addition, Electrolux strives to be an innovation driven company focused on the consumer. From an operational standpoint, it does this by maintaining a focus on the consumer during product development, design, production, marketing, logistics and service.

Because of this continued focus on improving the operating margin, one of the strengths of the company's operations is the diminishing cost of its supplier and production network. By the end of 2010, Electrolux will have moved 60% of its production to low-cost countries saving the company SEK 3 billion annually.[38] Another strength is that the company is not blindly relocating production facilities on the basis of price alone. Electrolux is making a strategic decision with each new production facility based on current and future costs of labor, transportation parameters, access to local suppliers and proximity to growing markets. Because of this, the company has made strategic decisions to keep some production in high or medium cost countries. For example, the company has determined that plants for built-in ovens and cookers for Europe must remain local due to advanced technology and high transportation costs. Likewise, refrigerators and washing machines must be produced close to the end market because the items are expensive to ship and labor costs make up a small fraction of the total cost of the product. The two production plants in Juarez, Mexico are a

prime example of this strategy. While Mexico is not a country with high labor costs, it is not considered low either. Two plants have been established in the country to serve the North American markets—one for kitchen appliances and one for washing machines and dryers. This helps to reduce the cost of labor but also maintain a facility in close proximity to the end market (See Exhibit 12). Conversely, vacuums are inexpensive to ship and labor makes up the bulk of the final price of the product. As such, 100% of Electrolux vacuum cleaners are made in low-cost countries—primarily Thailand. This represents a significant strength for Electrolux because it makes strategic decisions around its production facilities rather than constantly chasing the lowest cost labor.

Though Electrolux has been improving its operating position, the company still has a number of weaknesses. As mentioned above, the company has undergone a strategic initiative to significantly reduce its cost structure to achieve an operating margin of 6%. The company is nearing its goal with an operating margin of 4.82%. But even at 6%, Electrolux is well below the industry standard of 8.42%. This slim margin is a glaring weakness. Another weakness of Electrolux is that its margins are impacted greatly by an over reliance on low-cost items such as vacuum cleaners where margins are much tighter. As the company pushes toward the stated goal of a 6% operating margin, it will need to continue to emphasize high-end appliances over vacuums.

Marketing

A key strength for Electrolux is that after many years of continuously declining prices, the company managed to increase prices in Europe at the beginning of 2009 and at the same time maintained its price position in the American market. This is indicative of a strong brand that consumers are willing to pay a premium for—especially in the face of declining demand.[39] A second strength of the Electrolux marketing function is that the company has multiple customer touch points and entry points into the home, similar to GE. Also, the company has roots in door-to-door sales. This type of relationship selling is becoming even more crucial in today's market. While it's not door-to-door sales, consumers expect a one-to-one relationship with companies and are increasingly reluctant to engage with a brand that focuses on pushing messages to the masses. Electrolux is uniquely positioned in this regard. The company is also strongly positioned when it comes to sustainability initiatives. Many companies have jumped on the sustainability bandwagon, but few have done it with a clear plan on how they will cut energy consumption and how that will save the company resources in the long run. By year-end 2012, Electrolux factories, offices, and warehouses will use 15% less energy than in 2008. These reductions will result in CO_2 savings of over 73,000 tons—the equivalent of the yearly emissions from more than 32,000 cars. This reflects Electrolux's continued commitment to reducing energy use that has been ongoing and allow the company to save approximately $100 million per year.[40] Finally, the company's marketing function is strong in the fact that the department is engaged in the product development process from the start (see Exhibit 13). This helps to produce key innovations such as an induction cook top that can boil water in 90-seconds and a washer dryer that can complete a load of laundry in 36 minutes.

Because Electrolux is such a large company with several brands, a primary weakness of the marketing function is that the sub-brands are often more well-known than premium brands. For example, many people in the North American market are familiar with the Frigidaire brand but only have minimal awareness of the Electrolux brand outside of vacuum cleaners. This could pose a challenge for the company as it aims to move upstream and focus on high-end appliances. In addition, another key weakness of the Electrolux marketing team is its roots in door-to-door sales. While it is also a strength due to the heritage in relationship selling, it runs counter to the idea of a premium brand. When people think of high-end appliances, they don't immediately consider brands that sell vacuums door-to-door. If Electrolux hopes to move more squarely into the high-end appliance segment it will have to distance itself from this history.

Innovation

Electrolux's core competency is its unique focus on comprehensive innovation and ability to successfully create differentiated value in its products. Electrolux has been able to take cutting-edge technologies and integrate them into household appliances, catering to new consumer preferences and tastes. This ability to combine practicability and aesthetics has supported Electrolux as a prospector in the appliance industry.

The Ultra Silencer Green vacuum cleaner is a perfect example of combing the unique consumer tastes with new technologies. As previously described, the Ultra Silencer Green vacuum is comprised of 55% recycled plastic material and is the most energy efficient vacuum cleaner on the market. Its high-efficiency motor reduces the Ultra Silencer's energy consumption by 33% compared to the standard 2,000 watt vacuum cleaner.[41] With a sleek black finish, highlighted with green buttons, this vacuum cleaner sets the pace for an aesthetically pleasing model with the environment in mind.

Another example of Electrolux's focus on innovation is the new 200G Compass Control Electrolux industrial washer machine with the ability to send text message updates to users of the machine when cycles are completed.[42] With this, Electrolux has been able to capture more of an already mature market by introducing washers and dryers that clean clothes that would have normally only allowed for dry cleaning. The Electrolux Calima is a premium washing machine that is fitted with a fold-out heat map for sensitive garments such as woolen pullovers.[43] This ability to capture some of the substitute competitors market is a testament to Electrolux's ability to identify new opportunities in what was believed to be a mature market.

The supporting factor in Electrolux's core competency is its ability to listen to its customer and recognize evolving consumer demands and tastes. The Ultra Silencer vacuum cleaner originated from a comprehensive study that Electrolux completed in which consumers were surveyed and focus groups were assembled, to assess the most important variables in selecting vacuum cleaners. A growing factor in vacuum selection was noise level.[44] By focusing on the air-flow system of vacuum cleaners, Electrolux was able to take this growing trend and develop the Ultra Silencer which effectively eliminates all noise pollution from the vacuum cleaner. This technological advancement allows customers to play music and have a conversation with someone while vacuuming.

Although Electrolux has differentiated itself as a prospector and prided its business on innovation and incorporating cutting-edge technology, there are a few key weaknesses that negatively affect its potential. Electrolux has been unable to maintain sales of high-profit margin appliances in Germany, Spain, the UK and China.[45] Due to low-priced competition, and an inability to differentiate products such as refrigerators and dishwashers, Electrolux has squeezed only low profits from these mature markets. In relation to other markets and products offered, refrigerators and dishwashers sold in the aforementioned markets require significant company resources but return little in the form of profits.

In 2009, capacity utilization was only 60% for Electrolux.[46] With significant resources tied up in capital of production facilities, Electrolux suffers financially from high overhead costs and costs of goods sold. The return on the company's current manufacturing facility assets has declined significantly as a result of the past recession. Although Electrolux has closed 16 plants and cut back production in 5 others, low capacity utilization is still a major issue that Electrolux must resolve in order to compete on price against other low-priced competitors.[47]

Electrolux has always positioned itself as an appliance company focused on value over volume. Although the company chose to lower its production utilization and lessen its inventory levels, due to the abrupt decline of consumer demand during the last recession, Electrolux has been stuck with inventory in its factories.[48] Electrolux's competitors have experienced the same over production of products which leads to an industry wide problem of increased supply with decreased consumer demand. This basic economic dilemma leads to downward pressure on prices and lower profit margins for Electrolux.

Electrolux has not maintained the same level of innovation, value, and competitive advantage in all of its strategic business units. With multiple brands and hundreds of products, Electrolux has not been able to sustain high-profit margin products that are highly differentiated from its competitors. Although Electrolux excels in sales and profits in the Professional Products segment of the business, it falls behind its competitors in specific product categories like refrigerators.[49] Electrolux can be regarded as a prospector when it develops products like the Inspiro oven, but it can be seen as a defender in Europe with its line of standard, price-differentiated refrigerators. Electrolux must identify and strengthen its weaker strategic business units in order to maintain its competitive advantage.

Exhibit 1   2009 Sales by Product Category

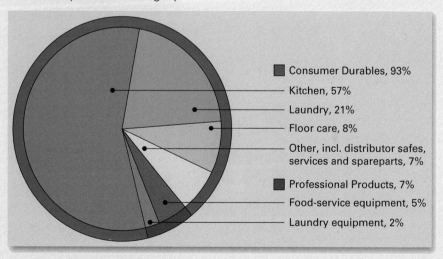

- Consumer Durables, 93%
- Kitchen, 57%
- Laundry, 21%
- Floor care, 8%
- Other, incl. distributor safes, services and spareparts, 7%
- Professional Products, 7%
- Food-service equipment, 5%
- Laundry equipment, 2%

Source: Electrolux 2009 Annual Operations Report

Exhibit 2   Sample of Electrolux Global Brands

Source: Electrolux Website

Exhibit 4   2009 Sales & Income by Region

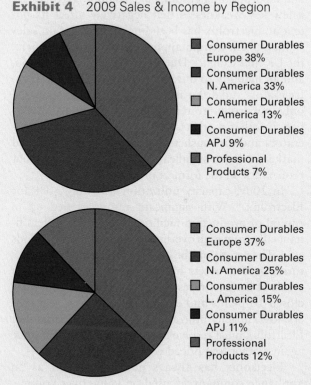

- Consumer Durables Europe 38%
- Consumer Durables N. America 33%
- Consumer Durables L. America 13%
- Consumer Durables APJ 9%
- Professional Products 7%

- Consumer Durables Europe 37%
- Consumer Durables N. America 25%
- Consumer Durables L. America 15%
- Consumer Durables APJ 11%
- Professional Products 12%

Exhibit 3

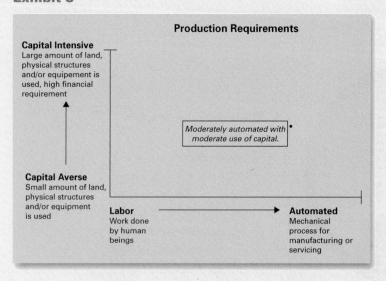

Production Requirements

Capital Intensive
Large amount of land, physical structures and/or equipement is used, high financial requirement

Moderately automated with moderate use of capital.

Capital Averse
Small amount of land, physical structures and/or equipment is used

Labor
Work done by human beings

Automated
Mechanical process for manufacturing or servicing

Exhibit 5 Sales & Net Income (8 year period)

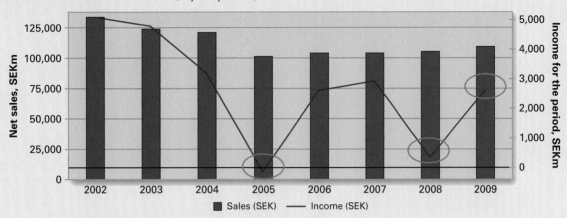

Exhibit 6 Quarterly Sales

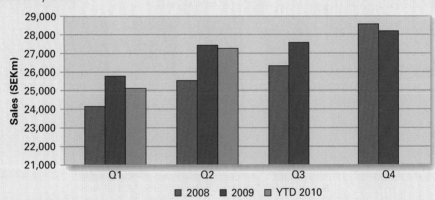

Exhibit 7 Cash & Long-Term Debt to Equity

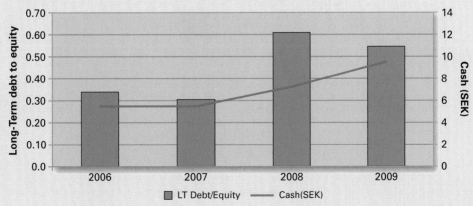

Exhibit 8   Operating Margin

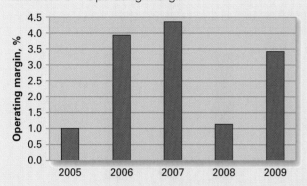

Exhibit 9   A/R, Inventory & Sales

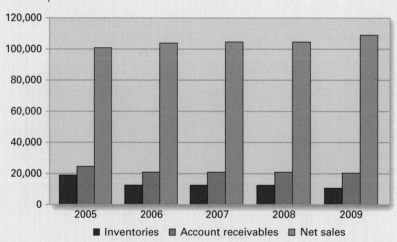

Exhibit 10   Electrolux 5 Year Stock Price Performance

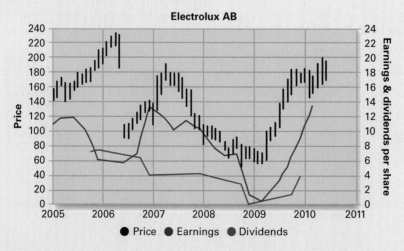

Exhibit 11   Electrolux Organization Structure

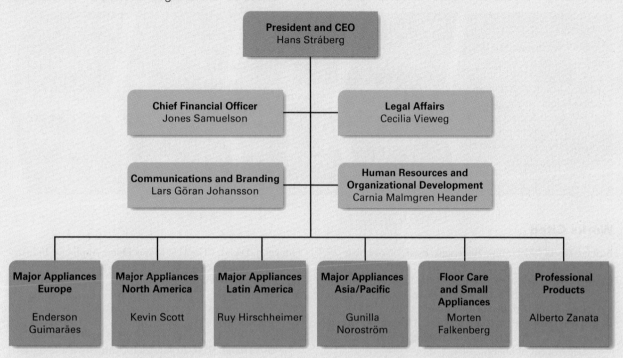

On August 4 Keith McLoughlin was appointed Chief Operations Officer Major Appliances. Keith McLoughlin was previously President and CEO of Major Appliances North America.

Exhibit 12   Manufacturing Footprint

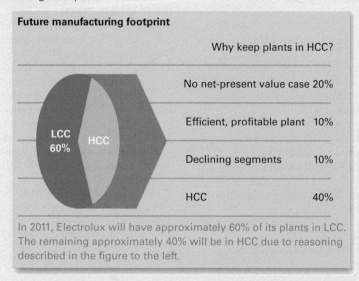

Future manufacturing footprint

Why keep plants in HCC?

No net-present value case 20%

Efficient, profitable plant 10%

Declining segments 10%

HCC 40%

In 2011, Electrolux will have approximately 60% of its plants in LCC. The remaining approximately 40% will be in HCC due to reasoning described in the figure to the left.

Exhibit 13 Electrolux Product Development Process

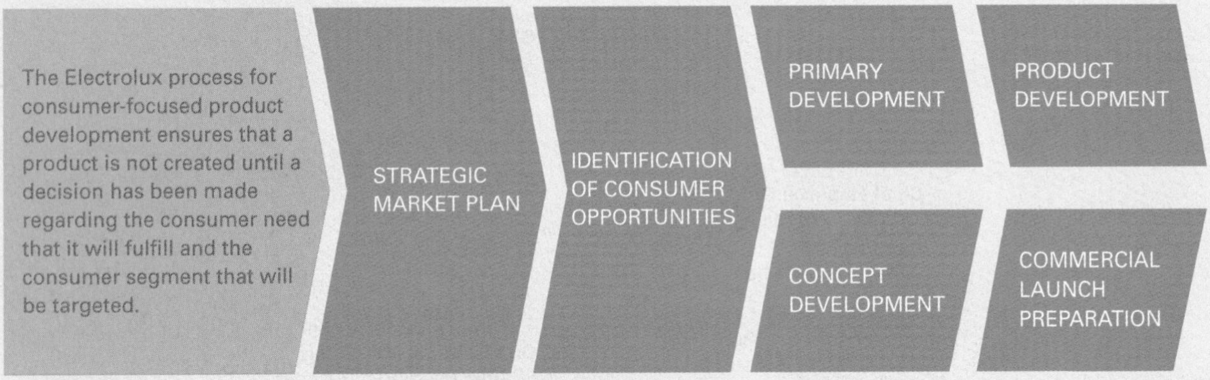

The Electrolux process for consumer-focused product development ensures that a product is not created until a decision has been made regarding the consumer need that it will fulfill and the consumer segment that will be targeted.

STRATEGIC MARKET PLAN

IDENTIFICATION OF CONSUMER OPPORTUNITIES

PRIMARY DEVELOPMENT

PRODUCT DEVELOPMENT

CONCEPT DEVELOPMENT

COMMERCIAL LAUNCH PREPARATION

Works Cited

BusinessWeek. "Electrolux Redesigns Itself." November 27, 2006.

China Daily. "No Cheap Labor? "China Increase Minimum Wages." July 2, 2010. <http://www.chinadaily.com.cn/china/2010-07/02/content_10053553.htm>.

Dale, Larry. Relative Price Elasticity of Demand for Appliances. Economic Analysis. Berkely: United States Department of Energy, 2008.

"ECOSAVINGS." *Welcome to Electrolux USA*. Web. 26 July 2010. <http://www.electrolux.com/ecosavings/>

Electrolux Annual Report 2009. <http://ir.electrolux.com/files/Elux_ENG_Ars09_Del1.pdf>.

Electrolux Blogspot. 18 March 2008. 15 July 2010 <http://electrolux-inspiro.blogspot.com/>.

GE Appliances. 20 July 2010 <http://www.geappliances.com/?cid=3113&omni_key=ge_appliances>.

Electrolux Company History. <http://www.electrolux.com/history_timeline.aspx>.

Electrolux Product Overview. <http://www.electrolux.com/node573.aspx>.

Electrolux. "Electrolux Professional Laundry Systems." *Electrolux Professional Laundry Systems—Home*. Web. 25 July 2010. <http://www.laundrysystems.electrolux.com/node237.aspx?lngNewsId=1122>.

GoldmanSachs."GlobalEconomicsPaperNo:170."7July2008. Web. <http://www2.goldmansachs.com/ideas/global-economic-outlook/expanding-middle.pdf>.

Google Finance Electrolux. 15 July 2010 <http://www.google.com/finance?q=eluxy>.

Google Finance GE. 10 July 2010 <http://www.google.com/finance?q=NYSE:GE>.

Google Finance Whirlpool. 20 July 2010 <http://www.google.com/finance?q=NYSE:WHR>.

Google Patents. July 2010 <www.google.com/patents>.

Hunger, J. David. "The U.S. Major Home Appliance Industry (1996): Domestic versus Global Strategies."

LG. 20 July 2010 <www.lg.com>.

Market Research. 1 February 2010. 7 July 2010 <http://www.marketresearch.com/product/display.asp?productid=2614446>.

"Microsoft Hohm." *Conserve Energy, Save Money—Microsoft Hohm*. Web. 26 July 2010. <http://www.microsoft-hohm.com/location/us/01701/default.aspx>.

Rising, Malin, "Electrolux Q2 Profits Rise, Helped by Cost Savings," iStockAnalyst. <http://www.istockanalyst.com/article/viewiStockNews/articleid/4319345>.

Sandstrom, Gustav. "Electrolux's Net Nearly Doubles—WSJ.com." *Business News & Financial News—The Wall Street Journal—WSJ.com*. Web. 26 July 2010. <http://online.wsj.com/article/SB10001424052748704335904574496642329931268.html>.

Schmit, Julie. USA Today. 23 February 2010. 20 July 2010 <http://www.usatoday.com/tech/news/2010-02-23-energyrebates23_ST_N.htm>.

Times Colonist. 3 July 2010. 20 July 2010 <http://www.timescolonist.com/technology/Electrolux+make+vacuums+from+plastic+ocean+trash/3232456/story.html>.

United States Department of Labor. "Thailand." <http://www.dol.gov/ilab/media/reports/iclp/sweat/thailand.htm>.

United States Government American Recovery and Reinvestment Act. <www.recovery.gov>.

Yahoo Finance. 2010. 8 July 2010 <http://biz.yahoo.com/p/310conameu.html>.

Yahoo Finance. 9 July 2010 <http://finance.yahoo.com/q/co?s=WHR+Competitors>.

Yahoo Finance Electrolux. 7 July 2010 <http://www.google.com/finance?q=PINK:ELUXY>.

Endnotes

1 Electrolux 2009 Annual Report. http://ir.electrolux.com/files/Elux_ENG_Ars09_Del1.pdf

2 Market Research, http://www.marketresearch.com/product/display.asp?productid=2614446

3 USA Today, http://www.usatoday.com/tech/news/2010-02-23-energyrebates23_ST_N.htm

4 Relative Price Elasticity of Demand for Appliances, Larry Dale

5 Appliances Industry Overview, http://biz.yahoo.com/ic/310.html

6 Whirlpool Competitors, http://finance.yahoo.com/q/co?s=WHR+Competitors

7 Appliances Industry Overview

8 Whirlpool Competitors

9 GE Appliances, http://www.geappliances.com/?cid=3113&omni_key=ge_appliances

10 Google Finance, http://www.google.com/finance?q=ge&rls=com.microsoft:en-us&oe=UTF-

11 Whirlpool Competitors

12 LG, www.lg.com

13 "United States Government American Recovery and Reinvestment Act." www.recovery.gov

14 *China Daily*. "No Cheap Labor? "China Increase Minimum Wages." July 2, 2010. http://www.chinadaily.com.cn/china/2010-07/02/content_10053553.htm

15 Goldman Sachs, http://www2.goldmansachs.com/ideas/global-economic-outlook/expanding-middle.pdf

16 Electrolux 2009 Annual Report

17 Electrolux 2009 Annual Report

18 Electrolux 2009 Annual Report

19 Electrolux 2009 Annual Report

20 Electrolux 2009 Annual Report

21 Electrolux 2009 Annual Report

22 Electrolux 2009 Annual Report

23 Electrolux 2009 Annual Report

24 Electrolux 2009 Annual Report

25 Electrolux 2009 Annual Report

26 Electrolux 2009 Annual Report

27 Electrolux 2009 Annual Report

28 Electrolux 2009 Annual Report

29 Electrolux 2009 Annual Report

30 Electrolux 2009 Annual Report

31 Electrolux 2009 Annual Report

32 Electrolux 2009 Annual Report

33 Electrolux 2009 Annual Report

34 Electrolux 2009 Annual Report

35 Electrolux 2009 Annual Report

36 Electrolux 2009 Annual Report

37 Electrolux 2009 Annual Report

38 Electrolux 2009 Annual Report

39 Electrolux 2009 Annual Report

40 Electrolux 2009 Annual Report

41 Electrolux 2009 Annual Report

42 Electrolux Professional Laundry Systems, http://www.laundrysystems.electrolux.com/node237.aspx?lngNewsId=1122

43 Electrolux 2009 Annual Report

44 Electrolux 2009 Annual Report

45 Electrolux 2009 Annual Report

46 Electrolux 2009 Annual Report

47 Electrolux 2009 Annual Report

48 Electrolux 2009 Annual Report

49 Electrolux 2009 Annual Report

CASE 17

American Airlines Since Deregulation: A Thirty-Year Experience, 1978–2007

Isaac Cohen

San Jose State University

Since the passage of the Airline Deregulation Act in 1978, eight major U.S. air carriers filed for bankruptcy. All were old, established carriers flying domestic as well as international routes. Three of the major carriers—Pan American Airways, Eastern Airlines, and Trans World Airways (TWA)—were eventually liquidated and their assets were sold to rival carriers. Two others—Continental Airlines and U.S. Air—filed for bankruptcy protection at least twice. And the remaining three—United, Delta, and Northwest Airlines—were operating in 2005–2006 under Chapter 11 of the Bankruptcy Code. Alone among all U.S. international majors, American Airlines (AA) had never filed for bankruptcy protection.

American's financial position was stronger than that of its competitors all through the era of deregulation. During the first two decades of the new era, Robert Crandall ran AA, first as President (1980–1985), and then as CEO (1985–1998). An executive widely regarded as the industry's most innovative strategist, Crandall introduced the frequent-flier program and the two-tier wage system, expanded American globally, formed alliances with other carriers, and established a successful regional airline affiliated with AA.

As Crandall retired in 1998, Donald Carty was selected CEO. An insider whose tenure was overshadowed by the terrorist attack of September 11, 2001, Carty was a lackluster leader, and his career ended in a public scandal that led to his replacement by Gerald Arpey in April 2003. Arpey needed to act quickly. Following the unprecedented losses incurred by American as a result of the September 11 attack—a loss of over $5 billion dollars during 2001 and 2002, and an additional loss of over $1 billion in the

first quarter of 2003—American Airlines was on the brink of bankruptcy.

What should Arpey do?

Should Arpey follow the strategies undertaken by Crandall to cut operating cost, improve AA's financial position, and turn the carrier profitable? Should Arpey, rather, reject some of the policies introduced by his predecessor? Or should he, instead, introduce brand new innovative strategies applicable to the airline industry in the 21st century?

To assess Arpey's strategic choices, this case looks back at the experience of his legendary predecessor. How precisely did Robert Crandall manage to turn American around?

The Airline Industry

The airline industry dates back to the Air Mail Service of 1918–1925. Using its own planes and pilots, the Post Office Department directly operated scheduled flights to ship mail. With the passage of the Air Mail Act (Kelly Act) of 1925, the Post Office subcontracted air mail transport to private companies and thereby laid the foundation of a national air transport system. The Post Office paid contractors substantial sums and encouraged them to extend their routes, buy larger planes, and expand their services.

The formative period of the private airline industry was the Great Depression. The five or six years following Charles Lindbergh's 1927 flight across the Atlantic were years of mergers and acquisitions in which every major carrier came into existence, mostly through the acquisition of smaller lines. American,

This case was presented in the October 2006 Meeting of the North American Case Research Association at San Diego California. Copyright Isaac Cohen and NACRA. I am grateful to the San Jose State University College of Business for its support.

United, Delta, Northwest, Continental and Eastern Airlines were all formed during this period. The increase in passenger transport during the 1930s led, in turn, to growing competition, price cutting, bankruptcies, and serious safety problems. It convinced the architects of the New Deal that the entire transport system—not just the air mail—required federal regulation. The outcome was the passage of the Civil Aeronautics Act (CAA) of 1938.[1]

The CAA had two major provisions. First, it prohibited price competition among carriers, and second, it effectively closed the industry to newcomers. The Civil Aeronautics Board (CAB) required that all air carriers flying certain routes charge the same fares for the same class of passengers. Similarly, the CAB required all applicants wishing to enter the industry to show that they were "fit, willing and able" to do so and that their service was "required by the public convenience and necessity." Typically, between 1950 and 1975 the board denied all 79 applications it had received from carriers asking to enter the domestic, scheduled airline industry.[2] The number of scheduled air carriers was reduced from 16 in 1938 to just 10 in the 1970s, following mergers, consolidations, and route transfers among carriers.[3]

By the mid-1970s, the airline industry had experienced serious financial troubles. Rising fuel prices, an economic recession, and the introduction of expensive wide-body aircraft (Boeing 747s, Lockheed L-1011s, and McDonnell Douglas DC-10s) led to climbing costs, higher fares, reduced traffic, falling revenues, and a growing public demand for opening up the airline industry to competition. As a result, in 1975, a Senate subcommittee chaired by Edward Kennedy held hearings on the airlines. Working closely with Kennedy was a Harvard law professor named Stephen Breyer, who later became a U.S. Supreme Court Justice. A specialist in regulation, the author of *Regulation and Reform*, and the Staff Director of the Kennedy hearings, Breyer helped Kennedy build up a strong case against airline regulation.

Together, Breyer and Kennedy contrasted intrastate air service—which had never been regulated by the CAB—with interstate service—which had been regulated since 1938. The figures were astounding. Air fares charged by an interstate carrier flying the New York-Boston route (191 miles) were almost double the fares charged by an intrastate carrier (Southwest Airlines) flying the Houston-San Antonio route (also 191 miles), and air fares charged

by an interstate airline servicing the Chicago-Minneapolis city pair market (339 miles) were more than double those charged by an intrastate airline (Pacific Southwest Airlines) serving the Los Angeles-San Francisco market (338 miles). The experience of Southwest Airlines in Texas—like that of Pacific Southwest Airlines in California—Breyer and Kennedy concluded, demonstrated the efficiency of the free market and the urgent need for deregulation.[4] Three years later, in 1978, Congress deregulated the airline industry.

Company Background

The early history of American Airlines dates back to 1929 when dozens of small airline companies merged together to form American Airways, a subsidiary of an aircraft manufacturing /airline service conglomerate called the Aviation Corporation (AVCO). From the outset, American Airlines shipped mail along the Southern sub-continental route from Los Angeles to Atlanta via Dallas. With the passage of the Air Mail Act of 1934, Congress prohibited aircraft manufacturing firms from owning airline companies and redistributed existing airmail contracts on a new, competitive bidding basis. To bid successfully on the new contracts, American Airways changed its name to American Airlines, and reorganized itself as stand alone company, independent of AVCO. Winning back its original government contracts, AA resumed its airmail operations and moved aggressively to expand its nascent passenger service.[5]

For the next 35 years, 1934–1968, a single CEO—Cyrus Rowlett Smith—ran American Airlines. A Texan, C. R. Smith managed to improve AA performance in the 1930s and led the company to sustained growth during the following three decades. He paid particular attention to two critical aspects of airline management, namely, aircraft technology and labor relations.

Smith played a key role in the introduction of the DC-3 aircraft in 1936, a well-designed, and efficient plane with two piston engines. The first commercially viable passenger aircraft ever produced, the DC-3 dominated the world's airways until after WWII. Because AA operated the largest fleet of DC-3s in the industry, it soon became the industry leader, carrying about 30% of the domestic passenger traffic in the late 1930s.[6]

Working together with Donald Douglas on the design and development of the DC-3, C. R. Smith lay the foundations for long lasting relations between AA and the Douglas (since 1967, McDonnell Douglas) Corporation. Not until 1955 did Smith select a Boeing model over a Douglas one [AA ordered its first jet—the B-707—from Boeing),[7] but soon thereafter American Airlines resumed its customer relations with Douglas. The two companies continued cooperating for decades. In 2005, long after C.R. Smith had retired, and nearly a decade after the Boeing Company bought the McDonnell Douglas Corporation, American Airlines' fleet was made up of 327 MD-80 McDonnell Douglas planes, and 320 Boeing planes (the B-737, 757, 767, and 777 models), a 46/45% mix which reflected AA's traditional ties with the McDonnell Douglas Corporation.[8]

C. R. Smith, in addition, played a central role in shaping AA's labor relations. AA employees, like the employees of virtually all other major airlines, had become highly unionized by the late 1940s, and subsequently, the company experienced growing labor troubles. Responding to two large-scale pilot strikes that shut down American airlines in 1954 and 1958, C. R. Smith proposed the establishment of a cooperative arrangement among air carriers known as the Mutual Aid Pact (MAP). Thinking in terms of the entire industry, Smith saw the pact as a self-protecting measure designed to check the rising power of unions. Originally established in 1958 by American and five other carriers (United, TWA, Pan American, Eastern, and Capital), the pact authorized airlines benefiting from a strike that shut down one or more carriers to transfer their strike-generated revenues to the struck carrier(s), an arrangement which reduced the financial losses of the struck carrier(s) and thereby increased management bargaining power across the industry. In its several different forms, the MAP survived for twenty years, providing AA and its rival carriers with a measure of protection against lengthy strikes.[9]

Smith's last four years at American Airlines, 1964–67, were AA's most profitable. In 1968, he retired, and was succeeded by George Spater, a corporate lawyer whose tenure at American was marred by recession and scandal. Spater not only failed to improve AA's performance during the recession of the early 1970s, but he also admitted making illegal corporate contributions to President Nixon's reelection campaign. As a result, the AA board forced

Spater to resign in 1973 and invited C.R. Smith to rejoin American as a caretaker for a short transitional period. Smith served just seven months until the board recruited Albert Casey, a media executive, to head the company.[10]

Casey's early years at American coincided with the political debate over airline deregulation. On the one side, AA financial results during these years were impressive: Casey turned a loss of $34 million in 1975 to a record profit of $122 million in 1978, and raised AA's cash position from $115 million in 1974 to $537 million in 1978. But on the other, Casey opposed deregulation. Casey's management team believed that airline deregulation would promote competition with low-cost carriers and shift passenger traffic away from transcontinental and semi-transcontinental routes—AA's most profitable ones—to short and medium haul routes. "We opposed [deregulation] all the way," Casey recalled years later. "We had the wrong route structure. We had the wrong aircraft . . . We weren't equipped right. [And w]e had very unfavorable union contracts."[11]

Notwithstanding his opposition to deregulation, Casey expected Congress to pass the deregulation act. To prepare for the passage of the act, Casey undertook two early initiatives which later contributed to AA's eventual success under deregulation. First, he established a major hub airport at Dallas/Fort Worth (D/FW) and moved the company's headquarters from New York to Dallas. Second, he promoted Robert Crandall to the presidency of American Airlines.

The Crandall Era, 1980–1998

Crandall's management style was distinctly different from that of Casey. Casey had a personable, relaxed, and jolly manner. Crandall was famous for his charismatic, intense, and combative style. Casey was diplomatic. Crandall was forthright, temperamental, and impatient. "The [airline] business is intensely, vigorously, bitterly, savagely competitive,"[12] Crandall once said, adding, "I want to crush all my competition. That is what competition is about."[13]

Crandall served as AA President for five years, and as CEO for 13 years. During the early period of 1980–1985, Casey turned over to Crandall the day-to-day operation of the company, and focused his attention on American's financial performance.[14]

During the later period, Crandall assumed full responsibility for AA's financial performance, becoming one of the industry's longest serving chief executives. As both President and CEO, Crandall developed a large body of corporate level strategies which helped American gain a competitive advantage over it rivals.

Developing the Hub and Spoke System

The hub and spoke system was the product of airline deregulation. During the regulatory era, government rules restricted the entry of carriers into new travel markets. With the coming of deregulation, such restrictions were removed, and airlines were free to establish their own connecting hubs for the purpose of transferring passengers from incoming to outgoing flights. Utilizing the hub-and-spoke system, carriers were able to cut costs in at least two ways. First, centralizing aircraft maintenance in hubs reduced the fleet's maintenance costs, and second, increasing the carriers' load factor and bringing it close to capacity resulted in a more efficient operation. In addition, the hub-and-spoke system resulted in greater flight frequency for passengers—a service benefit valued especially by business travelers.[15]

Throughout the first two years of his presidency, 1981–1982, Crandall added 17 new domestic cities to AA's D/FW hub, and seven new international destinations (in Mexico as well as the Caribbean). The sheer number of daily flights AA operated in D/FW climbed from 100 to 300 in 1981 alone. Building its central hub in D/FW, American shifted passenger traffic away from other carriers serving Dallas's outlaying cities, subjecting these carriers to relentless competitive pressure. Braniff International Airways is a case in point. The leading carrier serving the D/FW airport in the 1970s, Braniff filed bankruptcy and suspended operation in 1982 largely as a result of the cutthroat competition it was subject to by American Airlines in the Dallas area.[16]

Under Crandall's direction, AA expanded its hub and spoke operations in the 1980s, establishing major hubs in Chicago, Miami, and San Juan, Puerto Rico, and focusing on long-haul fights, the most profitable segment of the industry. By the mid 1990s, these new hubs—together with the D/FW one—had all become major international airports serving passengers flying to destinations in Europe, South America, Central America, and the Caribbean.[17]

Introducing the Two-Tier Wage System

Dubbed "the father of the two-tier pay scale," Crandall had little to do with the origins of the two-tier plan. The idea grew out of management's endless discussions of the need to achieve low cost growth. Rejecting employee concessions as an insufficient means to attain a low cost operation, Crandall nurtured the two-tier idea and transformed it from an abstract notion into a concrete policy—practical, consistent, and effective.[18]

The two-tier wage system distinguished between two types of employees: current employees paid by an A-scale and newly-hired employees paid by a B-scale. Initially, under the system established by Crandall at American, the two scales were not intended to merge at all; in other words, the top pay received by B-scale employees was expected to be significantly lower than the top pay received by A-scale employees. To persuade AA's labor unions to accept the two-tier plan, Crandall offered employees job security, job expanding opportunities, higher wages and benefits, and profit sharing. He also threatened to shrink the carrier unless the unions accepted the two-tier deal. Believing that lay-offs were eminent, American unionized employees agreed to the new wage structure, and in 1983, AA signed the industry's first two-tier contracts with its principal unions, the Allied Pilots Association (APA, representing the pilots), the Transport Workers Union (TWU, representing the machinists and other ground workers), and the Association of Professional Flight Attendants (APFA, representing the flight attendants). AA's major competitors—United, Delta, U.S. Air, and others—negotiated similar labor agreements. Consequently, the number of two-tier union contracts signed in the airline industry jumped from eight in 1983, to 35 in 1984, and then to 62 in 1985.[19]

AA's two-tier wage plan resulted in a significant pay gap between old and new employees. A newly-hired B-727 captain with a five year experience earned $68 an hour or less than half the $140 paid to his/her veteran counterpart. Such a wage gap led to substantial cost savings: between 1984 and 1989 American Airlines' labor cost fell from 37% to 34% of the carrier's total expenses.[20]

Creating a Holding Company

In 1982, Crandall oversaw the formation of the AMR Corporation—a holding company created "to provide [American] with access to sources of financing that otherwise might be unavailable."[21] AMR owned American Airlines together with several other non-airline subsidiaries, an arrangement which gave management greater flexibility in shifting assets among airline and non-airline subsidiaries, and in identifying new profit sources. Equally important was the protection AMR gave the airline from the swings of the business cycle: profits generated by AMR's nonairline units were expected to mitigate the impact of the industry's periodic downturns.

Consider the following example. During the downturn of 1990–1993, Crandall devised a "transition plan" that called for shifting assets from AMR's unprofitable airline operation to its profitable nonairline businesses. He even suggested leaving the airline business altogether. As AA's losses were mounting—and profits generated from AMR's non-airline units were increasing—Crandall threatened to sell AA and keep instead AMR's nonairline subsidiaries only.[22]

AMR's principal subsidiary—apart from AA—was the Sabre computer reservation system. Owned by AMR, Sabre (Semi Automatic Business Research Environment) had become AMR's most profitable unit during the 1990s, generating far higher returns on sales than the airline itself. In 1995, for instance, Sabre recorded total sales of $1.5 billion, or 9% of AMR revenues, and an operating profit of 19%.[23]

Building a Regional Airline

Another subsidiary of AMR was American Eagle. American Eagle was established in 1984 as AA's regional affiliate. Operating under the affiliate name, several small regional airlines were franchised by AA to supply connecting flights to American air services. From the start, American Eagle offered customers "seamless service," that is, assigned seats, boarding passes, and frequent flyer mileage. In 1987, AMR began acquiring American Eagle's franchised carriers, and in 1990, it consolidated these carriers into six airline systems that served the D/FW, Nashville, New York City, Chicago, Raleigh/Durham and San Juan regional markets. To better coordinate planning, operation, schedules, training, and marketing of commuter services, AMR sought further consolidation. Accordingly, in 1998, it merged the six regional airlines into a single entity carrier, the America Eagle Airlines, creating the world's largest regional airline system. Operating 1,450 daily flights to 125 destinations in the U.S., Canada, and the Caribbean; employing 10,000; and generating $1 billion in revenue, American Eagle was named "Airline of the Year" by *Commuter World* magazine in 1998.[24]

American Eagle's growth helped improve AMR's financial results. Originally, American Eagle operated as a regional carrier feeding passengers to American Airlines flights. But by the mid-1990s, Crandall had replaced a growing number of routes flown by AA pilots with routes flown by American Eagle pilots, a move which resulted in substantial labor cost savings, given the higher pay received by American than Eagle pilots (in 1997 AA pilots earned an average yearly pay of $120,000 and Eagle pilots $35,000).[25]

Upgrading the Computer Reservation System (CRS)

The Sabre computer reservation system was born in 1962, following a decade-long research effort carried out jointly by American Airlines engineers and IBM technicians. Initially, Sabre lagged behind comparable CRS systems used by its competitors, namely, United's Apollo, TWA's PARS, and Eastern Airlines' System One. But by the mid-1970s, with the appointment of Crandall to the position of AA's Vice President for Marketing, Sabre received a new lease of life. As marketing chief, Crandall controlled the company's budget for technology research and development. He recruited a strong team of Sabre computer engineers, and supplied the team with ample funding. At the same time, he launched a campaign to build an industry-wide CRS owned jointly by the major airlines, and used by travel agents. Confident that its own CRS was ahead of its competitors, United declined to join the industry-wide project, and instead, decided to sell its Apollo system's services directly to travel agents. Crandall reacted quickly. Implementing a carefully crafted back-up plan, he sent hundreds of sales people and technicians to travel agents all across the country, offering them a variety of Sabre services. Caught unprepared, United was unable to deliver its own computer reservation system's services until months later. The result was a swift victory of American over United in the race to wire travel agents.[26]

Sabre provided American Airlines with several information technology services. First, it calculated the yield of each American flight, setting and resetting the price of every seat sold. Second, it managed an inventory of close to one billion spare parts used by American's fleet in its maintenance facilities. Third, it directed the routing and tracking of all baggage and freight. And fourth, it supplied American with ongoing data on aircraft fuel requirements, take off weight, and flight plan.[27]

More important were Sabre's travel services. Sabre provided travel agents around the world with fares and schedules for flights offered by hundreds of carriers, not only American and American Eagle. In 1997, Sabre signed a comprehensive 25-year agreement to manage the information technology infrastructure of U.S. Air, and in addition, it renewed a five-year contract with Southwest Airlines to operate the carrier's reservation and inventory systems. Sabre and Canadian Airlines International signed a similar agreement in 1994.

Sabre's clients, it should be noted, were not limited to the airline industry. Both the London Underground and the French National Railway were Sabre's customers in the 1990s, the first contracted Sabre to manage its train and crew scheduling, the second, to design its computer reservation system. Under Crandall's leadership, furthermore, Sabre signed agreements with both Dollar Rent-a-Car and Thrifty Rent-a-Car to manage each company's reservation system.[28]

Under Crandall's leadership, Sabre had become the U.S. largest computer reservation system with a 40% share of all travel agent bookings in 1996. Nearly 30,000 travel agent offices in 70 countries subscribed to Sabre, and more than 2.5 million individual passengers subscribed to Travelocity, Sabre's Internet service. In 1995, the total value of travel-related products and services reserved through Sabre was estimated at $40 billion.[29]

Promoting Yield Management

Developing a revenue maximizing process called yield management was impossible without enhanced computer capabilities. To fill all empty seats on a given flight, American Airlines needed to obtain information pertaining to the desirable number of seats that could be sold at full versus discount fares, and the optimal mix of fares that could maximize the yield of a given flight. Obtaining such information required complex computer calculations based on the carrier's past performance. Hence the key role played by Sabre. Sabre could track any passenger on

any seat traveling any distance at any time. It could find out how early business travelers booked their flights, how far in advance coach passengers did so, and how sensitive each of these two groups was to fare price changes. With Sabre's growing computer capabilities, American began offering a large variety of discounted fares, as Don Reed, author of *Bob Crandall and American Airlines*, explained:

> Instead of offering first-class, coach, and one level of discount fares, American began offering several layers of discounts. The bigger the savings off full-fare prices, the more restrictions the tickets had. The more modest the savings, the fewer restrictions. So fourteen-day and seven-day advance purchase discount fares cost more than twenty-one-day fares, but they were less restricted. Because of this sliding scale of discounts, American could juggle the percentage of seats on any airplane allocated to one fare type or another. . . . By the late 1980s American would be able to, and often did, juggle the mix of fares right up until the moment of departure.[30]

Sabre's yield management system gave American a clear competitive advantage over its rivals. On any given flight, AA was able to offer a variety of discounted fares using projections based on past experience. Sabre's technology permitted Crandall to match or undercut the cheaper fares offered by competitors by simply lowering American's own discount prices for some seats and/or increase the number of seats available at the lowest price category. There was no need to reduce fares on all seats. While competitors lacking American's technology were unable to match AA's price flexibility, they soon introduced their own yield management systems; nevertheless, American Airlines managed to retain its leadership position in the field for decades.

Pioneering the Frequent-Flyer Program

Just as Sabre promoted the development of AA's yield management system, so did it facilitate the introduction of American's AAdvantage frequent flyer program, an innovation that allowed regular passengers to earn free tickets on miles traveled with American. And just as the hub-and spoke system was the outgrowth of deregulation, so was the frequent flyer program. While deregulation promoted competition, the frequent flyer program protected carriers from the competitive market forces by creating brand loyalty among travelers.

Crandall introduced the AAdvantage program—the first in the industry—in 1981, a year after he became president. Managed by Sabre, the frequent flyer innovation was an effective marketing program which lowered the advertising costs by targeting individuals AAdvantage card-holders reachable through mailing and/or email distribution lists. Sabre had been gathering information on passengers early on. As Mike Gunn, AA's Vice President for Marketing under Crandall noted: "one reason we were able to seize the competitive edge was that we already knew who many of our best customers were and how to reach them quickly. As other airlines struggled to match our initiative and identify their base of frequent-flyers, we were already placing AAdvantage cards and welcome letters in the hands of our best customers."[31]

More than one million passengers joined AAdvantage before the end of 1981, and another million joined the frequent flyer programs introduced by other airlines in 1981 in response to AAdvantage. Ten years later, 28 million travelers were card-carrying members of at least one frequent flyer program, and they held, on average, membership in 3.5 programs. American Airlines' program was the industry's largest. In 1991, American's frequent flier program had one million members more than that of its closest competitor, United, and four million more than Delta, the nation's third largest carrier.[32]

At the time Crandall left office in 1998, the frequent flyer program had become an airline industry standard feature. It impacted other industries as well and generated both revenues and profits for the airlines. American sold miles to a variety of companies which awarded, in turn, AA miles to loyal customers as an incentive. In 1998, over 2,500 companies awarded miles to customers using the AAdvantage Incentive Miles program, most of which were retail stores and food serving establishments.[33]

Expanding Internationally

Before the passage of the airline regulation act in 1978, American Airlines had virtually no international presence. The dominant U.S. international carriers at the time were TWA and Pan America World Airways, and neither United nor Delta Airlines served any foreign destinations.[34] The Deregulation Act removed government restrictions on entry into new travel markets, promoted the development of hub-and-spoke systems, and as such, prompted the leading domestic airlines—United, American, and Delta—to begin serving a growing number of international destinations.

From the outset, AA's domestic hub system supported international expansion, helping the carrier fill empty seats on overseas flights. In the early 1980s, Crandall extended AA's route network to Mexico and the Caribbean, but not until 1990 did he launch a massive drive at global expansion, adding many more overseas destinations in Europe and Latin America.

Crandall's decision to extend AA's international route network was informed by air-traffic projections. Over the ten-year period 1990–2000, U.S. air traffic was expected to grow at a modest rate of 3%-4% a year while transatlantic air traffic, as well as traffic between the U.S. and Latin America's destinations, was projected to increase at an annual rate of 6%-7%. To take advantage of these projections, Crandall committed $11 billion, or half of AA's investment budget, to global expansion over the five year period, 1990–1995. He also made two important acquisitions, both in 1989–1991. He first bought TWA's Chicago-London route in 1989, and six more TWA-London routes in 1991. He next acquired Eastern Airline's Latin America route system in 1990. In the Latin American market, AA used its strong Miami hub to handle traffic from 20 cities in 15 South and Central American countries. In the European market, Crandall embarked on what he called a "fragmentation strategy," namely, the break-up of the traditional route system linking one international city to another, for example, New York—London (and flying large commercial aircraft such as the 400-seat Boeing B-747), and replacing it with a route system that linked less congested cites like Chicago and Brussels or Chicago and Glasgow (and flying smaller 200-seat aircraft such as the Boeing B-767).[35]

Five years later, Crandall's plan achieved its main goals. By the mid-1990s, AA had become the dominant U.S. carrier serving Latin America, and the number two U.S. carrier serving Europe, closely behind Delta. In Latin America, AA carried 58% of all U.S. airline traffic to and from the region, served 27 nations, and opened two new U.S. gateway hubs, one in New York, the other in Dallas/Fort Worth, in addition to its principal one in Miami. In the transatlantic travel market, AA's share accounted for 23% of all airline traffic. In 1995, American derived 14%-15% of its airline revenues from the Latin America market, and 13% from the European market. As expected, both international markets were quite profitable: in 1996, AA generated an operating profit margin of 10% in Latin America, and 8% in Europe.[36]

Forming Alliances

Signing code-sharing agreements with foreign carriers was another growth strategy undertaken by Crandall. Code-sharing allowed American to assign its two letter code—AA—to flights operated by another carrier, thereby offering passengers flights to destinations not served by American. Enhanced by shared computer reservation systems and joint frequent-flyer programs, such agreements enabled American to increase its passenger traffic without extending its own route network, hence saving the carrier the expensive and risky cost of starting new international services.

American signed its first code-sharing agreement with Canadian Airlines International (CAI) in 1995. The agreement extended AA's route network to dozens of Canadian cities served by CAI and linked CAI route system to dozens of U.S. destinations served by AA. Seeking to extend AA's route structure to Asia, Crandall signed another code-sharing agreement with CAI in 1997. The 1997 agreement offered AA passengers trans-Pacific service on flights operated by CAI between Vancouver and Taipei. To further increase its Asia-bound traffic, American formed an alliance with China Eastern Airlines in 1998—the first code-sharing agreement between a U.S. carrier and an airline based in the People's Republic of China. Under the agreement's provisions, American placed its code on flights operated by China Eastern from Los Angeles and San Francisco to both Shanghai and Beijing, thereby offering passengers from destinations as distant as Latin America full service to Mainland China. Finally, in September 1998, a few months after Crandall stepped down, American Airlines announced the formation of OneWorld Alliance, a code-sharing agreement signed by five international carriers: American Airlines, British Airways, Canadian Airlines International, Qantas Airway (Australia), and Cathy Pacific Airlines (Hong Kong).[37]

Escalating the War with the Unions, 1990–1998

AA's labor relations under Crandall may be divided into two, distinctly different, periods: 1980–1989 and 1990–1998. In the 1980s, relations between labor and management at American were, for the most part, cooperative and peaceful. Crandall, as discussed, managed to convince the leadership of the pilots', flight attendants', and machinists' unions to negotiate and sign two-tier labor agreements which allowed management to place newly hired employees on a lower, B-type wage scale.

In the 1990s, by contrast, labor relations at American were stormy and contentious. Contract negotiations were long and difficult to conclude, and labor disputes triggered strikes, strike threats, and repeated instances of federal intervention to avert strikes. As a consequence, labor disputes were costly, resulting in revenue and income losses.

One major cause of the 1990s labor troubles was the lingering dissatisfaction—expressed by AA employees—with the two-tier wage system. For any unionized job, B-scale employees were paid much lower wages than their veteran counterparts, and over the years, these lower paid employees had turned extremely resentful toward management. As Crandall hired a growing number of B-scale recruits in the 1980s and 1990s, the "B-scalers" had eventually become the majority of all AA's unionized employees.

Two labor disputes at American during the 1990s stand out. The first involved a strike staged by the Professional Association of Fight Attendants. In 1993, 21,000 fight attendants struck American airlines during Thanksgiving Day weekend, crippling the carrier and ruining whatever prospects management had of posting profits that year (AA ended the year with a small loss of $110 million on $15.8 billion in revenues). Union leaders pointed out that Crandall's unwillingness to bend during negotiations precipitated the strike. Industry analysts agreed, noting Crandall's compulsion to keep labor cost-low. As the strike entered its fifth day, President Clinton intervened and pressured both sides to accept binding arbitration. The dispute was later settled, but the flight attendants remained disgruntled.[38]

A pilots' strike-threat underlay the second labor dispute. In November 1996, the Allied Pilots

Association's board of directors approved a tentative pilots' contract, and presented it to the union membership for ratification. Persuaded by a dissident group of grassroots union activists made largely of B-scale pilots, the membership rejected the contract by a margin of almost two to one. The union leadership, in turn, hardened it position, and threatened to strike the carrier. As the strike deadline approached, President Clinton intervened, invoking a rarely used provision of the 1926 Railway Act which empowered him to appoint a three-member emergency board to help settle the dispute. In the meantime American's losses were mounting. By April 1997, AA lost at least $100 million in advanced bookings, as passengers avoided flying an airline facing impending walkout days. The contract was eventually ratified, but here again, the pilots remained embittered, and they continued resenting Crandall's heavy-handed management methods.[39]

Improving Financial Results, 1985–1997

AA's financial performance under Crandall needs to be analyzed in conjunction with Crandall's evolving strategy. Serving as CEO for 13 years, Crandall shaped and reshaped his strategy, paying close attention to changes in the business cycle. In the 1980s, Crandall undertook a growth strategy that resulted in a rapid expansion of American Airlines' fleet, as well as workforce. The larger AA grew, the lower were its costs, the higher its revenues, and the larger its profits. In the early 1990s, as the air travel market slid into a protracted recession, and AA experienced four years of losses, Crandall embarked on a retrenchment strategy, laying off employees, grounding old planes, exiting unprofitable markets, and outsourcing selected services. Following the recession of 1990–1993, the industry expanded once again, and Crandall introduced a second growth plan. His renewed efforts at increasing revenues and improving profits were sustained by AA's industry-leading yield management system, its formidable AAdvantage frequent flyer program, and its extensive global route network. Notwithstanding the labor troubles of 1996–1997, the carrier had become profitable again, posting a net income of over $1 billion in 1996, close to $1 billion in 1997, and $1.3 billion in 1998, as Exhibit 1 shows, and reducing its debt as a percentage of capitalization from 83% in 1994 to 66% at the end of 1996.[40]

Exhibit 1   Robert Crandall's American Airlines Highlights of Financial Data, 1985–1998

	Revenues ($Mil.)	Net Income ($Mil.)	Income as % of Revenues
1985	6.131	346	5.6%
1986	6.018	279	4.6%
1987	7,198	198	2.8%
1988	8,824	477	5.4%
1989	10,480	455	4.3%
1990	11,120	(40)	—
1991	12,887	(240)	—
1992	14,396	(935)	—
1993	15,816	(110)	—
1994	16,137	228	—
1995	16,910	167	1.0%
1996	17,753	1,067	5.7%
1997	18,570	985	5.3%
1998	19,205	1,314	6.8%

Sources: "AMR Corporation," *Hoover's Handbook of American Business*, 1992, p. 110, 2002, p. 165.

Donald Carty and the September 11, 2001 Terrorist Attack

Donald Carty served as American Airlines CEO for five years. An AA's career executive, he was hand picked by Crandall to lead the carrier, first as President, and then, following Crandall's retirement in 1998, as CEO. Carty's five year tenure was marred by labor troubles, recession, and terrorism, and ended in a public scandal: as a result of the September 11, 2001 attack, American Airlines was losing several million dollars a day, yet in Spring 2003, at the time the carrier was inching towards bankruptcy, AA's senior executives—including Carty—received undisclosed bonuses and pension guarantees worth millions of dollars.

Carty's labor problems began early on. In 1999, he convinced the AMR board to acquire a small low-cost commuter airline called Reno Air. The proposed acquisition evoked a staunch opposition on the part of American pilots. Believing that Carty planed to replace them with low-paid Reno pilots, members of the Allied Pilots Association staged an 11 days sickout which forced American to cancel 6,700 fights, left 600,000 passengers stranded, and cost the carrier $225 million in lost earnings. Also in 1999, AA flight attendants rejected a tentative contract offer and threatened to strike the carrier. In 2001, AA's flight attendants agreed to accept a contract agreement only after exhaustive negotiations that ended hours before a strike deadline.[41]

Notwithstanding these labor differences, Carty moved to expand the airline by merger, purchasing TWA—a trunk-line carrier experiencing serious financial problems. Approved in April 2001, AA's merger with TWA created the nation's largest airline, adding 188 commercial airplanes to American's fleet (TWA's 104 McDonnell Douglas MD-80 jets fit nicely into AA's fleet), and providing American with a central hub at St. Louis. The cost of the transaction was just $742 million—a modest sum by any industry standards—and more important, the merger was supported by all major unions. Backed by the unionized employees of both carriers, Carty managed to integrate the two companies smoothly, earning the praise of industry analysts.[42]

Yet the TWA acquisition was untimely. The merger was approved at the time the entire airline industry was moving rapidly into a recession. Following the merger's approval in Spring 2001, business travel dropped precipitously, leisure travel fell too, and fuel prices were rising. As a result, AA lost $550 million during the first half of 2001.[43] Less than three months later, the 9/11 terrorist attack erupted, destroying two AA passenger jets at mid air, and shutting down all airline travel in the U.S. for two days.

The impact of the 9/11 attack on American's financial performance was long lasting. As shown in Exhibit 2, AA lost $1.8 billion in 2001, and a record $3.5 billion in 2002. In April 2003, following another loss of a billion dollar during the first quarter of the year, American Airlines was nearly bankrupt.

To avoid filing bankruptcy under Chapter 11, Carty asked the three unions representing the majority of AA employees to agree to major wage and benefit concessions. The leadership of each union accepted management's demand for a concessional contract and put the issue before the membership for a vote. Within two weeks, AA employees ratified a collective bargaining agreement that gave the carrier back a total of $1.8 billion, or 20% of the carrier's annual payroll.[44]

A day later the deal began to unravel. Following the contract ratification, union leaders, as well as members, learned from news reports that the AMR corporation awarded Cary and five other executives bonuses that equaled twice their annual salaries, and set aside a $41 million trust that was intended to protect the pensions of 45 executives in the event of bankruptcy. As it turned out, the carrier delayed filing a report detailing these executive compensation plans with the Security and Exchange Commission until after the contract vote was completed.[45]

The belated disclosure angered the employees and prompted two of the three unions to call for another contract vote. Carty, in turn, sent a letter to

Exhibit 2 Donald Carty's American Airlines Highlights of Financial Data, 1998–2002

	Revenues	Net Income	Income as	Stock Prices
	($Mil.)	($Mil.)	% of Revenues	FY Close
1998	19,205	1,314	6.8%	$26.54
1999	17,730	985	5.3%	29.95
2000	19,703	813	5.7%	39.19
2001	18,963	(1,762)	—	22.30
2002	17,299	(3,511)	—	6.60

Source: "AMR Corporation," *Hoover's Handbook of American Business,* 2005, p. 88.

AA employees apologizing for his conduct, and announcing the cancellation of the proposed bonuses: "My mistake was failing to explicitly describe these retention benefits . . . Please know that it was never my intention to mislead you."[46] The disclosure, in addition, surprised several members of the AMR board who felt misled by top management, believing that Carty had discussed the executive compensation package with the union leaderships prior to the contract vote. In response to the mounting public outcry over the disclosure, AMR board of directors sought Carty's resignation. Pressured by the board, Carty promptly stepped down, and the directors moved at once to elect a new CEO.[47]

The Future: Gerard Arpey's American Airlines, 2003—

A few board members suggested rehiring Robert Crandall. Others rejected Crandall's choice and sought instead a candidate that was likely to create a sense of management continuity in AA and act quickly to save the company from filing bankruptcy. Such a candidate, the majority of directors agreed, was American Airlines President Gerard Arpey. Elected by the board to replace Carty, Arpey had 24 hours to save the carrier. Crafting a revised labor management agreement that included the essential $1.8 billion cuts in wages and benefits, and offered the employees a number of additional nonmonetary gains, Arpey managed to convince the union leaderships to approve the new labor agreement and thereby save the carrier from filing for bankruptcy protection. Passing his first test as a chief executive, Arpey outlined a key management objective he would strive to accomplish throughout his tenure as AA CEO: "There is a definite need to rebuild trust [between management and labor] within the company. I hear that loud and clear. . .and I commit myself to earning everybody's trust."[48]

Gerard Arpey spent his entire career at American Airlines, joining the company as a financial analyst in 1982. Before accepting the top job, the 46 year old Arpey sought, and received, the approval of AA's union leaders: "He said he wouldn't take the position unless . . . he had our support, " John Darrah, President of the Allied Pilots Association recalled, adding, "I have a great deal of respect

for Mr. Arpey . . . I can honestly [say] there's not a person I have more respect for or trust in."[49]

Arpey's turnaround plan was based on several elements. First, Arpey believed that in order to compete successfully in the post 9/11 world, American Airlines needed to shift its strategic focus from revenue growth to cost reduction. To achieve this goal, he introduced a cooperative labor management scheme, a continuous improvement program, and other labor cost cutting-measures. Second, Arpey realized that American could take advantage of its global positioning to expand profitable international operation and curtail unprofitable domestic services. To achieve this goal, he sought to form closer alliances with foreign carriers. Altogether, Arpey embarked on four distinct strategies in his efforts to turn American around:

International Expansion. Referring to his plan to expand AA's international operation, Arpey explained:

> One of the things that we can capitalize on is the depth and breath of our network. Its one of the ways that we can compete more effectively with low-cost carriers that operate primarily in the domestic market . . . We have very aggressive plans internationally . . . Our strengths include a very broad network that spans the globe. . . the [industry's] largest frequent-flyer program, Admiral airport clubs, and a great first-class product. . . [W]e get more revenue per passenger than the low cost carrier[s and] . . . we can sustain a revenue premium.[50]

Arpey expected AA's international service to grow from over 30% of capacity in 2005 to 40% by the end of the decade. He planned to expand, above all, trans-Pacific travel service. In 2005, American introduced two nonstop services to Japan, operating flights between Chicago and Nagoya, and between Dallas and Osaka. Similarly, in 2005, AA started a nonstop service to India, flying the 7,500-mile route between Chicago and New Delhi, American's longest, in 14–15 hours. American also competed aggressively over the contested rights to serve China, planning to introduce a Chicago-Shanghai nonstop service as early as approval by the Chinese government was granted. Additionally, AA formed alliances with Aloha Airlines and Mexicana Airlines, on the one side, and consolidated its code sharing agreement with British airways, on the other.[51]

Labor-Management Cooperation. To improve his relations with the unions, Arpey instituted an open door policy. During his first two years in office, Arpey spent more time meeting union leaders than the time spent for this purpose by any other chief executive in the company's 75 years history. "You demonstrate commitment by where you put your time," he told a *Financial Times* reporter in 2005. "We are trying to make our unions our business partners."[52] Unlike Crandall and Carty, Arpey constantly highlighted the importance of getting AA employees involved in the business of airline management. Once elected CEO, he traveled widely, visited AA operations in one city after another, conducted town-hall meetings with AA employees, and solicited employee suggestions. "I try to spend as much time as I can [with the employees] when I travel," Arpey explained in a 2004 interview, "going to break rooms, talking to agents at the gate, talking to flight attendants on board [of] the airplane, riding jump seats, and . . . answering all the e-mail[s I] get."[53]

Still, Arpey was unable to change AA's climate of labor-relations single-handedly. He needed external help. To improve labor management relations at American, Arpey hired an employee-relations consultancy called the Overland Resource Group in Summer 2003. Instrumental in improving labor-relations at Boeing, Ford, and the Goodyear Corporation, the Overland group instructed AA managers to follow three fundamental principles, or maxims, in their relations with AA's employees: "Involve before Deciding," "Discuss before Implementing," and "Share before Announcing." More important, the Overland group created a Joint Leadership Team (JLT) chaired by Arpey and the national presidents of AA's three main unions (representing the pilots, flight attendants, and mechanics and ground workers), and attended by the company CFO as well as four vice presidents, on management side, and three representatives of each union, on labor side. The team met once a month to discuss issues ranging from AA's corporate-level strategies to union demands and grievances. The team also reviewed AA's financial data on a quarterly basis, an arrangement that helped senior union officials understand the airline business.[54] To help team members communicate, two Overland consultants attended all JLT meetings, acting as the dialogue facilitators. To ensure an honest, open, and free-flowing discussion with no fear of reprisal, each JLT participant signed a nondisclosure agreement.[55]

In addition to the team headed by Arpey and the union presidents, Overland facilitated the formation of seven regional JLTs located in different airports and maintenance bases throughout AA network. A local JLT met once a month to review the region's financial performance and to evaluate employee cost-saving ideas.[56]

Overland presence at AA enhanced employee motivation and morale. The higher level of employee motivation was reflected, first and foremost, in the growing number of cost savings suggestions initiated by employees. While AA management routinely ignored employee suggestions in the past [one union leader observed], Overland consultants now encouraged the adoption of such suggestions. And while Arpey's management team was actively soliciting employee ideas, no employee whose ideas were adopted received any compensation; on the contrary, helping the company was the employee's sole motivation.[57]

As a result of implementing employee-identified cost-saving ideas, AA saved about $100 million in 2004.[58] The overall decline in labor cost was larger. Partly as a consequence of introducing cost-saving ideas, and partly as a result of implementing the landmark concessional contract of April 2003, AA unit labor cost under Arpey declined by more than 20% in two years, as shown in Exhibit 3.

....

Exhibit 3 Labor Cost of U.S. Network Carriers, 4th Quarter 2002 and 4th Quarter 2004, Cents Per Available Seat-Mile (CASM)

Network	4Q-02 CASM	4Q-04 CASM
American	3.93	3.12
Continental	3.10	30.2
Delta	4.01	3.67
Northwest	3.98	3.82
United	4.51	3.25
U.S. Airways	4.15	3.11
Network	4.01	3.34

Sources: Eclat Consulting, *Aviation Daily*, May 4, 2004, p. 7, and May 26, 2005, p. 7

Continuous improvement

The Continuous Improvement (CI) program was implemented across all AA's maintenance facilities. During 2001–2004, United Airlines, Northwest Airlines, and U.S. Airways closed several of their maintenance bases, and sought instead to outsource heavy maintenance to outside contractors.[59] American Airlines, by contrast, kept maintenance work in house, and launch a massive drive at efficiency, seeking productivity gains in the shop floor.

The Continuous Improvement program had three main goals: the elimination of waste in any form, the standardization of maintenance work, and the optimal utilization of "human talent." The idea—and practice—of CI was based on the assumption that workers, not managers, were the real experts, and that employee empowerment was critical for building effective work teams. The CI program addressed a variety of issues ranging from shop floor reorganization to engine-overhaul turnover time reduction. To achieve these objectives, a "5S" technique ("sort, strengthen, standardize, shine, sustain") was introduced throughout AA's maintenance facilities. At American's largest maintenance base in Tulsa, Oklahoma, for example, Continuous Improvement teams in the avionic shop used the 5S technique to free nearly 12,000 sq. ft. of floor space and thereby save the company $1.5 million in inventory cost.[60]

Employee-identified CI ideas included new ways to reduce the cost of replacing aircraft parts and components. On the McDonnell Douglas MD-80 model, for instance, the cargo door torque (spring) tube needed to be replaced once a year. To do so, the company bought new tubes at a cost of $660 per tube. The CI team investigated the issue and ascertained that repairing broken tubes at a cost of only $134 per unit saved the company a total of $250,000 a year. On the Boeing 737, similarly, AA economized by replacing passenger light bulbs and cabin windows only when needed. In the past, AA replaced all light bulbs and cabin windows at the same time regardless of whether the bulbs were burned out or the windows worn out. The selective replacement of light bulbs and cabin windows saved AA $100,000 per year.[61]

American used CI teams to reduce engine overhaul times as well. One team of engine mechanics drafted a series of diagrams showing the most efficient way to disassemble a jet engine. Another devised a "point-of-use tool box" which contained all the tools necessary for an engine's assembly and dis-

assembly. Together, the two teams helped AA cut an engine's overhaul turnaround time from 53 days in 2003 to 40 days in 2004, an improvement of 25% in a single year.[62]

Continuous Improvement teams helped AA cut costs in still other ways. To service American Airlines fleet, company mechanics used thousands of drill bits monthly at a cost of $20 to $200 a piece. Two AA mechanics invented a drill bit-sharpening tool which refurbished bits for reuse at a cost saving of $300,000–400,000 a year. And in 2004, a CI team came up with the idea of reusing parts of obsolete DC-10 coffee makers on other AA airplanes, generating a one-time savings of $675,000.[63]

Taken together, all these improvements helped AA reduce its maintenance cost by 34% in two years (2002–2004). A comparison between American's maintenance cost reduction and that of five other U.S.-based network carriers shows that AA led the way, exceeding the industry average by 13 percentage points, and well ahead of any of its competitors (Exhibit 4).

Other Cost Cutting Measures. "Simplification and standardization drives efficiency,"[64] Arpey said in 2004, and he moved quickly to both simplify and standardize AA's fleet of aircraft. To simplify the fleet, Arpey reduced the number of aircraft types flown by American from 14 to 6, retiring many old models. The move reduced American spending on spare parts as well as crew training, especially pilots and

Exhibit 4 Maintenance Cost of U.S. Network Carriers, 4th Quarter 2002 and 4th Quarter 2004, Cents Per Available Swat Mile (CASM)

Network	4Q02 CASM	4Q04 CASM	% CASM
American	1.65	1.09	34%
Continental	0.96	0.93	3%
Delta	0.98	0.92	6%
Northwest	1.43	1.08	24%
United	1.41	1.24	12%
U.S. Airways	1.67	1.30	22%
Network	1.36	1.08	21%

Source: Eclat Consulting, *Aviation Daily*, May 4, 2004, p.7, and May 26, 2005, p.7

mechanics training. In addition, Arpey standardized aircraft seating, arranging all seats on a given aircraft type in a single configuration, as the two following examples suggest. Under Carty's leadership, the MD-80 fleet had two seating configurations, one designed to serve AA's business routes, the other to serve AA's low fare routes. Under Carty likewise, the B-777 had two seating configurations, one aimed at flights over the Pacific, the other at flights over the Atlantic. In an effort to simplify both aircraft maintenance and flight schedules, Arpey standardized all seating on the MD-80 and B-777 models in a single arrangement, a reconfiguration that resulted in substantial cost savings.[65]

Arpey reversed two other Carty's initiatives, first, the creation of more legroom for passengers, and second, the transformation of TWA's St. Louis hub into a major AA hub. In 2000, Carty launched the "More Room in Coach" marketing campaign in an attempt to increase revenues. AA, accordingly, removed more than 7,000 economy seats from its fleet, reducing the fleet's seating capacity by 6.4%. Carty's initiative, however, failed to generate the expected revenues, and therefore Arpey decided to undo it. In 2004, AA added two rows of seats to its fleet of 140 B-757s and 34 A-300s, and used both models to serve low-fare leisure markets. In 2005, AA added six more seats to its B-737 fleet, seven more to its fleet of MD-80s and B-767s, and nine more seats to its fleet of B-777s. The change in seating capacity was projected to generate a revenue increase of over $100 million a year.[66]

Lastly, Arpey announced early on his decision to scale back significantly AA's St. Louis operation. Expecting TWA's central hub in St. Louis to fit nicely into American route system, Carty, as noted, purchased TWA in 2001. Arpey, however, did not share Carty's vision. To improve AA's financial performance, Arpey shifted flights from routes out of the St. Louis hub to more profitable routes out of AA's Chicago and Dallas hubs. As a result, AA laid off more than 2,000 employees at the St. Louis airport in 2003 alone.[67]

Future Prospects and Concerns

One result of the successful implementation of Arpey's turnaround strategy was the deep decline in AA's operating costs. As shown in Exhibit 5, by 2005, American operating costs were lower than those of

Exhibit 5   Operating Cost of U.S. Network Carriers, 1st Quarter 2005, Cents in Available Seat Mile (CASM)

Network	1Q05 CASM
American	9.9
Continental	9.9
United	10.4
U.S. Air	10.7
Northwest	11.2
Delta	12.2

Source: Back-Aviation Solutions in Micheline Maynard and Jeremy Peters, "Circling a Decision," *New York Times*, August 18, 2005.

any other network carriers save Continental. American's stock prices too performed well. Following a sharp drop in AMR stock price during the post 9/11 years, AMR's stock more than doubled in value in 2005, rising 101% and outperforming the share prices of all major U.S. carriers, including Southwest Airlines. AA's cash position, furthermore, was stronger than that of other network carriers. AA managed to increase its cash surplus from $3 billion in 2004 to $4.3 billion in 2005, a margin sufficiently comfortable to give the carrier a greater staying power in the industry than its rivals.[68]

Nevertheless, American Airlines still faced a number of daunting challenges. First and most important was the need to achieve profitability. During Arpey's first three years in office, AMR continued to post large losses that amounted to $1.2 billion in 2003, $0.8 billion in 2004, and $0.9 billion in 2005. While analysts were impressed by AA's cost-cutting measures (as well as its collaborative labor management relations, strong cash position, rising fares, and trimmed capacity), and while AA stock doubled in value in 2005 in anticipation of profits in 2006, the continual increase in fuel costs during 2006 clouded AA's recovery prospects.[69]

Another concern pertained to labor relations. AA employees resented a stock-related bonus paid to American managers in 2006. The payout was authorized by an 18 year old "Long Term Incentive Program" which tied executive pay to AA's stock performance. Because AA's stock prices outperformed the stock prices of its five competitors (United, Delta, Continental, U.S. Air, Northwest) in 2005, American's top 1,000 mangers were eligible to share $80 million in cash. The payout, however, was viewed by American's unionized employees as extra compensation for managers not shared by other AA employees. A letter sent by top management to members of the Allied Pilots Association congratulating the pilots on saving $80 million in fuel cost in 2005—an amount equivalent to management's bonus—angered the pilots further, and threatened to undermine the cooperative labor relations at American.[70]

A final concern stemmed from AA's pension crisis. In 2005, American's pension plans were underfunded by about $2.7 billion. To be sure, AA's funding deficit was smaller than that of Delta ($5.3 billion) and Northwest ($3.8 billion), yet unlike Delta and Northwest, American's commitment to protecting its employees' pensions was embedded in a collective bargaining agreement: a key union demand incorporated into the 2003 labor agreement that saved AA from bankruptcy was the preservation of the carrier's pension plan intact. In 2006, Delta, Northwest, United, and other network carriers were all engaged in a process of converting their pension plans from defined benefit plans (plans that paid employees lifetime retirement pensions funded by the employer) to the less expensive defined contribution plans (plans that operated like retirement saving accounts funded by both the employee and the employer). American Airlines, accordingly, experienced a growing competitive pressure to convert its pension plans too, but such a move was likely to jeopardize the long-standing industrial peace at American which Arpey had worked so hard to craft and preserve.[71]

Endnotes

1 Henry Ladd Smith, *Airways: the History of Commercial Aviation in the United States* (1942, reprinted, New York: Russell and Russell, 1964).
2 Stephen Breyer, *Regulation and Its Reform* (Cambridge Mass.: Harvard University Press, 1982), p. 205.
3 Thomas K. McCraw, *Prophets of Regulations* (Cambridge Mass.: Harvard University Press, 1984), p. 3.
4 McCraw, *Prophets of Regulations*. pp. 266–67; Breyer, *Regulation and Its Reform*, pp. 204–5.
5 Smith, *Airways*, Chapters 12, 16, 22.
6 "AMR Corporation," *Hoover's Handbook of American Business 1992* (Austin: Hoovers Business Press, 1992), p. 110, "AMR Corporation," *International Directory of Company Histories* (Detroit: St. James Press, 1999). p. 23.
7 Robert Serling, *Eagle: The Story of American Airlines* (New York: At. Martin, 1985), p. 280.
8 "Carrier Profile," *Aviation Daily*, April 5, 2005.
9 Mark Kahn, "Airlines," in Gerald Somers, ed., *Collective Bargaining: Contemporary American Experience* (Bloomingdale, Illinois: Industrial Relations Research Association Series, 1980), pp. 354–58; Serling, *Eagle*, pp. 270–73, 304–306.
10 Dan Reed, *The American Eagle: The Ascent of Bob Crandall and American Airlines* (New York: St. Martin, 1993), Chapter 2.
11 Dan Reed, *American Eagle*, pp. 100–2. The quotation is on page 101.
12 Cited in Stewart Toy and Seth Payne, "The Airline Mess," *Business Week*, July 6, 1992, p. 50.
13 Cited in, "American Airlines Loses its Pilot," *Economist*, April 18, 1998, p. 58.
14 Reed, *American Eagle*, p. 207.
15 Steven Morrison and Clifford Winston, *The Evolution of the Airline Industry* (Washington D.C.: The Brooking Institution, 1995), pp. 44–45.
16 Reed, *American Eagle*, pp. 158–164, 174–175.
17 AA, in addition, established secondary hubs in Nashville, Tennessee, Raleigh/Durham, North Carolina, and San Jose, California, but following the recession of the early 1990s, American closed these three hubs, withdrawing from unprofitable short-hall travel markets. See Suzanne Loeffelholz, "Competitive Anger," *Financial World*, January 10, 1989, p. 31; and Perry Flint and Danna Henderson, "American at Bay," *Air Transport World*, March 1997. Online. ABI database, Start Page 28.
18 Dan Reed, *American Eagle*, pp. 204–205.
19 Seth Rosen, "A Union Perspective," in Jean McKelvey, Ed. *Cleared for Takeoff: Airline Labor Relations Since Deregulation* (Ithaca, New York: ILR Press, 1988), p. 22; Robert Crandall, "The Airlines: On Track or Off Course," in McKelvey, Ed. *Clear for Takeoff*, p. 352; Dan Reed, *American Eagle*, p. 202–204.
20 *Financial World*, January 10. 1989, pp. 29–30.
21 According to the company's annual report cited in "AMR Corporation," *International Directory of Company Histories*, p. 24.
22 Don Bedwell, *Silverbird: The American Airlines Story* (Sandpoint Idaho; Airway International Inc. 1999), pp. 137, 244.
23 Perry Flint, "Sabre Unlimited," *Air Transport World*, November 1996, p. 95.
24 Bedwell, *Silverbird*, p. 132, and Chapter 20.
25 Ronald Lieber, "Bob Crandall's BOO-BOOS," *Fortune*, April 28, 1997, p. 368; Don Lee and Jennifer Oldham,

"American Woos Wary Travelers," *Los Angeles Times*, Feb. 16, 1997.

26 Reed, *American Eagle*, Chapter 5; Bedwell, *Silverbird*, pp. 130–131, 250–251.

27 Kenneth Labich, "The Computer Network that Keeps American Flying," *Fortune*, September 24, 1990, p. 46.

28 Bedwell, *Silverbird*, p. 248.

29 *Air Transport World*, November 1996, p. 95.

30 Reed, *American Eagle*, p. 184.

31 Cited in Bedwell, *Silverbird*, p. 161.

32 Reed, *American Eagle*, pp. 176–177; Morrison and Winston, *The Evolution of the Airline Industry*, p. 59.

33 Bedwell, *Silverbird*, p. 161.

34 Seth Rosen, "Corporate Restructuring," in Peter Cappelli, ed., *Airline Labor Relations in the Global Era* (Ithaca, New York: ILR press, 1995). p. 33.

35 Kenneth Labich, "American Takes on the World," *Fortune*, September 24, 1990, pp. 41–42, Read, *American Eagle*, pp. 249, 251, 269, and "AMR Corporation," *International Directory of Company Histories*, p. 24.

36 *Air Transport World*, March 1997. Online. ABI Data Base. Start page 28.

37 Bedwell, *Silverbird*, pp. 233–236; "AMR Corporation," *International Directory of Company Histories*, p. 25.

38 Jeri Clausing, "Crandall's Hard-Ball Style Legendary," *Seattle Times*, November 25, 1993; James Peltz, "A 'Mellower AMR Chief?" *Los Angeles Times*, Feb. 14, 1997.

39 *Fortune*, April 28, 1997, p. 368; *Los Angeles Times*, Feb. 14, 1997; Scott McCartney, "The Deal Breakers," *Wall Street Journal*, Feb. 11, 1997; "American Airlines Loses its Pilot," *Economist* April 18, 1998, p. 58.

40 *Air Transport World*, March 1997, Start page 28.

41 Peter Elkind, "Flying for Fun & Profits," *Fortune*, Oct. 25, 1999, pp. 36–37; James Peltz, "Carty Has Been Forced to Guide AMR Through Turbulent Times," *Los Angeles Times*, Nov. 14, 2001; John Helyar, "American Airlines: A Wing and a Prayer," *Fortune*, Dec. 10, 2001, p. 182.

42 *Los Angeles Times*, Nov. 14, 2001; "American, TWA Deal Approved," *Aviation Daily*, April 10, 2001; and U.S. Senate. *TWA/American Airlines Workforce Integration*. Hearing before the Committee on Health, Education, and Pensions. 108thCong., 1ˢᵗ Sess., June 12, 2003, p. 24.

43 *Los Angeles Times*, Nov. 14, 2001.

44 Scott McCarthney, "At American, 48 Hours of Drama Help Airline Avert Bankruptcy, *Wall Street Journal*, April 28, 2003.

45 Brad Foss, "How It All Went Wrong," *Chicago Sun Times*, April 27, 2003.

46 Cited in *Chicago Sun Times*, April 27, 2003.

47 *Wall Street Journal*, April 28, 2003; and Edward Wong and Micheline Maynard, "A Taut, Last-minute Stretch to Save an Airline," *New York Times*, April 27, 2003.

48 Cited in the *Wall Street Journal*, April 28, 2003; but see also *New York Times*, April 27, 2003.

49 Cited in Eve Tahmincioglu, "Back from the Brink," *Workforce Management*, Dec. 2004. Online. ABI Data Base. Start page 32. See also Sara Goo, "Key Union Accepts Cuts at American," *Washington Post*, April 26, 2003.

50 Cited in Melanie Trottman, "Boss Talk," *Wall Street Journal*, Dec. 30, 2004.

51 David Field, "The American Way," *Airline Business*, Dec. 2004, p. 31; "American Enters India," *Aviation Daily*, July 13, 2005.

52 Cited in Caroline Daniel, "A Top Flight Employee Strategy," *Financial Times*, April 4, 2005.

53 Cited in the *Wall Street Journal*, Dec. 30, 2004.

54 *Financial Times*, April 4, 2005; *Workforce Management*, Dec. 2004, Start page 32.

55 *Workforce Management*, Dec. 2004, Start page 32.

56 *Financial Times*, April 4, 2005.

57 *Workforce Management*, Dec. 2004, Start page 32.

58 *Workforce Management*, Dec. 2004, Start page 32.

59 Perry Flint, "Rewired for Success: American Embraces Continuous Improvement," *Air Transport World*, August 2004, 39.

60 *Air Transport World*, August 2004, 39.

61 *Air Transport World*, August 2004, 39.

62 *Air Transport World*, August 2004, 39.

63 *Workforce Management*, Dec. 2004, Start page 32.

64 Cited in *Airline Business*, Dec. 2004, p. 31.

65 *Wall Street Journal*, Dec. 30, 2004; Michael Maynard, "No Longer on the Brink, American Air is Still in Peril," *New York Times*, March 18, 2004; Scott McCartney, "Low Cost Rivals Prompt American Airlines to Try Flying Like One of Them," *Wall Street Journal*, June 8, 2004; *Airline Business*, Dec. 2004, p. 31.

66 *Airline Business*, Dec. 2004, p. 33; Edward Wong, "American Air is Adding Seats," *New York Times*, May 22, 2003; "American Looks to Counteract $1.4 Billion Fuel Cost Increase," *Aviation Daily*, March 13, 2005.

67 *Wall Street Journal*, June 8, 2004; Edward Wong, "In a Sign of Stronger Finances, American Reports a Profit," *New York Times*, Oct. 23, 2003.

68 Melanie Trottman, "AMR Investors Bet on Clearer Skies Ahead," *Wall Street Journal*, Feb. 16, 2006; Caroline Daniel, "In Hard Times, Saving Dollars Makes Sense," *Financial Times*, March 15, 2005.

69 "AMR Company Records, Financials," *Hoovers*. Online. ABI Data Base. *Wall Street Journal*, Feb. 16, 2006.

70 Scott McCartney, "Airline Discord May Hurt Travelers," *Wall Street Journal*, Feb. 7, 2006.

71 Brad Foss, American Path Less Traveled," *Seattle Times*, June 11, 2005.

CASE 18

Blockbuster, Netflix, and the Media Entertainment Rental Industry in 2011

Gareth R. Jones
Texas A&M University

In July 2007, Jim Keyes, former CEO of the 7-Eleven retail chain replaced John Antioco as CEO of Blockbuster Inc. announcing that, "Blockbuster has a world-class brand and is a highly regarded leader in the home entertainment industry. I look forward to the opportunity to work with the Blockbuster team to better serve our customers and to position Blockbuster for profitable growth and an even stronger future." Yet Blockbuster's stock continued to fall—dropping 90% in 2009 alone—and it was forced to declare bankruptcy in September 2010. Why did Blockbuster's business model fail? What caused one of the most well-known media rental companies to fail in its battle to deliver media to customers in the 2000s? To answer this question, we need to look at the forces that propelled Blockbuster into becoming the number one distributor of movies and other entertainment media, and then how forces such as increasing competition and changing technology led to its decline and fall.

Blockbuster's History

David Cook, the founder of Blockbuster, took the skills he had developed in providing consulting and computer services to the petroleum and real estate industries and used them to entered the video-rental business based on a concept of an IT-enabled "video superstore." He opened his first superstore, called "Blockbuster Video," in Dallas in 1985.

Cook's idea for a video superstore resulted from his analysis of the changing forces in the video rental industry that were occurring during the 1980s. For example, the number of households that owned VCRs was rapidly increasing, and so were the number of video-rental stores being established to meet their needs. In 1983, 7,000 video-rental stores were in operation, by 1985 there were 19,000, and by 1986 there were over 25,000, of which 13,000 were individually owned. These "mom-and-pop" video stores offered a highly limited selection of videos and were often located in out-of-the-way strip shopping centers where rents were low. These small stores used little IT; usually customers brought an empty box to the video-store clerk who would exchange it for a tape if it was available—a procedure that was time-consuming, particularly at peak times such as evenings and weekends.

Cook realized that as VCRs had become more widespread, and the number of film titles available steadily increased, customers would begin to demand a larger and more varied selection of titles from video stores. Moreover, they would demand more convenient locations and quicker in-store service than mom-and-pop stores could offer. He realized that the time was right to develop the next generation of video-rental stores using advanced IT to speed customer transactions.

The Video Superstore Concept

Cook's business model for his new video superstores was based upon several different strategies. First, Cook decided that to give his superstores a unique identity that would appeal to customers, the stores should be highly visible stand-alone structures—rather than part of a shopping center. Also, superstores were to be large, between 4,000 and 10,000 square feet, well-lit and brightly colored, hence the bright blue and yellow "Blockbuster Video" sign. Each store would need ample parking and would be located in the vicinity of a large urban population to maximize its rental-customer base.

Second, each superstore was to offer a wide variety of videos, such as adventure, children's, instructional, and video game titles. Believing that movie preferences differ in different locations, Cook decided to allow each store to offer a different selection of 7,000–13,000 film titles, organized alphabetically in over 30 categories. New releases were stocked separately and alphabetically against the back wall of each store to make it easier for customers to make their selections. Cook's superstores also targeted the largest market segments, adults in the 18- to 49-year-old group, and children in the 6- to 12-year-old group. Cook believed that if his stores could attract children, their families probably would follow. New releases were carefully chosen based on reviews and box-office success to maximize their appeal to families.

Third, believing that many customers, particularly those with children, wanted to keep tapes for longer than a 1-day period, he created the concept of a longer, 3-day rental periods for $3. If the tape was available it was behind the cover box and customers would take the tape to the checkout counter where the clerk would scan the cassette and membership card. The rental amount was computed by the IT system and due at the time of rental. Movie returns were scanned and any late or rewind fees were recorded on the account and automatically charged the next time a member rented a tape. This system reduced customer checkout time and increased convenience, it also provided Blockbuster with marketing data on customer demographics. Finally, believing that customers wanted to choose a movie and quickly leave, Cook decided that his superstores would offer customers the convenience of long operating hours and quick service, generally from 10:00 A.M. to midnight 7 days per week.

These different strategies made Blockbuster's business model successful and customers flocked to its new stores. Wherever Blockbuster opened, local mom-and-pop stores were usually forced to close down because they could not compete with the number of titles and the quality of service that a Blockbuster store could provide due to its advanced IT.

By 1986, Blockbuster owned 8 stores and had franchised 11 more to interested investors who could see the potential of this new approach to video rental. Initially, the company opened stores in markets with a minimum population of 100,000; franchises were located in Atlanta, Chicago, Detroit, Houston, San Antonio, and Phoenix. New stores, which cost about $500,000 to $700,000 to equip, grossed an average of $70,000 to $80,000 a month. Their owners became millionaires within months.

Early Growth and Expansion

John Melk, an executive at Waste Management Corp., who had purchased a Blockbuster franchise in Chicago, changed the history of the company when, in 1987, he contacted H. "Wayne" Huizinga, a former Waste Management colleague, to tell him about the enormous revenue and profit his franchise was generating. Huizinga had experience in growing small companies in fragmented industries. In 1955, he quit college to manage a 3-truck trash-hauling operation; in 1962 he bought his first operation, Southern Sanitation and then merged it with other small sanitation companies such as Ace Partnership, Acme Disposal, and Atlas Refuse Service to form Waste Management in 1968. Huizinga continued to use Waste Management stock to buy more than 100 more companies that provided such services as auto-parts cleaning, dry cleaning, lawn care, and portable-toilet rentals, and used their cash flows to purchase hundreds more sanitation firms. By the time Huizinga sold his stake in Waste Management in 1984, it was a $6 billion *Fortune 500* company and Huizinga's stake made him a billionaire.

Huizinga had a low opinion of video retailers, but he agreed to visit a Blockbuster store where, instead of finding a dingy store renting X-rated movies, he found a brightly lit family video supermarket full of customers. Huizinga and other Waste Management executives saw the opportunity to make Blockbuster a national chain and agreed to purchase 33% of Blockbuster from Cook for $18.6 million in 1986. Then in 1987, CEO David Cook decided to resign and sell the majority of his stock to pursue other opportunities. Huizinga took over as CEO, and his goal was to make Blockbuster the industry leader in the U.S. video-rental market.

Blockbuster's Explosive Growth

Huizinga and his new top management team mapped out Blockbuster's new business model and strategies to grow the company. Store location was critical, and Huizinga moved quickly to obtain the best store locations in each geographic area into which Blockbuster expanded. They developed a "cluster strategy" whereby they targeted a particular geographic market, such as Dallas, Boston, or Los Angeles, and then opened up new stores one at a time until they had saturated the market. Thus, within a few years, the local mom-and-pop stores found themselves surrounded and unable to compete with Blockbuster, and closed down. As a result, its sales continued to soar and its cluster strategy eventually allowed Blockbuster into 133 major markets, where it reached over 75% of the U.S. population.

To further its marketing reach, it introduced "Blockbuster Kids," a promotion aimed at attracting the 6- to 12-year-old age group to strengthen the company's position as a family video store. It worked, and to further its family-oriented strategy, each store stocked 40 titles recommended for children, and a kids' clubhouse with televisions and toys so that children could amuse themselves while their parents browsed for videos. To attract customers and build brand recognition, Blockbuster also formed alliances with companies like Domino's Pizza, McDonald's, and PepsiCo.

Blockbuster made great progress on the operations side of the business to reduce its cost structure. Blockbuster's IT was constantly upgraded to allow it to provide fast checkout and effective inventory management. The company designed its point-of-sale computer system to make rental and return transactions easy; this system was available only to company-owned and franchised stores. To increase the speed at which individual stores received new movie titles, and to support its stores, Blockbuster opened a new 25,000-square-foot distribution center in Dallas where up to 200,000 videotapes at a time were removed from the original containers and affixed with security devices, bar-coded and then placed into a hard plastic rental case. In 1987, the physical facilities of the distribution center were expanded to double capacity to 400,000 videocassettes and Blockbuster began to open more distribution facilities around the country.

Blockbuster's growing buying power also helped reduce its costs, as the largest purchaser of videotapes, it was able to negotiate large discounts from retail prices charged by movie studios. At that time, cassettes were bought for around $40 each, and then rented for 3 nights for $3. Its cash investment on "hit" videotapes was recovered in a few months, then additional revenues were all profit. Blockbuster continued to developed its IT to create a highly efficient distribution system to move extra copies of movies that were declining in popularity at some stores to other stores where demand was increasing. The ability to transfer tapes to the location where they were most demanded was very important; customers wanted new tapes on the shelves when the movies were released. This is still true today as customers demand rapid access to their favorite movies and TV shows.

New-Store Expansion

With Blockbuster's functional-level competencies in place to facilitate rapid expansion, Blockbuster began to use its skills in store location, distribution, and sales. At first, Blockbuster focused on large markets, preferring to enter a market with a potential capacity for 500 stores—normally a large city. Later, Blockbuster decided to enter smaller market segments, such as towns with a minimum of 20,000 people within driving distance. All stores were built and operated using the superstore concept described earlier. Taking advantage of its rapidly developing functional skills, Blockbuster steadily increased its number of new-store openings until, by 1993, it owned more than 2,500 video stores.

Blockbuster's rapid growth also came from acquisitions, as it began to acquire many smaller, regional video chains to gain a significant market presence in a city or region. In 1987, for example, the 29 video stores of Movies To Go were acquired to expand Blockbuster's presence in the Midwest. Blockbuster then used this acquisition as a starting point for opening many more stores in the region. Similarly, in 1989, it acquired 175 video stores to develop a presence in southern California. In 1991, it took over 209 Erol's Inc. stores to obtain a stronghold in the Mid-Atlantic states.

Licensing and Franchising

Recognizing the need to rapidly build market share and develop a national brand name, Huizinga also increased Blockbuster's franchising program that helped.

Blockbuster to rapidly expand. By 1992, the company had more than 1,000 franchised stores compared to its 2,000 company-owned stores. However, despite its rapid growth, Blockbuster still controlled only about 15% of the market, and in 1993, Blockbuster announced plans for a new round of store openings and acquisitions that would give it a 25–30% market share within 2 or 3 years.

The Home-Video Industry

By 1990, revenues from video rentals exceeded the revenues obtained in movie theaters—something that is still true in 2011, hence the major competition between companies like Netflix, Amazon.com, and Apple to control movie and TV show distribution channels. Video rental revenues were $11 billion in 1991, compared to movie theaters' $4.8 billion.

Blockbuster's rapid growth had put it in a commanding position. By 1990, it had no national competitor and was the only company operating beyond a regional level. However, Blockbuster faced many competitors at the local and regional levels and competition in the industry was fierce because new competitors could enter the market with relative ease—the only purchase necessary was videotapes. However, unlike small video-rental companies, Blockbuster was able to negotiate discounts with tape suppliers because it bought new releases in such huge volumes.

However, an increasing problem facing Blockbuster in the 1990s was the variety of new ways in which customers could view movies and other kinds of entertainment because of the growth of digital technology spurred by the rapid popularity of PCs and gaming consoles. Blockbuster had always faced competition from specialized cable TV channels such as HBO, and, of course, movie theaters, but now digital technology began to give customers more ways to watch movies. New technological threats included pay-per-view (PPV) or video-on-demand (VOD) systems, digital compression, and direct broadcast satellites.

Pay-per-view movies seemed like a major threat to video-rental stores because PPV allows cable customers to pay their cable company a fee to watch a scheduled movie, concert, or sporting event on their TVs. Already, the prospect that customers would be able to access a "media provider" through some kind of digital device such as a PC or TV set-top box and choose to watch movies of their choice on their televisions for a fee seemed an increasing threat. Also, telephone companies such as AT&T and Verizon were realizing the potential for offering entertainment media including TV and movies through DSL networks of fiber-optic cables that were rapidly being installed throughout the country. Huizinga claimed Blockbuster was not overly concerned about the growth of digital methods of purchasing entertainment media because U.S. households had limited access to such services, and they were expensive. He was right because these kinds of digital networks did not take off in popularity until the late-1990s. But today, entertainment media are being increasingly routed to customers through either fiber-optic cables, phone lines, or satellite dishes, and these services bypass local video-rental stores. This has been a major factor in the decline of Blockbuster as discussed below.

Huizinga Sells Blockbuster to Viacom

Although Blockbuster, with its rapid growth and large positive cash flow, seemed poised to become an entertainment powerhouse, Huizinga knew there were real problems ahead. The rapid advances in digital technology, including faster broadband Internet access, meant that video-on-demand (VOD) was increasingly likely to become the way of the future. Some analysts were already suggesting that Blockbuster was a "dinosaur." Also, even within the video-rental business, new store chains such as Hollywood Video had begun to expand rapidly, not recognizing the threat from digital channels. Blockbuster faced increased competition even in its existing business.

Huizinga decided that the time was ripe to sell Blockbuster; his chaining and franchising strategies had made it the industry leader with a huge cash flow. His opportunity came when Sumner Redstone, chairman of Viacom, had become involved in an aggressive bidding war to buy the movie company Paramount Studios. Redstone recognized the value of Blockbuster's huge cash flow in helping to fund the debt needed to take over Paramount. Ignoring the risks involved in taking over Blockbuster, in 1994 Viacom acquired the company for $8.4 billion in stock (further details about the logic behind the acquisition are found in the Viacom case, and Huizinga cashed in his huge stockholdings—more billions for him).

Just the next year, in 1995, a tidal wave of problems hit the Blockbuster chain. First, a brutal price war hit the video-rental industry as new video chain start-ups fought to find a niche in major markets and increase their market share and revenues. Second, movie studios started to lower the price of tapes, realizing they could make more money by selling them directly to customers rather than letting companies like Blockbuster make the money through tape rentals. Third, as Blockbuster's video operations expanded, it had become obvious that the company did not have the materials management and distribution systems needed to manage the complex flow of products to its stores. Overhead costs started to soar, so that together with declines in revenues, the company turned from making a profit to a loss!

Blockbuster's Problems Grow By 2000

Blockbuster's falling cash flow was now a threat to Viacom, which was burdened by the huge debt it incurred to buy Paramount, and Viacom's stock price dropped sharply. Redstone reacted by firing its top managers and searching for an experienced executive to turn the Blockbuster division around. To control Blockbuster's soaring cost structure, Redstone looked for an executive with experience in low-cost merchandising, and in 1996, he pulled off a coup by hiring William Fields, who was expected to become Walmart's next CEO. An IT and logistics expert, Fields began to make plans for a huge state-of-the-art distribution facility that would serve all of Blockbuster's U.S. stores and replace its outdated facility. He also developed a new state-of-the-art point-of-sale merchandising information system that would give Blockbuster real-time feedback on which videos were generating the most money, and when they should be transferred to stores in other regions to make the most use of Blockbuster's stock of videos—its most important capital investment.

These moves increased costs, however, and Blockbuster's performance continued to decline in 1997 with a drop in profit of 20%. After only 13 months, Fields resigned and Viacom's stock fell to a 3-year low. Redstone argued that this was absurd because Blockbuster generated $3 billion in revenue and $800 in cash flow. However, the increasing threat of video-on-demand and Pay-per-view media streaming—something that only became a real threat in the 2010s—worried investors, and analysts wonder if Blockbuster could recover.

Once again, Redstone looked for a CEO who could turn Blockbuster around, and in the news was John Antioco, the head of PepsiCo's Taco Bell restaurant chain. In just 8 months, Antioco introduced a new menu, new pricing, and new store setup that had turned Taco Bell's mounting losses into rising profits. Antioco seemed the perfect choice as Blockbuster's new CEO, and after assessing the situation, he realized the need to focus on reorganizing Blockbuster's value chain to simultaneously reduce costs and attract more customers to generate more revenues.

Blockbuster's biggest expense was the capital invested in its videos; this was the logical place to start, and Antioco and Redstone examined the way Blockbuster obtained its movies. It was presently purchasing tapes from big studios such as MGM and Disney at the high price of $65, and this high price limited its ability to purchase enough copies of a particular hit movie to satisfy customer demand when the movie was released on tape. The result was that customers were left unsatisfied and major revenues were lost. Perhaps there was a better way to manage the process for both the movie studios and Blockbuster to raise revenues from movie tape rental?

Blockbuster proposed that it should enter into a revenue sharing agreement with the movie studios whereby the studios would supply Blockbuster with tapes at cost, around $8, therefore allowing it to purchase 800% more copies of a single title. Blockbuster would then split rental revenues with the studios 50/50! Their analysis suggested that this would grow the market for rental tapes by 20–30% each year, and revenues would increase for both Blockbuster and the movie studios.

While this deal was being negotiated in 1997, video rentals at Blockbuster dropped 4% more, and the studios that had hesitated to enter into this radically different revenue-sharing agreement came on board. The new revenue sharing agreement had amazing results, and the profitability for both parties increased dramatically as Blockbuster's market share increased from less than 30% to over 40% in the next 5 years, during which it once again became profitable—this was a major turning point for Blockbuster. Nevertheless, in the short run, this change hurt Blockbuster's performance, and in 1998, Viacom announced it would record a $437 million loss charge to write down the value of its Blockbuster videotape inventory. This write down wiped out Viacom's profits for 1998, and Redstone announced that a spinoff or initial public offering to make Blockbuster an independent company was likely because the unit was punishing Viacom's stock price and threatening its future profitability.

By the end of 1998, there were signs of a turnaround as the revenue sharing agreement drove revenues sharply higher, same-store video rentals increased by 13% in 1998, for example. The move to a revenue sharing agreement had allowed Blockbuster's managers to develop strategies to increase responsiveness to customers that allowed them to pursue their business model in a profitable way. With the huge increase in the supply of new tapes made possible by the revenue sharing agreement, Blockbuster was now able to offer the Blockbuster Promise to its customers, promising that their chosen title would be in stock or "next time, it's free." Also, lower prices could now be charged for older video titles to generate additional revenues without threatening profitability. It turned out that the real threat to Blockbuster in the late-1990s was *not* from new technologies like video-on-demand, but the lack of the right *product strategies* to keep customers happy—like having the products in stock that they wanted. Netflix did understand this, however, as discussed below, and this difference in their business models led to the dramatic change in their fortunes in the 2010s.

Blockbuster in the 2000s

Blockbuster's new business model was apparently working, and Viacom orchestrated a successful initial public stock offering in 1999 to divest the company. It turned out that 1999 was the first of 4 consecutive years of same-store sales increases at Blockbuster. A major reason was that in 2000, Blockbuster increased the number of DVDs titles it carried because they had much higher profit margins than VHS tapes—DVDs rented for a couple of dollars more. The result was dramatic as revenues soared, and in 2001, it eliminated 25% of its stock of

VHS tapes to focus on the booming market for DVD rentals. By the end of 2001, the company achieved record revenues, strong cash flow, and increased profitability while it lowered its debt by more than $430 million. Since 1997, Antioco had grown Blockbuster's revenues from $3.3 billion to over $5 billion and turned free cash flow from a negative position to over $250 million for 2001. Its stock had risen as investors realized that the company now had a business model that generated cash. By 2002, it was clear the future was in DVDs, and Blockbuster announced it was switching into DVDs and phasing out its VHS tapes. DVDs swept away VHS tapes much as CDs swept away vinyl records; DVD rentals increased 115% and in the spring of 2002, Blockbuster made $66 million in net income.

Antioco searched for more ways to broaden Blockbuster's product line to keep revenues increasing, and in 2002, he decided its stores should carry a full lineup of GameCube, Xbox, and PlayStation games to rent and sell video games in its stores. Renting games was attractive to customers because could try any game and decide whether they liked it before they were forced to pay the high price of buying the game. Video games seemed to be a natural, complementary product line, and in May 2002, Blockbuster announced that it wanted to become the biggest rental and retail source of video games. Blockbuster's new product line was a success, and it pushed to double its video game rentals by 2003. To help achieve this goal, in the summer of 2002, Blockbuster began to offer $19.95 monthly rental service for unlimited video game rentals. This fit well with Blockbuster's family profile, since parents could come into a store to rent a DVD while their children picked up a video game.

A major problem for Blockbuster developed in 2002, when movie studios began to sell DVDs of their new hit movies directly to the public, pricing the DVDs low to generate sales. DVD sales took off when it turned out customers liked the idea of a home-movie library and the movie studios generated billions in DVD sales. However, this was a major blow to Blockbuster as rentals of its new hit DVDs declined, and Antioco tried to make the best of it by starting to sell DVDs in its stores, too. However, movie studios obtained such high revenues from DVD sales, that they started to reduce their wholesale DVD prices for major low-cost retailers like Walmart and Best Buy. Within a few years, the price of DVDs had dropped dramatically as these stores started to discount DVD prices to sell millions of copies, and Blockbuster was forced to follow suit. Blockbuster's DVD revenues collapsed as both its DVD rentals and sales dropped sharply and its profits plunged as sales at Blockbuster stores fell by 6% in 2003.

Blockbuster had to find new ways to increase rental revenues, and quickly. To reduce customers' incentive to buy DVDs and build their own movie libraries, Blockbuster tested a new marketing strategy in 2004. For a monthly fee of $24.99, it offered unlimited DVD rentals in its stores. In another major move, it also announced in 2004 that it would end the expensive late fees when customers failed to return their tapes on time. This may have pleased customers, but it turned out that late fees were a major contributor to Blockbuster's revenues and profits; it was estimated that late fees accounted for over 35% of Blockbuster's profit! While it hoped no late fees would translate into more rentals, this did not happen and instead, actually reduced revenues in 2004 and 2005 while its profits turned into losses in 2004; it lost a staggering $1.25 billion during this time. To reduce its cost structure, Blockbuster closed almost a thousand of its weakest stores and took a huge tax write-off. By 2005, Blockbuster only operated 5,000 B&M stores, but this was still very expensive now that its revenues did not cover its costs, and were rapidly falling.

Growing Competition in Rental and Retail Movie and Game Entertainment

One major reason why Blockbuster's revenues continued to fall was because of increasing competition from other channels of distributing movies, and from the emergence of new competitors with newer business models.

The Growing Use of Broadband Distribution Channels

Since the early-2000s, new digital PPV and VOD technologies that involve the direct download or streaming of movies and TV shows to customers over cable, satellite, DSL, or other forms of broadband connection, had been a growing threat to Blockbuster's business model. These new technologies bypass the need for a bricks-and-mortar (B&M) rental store, and the potential effects of these new technologies on Blockbuster's revenues had depressed its stock price for years, despite not yet becoming a major threat.

However, Antioco was convinced that broadband competition was the major challenge facing the company and ignored the threat from emerging competitors such as Netflix and Redbox, which had developed business models focused upon gaining profits from the physical rental of DVDs (this is discussed in more detail below). As early as 2000, Antioco had announced that Blockbuster's goal was to be the dominant provider of streaming movies, and for its stores to gain a leadership position in a broadband world. To do this, he needed to from agreements with entertainment content providers—the movie studios—and gain more control of the content or "entertainment software" end of the business. In 2000, Blockbuster announced an agreement with MGM to digitally stream and download recent theatrical releases, films, and television programming from the MGM library to Blockbuster's Website for PPV consumption. It started to roll out its "Blockbuster on Demand" PPV, arguing that video rentals and PPV could exist side by side. Initial testing of the program started in 2001, and Blockbuster announced it would try to form similar agreements with other movie studios. It even signed a deal with TiVo, a maker of set-top digital recorders, to offer a VOD service through broadband using TiVo's recorders. TiVo agreed to put demonstration kiosks in over 4,000 Blockbusters stores to serve its 65 million customers. However, all these moves failed to establish Blockbuster as a major player in the PPV delivery market—it had no distinctive competence in this market.

The problem was that Antioco was too early to rush into the digital download market, which was still dominated by a swarm of competing technologies, all championed by different companies striving to gain the leadership position in the broadband market. There were no barriers to entry and no way for a company like Blockbuster that had no digital expertise to achieve a leadership position. This became clear in 2005, when 5 major movie studios—Sony, Time Warner, Universal, MGM, and Paramount—announced a plan to bypass powerful "middlemen" like Blockbuster and HBO and offer their own PPV service directly to customers. These companies were also too early because the technology they proposed to use was quickly superseded by advanced new ways of downloading digital content.

Eventually, in the late-2000s, these companies all took a stake in and signed up with a new kind of streaming video company—Hulu. In 2011, for example, Hulu had established itself as a leading entertainment streaming company, and it was rumored that Apple might buy it to complement its new iCloud digital entertainment download and storage service. Apple has clearly intended to try to establish itself as the leading PPV entertainment content download service provider. However, many other companies also offered similar services. In 2006, Amazon.com launched a form of PPV service which allowed its customers to download a wide range of movie content, and it has continued to develop its digital entertainment download business on its cloud service and launched the Amazon Kindle Fire in 2011, In 2010 Google announced it would use its advertising model to gain revenues from its popular YouTube channel to expand its media entertainment offerings and there was a rumor that both Google and Apple were interested in buying Hulu. Moreover, digital piracy was still a major problem as many Websites still offered illegal downloading of movie and TV shows free of charge.

Antioco's perception that digital downloads would become a major threat proved correct. By 2007, movie studios and distributors such as Amazon.com and Apple were fighting to become the hub of choice. Antioco, however, had staked Blockbuster's future on becoming the leader in the digital entertainment content world, but the company did not have the technology or the expertise to play this pivotal role any more than movie studios, new online dot.coms, cable operators, or satellite providers, could. Moreover, it was clear that entertainment content providers were willing to make agreements with any company that could provide them with revenues by distributing their digital content when they were losing billions because of illegal downloading. Essentially, it was the wrong strategy, not the wrong technologies that caused the crisis at Blockbuster, and by 2006, its stock dropped to a low of $5 as revenues plunged and losses dramatically increased (see Table 1).

Competition from New Online and B&M Retailers: Netflix and Redbox

Antioco was so fixated upon the digital download distribution channel that he discounted the fact that a combination of online and B&M, or just B&M, DVD rental stores could prove to be a profitable business model in the rapidly changing entertainment rental industry. Why would customers want DVDs by mail if they get them through its stores? In 2000, Antioco had been approached by Netflix CEO and cofounder Reed Hastings about forming a partnership. Reed proposed to Blockbuster that Netflix would use their brand name online and that they run the Netflix brand in its stores, but Blockbuster did not think Netflix would survive because a mail DVD distribution channel would only be a tiny market segment. Why?

Netflix was founded in 1997, and its business model was based upon customers ordering a DVD online and receiving it through the mail. This was a more convenient way to rent movies than to go to a B&M store. At first, this model did not work because just like Blockbuster, Netflix charged a set fee for each movie rented and this didn't prove popular. Then, Reed Hastings added a new strategy—one Blockbuster had adopted in 2004 when it offered customers unlimited in-store DVD rental for $19–95 a month. Reed Hastings changed Netflix' business model into a subscription model that allowed customers to pay a flat monthly fee of $17 a month, and they could keep as many as three DVDs at one time. Once they send the movies back, by popping them into a postage-paid envelope and dropping them in a mailbox, customers could immediately receive more DVDs; Netflix did not limit the number of DVDs that could be ordered in any one month.

Netflix kept DVDs in a warehouse and mailed them out as orders came in, but like Amazon.com, Netflix soon found that it needed a sophisticated regional distribution system to get DVDs to customers, and back from them quickly enough for the monthly service to work—to avoid customer complaints about slow delivery. It took Netflix several years to create the B&M infrastructure necessary to manage the huge inventory of DVDs necessary to ensure quick delivery of even the most popular recent movies. However, obviously, using the Internet and mail to deliver DVDs to customers is a far less expensive way to rent DVDs than managing a chain of B&M video stores. Netflix also went to work to attract customers, and through massive online advertising and mailing campaigns it began to attract increasing numbers of customers and became a real threat to Blockbuster. By 2004, Netflix had over 1.4 million customers, and the success of its business model showed Antioco he had made a mistake. Blockbuster had to respond, but it was too late as the revenues and profits of the two companies between 2004 and 2010 shown in the Table 1 confirm.

In late-2004, Blockbuster announced it would launch an online DVD rental service—*Blockbuster Total Access*—although Antioco still argued this segment would only ever reach about 3 million customers. Blockbuster claimed its new program would be better than Netflix' because customers who ordered DVDs online could then return them to Blockbusters stores if they chose. Antioco argued Blockbuster's business model was the best because it was the only company able to provide a simultaneous online *and* bricks-and-mortar service that would give customers more options and better service. For example, if Blockbuster customers returned DVDs to their local store, as part of its Total Access service they would then receive a coupon for a free in-store rental. Blockbuster hoped that by getting customers into its stores, it could generate more rental, sales, and revenues from selling other kinds of products such as candy.

Given that Blockbuster had 48 million members, this online DVD service seemed to be the right strategy to increase future revenues. However, in the short term, the problem for Blockbuster was that the new service required a major financial investment in order to set up the online infrastructure and national marketing campaign. This also led to its huge losses in 2004 and 2005, and its stock price fell from $20 a share to $10 share; investors became concerned it could not provide the online service in a cost-effective way. Analysts also wondered if Netflix had gained the first-mover advantage, making competition difficult.

By the end of 2006, Antioco announced that after a shaky start, Blockbuster had achieved its goal of 2 million subscribers to Total Access. Nevertheless, Netflix and Blockbuster were now locked in a vicious battle for subscribers, and both companies were paying heavily for online ads on major Websites such as eBay and Yahoo!. Once again, Antioco argued that because customers no longer had to choose between renting online or renting in-store, they never needed to be without a movie, and this would make Blockbuster.com the fastest growing online DVD rental service in 2007. As Table 1 suggests he was wrong, in fact, the highest number of subscribers the total access program achieved was 3 million, and the new service was never profitable; it simply drained away Blockbuster's scarce resources.

Table 1 Blockbuster Versus Netflix Revenues and Profits 2004–2010 (All data in millions of dollars)

Year	Blockbuster Revenue	Blockbuster Net Income	Netflix Revenue	Netflix Net Income
2004	6,053	−1,250	506	22
2005	5,864	−588	682	42
2006	5,523	55	997	49
2007	5,542	−74	1,205	70
2008	5,290	−374	1,365	83
2009	5,065	−310	1,670	116
2010	4,062	−558	2,660	214

DVD Rental Kiosks

A second major source of B&M competition emerged in 2004 when Redbox, a division of Coinstar, best known for its coin-money counting machines, began offering video rentals for $1 a night through vending machines at fast-food restaurants, grocery stores, and other retail outlets. This was a low cost channel of distribution and a way of stealing away Blockbuster customers; overhead costs were a fraction of those involved in running a huge chain of B&M stores. Blockbuster responded by opening its own line of Blockbuster Express kiosks, made by NCR, the well-known maker of cash registers, and by 2010, there were 15,000 kiosks in operation compared to the 24,000 operated by Redbox. However, as its profitability collapsed, Blockbuster could not afford to run the kiosks, and licensed the ownership of the kiosks back to NCR, which ran them in 2011. These kiosks generated substantial revenues and in 2010, Coinstar announced that revenues from its Redbox kiosks had increased by 38%. In 2011, after Blockbuster's bankruptcy and purchase by DISH Network Corp., discussed below, DISH sued NCR, arguing that NCR had lost the right to use the Blockbuster brand name. NCR put the Blockbuster kiosks up for sale, and in 2011 it seemed that either DISH or Coinstar was the most likely buyer for the kiosks.

The Future of the Rental Entertainment Industry

As the figures in the table suggest, Blockbuster's losses continued to increase and it was forced to enter Chapter 11 bankruptcy in September 2010. Blockbuster had failed in its battle with Netflix, which had over 17 million subscribers by 2010, increasing profits, and a soaring stock price that reached more than $300 by June 2011. By 2010, it also had no cash to continue to operate its chain of 5,000 stores, or its rental kiosks and its digital broadband download strategy was history. In late-2007, it had replaced Antioco as CEO with James Keyes, who decided to focus Blockbuster's strategy on building in-store sales. With this in mind, Keyes proposed that Blockbuster should acquire Circuit City, the electronics retailer, which also had a failed business model, while he gave control of Blockbuster's profitable kiosk rental operations back to NCR. Analysts laughed at

this acquisition—why would merging the operations of two failing retailers result in a turnaround?

Also, the increasing competition between companies such as Amazon.com, Apple, and Hulu to dominate the digital entertainment streaming industry added to Blockbuster's problems and those of Netflix. Netflix, like Blockbuster, was now confronted with the need to offer a digital movie and streaming TV download service as DVDs, now superseded by the unpopular high-definition "Blue-ray" format, were threatening its DVD format model. One reason its stock price soared in 2010 was that Netflix announced its own entertainment streaming service as a part of its DVD service for as low a price as $10 month. Netflix, however, like all other entertainment channel providers, had to negotiate prices with the content providers—movie studios and TV channels. In June 2011, Netflix announced a 60% increase in the price of its combined DVD/streaming service to pay for the costs of this content and to build the infrastructure necessary to operate digital streaming. It stock price plunged as analysts decided the jump to $16 for both plans might cost it 2–3 million customers, and they saw no reason why content providers would continue to form alliances with the company—just as they had abandoned Blockbuster years before. However, CEO Reed Hastings, following the approach of Steve Jobs of Apple, had focused his efforts on developing close personal relationships with its content providers, and the 17 million subscribers who paid money for their content, was a major force to reckon with—especially now that Blockbuster was in Chapter 11.

As for Blockbuster, in May 2011, it was bought by the DISH satellite network for a few hundred million dollars. Analysts were unclear why DISH decided to purchase the chain as it would now have to fund the costs of running its B&M stores, and Blockbuster's assets seemed to offer few ways to complement its satellite TV and movie distribution channel. However, in the 1990s, DISH and Blockbuster had formed an alliance to sell DISH satellite packages in its stores and to share video-on-demand revenues, although Blockbuster never gained control of this market. By July 2011, DISH announced that it would be able to continue to operate 1,500 Blockbuster stores that would serve 100 million customers; it had hoped to continue to operate 3,000 stores, but their franchisees decided to liquidate. As noted earlier, it also started a legal battle over the rights to control the Blockbuster name in its DVD kiosk business with NCR. Because Blockbuster's major B&M competitors such as Hollywood Video had also been forced into bankruptcy in the 2000s, it was the only B&M rental chain left.

In September 2011 DISH announced it would offer its subscribers a media download rental system similar to Netflix's that would be available to its subscribers at a discount price. It also boosted Blockbusters media download rental offerings to ordinary customers in October 2011 to attract new users. Something that became possible after Netflix's disastrous change in rental strategy that by November had wiped $10 billion off its market value—dropping the value of the company from $16 to $6 billion!

The Netflix Fiasco   Riding its wave of success by the summer of 2011 Netflix's share price had soared to over $300 as investors became convinced it would be company the industry leader in the DVD and media entertainment download industry. However, Netflix, like Blockbuster before found itself dependent on the suppliers of entertainment content and of course they wanted to charge the highest price they could for their media content. To keep their business Netflix had to agree to pay higher prices but the result of this was that it was forced to charge higher prices to its subscribers. In August 2011 it announced large increases in monthly fees that generated an enormous amount of customer protest. Even though it was still relatively inexpensive, Netflix learned the hard way that customers do not like to pay for online digital content. As the number of its subscribers plummeted Hastings announced the company would separate into two different companies—Netflix would now become the supplier of digital download media, while a new company called "Quickster" would take over as the supplier of DVD rentals.

Although designed to allow subscribers to reduce their monthly rentals this new strategy was a disaster; Netflix would have to manage two different groups of customers and sacrifice any gains by offering some combination of DVD plus digital media downloads. Within weeks, Hastings announced this new strategy was dead—Netflix would continue to offer both kinds of media rental services—but its subscribers were by now totally confused and angry at the changes it had made to its services.

Netflix's share price began to plunge in September 2011. And then when in late October 2011 it announced that it had lost 800,000 U.S. subscribers, and that the costs of entering global markets in Europe and Central America would result in losses in 2012, its stock price plunged by 35% on October 25th 2011—from over $300 to $75 a share in a few months! Its new strategy had resulted in a major disaster and this opened the way for new competitors to enter the market and try to take away its dominant position.

As noted earlier, competitors such as Amazon.com, Apple, Hulu, and Google have also invested major capital resources to become the future leaders in digital entertainment media downloading. Also, DISH is seeking to rebuild its Blockbuster franchise. The fight continues for companies to become a major players in this very profitable industry, as digital technology continues to improve and change every company's competitive advantage and position. As Blockbuster—and then Netflix—learned, new technology is not enough to succeed. A company must develop the business model and strategies necessary to profit from changing industry opportunities to become a major player in the digital entertainment market, or to become a leader in a niche, such as Redbox in the DVD rental kiosk segment. There are many ways to make money—and lose money quickly—in the rapidly changing media entertainment rental industry.

Endnotes

www.blockbuster.com, 1990–2010.
blockbuster.com, Annual and 10K Reports, 1990–2010.

www.netflix.com, 1998–2011.
Netflix.com, Annual and 10K Reports, 1998–2010.

CASE 19

How SAP's Business Model and Strategies Made it the Global Business Software Leader—Part 1

Gareth R. Jones
Texas A&M University

In 1972, after the project they were working on for IBM's German subsidiary was abandoned, 5 German IBM computer analysts left the company and founded Systems Applications and Products in Data Processing, known today as SAP. These analysts had been involved in the provisional design of a software program that would allow information about cross-functional and cross-divisional financial transactions in a company's value chain to be coordinated and processed centrally—resulting in enormous savings in time and expense. They observed that other software companies were also developing software designed to integrate across value-chain activities and subunits. Using borrowed money and equipment, the 5 analysts worked day and night to create an accounting software platform that could integrate across all the parts of an entire corporation. In 1973, SAP unveiled an instantaneous accounting transaction processing program called R/1, one of the earliest examples of what is now called an enterprise resource planning (ERP) system.

Today, ERP is an industry term for the multimodule applications software that allows a company to manage the set of activities and transactions necessary to manage the business processes for moving a product from the input stage, along the value chain, and to the final customer. As such, ERP systems can recognize, monitor, measure, and evaluate all the transactions involved in business processes such as product planning, the purchasing of inputs from suppliers, the manufacturing process, inventory and order processing, and customer service. Essentially, a fully developed ERP system provides a company with a standardized information technology (IT) platform that provides managers with complete information about all aspects of its business processes and cost structure across all functions and divisions. This allows managers at all levels to (1) continually search for ways to perform these processes more efficiently and lower its cost structure, and (2) improve and service its products and raise their value to customers. For example, ERP systems provide information that allows for the redesign of products to better match customer needs and that result in superior responsiveness to customers.

To give one example, Nestlé installed SAP's newest ERP software across its more than 150 U.S. food divisions in the 2000s. Using its new IT platform, corporate managers discovered that each division was paying a different price for the same flavoring—vanilla. The same small set of vanilla suppliers was charging each individual division as much as they could, and different divisions paid prices that varied widely depending upon their bargaining power with the supplier. Before the SAP system was installed, corporate managers had no idea this was happening because their old IT system could not compare and measure the same transaction—purchasing vanilla—across divisions. SAP's standardized cross-company software platform revealed this problem, and hundreds of thousands of dollars in cost savings were achieved by solving this one transaction difficulty alone. This is why ERP systems can save large companies hundreds of millions and billions of dollars over time, and explains why SAP's ERP became so popular.

Focus on Large Multinationals

SAP first focused its R/1 software on the largest multinational companies with revenues of at least $2.5 billion because they would reap the biggest cost savings there. Although relatively few in number, these companies, mostly large global product manufacturers stood to gain the most benefit from ERP, and they were willing to pay SAP a premium price for its product. Its focus on this influential niche of companies helped SAP develop a global base of leading companies. Its goal, as it had been from the beginning, was to create the global industry standard for ERP by providing the best business applications software infrastructure—and it succeeded in 2011—it still has the largest installed base of the world's most well-known companies.

ERP and Consulting

In its first years, SAP not only developed ERP software, but it also used its own internal consultants to physically install it on-site at its customers' corporate IT centers, manufacturing operations, and similar locations. Determined to increase its customer base quickly, however, SAP switched strategies in the 1980s. It decided to focus primarily upon the development of its ERP software and to outsource (to external consultants), more and more of the highly complex implementation consulting services needed to install and service its software on-site in a particular company. It formed a series of strategic alliances with major global consulting companies such as IBM, Accenture, and Cap Gemini to install its R/1 system in its growing base of global customers.

ERP installation can often be a long and complicated process. A company cannot simply adapt its information systems to fit SAP's software; it must rework the way it performs its value-chain activities so that its business processes—and the IT system that measures and evaluates these business processes—can become compatible with SAP's software. SAP's claim to fame was that by modeling its business processes on its ERP platform, which contains the solutions needed to achieve best industry practices across its operations, a large company could expect a substantial increase—often 10% or more in performance. However, the more a particular company's managers wanted to customize the SAP platform to fit their own internal business processes, the more difficult and expensive the implementation process would become—and the harder it would, in turn, become for companies to realize the potential gains from cost savings and value added to the product by SAP's software.

SAP's outsourcing consulting strategy allowed it to penetrate global markets quickly and eliminated the huge capital investment needed to employ the thousands of consultants required to provide this service on a global basis. On the other hand, for consulting companies, the installation of SAP's popular software became a major money-spinner and they earned billions by learning how to install its ERP system. Consequently, SAP did not enjoy the huge revenue streams associated with providing software consulting services, such as the design, installation, and maintenance of an ERP platform on an ongoing basis. It earned only a small amount of revenue by training external consultants in the intricacies of how to install, customize, and maintain its ERP systems within its customer base. This was a major error because revenues from consulting over time are often as great as that those that can be earned from selling complex software applications. By focusing on ERP software development, SAP could forfeit high consulting profits and also become dependent upon consulting companies that were now the experts in the installation/customization arena—such as Accenture and IBM.

The Changing Global Landscape

This decision had unfortunate long-term consequences because SAP began to lose first-hand knowledge of its customers' emerging problems and an understanding of the changing needs of its customers—something especially important as growing global competition, outsourcing, and the increasing use of the Internet to facilitate cross-company commerce had become major competitive factors changing the ERP industry and software applications market. For a company with a goal to provide a standardized platform across functions and divisions, this outsourcing consulting strategy seemed like a major error to many analysts. SAP's failure to work quickly to expand its own consulting operations to run parallel to those of external consultants, rather than providing a training service to these consultants to keep them informed about its constantly changing ERP software, left the door open for IBM and Accenture to dominate the software consulting industry—and they still do today.

To some degree, SAPs decision to focus upon software development and outsource more than 80% of installation was a consequence of its German founders' "engineering" mindset. Founded by computer program engineers, SAP's culture was built upon values and norms that emphasized technical innovation, and the development of leading-edge ERP software algorithms and best practices. SAP's managers poured most of its profits into research and development (R&D) to fund new projects that would increase its ERP platform's capabilities; they had little desire to spend money on developing its consulting services. Essentially, SAP became a *product-focused*, not a customer–focused company since it believed R&D would produce the technical advances that would be the source of its competitive advantage and allow it to charge its customers a premium price for its ERP platform. By 1990, SAP spent more than 30% of gross sales on R&D.

Global Sales and Marketing Problems

SAP's top managers, who had focused on developing its technical competency, had another unfortunate consequence. They underestimated the enormous problems involved in developing and implementing its global marketing and sales competency to increase its large customer base—and to attract new kinds of customers—especially smaller companies. The need to build an efficient global structure and control system to effectively manage its own operations was largely ignored because managers believed the ERP platform would sell itself! Indeed, SAP's focus on R&D and neglect of its other functions made its sales, marketing, and internal consultants and training experts feel as if they were second-class citizens—despite the fact that they brought in new business and were the people responsible maintaining good relationships with SAP's growing customer base.

The classic problem of managing a growing business from the entrepreneurial to the professional management phase was emerging in SAP and its revenues and profits were slowing as a result. SAP's top managers were not experienced business managers who understood the problems of implementing a rapidly growing company's strategy on a global basis; the need to develop a sound corporate infrastructure was being shoved aside—something that had cost it billions of dollars in lost profits over the decades.

The Second Generation R/2 ERP Platform

In 1981, SAP introduced its second-generation ERP software, R/2. Not only did it contain many more value-chain/business process software modules, but it also linked its ERP software seamlessly to the existing or legacy databases and communication systems used on a company's mainframe computers. This allowed for greater connectivity and ease of use of ERP throughout a company at all levels and across all subunits. The R/1 platform had largely been a cross-organizational accounting/financial software module; the new software modules could handle procurement, product development, and inventory and order tracking. Of course, these additional components needed to be compatible with one another so that they could be seamlessly integrated together on-site, at a customer's operations, and with its existing or legacy IT system.

SAP did not develop its own database management software package; its system was designed to be compatible with Oracle's database management software, the global leader in this segment of the software applications industry. Once again, this would have repercussions later, when Oracle began to rapidly develop its own ERP software platform during the 2000s, essentially moving from database software into ERP and other kinds of business software applications. As part of its push to make its R/2 software the global industry standard for the next decades, SAP also developed new "middleware" software that will allow the hardware and software made by different global computer companies to work seamlessly together on any particular company's IT system. This is also an industry in which Oracle competes.

Recognizing that the way value-chain activities and business processes are performed differs *from industry to industry* because of differences in manufacturing and other business processes. SAP also spent a lot of time and money customizing its basic

ERP platform to accommodate the needs of companies in different kinds of industries. Increasingly, over time, ERP companies recognized that their long-term competitive advantage depended upon being able to provide the ERP software solutions that must be customized by industry to perform most effectively. Its push to become the ERP leader across industries, across all large global companies, and across all value-chain business processes required a huge R&D investment.

SAP Becomes a Global Leader

In 1988, SAP went public on the Frankfurt stock exchange to raise the necessary cash to fund its growing global operations, and by 1990, it had become a global leader of business applications software as its market capitalization soared. SAP now dominated ERP software sales in the high-tech and electronics, engineering and construction, consumer products, chemical, and retail industries. Its product was increasingly being recognized as superior to the other ERP software being developed by companies such as PeopleSoft, S. D. Edwards, and Oracle. The main reason for SAP's increasing competitive advantage was that it was the only company that could offer a potential customer a broad, standardized, state-of-the-art solution that spanned a wide variety of value-chain activities spread around the globe. By contrast, its competitors, like PeopleSoft, offered more-focused solutions aimed at one business process, such as human resources management.

SAP Introduces the R/3 Solution

SAP's continuing massive investment in developing new ERP software resulted in the introduction of its R/3, or third-generation, ERP solution in 1992. Essentially, the R/3 platform expanded upon its previous solutions; it offered seamless, real-time integration for over 80% of a company's business processes. It had also embedded in the platform hundreds, and then thousands, of industry best practice solutions, or templates, that customers could use to improve their operations and processes. The R/3 system was initially composed of seven different modules corresponding to the most common business processes: production planning, materials

management, financial accounting, asset management, human resources management, project systems, and sales and distribution. R/3 was designed to meet the diverse demands of its previous global clients. It could operate in multiple languages, convert exchange rates, and additional functions, on a real-time basis.

By the 1990s, however, as it now dominated the ERP market for large companies, SAP realized that for its sales to expand quickly it also needed to address the needs of small- and medium-sized businesses (SMBs). Recognizing the huge potential revenues to be earned from SMB customers, SAP's engineers designed the R/3 platform so that it could be configured for smaller customers as well as customized to suit the needs of a broader range of industries in which they competed. Furthermore, SAP designed R/3 to be "open architecturally," meaning that using its middleware, the R/3 could operate with whatever kind of computer hardware or software (the legacy system) a SMB was presently using.

Finally, in response to customer concerns that SAP's standardized system meant huge implementation problems in changing their business processes to match SAP's standardized solution, SAP introduced some limited customization opportunity into its software. Using specialized software from other companies, SAP claimed that up to 20% of R/3 could now be customized to work with the company's existing operating methods and thus would reduce the problems of learning and implementing the new system. However, the costs of doing this were extremely high and became a huge generator of fees for consulting companies. SAP used a variable-fee licensing system for its R/3 system; the cost to the customer was based upon the number of users within a company, upon the number of different R/3 modules that were installed, and upon the degree to which users utilized these modules in the business planning process.

SAP's R/3 far outperformed its competitors' products in a technical sense and once again allowed it to charge a premium price for its new software. Believing that competitors would take at least 2 years to catch up, SAP's goal was to get its current customers to switch to its new product and then rapidly build its customer base to penetrate the growing ERP market. In doing so, it was also seeking to establish R/3 as the new ERP market standard in order to lock in customers before competitors could offer viable alternatives. This strategy was vital to its future success because, because of the way an ERP system changes the nature of a customer's business processes once it is installed and running; there are high switching costs involved in moving to another ERP product, costs that customers want to avoid.

SAP's Growing Global Implementation Problems

R/3's growing popularity led SAP to decentralize more and more control of the marketing, sale, and installation of its software on a global basis to its overseas subsidiaries. While its R&D and software development remained centralized in Germany, it began to open wholly-owned subsidiaries in most major country's markets. By 1995, it had 18 national subsidiaries; today, it has over 50. In 1995, SAP established a U.S. subsidiary to drive sales in the huge and most profitable market—the U.S. market. Its German top managers set the subsidiary a goal of achieving $1 billion in revenues within 5 years. To implement this aggressive growth strategy, and given that R/3 software needs to be installed and customized to suit the needs of particular companies and industries, several different regional SAP divisions were created to manage the needs of companies and industries in different U.S. regions. Also, the regional divisions became responsible for training an army of both internal and external consultants on how to install and customize the R/3 software. For every internal lead SAP consultant, there were soon about 9–10 external consultants working with SAP's customers to install and modify the software—which again boosted IBM and Accenture's profits.

Problems with its U.S. Operations

The problems with its policy of decentralization soon caught up with SAP, however. Because SAP was growing so fast, and demand for its product was increasing so rapidly, it was hard to provide the thorough training consultants needed to perform the installation of its software. Often, once SAP had trained an internal consultant, that consultant would leave to join the company for which he or she was performing the work, or even to start an industry-specific SAP consulting practice! The result was that

SAP customers' needs were being poorly served and the number of complaints about the cost and difficulty of installing its ERP software was increasing. Since large external consulting companies made their money based upon the time it took their consultants to install a particular SAP system, many customers complained that consultants were deliberately taking too long to implement the new software to maximize their earnings and were even pushing inappropriate or unnecessary R/3 modules. For example, Chevron spent over $100 million and 2 years installing and getting its R/3 system operating effectively. In one well-publicized case, FoxMeyer Drug blamed SAP software for the supply chain problems that led to its bankruptcy and the company's major creditors, and sued SAP alleging that the company had promised R/3 would do more than it could. SAP responded that the problem was not the software but the way the company had installed it, but SAP's reputation was harmed nevertheless.

SAP's policy of decentralization was also somewhat paradoxical because the company's mission was to supply software that linked functions and divisions rather than separated them, and the characteristic problems of too much decentralization of authority soon became evident throughout SAP. In its U.S. subsidiary, each regional SAP division started developing its own procedures for pricing SAP software, offering discounts, dealing with customer complaints, and even rewarding its employees and consultants. There was a complete lack of standardization and integration inside SAP America and between SAP's many foreign subsidiaries and their headquarters in Germany. This meant that little learning was taking place between divisions or consultants, there was no monitoring or coordination mechanism in place to share SAP's *own* best practices between its consultants and divisions, and organizing by region in the U. S. was doing little to build core competences. For example, analysts were asking: "If R/3 has to be customized to suit the needs of a particular industry, why didn't SAP use a market structure and divide its activities by the needs of customers based in different industries?" These problems slowed down the process of implementing SAP software and prevented quick and effective responses to the needs of potential customers.

SAP's R/3 was also criticized as being too standardized because it forced all companies to adapt to what SAP had decided were best industry practices.

When consultants reconfigured the software to suit a particular company's needs, this process often took a long time, and sometimes the system did not perform as well as had been expected. Many companies felt that the software should be configured to suit their business processes and not the other way around, but again SAP argued that such a setup would not lead to an optimal outcome. For example, SAP's retail R/3 system could not handle Home Depot's policy of allowing each of its stores to order directly from suppliers, based upon centrally negotiated contracts between Home Depot and those suppliers. SAP's customers also found that supporting their new ERP platform was expensive and that ongoing support cost 3–5 times as much as the actual purchase of the software, although the benefits they received from its R/3 system usually substantially exceeded these costs.

The Changing Industry Environment

Although the United States had become SAP's biggest market, the explosive growth in demand for SAP's software had begun to slump by 1995. Competitors such as Oracle, Baan, PeopleSoft, and Marcum were catching up technically, often because they were focusing their resources on the needs of one or a few industries, or on a particular kind of ERP module (for example, PeopleSoft's focus on the human resources management module). Indeed SAP had to play catch-up in the HRM area and develop its own to offer a full suite of integrated business solutions. Oracle, the second largest software maker after Microsoft, was becoming a particular threat as it expanded its ERP offerings outward from its leading database knowledge systems and began to offer more and more of an Internet-based ERP platform. As new aggressive competitors emerged and changed the environment, SAP found it needed to change as well.

Competitors were increasing their market share by exploiting weaknesses in SAP's software. They began to offer SAP's existing and potential customers ERP modules that could be customized more easily to their situation and that were less expensive than SAP's. SAP's managers were forced to reevaluate their business model, and their strategies and the ways in which they implemented this model.

New Implementation Problems

To a large degree, SAP's decision to decentralize control of its marketing, sales, and installation to its subsidiaries was due to the way the company had operated from its beginnings. Its German founders had emphasized the importance of excellence in innovation as the root value of its culture, and SAP's culture was often described as "organized chaos." Its top managers had operated from the beginning by creating as flat a hierarchy as possible to create an internal environment where people could take risks and try new ideas of their own choosing. If mistakes occurred or projects didn't work out, employees were given the freedom to try a different approach. Hard work, teamwork, openness, and speed were the norms of their culture. Required meetings were rare and offices were frequently empty because most of the employees were concentrating on research and development. The pressure was on software developers to create superior products. In fact, the company was proud of the fact that it was product driven, not service oriented. It wanted to be the world's leading innovator of software, not a service company that installed it.

Increasing competition led SAP's managers to realize that they were not capitalizing on its main strength—its human resources. In 1997, it established a human resources management (HRM) department and gave it the responsibility to build a more formal organizational structure. Previously it had outsourced its own HRM. HRM managers started to develop job descriptions and job titles, and put in place a career structure that would motivate employees and keep them loyal to the company. They also put in place a reward system, which included stock options, to increase the loyalty of their technicians, who were being attracted away by competitors or were starting their own businesses because SAP did not then offer a future: a career path. For example, SAP sued Siebel Systems, a niche rival in the customer relationship software business, in 2000 for enticing 12 of its senior employees, who it said took trade secrets with them. SAP's top managers realized that they had to plan long term and that innovation by itself was not enough to make SAP a dominant global company with a sustainable competitive advantage.

At the same time that it started to operate more formally, it also became more centralized to encourage organizational learning and to promote the sharing of its own best implementation practices across divisions and subsidiaries. Its goal was to standardize the way each subsidiary or division operated across the company, thus making it easier to transfer people and knowledge where they were needed most. Not only would this facilitate cooperation, it would also reduce overhead costs, which were spiraling because of the need to recruit trained personnel as the company grew quickly and the need to alter and adapt its software to suit changing industry conditions. For example, increasing customer demands for additional customization of its software made it imperative that different teams of engineers pool their knowledge to reduce development costs, and that consultants should not only share their best practices, but also cooperate with engineers so that the latter could understand the problems facing customers in the field.

The need to adopt a more standardized and hierarchical approach was also being driven by SAP's growing recognition that it needed more of the stream of income it could get from both the training and installation sector of the software business. It began to increase the number of its consultants. By having its consultants work with SAP's software developers they became the acknowledged experts and leaders when it came to specific software installations and could command a high price. SAP also developed a large global training function to provide the extensive ERP training that consultants needed and charged both individuals and consulting companies high fees for attending these courses so that they would be able to work with the SAP platform. SAP's U.S. subsidiary also moved from a regional to a more market-based focus by re-aligning its divisions, not by geography, but by their focus on a particular sector or industry, for example, chemicals, electronics, pharmaceuticals, consumer products, and engineering.

Once again, however, the lines of authority between the new industry divisions and the software development, sales, installation, and training functions were not structured well enough, and the hoped-for gains from increased coordination and cooperation were slow to be realized. Globally, too, SAP was still highly decentralized and remained a product-focused company, thus allowing its subsidiaries to form their own sales, training, and installation policies. Its subsidiaries continued to form strategic alliances with global consulting companies,

allowing them to obtain the majority of revenues from servicing SAP's growing base of R/3 installations. SAP's top managers, with their engineering mindset, did not appreciate the difficulties involved in changing a company's structure and culture, either at the subsidiary or the global level. They were disappointed in the slow pace of change because their cost structure remained high, although their revenues were increasing.

New Strategic Problems

By the mid-1990s, despite its problems in implementing its strategy, SAP was the clear market leader in the ERP software industry and the 4th largest global software company because of its recognized competencies in the production of state-of-the-art ERP software. Several emerging problems posed major threats to its business model, however. First, it was becoming increasingly obvious that the development of the Internet and broadband technology would become important forces in shaping a company's business model and processes in the future. SAP's R/3 systems were specifically designed to integrate information about all of a company's value-chain activities, across its functions and divisions, and to provide real-time feedback on its ongoing performance. However, ERP systems focused principally on a company's internal business processes; they were not designed to focus and provide feedback on cross-company and industry-level transactions and processes on a real-time basis. The Internet was changing the way in which companies viewed their boundaries; the emergence of global e-commerce and online cross-company transactions was changing the nature of a company's business processes both at the input and output sides.

At the input side, the Internet was changing the way a company managed its relationships with its parts and raw materials suppliers. Internet-based commerce offered the opportunity of locating new, low-cost suppliers. Developing Web software was also making it much easier for a company to cooperate with suppliers and manufacturing companies and to outsource activities to specialists who could perform the activities at lower cost. A company that previously made its own inputs or manufactured its own products could now outsource these value-chain activities, which changed the nature of the ERP systems it needed to manage such transactions. In general, the changing nature of transactions across the company's boundaries could affect its ERP system in thousands of ways. Companies like Commerce One and Ariba, which offered this supply-chain management (SCM) software, were rapidly growing and posing a major threat to SAP's "closed" ERP software.

At the output side, the emergence of the Internet also radically altered the relationship between a company and its customers. Not only did the Internet make possible new ways to sell to wholesalers, its largest customers, or directly to individual customers, it also changed the whole nature of the company—customer interface. For example, using new customer relationship management (CRM) software from software developers like Siebel Systems, a company could offer its customers access to much more information about its products so that customers could make more-informed purchase decisions. A company could also understand customers' changing needs so it could develop improved or advanced products to meet those needs; and a company could offer a whole new way to manage after-sales service and help solve customers' problems with learning about, operating, and even repairing their new purchases. The CRM market was starting to boom.

In essence, the Internet was changing both industry- and company-level business processes and providing companies and entire industries with many more avenues for altering their business processes at a company or industry level, so that they could lower their cost structure or increasingly differentiate their products. Clearly, the hundreds of industry best practices that SAP had embedded in its R/3 software would become outdated and redundant as e-commerce increased in scope and depth, and offered improved industry solutions. SAP's R/3 system would become a dinosaur within a decade unless it could move quickly to develop or obtain competencies in the software skills needed to develop Web-based software.

These developments posed a severe shock to SAP's management, who had been proud of the fact that, until now, SAP had developed all its software internally. They were not alone in their predicament. The largest software companies, Microsoft and Oracle, had been caught unaware by the quickly growing implications of Web-based computing. The introduction of Netscape's Web browser had led to a collapse in Microsoft's stock price because investors saw Web-based computing, not PC-based computing, as the choice of the future. SAP's stock price also began to reflect the beliefs of many people that expensive, rigid, standardized ERP systems would not become the software choice as the Web developed. One source of SAP's competitive advantage was based on the high switching costs of moving from one ERP platform to another. However, if new Web-based platforms allowed both internal and external integration of a company's business processes, and new platforms could be more easily customized to answer a particular company's needs, these switching costs might disappear. SAP was at a critical point in its development.

The other side of the equation was that the emergence of new Web-based software technology allowed hundreds of new software industry start-ups, founded by technical experts equally as qualified as those at SAP and Microsoft, to enter the industry and compete for the wide-open Web-computing market. The race was on to determine which standards would apply in the new Web-computing arena, and who would control them. The large software makers like Microsoft, Oracle, IBM, SAP, Netscape, Sun Microsystems, and Computer Associates had to decide how to compete in this totally changed industry environment. Most of their customers, companies large and small, were still watching developments before deciding how and where to commit their IT budgets. Hundreds of billions of dollars in future software sales were at stake, and it was not clear which company had the competitive advantage in this changing environment.

Rivalry among major software makers in the new Web-based software market became intense. Rivalry between the major players and new players, like Netscape, Siebel Systems, Marcum, I2 Technology, and SSA, also intensified. The major software makers, each of which was a market leader in one or more segments of the software industry, such as SAP in ERP, Microsoft in PC software, and Oracle in database management software, sought to showcase their strengths to make their software compatible with Web-based technology. Thus, Microsoft strove to develop its Windows NT network-based platform and its Internet Explorer Web browser to compete with Netscape's Internet browser and Sun Microsystems' open-standard Java Web software programming language, which was compatible with any company's proprietary software, unlike Microsoft's NT.

SAP also had to deal with competition from large and small software companies that were breaking into the new Web-based ERP environment. In 1995, SAP teamed with Microsoft, Netscape, and Sun Microsystems to make its R/3 software Internet-compatible with any of their competing systems. Within one year, it introduced its R/3 Release 3.1 Internet-compatible system, which was most easily configured, however, when using Sun's Java Web-programming language. SAP raised new funds on the stock market to undertake new rounds of the huge investment necessary to keep its Web-based R/3 system up to date with the dramatic innovations in Web software development, and to broaden its product range to offer new, continually emerging Web-based applications, for example, applications such as the corporate intranets, business-to-business (B2B) and business-to customer (B2C) networks, Website development and hosting, security and systems management, and streaming audio and video teleconferencing.

Because SAP had no developed competency in Web software development, its competitors started to catch up. Oracle emerged as its major competitor; it had taken its core database management software, which was used by thousands of large companies, and overlaid it with Web-based operating and applications software. Oracle could now offer its huge customer base a growing suite of Web software, all seamlessly integrated. The suite of software also allowed them to perform Internet-based ERP value chain business processes. While Oracle's system was nowhere near as comprehensive as SAP's R/3 system, it allowed for cross-industry networking at both the input and output sides, it was cheaper and easier to quickly implement, and it was easier to customize to the needs of a particular customer. Oracle began to take market share away from SAP.

New companies like Siebel Systems, Commerce One, Ariba, and Marcum, which began as niche players in some software applications such as SCM, CRM, intranet, or Website development and hosting, also began to build and expand their product offerings so that they now possessed ERP modules that competed with some of SAP's most lucrative R/3 modules. Commerce One and Ariba, for example, emerged as the main players in the rapidly expanding B2B industry SCM market. B2B is an industry-level ERP solution that creates an organized market and thus brings together industry buyers and suppliers electronically, and provides the software to write and enforce contracts for the future development and supply of an industry's inputs. Although these niche players could not provide the full range of services that SAP could provide, they had become increasingly able to offer attractive alternatives to customers seeking specific aspects of an ERP system. Also, companies like Siebel, Marcum, and I2 claimed that they had the ability to customize their low-price systems, and prices for ERP systems began to fall.

In the new software environment, SAP's large customers started to purchase software on a "best of breed" basis, meaning that customers purchased the best software applications for their specific needs from different, leading-edge companies rather than purchasing all of their software products from one company as a package—such as SAP offered. Sun Microsystems began to promote a free Java computer language as the industry "open architecture" standard, which meant that as long as each company used Java to craft their specific Web-based software programs, they would all work seamlessly together, and there would no longer be an advantage to using a single dominant platform like Microsoft's Windows or SAP's R/3. Sun Microsystems was (and still is) trying to break Microsoft's hold over the operating system industry standard, Windows. Sun Microsystems wanted each company's software to succeed because it was "best of breed," not because it locked customers in and created enormous switching costs for them should they contemplate a move to a competitor's product.

All these different factors caused enormous problems for SAP's top managers. What strategies should they use to protect their competitive position? Should they forge ahead and offer their customers a broad, proprietary, Web-based ERP solution and try to lock them in to continue to charge a premium price? Should they move to an open standard and make their R/3 ERP Internet-enabled modules compatible with solutions from other companies, and forge alliances with those companies to ensure that the software seamlessly operated together? Since SAP's managers still believed they had the best ERP software and the capabilities to lead in the Web software arena, was this the best long-run competitive solution? Should SAP focus on making its ERP software more customizable to its customers' needs, and make it easier for them to buy selected modules to reduce the cost of SAP software? This alternative might also make it easier for them to develop ERP modules that could be scaled back to suit the needs of medium and small firms, which were increasingly becoming the targets of its new software competitors. Once these new firms established toeholds in the market, it would only be a matter of time before they improved their products and began to compete for SAP's installed customer base. SAP realized that it had to refocus its business model, especially because rivals were rapidly buying niche players and, at the same time, filling gaps in their product lines to be able to compete with SAP.

Protecting its Competitive Position

In 1997, SAP sought a quick fix to its problems by releasing new R/3 solutions for ERP Internet-enabled SCM and CRM solutions, which converted its internal ERP system into an externally based network platform. SCM, now known as the "back end" of the business, integrates the business processes necessary to manage the flow of goods, from the raw material stage to the finished product. SCM programs forecast future needs, and plan and manage a company's operations, especially its manufacturing operations. CRM, known as the "front-end" of the business, provides companies with solutions and support for business processes directed at improving sales, marketing, customer service, and field service operations. CRM programs are rapidly growing in popularity because they lead to better customer retention and satisfaction and higher revenues. In 1998, SAP followed with industry solution maps, business technology maps, and service maps, all of which were aimed at making its R/3 system dynamic and responsive to changes in industry conditions.

Also in 1998, recognizing that its future rested on its ability to protect its share of the U.S. market, SAP listed itself on the New York Stock Exchange and began to expand the scope of its U.S. operations, both to encourage internal "organic growth," meaning growth through internal new venturing, and to allow it to develop a U.S. top management team that could develop the strategies and business model necessary to allow it to respond to the growing competition it was facing. As with all growing businesses, the need to manage the fit between its strategy and structure had become its major priority—SAP's R&D culture was hurting it in its battle with agile competitors, and had to be changed.

Endnotes

www.sap.com, 1988–2011.
SAP Annual Reports and 10K Reports, 1989–2011.
SAP 10K Reports, 1989–2011.

CASE 20

SAP and the Evolving Global Business Software Industry in 2011—Part 2

Gareth R. Jones
Texas A&M University

As Part 1 discusses, by 1997, SAP realized the need to release new Internet-enabled ERP R/3 solutions, which converted its internal ERP system into an externally-based network platform, to satisfy customers needs for SCM and CRM. Recall that SAP's Supply Chain Management (SCM) integrates the business processes necessary to manage the flow of goods from the raw material stage to the finished product—it is a set of supply value-chain solutions designed to control costs and increase differentiation over the product life-cycle. By, for example, forecasting future product developments, and then devising solutions to more effectively manage a company's value-chain operations, especially its manufacturing operations, to increase performance. Customer Relationship Management (CRM), at the front-end of the value chain, provides companies with solutions and support for business processes directed at improving sales, marketing, customer service, and field service operations. By 2000, CRM programs were rapidly growing in popularity because they lead to better customer retention and satisfaction and higher revenues and profits for the companies that make them part of their IT system.

The mySAP.com Initiative

Like most software applications companies, SAP had been slow to recognize the enormous potential of the Internet to build a company's global competitive advantage in so many different ways. In 1999, however, SAP's realization of the growing importance of the Internet was made apparent by major changes to its business model and strategies when it introduced its mySAP.com (mySAP) initiative. The strategy behind mySAP was to allow the company to regain leadership of the Internet Web-based ERP, SCM, and CRM markets, and to promote its ability to develop new Internet-based software applications as they have evolved over time. In essence, the mySAP initiative was a comprehensive ebusiness platform designed to promote internal collaboration inside a client company, and collaboration with other companies in its supply chain. mySAP demonstrated several elements of top managers changing strategic thinking for how to succeed in the 2000s.

First, to meet its customers' needs in a new electronic environment, SAP used the mySAP platform to change itself from a vendor of ERP components to a provider of ebusiness solutions. The platform would be the online portal through which customers could view and understand the way its Internet-enabled R/3 modules could match their evolving needs. Customers wanted to be able to leverage new ebusiness technologies to improve basic business goals like increasing profitability, improving customer satisfaction, and lowering overhead costs. In addition, customers wanted total solutions that could help them manage their relationships and supply chains.

mySAP would offer a total solutions ERP package, including SCM and CRM applications that would no longer force customers to adapt to SAP's standardized architecture. Rather, mySAP software was designed to help facilitate a client company's transition into ebusiness and provide them with the advantages offered by the Internet. Of course, mySAP solutions would also create value for clients by building on

SAP's established core competencies, including its industry best practices. In addition, mySAP solutions would also allow a client company to leverage its own core competencies and build its competitive advantage from within, SAP created a full range of front- and back-end ERP products available through its mySAP.com portal that were specific to different industries and manufacturing technologies. These changes meant that it could compete in niche markets and make it easier to customize a particular application to an individual company's needs. mySAP showed it was offering customers not product-based solutions but customer-based solutions. Its mySAP ebusiness platform solutions are designed to be a scalable and flexible architecture that supports databases, software applications, operating systems, and hardware platforms from almost every major vendor.

Second, mySAP provided the evolving IT platform that would allow SAP's own product offerings—software applications—to expand and broaden over time, something especially important because Web-based applications software was evolving in ever more varied and unexpected ways as new high-tech software companies recognized a new niche in the market and were striving to develop software applications that companies would want to buy and use. In essence, SAP had begun to pursue related diversification, and other major software applications makers, such as rivals Oracle and Microsoft, were, too. All these competitors were branching out into more segments of the software industry to capitalize on higher-growth emerging software segments, and to fill the niches to keep potential competitors from invading their core software markets and stealing away their customers.

Third, SAP realized that price was becoming a more important issue because both large software companies and new software startups competition were increasingly offering companies lower-priced software solutions and solutions to persuade these companies to shift their loyalties and abandon SAP's software platform. Major rivals, Oracle and Microsoft had begun to offer good deals to companies to build their market share; they offered their software at discount prices or packed their ERP software with their other software such as database or PC software to generate demand for their product. SAP focused on making mySAP more affordable by breaking up its modules and business solutions into smaller, separate products. Customers could now choose which particular solutions best met their specific needs; they no longer had to buy the whole package. At the same time, all mySAP offerings were fully compatible with the total R/3 system so that customers could easily expand their use of SAP's products. SAP was working across its entire product range to make its system easier and cheaper to use. SAP realized that repeat business is much more important than a 1-time transaction, so they began to focus on seeking out and developing new, related solutions for their customers to keep them coming back and purchasing more products and upgrades.

Fourth, SAP was announcing that in the future, its mySAP solutions would be designed to fit and support the needs of large, medium, and small companies, and it intended to compete in all market segments. SAP would broaden its mySAP ebusiness solution packages so it would target not only large corporations, but also small- and medium-sized business enterprises (SMEs). mySAP allowed SAP to provide several simpler and cheaper versions of its application software, such as low-cost ERP solutions that could be scaled down to suit the needs of smaller firms. Also, for SMEs that lacked the internal resources to maintain their own business applications on-site, mySAP offered hosting for data centers, networks, and applications. Small businesses could greatly benefit from the increased speed of installation and reduced cost possible through outsourcing and by paying a fee to use mySAP in lieu of purchasing SAP's expensive software modules. SAP also focused on making its R/3 mySAP offerings easier to install and use, and reduced implementation times and consulting costs in turn reduced the costs of supporting the SAP platform for both small and large organizations.

To support its mySAP initiative, SAP had continued to build in-house training and consulting capabilities to increase its share of revenues from the services side of its business. SAP's increasing Web-based software efforts paid off because the company was now better able to recognize the problems experienced by customers. This result led SAP to recognize both the needs for greater responsiveness to customers, and customization of its products to make their installation easier. Its growing customer awareness had also led it to redefine its mission as a developer of business solutions, the approach embedded in mySAP, rather than as a provider of software products.

To improve the cost effectiveness of mySAP installations, SAP sought a better way to manage its relationships with consulting companies. It moved to a parallel sourcing policy, in which several consulting firms competed for a customer's business, and it made sure an internal SAP consultant was always involved in the installation and service effort to monitor external consultants' performance. This helped keep service costs under control for its customers. Because customer needs changed so quickly in this fast-paced market and SAP continually improved its products with incremental innovations and additional capabilities, it also insisted that consultants undertake continual training to update their skills, training for which it charged high fees. In 2000, SAP adopted a stock option program to retain valuable employees after losing many key employees—programmers and consultants—to competitors like IBM.

Indeed, strategic alliances and acquisitions became increasingly important parts of its strategy to reduce its cost structure, enhance the functionality of its products, and build its customer base. Because of the sheer size and expense of many Web-based software endeavors, intense competition, and the fast-paced dynamics of this industry, SAP's top managers began to realize they could not go it alone and produce everything in-house. SAP's overhead costs had rocketed in the 1990s, as it pumped money into building its mySAP initiative. Intense competition seemed to indicate that continuing massive expenditures would be necessary. SAP's stock price had decreased because higher overhead costs meant falling profits despite increasing revenues. SAP had never seemed to be able to enjoy sustained high profitability because changing technology and competition had not allowed it to capitalize on its acknowledged position as the ERP industry leader.

Given existing resource constraints and time pressures and the need to create a more profitable business model, in the 2000s, SAP's managers realized that they needed to partner with companies that had developed the "best of breed" software applications in various niches of the Web software market. Now SAP could avoid the high R&D outlays necessary to develop new software itself. In addition, synergies with its software partners might make it possible to bring new mySAP products to the market more quickly and efficiently.

SAP also began to use acquisitions to speed its entry into crucial new segments of the Web software market. For example, SAP acquired Top Tier Software Inc. in 2001 to gain access to its iView technology. This technology allows seamless integration between the Web software of different companies and is critical for SAP because it lets customers drag-and-drop and mix information and applications from both SAP and non-SAP platform-based systems. Top Tier was also an enterprise portal software maker, and in 2001, SAP used these competencies to create a new U.S. subsidiary called SAP Portals, which would deliver state-of-the-art enterprise portal products that would result in greater business efficiency and attract more customers. It also opened SAP hosting to provide hosting and Web maintenance services to its new portal customers.

By 2002, SAP believed that its alliances and acquisitions had given it a competitive advantage it could use to sustain its position as the dominant business applications software company. Its alliances with other software makers promoted mySAP as the industry standard and the dominant player in the ERP Web software market. SAP's managers were therefore shocked when it became clear that Microsoft, which also recognized the enormous potential of Web software ERP sales, particularly in the SME segment of the market, was also planning to compete in this fast-growing market segment. In 2002, Microsoft had bought two companies that competed in the SME segment to bolster its own Web software offerings such as its suite of office products including email, word processing and other important applications that it could now bundle with its ERP offerings to SMEs. Microsoft's goal was clearly to become a formidable competitor for SAP, and with its competencies in a wide area of software products and huge resources, it could quickly and easily develop an ERP system with Web-based solutions that integrated with its other applications software.

SAP's number of global software installations and customers increased steadily between 1998 and 2002 when SAP was still the industry leader with a worldwide market share of over 30%. Oracle was next with a 16% share of the market, and Microsoft had around 7%. SAP claimed that it had 10 million users and 50,000 SAP installations in 18,000 companies in 120 countries in 2002, and that 1/2 of the world's top 500 companies used its software.

Implementing mySAP

SAP's problems were not just in the strategy area, however. Its mySAP initiative had increased its overhead costs dramatically, and it still could not find the appropriate organizational structure to make the best use of its resources and competencies. It continued to search for the right structure for servicing the growing range of its products and the increasing breadth of the companies, in terms of size, industry, and global location, it was now serving.

Recall that in the mid-1990s, SAP had begun to centralize authority and control to standardize its own business processes and effectively manage knowledge across its organizational subunits. While this reorganization helped reduce costs, unfortunately it also lengthened the time it took SAP to respond to the fast-changing Web software ERP environment. To quickly respond to changing customer needs, the needs for product customization, and the actions of its rivals, SAP now moved to decentralize control to teams of software engineers who were experts in a business process or in a particular industry, and who now worked with its local salesforce to manage customer problems where and when they arose. SAP's managers felt that in a market dominated by high rivalry among ERP vendors and in which customers had more bargaining power to obtain software and services cheaper and easier to use, it was important to get close to the customer. SAP had now put into place its own applications software to integrate across its operating divisions and subsidiaries and allow them to share best practices and new developments. Thus, it hoped to avoid the problems it had experienced in the past when it had decentralized too much authority.

SAP also changed the way its three German engineering groups worked with the different mySAP products groups. Henceforth, a significant part of the engineering development effort would take place inside each mySAP product engineering group so that the software engineers, who write and improve the specific new mySAP software applications, were joined with the sales force for that group. Now they could integrate their activities and provide better customized solutions. The software engineers at its German headquarters, besides conducting basic R&D, would be responsible for coordinating the efforts of the different mySAP engineering groups, sharing new software

developments among groups, providing expert solutions, and ensuring all the different mySAP applications seamlessly worked together.

Each mySAP product group is now composed of a collection of cross-functional product development teams focused on their target markets. Teams are given incentives to meet their specific sales growth targets and to increase operating effectiveness, including reducing the length of installation time. The purposes of the new product group/team approach was to decentralize control, make SAP more responsive to the needs of customers and to changing technical developments, and still give SAP centralized control of development efforts. To ensure that its broadening range of software was customizable to the needs of different kinds of companies and industries, SAP enlisted some of its key customers as "development partners" and as members of these teams. Customers from large, mid-sized, and small companies were used to test new concepts and ideas. Within every mySAP product group, cross-functional teams focused upon customizing its products for specific customers or industries.

At the global level, SAP grouped is national subsidiaries into 3 main world regions: Europe, the Americas, and Asia/Pacific. This grouping made it easier to transfer knowledge and information between countries and serve the specific demands of national markets inside each region. Also, this global structure made it easier to manage relationships with consulting companies and to coordinate regional marketing and training efforts, both under the jurisdiction of the centralized marketing and training operations.

Thus, in the 2000s, SAP had begun to operate with a loose form of matrix structure. To increase internal flexibility and responsiveness to customers while at the same time boosting efficiency and market penetration, the world regions, the national subsidiaries, and the salespeople and consultants within them constitute one side of the matrix. The centralized engineering, marketing, and training functions and the 20 or so different mySAP product groups compose the other side. The problem facing SAP is to coordinate all these distinct subunits so they will lead to rapid acceptance of SAP's new mySAP platform across all the national markets in which it operates.

In practice, a salesperson in any particular country will work directly with a client to determine what type of ERP system he or she needs. Once it is determined which system will be used, a project manager from the regional subsidiary or from one of the mySAP groups is appointed to assemble an installation team from members of the different product groups that have the expertise required to implement the new client's system. Given SAP's broad range of evolving products, the matrix structure allows SAP to provide those products that fit the customer's needs in a fast, coordinated way. SAP's policy of decentralizing authority and placing it in the hands of its employees enables the matrix system to work. SAP prides itself on its talented and professional staff that can learn and adapt to many different situations and networks across the globe.

Developments in the Early-2000s

In April 2002, SAP announced that its revenues had climbed 9.2%, but its first-quarter profit fell 40% because of a larger-than-expected drop in license revenue from the sale of new software. Many customers had been reluctant to invest in the huge cost of moving to the mySAP system and the 2000 economic recession reduced IT expenditures. SAP announced it had several orders for mySAP in the works, however, and that it believed the 18,000 companies around the world using its flagship R/3 software would soon move to mySAP once their own revenues and profits recovered. In the meantime, SAP announced that it would introduce a product called R/3 Enterprise that would be targeted at large R/3 customers to show them what mySAP can accomplish once it is up and running in their companies.

SAP's managers believed these initiatives would allow the company to jump from being the third largest global software company to being the second, ahead of main competitor Oracle. They also wondered if they could use its mySAP open system architecture to overcome Microsoft's stranglehold on the software market and bypass the powerful Windows standard. Microsoft is the largest global software company.

Pursuing this idea, SAP put considerable resources into developing a new business computing solution called SAP NetWeaver that is a Web-based, open integration and middleware application platform that serves as the foundation for enterprise service-oriented architecture (Enterprise SOA) and allows the integration and alignment of people,

information, and business processes across business and technology boundaries. Enterprise SOA utilizes *open standards* to enable the integration of the software applications of most different software companies no matter upon what particular technology, for example, JAVA or LINUX, it is based. SAP NetWeaver is now the foundation for all Enterprise SOA SAP applications and mySAP Business Suite solutions; it also powers SAP's partners' solutions and custom-built applications. Also NetWeaver integrates business processes across various systems, databases, and sources—from any business software supplier—and is marketed to large companies as a service-oriented application and integration platform. NetWeaver's development was a major strategic move by SAP to drive companies to run all their business software using a single SAP platform.

Although SAP was developing and upgrading its products at a fast pace throughout the early-2000s, the continuing worldwide recession continued to limit or reduce the company's IT expenditures. SAP, like all other computer hardware and software companies, suffered as its revenues fell and SAP's stock price plunged in 2002 from $40 to almost $10 as the stock market crashed. However, while SAP's revenues fell by 5% in 2003 because of lower ERP and consulting sales, its profit doubled because it had finally brought its global cost structure under control and was making better use of its resources. Strict new controls on expenses had been implemented, a hiring freeze imposed, and the company was focusing its German programmers to work on urgent problems. Consequently, its stock was back up to $35 by the end of 2003 as its future growth prospects looked good.

As a part of its major push to reduce costs, SAP began to outsource the enormous amount of routine programming involved in improving and creating advanced applications to low-cost countries overseas, such as India. In 2003, SAP recruited 750 software programmers in India, this number grew to 1,500 in 2004, and 5,000 in 2006. SAP used its growing army of low-cost Indian programmers to work the bugs out of its mySAP modules and to increase their reliability when they were installed in a new company. This prevented embarrassing blows-ups that sometimes arose when a company implemented SAP's ERP for the first time. Fewer bugs also made it easier to install its modules in a new company, which reduced the need for consulting and lowered costs, leading to more satisfied customers. Increasingly,

SAP also began to use the advanced skills of its Indian research center programmers to cooperate in the development of new mySAP ERP modules to serve new customers in an increasing number of industries or "vertical markets." By 2006, SAP's Indian research group was bigger than its research group in Waldorf, Germany and has been growing ever since. Outsourcing has saved the company billions in development costs and had continuously contributed to its rising profitability in the 2000s.

The Growing Small- and Medium-Enterprise Market

In 2003, SAP changed the name of its software from mySAP.com to mySAP Business Suite because more customers were now licensing its software suite rather than purchasing it. Part of this change occurred because of the many upgrades SAP was continuously releasing, and in a licensing arrangement, its clients could expect continual free upgrades as it improved its ERP modules as a part of their contract. However, while SAP continued to attract new, large business customers, the market was becoming increasingly saturated; it already had around 50% of the global large business market by 2003. To promote growth and increase sales revenues, SAP began a major push to increase its share of the SME market segment of the ERP industry.

The small size of these companies, and so the limited amount of money they had to spend on business software, was a major challenge for SAP, which had primarily worked with multinational companies that had huge IT budgets. Also, there were major competitors in this market segment that had specialized in meeting the needs of SMEs to avoid direct competition with SAP—and they had locked up a significant share of business in this ERP segment. By focusing primarily on large companies, SAP had left a gap in the SME market. Other large software companies, such as Oracle and Microsoft, but also newcomers such as Siebel, PeopleSoft, and salesforce.com, rushed to develop their own SME ERP products and services to compete for revenues in the fast-growing SME market segment—worth billions of dollars.

To attract SME customers as quickly as possible, SAP decided to develop two primary product offerings customized to their needs: SAP All-in-One and SAP Business One. SAP All-in-One is a streamlined version of its R/3 mySAP Business Suite; it is much easier to install and maintain and much more affordable for SMEs. To develop All-in-One, SAP's software engineers took its mySAP Business Suite modules designed for large companies and scaled them down for users of small companies. All-in-One is a reduced version of SAP's total range of products such as SAP Customer Relationship Management, SAP ERP modules, SAP Product Lifecycle Management, SAP Supply Chain Management, and SAP Supplier Relationship Management. Despite its reduced size, it is still a complex business solution and one that requires a major commitment of IT resources for a SME.

Recognizing the need to provide a much simpler, limited, and affordable ERP solution for smaller companies, SAP decided to also create a second SME ERP solution. SAP decided not to begin anew to develop a software package based on its R/3 platform, as it did with its All-in-One solution. Rather, it took a new path and bought an Israeli software company called TopManage Financial Solutions in 2002, and rebranded its system as SAP Business One. SAP Business One would be a much more limited ERP software package that integrates CRM with financial and logistic modules to meet a specific customer's basic needs. However, it still provides a powerful, flexible SME solution and is designed to be easy to use and affordable. Business One works in real time, the software suite manages and records the ongoing transactions involved in a business such as cost of goods received, through inventory, processing and sale, and delivery to customers, and automatically records transactions in a debit and credit account. In 2005, SAP began reporting revenues from the SME market segment separately from revenues for its larger customers, one way of showing its commitment to SME customers.

The Changing Competitive Environment

By 2004, achieving rapid growth by increasing the number of new large business customers was becoming more and more difficult, simply because SAP's share of the global ERP market had now grown to 58%—one of the major reasons it entered the SME ERP market. SAP reported that because of slowing ERP sales it expected single digit growth in the next few years—growth worth billions in revenues, but still growth that would not fuel a rapid rise in its stock price.

However, competition in the SME market was also increasing as its business software rivals watched SAP develop and introduce its All-in-One and Business One solutions. SAP's rapid growth in this segment led to increasing competition and to a wave of consolidation in the ERP industry. In 2003, PeopleSoft, the leader in the HRM software module segment, bought J. D. Edwards & Son, a leader in SCM, to enlarge its product offerings and strengthen its market share against growing competition from SAP and Oracle. However, Oracle, the leading database software management company also realized the stakes ahead in the rapidly consolidating business applications software market.

Essentially, the problem was that all the major competitors needed to be able to offer potential customers—large or small—a broad range of business software applications so that it could bundle them together and offer them at a reduced price. For example, most large companies already were using Oracle's database software, if it could provide them with an ERP solution to meet their needs at a lower cost than SAP or Microsoft, it could grow its market share. While SAP had never made billion-dollar acquisitions, preferring "organic growth" from the inside or small acquisitions, the opposite was the case with Oracle.

Its CEO Larry Ellison decided that to compete with SAP in the ERP market, Oracle would have to make major acquisitions to rapidly expand Oracle's range of business modules to complement the suite of ERP modules it had been internally developing, and gain market share. Only through acquisitions could it quickly develop an ERP suite with the breadth of SAP's to meet the needs of SMEs. Also, Ellison decided it could use its new competencies, combined with its existing database competences to attack SAP in the large company segment that Oracle now also regarded as a major growth opportunity.

In 2004, Oracle had begun a hostile takeover of PeopleSoft, which had also acquired several other ERP companies to build its competitive advantage. PeopleSoft's top managers battled to prevent the takeover, but Oracle offered PeopleSoft's customers special low-cost licensing deals on Oracle database software and guaranteed them the changeover to its software would be smooth. It finally acquired PeopleSoft—and the resources and customers necessary to gain a large market share in the SME segment at the expense of SAP and Microsoft—in 2005.

Oracle kept up the pressure. Between January 2005 and June 2007 it acquired 25 more business software companies in a huge acquisition drive to build its distinctive competencies and market share in ERP software. PeopleSoft brought Oracle expertise in HRM solutions, and J. D. Edwards' expertise in SCM solutions. Then in a major acquisition of Siebel Systems, Oracle bought a leading CRM software developer. These acquisitions allowed Oracle to dramatically increase its range of ERP offerings and build market share with small- and medium-sized businesses. Before purchasing Seibel, for example, Oracle had a 6.8% share of this market; now it could add Seibel's 11% market share to become one of the top 3 CRM suppliers—alongside SAP and Salesforce.com.

Oracle, already a major supplier of middleware, also wanted to be able to offer companies middleware that allowed them to seamlessly connect different ERP software packages from different companies. In turn, it developed a new ebusiness suite called Oracle Fusion middleware that would allow companies to leverage their existing investments in the software applications of other companies, including SAP, so that they work seamlessly with Oracle's new ERP modules. Fusion is Oracle's answer to SAP's NetWeaver because it gives SME customers no incentive to move to SAP's All-in-One or Business One suite. Indeed, Fusion became a threat to SAP because many of oracle's ERP modules such as its CRM and HRM solutions often better fit the needs of SMEs than SAP's. Thus, many companies decide to keep their existing PeopleSoft installations and then choose more offerings from Oracle's growing array business applications.

The third leading SME ERP supplier, Microsoft, is also keeping up the pressure. Using the competencies from its acquisition of Great Plains and Navision, it released a business package called Microsoft Dynamics NAV, ERP software that can be customized to the needs of SME users, to their industries, and scaled to their size. Microsoft's advantage lies in the compatibility of its ERP offerings with the Windows platform, which is still used by more than 85% of SMEs, especially as it can offer substantial discounts when customers choose both types of software. Also, as Microsoft continues to introduce new versions of its Windows and Office software, such as Windows 8, it can use low-cost pricing to convince its customers to upgrade to its new ERP software.

SAP has worked hard to develop strategic alliances with all kinds of software companies to respond to the challenge from Oracle and Microsoft. By 2007, it had formed contracts with over 1,000 independent software vendors (ISVs) that have helped it expand its offerings, and it has jointly developed 300 new ERP solutions for the 25 industries it now serves, and all these applications are all powered by SAP NetWeaver. An important alliance was announced with IBM in 2006, IBM would invest $40 million over the next 5 years to develop the capabilities necessary to install SAP's new software. Also, SAP will integrate NetWeaver with IBM's new cloud computing data storage offerings for large companies.

SAP also made many small acquisitions to improve its competitive position in various industries and to develop Web-based products to help companies utilize the Internet more effectively. For example, in the retail software industry, it acquired companies like Triversity and Khimetrics. Triversity provides point of sales, store inventory, customer relations and service solutions for retail companies, and Khimetrics helps retailers price and position products to manage demand, improve margins, and predict sales and income. It also acquired TomorrowNow, that specialized in providing maintenance and support services for PeopleSoft and J. D. Edwards & Company customers (that were now Oracle clients). SAP also created "safe passage programs" designed to help companies switch to SAP solutions from software applications now owned by Oracle. SAP also planned to develop a variety of new-generation products, including new SAP industry solutions, and more applications for SMEs—in a direct challenge to Oracle's Fusion software.

Strategic Moves 2006–2008

In 2006, SAP's CEO Henning Kagermann announced 4 major priorities for the next decade—to increase market share, especially in SME; to increase profitability by improving productivity and efficiency; to better serve SAP users with new software applications products and expand to new industries; and to help customers transition to and gain benefits from the rapidly developing software on-demand or software as a service (SaaS) segment of the Web-based applications segment.

SAP's need to focus upon the on-demand applications segment reflected its rapid rise in importance by the mid-2000s. New Internet companies, such as salesforce.com (which had become a major software as a service (SaaS) competitor to SAP by 2011), were offering SMEs the ability to license ERP modules services, especially CRM modules, and then access these modules online and store their databases on the Internet hosting company's Website. This was a game changing move for large ERP companies because it signaled to SMEs that on-demand Internet providers such as salesforce.com could offer much lower prices—even if they were less customized. SAP's answer was to introduce a SaaS platform available to customers through on-demand and hosted delivery—and since 2007, SAP had been expanding the number of ERP modules it had offered through its "Business by Design" software suite, that by 2011, had become a part of its cloud computing services. Its SaaS service that will use its NetWeaver middleware also allowed customers to seamlessly integrate the software of different vendors and make possible real-time upgrades and improvements.

In 2007, Henning Kagermann, who was now partnered at the top by deputy CEO Leo Apotheker, now embarked upon a major change in strategy. As noted earlier, SAP was proud of its "organic growth" or internal R&D to develop new software products. However, in March 2007, Oracle announced it would acquire Hyperion Solutions, a global provider of business intelligence software that provided performance-enhancing solutions for $3.3 billion. In doing so, it was entering a new segment of the applications software market—one that might prove to be disruptive. The growing power of mathematical algorithms to offer radical changes to a company's strategy to enhance performance seemed to fit well with the products of an ERP company that was continuously trying to improve best practices. SAP thought this might be a disruptive game-changing move by Oracle, and determined to respond quickly, it was forced to acquire the leading company in the Business Intelligence segment, Business Objects, for $6.8 billion. Today, SAP Business Objects has become the fastest growing of SAP's different software businesses, business intelligence (BI) and the industry leader—outcompeting Oracle's BI applications obtained through its acquisition of Hyperion. Oracle does not have the complementary skills needed to push the boundaries in BI. While BI generated only 7% of SAP's revenues in 2007, it is expected to generate over 15% in 2011. SAP has leveraged all its existing competences and applied them to Business Objects—and vice-versa—to increase the value of its BI services to customers. In addition, in 2010 SAP Business Objects announced a revolutionary new "in-memory computing solution" that speeds the processing of real-time information in ways that lead to new solutions and practices that can dramatically increase performance. SAP claims that this is a disruptive technology and one that will change the BI and ERP markets and give it a competitive advantage over its rivals.

Apotheker is Replaced by Two Co-CEOs

In 2008, Leo Apotheker became CEO of SAP, and because of the new global recession, he presided over the first annual drop in revenue at SAP since 2003, as customers refrained from purchasing new software. Moreover, SAP's global cost structure had soared as its workforce increased and it entered new markets like Business Intelligence. At the same time, Oracle had, since 2005, spent more than $42 billion to acquire additional ERP and business applications software, and claimed it was winning market share at the expense of SAP, by becoming a one-stop shop for customers—beginning with the PeopleSoft acquisition. Microsoft was also claiming gains in market share in the SME segment, and so were smaller players such as salesforce.com in CRM, and Sage another niche player in the growing global ERP market. Oracle's sales almost doubled to $23.3 billion between 2005 to 2009, while SAP's sales rose 42%.

SAP's board of directors decided that change was necessary; in 2010, he was replaced by dual CEOs, Bill McDermott, who took control of SAP global field operations, and Jim Hagemann Snabe, who took control of business solutions and technology. Their dual roles reflect SAP's continuing need to coordinate its global matrix structure to manage its growth across world regions, countries, and the large and SME customer's segments, while providing the business applications package best tailored to the needs of different customers in different countries.

By 2010, it had become clear that three major strategic priorities were now facing all ERP companies. First, the need to provide the best-customized suite of business solutions to companies, especially large companies, that wanted to install and implement SAP's software applications "on premise" meaning that the software installation was maintained and upgraded across a company's global facilities. Second, the need to provide a suite of software applications, especially CRM solutions that could be obtained on-demand, the SaaS solution that allowed SMEs to lease an SAP business solution package and use it to process and store their data on the Internet or in the cloud, as described earlier. And, third, to provide SAP solution's "on device," meaning that SAP's customers could access its solution from their laptops, smartphones, and other mobile devices.

The last "on device" method of delivering SAP's services was most problematic since it lacked advanced capabilities in mobile software applications. In 2010, co-CEOs, McDermott and Snabe decided that a major new acquisition was necessary if SAP was to keep up with Oracle and Microsoft, which already had their own mobile platforms up and running. In 2010, they decided to acquire Sybase, a leader in the kind of software that helps corporate customers run applications on mobile devices for $5.8 billion, which would allow its corporate customers to run SAP applications, and link into their company's database on mobile devices from anywhere in the world. SAP will use the purchase to cater to customers that want employees to use tablets and smartphones while working: "This will literally connect the shop floor to the corner office," CEO McDermott announced. Also, Sybase is strong in the telecom and financial sectors where SAP is weak, so that it will be able to expand its existing client base. Sybase CEO John Chen will continue to run Sybase as an independent unit complementing all of SAP's other software services. SAP Sybase is expected to contribute significantly to SAP Business Objects' revenues and profits over time, and give it one more competitive advantage over Oracle, which was fighting to develop a major presence in mobile computing applications in 2011. Sybase can work with Microsoft's mobile platform as well as Apple's iPhone and Google's Android systems.

Competitive Advantage in 2011

In 2011, SAP was working closely with customers and partners worldwide, to develop a product and services strategy that would enable customers to use its enterprise application software wherever and whenever they need it–on premise, on demand, or on device. SAP's NetWeaver technology platform will serve as the foundation for all its SAP Business Suite applications.

SAP "Business Suite" that contains a complete set of software solutions aimed at large customers; SAP "All in One Suite" that can be tailored to the needs of companies with 100–2500 employees; and SAP "Business One" and "Business By Design" that essentially offer a cost-effective package of on-demand business solutions that can be hosted on SAP's remote cloud computing network.

SAP is also working to be able to offer all its customers the advantage of cloud computing as it advances, and as it becomes more reliable and secure. SAP Business Objects solutions are continually being upgraded and developed to help companies optimize business processes on premise, on demand, and on device.

SAP believes that it is has developed a competitive position in these three areas, and developed a suite of software applications suited to the needs of different sized companies that will allow it to compete effectively against Oracle, now it major rival, in the next decade. However, many analysts believe that its share of the large and SME segments, particularly in CRM, may decline by 2–5% in the next 2–3 years; it is expected to more than double its share of the growing BI market. If it can develop and leverage its competencies in BI solutions and its Sybase mobile platform applications across market segments—and develop first-rate cloud computing solutions—it may be able to gain 2–5% market share.

SAP's ability to retain and grow its market share is critical because this determines how well its stock price will perform in the 2010s. The higher its stock price rises, the more existing and new global customers will be attracted to use its growing business software applications; stock increases show it has achieved sustainable competitive advantage. In July 2011, SAP announced record revenues for the quarter and that it would exceed its profit forecast for the year as its software and service licenses soared.

It also announced that its profits would exceed its previous forecast as it was taking market share away from Oracle as its second-quarter software license sales grew 26%, compared to Oracle that reported a 19%. Its stock price also soared as investors now believed SAP was developing the right business model and strategies to beat Oracle and maintain its dominance as the biggest global business software maker.

SAP's Co-CEOs Bill McDermott and Jim Hagemann Snabe announced that their goal was to increase SAP's profits by 10% per year, driven by increases in its mobile products, on-demand services, and its new real-time business solution analytics technology "Hana." "The pipeline for Hana is the biggest in the history of SAP," McDermott proudly announced, "The Hana in-memory product, or High-Performance Analytic Appliance, is designed to speed up analysis of business data. It comes on servers from companies such as Hewlett-Packard Co., International Business Machines Corp., Dell, and Cisco Systems Inc." McDermott also said SAP was benefiting from the use of Apple's iPad tablet among executives, who can use the device to take advantage of SAP's software that provides them with mobile access to real-time business analytics. "By 2014, 6.5 billion workers worldwide will be on mobile devices. What you are seeing is a generational change," he announced.

Indeed, SAP provides the software for the order fulfillment process behind Apple's iTunes download system and Apple, and other large companies are experimenting with its Hana in-memory technology. SAP formed alliances with major companies such as Verizon, Dell, and Amazon.com, to sell its mobile products, Hana, and its SOA software as a service. McDermott also announced that unlike Oracle, SAP's future focus would be on organic growth from internal new venturing across its software divisions. Clearly, that battle in the business software industry is escalating. In July 2011, Oracle also announced many improvements to its software suite for businesses of all sizes, and niche players such as salesforce.com continue to grow their sales.

Endnotes

www.sap.com, 1998–2011.
SAP Annual Reports and 10K Reports, 1998–2011.
SAP 10K Reports, 1998–2011.

CASE 21

How Amazon.com Became the Leading Online Retailer by 2011

Gareth R. Jones
Texas A&M University

Since its founding in 1995, Amazon.com (Amazon) has grown from an online bookseller to a virtual retail supercenter selling products as diverse as books, toys, food, and electronics for which it is best known today. On Amazon's main storefront, customers can discover anything they might want to buy online and it endeavors to offer customers the lowest possible prices. However, its less well-known that by 2010 it had become the world's biggest provider of service oriented software (SOA), combined with cloud computing solutions that can be accessed by all kinds of customers including individuals, small- and medium-sized businesses, and large corporations—just one more kind of online retail storefront for virtual products such as data processing and storage. In 2011, its business mission states that its goal is to be "Earth's most customer-centric company" for three primary customer groups: consumer customers, seller customers, and developer customers.

In many ways, the last decade has been a wild ride for Amazon as its revenues, profits, and stock price initially soared and then plunged as a result of the dot-com boom and then bust of the early-2000s. But, since hitting a low of $8 in 2001, in the last decade—and especially in the last 3 years—its stock has soared. It was over $210 in July 2011—an incredible increase. It has also been a wild ride for Amazon's founder, Jeff Bezos, who through all the turmoil in its performance, consistently championed his company and claimed investors had to look long term to measure the success of Amazon's business model. He originally said he did not expect his company to become profitable for several years, and his forecast turned out to be correct. But, his claims are correct, and every year in his annual letter to shareholders, he includes his 2007 letter that stated why its business model would succeed (see his 2010 letter on the Amazon.com investors' Webpages).

Amazon's Beginnings: The Online Bookstore Business

In 1994, Jeffrey Bezos, a computer science and electrical engineering graduate from Princeton University, was growing weary of working for a Wall Street investment bank. Seeking to take advantage of his computer science background, he saw an entrepreneurial opportunity as he observed that Internet usage was enormously growing every year as tens of millions of new users were becoming aware of its potential uses. Bezos decided the bookselling market offered an excellent opportunity for him to take advantage of his IT skills in the new electronic, virtual marketplace. His vision was an online bookstore that could offer millions more books to millions more customers than a typical brick-and-mortar (B&M) bookstore. To act upon his vision, he packed up his belongings and headed for the West Coast to found his new dot-com start-up. On route, he had a hunch that Seattle, the hometown of Microsoft and Starbucks, was a place where first-rate software developers could be easily found. His trip ended there, and he began to flesh out the business model for his new venture.

What was the vision for his new venture? To build an online bookstore that would be customer-friendly, easy to navigate, provide buying advice, and offer the broadest possible selection of books at low prices.

Bezos' original mission was to use the Internet to offer books "that would educate, inform and inspire." From the beginning, Bezos realized that, compared to a physical B&M bookstore, an online bookstore could offer customers a much larger and much more diverse selection of books. There are about 1.5 million books in print, but most B&M bookstores stock only around 10,000 books; the largest stores in major cities might stock 40,000 to 60,000. Moreover, online customers would be able to easily search for any book in print using computerized catalogs. There was also scope for an online company to find ways to tempt customers to browse books in different subject areas, read reviews of books, and even ask other shoppers for online recommendations—all of which would encourage people to buy more books. One of Amazon's popular features is the users' ability to submit product reviews on its Website. As part of their reviews, users rate the products on a scale from 1 to 5 stars and then provide detailed information that helps other users decide whether to purchase the products. In turn, the users of these ratings can then rate the usefulness of the reviews, so the best reviews are those that rise to the top and are read first in the future!

Operating from his garage in Seattle with a handful of employees, Bezos launched his online venture in 1995 with $7 million in borrowed capital. Because Amazon was one of the first major Internet or dot-com retailers, it received an enormous amount of free national publicity, and the new venture quickly attracted an increasing number of book buyers. Book sales quickly picked up as satisfied Internet customers spread the good word and Amazon became a model for other dot-com retailers to follow. Within weeks, Bezos was forced to relocate to larger premises, a 2,000-square-foot warehouse, and hire new employees to receive books from book publishers and fill and mail customer orders as book sales soared. Within 6 months, he was once again searching for additional capital to fund his growing venture; he raised another $7 million from venture capitalists, which he used to move to a 17,000-square-foot warehouse that was now required to handle increasing book sales. As book sales continued to soar month by month over the next 2 years, Bezos decided that the best way to raise more capital would be to take his company public and issue stock. This, of course, would reward him as the founder and the venture capitalists who had funded Amazon because

they would all receive significant percentages of the company's stock. In May 1997, Amazon.com's stock began trading on the NASDAQ stock exchange.

Building Up Amazon's Value Chain

Amazon's rapid growth continued to put enormous pressure on the company's physical warehousing and distribution capabilities. The costs of operating an online Website, for example, continuously improving the capabilities of the Website's software, and maintaining and hosting the computer hardware and Internet bandwidth connections necessary to serve customers, are relatively low given the hundreds of millions of visits to its Website and the millions of sales that are completed. However, Bezos soon found out that the costs of developing and maintaining the physical B&M infrastructure necessary to obtain and stock supplies of books and then package and ship the books to customers, were much higher than he had anticipated—as was the cost of the employees required to perform these activities.

Soon, developing and maintaining the physical B&M side of Amazon's value chain became the source of the greatest proportion of its operating costs, and these high costs were draining its profitability—given the low prices at which it was selling its books. Also, price competition was also heating up because of new competition from B&M booksellers such as Barnes & Noble and Borders, that had been late to recognize the potential of the Internet and now opened their own online bookstores to compete with Amazon. In fact, in 1997, as it passed the 1-million-different-customers-served point, Amazon was forced to open up a new 200,000-square-foot warehouse and distribution center and expand its old one to keep pace with demand.

Bezos then sought ways to increase the motivation of his employees across all the company. Working to quickly fill customer orders is vital to an online company; minimizing the wait time for a product like a book to arrive is a key success factor in building customer loyalty. On the other hand, motivating Amazon's rapidly expanding army of software engineers to develop innovative customer-oriented software, such as its patented 1-Click (SM) Internet ordering and payment software, was also vital to sustaining its competitive advantage. To ensure good responsiveness to customers, Bezos implemented a policy of decentralizing significant decision-making authority to employees and empowered them to find ways to meet customer needs quickly. Because Amazon.com employed a relatively small number of people—about 2,500 worldwide in 2000—Bezos also empowered employees to recruit and train new employees to quickly learn their new jobs. And to motivate employees, Bezos decided to give all employees stock in the company. Amazon employees own over 10% of their company, a factor behind Amazon.com's rapid growth.

In fact, Jeff Bezos is a firm believer in the power of using teams of employees to spur innovation. At Amazon, teams are given considerable autonomy to develop their ideas and experiment without interference from managers. Teams are kept deliberately small, and, according to Bezos, no team should need more than "two pizzas to feed its members"; if more pizza is needed, the team is too large. Amazon's "pizza teams," which usually have no more than about 5–7 members, have come up with many innovations that have made its site so user-friendly. For example, one team developed the "Gold Box" icon that customers can click on to receive special offers that expire within an hour of opening the treasure chest; another developed "Bottom of the Page Deals," low-priced offers for products such as batteries and power bars, and one more team developed the "Search Inside the Book" feature discussed later. These teams have helped Amazon expand into many different retail storefronts and provide the wide range of IT services it does today. Indeed, Bezos and his top managers believe that Amazon is a *technology company* first and foremost, and its mission is to use and develop its technological expertise to sell more and more goods and services in ways that satisfy customers and keep its profit growing. Hence, the enormous buildup of its SOA software services and on-demand cloud computing services as discussed below.

Since the beginning, Bezos has personally played a very important part in energizing employees and representing his company to customers. He is a hands-on, articulate, forward-looking executive who puts in long hours and works closely with employees to find innovative and cost-saving solutions to problems. Moreover, Bezos has consistently acted as a figurehead for his company and has become a national

media celebrity as he worked to further Amazon's visibility with customers. He spends a great deal of time flying around the world to publicize his company and its activities, and he has succeeded because Amazon is in the top five of the best recognized dot-com companies.

The Amazon Associates program, created in 1996 to attract new customers to its retail storefront and grow sales, is another important strategy. Any person or small business that operates a Website can become affiliated to Amazon by putting an official Amazon hyperlink to Amazon's Website on its own Website. If a referral results in a sale, the Associate receives a commission from Amazon. By 2004, Amazon had signed up over 1 million Associates and by 2007, about 40% of Amazon's revenues were generated from the sales of its Associates, who pay a commission to Amazon to advertise and sell their products on its Website.

By 1998, Amazon could claim that 45% of its business was repeat business, which translated into lower marketing, sales, and operating expenses, and higher profit margins. By using all his energies to act on the online bookselling opportunity, Bezos had given his company a first-mover advantage over rivals, which has been an important contributor to its strong position in the marketplace. Nevertheless, Amazon still had yet to make a profit, just as Bezos had predicted.

The Bookselling Industry Environment

The book distribution and bookselling industry was changed forever in July 1995 when Jeff Bezos brought virtual bookseller Amazon.com online. His new company changed the entire nature of the environment. Previously, book publishers had indirectly sold their books to book wholesalers that supplied small bookstores, directly to large book chains like Barnes & Noble or Borders, or to book-of-the month clubs. There were so many book publishers and so many individual booksellers that the industry was relatively stable, with both large and small bookstores enjoying a comfortable, nonprice competitive niche in the market. In this stable environment, competition was relatively low, and all companies enjoyed good revenues and profits.

Amazon.com's Web-based approach to buying and selling books changed all this. First, since it was able to offer customers quick access to all of the 1.5 million plus books in print and discount the prices of its books, a higher level of industry competition immediately developed. Second, it also negotiated directly with the large book publishers over price and supply because it wanted to quickly get books to its customers; the industry value chain and Amazon, therefore, gained more power over publishers because it is a powerful buyer. All players—book publishers, wholesalers and bookstore chains had to rethink their strategies. Third, as a result of these factors and continuing improvements in IT and the speed of the Internet, the competitive forces in the bookselling business began to rapidly change and lower prices became a major priority.

As the first in the online bookselling business, Amazon was able to capture customers' attention and establish a first-mover advantage. Its entry into the bookselling industry using its new IT posed a major threat for B&M bookstores, and Barnes & Noble, the largest U.S. bookseller, and Borders, the second largest bookseller, realized that with its competitive prices, Amazon would be able to siphon off a significant percentage of industry revenues. These B&M bookstores decided to launch their own online ventures to meet Amazon's challenge and to convince book buyers that they, not Amazon, were still the best places to shop for books. However, being first to market with a new way to deliver books to customers resulted in satisfied customers who became loyal customers. Once a customer had signed up as an Amazon customer, it was often difficult to get that person to register again at a competing Website.

Amazon's early success also made it difficult for the hundreds of new "unknown" online booksellers who entered the market to survive because they faced the major hurdle of attracting customers to their Websites rather than to Amazon.com's. Even the major B&M competitors such as Barnes & Noble and Borders that now imitated Amazon's online business model faced major problems in developing a major online presence let alone attracting away Amazon's customer base.

If large B&M bookstores had problems attracting customers, small specialized B&M bookstores were in desperate trouble. Their competitive advantage has been based on providing customers with hard-to-find books, a convenient location, and good customer service. Now they were faced with competition from an online bookstore that could offer customers all 1.5 million books in print at significantly lower prices. Thousands of small, specialized B&M bookstores closed their doors nationwide in the 2000s, as the large B&M bookstores struggled to compete.

Competition increased by 2000 as large B&M bookstores began a price war with Amazon that resulted in falling book prices; this squeezed Amazon's profit margins and put more pressure on it to contain its increasing operating costs. Amazon and its largest competitors, Barnes & Noble and Borders, announced a 50% discount off the price of new best-selling books to defend their market shares; they were locked in a fierce battle to see which company would dominate the bookselling industry in the new millennium. Barnes & Noble did manage to establish an online presence and its storefront has continued to exist into the 2010s, although it has never regained market share from Amazon. Border's online bookstore was a complete failure, and in 2002, it announced all referrals to its online storefront would be referred to Amazon, for which it would receive a commission. This arrangement was a disaster for now Border's had given up on online retailing, as a B&M bookstore. Its performance continued to decline, its agreement with Amazon was ended in 2008, and in 2011, Border's liquidated and its stores were closed. By 2011, the value of Barnes & Noble, also suffering heavily from competition from Amazon, had dropped to $1 billion from over $30 billion, and many analysts wondered how long it would survive as Amazon became the online portal of choice for most major book publishers as the digital downloading book business became the way of the future as discussed below.

From Online Bookstore to Internet Retailer

Although Bezos initially focused on selling books, he soon realized that Amazon's rapidly developing IT competences could be used to sell many other kinds of products online. But, he was cautious because he also now understood how high were the value-chain costs involved in stocking and delivering a wide range of different products to customers. However, Amazon's slowing growth in the late-1990s led many of its stockholders to complain that the company was not on track to becoming profitable fast enough, so Bezos began to search for other products that could profitably be sold over the Internet. One growing online business was music CDs, and he realized CDs were a good fit with books, so in 1999, Amazon announced its intention to become the "earth's biggest book and music store." The company used its IT competences to widen its product line by selling music CDs on its retail Website. The strategy of selling CDs also seemed like a good move because the leading Internet music retailers at this time, such as CDNow, were struggling—they had also discovered the high physical costs associated with delivering products bought online to customers. Amazon now had built up its skills in this area, and its online retail competencies were working to its advantage; for example, its IT now allowed it to constantly alter the mix of products it offered on its storefront to keep up-to-date with changing customer needs.

Amazon also took many more steps to increase the usefulness of its retail sites to attract more customers and get its established customers to spend more. For example, to entice customers to send books and CDs as presents at important celebration and holiday shopping times such as birthdays, Christmas, and New Year's, Amazon opened a holiday gift store. Customers could take advantage of a gift-wrapping service as well as using a free greeting card e-mail service to announce the arrival of the Amazon gift. Amazon began to explore other kinds of online retail ventures; for example, recognizing the growing popularity of online auctions pioneered by eBay, Bezos moved into this market by purchasing Live-bid.com, the Internet's only provider of live online auctions at that time. Also in 1999, it entered into an agreement with Sotheby's, the famous auction house, to enter the high end of the online auction business. In making these moves, it was attempting to compete in eBay's auction segment of the market—a move that not only failed because eBay had the first mover advantage, but also because, fixed-price sales were becoming the most popular segment of the market, as discussed later.

Nevertheless, starting in 2000, Amazon's stock price fell sharply as investors believed that intense competition from Barnes & Noble and other online retailers like eBay might keep its operating margins low into the foreseeable future. Despite his company's moves into CDs and the auction business,

Bezos was being increasingly criticized as much too slow to take advantage of Amazon's brand name and core skills and to use them to sell other kinds of products online—much like a general B&M retailer sells many different kinds of products in the same store. Bezos responded that he had to make sure his company's business model would successfully work in book retailing before he could commit his company to a widespread expansion into new kinds of retail ventures. However, Amazon's plunging stock price forced him into action, and from 2000 forward, it expanded its storefronts and began to sell a wider range of electronic and digital products, such as cameras, DVD players, and MP3 players. To achieve a competitive advantage in these new product categories, Amazon used its expertise in retailing software to provide customers with more in-depth information about the nature of the products they were buying and to offer users better ways to review, rank, and comment on the products they bought on its Website. Customers were increasingly seeing the utility of Amazon's service—especially because of its low prices.

Bezos pushed Amazon and its "pizza teams" to find new ways to use its core skills to expand into different kinds of retail segments, and by 2003, it had developed 23 different storefronts. By 2006, Amazon had 35 storefronts selling products as varied as books, CDs, DVDs, software, consumer electronics, kitchen items, tools, lawn and garden items, toys and games, baby products, apparel, sporting goods, gourmet food, jewelry, watches, health and personal-care items, beauty products, musical instruments, and industrial and scientific supplies. Increasingly consumers came to see Amazon as the low-price retailer for many products. Customers began to visit B&M retail stores to view the physical product, but then they would go online to buy from Amazon. Customers can avoid paying state sales tax when they buy online, and for high-ticket items, this is an important savings, often amounting to a 10% price advantage (although sometimes there are shipping costs).

New Problems

As time went on, however, customers increasingly began to compare the prices charged by different online retail Websites to locate the lowest priced product, and many dot-coms, desperate to survive in a highly competitive online retail environment, undercut Amazon's prices and put more pressure on its profit margins. To strengthen Amazon's competitive position and make it the preferred online retailer, Bezos moved aggressively to find ways to attract customers, such as by offering them free shipping or "deals of the day." To make its service more convenient, Amazon also began to forge alliances with B&M companies like Toys"R"Us, Office Depot, Circuit City, Target, and many others. Now, customers could buy products online at Amazon's Website, but if they wanted their purchases immediately, they could pick them up from these retailers' local B&M stores. Amazon had to share its profits with these retailers, but it also avoided high product stocking and distribution costs. These alliances also helped Bezos quickly transform his company from "online bookseller" to "leading Internet product provider." His goal was for Amazon to become the leading online retailer across many market segments and drive out the weaker online competitors in those segments, consolidating many segments of the online retail industry. As it happened, he also drove out the weakest B&M retailers, such as Circuit City and Border's, which were giving up on online operations, and forced to liquidate.

Amazon's Online Retail SOA Software Platform

Small- and medium-sized businesses quickly discovered the high costs of operating the value chain functions necessary to deliver products to customers, which helped Bezos. Increasingly, Amazon began to offer its online services to these companies, such as Borders and Waldenbooks in the book business, but also to Sears and Target; as noted above, these booksellers were also eventually forced to close down their B&M operations. Weaker companies became Amazon Associates and began directing Internet traffic from their Websites to Amazon's instead in return for sales commissions.

Amazon soon realized the important revenues associates could bring in, and began offering all kinds of small- and medium-sized companies the opportunity to establish storefronts on Amazon.com, and offer their products—many of which are often sold in direct competition with Amazon's own products as its service operations software brings up the offerings of all sellers for a particular product. However, this has proved to be a major advantage, and in 2011, 40% of Amazon's sales revenue was generated by the millions of associates who pay to establish storefronts on its Website and pay it fees when their products are sold on its Website. The Internet bubble burst in the early-2000s strengthened Amazon's competitive advantage; thousands of cut-price online retailers went out of business—because they had no source of competitive advantage. Despite that its own stock price plunged too, Amazon was now the strongest dot-com in the most important retail segment—the fixed-price segment.

Many well-known B&M retailers that had also established virtual storefronts found they could not make their online storefronts profitable in the 2000s because of high operating costs. The few that did succeed, such as Lands' End, did so because they already possessed well-developed catalog operations that were obviously suited to Internet retailing—paradoxically Sears, which had been the strongest in catalog sales, had shut down its operations by the 1990s when shopping malls and chain stores like Walmart had come to dominate U.S. retailing.

Over the 2000s, tens of thousands of other established B&M companies that found online retailing too complex and expensive also formed agreements with Amazon (or eBay) to operate their online stores. As noted earlier, Amazon seized this opportunity to get into the new business of using its proprietary retail IT to design, operate, and host other companies' online storefronts for them for a fee. By 2007, Amazon also had many online storefronts developed to sell its SOA retail solutions. Amazon had become an IT services company as well, and today its other Websites such as its major IT SAO service site (www.amazonservices.com) and its affiliates program (https://affiliate-program.amazon.com/), detail the enormous range of services that it offers to potential sellers, or "developers," as Amazon often calls them. A noted above, its SOA software services division has become a major source of its rapidly rising revenues and profits—and it continues to expand its retail IT activities as it moves to become a leader in cloud computing and storage.

Branching off into these new retail market segments also allowed Amazon to more fully utilize its expensive warehouse and distribution system; faster sales across product categories increased inventory turnover and reduced costs. Moreover, its alliances with retailers to sell their products on its Website allowed it to reduce the quantity of expensive merchandise it needed to purchase and warehouse until sold, which, in turn, helped its profit margins. In addition, by offering many different kinds of products for sale, customers could now "mix" purchases and add a book or CD to their electronic product order, and so on, which led to economies of scale and scope for Amazon. Essentially, Amazon was pursuing related diversification, by giving customers more and more reasons to visit its site, and hoped to drive business and sales across all its product categories, using its 1-Click system to make the transactions as easy as possible for consumers.

However, from the beginning, to keep its operating costs low, Amazon adopted a low-key approach to providing customer service; it did not reveal a customer service telephone number anywhere on its U.S. Website. However, as the complexity of its business has grown and fraud has increased, it recognized the need to provide some level of service, and in 2006, Amazon added to its Website an e-mail link. Using this link, customers provide their phone numbers, and Amazon customer service reps make outbound calls to provide whatever help is needed, for example, with parcel tracking information. Customer service is handled by datacenters in different countries all around the world and Amazon has outsourced most of this activity to minimize costs.

Amazon's venture into the online auction market failed in the early-2000s and was shut down, but now its top managers can focus all their energies on building its competences in the fixed-price retailing market, and by expanding into new kinds of retail formats. In 2001, Amazon added a new retail service that turned out to be highly profitable and important to maintaining its leadership position in online retailing. Amazon launched zShops, a fixed-price retail marketplace that became the foundation of its highly successful Amazon Marketplace Service. This retail service allows customers to sell their used books, CDs, DVDs, and other products alongside the identical brand-new products that Amazon offers on the product pages of its retail Website. This significantly added to its sales revenues, and Amazon has continually added to its offerings over the 2000s. Today, its marketplace services retail storefront is part of its amazonservices.com Website reflecting its move into related diversification by its continual effort to share and leverage its core IT competences across its different storefronts. eBay bought a company called half.com to compete with Amazon Marketplace, and today it is Amazon's main rival as both companies compete to provide a profitable fee-based service to sellers of used products.

In the 2000s, as Amazon became the acknowledged leader in Internet retailing, it took advantage of its skills to offer a SOA consulting service to virtual and B&M retailers and to create for them a unique, customer-friendly storefront using Amazon's proprietary IT. As discussed above, this consulting service has proved to be a very profitable business activity, especially because in the process of designing storefronts and SOA services for other companies, Amazon's software engineers found new opportunities to improve its own IT software services by learning from its "leading customers." However, to protect its competitive advantage and proprietary IT, Amazon also started lawsuits against other virtual or B&M companies that had started to imitate services such as its 1-Click checkout system and infringe other proprietary software it claims is protected by patents. By 2011, many high-tech companies had begun to launch lawsuits claiming others had infringed on their patents; this became a multibillion dollar issue by 2011 as Google, Apple, and Oracle fought to claim the ownership of touch-screen, mobile payment, and other kinds of software services.

Global Expansion

Since IT is not specialized to any one country or world region, a virtual company can use the Internet and WWW to sell to customers around the globe—providing, of course, that the products it sells meet the needs of overseas consumers. Bezos was quick to realize that Amazon's IT could be profitably transferred to other countries to sell books. However, the ability to enter new overseas markets was limited by one major factor: Amazon.com offered its customers the biggest selection of books written in the *English* language, so overseas customers had to be able to read English. Where to locate them?

An obvious first choice would be the United Kingdom, followed by other English-speaking nations such as Australia, New Zealand, India, and Germany (of any nation in the world, Germany has one of the highest proportion of English-as-a-second-language speakers because English is taught in all its schools). To speed entry into overseas markets, Amazon searched for Internet book retailers that had gained a strong foothold in their local domestic market and acquired them. In the UK, Amazon bought Bookpages.com in 1996, installed its proprietary IT, replicated its value creation functions, and renamed it Amazon.co.uk. In Germany, it acquired a new online venture, ABC Bücherdienst/Telebuch.de, and created Amazon.de in 1998. Amazon continued its path of global expansion, and by 2006, it also operated retail Websites in Canada, France, China, and Japan, and shipped its English language books to customers anywhere in the world. All these ventures have been tremendously successful and have significantly added to its revenues and profits.

To facilitate the growth of its global IT and distribution retail systems across all market segments, Amazon also established SOA software product and service development centers in England, Scotland, India, Germany, and France. Just as Amazon expanded the range of products/software services it sold on its U.S. Websites, it also increased the range of products/services it sold abroad as its warehouse and distribution systems became strong enough to sustain its expansion and its local managers selected the product mix best suited to the needs of local customers.

Developments in the 2000s

Amazon finally turned its first profit in the fourth quarter of 2002—a meager $5 million, just $0.01 per share on revenues of over $1 billion—but this was an important signal to investors. In fact, Amazon's stock price soared again in the early-2000s as investors believed its business model would enable it to become an online retail leader. Its stock price increased from $6 in 2001 to $60 by 2004. Amazon's net profits also increased to $35 million in 2003 and to $588 million in 2004, while its revenues more than doubled to $7 billion in the same period. Amazon's future looked bright as it became the largest Internet retailer and achieved a dominant position in many market segments.

New Acquisitions and Business Opportunities

To make better use of its resources and capabilities and to maintain its profit growth, Amazon began to acquire many small specialized retail and IT companies. Its strategy to acquire small IT companies was to strengthen its distinctive competencies in SOA IT and to develop more kinds of Web-based IT commercial services that it could sell to both B&M and online companies. Bezos has always preached that Amazon is first and foremost a *technology company* and that its core skills drive its retail mission. Its goal in buying small retail companies was to find new opportunities to increase sales of its existing retail storefronts and to allow it to establish storefronts in new segments of the retail market. Some acquisitions have been successful, and some have not.

For example, Amazon bought Internet Movie Database (www.IMDb.com), a company that hosts a comprehensive list of all movies in existence. Amazon transformed it into a commercial venture whose function is to help customers easily find and identify DVDs to purchase and to make related suggestions to encourage additional purchases on its Website. Similarly, Amazon acquired Exchange.com, which specialized in hard-to-find book titles at its Bibliofind.com Website, and hard-to-find music titles and memorabilia at MusicFile.com. The acquisition also helped Amazon develop user-friendly search engines to help customers identify and buy its products, once again using its 1-Click system.

Amazon bought PlanetAll.com, which operated a Web-based address book, calendar, and reminder service that had over 1 million registered users, and Junglee.com, an XML-based data-mining start-up that had technology for searching and tracking Internet users' Website visits based on their personal interests. As it purchased these companies, Amazon absorbed these technologies and employees into its IT operations to improve its retail software services. For example, PlanetAll's "relationship-building" software applications were folded into Amazon's Friends and Favorites area, and its new employees went on to build community-focused features for Amazon's Website including the Amazon.com Marketplace and Amazon.com Purchase Circles. Amazon was driven by the goal of developing superior Web-based techniques for attracting and keeping

Internet customers when rivalry with eBay, Apple, and Google increased because these companies started to enter each other's businesses. For example, the online download music business when Apple introduced its online music download iTunes store, and thus leapfrogged over Amazon to control this market—although Amazon still controls the online sales of music CDs.

Amazon started its own online music store in 2007 selling downloads in the MP3 format after securing agreements with the four major record companies, however, its music download service never obtained the success of Apple's iTunes, which has prospered because of its link to the iPod and now the iPhone. In another venture into entertainment content, Amazon launched a digital download video service called Amazon Unbox in 2007. This new download service offered customers thousands of television shows, movies, and other video content from more than 30 studio and network partners from Hollywood and around the world. Unbox claimed to be the only video download service to offer DVD-quality pictures, however, within weeks this new download service had generated negative comments from users; the number of movies downloaded was disappointingly few because the service's poor software caused many glitches and very slow—hours—of download time. Essentially, Amazon was too early to enter this vital Movie/TV Content Streaming Download Service. Even in 2011, it was still uncertain which company and which digital format would prevail, and customers were confused as competitors such as Google's YouTube, Netflix's streaming offerings, Hulu's content, and Apple's new video content services, were competing to be the next industry standard. In addition, many Websites still offered illegal downloading free of charge. The online entertainment streaming market segment is a complex one in which to compete, but also a vital one given the enormous growth in downloading using smartphones and tablet computers that has occurred in the 2010s.

Amazon also acquired several companies to enter and grow in the search engine market to find ways to track its customers across the WWW to personalize the retail service it could offer and, therefore, boost sales. However, it did not understand that Google's search engine business model was based on increasing online advertising revenues—not offering them actual products—and its efforts failed. Customers do not like to be tracked across the WWW and efforts to prevent Web tracking have increased in the 2010s. Even Amazon's own efforts are considered invasive by many people as it stores personal information in order to offer customized product choices.

In the effort to keep its customers loyal, Amazon began providing a range of new customer services. In 2006 it launched Amazon Prime, a $79 per year service that allows users to get unlimited free two-day shipping for a year on all eligible items bought from its storefronts. Also, in 2006, it began its first cloud computing data storage product called Amazon S3 that allows users to store data for $0.15 per gigabyte per month—something that was soon rendered useless when Google began to offer its customers free online data storage that has expanded to hundreds of gigabytes. In 2007, Amazon entered the grocery delivery business when it launched Amazon Fresh, a new grocery storefront that sold a wide variety of nonperishable food and household items that, once ordered, can be reordered using Amazon's shopping-list software. To ensure competitive pricing with B&M grocery stores, customers receive free shipping on purchases of canned and packed food products over $25.

In the 2000s, Amazon continued to refine its SOA business software solutions to make it easier and faster for businesses to take advantage of its expanding array of services. By 2010, its increasing expertise made it simple for small or large businesses to use services such as Fulfillment by Amazon and WebStore by Amazon to manage many aspects of their value chains. Essentially, Amazon was offering companies a value-chain outsourcing service. For example, Fulfillment by Amazon allows small businesses to use Amazon's own order fulfillment and after-order customer services, and gives their customers the ability to benefit from Amazon's shipping offers. Fulfillment by Amazon performs the value chain activities that allow small online businesses to minimize the costs required to store, pick, pack, ship, and provide customer service for the products they sell online. After paying Amazon's service fee, small businesses ship their products to an Amazon fulfillment center that stores and sends those products to customers who order them on the small business' or Amazon's storefront. Amazon also manages post-order customer service such as customer returns and refunds for businesses that use Fulfillment by Amazon. Small businesses benefit from the cost savings that result when Amazon's service fees are lower than the costs of performing the value chain service themselves.

WebStore by Amazon allows businesses to create their own privately branded e-commerce Websites using Amazon technology. Businesses can choose from a variety of Website layout options and can customize their sites using their own photos and branding. For example, Seattle Gift Shop now has its own WebStore at www.seattlesgifts.com. WebStore by Amazon users pay a commission of 7% (price includes credit card processing fees and fraud protection) for each product purchased through their site and a monthly fee of $59.95. As one business owner commented, "Not only has WebStore increased my sales dramatically, but also its easy-to-use tools give me complete control of the look and feel of my site." WebStore allows small businesses to build their brand name while using Amazon's easy-to-use flexible "back-end" technology—including Amazon's 1-Click checkout system—and allows them to refer customers through the Amazon Associates program if they choose.

Amazon's Growing Dominance in the Retail Sector

All of Amazon's expenditures to develop the new IT platforms necessary to launch complex digital storefronts that sell books, music, and video, and build the SOA services side of its business increased its operating costs and reduced its profit margins in 2007. So, too, did Amazon's need to open enormous new warehouses or "fulfillment" centers in many different states during the late-2000s. In 2011, for example, it announced it would open a fourth 1.2 million square-foot facility in Phoenix, Arizona, bringing its total capacity in that state to over 4 million square feet. Rising costs, together with increasing competition from Apple, eBay, and especially Google led many analysts to wonder if Amazon could maintain its rapid growth—something that led to Bezos' 2007 letter to shareholders, pointing out that once again his company's strategy was to build the infrastructure that would lead to long-term growth and profits and that short term results were

meaningless (see Appendix). Proof that its business model was working, and one measure of Amazon's growing dominance, was the increase in the number of repeat customers—from 45% in 2005, to 59% in 2007, and to over 70% by 2010. Repeat business is a major indicator of a company's ability to grow its business and profit growth.

The Amazon's Kindle Reader Arrives

In 2007, Amazon pushed to dominate the online the online book-downloading business when it announced its new Kindle book reader. Its new $399 3G device with free Internet connection was based on technology developed by a company it had acquired in 2005. The Kindle allows customers to download digital versions of books in print and also allows Amazon to offer these digital books at greatly discounted prices—including new books and bestsellers. By 2008, Amazon announced that the Kindle had become its best selling product and that digital downloads were increasing rapidly; spurred by the acceptance of the Kindle, it offered a cheaper non-3G version. By 2011, its special offer Kindle was selling for $114 and $139, its free 3G version for $189, and its top-of-the-line DX version for $379. Why the fall in price? Apple's iPad tablet computer was overshadowing the Kindle's amazing popularity and growing dominance. The Kindle was a black and white reader optimized for reading print in all lighting conditions; the iPad was a full-color touch screen device that could access the Internet and download all kinds of digital applications, not just eBooks.

Nevertheless, many analysts claimed that Amazon realized too late that the money to be made was not in the hardware itself, but in the money it received from the digital content—books and magazines that users downloaded. In 2010, Amazon announced that for the first time its Kindle digital books sales exceeded that of its paper-based books. Some analysts wondered why Amazon was not giving away its reader free of charge, but there was speculation in 2011 that Amazon was planning to introduce a new advanced color version of the Kindle to rival the iPad. But in July 2011, Amazon announced that it would begin to allow students to rent textbooks in e-book format for its Kindle readers for as much as 80% off the list price, and that the three major textbook companies had signed up for this service.

A sign of Bezos' commitment to this product came in his 2010 letter to shareholders, where demonstrating the prowess of Amazon's software engineers, he announced a new Kindle application Whispersync, a "Kindle service designed to ensure that everywhere you go, no matter what devices you have with you, you can access your reading library and all of your highlights, notes, and bookmarks, all in sync across your Kindle devices and mobile apps. The technical challenge is making this a reality for millions of Kindle owners, with hundreds of millions of books, and hundreds of device types, living in over 100 countries around the world—at 24/7 reliability." To enlarge the content for its Kindle device, Amazon announced in 2011 that it had acquired The Book Depository, an online bookseller that offers 6 million specialized books for delivery worldwide.

More Moves in SOA and Cloud Computing

In March 2011, Amazon launched Cloud Drive, Amazon Cloud Player for the Web, and Amazon Cloud Player for Android. Together, these services enabled individual customers to securely store music in the cloud and play it on any Android phone, Android tablet, Mac or PC, and now iPad, wherever they are located. Customers can easily upload their music library to Amazon Cloud Drive and can save any new Amazon MP3 purchases directly to their Amazon Cloud Drive for free. In July 2011, Amazon announced three improvements to Amazon Cloud Drive and Cloud Player to better compete with Google and Apple's alternatives: storage plans that include unlimited space for music for $20 a year, free storage for all Amazon MP3 purchases and a Cloud Player iPad application. It also offered any customer 5GBs of free storage to encourage customers to try out its new services.

By 2010, Amazon's engineers had developed advances in data management, which led to new architectures and cloud storage and data management services that could be scaled to the needs of companies from small, to medium to large. It renamed its IT customer storefront Amazon Web Services (AWS) and analysts expect it to become its next billion dol-

lar business. Of course, this also meant large expenditures on servers and datacenters to support AWS expansion, but this is completely in keeping with Bezos's 2007 letter to shareholders. Amazon believes revenues may reach $3 billion by 2015 as individuals and companies outsource more of their data center needs. The growing popularity of AWS is that it is "on-demand" software and services; business customers are charged a fee based on how much they use its SOA and there are no upfront costs to prevent potential customers from trying out its services.

Amazon's Future Prospects

Jeff Bezos and his top management team seem committed to leveraging Amazon's core competencies in whatever ways they can to find to realize the value of the company's assets. The range of possible services Amazon can offer appears endless. Today, Amazon is the leading fixed-price product Internet retailer. It has over 34,000 employees and in 2010 it earned $700 million on $10.7 billion revenues. This was a huge increase in profit from the year before, and its stock price soared in early-2011 as investors became convinced it would remain the industry leader. Only eBay was now a major competitor, but its failure to enter and capitalize on the fixed-price market sooner had resulted in a major decline in its stock price as the growth of the online auction market slowed in the 2000s. Customers today favor the fixed-price format as long as they are offered lower prices than they can get in B&M stores. Also, customers like the daily deal kind of online offers pioneered by Groupon and other companies such as LivingSocial that has Amazon as a major investor.

Record Sales in 2011

Finally, another sign that Amazon's business model and strategies are working came in July 2011 when Amazon reported its second quarter results. Its revenues had increased by 50% compared to the same quarter in 2010 as its product sales increased and its Kindle e-reader and digital-media services revenues soared. However, its profit also dropped by 8% because operating expenses rose by 54%. Why? Following its business model, Amazon has been spending billions to build its IT infrastructure to build its cloud computing and entertainment streaming services IT infrastructure to serve both individual and business customers. And, investing a billion more to build new state-of-the-art fulfillment centers to be able to distribute the products that it sells under its own name, and under the names of the millions of companies that now use its services to sell their products on its Website.

The Kindle Fire: Building New Opportunities and Threats

Then, at the end of September 2011 the long awaited new color Kindle download media device that would rival Apple's iPad was introduced by Bezos to wide acclaim. Amazon decided to sell the new Kindle Fire for $199, lower than it cost to produce, because Bezos believes that Amazon will make its profits from all the books, magazines, movies, music, and TV shows that users can now download to its new touch screen device. Amazon controls important

media content—much more so than Apple and the Market for tablets computers was weakening in late 2011 as customers were wondering exactly what they were buying as new much more powerful and lightweight laptops were being introduced.

Nevertheless, when on October 25th 2011 Amazon reported that its third quarter profit had plunged by 73% because of the high costs necessary to create the new Kindle Fire and the IT infrastructure to support it—plus its huge investment in IT cloud computing—investors immediately reacted be sending its stock price down by $30 or 15%. Throughout its history its stock price has soared or plunged as investors try to evaluate the future results of its strategy; but its CEO Jeff Bezos just seems to be having fun as he strives to create the most successful company he can—the one that adds the most value for its customers and stockholders.

What new strategies will Bezos pursue to take Amazon to the next level? Are any new mergers and acquisitions on the horizon? How many more B&M companies will Amazon drive out of business?

APPENDIX ADAPTED FROM AMAZON.COM 2007 LETTER TO SHAREHOLDERS

We believe that a fundamental measure of our success will be the shareholder value we create over the *long term*. This value will be a direct result of our ability to extend and solidify our current market leadership position. The stronger our market leadership, the more powerful our economic model. Market leadership can translate directly to higher revenue, higher profitability, greater capital velocity, and correspondingly stronger returns on invested capital.

Our decisions have consistently reflected this. We first measure ourselves in terms of the metrics most indicative of our market leadership: customer and revenue growth, the degree to which our customers continue to purchase from us on a repeat basis, and the strength of our brand. We have invested and will continue to invest aggressively to expand and leverage our customer base, brand, and infrastructure as we move to establish an enduring franchise. Because of our

emphasis on the long term, we may make decisions and weigh tradeoffs differently than some companies.

Accordingly, we want to share with you our fundamental management and decision-making approach so that you, our shareholders, may confirm that it is consistent with your investment philosophy:

- We will continue to focus relentlessly on our customers.
- We will continue to make investment decisions in light of long-term market leadership considerations rather than short-term profitability considerations or short-term Wall Street reactions.
- We will continue to measure our programs and the effectiveness of our investments analytically, to jettison those that do not provide acceptable returns, and to step up our investment in those that work best. We will continue to learn from both our successes and our failures.

- We will make bold rather than timid investment decisions where we see a sufficient probability of gaining market leadership advantages. Some of these investments will pay off, others will not, and we will have learned another valuable lesson in either case.
- When forced to choose between optimizing the appearance of our GAAP accounting and maximizing the present value of future cash flows, we'll take the cash flows.
- We will share our strategic thought processes with you when we make bold choices (to the extent competitive pressures allow), so that you may evaluate for yourselves whether we are making rational long-term leadership investments.
- We will work hard to spend wisely and maintain our lean culture. We understand the importance of continually reinforcing a cost-conscious culture, particularly in a business incurring net losses.
- We will balance our focus on growth with emphasis on long-term profitability and capital management. At this stage, we choose to prioritize growth because we believe that scale is central to achieving the potential of our business model.
- We will continue to focus on hiring and retaining versatile and talented employees, and continue to weight their compensation to stock options rather than cash. We know our success will be largely affected by our ability to attract and retain a motivated employee base, each of whom must think like, and therefore must actually be, an owner.

Selected Sources

www.amazon.com, 2011.
Amazon.com, Annual and 10K Reports, 1997–2011.

eBay and the Online Auction and Retail Sales Industry in 2011

Gareth R. Jones
Texas A&M University

With almost 18,000 employees, eBay, headquartered in San Jose, California, manages and hosts the well-known global online auction and shopping Website that people all around the world visit to buy and sell goods and services. In 2010, eBay generated $9.5 billion in revenue, up from $4.5 billion in 2005, but it generated only $3.5 billion in earnings (measured by EBITDA) compared to $2.1 billion in 2005. Prior to 2007, eBay had been a stellar performer on the stock exchange under the guidance of Meg Whitman, its first CEO; the company's stock market valuation was $46 billion in 2007, making investors extremely happy. But since 2007, eBay has experienced increasing competition and so many problems that its stock price has dramatically fallen—so much so that in July 2011, its market valuation had dropped to $43 billion. Why? Investors became worried its business model would not be so profitable in the future because the online auction market was becoming mature and opportunities for growth were declining. In addition, the nature of competition in online retailing was changing and Amazon.com had emerged as the top online retail portal. Its stock plunged in value as it seemed likely that eBay's business model had run out of steam. But to understand the sources of eBay's success and the current challenges it faces, it is necessary to explore the way eBay's business model and strategies have changed over time.

eBay's Beginnings

Until the 1990s, the auction business was largely fragmented; thousands of small city-based auction houses offered a wide range of merchandise to local buyers. And a few famous global houses, such as Sotheby's and Christie's, offered carefully chosen selections of high-priced antiques and collectibles to limited numbers of dealers and wealthy collectors. However, the auction market was not very efficient, for there was often a shortage of sellers and buyers, and so it was difficult to determine the fair price of a product. Dealers were often able to influence auction prices and obtain bargains at the expense of sellers. Typically, dealers were able to buy at low prices and then charge buyers high prices in the bricks-and-mortar (B&M) antique stores that are found in every town and city around the world; they reaped high profits. The auction business was changed forever in 1995, when Pierre Omidyar developed innovative software that allowed buyers around the world to bid online against each other to determine the fair price for a seller's product.

Omidyar founded his online auction site in San Jose on September 4, 1995, under the name "Auction Web." A computer programmer, Omidyar had previously worked for Microsoft, but he left that company when he realized the potential opportunity to develop new software that provided an online platform to connect Internet buyers and sellers. The entrepreneurial Omidyar changed his company's name to eBay in September 1997, and the first item sold on eBay was Omidyar's broken laser pointer for $13.83. A frequently repeated story that eBay was founded to help Omidyar's fiancée trade PEZ Candy dispensers was fabricated by an eBay public relations manager in 1997 to interest the media. Apparently the story worked, for eBay's popularity grew quickly by word of mouth, and the company did not need to advertise until the early-2000s. Omidyar had tapped into a huge unmet buyer need and people flocked to use auction software platform. Another major reason eBay did not advertise in its early years was that its growing global popularity had put major pressure on its internal computer information systems, both its hardware and software. In particular, the technology behind its search engine—which was not developed by Omidyar but furnished by independent specialist software companies–could not keep pace with the hundreds of millions of search requests that eBay's users generated each day. eBay was also installing powerful servers as quickly as it could to manage its fast-growing global database, and it was recruiting computer programmers and IT managers to run its systems at a rapid rate.

To finance eBay's rapid growth, Omidyar turned to venture capitalists to supply the hundreds of millions of dollars his company required to build its online IT infrastructure. Seeing the success of his business model, he was quickly able to find willing investors. As part of the loan agreement, however, the venture capitalists insisted that Omidyar give control of the running of his company to an experienced dot.com top manager. They were very aware that founding entrepreneurs often have problems in building and implementing a successful business model over time. They recommended that Meg Whitman, an executive who had had great success as a manager of several software start-up companies, be recruited to become eBay's CEO, while Omidyar would assume the role of chairman of the company.

eBay's Evolving Business Model

From the beginning, eBay's business model and strategies were based on developing and refining Omidyar's auction software to create an easy-to-use online market platform that would allow buyers and sellers to meet and transact easily and inexpensively. eBay's software was created to make it easy for sellers to list and describe their products, and easy for buyers to search for, compare, and bid on the products they wanted to purchase. The magic of eBay's software is that the company simply provides the electronic conduit between buyers and sellers; it never takes physical possession of the products that are listed, and their shipping is the responsibility of sellers and payment the responsibility of buyers.

Thus, eBay does not need to develop all the high-cost functional activities like inventory, shipping, and purchasing to deliver products to customers, unlike Amazon.com, for example. So, eBay operates with a low cost structure given the huge volume of products it sells and sales revenues it generates—hence the high revenues and profits it earned before until 2007, as mentioned earlier. Also, word of mouth enabled eBay to avoid paying high advertising costs, an especially important consideration early on because these are a major expense for many online portals seeking to gain a reputation. And, as far as buyers are concerned, eBay is also low cost, for under current U.S. law, sellers located outside a buyer's state do not have to collect sales tax on a purchase. This allows buyers to avoid paying state taxes on expensive items such as jewelry and computers, which can save them tens or even hundreds of dollars, and makes purchasing on eBay more attractive.

To make transactions between anonymous Internet buyers and sellers possible, however, Omidyar's software had to reduce the risks facing buyers and sellers. In particular, it had to convince buyers that they would receive what they paid for, and that sellers would accurately describe their products online. Also, sellers had to be convinced that buyers would pay for the products they committed to purchase on eBay, although of course they were able to wait for the money to arrive in the mail, so their risk was lower; however, many buyers do not pay or pay extremely late. To minimize the ever-present possibility of fraud from sellers misrepresenting their products, or from buyers unethically bidding for pleasure and then not paying, eBay's software contains a method for building and establishing trust between buyers and sellers—building a reputation over time.

After every transaction, buyers and sellers can leave online feedback about their view of the other's behavior and the value of the transaction they have completed. They can fill in an online comment form, which is then published on the Web for each seller and buyer. When sellers and buyers consistently act in an honest way in more and more transactions over time, they are able to build an increasingly stronger positive feedback score that provides them with a good reputation for honesty. More buyers are attracted to a reputable seller, so the seller obtains higher prices for their products. Sellers can also decide if they are dealing with a reputable buyer—one who pays promptly, for example. Over time, this became more difficult because new "unknown" buyers come into the market continuously, so eBay developed online mechanisms so sellers can refuse to deal with any new or existing buyer if they wish, and can remove that buyer's bid from an auction.

eBay generates the revenues that allow it to operate and profit from its electronic auction platform by charging a number of fees to sellers (buyers pay no specific fees). In the original eBay model, sellers paid a fee to list a product on eBay's site and paid a fee if the product was sold by the end of the auction. As its platform's popularity increased and the number of buyers grew, eBay increased the fees it charged sellers. The eBay fee system is quite complex, but in the United States in 2006, eBay took between $0.20 and $80 per listing, and 2%–8% of the final price, depending on the particular product being sold, and the format in which the product sold. In addition, eBay acquired the PayPal payment system that charges substantial fees of its own; this is discussed in detail below.

This core auction business model worked well for the first years of eBay's existence. Using this basic software platform, every day tens of millions of products such as antiques and collectibles, cars, computers, furniture, clothing, books, DVDs and a myriad of other items are listed by sellers all around the world on eBay and bought by the highest bidders. The incredible variety of items sold on eBay suggests why eBay's business model has been so successful—the same set of auction platform programs, constantly improved and refined over time from Omidyar's original programs, can be used to sell almost every kind of product, from low-priced books and magazines costing only cents, to cars and antiques costing tens or hundreds of thousands of dollars. Some of the most expensive items sold include a Frank Mulder 4 Yacht Gigayacht ($85 million), a Grumman Gulfstream II jet ($4.9 million), and a 1993 San Lorenzo 80 Motor Yacht (just under $2 million). One of the largest items ever sold was a World War II submarine that had been auctioned off by a small town in New England that decided it did not need the historical relic anymore.

Meg Whitman's biggest problem was to find search engine software that could keep pace with the increasing volume of buyers' inquiries. Initially, small independent suppliers provided this software; then IBM provided this service. But as search technology advanced in the 2000s, eBay recruited its own search experts from other companies such as Yahoo! and Google. Today, it has its own in-house search technology teams who continually refine and improve its own proprietary search engine software to make it more appealing to its sellers and buyers—and to keep up with competitors. CEO Whitman looked for new ways to improve eBay's business model, while the most pressing concerns were keeping the eBay Website up and running 24 hours per day, and keeping its online storefront meeting the needs of its rapidly increasing number of buyers and sellers.

First, to take advantage of the capabilities of eBay's software, the company began to expand the range and categories of the products it offered for sale to increase revenue. Second, it increased the number of retail or "selling" formats used to bring sellers and buyers together. For example, its original retail format was the 7-day auction format, where the last bidder within this time period "won" the auction, provided the bid met the seller's reserve or minimum price. Then, it introduced the "buy-it-now" format where a buyer could make an instant purchase at the seller's specified price, and later a real-time auction format in which online bidders, and bidders at a B&M auction site, compete against each other in real time to purchase the product up for bid. In this format, a live auctioneer, not the eBay auction clock, decides when to close an auction.

Beyond introducing new kinds of retail formats, over time eBay continuously strived to improve the range and sophistication of the information services it provides its users—to make it easier for sellers to list, describe, present, and ship their products, and for buyers to make better purchasing decisions. For example, software was developed to make it easier for sellers to list their products for sale and upload photographs and add or change information to the listing—however eBay began to charge more for these services. Buyers were also able to take advantage of the new services offered in what is called My eBay; buyers can now keep a list of "watched" items so that over the life of a particular auction they can see how the price of a product has changed and how many bidders are interested in it. This is a useful service for buyers because frequently bidders for many items enter in the last few minutes to try to "snipe" an item or obtain it at the lowest possible cost. As the price of an item becomes higher, this often encourages more buyers to bid on it, so there is value to buyers (although not sellers, who want the highest prices possible) to wait or just bid a minimal amount so they can easily track the item.

By creating and then continually improving its easy-to-use retail platform for sellers and buyers, eBay revolutionized the auction market, bringing together international buyers and sellers in a huge, never-ending yard sale. eBay became the means of cleaning out the "closets of the world" with its user-friendly platform.

New Types of Sellers

Over time, eBay also encouraged the entry of new kinds of sellers into its electronic auction platform. Initially, it focused on individual, small-scale sellers; however, it then sought to attract larger-scale sellers using its eBay Stores selling platform, which allows sellers to list not only products up for auction but also all the items they have available for sale, perhaps in a B&M antique store or warehouse. Store sellers then pay eBay a fee for these "buy it now" sales. Hundreds of thousands of eBay stores became established in the 2000s, greatly adding to eBay's revenues.

Also, during the 2000s, small specialized online stores and large international manufacturers and retailers such as Sears, IBM, and Dell began to open their own online stores on eBay to sell their products using competitive auctions for "clearance goods" and fixed-priced buy-it-now storefronts to sell their latest products. By using eBay, these companies established a new delivery channel for their products, and they were able to bypass wholesalers such as discount stores or warehouses that take a much larger share of the profit than eBay does through its selling fees.

Software advances arrived faster and faster in the 2000s, in part due to eBay's new Developers Program that allowed independent software developers to create new specialized applications that seamlessly integrate with eBay's electronic platform. By 2005, there were over 15,000 members in the eBay Developers Program, comprising a broad range of companies creating software applications to support specialized eBay sellers and buyers, as well as eBay Affiliates. All this progress helped speed and smooth transactions between buyers and sellers and drove up eBay's revenues and profits, something that resulted in a huge increase in the value of its stock.

Competition in the Retail Auction Industry

eBay's growing popularity and growing user or customer base made it increasingly difficult for the hundreds of other online auction houses that had also come online to compete effectively against it. Indeed, its competitive advantage was increasing because both sellers and buyers discovered that they were more likely to find what they wanted and get the best prices from a bigger auction Website's user base or market. And, from the beginning, eBay controlled the biggest market of buyers and sellers, and new users became increasingly loyal over time. So even when large, well-known online companies such as Yahoo! and AOL attempted to enter the online auction business, and even when they offered buyers and sellers *no-fee* auction transactions, they found it was impossible to grow their user bases and establish themselves in this market. From network effects, eBay had obtained a first-mover advantage and was benefiting from this.

The first-mover advantage eBay gained from Pierre Omidyar's auction software created an unassailable business model that effectively gave eBay a monopoly position in the global online auction market. Even today, there are few online or B&M substitutes for the auction service that eBay provides. For example, sellers can list their items for sale on any kind of Website or bulletin board, and specialist kinds of Websites exist to sell highly specialized kinds of products like heavy machinery or large sailboats, but for most products, the sheer reach of eBay guarantees it a dominant position in the marketplace. Because there has been little new entry into the online auction business, the fees eBay charges to sellers steadily increased as it grew, and skimmed off ever more of the profit in the auction value chain. eBay decided it did not have to worry about the power of buyers or sellers to complain about fee increases because it has access to millions of individual buyers and sellers. Sellers would only be a threat to eBay if they could band together and demand reductions in eBay's fees and charges.

This happened first during the early-2000s. Meg Whitman, desperate to keep eBay's revenues growing to protect its stock price, started to continuously increase the fees charged to eBay stores to list their items on eBay. Store sellers rebelled and used the eBay community bulletin boards and chat rooms to register their complaints. eBay realized there was a limit to how much it could charge sellers. It would have to find new ways to attract more buyers to the sellers' products, and get them better prices, if was going to be able to increase the fees it charged sellers. Or it would have to find new ways to extract profit from the auction value chain.

New Ways to Grow eBay's Value Chain

Meg Whitman always preached to eBay's employees that to maintain and increase the value of its stock (and many employees own stock options in the company), eBay must (1) continually attract more buyers and sellers to its auction site, and (2) search for ways to generate more revenue from these buyers and sellers. To create more value from its auction business model, eBay has adopted many other kinds of strategies to grow profitability over time.

International Expansion

Online, buyers from any country in the world can bid on an auction, and so it became clear early on that one way to grow eBay's business would be to replicate its business model in different countries around the world. Accordingly, eBay quickly moved to establish storefronts around the world customized to the needs and language of a particular country's citizens. Globally, eBay established its own online presence in countries like the United Kingdom and Australia, but in other countries, particularly non-English-speaking countries, it often acquired the national start-up online auction company that had stolen the first-mover advantage in a particular country. In 1999, for example, eBay acquired the German auction house Alando for $43 million and changed it into eBay Germany. In 2001, eBay acquired MercadoLibre, Lokau, and iBazar, Latin American auction sites, and established eBay Latin America. In 2003, eBay acquired

EachNet, a leading e-commerce company in China, for $150 million to enter the Chinese market. And, in 2004, it bought Baazee.com, an Indian auction site, and took a large stake in Korean rival Internet Auction Co. In 2006, eBay acquired Tradera.com, Sweden's leading online auction-style marketplace, for $48 million, in 2009 it acquired Gmarket, Korea's leading online marketplace.

All these global acquisitions helped eBay to retain its dominant presence in the global online auction business to facilitate transactions both inside countries and between countries to build up revenue. Once eBay was up and running in a particular country, network dynamics took effect, and it became difficult for a new auction start-up to establish a strong foothold in its domestic online auction market. But, eBay has faced serious competition in countries such as Japan and Hong Kong, where Yahoo! gained a head start over eBay and thus gained the first-mover advantage in these countries; in China, too, eBay has run into major opposition. Thus, by 2011, significant global expansion was difficult because the cost of overseas online auctions sites had become extremely expensive and eBay's goal was to protect its market share around the world.

Expanding its Value Chain Activities

Providing more kinds of value-chain services that add value and create revenue and profit at different stages of the online auction and retail value chain is a second way in which eBay has grown the revenues from its auction model. This strategy emerged gradually as it sought new sources of revenues to bolster its bottom line.

eBay Drop-Off Stores

One service it created in the early-2000s to encourage more business from individuals who want to sell their goods online—but lacked the computer skills to do so—was eBay Drop Off. eBay licenses reputable eBay sellers that have consistently sold hundreds of items using its platform to open B&M consignment stores in cities where anybody can "drop off" the products they want to sell. The owner of the

Drop-Off Store describes, photographs, and lists the item on eBay and then handles all the payment and shipping activities involved in the auction process. The store owner receives a commission, often 15% or more of the final selling price (not including eBay's commission) for providing this service. These stores have proved highly profitable for their owners and thousands have sprung up across the United States and the world (a search request on eBay's site allows buyers to identify the closest eBay Drop-Off Store). The advantage for eBay is that this drop-off service gives it access to the millions of people who have no experience in posting photographs online, organizing payment, or opening an eBay account and learning how to list an item, and so eBay gains from increased listing fees.

Increased Advertising

To promote the millions of products it has for sale on its site, eBay increased its use of advertising—on television, newspapers, and on popular Websites—to expand its user base in the 2000s. Its goal was to make eBay *the* preferred place to shop online by demonstrating two things: first, the incredible diversity of products available for purchase on its site, and second, the fact that its products generally cost less than buyers would pay in B&M stores—or even on other online stores. New and used DVDs, books, designer clothing, electronics and computers are some of the multitude of products that can be obtained at a steep discount on eBay. Thus, while the range of the products eBay sells provides it with a differentiation advantage, the low prices that buyers can often obtain gives it a low-price advantage too—provided buyers are prepared to wait a few days to receive their newly purchased products.

PayPal Payment Service

Meg Whitman was also working to find ways to make transactions easier for eBay buyers and sellers to increase the ease, security, and volume of online sales. One way to do this was to get involved in an extremely profitable part of any company's value chain activity—the payment system involved in managing the financial transactions necessary to complete online transactions—to both purchase and sell products online. The effective management of financial transactions is vital in online transactions for this poses the greatest risks to buyers, who may be taken advantage of by unscrupulous or fraudulent sellers who take money and then fail to deliver the expected product. Sellers also faced problems. When eBay first started, sellers usually demanded money orders or bank cashiers' checks as secure forms of payment from buyers, or insisted that ordinary checks had to be cleared through their accounts before mailing the product to customers. This increased the length of time and effort involved in a transaction for sellers and buyers and led to lost sales—customers don't like to wait a long time to receive their purchases.

By the early-2000s, online companies like PayPal and Billpoint had emerged that offered secure online electronic payment services that greatly facilitated online commerce. To work efficiently, these services require sellers and buyers to register and enter a valid bank account number, and usually a credit card number, to authenticate the sellers' and buyers' identities and their ability to pay for the items purchased. Now payment became instantaneous; the money was taken directly from the buyer's bank account or paid for by credit card. Buyers could now purchase on credit, while sellers could immediately send off the product to the buyer. When buyers paid sellers, the online payment company collected a 3% commission, which was taken from the seller's proceeds—a very profitable source of revenue.

eBay recognized this was highly profitable value-chain activity because by becoming involved in online payment services it would increase its share of the fees involved in eBay transactions. But, eBay also realized that ownership of a secure online payment system would reinforce its attempts to increase the reputation of both buyers and sellers to encourage the growth of online sales by preventing fraud. Major synergies between selling and payment activities were possible. Since it was late to enter this business and would take a long time to develop its own payment service from scratch, eBay acquired the online payment service Billpoint and worked to get eBay buyers and sellers to register with Billpoint. However, eBay found itself running up against a brick wall; just as eBay had gained the first-mover advantage in the auction business, so PayPal had gained it in the online payment business. Millions of eBay users were already signed up with PayPal. After failing to make Billpoint the market leader, in 2002 eBay acquired PayPal for $1.5 billion in stock—a great return for PayPal's stockholders. Then, to reduce costs, eBay switched all Billpoint customers to PayPal and shut down Billpoint. This purchase has been very profitable for eBay, for it now owns the world's leading online payment system. The PayPal acquisition has paid for itself many times over, as discussed below.

More Retail Formats

eBay also began to make many acquisitions to facilitate its entry into new kinds of specialized retail and auction formats to increase its market reach—and its revenues and profits. In 1999, it acquired the well-known auction house Butterfield & Butterfield to facilitate its entry into the auctioning of high-priced antiques and collectibles and compete with upper-end auction houses such as Sotheby's and Christie's. However, eBay's managers discovered that a lot more involvement was needed to correctly identify, price, list, and then auction rare, high-priced antiques, and it exited the upper-end auction niche in 2002 when it sold Butterfield & Butterfield to Bonhams, an upscale auction house that wanted to develop a much bigger online presence.

To further its expansion into the highly profitable motor vehicle segment of the market, in 2003 eBay acquired CARad.com, an auction management service for car dealers, to strengthen eBay Motors. Now eBay controls the auctions in which vehicle dealers bid on cars that they then resell to individual buyers, often on eBay Motors. In another move to enter a new retail market in 2004, eBay acquired Rent.com for $415 million. This online site offers a completely free rental and roommate search service; it offers to pay users who have signed a new lease at a property found on its Website $100 when they inform Rent.com. Once again, the "sellers" of the rentals on its Websites are charged the fees; the online roommate search is free. Rent.com has millions of up-to-date rental listings, with thousands added every day; listings include a property's address and phone number, a detailed description, photos, floor plans, and so on, which makes it easier for prospective renters to research and select a rental.

In 2000, eBay acquired Half.com for $318 million. Half.com is an online retail platform that specializes

in the sale of new and used fixed-price consumer products such as books, movies, video games, DVDs, and so on that are offered at a fixed price and sold on a first-come-first-served basis, not by auction. eBay's "Buy It Now" feature is similar, although sellers are allowed to set a lower start price than the buy-it-now price, and the selling process can develop into an auction if bidders start to compete for the product. In the 2000s, the popularity of fixed-price online retailing led to a significant expansion in eBay's activities in this segment of the retail market. In 2006, eBay opened its new eBay Express site, which was designed to work like a standard Internet shopping site to consumers with U.S. addresses. Select eBay items are mirrored on eBay Express, where buyers use a shopping cart to purchase products from multiple sellers. A UK version of eBay Express is also in development.

In 2005, eBay acquired Shopping.com, an online price-comparison shopping site, for $635 million. With millions of products, thousands of merchants, and millions of reviews from the Epinions community, Shopping.com empowers consumers to make informed choices and, as a result, encourages more buyers to purchase products. Information provided by Shopping.com also facilitates eBay sellers' pricing knowledge about their online competitors and helps them price their products competitively so that they can sell them more quickly. The site also allows customers to purchase products from various eBay retail formats.

In the 2000s, online local classifieds have become an increasingly popular way for people to sell their unwanted products, especially because there are usually no fees associated with them. Local classifieds are very popular for bulky products like furniture, appliances, exercise equipment, and so on, where high transportation costs represent a significant percentage of the purchase price. In 2004, to ensure its foothold in this online retail segment, eBay bought a 25% stake in the popular free online classifieds Website Craigslist by buying the stock of one of Craigslist's founders.

These free local classified services have been hurting newspapers whose classified sales have sharply decreased. It remains to be seen in the future whether these classified services will remain free or whether they will also be charging fees. Clearly, eBay would like to charge a fee if it owned a controlling stake in Craigslist. Perhaps preparing for the future when money will be made from online classifieds, in 2004, eBay acquired Marktplaats, a Dutch competitor that had achieved an 80% market share in the Netherlands by focusing on small fixed-price ads, not auctions. Then, in 2005, eBay acquired Gumtree, a network of UK local city classifieds sites; the Spanish classifieds site, Loquo; and the German language classifieds site, Opus Forum. In 2005 eBay launched Kijiji, a local classifieds site it made available in nearly a dozen countries to try to dominate this growing retailing market.

The Skype Acquisition

Perhaps going furthest away from its core business, in 2005, eBay acquired Skype, the dominant Voice-Over-Internet-Provider (VOIP) telephone company, for $2.6 billion. Meg Whitman's rationale for this expensive purchase was that Skype would provide eBay with the ability to perform an important service for its users, specifically, to give them a quick, inexpensive way to communicate and exchange the information required to complete online transactions. Skype's software allows users to make free calls from their computers over the Internet to anyone, anywhere in the world. Skype boasts superior call quality and the ability to allow users not just to make phone calls but also to send instant messages, transfer big files, chat, and make video conference calls. It is a full-scale online communications company.

According to Whitman, Skype would help eBay sellers build their online businesses. Using Skype, buyers can contact sellers anytime on their Skype phone number. Sellers can also call regular phone numbers anywhere in the world using SkypeOut at very low rates, and with a SkypeIn phone number, buyers can call a regular telephone number wherever the seller is in the world. Also, in the case of large sellers, Skype allows continuous contact between all the members of the store with SkypeIn numbers and Skype Voicemail. For buyers, Skype allows them to get all the product information they need to buy with confidence and to get answers immediately, without waiting for e-mail.

Many analysts believed it was questionable whether eBay needed to buy a VOIP company given that so many alternative methods of instant communication were offered by so many online companies as AOL, MSN, Yahoo!, Google, and so on. Nevertheless, eBay quickly developed strategies to get

sellers to integrate Skype into their storefronts and to find new ways to include it in the regular transaction process just as it was doing with its PayPal service.

eBay ProStores

Another strategy eBay has used to grow its revenues was to create a new online retail consulting service called ProStores in 2005 that allows potential sellers to utilize eBay's functional competencies in online retailing to create their own online storefront using eBay's software—for a fee of course. ProStores offers sellers a fully featured Web store that can be customized specifically for each online seller and that is then maintained and hosted by eBay. Sellers using the ProStores service might be specialist B&M stores searching for a quick and easy way to establish an online presence, or any entrepreneur who wishes to start an online store. The difference between eBay ProStores and regular eBay Stores is that ProStores sites are accessed through a URL unique to each seller and are not required to carry eBay branding. ProStores sellers are responsible for driving their own store traffic. While items on ProStores sites sell at fixed prices only, they can be simultaneously listed on the eBay marketplace in either the auction or fixed-price formats.

ProStores provides all software needed to build a storefront and then create the listing, promotion, and payment systems needed to make it work. ProStores uses templates and wizards that allow users to quickly and easily build an attractive, feature-rich store with no technical or design skills whatsoever. In return, eBay charges two basic fees to all sellers who purchase a ProStores Web store: (1) a monthly subscription fee and (2) a monthly successful transaction fee calculated as a percentage of the sales price of items sold in the store. The subscription fee ranges from $6.95 to $249.95, depending on the size of the store. The successful transaction fee varies between 1.5 and 2.5%.

eBay Express

Finally, reacting to growing buyer demand for a discounted, fixed-price retail format, in 2006, eBay established eBay Express, where a vast inventory of brand-new, brand-name, and hard-to-find products are offered at fixed prices by top eBay sellers. Buyers are able to obtain the products they want with no bidding and no waiting; they can fill their shopping carts from multiple eBay merchants and pay for everything, including shipping, in a single, secure payment using PayPal. eBay is touting that every transaction is safe, secure, and fully covered by free buyer protection from PayPal. eBay Express was eBay's first major move to react to the growing threat it was facing from Amazon.com, whose rapid growth was based on the growing popularity among online customers for fixed-price retailing. As discussed below, eBay was too late to enter fixed-price retailing because Amazon.com had now gained the first mover advantage and this has resulted in growing problems, as discussed next.

New Problems for eBay

Despite adopting all these new strategies to strengthen its business model, in the 12 months ending August 2006, eBay's stock declined 30% from its lofty height, while the stock market had risen about 8%. Why? The first major problem facing eBay was that while the number of its global users was increasing, it was increasing at a decreasing rate—even after all its promotional and advertising efforts and its emphasis on introducing new site features, functionality, retail formats and international expansion. Similarly, although the number of items listed on eBay's retail platforms was increasing (by 45% in 2004 and 33% in 2005), growth was also slowing. In fact, in eBay's U.S. retail segment, net transaction revenues increased only 31% in 2005 and 30% in 2004, compared to 43% in 2003, while gross merchandise volume increased 19% in 2005 and 27% in 2004, compared to 41% in 2003. eBay's revenue growth was slowing, and it seemed clear to investors that despite all its new strategies and entry into online payment and communications activities would not be able to sustain its future growth—and so justify its lofty stock price.

A second major problem was its failure to recognize the potential of online advertising revenues. By 2006, it was clear that leading Internet companies like Yahoo!, Microsoft, and eBay were all facing a major threat from Google, which was perfecting its incredibly lucrative online search and advertising model. Google was now the "new eBay" in terms of stock appreciation because of the way it was able to implant its advertising search software into its own

and any other Internet Website willing to share advertising revenues with Google. In fact, because eBay is one of the world's biggest buyers of Web search terms, it is one of Google's largest customers. eBay manages a portfolio of 15 million keywords on different search sites, such as Google, Yahoo!, and AOL. These searches are aimed at attracting bidders to one of eBay's retail formats, which is why eBay, or one of its subsidiaries, often comes up first on a search inquiry.

All the large Internet companies realized they had underestimated the enormous potential revenues to be earned from Internet advertising and were anxious to get a bigger share of the pie and copy Google's approach. eBay, which had not placed ads on its pages in the past to allow its users to focus on the products for sale, now began to have banner ads, pop-ups, and the other obtrusive and annoying ways of advertising developed by software advertising engineers. By 2007, it had placed several ads on each page in its desperate hurry to increase revenues. eBay became concerned Google would start to drain away even more of its revenues and customers, and it searched for ways to counter Google's threat. However, analysts noted that eBay could not abandon its "friendly" relationship with Google because Google is the most popular search engine on which eBay promotes its retail storefronts.

Third, in another controversial move, in the spring of 2006, eBay decided to sharply increase the fees it charged its fixed-cost storefronts to advertise on its site. By 2006, sales of fixed-price products, which carried smaller margins than auction products, had grown to over 80% of total retail sales. In charging higher fees, eBay risked alienating large fixed-cost sellers, which would be forced to pass on these increases to customers, and of alienating customers who now could choose a popular shopping comparison tool like eBay, MSN, or Google's shopping-specific Websites, all of which attempt to locate the lowest-priced products. They could also go and shop at Amazon.com. Analysts questioned if this strategy would backfire—and it did as discussed below.

A 2007 Turnaround?

In 2007, eBay announced some impressive financial results that provided a lift to its stock price that had fallen from $60 in 2005 to a low of $25 in 2006. Shares of eBay jumped by 8% in February 2007 when eBay reported a fourth-quarter profit that climbed 24% as sales rose more than expected, helped by a surge in its PayPal electronic payments business and higher prices for the items eBay sells online. Net income for the fourth quarter rose to $346 million, or $0.25 a share, from $279 million, or $0.20, a year earlier. Revenue from eBay's PayPal payments business rose 37% to $417 million, or 1/4 of the company's total, while sales in its online marketplace business rose 24%. These results suggested that eBay's decision to raise its charges to list items in eBay stores to some of its highest-volume sellers had paid off, the quality of the listing had improved, and more of these sellers had been encouraged to use the higher fee-paying auction method. eBay's stock price climbed to $40 by October 2007, and that once again seemed to suggest to investors that its competitive advantage was secure, even in the face of challenges from Google and Amazon.com. However, the turnaround was short-lived.

A New CEO and New Problems and Strategies

When eBay reported results in the next two quarters, however, it was clear that all was not well as its core auction business experienced sequential declines in listings. It was becoming clear that the company's growth was still slowing despite all of Meg Whitman's efforts to expand its sales and retail channels, payment services, and communication through Skype. When the company's stock had dropped back to $26 by March 2008, Whitman decided to resign and a new CEO, John Donahoe, who had been president of eBay Marketplaces and its retail channels, was named to succeed her.

In one of his first press conferences as CEO, Donahoe announced that eBay's biggest problem was that it was lagging behind in its attempts to develop an advanced search engine that would let users find the products they want: "Today our buyers tell us that we know you have unmatched selection, but we can't always find what we want and find values as fast as we want," Donahoe said. Donahoe's new goal for eBay's retail channels was to use its massive database on seller and buyer transactions to provide the most relevant search experience possible, Donahoe

also proposed to develop a much clearer way of combining fixed-price listings, which are appropriate for new current-model products, and auctions, which are the best way to find prices for unique, older and used merchandise. In 2008, buyers could purchase fixed-price goods on the main eBay site, as well as on its eBay Express site and Shopping.com site. In the future, Donahoe wants all these different options to be presented on a single page of search results from eBay's main site. This was an ambitious goal as the changes eBay's software designers had been making over time were often not well received by buyers or sellers, who had not liked the changes eBay had been making to its search engine. However, eBay was now increasingly under attack from Google and Amazon.com, that had been developing much more advanced search engines and were attracting more customers as a result.

Donahoe also noted that an increasing percentage of eBay's revenues and profits were coming from its PayPal operations and that one of his major priorities would be to promote the use and scale of PayPal's financial operations. On the other hand, he also noted that the Skype acquisition was not increasing the profitability of eBay's value-chain operations, and that he would look at the pros and cons of divesting it to free up working capital to be invested in eBay's Marketplaces retail channels.

Donahoe also announced that eBay would be creating a new fee structure for sellers that would reduce the initial cost of listing an item, including the cost of putting photographs on the listing, and shifting the burden to an increased percentage of the final sale price. He claimed that, as Amazon.com was doing, sellers prefer this model that only charges a fee when a sale is made because it involves less risk to them. However, as he said: "There definitely will be those that are concerned or upset about these changes, our clear belief is what's good for buyers is good for sellers, and is good for eBay." Little did he know what was in store for eBay.

eBay's Seller's Revolt

As noted earlier, since its founding, eBay has sought to cultivate good relationships with the millions of sellers that advertise their goods on its Website. But, at the same time, to increase its revenues and profits it steadily increased the fees it charges sellers to list and promote their products on its sites, to use its PayPal payment service, and so on. This had caused some grumbling and problems with sellers in the past because it reduced their profit margins. However, eBay had been increasing its advertising and developing new retail channels to attract millions more buyers to its Websites so sellers would receive better prices and this would offset their higher costs. As a result, sellers tolerated eBay's fee structure.

This all changed in February 2008 when Donohue's new fee structure took effect. For its small-scale sellers that already had thin profit margins the fee hikes that increased back-end commissions on completed sales and payments were painful. In addition, in the future, eBay announced it would block sellers from leaving negative feedback about buyers—feedback such as buyers who didn't pay for the goods they purchased or took too long to do so. Donohue's claimed this change was to improve the buyer's experience because many buyers had complained that if they left negative feedback for a seller—the seller would then leave negative feedback for the buyer!

Together, however, these changes resulted in a blaze of conflict between eBay and its millions of sellers who thought they were being harmed by these changes, that they had lost their prestige and standing at eBay, and their bad feelings resulted in a revolt. Blogs and forums across the Internet were filled with messages expressing feelings that eBay had abandoned its smaller sellers and was pushing them out of business in favor of high-volume "powersellers" who contributed more to eBay's profits. eBay and Donohue received millions of hostile e-mails and sellers threatened they would move their business elsewhere, such as onto Amazon.com. Sellers even organized a 1-week boycott of eBay during which they would list no items with the company to express their hostility. Many sellers did shut down their eBay online storefronts and moved to Amazon.com, which claimed in 2009 that for the first time its network of retail sites had overtaken eBay in monthly unique viewers or "hits." One informal survey found that while over 50% of buyers thought Amazon.com was an excellent sales channel, only 23% regarded Bay as being excellent.

Realizing his changes had backfired, Donohue reversed course in 2009 and eliminated several of eBay's fee increases and revamped its feedback system so that buyers and sellers can now respond to one another's comments in a fairer way. These moves

did smooth over the bad feeling between sellers and eBay, but the old "community relationship" it had enjoyed with sellers largely disappeared.

Improving Retail Channels and Product Search

Clearly, Donahoe would not be able to significantly increase eBay's revenues by increasing fees to sellers in the future, so his focus now was on expanding and improving its retail channels and product search capabilities to increase revenues. In 2007, eBay had acquired StubHub, the world's largest online ticket marketplace, and Donahoe worked to increase its market share and profits, once again by increasing fees, but also by improving its search software capabilities. eBay has also launched its Kijiji classified sites in 200 U.S. cities during 2007, but had not had the success it expected. In 2010, eBay relaunched its Kijiji classifieds site as eBayClassifieds.com with major software enhancements that it claimed would create industry-leading standards in trust and safety, customer service and user experience. In 2008, eBay Marketplaces introduced gift cards to capitalize on the growing popularity of "private" credit cards.

In 2009, eBay introduced "Daily Deals" to compete with Groupon and Living Social, backed by Amazon.com. This new online coupon retail channel connects buyers with sellers faster than ever, and its popularity has exploded. In 2011, eBay launched a new home page design that offers more deals and personalization—especially for fixed-price goods the latest step in Donahoe's attempts to improve its search engine capabilities. Also, in 2011, it acquired local product search company, Milo.com, to enhance its daily deal channel offerings.

New Moves with PayPal

Over the last several years, PayPal was contributing more and more to eBay's profits as the number of its active users, compared to eBay users, and the volume and value of PayPal's transactions increased (See Exhibit 1).

eBay has been working hard to make PayPal a financial powerhouse, and a leading conduit through which buyers and sellers can transact internationally,

---

Exhibit 1   Changes in eBay and PayPal Users and PayPal Payments 2006–2010

	2006	2007	2008	2009	2010
Number of Active Global eBay Users (in millions)	82	85	88	90	94
Number of Active Global PayPal Users (in millions)	49	57	70	81	94
Total PayPal Payment Volume (in billions)	$366	$486	$606	$726	$926

© Cengage Learning 2013

something that often involves high fees for buyers and sellers. PayPal also issues eBay credit cards and it has become another important means to reassure buyers that sellers are honest and reputable. During the last decade complaints about fraud on eBay have received increasing publicity as the scams practiced by unethical sellers have been revealed. PayPal allows eBay to offers buyers who use PayPal to pay for their products free product insurance protection in the event that their purchases are either fraudulent or misrepresented. It also reassures sellers that they can trust buyers. Through PayPal, eBay can police sellers and buyers and suspend their accounts if necessary to increase the reliability and quality of its performance. Today, the eBay Buyer Protection program offered through PayPal is the most comprehensive online consumer protection provided by a global retailer.

eBay has also been working to expand PayPal's appeal in many other ways to make it the leading online payment company. In 2005, PayPal launched its Merchant Services division that allows sellers of all sizes to easily and securely accept payments across the Internet. In 2006, PayPal launched a mobile application that allows PayPal users to send money via their mobile phones. By 2008, 8% of all e-commerce worldwide was transacted via PayPal. In 2009, PayPal acquired Israel's Fraud Sciences Ltd. to enhance its security and fraud management systems. Also in 2009, eBay launched its iPhone application, giving millions of buyers mobile access to eBay so that they could buy their items and then pay for them online. To allow its customers more credit facilities, eBay also acquired "Bill Me Later," a leading online-oriented payments brand and began to offer Bill Me Later as an option to customers during checkout.

In 2009, PayPal also opened its platform, PayPal X to become the first major global payments company that was open to third-party development so

other companies could link in directly to the PayPal system and customize their payment approach. For example, in 2010

Facebook users became able to use PayPal to pay for Facebook Ads through the company's online advertising tool and for gaming services such as Zynga's Cityville and Farmville. In 2011, PayPal launched a new service that lets digital-game players pay for digital goods without leaving the content site—and it has already processed $3.4 billion in digital-goods payments.

Given the growing importance of secure mobile payments in the 2010s as Apple and Google also began offering their own mobile online payments system, in 2011 eBay acquired privately-held Zong Inc. for $240 million to strengthen PayPal's position in the fast-growing mobile payments and digital goods market. Zong allows consumers to pay for purchases from their mobile phones (or direct-carrier billing) on the Internet and offers a secure connection to more than 250 mobile operators in 45 countries. PayPal President Scott Thompson said that eBay expects that "Zong will strengthen PayPal's value by helping us reach the more than 4 billion people who have mobile phones, giving them more choice and security when they pay."

The Skype Divestiture

Meg Whitman's strategy that Skype, by providing easy and free global communication, would speed information flow between sellers and buyers and drive eBay's global sales and revenues was not realized—most eBay users stayed with their own e-mail or SMS providers. Consequently, in 2009 announced that it would sell about 70% of Skype to a group of private investors for $2.75 billion, which it bought for about $3.1 billion in 2005. While this seemed to be a poor return on eBay's investment, it received a pleasant surprise in 2011 when Microsoft announced that it was acquiring Skype for $8.5 billion; that gave eBay a quick $1.4 billion profit on its remaining 30% stake.

A 2011 Turnaround?

After all these strategic changes to its business model, by October 2010, Donahoe's turnaround plan for eBay was showing signs of success; 2009 revenues were $8.7 million, or 14% higher than before Donahoe took over in 2008, and in 2010, revenues were $9.5 billion while profit had also increased fueled by the Skype sale, growth in PayPal and growth in revenues from increased sales from its online retail channels." CEO John Donahoe announced that he was pleased with the progress that buyers and sellers were noticing, but also that there was still a lot of work to do. eBay's biggest challenge is still how to manage the threats posed by Amazon.com and Google, which have also been changing their business models to outcompete eBay.

One strategy eBay announced in July 2011 was that it was going to start rolling out a fulfillment service for its merchants, similar to Amazon.com's Marketplace service, and this will handle the storage and shipping of inventory of the merchants who sell their products on its Websites. Merchants who use Amazon.com's value-chain services benefit enormously from its huge supply chain and the economies of scale that come with it, such as not having to handle inventory, and fast and often free shipping. In the past, eBay appeared to have a stronger business model than Amazon.com's because, unlike Amazon.com, it did not have to bear the costs of warehouses, inventory, and shipping. It provided the marketplace for buyers and sellers to meet, and then, of course, also provided the profitable PayPal payment service that has allowed it to take a greater percentage of the revenues from online transactions on its Website. However, Amazon.com, has shown that by using IT to manage the huge supply chain infrastructure of warehouses necessary to control transactions along the value chain it can provide a better experience for merchants and customers—driving merchants to sell through Amazon.com instead of eBay. Recall, that in the late-1990s Amazon.com tried to take on eBay in auctions and failed. Now eBay is playing catch-up to Amazon.com in the fixed-price product market and is establishing its own physical value chain. Will this work? In 2011, more and more of eBay's profits were coming from expanding its PayPal financial services and analysts worried that this was not a good strategy to increase the profitability of its business model.

Endnotes

www.ebay.com, press releases 1997–2011.

eBay Annual and 10K Reports, 1997–2011.

Belbin, David, *The eBay Book: Essential Tips for Buying and Selling on eBay.co.uk*, (London: Harriman House Publishing, 2004).

Cihlar, Christopher, *The Grilled Cheese Madonna and 99 Other of the Weirdest, Wackiest, Most Famous eBay Auctions Ever*, (New York: Random House, 2006).

Cohen, Adam, *The Perfect Store: Inside eBay*, (Boston: Little, Brown & Company, 2002)

Jackson, Eric M., *The PayPal Wars: Battles with eBay, the Media, the Mafia, and the Rest of Planet Earth*, (Los Angeles: World Ahead Publishing, 2004).

Nissanoff, Daniel, *FutureShop: How the New Auction Culture Will Revolutionize the Way We Buy, Sell and Get the Things We Really Want*, London: The Penguin Press, 2006).

Spencer, Christopher Matthew, *The eBay Entrepreneur*, New York: Kaplan Publishing 2006).

Is Yahoo!'s Business Model Working in 2011?

Gareth R. Jones
Texas A&M University

In 2006, Yahoo! was the world's most-visited interactive Web portal or entryway into the World Wide Web (WWW). It averaged over 144 million page views per day, earned $2 billion on revenues of $6.4 billion in 2006, and its stock price was around $30 (down from its all time high of $100 before the 2000 dot.com bust led its stock price to plunge in value to $4.40!). By 2010, Yahoo! was still the third most-visited Web portal, despite that both Google and Facebook surpassed it in their numbers of daily page views. Moreover, its share of the search engine market had dramatically plummeted from over 30% to around 12% while Google search increased its share to a whopping 65%. The result of these changes was that in 2011, Yahoo!'s stock price averaged around only $15—it had lost over half its value in the last 5 years. What went wrong? Why had Yahoo!'s business model been performing so poorly; why were its strategies not working in the rapidly evolving Internet content provider industry?

Yahoo!'s Beginnings

The Yahoo! portal has its origins in the Website directory created as a hobby by its two founders, David Filo and Jerry Yang. Filo and Yang, two Ph.D. candidates in electrical engineering at Stanford University. They wanted a quick and easy way to remember and revisit the Websites they had identified as the best and most useful from the hundreds of thousands of sites that were quickly appearing on the WWW in the early-1990s. They soon realized that as the list of their favorite Websites grew longer and longer, the list began to lose its usefulness, as they had to wade through a longer and longer list of URLs (Website addresses) to find the specific

site they wanted. So to reduce their search time Filo and Yang decided to divide their list of Websites into smaller and more manageable categories according to each one's specific content or subject matter, such as sports, business, politics, or culture. In 1994, they published their Website directory online calling it "Jerry's Guide to the WWW" for their friends to use. Soon, hundreds—then thousands—of people located and clicked on their Website because it saved them time and effort to identify the most useful sites— their Website went viral.

As they continued to develop their directory, Filo and Yang found that each of the directory's subject categories were also quickly becoming large and unwieldy to search, so they further divided them into subcategories. Now, their directory organized Websites into a hierarchy, rather than a searchable index of pages, so they renamed their directory "Yahoo!" supposedly short for "Yet Another Hierarchical Officious Oracle," and the Yahoo! search engine was born. However, Filo and Yang insisted they selected the name because they liked the word's general meaning as originated by Jonathan Swift in *Gulliver's Travels* as someone or something that is "rude, unsophisticated, and uncouth"; their goals was, after all, to continuously improve the site over time. As their directory grew, they realized they could not possibly identify all the best Websites that were appearing in the WWW, so they recruited human volunteers to help them improve, expand, and refine their directory and make it a more useful, laborsaving search device.

By 1994, hundreds of thousands of users were visiting Yahoo! every day; it had quickly become the primary search portal of choice for people surfing the Web to help them find the sites that provided the most useful, interesting and entertaining content.

By 1995, Yahoo! recorded over a million "hits" or user visits per day as word kept spreading about the utility of their search engine. The increasing size of their search engine had outgrown the limited hosting capacity of their Stanford University account so they arranged to borrow server capacity from nearby Netscape, which had developed the first Web browser. Yang and Filo decided to put their graduate studies on hold and turn their attention and skills to work on building Yahoo! into a business.

When they created their directory, Filo and Yang had no idea they had a potential gold mine at their fingertips. They enjoyed surfing the Web and were interested in making it easier for ordinary people to do so as well. But, by 1994, it became clear that they could make major money from their directory if they allowed companies to advertise their products on the site in order to attract more sales. Of course, all along, the Internet had been rapidly expanding, and Filo and Yang realized they had to move quickly to capitalize on Yahoo!'s popularity—in any market there are always several other entrepreneurs who are pursuing a similar idea, and the race is on to become the first to successfully develop a new product and make it a success. Although their search engine was the first of its kind to be up and running, they knew it could be imitated. Indeed, competitive Web-crawling search engine companies like AltaVista that used mathematical algorithms to detect the most relevant Websites had already emerged. At this time, Yahoo!'s advantage was that it was a human-powered search engine where real people did the legwork for ordinary Internet surfers, and listed sites handpicked for their usefulness. The new mathematical algorithms being developed at this time could not match Yahoo!'s ability to select relevant results for specific user inquiries—however, technology quickly improved, and Filo and Yang's human-powered search engine was already on the way to becoming a dinosaur because of the incredible growth of the Internet and WWW that would occur in the next decade.

Nevertheless, as visits to Yahoo!'s hits continued to increase, so did requests by companies to advertise on its Web portal, and its advertising revenues rapidly increased, which paid for the rocketing costs of hosting their online directory on computer servers. With a hot new business on their hands, Yang and Filo's business model was to generate revenues by renting advertising space on the rapidly expanding Web pages of their search engine. When a user clicked on an ad, this "click impression" became a charge to the advertiser's account, and the greater the number of impressions the greater the advertising fees. As their fledgling company grew and the number of user visits soared, Filo and Yang realized they needed to find new sources of funding to develop a sophisticated IT infrastructure to support their portal's growth. Searching for backing from venture capitalists, they soon struck a deal with Sequoia Capital, a Silicon Valley firm that had supported Apple and Oracle among other high-tech companies. Using the $2 million seed capital to build their company's IT systems, their portal continued to soar in popularity, and in 1996, this success led to Yahoo!'s initial public stock offering that raised $338 million by selling 2.6 million shares at $13 each, to allow it to fund future growth.

Sequoia Capital understood the problems facing new startups and entrepreneurs and insisted that Filo and Yang, who had no business background, should hire experienced executives to develop Yahoo!'s business model. Sequoia's partners had learned that the skills needed to be a successful manager often diverge from those necessary to develop successful business strategies, especially if entrepreneurs are driven by their technical or scientific background and do not understand the realities of industry competition. Filo and Yang hired Tim Koogle, an experienced ex-Motorola executive with an engineering background to be Yahoo!'s new CEO. Filo and Yang became joint co-chairmen of Yahoo! with the title of "Chief Yahoo!".

Developing Yahoo!'s Business Model

Koogle started to build Yahoo!'s business model by focusing on recruiting marketing experts and increasing the company's advertising function to strengthen Yahoo!'s core competences and increase ad revenues to fund the company's further growth. At the same time, Koogle decided revenue growth should be driven by increasing the number of site users, and so the need to continuously improve Yahoo!'s search engine—and find new ways to attract visitors—was vital.

Filo and Yang took responsibility for improving the search engine but now hired many experts such as Srinija Srinivasan or "Ontological Yahoo!" as she became known in the company's early days because of her crucial role in refining and developing the classification system that was the hallmark of Yahoo!'s search engine. She helped Filo and Yang hire hundreds more software engineers to broaden and increase the reach and usefulness of Yahoo!'s search engine, and to manage its fast-growing IT infrastructure that was being continuously upgraded to handle the tens of millions of daily user requests the company was now receiving. By 1996, Yahoo! listed over 200,000 individual Websites in over 20,000 different categories. Hundreds of companies had signed up with Yahoo! to advertise their products on its portal to reach its millions of users.

Another strategy Koogle developed was to take Yahoo!'s business model and replicate it around the world—to increase global advertising revenue. By the end of 1996, there were 18 Yahoo! portals using 12 languages operating outside the United States. In each country, Yahoo!'s portal and Web directory was customized to the tastes and needs of local users. However, there was considerable overlap between countries in terms of popular global news, politics, media, and entertainment Websites, which also helped Yahoo! to find new attractive Websites and strengthen its U.S. search engine. This, of course, led to the development of new Web pages that helped increasing its advertising revenues.

Yahoo!'s success with its growing global Internet search operations convinced Koogle to craft a new vision and business model for Yahoo!. The company would no longer operate only as a search engine, but would now develop new media and entertainment services to allow it become the dominant global communication, media entertainment, and retail company. Yahoo! would become a portal that could be used to enable anyone to connect with anything or anybody on the Internet.

In the vision its top executives crafted, Yahoo! would not only continue to generate increasing revenues from the sale of advertising space on its search engine pages, it would also earn significant revenues from engaging in e-commerce transactions—buying and selling between Internet users—and take a percentage of the value of each transaction executed using its portal as its fee. Of course, other companies such as eBay and Amazon.com were also quickly developing this kind of Website service. In 1998, Yahoo! acquired the Internet shopping por-

tals Viaweb and Yoyodyne to create its new retail-shopping platform, Yahoo! Stores. Its new online services would enable new and existing businesses to quickly create and manage secure online stores to market and sell their products. After launching their store, these merchants were also included in searches on Yahoo! Shopping, one of the increasingly popular shopping portals that provided potential customers with price comparisons of the products in which they are interested, and so helped to determine the online store from which they would purchase.

To build brand awareness and make it the portal of choice for all kinds of Internet-based services Yahoo! spent heavily on advertising, using radio and television ads targeted at mainstream America. To make its portal more useful, Koogle pioneered Yahoo!'s strategy of expanding the range of content and services of the Internet communication services it provided to its users to make the portal more useful to them. Over the next decade, Yahoo! continuously developed its technology and made many (expensive) acquisitions that allowed users to access services such as e-mail, instant and text messaging, news, stock alerts, personals, and job placement services. Moreover, it made these services available over a rapidly expanding array of digital and computing devices or channels from desktop PCs to wireless laptops, and eventually to mobile computing devices such as PalmPilots and smartphones.

Yahoo! also began to work with media and entertainment content providers to help them build and improve their own online content and ability to work on Yahoo!'s digital platform. This increased the value of Yahoo!'s portal to users who could access any content or merchants they needed through Yahoo!. Its goal was to become the portal of choice—the place where Internet users would routinely visit to enjoy and complete online transactions.

At the same time, these moves made Yahoo! increasingly valuable to companies anxious to advertise on the Internet to grow their business. Each specific new online service Yahoo! offered allowed advertisers to better target their advertising message to specific demographic groups, for example, sports fans, teens, game players, or investors. Online brokers such as E*Trade and Ameritrade started to heavily advertise on Yahoo!'s popular financial pages; similarly, sports magazines, eBay, and Blockbuster focused on the best way to spend their ad dollars on its shopping and news pages. Targeted advertising increased the rate at which a user clicks on ads, which translated into more completed online transactions, therefore increasing the yield (or return) of online advertising to merchants. (This is something Google understood much better than Yahoo! and the reason why Google is the leader in online advertising today.)

The result of Koogle's new business model and strategies was spectacular. By the end of 1998, the company had 50 million unique users, up from 26 million in the prior year; 35 million of these were now registered Yahoo! users who had created e-mail, gaming, and other kinds of accounts with the company. Moreover, 3,800 companies were advertising on Yahoo!'s pages up from 2,600 in 1997, and 700 in 1996. By 1999, 5000 merchants were selling products on the Yahoo! Shopping page up from 3,500 in 1998, and the company's revenues had grown from $21.5 million in 1996 to $203 million in 1998!

Building a Stronger Business Model: More Content and Channels

To keep Yahoo!'s profits growing, it was necessary to drive an increasing number of users to its portal, and Koogle's new strategies revolved around making Yahoo! a "megabrand" by "becoming the most useful and well-known Web portal on the Internet." His entire focus was to create compelling news, media, shopping, and entertainment content by adding additional Yahoo! channels, which had more services and features to increase its value to users, and encourage them to become regular registered users. The ability to attract and retain customers is a major metric used by investors to evaluate a company's value, not only Internet content providers but also cable TV providers, wireless phone providers, and so on. Yahoo!'s goal was to lock in users and increase their switching costs of turning to a new portal.

To facilitate this process, Yahoo! provided features that made it possible for users to customize Yahoo!'s Web pages and services to better meet their specific needs. For example, Yahoo!'s registered users could customize its popular news service to show the specific news sections they were the most interested in, such as technology or entertainment, or users could input their personal portfolios into its

financial Web page and track their portfolio's value over time. The financial Webpage also provided links to message boards where individual investors can jointly discuss a company's prospects. The ability to create a high level of customization created major switching costs for customers. Once users created their portfolios, personal pages, shopping lists, and other profiles, they would be much less likely to want to repeat this process by signing up at another Web portal—unless it offered some other "killer application," or compelling content, which of course is what Google and Facebook have been able to offer in the 2000s.

Yahoo! worked hard to remain the Web portal of choice by continuing to introduce additional kinds of online services as soon new startup Internet companies had showed their services were popular among online users. It developed a strategy of acquiring the leading Internet company in a particular online area, for example, online dating, to extend its portfolio of services, and keep its leadership as an online portal, thereby increasing its value to its users. In 1999, for example, it made three important acquisitions, RocketMail, an e-mail service provider that became the basis for Yahoo! Mail; GeoCities that provided a free Web-hosting service to registered users, which allowed them to publish their own personal homepages (containing material of their own choice) and to share it with friends and any other interested parties. Lastly, it bought Broadcast.com, an early leader in online streaming digital audio and video programming that allowed Yahoo! to broadcast audio and video content on all its channels to users. Yahoo!'s goal was to make its services even more valuable to its users—and thus to its advertisers as well—so that these acquisitions would result in increasing advertising revenues. Then, in 2000, Yahoo! acquired eGroups, a free social group/mailing list hosting service that allowed registered users to set up any kind of online group of their choice, and use it as a forum to attract other Internet users that shared their interests; soon hundreds of thousands of specialized groups had been established. Yahoo! integrated eGroups into its successful Yahoo! Groups service to develop and strengthen its services, and today it has millions of registered groups of users and is a popular mailing list service for all kinds of social networking purposes. Yahoo! paid billions to acquire these companies, however, because this was the time of the dot.com bubble;

afterwards the value of these acquisitions plunged—as did Yahoo!'s stock.

In addition to the services just mentioned, Yahoo! also now provided services such as Yahoo! Messenger, an instant messaging client that allowed for on-line chat; Yahoo! Games, a successful game-playing service; and various specialized online retail sites, including an online auction service it had started to compete with highly-profitable eBay. Its original search engine had, by this time, become just one of the many services it provided. As it turned out, Koogle's (and Filo and Yang's) failure to realize the central importance of Internet searching was a major factor that led to Yahoo!'s later problems—just as this same error hurt Microsoft, AOL, and all the other major search portals. Google was the exception, as it was focusing its efforts on search capabilities, although its reasons were not obvious until the early-2000s.

Nevertheless, as Koogle hoped, as the range of services Yahoo! offered expanded, its popularity increased as it became a "one-stop shop" that could cater to most kinds of services that Internet users' needed—information, entertainment, and retail, for example. Its expanding business model seemed to be working. Most of its services were provided free to Yahoo! users because the advertising revenues it earned from the ads on the millions of Web pages on its portal were the primary source of revenues in its profitable business model. In addition, it earned some revenues from the fees it charged sellers and buyers on its shopping and specialized retail sites. Also, Yahoo! charged for specialized services such as its personals dating service, a streaming stock quotes service, a job hunting service, and various premium e-mail and Web storage options that provided users with more kinds of value-added solutions. This also helped to increase revenues and earnings.

The success of its strategy of bundling online services to attract ever-greater numbers of users became clear as Yahoo!'s user base exploded. By the end of the 1990s, 15 million people a day were visiting Yahoo! and it had become the most visited portal on the WWW. Its business model, based on the idea that the more services it offered, the greater the number of Internet users it would attract, (and the higher would be the advertising fees it could charge companies) seemed to be working. In 2000, Yahoo!'s stock price reached the astronomical height of $237, its market value was $220 billion!

Big Problems Face Yahoo!

Just 2 years later, however, Yahoo!'s stock had plummeted to just $9 a share, which valued the company at less than $10 billion. Why? Because the dot.com bust sent thousands of Internet companies into bankruptcy and caused an across-the-board plunge in their stock prices. However, Yahoo! was still regarded as a dot.com powerhouse and many analysts put some of the blame for the fall in its stock price (eBay's did not fall greatly) on managerial mistakes at the top of the company—in particular on the way Yahoo!'s business model had developed over time.

CEO Tim Koogle had staked Yahoo!'s continuing success on its ability to develop an increasing range of compelling Web content and services to drive increased visits to its portal and generate more advertising and e-commerce revenues. The problem with this business model was that it made Yahoo!'s profitability (and stock price) totally dependent upon how fast advertising revenues increased—or how fast they fell. The dot.com bust and the economic recession that followed in the early-2000s led to a huge fall in the amount large and small companies were willing to spend on Internet advertising. As its advertising revenues plunged, Yahoo!'s stock price plummeted, and its investors' hopes of increasing revenue growth disappeared. Moreover, it turned out that Koogle had spend far too much money—billions too much—to pay for acquisitions such as GeoCities and eGroups (especially given that these companies profits were also highly dependent on Internet advertising!). Had these companies remained independent, they would now be valued at a fraction of the price Yahoo! paid for them.

Advances in Internet and Digital Technologies

At the same time, Internet and digital technologies were continually advancing and improving, and that lowered the value of the acquired companies' distinctive competencies, and therefore their competitive advantage in providing a specific online service—the primary reason why Yahoo! acquired them. Technological advances had made it easier for entrepreneurs to start new dot.coms that could provide similar kinds of specialized Internet services that Yahoo! offered—but which also had a new twist or killer application that was better than Google's. Thus in the 2000s, competitors like Monster.com, MySpace, and YouTube emerged offering digital services that proved so attractive they also became leading Web portals in providing a particular kind of online application: job hunting, social networking, and online video, respectively. These portals became major threats to Yahoo! because they siphoned off its users, and reduced its advertising revenues, which at that time were mainly based on the number of users visiting a Website. Now, Yahoo! lacked the resources to buy these portals, it had spent its cash and its stock price was low.

Search Engine's Become More Powerful: The Growing Threat from Google

On the search engine front as well, the search information service that had been the key to Yahoo!'s rise and its original distinctive competence was also experiencing a new threat. Yahoo! was experiencing increased competition because of the growing popularity of Google, a small, relatively unknown search engine company in 2000. By the early-2000s, however, it became obvious to Web watchers that Google was pioneering advances in WWW search technology that was making Yahoo!'s hierarchical directory classification obsolete! Yahoo!, like other major Web portals such as Microsoft's MSN and AOL had failed to realize how the search function would increase so much in importance as the breadth and depth of information on the WWW increased. It had become increasingly difficult for Internet users to locate the specific information they needed. The search engine that can find the specific information users want in the fastest time is the one that wins the search engine war, and Google's proprietary technology was attracting more and more users by word of mouth— just as Yahoo!'s directory had grown in popularity so fast in the 1990s. Yahoo! had been providing more and more kinds of online services but in the process had forgotten—or lost—the reason for its original success. Perhaps a professional manager at the helm was not such a good idea in the first place. Or, perhaps Filo and Yang were simply enjoying their newfound wealth and had not worked to improve

Yahoo!'s search engine technology because it had become a portal providing so many different kinds of information services.

The Web Portal Industry

To appreciate the problems Yahoo! was now facing, it is necessary to understand how the incredible growth in the 1990s of the Internet and WWW, and rapid advances in Internet hardware and software, changed the function of Web portals dramatically over the 2000s.

Internet Service Provider Portals

The first commercial portals were entry or access portals called Internet Service Providers (ISPs) that provided people with a way to log on to the Internet. For example, companies such as CompuServe, MSN, and AOL offered customers e-mail service and access to the WWW for time-related fees. Slow dial-up connections meant high monthly fees, and early on, ISPs charged users for each individual e-mail they sent! Moreover, once on the WWW, users were hampered by the fact that there was no Internet Web browser available to help them easily find and navigate to the thousands (and then millions) of Web pages and Websites that were emerging. Yahoo!'s directory, and then Netscape's Internet browser (introduced in 1994), changed all this. So did the growth in the number of search engines, including early leaders such as AltaVista, Inktomi, and Infoseek, that were all available to help users surf the Web. Typically, a user would connect to the Web through an access portal, and then go to their specific search engine of choice to identify Websites of interest, which they could then bookmark as favorites using Netscape's Web browser.

Product Bundling Portals

When Yahoo! became the leading search engine, this began the second phase of portal development, the product bundling or aggregation phase. Dot.coms such as Yahoo!, AOL, MSN, and hundreds of other now defunct Web portals were competing to attract Internet users and become the main portal of choice—to obtain advertising revenues. Now differences in the business models of different portals became increasingly clear, for example, portals like Yahoo! focused on offering users the widest possible selection of free Internet services to create switching costs and develop brand loyalty. Others, like AOL and MSN, adopted the fee-paying model, in which users paid to access the Web through a dial-up connection their portals provided, then they could use the range of services they offered free or for a charge for a premium service, like personals.

Competition between these combined access/aggregation portals increased as they strived to attract the tens of millions of new Internet users who were coming online at this time. The bigger their user base, the higher the potential fees and advertising revenues they could collect, so the price of Internet service quickly fell. By the mid-1990s, AOL made a major decision to offer its users unlimited Internet connection time for $19.95 a month. In the U.S., this attracted millions of new customers, and AOL became the leading access and aggregation portal with over 30 million users at its height, followed by MSN, and many other smaller ISPs.

The competitive problem these ISP/aggregated service portals like AOL faced from the beginning was that once their users were online, they would search out the "best of breed" Web portal that could provide them with the particular kind of information service they most wanted. So, millions of AOL subscribers, for example, used the portal to get online, but then used the myriad of services available on Yahoo! and other portals. The business model used by AOL, MSN, and others was to improve their content to keep subscribers on their portals in order to obtain the vital advertising and e-commerce revenues that Yahoo! was enjoying.

The problem soon facing the ISP/aggregation portals was that new companies started to offer lower-priced Internet access service, and, especially, that developing broadband technology had started to rapidly grow in popularity because of the speed it offered in using and downloading the WWW services or content that users wanted. This worked in favor of free portals like Yahoo! that did not generate revenues from getting users online. But, it began to hurt fee-based portals such as AOL and MSN that soon experienced falling revenues as new and existing Internet users chose faster broadband ISP connections, and users continued to gravitate to portals such as Yahoo!, eBay, Amazon.com, MySpace, YouTube, and other similar sites.

Customized Portals

In fact, the next major development in Web portals arrived when some Web portals started to specialize in developing "deeper" relationships with their users. Their goal was to offer their users an increasingly customized online experience that set out to help users make better or more informed choices when buying goods or services. Internet book-selling Amazon.com was one of the first portals to pioneer the development of the personalized or customized shopping experience. Amazon.com's software focused upon providing more information to users by, for example, allowing people who had bought books to provide detailed feedback to users about a particular book—and subsequently all kinds of products that it sold. Similarly, one of Amazon.com's central goals became to track its users around its site to help them find other products that they might be attracted to. Amazon.com's database recorded each user's buying preferences to help them make better buying decisions, and in the 2000s, its tracking technology became so invasive it developed software to track its users as they surfed the Web on other sites to find new products to offer them. Not surprisingly, many of its users thought this was an invasion of their privacy, but in the last decade these new tracking technologies have proliferated, and few ordinary Internet users today are aware of how much information is being collected about them by tracking companies that can sell this information to advertising companies.

All the major portals began to realize the importance of offering users a customized online experience, to increase their switching costs, and to keep them loyal, repeat users so their purchases and use could be tracked. Yahoo!, for example, uses "beacons" that allow it to follow its users around the WWW unless they choose to turn off this feature to increase their privacy. All the major portals began to make the "My" personal preferences choices on their portals a more important part of their service such as "MyAOL and MyYahoo! in order to be able to increasingly target advertising toward specific customer groups and make their portals easier to use by, for example, offering easy online payment checkout services.

However, it became increasingly apparent that the "best of breed" or leading category Web portals were quickly developing a first-mover advantage and strong brand loyalty. Amazon.com's stock price had also plunged after the dot.com bust, but it still pursued its business model to develop the online software that would attract the most customers and allow it to become the leader in Internet retailing. It succeeded, and was able to withstand the challenge from the thousands of other shopping portals that had sprung up in the 2000s, but Amazon.com also crushed the shopping channels of leading portals such as Yahoo! and AOL. Similarly, Yahoo!'s online auction service, despite that it was *free* to its registered users, could not compete with online auction leader eBay because eBay had gained the first-mover advantage, and its popularity allowed it to offer buyers and sellers a much larger market (and therefore a much better selection and higher prices).

Yahoo! Problems Increase throughout the 2000s

In the 2000s, it became clear that the two biggest sources of revenue and profit for Web portals were those gained from e-commerce, for example, from online retail and auction sales, which has been the source of Amazon.com's success in the 2010s; and to the generation of and sale of online advertising revenues. In the search engine segment of the market, the search engine company that could quickly provide online customers with the specific information necessary for them to make the best purchase possible, attracted the most advertisers, and could charge higher advertising rates. Google's strategy to continuously increase its competencies to provide fast, relevant information has, of course, been the business model behind its huge success, and the failure of most other search engine companies, including Yahoo! and MSN. However, customized portals like Facebook that provide specialist services such as social networking, could also earn high advertising and e-commerce revenues. Facebook's software platform and huge user base has allowed it to collect detailed information about its users that it can sell to generate

targeted advertising revenues. In addition, its online games, such as CityVille, provided by Zynga, allow it to generate revenues from the fees it can charge game providers, retail providers, and others.

Many analysts argued that when Yahoo!'s stock price was at its peak, it should have purchased other e-commerce companies that were generating revenue by other means than advertising—such as eBay—so that it could have broadened the source of its revenues and reduced its dependency on advertising revenues. If advertising revenues decreased, Yahoo!'s profitability and stock price would plunge. In the early-2000s, Yahoo!'s stock price plummeted as the dot.com bust led to a huge fall in advertising revenues, and investors began to realize the weaknesses associated with its business model.

Yahoo!'s disastrous performance convinced its board of directors that new leadership was needed, and Tim Koogle was replaced as CEO by Terry Semel, an experienced Hollywood media executive who had once controlled Warner Brothers. To change Yahoo!'s business model, especially as it could no longer afford to acquire specialized Web portals, Semel adopted new strategies to generate increased online revenues.

First and foremost, Yahoo! needed to improve its search engine technology, a major portal attraction, to generate more users and advertising revenues. As time went on, and the success of Google's business model became increasingly obvious, Yahoo! focused upon improving its search software to beat Google at its own game and develop the ability to offer high-quality targeted advertising. Also, Semel decided to pursue a new content-driven strategy, and Yahoo! internally developed new kinds of services, and acquired small specialist Internet companies that could provide it with the new competencies it needed to compete in new emerging online information and media market segments. For example, Yahoo! acquired HotJobs, a leading Internet job hunting and placement company, and it began to expand its global news and media services operations.

Recognizing the growing importance of digital communications media to generate advertising revenues, it established a new Media Group function to develop advanced imaging and video news content to take advantage of increasing broadband Internet access. Yahoo! launched its own video search engine service in 2005, and revamped the Yahoo! Music download service; it also acquired Flickr, a leading photograph hosting and sharing site. All these strategies were designed to become a part of its new social networking strategy in order to compete with MySpace, YouTube, and Facebook. In fact, Yahoo! lost its battle to acquire YouTube to Google in 2006, and, of course, the fast growth of Facebook destroyed its chances to develop a popular social networking site, as Facebook overpowered MySpace, which had been purchased by News Corp. The fast-changing fortunes of Web portals is shown by the change in MySpace's fortunes; in 2005 it was valued at $3 billion, but its owner New Corp. was happy to divest it in 2011 for $100 million.

Semel continued to try to make new acquisitions to revitalize the appeal of Yahoo!'s hundreds of different online content and media services to create a more customized, social network-like appeal to its users. Yahoo! launched a personalized blogging and social networking service Yahoo! 360°, revamped its MyWeb personal Web hosting service, created a new PhotoMail service, and purchased online social event calendar company Upcoming .org to compete with Google's new online calendar service. Continuing its push to strengthen its social networking services. Yahoo! acquired blo.gs, a service based on RSS feed aggregation and del.icio.us, which allows registered users to create a scrapbook or notebook of information they wish to keep from the Websites they visit, similar to Google's notebook service.

Semel's content-driven strategy was to make Yahoo!'s media and entertainment services so useful and attractive to online customers that they would be willing to pay for them—in the form of once-and-for-all or monthly fees for services. For example, monthly fees for personal ads in its dating site, or ads to sell or rent merchandise like cars or homes, and fees that provided premium services in areas such as e-mail, data storage, photo sharing, e-commerce, message boards, and similar services. Also, it followed Amazon.com's initiative and worked to provide online software to generate fees from small businesses that wished to link to its Web portal and use Yahoo!'s specialist services to create, host, and manage their retail stores. Through these moves, Yahoo! kept its position as the most popular portal; its revenue more than tripled from 2003 to 2006 to over $6 billion, and its stock price recovered somewhat in the first half of 2006.

New Problems with a Content-Driven Strategy

By the summer of 2006, things were not so rosy, and major questions were surfacing about how Yahoo!'s content-driven strategy could continue to drive its revenues in the future as competition, especially as Google's and Facebook's popularity increased. Yahoo!'s stock fell 25% in the last half of 2006, and analysts worried that these popular search engine and social networking portals were stealing away its users, and that advertising revenues and user fees would fall in the future. For example, Google was now offering an ever-increasing number of free online services such as e-mail, chat, storage, and word processing software to compete with MSN as well as Yahoo!

In an internal e-mail leaked to the media, one of Yahoo!'s top managers expressed concern that many of its new investments in content and services were too expensive, unlikely to generate much profit, and it would not be able to keep up with agile new specialist portals; Google was becoming an Internet Giant. In the "Peanut Butter" memo, senior executive Brad Garlinghouse described Yahoo! as a company in search of a successful business model and strategies: "I've heard our strategy described as spreading peanut butter across the myriad opportunities that continue to evolve in the online world. The result: a thin layer of investment spread across everything we do and thus we focus on nothing in particular. I hate peanut butter. We all should." He had good reasons for his concern because the new specialist portals were more popular than Yahoo!'s own instant messaging and e-mail service, and, especially, in online imaging and video that had become increasingly important to Internet users. For example, Google drew further ahead of Yahoo! after its purchase of YouTube in 2006.

Nevertheless, Yahoo! still had impressive content covering sports, entertainment and finance, in particular. Also, it had embarked upon a major push to enhance the mobile delivery of all its services to better meet the needs of people on the go as the number of people using mobile-computing devices such as smartphones soared through the end of the 2000s, and is still growing in 2011. By 2008, for example, mobile video was a killer application, and to compete with Google, Yahoo! had heavily invested to upgrade this service—but eventually Yahoo! was forced to shut down its video service to cut costs.

The problem for Yahoo! was that its cost structure was increasing and it had lost its first-mover advantage to its new rivals—not a good position in the fast-changing online world.

The Search Engine Dilemma

A discussed earlier, for online digital media companies it had become essential to improve their search engine capabilities. Only Google had understood the crucial strategic relationship between providing users with fast, accurate search results, and the search engine provider that gives the ability to generate increasing advertising revenues. Google's business model was based upon providing better search capabilities and then providing an increasing number of free online services to attract more users and develop brand loyalty. To achieve significant revenue and profit growth, Semel recognized that Yahoo! also had to increase the capabilities of its search engine and generate the high volume of user visits that lead to increased revenues from online advertising and facilitating e-commerce transactions. Semel began to look for acquisitions to strengthen and improve Yahoo!'s search engine, and it bought several search companies such as Inktomi and Overture to improve its search competences. However, Google was unbeatable; its share of the search engine market was double that of Yahoo!'s—49% compared to Yahoo!'s 24% in 2006—and Microsoft's own search engine also plunged in popularity.

To meet Google's challenge, Semel combined the distinctive competencies of Inktomi and Overture, with its own in-house technology, to develop an improved search engine that would allow Yahoo! to offer a much more targeted online advertising program to compete with Google's—*Project Panama*. This huge, expensive project soon fell behind schedule, the company failed to launch it according to schedule, and Yahoo!'s stock price continued to plunge as it played catch up to Google and the other specialized Web portals. In fact, in 2005, Yahoo! and Google were neck-and-neck and each had about 18% of total online advertising revenues. By the end of 2006, Google's revenue had grown to 25% and Yahoo!'s had dropped to less than 14%.

In 2007, Semel reorganized Yahoo!'s management structure to allow it to better implement its business model and compete with its rivals—a shakeup sparked by the peanut butter memo. The new streamlined organizational structure grouped Yahoo!'s services into three primary product divisions, one focused upon satisfying the needs of its Website users, one upon finding better ways to service the needs of its advertisers, and one upon developing new technology. Semel hoped the reorganization would make Yahoo! more proficient at delivering online services and ads to capture the attention of online users. In 2007, Yahoo! rolled out its new targeted advertising system and announced that it expected major improvements in advertising revenues by the summer. Revenue per search query may grow by 10% or more in the second half of the year, and Semel said, "We believe this will deliver more relevant text ads to users, which in turn should create more high-quality leads. By the time we get to 2008 and beyond, this is a very, very, significant amount of additional profit and I'm pleased with the tangible progress we have made. I'm convinced we're on the right path." Yahoo!'s stock increased by over 10% as investors bet that this would be a turnaround moment in Yahoo!'s battle with Google.

Jerry Yang Takes Over as CEO

Semel and Yahoo! Investors were wrong. The number of users, including registered Yahoo! users, of Google's advanced search engine and other services, and the rapid development of popular specialized portals such as YouTube, and social networking Websites like Facebook, continued to siphon off millions of visits to Yahoo!'s Website. At the same time, the number of Yahoo! employees needed to provide the new advanced media services it was trying to offer soared, and so did its R&D costs; its cost structure increased. Also, at the same time, Microsoft recognized it had been slow to develop its search competencies and it began to pour billions into developing an advanced search engine called "Bing" that emerged at the end of the 2000s.

Investors lost confidence in Semel, who was forced out in 2008, and Yahoo!'s new CEO was now one of its original founders Jerry Yang. Yang spent the next 8 months streamlining Yahoo!'s business model, prioritizing the importance of its vast array of online services, and improving its search and advertising competences, while reducing its workforce to cut costs. But the Google Juggernaut was roaring ahead, and the value of Yahoo!'s stock continued to fall, so much so that in late-2008, Microsoft announced that it wanted to acquire Yahoo! for $40 billion, a huge premium over its stock price, before the bid and Yahoo!'s stock soared in value. Microsoft's logic was that its new search engine technology was now mature enough to replace Yahoo!'s and that in combining their search engines and online advertising functions, the merger would reap billions of dollars in cost savings. Furthermore, the merger would allow it to combine its MSN online service with Yahoo!'s so its registered customer base would soar, as would the number of users of its new combined Web portal. $40 billion was a lot of money, however.

After the bid, CEO Yang announced that Microsoft's offer to buy Yahoo! was a "galvanizing" event for his beleaguered company. However, he also made it clear that he was not interested in the takeover bid, and that he would meet with its board of directors to defend against what he expected would turn into a hostile bid. The battle raged for months during which Yang said he was holding out for a higher offer than the current bid that substantially undervalued Yahoo!'s assets. However, many analysts claimed that Yang was dreaming, and that the company's founder was not the right person to be in charge of making such an important decision.

Yang was supported by the board, and continued to reject repeated buyout and search-ad deal offers from Microsoft throughout 2008; eventually Microsoft announced it was withdrawing its bid for the company—upon which the value of the company's stock plunged and irate stockholders demanded that Yang be replaced. During this crucial year, Yang had been distracted by the takeover bid from streamlining the company's business model, so its performance had continued to fall! An exhausted Yang, whose resistance to the merger had personally cost him billions of dollars, decided that his future as CEO looked bleak and he handed over the reins to former Autodesk CEO Carol Bartz who became Yahoo! CEO in January 2009.

Bartz Reorganizes Yahoo!

Bartz has a long history of success in managing online companies and she moved quickly to find ways to reduce Yahoo!'s cost structure and simplify its operations to maintain its strong online brand identity. Bartz decided that the best way to restructure Yahoo! to gain more control over its business units and reduce operating costs was to centralize functions that had previously been performed by Yahoo!'s different business units, such as product development and marketing activities. For example, all the company's online publishing and advertising functions were centralized and put under the control of a single executive. Yahoo!'s European, Asian, and emerging markets divisions were combined and centralized under the control of another top executive. Bartz was astonished to find that Yahoo!'s talented programmers and engineers, who worked in different business units, didn't talk to each other, and she brought them all under the centralized control of a new executive in charge of product development, Chief Technology Officer Ari Balogh.

Bartz' cost-cutting efforts helped Yahoo! satisfy investors when, in the Spring of 2009, she announced plans to cut 5% more of Yahoo! staff, on top of 1,600 job cuts that had been made in December 2008. However, the way she would grow its revenues was not clear, especially as she assumed control when the financial crisis and recession had begun in 2009, and online advertising revenues plunged. Bartz said brand marketers put the brakes on ad spending, especially on display ads; the pictorial banners that were Yahoo!'s chief source of business and revenues fell 13% in 2009. Also, Yahoo!'s search engine advertising business fell 3% after having made progress in the last few years—Google kept powering ahead. Nevertheless, she had reduced operating expenses by 4% and had not cut employees in key functions such as product development and marketing. Yahoo!'s stock price rose 5% in the middle of 2009.

Although Yang had refused to sell the company he founded, Bartz made it clear that the company was still for sale—at the right price. Microsoft, however, was no longer interested in a takeover as the power of specialized portals such as Facebook, YouTube, and Amazon.com had by now become apparent—being a generalist and offering all things to all users was no longer possible. Nevertheless, the possibility of a major strategic alliance between the companies, so both could enjoy cost savings from economies of scale and scope in combining their search engine and online-targeted advertising functions, still existed. Essentially, Microsoft sought to obtain many of the advantages it had sought to achieve from acquiring Yahoo! by forming a strategic alliance. Now, Yahoo!'s position was considerably weaker as Bartz had to find ways to reduce costs given that Yahoo!'s revenues were stagnant or declining in many areas. She needed to keep up the company's stock price, in part, to still make it an attractive acquisition despite the fact that its market value had now plunged below $30 billion—over $10 billion less than Microsoft had offered for the company. In addition, Bartz announced that when the economy turned around, Yahoo!'s strategy for restoring growth would capitalize upon its online brand name and large size, and focus on "creating kick-ass products" to drive its growth.

The Agreement with Microsoft

In 2009, Yahoo! and Microsoft announced they had formed a strategic alliance that would benefit both companies in their battle with Google and Facebook. Yahoo! agreed to outsource its back-end search functions such as Web crawling, indexing and ranking to Microsoft to save money and use its Bing search engine to enhance its competitive position. In exchange, Yahoo! agreed to pay Microsoft a commission for paid search ads sold on Yahoo! and Yahoo! partner sites. Yahoo! estimated that this alliance would boost its annual operating income by about $500 million and reduce costs by about $200 million. Nevertheless, Bartz noted that "Search is a very valuable business for Yahoo!; we need to retain some stake in search to help it target display ads better. Search is important to our users and search is important to our advertisers."

At the same time, Bartz continued to prune Yahoo!'s unprofitable online services to reduce costs and focus its efforts upon the fastest growing, most profitable ad display markets. Yahoo! also announced continuing job cuts throughout 2009 and 2010 to reduce its workforce to under 14,000 and bring costs back under control.

Yahoo! in 2011

In June 2011, Yahoo! announced some disappointing results, in the most recent quarter its revenues had dropped by 23% compared to a year ago while Google announced that its revenues had increased by 32%. In the past year, Yahoo!'s 14,000 employees had generated $5.6 billion in revenues and $1.2 billion in

profit, while Google's 29,000 employees had generated $33 billion in revenues and $9 billion in profit. Why?

First, Yahoo! had not obtained the potential benefits it had expected to receive from its deal with Microsoft; although it was guaranteed a minimum payment of $450 million per year, the alliance had not generated a major increase in the number of visits to its search engine. However, Bartz said she expected revenues to substantially increase by the end of 2011 as the Bing search engine used by Yahoo! was increasing in popularity.

Second, Yahoo!'s targeted display advertising business had not performed as well as expected and profits had significantly fallen. However, Bartz announced that the costs of upgrading Yahoo!'s advertising platform and making it consistent across its global Websites was the main reason for this. With its new systems in place, Yahoo! would be able to deliver targeted advertising faster across all its different online services globally, and to provide companies with more effective advertising. Also, Yahoo! could now deliver its content and ads on all kinds of mobile computing devices, not just desktops, and Bartz stressed Yahoo!'s leading position in the U.S. and abroad in important content channels such as news and finance. However, Yahoo! has faced increasing competition from Facebook and Google, and investors worried if it could recover revenue in this highly lucrative market segment.

Yahoo!'s stock fell after this report, especially because it also announced lower revenue guidelines for the rest of 2011. But, its stock also took a major hit in June 2011 when it was announced that Alibaba, a huge Chinese Web portal, in which Yahoo! owns a 40% stake, had spun off its Alipay online payment service into a new company—without securing agreement from Yahoo!. Alibaba is worth many billions to Yahoo!, so this seemed to wipe off billions more of its market value and its stock plunged again. In August 2011, Bartz announced that Yahoo! would receive between $2 and $6 billion if and when the Alipay service was eventually spun off in an initial public offering, but this further reduced the value of its Alibaba investment and damaged Bartz' position. In August 2011, Yahoo!'s market value was about $18 billion, and 2/3 of that value was made up of its Asian assets valued at $9 billion, its $3 billion in cash; what was left was Yahoo!'s global online assets, now valued at around $6 billion. Microsoft had offered to pay $40 billion for its assets just a few years ago!

Thus, in August 2011, Yahoo! analysts could not decide if Yahoo! was undervalued because its online properties still offered the possibility of generating substantial revenue from search and advertising. Or, if its value might decline further in the future because it now had given up its online search expertise to Microsoft? It could not counter the strategies of Google and Facebook, and there was still no pipeline of innovative products to attract new users. Bartz' turnaround plan for Yahoo! had kept the company profitable because it had reduced costs, but what was its future vision and mission?

Yahoo! Fires Bartz

In September 2011, Yahoo!'s board of directors decided to fire Bartz—over the phone—claiming she had not found the right strategies to turn around the company. Yahoo! was in disarray in October 2011 as no new strategic leadership had emerged to orchestrate the company's turnaround and a stunned Bartz tweeted through her iPad that "Yahoo has. . . . me over." It seems that Yahoo!'s dysfunctional board is desperately trying to find a buyer for the company in order to provide stockholders with the most value for their investment.

In October, Microsoft, Google, and private investment funds had all been suggested as potential buyers for the company at a price around $20 billion—half of Microsoft's original offer. The company was still for sale—but the billion dollar question is at what price? The longer it takes to find a new buyer the less valuable Yahoo! is likely to be in the future—unless it can find some visionary CEO that can provide the company with a new vision and mission.

Endnotes

www.yahoo.com, 1990–2011.
Yahoo! 10K Reports, 1990–2011.

CASE 24

Viacom is Successful in 2011

Gareth R. Jones
Texas A&M University

CBS Broadcasting established Viacom as an independent company in 1970 to comply with regulations set forth by the U.S. Federal Communications Commission (FCC) barring television networks from owning cable TV systems, or from syndicating their own programs in the United States. The increasing spread of cable television and the continuing possibility of conflicts of interest between television networks and cable television companies made the spinoff necessary, and Viacom formally separated from CBS in 1971, when Viacom's stock was distributed to CBS shareholders.

Viacom quickly became one of the largest cable operators in the United States, with over 90,000 cable subscribers. It also owned the syndication rights to a large number of popular, previously run CBS television series that it made available for syndication to cable TV stations. In 1976, to take advantage of Viacom's experience in syndicating programming to cable TV stations, its managers decided to establish the Showtime movie network to directly compete with HBO, the leading outlet for films on cable television. In 1977, Viacom earned $5.5 million on sales of $58.5 million. Most of its earnings represented revenues from the syndication of its television series, but they also reflected growth of its own cable TV systems, which at this time had about 350,000 subscribers. Recognizing that both producing and syndicating television programming could earn greater profits, Viacom's managers decided to produce their own television programs in the late-1970s and early-1980s. Their efforts produced only mixed results, however, no hit series resulted from their work, and the Big Three television networks of ABC, NBC, and CBS continued to dominate the airwaves.

During the early-1980s, the push to expand the cable television side of its business was Viacom's managers' priority, and it rapidly grew its subscriber base. Viacom's managers, however, believed that its core cable operations were not a strong enough engine for future growth. Cable TV prices were regulated at this time, so cable companies had limited ability to increase prices, but its managers believed that real profit growth would come from providing the *content* of cable programming—television programs—not from just cable television service. Given that Viacom had failed to make its own successful new TV programs, its managers sought to acquire companies that made entertainment programs—the content. In 1981, Viacom started in a small way by buying a stake in Cable Health Network, a new advertiser-supported television network. Then, in September 1985, in a stroke of fortune, it made the acquisition that would totally change the company's future. Viacom purchased the MTV Networks from a competitor, Warner Bros., that desperately needed cash to invest in its own cable TV system to keep it viable. As it turned out, Warner Bros. had sold the jewel in its crown.

The MTV Networks included MTV, a new popular music video channel geared toward the 14–24 age groups; Nickelodeon, a channel geared toward children; and VH-1, a music video channel geared toward an older 25–44 age audience. MTV was the most popular property in the MTV Network. Its quick pace and flashy graphics attracted young television viewers who were a major target for large advertising companies, and the popularity of a TV station's programming determines how much a broadcast network can charge for advertising—which is why Super Bowl ads cost millions. MTV was performing well, but Nickelodeon had been less successful and had not achieved much of a following among young TV viewers, which limited its advertising revenues. Viacom's managers moved quickly to revamp Nickelodeon and give it the slick, flashy look of MTV. They developed unique programming to appeal to children—programming a very different aesthetic than *The Mickey Mouse Show*, which competitors like the Disney Channel offered. In the next few years, Nickelodeon went from being the least popular children's cable TV channel to being the most popular! Viacom's managers were confident that they had the foundation of a new content programming strategy to complement its cable TV interests to increase the company's profit growth.

Enter Sumner Redstone

Viacom's hopes were shattered when its Showtime channel lost 300,000 subscribers by 1986 because of intense competition from HBO, which, under its CEO Frank Biondi, had become the dominant subscriber movie channel. Viacom's cash flow plunged, it reported a loss in 1986, and, weakened by the $2 billion debt incurred to fund its growth, it became a takeover target.

After a 6-month battle to acquire the company Sumner M. Redstone bought Viacom for $3.4 billion in 1986. Redstone was the owner of National Amusements Inc. that owned and operated 675 movie theatres. Redstone had built NAI from 50 drive-in movie theaters to a modern theater chain and is credited with pioneering the multiplex movie theater concept. However, running a chain of movie theaters is very different from running a debt-laden media company like Viacom. Many analysts believed Redstone had overpaid for Viacom—but he saw a great potential for growth.

Aside from its cable television systems and syndication rights, which now included the popular TV series *The Cosby Show*, Redstone recognized the potential of its MTV and Nickelodeon channels. Also, Viacom had acquired 5 television and 8 radio stations in major markets that were also valuable properties. Redstone quickly moved to solve Viacom's problems and with his "hands-on," directive management style, he fired Viacom's top managers and searched for more capable managers who would be loyal to him. To turn Showtime around, he hired Frank Biondi, who had made HBO the major pay movie channel, as CEO of Viacom.

Viacom Speeds Up

Redstone bought Viacom because he believed that cable TV programming would become the main channel to deliver customers with entertainment content in the future. Redstone believed Viacom's MTV and Nickelodeon networks were its "crown jewels," they provided half the company's revenues and profits, which came both from subscribers (the cable companies that bought the programming) and from advertisers (who advertised on these channels). To strengthen these networks and build their brand name, Redstone hired a more aggressive advertising and sales management team, and against the expectations of industry analysts MTV and Nickelodeon experienced continuing growth and profitability. In 1989, for example, the MTV Networks won 15% of all dollars spent on TV cable advertising. Also, MTV was rapidly expanding throughout the world—broadcasting to Western Europe, Japan, Australia, large portions of Latin America, and eventually to countries in Asia.

Viacom in the 1990s

The problem facing Redstone and Biondi was how to position Viacom for profitable growth in the 1990s. Both executives felt that developing and expanding Viacom's strengths in developing entertainment content was the key to its future success, although this is a very expensive process. They believed that the message or content that is sent is what really mattered, not the distribution channel carrying it. As Biondi put it, "In the end, a pipe is just a pipe. The customer doesn't care how the information is obtained; all that matters is "the message." To build its entertainment programming strengths, Biondi worked hard to expand the success of Viacom's MTV channels. His goal was to promote the MTV networks as global brands that were perceived as having something unique to offer. Since MTV's viewers dominate the record-buying audience, Biondi sought to negotiate exclusive contracts that gave MTV the first crack at playing most major record companies' music videos—thus making it unique. At the same time, MTV went from being a purely music video channel to a channel that championed new kinds of innovative programming to appeal to a younger audiences, such as *Beavis and Butthead,* and *Road Stories,* that were interspersed with music videos.

In developing its programming strategy, however, Viacom's interest was not in promoting certain specific programs or stars—all of which may have short-lived popularity of fame—but in building its networks as unique brands. For example, on the MTV channel, the goal was to attract viewers because of what the channel as a whole personified— an appeal to youth. Soon, MTV reached 250 million households in 74 countries. Viacom began to perform much better: in 1992 it made profits of $48 million on sales of $1.86 billion, and in 1993 it made profits of $70 million on sales of $2 billion. While the development of innovative programming was one reason for Viacom's return to profitability, a second reason was Redstone's emphasis on keeping costs under control. Redstone is well known for his frugal way of doing business. He runs Viacom in a cost-conscious manner and this is evident throughout the organization. For example, costs soared in Hollywood studios and television networks as movie stars, writers, and production companies demanded ever increasing prices for their services. At Viacom, Redstone demanded that its own programming should be made by using low-cost, homegrown talent. An example of this is in the production of its MTV shows—most of its homegrown hosts are paid little compared to employees at well-known networks that are often paid millions of dollars per year.

Changes in the Media and Entertainment Industry

Although focused on building Viacom's programming strengths, Redstone and Biondi realized the entertainment industry was rapidly changing and that it was not at all clear how entertainment programming would be delivered, that is, through which distribution channels, in the future. In the 1990s, the U.S. cable television industry was in a state of flux as emerging technologies such as wireless satellite TV and Internet broadband threatened to bypass traditional cable systems—making Viacom's investment in wired cable much less valuable. Also, pressures were building to deregulate the industry so that by the end of the 1990s, companies in different industries—cable companies, telephone companies,

Internet service providers (ISPs), radio stations, and others, were allowed to enter each other's markets. These changes led to industry consolidation and the emergence of new giants such as Time Warner, News Corp., Comcast, and Disney, companies that were now all competing to offer the best selection of entertainment content or programming "software" as well as the best way to distribute this content through channels such as cable, wireless, or the Internet, the "hardware" side of the business.

Viacom's business model was based on the premise that to prosper in the fast-changing entertainment industry, a company needed to be the provider of the entertainment to all the different distribution channels. In other words, the most successful entertainment companies would be those that could offer programming suitable for any channel, and be the primary software providers—not the hardware providers that provided the infrastructure to bring entertainment into peoples' homes. With its well-known channels such as MTV, Nickelodeon, Showtime, and its syndicated programming, Viacom should base its strategy on forming alliances with the companies that provided the "hardware" channels into peoples' homes. Viacom's revenues would come both from the fees it charged to the hardware providers for its entertainment channels and most importantly, from the huge revenues it would obtain from selling advertising spots on its many popular TV shows, revenues that are determined by the size of the viewing audience. However, the issue was how to obtain high-quality programming at a price lower than the revenues to be earned from advertising and distributing its programs to maximize profits in an industry in which the value of entertainment and media companies was rocketing as stock prices increased.

The Paramount and Blockbuster Acquisitions

Viacom's new mission was to become an entertainment software-driven company with the goal to drive its entertainment content through every distribution channel possible, and to every world region to maximize revenues and profits. To achieve this mission, Viacom needed to acquire companies that could produce unique entertainment programming content for worldwide distribution. In particular, Viacom needed an entertainment company that had an established film/TV studio and library that could round out Viacom's current programming portfolio by supplying old feature films and TV shows to its television channels. Paramount Pictures provided an opportunity for this when it became an acquisition target in 1993.

Paramount's many businesses included entertainment including the production, financing, and distribution of motion pictures, television programming, the operation of movie theaters, independent television stations, regional theme parks, and Madison Square Garden. Paramount also owned a large library of movies. Redstone and Biondi began to picture the extensive synergies that a merger with Paramount would provide Viacom in the future. As Redstone told reporters, "This merger is not about two plus two equaling four, but six, or eight, or ten." Together Viacom and Paramount would be a much more efficient and profitable organization because, for example, Paramount could make films that featured MTV characters like Beavis and Butthead and new cable TV channels supported by Paramount's library of 1,800 films and 6,100 television programs. In 1993, after behind-the-scene talks between Redstone and Paramount executives, Paramount announced an $8.2 billion merger with Viacom. However, a bidding war for Paramount started when Barry Diller, CEO of QVC Network Inc., another large entertainment company, announced a hostile bid for Paramount. On September 20, 1993, QVC announced an $80 per share or $9.5 billion bid for Paramount, and the battle between Viacom and QVC for ownership of Paramount Communications Inc. had begun.

This unwelcome bid from QVS was a major problem for Redstone because Viacom still had a substantial debt due to the original 1987 acquisition of Viacom, and the expenses incurred to rapidly develop its own TV programming. Redstone could not afford to counter QVS's bid unless he obtained other sources of financing and cash flow. At the same time, Blockbuster Video's energetic CEO, Wayne Huizinga, who had made it the largest chain of video stores in the nation, was also on the market. Blockbuster was cash rich because of its rapid growth, but Huizinga recognized the growing threat that digital electronic entertainment channels, such as pay-per-view, wireless cable, and the

Internet, could pose to the sale and rental of movies and games in the future was looking for a buyer for Blockbuster. Redstone also knew that Blockbuster's future was in doubt because of the development of new digital entertainment distribution technologies, but now Redstone was in a war with Diller to acquire Paramount, and offers for the company soared. In January 1994, Viacom announced an $8.4 billion merger with Blockbuster; it also announced a higher bid for Paramount of $105 a share—a huge premium price—but this bid allowed Viacom to acquire Paramount in July 1994. Redstone hailed the new Viacom as an "entertainment colossus" and "a massive global media company."

Explosive Growth

In a few short years, Redstone had gone from controlling several hundred movie theaters to controlling the properties and franchises of three *Fortune 500* companies—Viacom, Blockbuster, and Paramount. By engineering the 3-way merger of Viacom, Paramount, and Blockbuster Entertainment, Redstone created one of the three largest global media empires (the others were Disney/Capital Cities ABC, and AOL Time Warner) each with annual revenues in excess of $10 billion. This was a large jump from the $2 billion revenue that Viacom had generated just before its new acquisitions. It was clear that Redstone and Biondi faced several major challenges to manage Viacom's new entertainment empire to allow it to achieve profitable growth.

Engineering Synergies

To justify the expensive purchase of Paramount and Blockbuster, it was essential that CEO Biondi engineer synergies between Viacom's different entertainment properties, each of which was now organized as a separate business division. Efforts began immediately, Paramount executives were instructed to evaluate the potential of new shows developed by MTV and Nickelodeon to sell to television networks. Viacom launched a new TV channel, the United Paramount Network (UPN) in 1995 to take advantage of its new programming resources across its entertainment divisions. For example, MTV executives were instructed to quickly begin developing programming for UPN.

In another attempt to create synergies, Paramount executives were instructed to make their moviemaking skills available to the MTV Network, and to help it make inexpensive movies that could be distributed through Paramount. One result of this was a "Beavis and Butthead" movie produced by Paramount that proved very successful when it was launched in theatres in 1996. To keep costs low, Redstone's strategy was to boost the output of movies at Paramount, while at the same time keeping its budget under control and forcing its managers to find ways to make low-budget successful movies—not an easy task. Redstone and Biondi also searched for synergies between Blockbuster and Viacom's other divisions, hoping that Blockbuster could link its retail stores with Viacom's cable networks and Paramount's extensive film library. Perhaps Blockbuster could sell copies of Paramount's vast library of movies to encourage people to create their own DVD collections. Also, the release of a new Paramount movie on DVD could be timed to coincide with a major advertising campaign in Blockbuster stores to promote the launch. Finally, the launch of new movies could be timed to accompany a major advertising blitz on the MTV channel—something that happened when Paramount released *Mission Impossible* in 1996. Redstone claimed that: "Viacom through its new combination of assets is poised to participate in, and in many ways define, the entertainment and information explosion about to engulf the globe." As events turned out, however, few potential synergies emerged between Viacom's various divisions to help boost revenues and profits.

Media and Entertainment Industry Challenges

The fast-changing entertainment and media industry created many challenges for Redstone and Biondi especially because the major U.S. entertainment companies were all rapidly expanding and the industry was consolidating. Seven major studios dominated movie production and the "Big Three" networks—ABC, CBS, and NBC—had for years dominated the production of TV programming for the mass audience. The growing strength of Viacom spurred industry consolidation; in 1995 AOL Time Warner announced that it would merge with Turner Broadcasting; Disney announced that it would merge with Capital Cities/ABC; and News Corp. that had established the Fox channel and owned the 20th Century Fox was also buying new entertainment channels—especially online digital channels. As a result, the industry was now composed of four major players: Disney, AOL Time Warner, News Corp., and Viacom, which was the fourth biggest company.

A major threat by the mid-1990s was that the number of entertainment distribution channels was exploding as government regulations prevented broadcast networks from owning TV programming companies and so on were phased out. Viacom's strategy to develop a full line of movie and TV entertainment programming had also spurred changes in the competitive dynamics of the entertainment and media industry as many new small independent movie and TV studios, such as Pixar and DreamWorks, were established to provide attractive new programming that could be sold to movie distributors and cable TV providers.

The industry was also experiencing rapid globalization as U.S. movies, news, and TV shows were now being shown around the world. A major challenge facing Viacom was to obtain access to the global marketplace to increase revenues and profits, for example, there was a potential market of over a billion viewers in India and China. As one example of Viacom's global strategy in 1995, Viacom won a cable television license to launch its Nickelodeon and VH-1 channels in Germany, Europe's biggest and potentially most lucrative media market, to complement the MTV pop music network that had operated in Europe since 1987. However, all this global expansion was expensive and Viacom's cost structure increased, which resulted in lower profits.

New technology challenges also confronted Viacom and the media industry because advances in digital technology, including streaming audio and video over the Internet began to offer online companies viable new channels to distribute entertainment content. Just as the dominance of the Big Three networks had been eroded by the growth of companies like Viacom with its new programming networks, so now new channels to distribute content to consumers were now threatening major entertainment companies. Moreover, digital piracy had become a major threat to these companies, as Websites such as Napster and LimeWire were developed to exchange digital music and movie files. This was also a major threat to revenues and profits and by the 2000s digital piracy resulted in major entertainment companies losing billions in potential revenues—even new movie releases were often available illegally online for download just days after being introduced in movie theaters.

Major Problems for Viacom

Soon after Redstone's expensive decision to buy Paramount, its new movie *Forrest Gump* became a surprise hit that generated over $250 million for Viacom and silenced analysts who argued that he had spent far too much to purchase the movie studio. Viacom's managers began to feel like *Forrest Gump* with his philosophy that: "Life is like a box of chocolates: You never know what you're going to get." It seemed that Redstone and Viacom had been in the right place at the right time and had made a profitable acquisition. Just as Redstone had sensed the potential of MTV, he had also sensed the potential of Paramount and Blockbuster. By the end of 1995, however, the selection of chocolates in Viacom's box had gone downhill as many of the hoped-for synergies were not obtained. Before the merger, Redstone claimed that Blockbuster would be valuable to Viacom as a distributor of its creative programming—but few benefits of this kind were achieved. Analysts argued that Paramount had to cooperate more closely with Viacom's cable TV channels and Blockbuster to achieve synergies.

Most importantly, both the Paramount and Blockbuster divisions' performance had proved disappointing. The Gump smash hit was followed by a string of expensive failures that lost hundreds of millions, and Redstone began to realize that making hit movies is a highly risky business—past successes are no indication of future success. Paramount's share of box office revenues dropped by 5% during 1995, but the marketing and production costs to make its movies were rapidly increasing. Paramount's poor performance hurt Viacom's cash flow and ability to pay its huge debts.

Viacom's situation was made worse because Blockbuster was also not performing well. Redstone bought Blockbuster at the peak of its success—when its revenues were doubling every year and its free cash flow was a valuable asset. But after the acquisition, Blockbuster ran into increased competition from new rival video chains, such as Hollywood Video, that were creating a price war in some markets, while pay-per-view and on demand television was spreading rapidly in large urban markets. Blockbuster's revenues were flat; its costs were increasing and the hoped-for growth in cash flow to service Viacom's debts did not occur.

Redstone fell out with the top management teams of Paramount and Blockbuster that he thought were doing a poor job; he forced the resignations of key executives and went in search of new leadership talent. Then, in 1996, he announced that he was firing his second-in-command Frank Biondi because Biondi did not have the "hands-on skills" needed to manage the kinds of problems that Viacom was facing. Redstone felt that Biondi's decentralized management style was out of place in a company actively searching for synergies and cost reductions. In place of Biondi he promoted his two lieutenants, Philippe Dauman and Tom Dooley, to orchestrate Viacom's strategy despite that they had little direct experience with the entertainment business.

Viacom's New Moves

In 1996, Redstone hired William Fields, a senior Walmart manager who had extensive experience using IT to run efficient retail operations, to be Blockbuster's new CEO. Redstone hoped he could find a way to transform the Blockbuster Video stores into broader based entertainment-software stores because video cassettes were being replaced by DVDs, and new wireless cable, DSL telephone, and direct broadcasting technologies, such as the DISH network, were rapidly expanding.

However, it was too late; in early-1996 Viacom's stock price plunged from $55 to $35 as investors fled the stock because of problems at Blockbuster and Paramount. By summer of that year, after a string of flops, Redstone announced plans to cut back the number of movies Paramount would make and to reduce its production costs as he searched for a new strategy. Chief among Viacom's problems was its huge debt that had to be pruned by selling its assets. Also, Viacom had to find ways to reduce rising operating costs as well new ways to leverage resources and competences across divisions to increase revenues and build cash flow. Flat revenues and soon-to-be losses at Blockbuster and Paramount were pulling down the performance of the whole corporation.

Blockbuster was now a growing liability, and Field's efforts were not bearing quick results.

In fact, Blockbuster's revenues were falling, and in 1997, Fields left and Redstone brought in a new CEO, John Antioco, and they streamlined Blockbuster's operations. (See the Blockbuster case for detailed information on its new strategy.) They also introduced the radical idea of video-rental revenue sharing with the movie studios, and within a few years, Blockbuster's revenue stream was increasing again.

On the revenue side, there were signs that some potential synergies were emerging. Paramount did produce successful *Beavis and Butthead* movies. Viacom's global presence was widening as its TV studios developed new and customized channels to meet the demands of customers in different countries around the world. In 1997, growing demand for its entertainment content led Viacom to buy the rest of Spelling Entertainment, with its *Star Trek* franchise, to help its struggling UPN network that was failing (it became part of CBS in 2006). Redstone integrated Spelling Entertainment into Paramount's TV operations to obtain economies of scale and scope in the production of new television programming—such as new *Star Trek* programming that has proved to be highly profitable.

Although Redstone was focused on creating long-term benefits from his entertainment empire, the poor performance of Viacom's stock was a continual embarrassment to him because he had not been able to realize the potential of Viacom's entertainment assets. However, Blockbuster enjoyed increasing revenues in 1999 because of its revenue sharing agreement, and this gave Redstone the opportunity he needed to dispose of this risky asset. Viacom announced that Blockbuster stock would be listed separately from Viacom's so its performance could be evaluated separately. Approximately 18% of Blockbuster's stock was sold at $16 to $18 a share, and this raised over $250 million that was used to pay off Viacom's debt.

Also in 1999, Redstone hired the experienced media and entertainment manager, and former head of CBS, Mel Karmazin, as Viacom's CEO to help solve its ongoing problems. Karmazin had made his reputation by selecting hit TV programming, and for his hands-on ability to find ways to leverage resources to increase profitability. He set to work to restructure Viacom's different entertainment assets to engineer cross-divisional synergies, create new programming content, and enhance its revenue and earnings.

Both Redstone and Karmazin understood that the most important source of profits from owning an entertainment empire was to achieve economies of scale and scope that arise when a company is able to offer large companies the opportunity to advertise their products across multiple channels that attract different kinds of viewers. In other words, a potential advertiser could produce one or more themed commercials to run across all of Viacom's different TV networks as well as its movies, theme parks, and other channels. Redstone noted that Disney merged with the Capital/ABC networks to provide it with important new distribution and advertising channels for the Disney franchise.

Since the majority of Viacom's future revenue stream would come from the success of its advertising, Redstone established a new unit, Viacom Plus, to provide a centralized advertising service to manage relationships with large companies and handle advertising for *all* of Viacom's divisions. For example, in 2001, Procter & Gamble (P&G) and Viacom Plus negotiated a new cross-channel deal whereby P&G would pay $300 million for advertising spread across 9 of Viacom's major divisions. This deal worked out so well for P&G it paid $350 million in 2002 for advertising spread across 14 of Viacom's divisions. P&G could obtain a much better deal than if it negotiated with each Viacom channel separately and Viacom Plus had reduced the costs of managing the vital advertising process across the company. Other companies followed P&G's lead to "scatter" their advertising dollars across Viacom's different channels and reach different demographic groups including children who watched Nickelodeon, teens who tuned into MTV, and different groups of adults who watched its different network programming. The future of the Viacom advertising platform looked bright indeed, perhaps it could provide the platform for giving the company the synergies it needed to boost revenues and profits.

The CBS Acquisition

To capitalize on advertising synergies, a new opportunity arose in 1999 when CBS was in trouble because of falling ratings, and its managers were interested in merging with another entertainment company. Redstone decided that CBS's entertainment assets would give Viacom access to a much larger number of channels to reach the greatest number of viewers and listeners (CBS-owned Infinity Radio Broadcasting) of any media enterprise, spanning all ages and demographics from "cradle to cane." This would allow Viacom to become the premier outlet for large companies around the world because it could offer them the opportunity to achieve huge economies of scale and scope when spending their advertising dollars. Advertising content could be driven and promoted across all media segments, including broadcast and cable television, radio, outdoor advertising and new digital media. Also, channels such as MTV, MTV2, VH-1, and CMT could now be broadcast over Trinity's radio stations and over the Internet, and CBS's high-quality content, such as its news and sports programming, could be broadcast over all Viacom's properties. After the merger, Viacom's bigger empire would also give it more bargaining power with programming suppliers (to reduce programming costs) and allow it to maximize the effectiveness of its advertising salesforce across all its divisions. Perhaps Viacom's problem was that it was simply not big enough to generate higher revenues and profits?

In 2000, Viacom and CBS Corp. began the process of merging the operations of the two companies to create the largest global media company, because they believed that "biggest is the best." The range of Viacom's properties was now staggering in its scope, especially because CBS had acquired radio station owner Infinity Broadcasting and King World productions that syndicated such programs as *Jeopardy* and the *Oprah Winfrey Show*. Karmazin now gave his full attention to structuring and managing Viacom's new assets to realize the gains from sharing and leveraging the competencies of its divisions across all its entertainment operations—not an easy thing to do given all the uncertainties involved in managing their different business models and a rapidly changing industry environment.

However, it began to appear that the CBS acquisition had given Viacom the critical mass it needed to achieve advertising synergies and cost savings. Karmazin integrated Paramount's and CBS' television groups, and the new division consisted of 35 television stations reaching 18 of the top 20 U.S. television markets. CBS would now function as a local as well as a national broadcaster, and it could

leverage its news, sports, and other programming across many more of Viacom's channels. Viacom's TV studios also formed a unit called MTV Films to produce movies for Paramount. Some of its low-budget movies made a profit including *The Rugrats* and *Beavis and Butthead Do America*.

In yet another move to make it the number 1 advertising platform in the world for advertisers with programming that appealed to every demographic category, in 2001, Viacom acquired Black Entertainment Television (BET) for $3 billion. The BET network reaches 63.4 million U.S. households, and its other channels, like BET on Jazz and BET International, reach 30 countries in Europe and 36 in Africa. Continuing its strategy of leveraging value from its properties, BET began to seek ways to integrate its activities with other Viacom properties, both by customizing various Viacom TV programming for BET's channels, and vice versa, such as its popular shows and also news and sports programming.

Karmazin instructed all of Viacom's networks to follow MTV's lead and develop a global strategy to locally produce content in each country in which they were broadcasting in order to increase the company's global viewing audience. MTV, for example, has a presence in most of the world's major markets; it reaches a billion households and generates crucial revenues for Viacom today. And, while it broadcasts its U.S. programming in countries abroad, it had also produced successful shows in countries abroad that are customized to local tastes; these have proved so popular that they have been successfully transferred to the United States and other countries.

Viacom's stock climbed in 2002 despite the huge fall in advertising revenues caused by the 2000 recession that caused the earnings of its broadcast networks to drop by 20%. Nevertheless, analysts believed that Viacom was the best-positioned media company to benefit from the upswing in advertising that was expected in the 2000s because of its combination of large-scale operations and leading brands. Reeling from the downturn in advertising revenues, Redstone and Karmazin continued to seek ways to counter future threats to the Viacom empire particularly because the threat from digital and broadband technology was directly impacting its Blockbuster unit, and would in the future, threaten Viacom's distribution channels.

Indeed, many analysts reported that Mel Karmazin and Redstone had locked heads on many occasions about emerging strategic issues having to do with digital and programming content. Karmazin was especially critical of Redstone's expensive acquisitions that increased debt, but had not yet realized the benefits that had been expected. Karmazin also argued that Viacom needed to increase its online presence as quickly as possible. However, in 2002, the increased revenues and profits resulting from the CBS and BET acquisitions suggested that Redstone's "growth-by-acquisition" strategy was working. Karmazin joked that their management styles were complementary, and that he was in no rush to assume leadership of Viacom, especially since the 79-year-old Redstone was "good for another 30–40 years—at least!" Redstone, however, joked that when Karmazin's contract expired in 2003, Karmazin "might want to retire." Karmazin's response? "Never, never, never."

New Problems for Viacom

In the early-2000s, Viacom made no significant acquisitions, Redstone felt his company has all the right pieces of entertainment property in place and the company still had a huge debt load. Redstone believed the primary strategic problem facing Karmazin was to manage Viacom's assets to realize the huge potential stream of advertising revenues and profits locked up in its entertainment assets. Operating revenues from its entertainment division, which included Paramount Pictures and theme parks, rose by 46% in 2003, and its operating income was up 15% to $66 million as a result of higher movie ticket sales and stronger sales of DVDs. Its Viacom Plus unit continued to aggressively market its "one-stop-shopping approach across all marketing channels," and as the economy picked up in 2003, advertising revenues rebounded. In 2004, Viacom announced its overall revenues were up 11% and half the increase was due to increased advertising revenues.

The Growing Use of the Internet

While national advertising revenues on Viacom's many cable channels rebounded, however, local advertising revenues from its TV stations, including the CBS network, and from its radio stations were falling and hurting the company's performance; fewer and fewer people were watching or listening to local

channels—preferring to watch their favorite cable channels or to surf the Web. Slowly but steadily, the growing use of the Internet and new online digital media properties were taking away advertising revenues and Viacom was slow to realize the dangers the Internet posed as a major alternative entertainment channel. Competition began to increase as new Websites that offered specialist services, such as www.rottentomatoes.com (a movie review Website owned by News Corp.), video Websites such as YouTube, and a host of illegal Websites that offered free downloading of video content, had emerged. Viacom's revenues fell, but perhaps this was a temporary phenomenon because Redstone and Karmazin announced they expected major increases in revenues and profits in the future.

Problems at CBS

Another major problem for Viacom was that its acquisition of CBS was not generating the hoped for cost savings or synergies that drive revenue growth. When a company buys different kinds of media properties and channels, it also enters new industries and faces different sets of competitive opportunities and threats! Investors became increasingly wary of Viacom's stock because they no longer believed Redstone or Karmazin could manage its new assets—and they found it much more difficult to evaluate the real value of each of its many media properties and channels, especially its Blockbuster division.

Spinning off Blockbuster into a separate company would eliminate this source of uncertainty; in 2004, when Blockbuster's stock was trading at a recent new high of $20, Viacom announced it would divest its remaining shareholding in Blockbuster. By making the deal attractive to Viacom stockholders, Redstone was finally able to divest the unit which became an independent company headed by its CEO John Antioco. (See the Blockbuster case for what has happened since.)

Viacom's Failing Business Model: Bye Bye CBS

Viacom had failed to realize the importance of building strong online entertainment assets when they were cheap, and it now lagged behind major competitors like Disney and News Corp. At the same time, despite having spent 5 years developing strategies to realize the value from the 2000 CBS acquisition, it was clear that Redstone and Karmazin had failed. Adding TV and radio stations and a host of other media assets to Viacom's TV channel and movie programming empire had increased the strategic problems associated with managing its empire of media assets. Redstone learned the hard way that the different divisions of a company grow at different rates, and the performance of the weakest division pulls down the performance of the whole company—and Viacom's growth was slowing fast. Its CBS assets, like Blockbuster had before, could not meet Viacom's aggressive growth targets. Redstone was frustrated once again that Viacom's underperforming assets were dragging down its stock price, which by 2004, was almost half of its 2000 stock price! Karmazin had warned Redstone about this, and the personal relationship between Redstone and Karmazin now deteriorated fast. Redstone fired Karmazin (who was the CEO of SiriusXM Radio in 2011).

In 2005, to improve Viacom's future growth, Redstone announced that he would split the $60 billion conglomerate into two smaller, separately traded companies. CBS would be allocated Viacom's slow and steady growth properties and channels, such as CBS TV programming and TV and radio stations, Showtime, outdoor advertising, and so on. The future Viacom would be made up of high potential growth properties and channels such as MTV, Nickelodeon, BET Networks, and Paramount Studios—essentially the company's focus after it divested Viacom, and before it merged with CBS. CBS was also allocated slow-growth Paramount Parks, which it later sold to amusement park operator Cedar Fair in 2006. The split took effect at the beginning of 2006 and effectively retracted the Viacom/CBS merger.

The New Viacom Business Model

After a decade of growth by acquisition, Viacom, like other media conglomerates, such as Sony, Disney, and Time Warner, began to reconfigure its business model. These companies were now being pushed hard by new Internet technologies and changing customer viewing habits that had altered the channels on which they could hope to obtain maximum advertising revenues—still the main source of revenues upon which most entertainment companies depended. By the 2000s, the cookie-cutter business model, whereby a media giant could simply add new media properties to its existing ones to increase profitability, had been shown to be a failure—at least in terms of generating consistent increases in a company's stock price.

As noted above, Redstone's focus upon fixing the ongoing problems with his media empire also delayed his recognition of the growing importance of the Internet as an entertainment distribution channel and the threat of competition from (illegal) digital video downloading and streaming media. In the mid-2000s, Viacom moved to acquire some small Internet media properties such as Neopets, a virtual pet Website, and Xfire, iFilm, Quizilla.com, Harmonix Music Systems, and Atom Entertainment, that served niche markets. However, these acquisitions didn't have the reach of News Corp.'s acquisition of the social networking company MySpace, which was valued at $3 billion (although it had been bought for only a few hundred million in 2004). Viacom was much slower than its rivals to react to the changes in digital and Internet technologies taking place, and its stock price continued to suffer. The entertainment company with the best digital strategy in the 2000s had been News Corp.

As the "unknown" names of its Internet acquisitions suggest, Viacom was failing in its attempt to develop a strong, coherent Internet strategy. This strategic failure hurt its stock price, which had risen to $45 after the 2005 split, but now plunged to $35 in 2006. Redstone, as usual, responded by firing Viacom's CEO, blaming him for the company's poor performance, and appointed Philippe Dauman as the new CEO of Viacom. Dauman had been one of Redstone's top strategists for decades, and a top Viacom executive from 1994 to 2000— he was now in charge of maximizing the value from Viacom's assets.

In his first public statement, Dauman claimed he had free reign to develop a new business model, and that he wasn't simply a pawn for Redstone to use and then discard. If Redstone attempted to micromanage or meddle in operational issues Dauman said, "I can push back." He also indicated he would work to create a new business model based on "creative excellence" and focus on strategic movie, TV channel and Internet internal ventures and acquisitions. Dauman claimed Viacom still had an enormous potential for achieving internal "organic growth," meaning that it could innovate new entertainment products internally and increase the value from its first-class set of entertainment properties and channels. He noted that BET and Comedy Central had a huge future potential and that even established brands such as MTV and Nickelodeon could be developed to offer a much wider range of programming to attract different kinds of customers. As a result, Viacom would be able to increase its advertising revenues by offering large companies the opportunity to reach the mass audience, and targeted marketing toward specific customer groups, which was becoming increasingly important in the 2000s. Once again, a division similar to Viacom's centralized marketing division, which had been closed down, was reactivated to focus on increasing advertising revenues. If this failed, then further divestitures seemed likely because the new Viacom had to realize the value from its assets in order to pay down its huge debt.

In late-2006, Viacom reported a 16% fall in third-quarter profit as weakness at the box office from unprofitable movies offset strength in cable and higher advertising revenues. Viacom's recovering share price plunged; as usual, Redstone fired someone, this time its chief financial officer, and he said that Viacom would now "move rapidly to the forefront of emerging digital markets, keeping us on the path to outstanding long-term financial performance and free cash flow generation." Clearly, even managing a smaller, more focused media company to achieve profitable growth is a difficult task—especially when each of its different divisions face complex problems and agile competitors.

Dauman's Creates a Successful Business Model for Viacom

In 2007, CEO Dauman faced difficult choices in deciding upon the right corporate and business strategies to pursue to create a profitable future business model for the company. Having an 83-year-old owner in charge was probably not the best thing for Dauman, or for Viacom's shareholders, apart from Redstone himself, of course. Dauman set to work after observing the reasons for the failures and firings of its several last CEOs. Since 2007, Dauman has made few acquisitions, although it bought

RateMyProfessors.com in 2007, and acquired the global franchise for *Teenage Mutant Ninja Turtles* in 2009. He did however, form several strategic alliances to increase the value of Viacom's assets such as several joint ventures with Indian companies to expand its presence in a country with almost a billion viewers, and with U.S. media companies to find better ways to make use of their resources. He also sold some of its little-known online assets such as Harmonix Music Systems and Famous Music to Sony to exit the music business.

His new focus was upon finding ways to use Viacom's assets in creative ways. For example, he created a new specialty movie division called Paramount Vantage, and Paramount decided to take control of distributing its own movies in the 15 major markets outside the United States. Also, a major rebranding of its TV networks took place as the company developed increasing numbers of TV channels to further segment its network viewing audience to directly target specific customer groups. For example, its Nickelodeon network now includes channels such as Nickelodeon, Nick at Night, Nick.com, Nick Jr., Teen Nick, Nickelodeon Kids, Nick Toons, Nickelodeon Virtual Worlds, and Family Games! The costs of such increased differentiation and market segmentation has been spurred by the development of digital technologies that dramatically reduce the costs involved in creating new channels. At the same time, differentiation provides a way to attract advertisers, who wish to focus on a specific market segment and are willing to pay for it. It has made the same kinds of changes to its global MTV networks that today allow for increasing customization of programming, both between and within countries, and new ideas are quickly transferred around the world and have resulted in several hit new shows.

Most importantly, Dauman recruited a top management team of media experts to develop hit new shows for its networks, shows that could be made at relatively low costs, such as reality programming. In the last 5 years, Viacom has excelled at creating new shows that have resulted in major increases in its advertising revenues and profits. At the same time, Dauman has been vigilant to protect the value of Viacom's digital content, and in 2009, it sued Google because it claimed its YouTube channel was allowing the streaming of thousands of its TV shows and movies. It lost the suit, but Google has been forced to more closely monitor the content being uploaded onto YouTube. In addition, realizing it was too late to establish its own online entertainment distribution channels, Dauman has been increasingly working to form strategic alliances with distribution companies such as Netflix and Hulu and license the rights to show its programming content in return for a share of the revenues. Given that once the programming has been made and shown on its own networks, where it receives advertising revenues to cover the costs of production and make a profit, almost all the revenues it makes from online streaming agreements translate into profits. This is also true of streaming its Paramount movies through other distribution channels, where it can at least obtain some revenue by attracting customers that dislike illegal downloading, and are willing to pay a modest fee to obtain Viacom's content in a safe and legal manner. Every dollar Viacom obtains from licensing its content results in 90% profit because the costs of making its content available to Internet distributors are extremely low.

Viacom in 2011

How well has Dauman's new business strategy succeeded? Perhaps the best way to evaluate this is to look at Viacom's financial results released in August 2011, and the new business model behind the company. Viacom announced that its third-quarter earnings grew 37% because its portfolio of entertainment properties resulted in growing advertising sales and higher fees from cable TV companies that wish to show its programming, and by online companies, such as Netflix, that want to stream its content. The media company earned $574 million, or $0.97 per share, up 37% from $420 million (or $0.69 per share) a year earlier.

Advertising and programming revenues grew because of the success of its new movies, TV networks and its new TV shows such as "Jersey Shore" and "16 and Pregnant." CEO Dauman said the "breadth of hit programming found across Viacom's

media network portfolio was the major contributor to its strong advertising growth. In a press release, Dauman said: "Our media networks are creating hit after hit, sought after by both audiences and advertisers, and Paramount Pictures is putting together a truly unprecedented year of box office success." Viacom said revenue from its media or TV networks division that includes MTV, Nickelodeon and other channels grew 16%; revenues from its Paramount film division increased by 13%, thanks to gains in DVD sales and TV license revenue. At the same time, global advertising revenue grew by 14%, which was more than in the previous quarter—a sign that the global advertising market was improving.

In addition, Viacom's efforts to secure more revenues from the cable and wireless TV providers, and online digital providers that want to show its entertainment content, also increased by 19%. This includes revenues from Viacom's older TV shows such as "SpongeBob SquarePants," and especially from new shows such as "Jersey Shore" and Comedy Central's "The Sarah Silverman Show." Its agreement with Hulu and Netflix significantly boosted revenues. Its blockbuster film *Transformers: Dark of the Moon* was released too late to contribute to its reported profits, so it expects a continuing improvement in revenues through 2011.

In 2011, it seemed that Dauman had been able to realize the value in Viacom's assets, and had been able to develop new potential sources of revenue. He had also kept the company's cost structure under control while pursuing new low-cost digital avenues to expand its revenues. How well has Viacom performed compared to its competitors over the last 5 years? In August 2011, while its stock price had increased by 150%, Disney's had increased by 20%, while News Corp. had fallen by 16%, and Time Warner's had fallen by 38%. Under Dauman, Viacom finally appears to be managing its entertainment assets and channels to add value to the company; if its good performance continues, it will be able to reduce its debt and develop new entertainment content that will provide new sources of revenue and profit for the future.

Endnotes

www.amazon.com, 1997–2011.
Amazon.com, Annual and 10K Reports, 1997–2011.

CASE 25

Ecomagination: Driving Sustainable Growth for GE

"GE should be commended for a bold approach to climate issues. However, the company has a long way to go before it can legitimately claim to be an environmentally progressive company."[1]
—**Jeff Jones, Communications Director, Environmental Advocates of New York,**[2] in 2009.

Green Can Be Green!

On June 24, 2009, US-based technology giant General Electric Company (GE), surpassed its target of investing US$5 billion in research and development in its environmental initiative, Ecomagination. GE had earlier set 2010 as the target for achieving this goal but reached it a year ahead of schedule.[3] The company planned to invest an additional US$10 billion in R&D by 2015. It was also on its way to achieving the US$20 billion mark in revenues from Ecomagination products, having generated US$18 billion in 2009, an increase of 6%. GE expected the Ecomagination revenue to grow at twice the rate of the total company revenue by 2015, which would give Ecomagination an even larger share of the total company sales. According to Steve M. Fludder (Fludder), vice president, Ecomagination, "We have grown Ecomagination revenue and research and development every year, even in challenging economic times. Given our success, we are committing to do more. The vision of a cleaner, affordable, secure, and globally accessible energy infrastructure inspires and motivates us."[4]

Established in 1892, GE is a diversified conglomerate with products and services ranging from aircraft engines and power generation to business and consumer financial services, healthcare, and television programming. Started in 2005, Ecomagination embodied GE's commitment to building innovative clean energy technologies and meeting customers' demands for more energy-efficient products and bringing reliable growth for the company. The main objectives of this green initiative were to reduce greenhouse gas (GHG) emissions, increase energy efficiency of GE operations, improve water use, double the investment in R&D for cleaner technologies, and keep the public informed about its Ecomagination efforts.

Through Ecomagination, GE developed products and services with lower environmental impact, such as energy-efficient engines, appliances, locomotives, and wind turbines. According to some analysts, Ecomagination was a business opportunity for GE to increase revenues by introducing energy-efficient products to customers.

However, some critics felt that Ecomagination was just a business savvy move by the company, aimed at resurrecting its image as an environment friendly company. Behind the façade of environmental sustainability and green technologies was GE's corporate goal of increasing profits, they alleged. Critics felt that the initiative was over-hyped and that GE was pursuing profits in the name of clean technologies. According to Kavita Prakash Mani, vice president of SustainAbility,[5] "GE has invested billions of dollars in Ecomagination, but it hasn't really changed the rest of its business. It's made out to be bigger than it actually is."[6] Executives from GE, however, maintained that Ecomagination was not a brand building exercise; it was a good business opportunity for GE to make money while at the same time contributing to environmental sustainability. "It's not an advertising ploy or marketing gimmick. GE wants to do this because it is right, but also we plan to make money while we do so,"[7] said Peter O'Toole (O'Toole), director of public relations at GE.

This case was written by Syeda Maseeha Qumer, under the direction of Debapratim Purkayastha, IBS Center for Management Research. It was compiled from published sources, and is intended to be used as a basis for class discussion rather than to illustrate either effective or ineffective handling of a management situation.

About GE

GE was formed in 1892 by the merger of the Edison General Electric Company (EGEC) and the Thomas-Houston Electric Company[8] (TEC). By the 1950s, GE had grown into a large industrial conglomerate with interests in diverse businesses. In the late 1960s, GE had 46 Strategic Business Units (SBUs) within the company and also diversified into other new businesses like computers, nuclear power, and aircraft engines. In 1977, GE's earnings crossed the US$1 billion mark.

In 1981, an important phase began in GE's history when Jack Welch (Welch) was appointed as CEO. One of Welch's core strategies was the Number One Number Two strategy.[9] In 1995, GE's market value exceeded US$100 billion. In 1996, GE completed 100 years on the Dow Jones Industrial Average,[10] the only company remaining from the original list of 12 stocks, first published on May 26, 1896.

In mid-2001, Jeffrey R. Immelt (Immelt) succeeded Welch as the Chairman and CEO of GE. Within days of his taking over, the September 11, 2001 terrorist attacks occurred. As a result, GE too was affected by the changes in the business environment. Immelt then brought in several changes at the company in order to win investor confidence. The company was listed on the Dow Jones Sustainability Index in late 2004.[11] In the fiscal year ended December 2005, GE posted revenues of more than US$149 billion.

In 2009, *Forbes* ranked GE as the world's largest company with over 300,000 employees in its various business units. At the end of 2009, GE had six core business units and was the biggest manufacturer of power plants, jet engines, locomotives, and medical equipment worldwide[12] (Refer Exhibit I). GE Global Research consisted of more than 3,000 employees working in four state-of-the-art facilities at Niskayuna (New York), Bangalore (India), Shanghai (China), and Munich (Germany). In 2009, despite the tough economic climate, GE reported earnings of US$11.2 billion (Refer Exhibit II and III). In 2010, GE was ranked among *Fortune's* 'Most Admired Companies in the World' for the 5th consecutive year. In the second quarter ended June 2010, the company's revenues fell by 4% to US$37.4 billion. Industrial sales were US$24.4 billion, down 6% compared to corresponding period of the previous year.

Winds of Change at GE

According to some analysts, GE had not been known over the years as a particularly environment-friendly company. In fact, it was considered for a long time as one of the biggest corporate polluters in the US. Though the company delivered outstanding returns to shareholders, it lagged behind on the social responsibility front. GE was criticized on several occasions for its lack of social responsibility. However, the company chose to ignore its critics and gave precedence to profitability and financial goals rather than social and environmental objectives, added experts.

During the 1980s and 1990s, GE stonewalled and delayed most of its environmental initiatives, and this led to significant negative equity among many in the environmental community. One of the biggest environmental controversies involving GE was related to the pollution of the Hudson and Housatonic rivers in the US. In the early-1980s, GE was indicted for dumping several million of pounds of polychlorinated biphenyls (PCBs)[13] into stretches of the two rivers from its factories located along their banks. In 1977, after the US Congress passed the Clean Water Act,[14] the US Environment Protection Agency (EPA)[15] banned the production of PCB. Since most of GE's PCB dumping had been done before 1972, when the substance was not banned by law, the company argued that it was not responsible for the sediments already present in the rivers. But environmentalists argued that the dangerous nature of PCBs had been well known even before the law had been passed, and that GE had acted irresponsibly in dumping the chemicals in the rivers.

Between 1991 and 1996, EPA charged GE with 23 violations when toxic releases from its plants went unreported. In March 1992, the Nuclear Regulatory Commission (NRC)[16] slapped a fine of US$20,000 on GE for violating regulations at its fuel fabrication plant in Wilmington, North Carolina. It was reported that workers at the plant had accidentally moved about 320 pounds of uranium to a waste treatment tank, which could have led to a nuclear accident. Later, the NRC found that the mistake had been made because of lax safety controls at the plant. Again in March 1998, GE was fined US$92,000 for violations of environmental reporting requirements for toxic releases at its silicone manufacturing plant in Waterford, New York.

Though GE gave more significance to profitability than to social responsibility, the business environment prevailing in the early-2000s made companies look beyond financial goals. Sustainability became critical for business success as climate change, water scarcity, and poverty were seen as profound challenges for the global economy. During this time, the Kyoto Protocol[17] was a much discussed subject, and at global forums like the G8[18] and WTO[19] meetings, environmental sustainability became a hot topic. Moreover, as consumers and investors became more environmentally conscious than before, it became more important for companies to consider environmental sustainability in their operations.

In 2001, when Immelt succeeded Welch, the company started to focus more on addressing environmental challenges. Immelt felt that sustainability was a profitable business opportunity rather than a cost and hence seized on the idea of greening GE's technology and turning it into a corporate-wide strategy for growth. He felt that with creativity and imagination, it was possible to solve some of the world's most difficult environmental problems and make money while doing it. Immelt's new slogan was "green is green," meaning that green business equaled green money.

Immelt wanted GE to support climate change and invest in creating new markets for cleaner fuels and technologies as they offered opportunities for product innovation. He consulted executives from other companies who had launched environmental programs such as DuPont[20] Chairman and CEO, Charles Holliday Jr. They advised him to solve the company's earlier environmental problems and then go ahead with green product ideas.

In 2002, a large team of executives from GE attended a training session on CSR at Crotonville. As part of the training, the executives visited several companies that dealt with social and environmental issues such as IBM,[21] Eli Lilly,[22] BP,[23] and Nike.[24] They also interacted with regulators, activists, and investors, who had an interest in CSR. During the course of their training, the executives found that though GE was well known for its management quality and operations, it ranked low on the social responsibility aspect. They felt that for GE to maintain its position in the global economy, immediate steps had to be taken to build its image as an environmentally-friendly company.

In 2002, Christine Todd Whitman, the then EPA Administrator, issued a ruling related to the Hudson river clean-up that gave GE two options—to agree to an out of court settlement, or pay fines of up to US$2 billion.[25] In 2005, GE entered into an agreement with the EPA and the US Department of Justice to carry out a two stage clean-up of the Hudson River at an estimated cost of around US$750 million.[26]

In the early 2000s, GE launched several global initiatives in order to make the company more socially responsible. For instance, it started conducting audits on its suppliers to ensure that they were complying with globally accepted labor, environmental, health, and safety standards in their operations. In 2002, Immelt appointed Bob Corcoran, a long-time GE employee, as the company's first vice president for corporate citizenship. Immelt also restructured GE's business portfolio to include more companies operating in emerging industries and acquired companies such as Enron Wind Corp.,[27] Ionics Inc.,[28] Osmonics Inc.,[29] and AstroPower Inc.[30] The company began to invest in new technologies. For instance, in 2004, GE invested in a new coal technology called Integrated Gasification Combined-Cycle (IGCC), which filtered out GHG and pollutants when coal was burned for energy.[31]

As part of the green drive, Immelt began delegating preliminary tasks to various teams within the company like researching greenhouse legislation, formulating metrics, conducting customer surveys, prototyping new products, formulating cross-company guidelines, etc. The company's marketing team identified a B2B[32] market opportunity for green products and outlined the monetary benefits of these products to its customers.

In late 2004, a senior-level brainstorming session at GE set the stage for the companywide environmental initiative, Ecomagination. The initiative was initially greeted with skepticism by a majority of the senior level management as they felt that it would require huge investments. Senior executives posed questions such as "Do we want to attract attention?" and "Will this create problems around the Hudson River [issue]?" during internal discussions. Instead of stepping back, Immelt drew on the trust and support he had earned from his team and went ahead with the proposal. Since GE comprised many businesses, convincing the heads of each business unit was one of the toughest parts of the execution process. According to O'Toole, "Ecomagination had to enable our business leaders to work better with their customers. It couldn't be an 'unfunded mandate' from corporate. So there had to be give-and-take with our top leaders to ensure we were helping our customers."[33]

Some environmentalists too supported the initiative as it addressed environmental challenges such as global warming and climate change. According to Eileen Claussen, president of the Pew Center for Climate Change,[34] "We are still quite politically polarized on the issue of climate change in this country. The fact that a company that size wants to take a very public position to talk about their products in terms of climate change and then, most important of all, to say they want to be part of the policy dialogue, which is very difficult in the United States at this moment, is an act of courage."[35]

The Launch of Ecomagination

On May 9, 2005, Immelt announced the launch of the US$ 150 billion environmental initiative. According to GE's Ecomagination Website, Ecomagination is "a business initiative to help meet customers' demand for cleaner and more energy-efficient products and to drive reliable growth for GE."[36] Commenting on the initiative, Immelt said, "It's no longer a zero-sum game—things that are good for the environment are also good for business. We are launching Ecomagination not because it is trendy or moral, but because it will accelerate our growth and make us more competitive."[37]

The name 'Ecomagination', which was derived from GE's "Imagination at Work" slogan, addressed challenges such as the need for cleaner and more efficient sources of energy, reduced emissions, and new sources of clean water. Through Ecomagination, GE aimed to focus on its energy, technology, manufacturing, and infrastructure capabilities to develop new sustainable solutions and invest in technologies such as solar energy, hybrid locomotives, wind power generation, fuel cells, lower emission aircraft engines, efficient lighting, and water purification technologies and appliances.

Through Ecomagination, GE planned to invest in technologies such as biomimicry, nanotechnology, and other emerging clean technologies. Experts were of the view that at a time when most other companies were cutting back on R&D funding for projects that lacked clear market application with customers, GE, through the initiative, had created options to develop radical technologies which would take longer to develop but deliver results with large payoffs. According to Lorraine Bolsinger (Bolsinger), president and CEO of GE Aviation Systems LLC, "Ecomagination is for us, above everything else, a growth strategy. It is a business strategy based on the idea that by investing in technologies to help customers solve these big megatrends that we're seeing, to help them grow sustainably in this world—where there is more regulation, more scarcity, higher energy costs—that we can grow sustainably as well."[38]

As part of the initiative, GE committed itself to doubling its annual research investment in cleaner technologies, from US$700 million in 2004 to US$1.5 billion in 2010.[39] During the same period, GE aimed to double its revenue from Ecomagination products and services to US$20 billion annually and expected more than half of its product revenue to come from such products by 2015. GE set a target to reduce GHG emissions from its factory operations by 1% by 2012 from a 2004 baseline and to improve energy efficiency by 30% by the end of 2012.[40]

GE promoted Ecomagination widely through advertisements and other promotion campaigns, as part of its 'keeping the public informed' objective. It launched an integrated advertising campaign in the television, print, and online media to make consumers aware of the company's energy-efficient products available in the market. Besides advertisements, GE also launched an exclusive Website and several short online films. In October 2005, GE partnered with Dow Jones to launch a US$50,000 prize competition called "ECOnomics: The Environmental Business Plan Challenge" which invited entrepreneurs, executives, and students to submit eco-friendly business ideas. In September 2006, GE in association with MtvU[41] rolled out the "MtvU GE Ecomagination Challenge" wherein college students across the US were asked to submit innovative ideas for projects that would make their institutions more environmentally responsible. In 2008, GE launched a comprehensive campaign to promote its Smart Grid technology. According to Jeff Renaud, Director of GE's Ecomagination program, "Looking at GE's overall advertising and digital media efforts, it's clear that Ecomagination is a core element . . . We also believe that Ecomagination has had and will continue to have a positive impact on GE's overall brand value."[42]

Ecomagination at Work

One of the vital components of GE's Ecomagination program was to build strategic partnerships with corporations and governments around the world, universities, and research institutions to solve energy needs.

In 2005, GE Energy Financial Services entered into a partnership with AES Corporation[43] to develop a venture called Greenhouse Gas Services[44] in the US. The goal of the partnership was to offset the equivalent of an annual production volume of 10 million metric tons (MMT) of carbon dioxide gas by 2010 through the reduction of methane emissions from landfill gas, coal mines, and agricultural waste. In 2008, Greenhouse Gas Services joined with Google, Inc.[45] to codevelop a GHG reduction project[46] at a landfill in Caldwell County, North Carolina.

According to GE's 2005 Ecomagination Report, in 2004 and 2005, the company had undertaken nearly 500 global energy conservation projects which had led to substantial energy cost savings and a reduction of more than 250,000 tons of GHG emissions, equivalent to keeping nearly 50,000 cars off the road.[47] Between 2005 and 2009, GE financed and invested in 247 megawatts of solar projects, including one of the world's largest, the 11-megawatt Serpa solar plant in Portugal. The company focused not only on individual projects but also invested capital in other companies that were developing solar power around the world. For instance, GE Oil & Gas Ecomagination technology played a vital role in the development of Asia's natural gas pipeline infrastructure to supply gas from Uzbekistan and Kazakhstan to China for meeting China's rising energy demands.

In May 2006, GE launched Ecomagination in China followed by its launch in Australia five months later. According to GE, China Ecomagination products brought significant growth to GE's business in China. In the first three quarters of 2009, GE's Ecomagination revenues in China reached US$656 million, an increase of 50% compared to the previous year. In 2009, GE signed 20 memorandums of under standing (MOUs) with central and local government bodies and 10 MOUs with state-owned-enterprises and Chinese universities to develop energy-efficient solutions in areas such as biogas solutions, wind power, clean coal technology, industrial emissions reduction, aircraft engines, locomotives, etc.[48]

In February 2007, GE Aviation signed an MOU with Air India,[49] to make Air India's operations more sustainable by providing the airline's fleet with fuel-efficient engines. By using these engines, the airline was expected to save US$150 million over the next 15 years while establishing itself as an environmentally friendly service. In 2007, to combat severe potable water shortages in countries in Southeast Asia, Africa, and Latin America, GE provided solar energy modules and water filtration technologies to rural areas in these regions. In Africa, GE partnered with the Algerian government and the Algerian Energy Company to build the continent's largest desalination plant at Hamma.

GE also collaborated with end users and external partners to identify energy-saving lighting projects. In 2007, Wal-Mart[50] fitted refrigerated display cases with GE's light emitting diodes (LEDs) to reduce energy consumption in more than 500 of its retail stores. The same year, oil giant BP also formed a global alliance with GE to develop about 15 hydrogen power projects in order to cut GHG emissions from electricity generation.[51] Besides big companies, GE also partnered with non-profit organizations such as the World Resources Institute[52] and the Pew Center on Global Climate Change to check GHG emissions. According to Beth Comstock (Comstock), Chief Marketing Officer of GE, "Ecomagination has been strengthened by input from a variety of partners . . . When you're teamed with a partner who shares a common vision and commitment and complementary capabilities, a new kind of energy is created."[53]

As part of the Ecomagination initiative, GE rolled out several energy efficient and renewable energy technologies at its facilities too, including products such as solar panels and advanced lighting systems which it manufactured itself. Within the company, GE began engaging employees to see where energy savings could be achieved. It implemented initiatives such as turning off the lights when a factory was idle, installing LED lights on factory floors, recycling water at nuclear facilities, etc. GE installed solar panels on many buildings, including its headquarters, and energy efficient light bulbs in many of its factories. "Leading by example is the essence of Ecomagination. If we are proposing that customers and enterprises around the world use GE solutions to reduce their emissions, then we should do the same,"[54] said Fludder.

To reduce energy usage and GHG reductions, GE made use of the "Energy Treasure Hunts"[55] developed by Toyota.[56] GE carried out regular treasure hunt sessions from 2005 to identify energy-efficiency savings at a specific manufacturing site. For instance, at its, locomotive operations in Erie, Pennsylvania, GE switched to natural-gas fired power from oil, saving money and cutting emissions in the manufacture of locomotive engines. As of July 2010, GE had conducted 200 internal treasure hunts, which helped the company save more than US$130 million annually and contributed to reductions in excess of 250,000 metric tons of CO_2.[57]

In 2007, GE Transportation partnered with Union Pacific,[58] to launch hybrid locomotives capable of recycling thermal energy as stored power in on-board batteries. The energy stored in the batteries could reduce fuel consumption and emissions by as much as 10% compared to ordinary freight locomotives. In the automotive sector, GE Energy Financial Services[59] invested in the battery company, A123 Systems Inc.,[60] to develop the next generation of battery technology for hybrid and plug-in hybrid electrics. For instance, GE made an investment to help A123Systems roll out batteries for Norwegian electric car manufacturer Think Global.[61] Besides providing capital, GE, through GE Global Research, offered system design expertise and supported A123's power product development for electric grid applications, and designed battery system components for A123's automotive programs.

In May 2007, GE's media arm, NBC Universal[62] (NBCU), announced its "Green is Universal" initiative to bring about environmental awareness and educate consumers about environmental sustainability. NBCU aimed to reduce its GHG emissions at least 1% by 2012. As part of this effort, NBCU aired environmentally themed content through its on-air networks and online platforms during its Green Week (in November) and Earth Week (in April). In November 2009, NBCU's "Make Green Count" campaign was launched. This campaign encouraged audiences to make one small green change to their daily lives such as turning the lights off or walking to work.

Ecomagination Products

To ensure that Ecomagination products and services improved environmental performance, GE employed a rigorous review and qualification procedure known as the Ecomagination Product Review (EPR) process to assess which products and services should be included in the Ecomagination portfolio. The EPR process was carried out by the Ecomagination team comprising environmental health and safety counsel product marketing teams from the GE business units and corporate legal counsel. The evaluation process was audited by a third party. Product characteristics considered during the EPR process included environmental factors such as energy consumption, GHG emissions, and water usage, in addition to the financial benefits of the product to customers.

For products to be included in the Ecomagination portfolio they had to be better in terms of operating as

well as environmental performance, support growth of new technologies, and drive a more sustainable form of development. Talking about the product verification process, Bolsinger said, "If we got this great green technology, but it's totally unaffordable, we say no, that's not ready to be an ecoproduct. It has to be better, in terms of operating performance for the customer—to give them some economic return—as well as the environmental piece of it."[63]

As part of the EPR process, GE analyzed the environmental attributes of its products relative to benchmarks such as competitors' products, regulatory standards, and historical performance. It ensured that all Ecomagination products met the required criteria and that the product marketing was clear and substantiated. To provide independent, quantitative environmental analysis and verification of GE's product claims, GE partnered with GreenOrder.[64] The firm verified the product information and advised GE on the associated marketing claims of the products. For this purpose, GreenOrder developed a scorecard system for evaluating Ecomagination products and technologies. For each product, an extensive scorecard was created quantifying the product's environmental attributes, impact, and benefits relative to comparable products. The scorecards were then used to create product marketing claims. "This process is flexible enough to cover incredibly diverse industries, since Ecomagination creates, compares, measures, and launches products as small as a light bulb or as big as a jet engine,"[65] said Comstock.

As of June 2010, GE was marketing 90 Ecomagination certified products ranging from compact fluorescent lighting, smart grid components, and wind turbines, to smart appliances, aircraft engines, and water treatment technologies (Refer to Exhibit IV). Products developed under the Ecomagination umbrella were not limited to GE's manufacturing businesses alone but was also extended to the company's financial business. Once a product became a part of the Ecomagination portfolio it was reviewed regularly to ensure that performance claims were based on the latest relevant information and reflected any changes to the product itself or its market. R&D funding for Ecomagination products was provided by GE's four Global Research Centers and some major businesses of the company.

Between 2002 and 2005, GE invested more than US$350 million to develop high efficiency appliance products and to meet the ENERGY STAR[66] qualification for as many of its Consumer & Industrial products as possible. In 2005, GE invested more than US$60 million to develop 164 new ENERGY STAR qualified appliances. Again in 2007, the company invested approximately US$47 million to create 215 new ENERGY STAR qualified appliance models. In recognition of GE's commitment to developing high-efficiency appliance products, the US Department of Energy and the EPA awarded GE the ENERGY STAR Partner of the Year "Sustained Excellence" award for three consecutive years (2006–2008).[67]

In May 2007, GE launched 11 new Ecomagination products and services including a hybrid locomotive[68] and a carbon offset company. In July 2007, GE Money[69] launched the first-ever US credit card with a reward program known as GE Money Earth Rewards.[70] The program offered cardholders an easy way to offset their carbon impact and reduce carbon emissions by contributing up to 1% of their net spend to buy carbon offsets. On May 24, 2007, the GE and Masco Contractor Services[71] (MCS) Environments for Living division announced the Ecomagination Homebuilder Program to help residential developers and builders design homes which were are not only comfortable, but also more efficient in their energy consumption and indoor water consumption. Homes built under this program resulted in at least 20% saving in household energy, water consumption, and emissions compared to industry accepted new homes. In 2008, for the first time, GE Healthcare products joined the Ecomagination portfolio. These products not only provided outstanding clinical performance, but also offered significant savings. In 2010, GE launched two new products in the Ecomagination portfolio—the WattStation electric vehicle charger[72] and the Nucleus,[73] a real-time home energy monitor.

On July 13, 2010, GE launched a US$200 million global innovation challenge called the GE Ecomagination Challenge: Powering the Grid to create and adopt more efficient and economically sustainable electric grid technologies. The challenge invited technologists, entrepreneurs, and startups to design innovative business models, technologies, and processes that would bring clean, usable energy to the market through renewable energy, power grid efficiency, and eco homes. Co-funded by four venture capital firms,[74] the challenge aimed to leverage on GE's technical expertise and bring new ideas to market quickly. Until September 30, 2010, participants could submit proposals in three general categories—Renewable Energy, Grid Efficiency, and EcoBuildings/Homes. Each of the five innovation challenge award winners would receive US$100,000 in cash and bag a partnership deal with GE to develop and distribute the technology.

Results

According to analysts, Ecomagination was a turning point for the company, which had been grappling with the problem of an inconsistent green image. Since its launch in 2005, the initiative paid off in a big way as it helped GE to evolve as a sustainable enterprise and contributed to the rise in its brand value, they said. Talking about the success of the program, Immelt said, "Ecomagination is one of the most successful cross-company business initiatives in our recent history. It is a clear amplifier of our strong reputation for innovation and execution, harnessing the strength of every GE business to maximize returns for GE investors while minimizing our own energy use and greenhouse gas emissions."[75]

In 2005, revenues from the sale of Ecomagination products and services reached US$10.1 billion compared to US$6.2 billion in 2004.[76] Orders and commitments doubled to about US$17 billion. In 2006, revenues from the Ecomagination portfolio of products and services surged past US$12 billion, up 20% from 2005, while the order backlog increased to US$50 billion.[77] In 2007, Ecomagination revenues crossed US$14 billion, an increase of 15% from 2006.[78] For the first time, GE's investment in cleaner technology R&D crossed US$1 billion in 2007. In 2008, GE's revenues from Ecomagination grew by 21% to US$17 billion.[79] The company increased its investment in R&D of clean tech solutions by 27% to US$ 1.4 billion, up from US$750 million in 2005. In 2008, GE reduced GHG intensity by 41%, surpassing its goal of reducing it by 30%.

In the year 2009, which marked the fifth anniversary of the Ecomagination program, revenues from Ecomagination products and services grew by 6% to cross US$18 billion despite the global economic recession.[80] In 2009, GE invested US$1.5 billion on Ecomagination R&D. In 2009 GE's GHG emissions were 22% below its 2004 baseline and water consumption reduced by 30% compared to a 2006 baseline, surpassing the original goal of 20% by 2012. According to GE statistics, since the inception of Ecomagination, the company had invested a total of US$5 billion in its R&D investment and generated a total of US$70 billion in revenues through the end of 2009.[81] "Ecomagination is one of our most successful cross-company business initiatives. If counted separately, 2009 Ecomagination revenues would equal that of a Fortune 130 company and Ecomagination revenue growth equals almost two times the company average,"[82] said Immelt.

The Other View

Despite the positive aspects of this green initiative, some experts felt that GE could not call itself an eco-friendly company because of its history of pollution, particularly the dumping of PCBs in the Hudson River and the delay in cleaning it up. Some analysts charged that despite making tall claims about its products being environmental friendly, GE continued to sell coal-fired steam turbines and was involved in oil and gas extraction.

Some analysts accused GE of greenwashing as they felt that the Ecomagination initiative was meant to divert people's attention from the company's negligent stance toward environmental matters. Ecomagination was an attempt to cover up GE's poor environmental image and its continuing obsession with profit at the expense of the environment, they charged. According to Chris Ballantyn, director of the Hudson River Program, "Actions speak louder than words. When you scratch beneath the public relations surface, I'm afraid they have unfinished business in terms of environmental protection."[83]

Moreover, GE's annual US$1 million investment in marketing Ecomagination was criticized as an expensive branding exercise which amounted to greenwashing. Some experts were of the view that Ecomagination did not address all of the company's environmental problems and was risky as companies were generally reluctant to play up their products' environmental benefits fearing that their green claims would not able to match the company's overall environmental footprint. They observed that sustainability as a corporate strategy worked only if it was made a company-wide initiative. If it remained restricted to a few products, its impact would be limited. "Even at $20 billion, Ecomagination is only about 10 percent of GE. It's a very creative way to drive and differentiate the company, but it's not going to make, break, or save GE,"[84] said William Rothschild, a Consultant at Rothschild Strategies Unlimited.[85]

According to some experts, Ecomagination products and technologies focused on large scale, centralized solutions and were mostly capital-intensive applications based on existing business models. Little attention was paid to small-scale standalone applications that might address distinct market needs and customers, they said. Industry observers felt that Ecomagination products mostly served the needs of customers at the top of the economic pyramid[86] and ignored the requirements of customers at the base of the pyramid who lacked reliable and affordable solutions related to energy, transportation, water, materials, and financial services.

Commenting on the criticism related to the initiative, Bolsinger said, "I think the skepticism piece was never a big deal for me because (Ecomagination) was never based on "we're doing this for philanthropy" or "we're doing this to make the world safe." We're glad to be doing that as a result of making money. It's a different lens that informs your decisions about where to spend money and what resources you're going to invest."[87]

Looking Ahead

According to GE, Ecomagination was not a short-term proposition and the company planned to make it a part of its identity and market the brand aggressively to the world. GE planned to increase revenues from Ecomagination products and services to at least US$25 billion by the end of 2010.[88] GE committed itself to reducing its GHG emissions by 1% by 2012 and to improving energy efficiency by 30% by the end of 2012 compared to the 2004 baseline. GE aimed to achieve its commitment to double annual investment in clean tech R&D to US$ 1.5 billion by 2010.[89] It also planned to invest an additional US$10 billion in Ecomagination R&D by 2015, particularly in the development of low-carbon products.

The company committed itself to ensuring that by 2015, Ecomagination revenue would grow at twice the rate of total company revenue and planned to improve the energy intensity of its operations by 50% and reduce its absolute GHG emissions by 25%, both against the 2004 baseline.[90] The company also altered its goal of reducing freshwater consumption by 20% by 2012 from the 2006 baseline to 25% by 2015. As part of its public awareness, GE planned to increase its interactions with the public and revamp its Website to enable people to put forward their questions and queries.

In the future, under the Ecomagination program, GE planned to build a massive battery plant in New York and a US$2 billion wind project in Oregon and to launch a series of high-end energy-efficient front-load washers and dryers. In June 2010, GE Energy Financial Services entered into an agreement with a Spanish renewable energy company Abengoa,[91] to develop the largest cogeneration[92] power plant in Mexico. The companies were to invest US$180 million in the project expected to be commercially operational by 2012. The 300 megawatt plant was to supply electricity and steam over the next 20 years and help the Mexican government meet its energy efficiency targets by reducing GHG emissions by 50% in comparison with 2002 by 2050. GE identified China and South Korea as countries where the company expected green technology to thrive in the future.[93]

GE said while it would continue to invest in products like energy efficient turbines, green locomotives, and sodium batteries in the future, it would also focus on bringing more intelligence and networking to its existing product categories. For instance, it planned to roll out software applications for monitoring flight paths, take-offs, and landings for airplanes in order to reduce the time that planes had to spend circling airports. This would help cut fuel consumption. "It is a cost savings to the airlines and it is a huge comfort factor for customers. These are the kind of IT-enabled solutions we will invest in,"[94] said Fludder.

According to industry observers, Ecomagination was a good platform for GE to make investments in new technologies while making money at the same time. They felt that the initiative had huge scope for expansion in the future as more green technologies would be able to address new problems, create new markets, and reach underserved customers. While there were some discordant notes as well, the company said it was committed to taking this initiative forward. According to Comstock, "With Ecomagination, we've learned that sustainability is as much a change-management challenge as it is a business or scientific challenge . . . Change happens when others see opportunity—and change their behavior, join in, and make it their own. Ecomagination's mantra is no longer just GE's. And that's just fine with us."[95]

Exhibit I GE-Business Groups

Energy

- Digital Energy
- Electrical Distribution
- Energy
- Oil & Gas
- Sensing & Inspection
- Water & Process Technologies

Technology Infrastructure

- Aviation
- Healthcare
- Transportation

GE Capital

- Commercial Lending & Leasing
- Consumer Financing
- Energy Financial Services
- GE Capital Aviation Services
- Real Estate Financing
- Worldwide GE Capital Locations

NBC Universal

- Cable
- Film
- Networks
- Parks & Resorts

GE Home & Business Solutions

- Appliances
- Consumer Electronics
- Intelligent Platforms
- Lighting

Source: http://www.ge.com/products_services/directory/by_business.html

Exhibit II   General Electric Company-Consolidated Statement of Earnings
For the years ended December 31
Dollar amounts and share amounts in millions; per-share amounts in dollars

	2009	2008	2007
Revenues			
Sales of goods	65,068	69,100	60, 670
Sales of services	38,709	43,669	38,856
Other income	1,006	1,586	3,019
GECS earnings from continuing operations	—	—	—
GECS revenues from services	52,000	68,160	69,943
Total Revenues	156,783	182,515	172,488
Costs and expenses			
Cost of goods sold	50,580	54,602	47,309
Cost of services sold	25,341	29,170	25,816
Interest and other financial charges	18,769	26,209	23,762
Investment contracts, insurance losses and insurance annuity benefits	3,017	3,213	3,469
Provision for losses on financing receivables	10,928	7,518	4,431
Other costs and expenses	37,804	42,021	40,173
Total costs and expenses	146,439	162,733	144,960
Earnings (loss) from continuing operations before income taxes	10,344	19,782	27,528
Benefit (provision) for income taxes	1,090	(1,052)	(4,155)
Earnings from continuing operations	11,434	18,730	23,373
Loss from discontinued operations, net of taxes	(193)	(679)	(249)
Net earnings	11,241	18,051	23,124
Less net earnings (loss) attributable to non controlling interests	216	641	916
Net earnings attributable to the Company	11,025	17,410	22,208
Preferred stock dividends declared	(300)	(75)	—
Net earnings attributable to GE common shareowners	10,725	17,335	22,208
Amounts attributable to the Company:			
Earnings from continuing operations	11,218	18,089	22,457
Loss from discontinued operations, net of taxes	(193)	(679)	(249)
Net earnings attributable to the Company	11,025	17,410	22,208
Per-share amounts—net earnings			
Diluted earnings per share	1.01	1.72	2.17
Basic earnings per share	1.01	1.72	2.18
Dividends declared per common share	0.61	1.24	1.15

Source: GE 2009 Annual Report

Exhibit III   Top 10 in Fortune's Ranking of America's Largest Corporations (2010)

Rank	Company	Revenues (US$ millions)	Profits (US$ millions)
1	Wal-Mart Stores	408,214.0	14,335.0
2	Exxon Mobil	284,650.0	19,280.0
3	Chevron	163,527.0	10,483.0
4	General Electric	156,779.0	11,025.0
5	Bank of America Corp.	150,450.0	6,276.0
6	ConocoPhillips	139,515.0	4,858.0
7	AT&T	123,018.0	12,535.0
8	Ford Motor	118,308.0	2,717.0
9	J.P. Morgan Chase & Co.	115,632.0	11,728.0
10	Hewlett-Packard	114,552.0	7,660.0

Adapted from http://money.cnn.com/magazines/fortune/fortune500/2010/full_list/

Exhibit IV   Ecomagination Statistics

	Total Products	Investment in R&D	Greenhouse Gas (GHG) emissions	Revenues
2005	GE has increased its Ecomagination pipeline by 75% over the last year—from 17 products to 30.	GE invested US$700 million in cleaner technologies in 2005.	GHG emissions from operations remained relatively flat in 2005 compared to 2004, while GHG intensity was reduced by 10% and energy intensity was reduced by 11%.	GE's revenues from Ecomagination products and services reached US$10.1 billion. Orders and commitments nearly doubled to US$17 billion. Revenues for 2005 were at US$10.1 billion; orders went up 93% from 2004, nearly doubling to US$17 billion.
2006	GE has increased its Ecomagination pipeline by 50% over the last year—from 30 products to 45.	GE invested US$900 million in cleaner technologies in 2006.	GHG emissions in 2006 from operations have been reduced by about 4% from the 2004 baseline. GHG and energy intensity have been reduced by 21% and 22% respectively compared to 2004.	In 2006—GE's revenues grew from US$10 billion in 2005 to US$12 billion, delivering a 20% increase in revenue. 2006 revenues at US$12 billion; orders and commitments have increased to US$50 billion.

	Total Products	Investment in R&D	Greenhouse Gas (GHG) emissions	Revenues
2007	GE increased the number of Ecomagination-certified products by 38 percent over last year—from 45 to 62 products.	It invested US$1.1 billion in cleaner technology research and development.	It reduced its greenhouse gas (GHG) emissions by about 8% in 2007 from the 2004 baseline, while reducing GHG and energy intensity by 34% and 33% respectively.	It increased its revenues from Ecomagination products with US$14 billion in revenues from Ecomagination products and services in 2007.
2008	GE increased its Ecomagination portfolio—from 17 products in 2005 to more than 80 products today.	GE invested US$1.4 billion in cleaner technology research and development in 2008, up from US$750 million in 2005.	GHG emissions from operations reduced by about 13% from the 2004 baseline. GHG and energy intensity reduced by 41% and 37%, respectively, compared to 2004.	GE reported US$17 billion in revenues from Ecomagination products and services in 2008, an increase of 21% over the previous year.
2009	Products grew to 90.	It invested US$1.5 billion in cleaner technologies, achieving its 2010 goal one year ahead of schedule.	Reduced greenhouse gas emissions from operations approximately 22% from the 2004 baseline. GHG and energy intensity reduced by 39% and 34% respectively.	Revenues grew by 6% to US$18 billion.

Compiled from various sources

References:

1. Ariel Schwartz, "GE Boosts Ecomagination Initiative with an Extra $10 Billion," www.fastcompany.com, June 25, 2010.
2. Candace Lombardi, "GE to Invest $10 billion in Ecomagination Initiative," http://news.cnet.com, June 24, 2010.
3. "Ecomagination at 5: Unleashing Action & Measurement," www.gereports.com, June 24, 2010.
4. "GE Surpassed $5 Billion in Research & Development Investment in Ecomagination Technology," www.genewscenter.com, June 24, 2010.
5. Michael Kaneloss, "GE Looks to Smart Grids for Airports, Railroads in Ecomagination 2.0," www.greentechmedia.com, June 24, 2010.
6. "GE's Ecomagination Business in China Records 50% Growth," www.reliableplant.com, 2010.
7. Caylena Cahill, "Problems in Green Marketing," fuse.ithaca.edu, December 2009.
8. James Murray, "GE Talks up Ecomagination Success," www.businessgreen.com, May 28, 2009.
9. "GE's Ecomagination Team Unveils its Annual Scorecard," www.gereports.com, May 27, 2009.
10. "GE Ecomagination Revenue Grows 21% to $17B," www.environmentalleader.com, May 27, 2009.
11. GE 2009 Annual Report.
12. GE 2009 Ecomagination Report.
13. Lisa Roner, "GE: Runaway Ecomagination is Not Enough," www.climatechangecorp.com, June 4, 2008.
14. "GE's_Ecomagination' Business Grows to $14 billion; Revenue Target Raised to $25 billion as Orders Top $70 billion," www.domain-b.com, May 29, 2008.
15. "GE's_ecomagination' business grows to $14 billion; revenue target raised to $25 billion as orders top $70 billion news," www.domain-b.com, May 28, 2008.
16. Martin LaMonica, "GE to Lower Water Use, Raise Ecomagination Target," http://news.cnet.com, May 28, 2008.
17. Douglas MacMillan, "The Analysis: In Immelt We Trust," www.businessweek.com, March 4, 2008.
18. GE 2008 Ecomagination Report.

19. Lucy Aitken, "Wiping out _Greenwash," www .guardian.co.uk, November 19, 2007.
20. Martin LaMonica, "Stirring GE's Ecomagination," http://news.cnet.com, October 26, 2007.
21. "GE's Jeff Renaud Discusses Ecomagination and Transparency," www.environmentalleader.com, August 22, 2007.
22. Mary Milliken, "GE "Green" Ecomagination Unit Gaining Ground: CEO," http://uk.reuters.com, May 24, 2007.
23. GE 2007 Ecomagination Report.
24. Amanda Griscom Little, "GE's Green Gamble," Vanity Fair, July 12, 2006.
25. GE 2006 Ecomagination Report.
26. Elizabeth M. Whelan, "Public Health Absurdities," The Washington Times, December 30, 2005.
27. Brett Clark, "General Electric's Ecomagination: New Veneer, Same Propaganda," http://mrzine.monthlyreview .org, August 2, 2005.
28. Ron Irwin, "GE Imagines a Greener Future," www .brandchannel.com, July 11, 2005.
29. Greg Schneider, "GE Determined to Show More_ Ecomagination," www.washingtonpost.com, May 10, 2005.
30. "Global Environmental Challenges," www.ge.com, May 9, 2005.
31. Joel Makeower, "Ecomagination: Inside GE's Power Play," www.worldchanging.com, May 8, 2005.
32. GE 2005 Ecomagination Report.
33. www.ecomagination.com
34. www.ge.com.
35. www.hoovers.com

Endnotes

1 Caylena Cahill, "Problems in Green Marketing," www .fuse.ithaca.edu, December 2009.
2 Environmental Advocates of New York is a watchdog group on environmental issues affecting New York.
3 "GE Surpassed $5 Billion in Research & Development Investment in Ecomagination Technology," www .genewscenter.com, June 24, 2010.
4 Ibid.
5 SustainAbility is an independent think tank and strategy consultancy.
6 Lucy Aitken, "Wiping out 'Greenwash'," www.guardian .co.uk, November 19, 2007.
7 Ron Irwin, "GE Imagines a Greener Future," www .brandchannel.com, July 11, 2005.
8 The Thomas-Houston Electric Company was founded in 1879. It was a competitor to EGEC until the merger of the two companies.
9 As per the 'Number One Number Two' strategy GE had to be either the number one or number two player in every segment it operated. If any business failed to meet this criterion, it was shut down or sold off.
10 The Dow Jones Industrial Average (DJIA) is the average value of 30 large, industrial stocks. These market averages help investors know how companies traded on the stock market are performing in general.
11 Launched in 1999, the Dow Jones Sustainability Indexes are a group of indexes which track the financial performance of companies that fulfill criteria for environmental, social, and financial sustainability.
12 Amanda Griscom Little, "GE's Green Gamble," Vanity Fair, July 12, 2006.
13 PCBs are chemical compounds with low water solubility and environmental degradability, and studies have shown that people exposed to them could suffer several adverse effects.
14 Established in 1972, The Clean Water Act is a primary federal law in the US governing water pollution.
15 EPA is an agency of the US federal government responsible for protecting human health and safeguarding the natural environment.
16 Formed in 1975, NRC is a US government agency responsible for overseeing the civilian use of nuclear materials in the US.
17 The Kyoto Protocol is an agreement made under the UN Framework Convention on Climate Change concerning issues related to global warming. The countries that ratify the protocol commit themselves to reducing their emissions of carbon dioxide and five other greenhouse gases, or to engage in emissions trading if they maintain or increase emissions of these gases. The treaty was negotiated in December 1997 and came into force on February 16, 2005. As of July 2010, there were 192 signatories to the treaty.
18 The G8 or the Group of Eight is an annual political summit meeting of the heads of government of eight of the most powerful countries in the world. The members are: Canada, France, Germany, Italy, Japan, Russia, the UK, and the US.
19 Headquartered in Geneva, Switzerland, the WTO (World Trade Organization) is an international, multilateral organization, which sets the rules for the global trading system and resolves disputes between its member states.
20 Founded in 1802, DuPont is a science-based products and services company operating in 80 countries worldwide.
21 IBM Corporation is a multinational computer, technology, and IT consulting company headquartered in Armonk, New York.
22 Headquartered in Indianapolis, Eli Lilly and Company is a global pharmaceutical company.
23 Headquartered in London, UK, BP Plc is one of the largest oil and gas companies in the world with operations in over 100 countries.

24 Nike, Inc is a leading US-based sportswear and equipment manufacturer and supplier.

25 Ibid

26 Elizabeth M. Whelan, "Public Health Absurdities," *The Washington Times*, December 30, 2005.

27 Enron Wind Corp was a global supplier of wind turbine generators.

28 Ionics, Inc provided water and water treatment equipment through the use of proprietary separation technologies and systems.

29 Osmonics, Inc designed, manufactured, and marketed a wide range of products used in the filtration, separation, and processing of fluids.

30 AstroPower Inc was one of the biggest manufacturers of solar energy equipment in the US.

31 Ibid

32 The Business-to-Business (B2B) market involves transactions between businesses, such as between a manufacturer and a wholesaler, or between a wholesaler and a retailer.

33 Douglas MacMillan, "The Analysis: In Immelt We Trust," www.businessweek.com, March 4, 2008.

34 Established in 1998, The Pew Center on Global Climate Change is a nonprofit, independent organization dedicated to providing credible information and solutions related to global climate change.

35 Greg Schneider, "GE Determined to Show More 'Ecomagination'," www.washingtonpost.com, May 10, 2005.

36 www.ge.com/in/company/factsheet_in.html.

37 "Global Environmental Challenges," www.ge.com, May 9, 2005.

38 Martin LaMonica, "Stirring GE's Ecomagination," http://news.cnet.com, October 26, 2007.

39 GE 2005 Ecomagination Report.

40 "GE's 'Ecomagination' Business Grows to $14 billion; Revenue Target Raised to $25 billion as Orders Top $70 billion," www.domain-b.com, May 29, 2008.

41 MtvU is MTV Networks' 24-hour television network just for college students in the US. It is broadcast to more than 750 college campuses and 700 college communities in the US.

42 "GE's Jeff Renaud Discusses Ecomagination and Transparency," www.environmentalleader.com, August 22, 2007.

43 Headquartered in Arlington, Virginia, AES Corporation is a global power company involved in generation and distribution of electric power.

44 Greenhouse Gas Services builds a portfolio of projects that reduce, avoid, or destroy gases that directly contribute to global warming.

45 Google Inc. is a global technology company that provides a Web-based search engine through its Website. The company offers a wide range of search options, including Web, image, groups, directory, and news searches.

46 Through the project, Greenhouse Gas Services would capture and destroy methane gas emitted from the landfill to generate about an estimated 110,000 tons of carbon credits over a ten-year timeframe. Google would use a percentage of the credits to achieve carbon neutrality.

47 Ibid

48 "GE's Ecomagination Business in China Records 50% Growth" www.reliableplant.com, 2010.

49 Air India is the state owned domestic airline of India.

50 Wal-Mart Stores, Inc. is a US based chain of large retail discount department stores.

51 Mary Milliken, "GE "Green" Ecomagination Unit Gaining Ground: CEO," http://uk.reuters.com, May 24, 2007.

52 Based in Washington, The World Resources Institute (WRI) is an environmental think tank which protects the earth and improves people's lives.

53 "Ecomagination at 5: Unleashing Action & Measurement," www.gereports.com, June 24, 2010.

54 "GE's Ecomagination Team Unveils its Annual Scorecard," www.gereports.com, May 27, 2009.

55 The Energy Treasure Hunt process created by Toyota Motor Manufacturing North America identifies projects that drive energy efficiency.

56 Headquartered in Japan, Toyota Motor Corporation is one of the largest automakers in the world.

57 GE 2009 Ecomagination Report

58 Union Pacific Corporation is one of the leading transportation companies and the operator of one of the largest railroads in North America.

59 GE Energy Financial Services, a division of GE, provides financial and technological investment in energy infrastructure projects around the world. In renewable energy, GE Energy Financial Services is growing its portfolio of more than US$4 billion in assets in wind, solar, biomass, hydro, and geothermal power.

60 Founded in 2001, A123Systems develops and manufactures advanced lithium-ion batteries and battery systems for the transportation, electric grid services, and portable power markets.

61 Founded in 1991, Think Global is a Norwegian electric car company which manufactures cars under the TH!NK brand.

62 NBC Universal is one of the world's leading media and entertainment companies involved in the development, production, and marketing of entertainment, news, and information.

63 Ibid

64 Established in 2000, GreenOrder is a US-based sustainability strategy consulting firm.

65 Ibid

66 ENERGY STAR, a joint program of the U.S. Environmental Protection Agency and the US Department of Energy, is an international standard for energy efficient consumer products. It was created in 1992 as a US government program and was subsequently adopted by Australia, Canada, Japan, New Zealand, Taiwan, and the European Union.

67 The Sustained Excellence award recognizes GE's achievement in developing high-performance household appliance and lighting products, which help reduce energy spending and protect the environment.

68 GE engineers designed a hybrid diesel electric locomotive that captures the energy dissipated during braking and stores it in a series of batteries which can be used by the crew on demand. The electric locomotive reduces fuel consumption by as much as 15% and emissions by about 50% compared to normal freight locomotives.

69 Headquartered in London, GE Money is part of GE Capital operating division of GE.

70 Under the GE Money Earth Rewards program, cardholders were able to automatically contribute up to 1% of their purchases to buy carbon offsets. The credit card rewards accrued over the course of the year and could be redeemed for emissions credit on each Earth Day (April 22).

71 Based in Florida, Masco Contractor Services provides products and installation services for residential and commercial builders.

72 Named the GE WattStation, the electric-vehicle charging station was designed to charge an electric vehicle in four to six hours. The charging station, as tall as a bar stool. featured a sleek silver column equipped with a retractable cord. The electric vehicle charger not only significantly decreased the time needed for charging, but its smart grid technology let utilities manage the impact on local and regional grids.

73 Nucleus is an in-home energy consumption tracking device that communicates with GE appliances and allows consumers to track their energy usage through a display or Website.

74 The venture capital firms included Emerald Technology Ventures, Foundation Capital, Kleiner Perkins Caufield & Byer and RockPort Capital.

75 Martin LaMonica, "GE to Lower Water Use, Raise Ecomagination Target," http://news.cnet.com, May 28, 2008.

76 Ibid

77 GE 2006 Ecomagination Report.

78 Ibid

79 GE 2008 Ecomagination Report.

80 Ibid

81 Candace Lombardi, "GE to Invest $10 billion in Ecomagination Initiative," http://news.cnet.com, June 24, 2010.

82 Ibid

83 Ibid

84 Lisa Roner, "GE: Runaway Ecomagination is Not Enough," www.climatechangecorp.com, June 4, 2008.

85 Rothschild Strategies Unlimited, is a US-based consulting firm specializing in strategy development, review and human resources.

86 An economic pyramid depicts the distribution of wealth among the world's population. The bottom rung of the economic pyramid comprises low income group people whereas high earners are placed at the top of the pyramid.

87 Martin LaMonica, "Stirring GE's Ecomagination," http://news.cnet.com, October 26, 2007.

88 Ibid

89 Ibid

90 Ibid

91 Abengoa SA is a technology company that applies innovative solutions to sustainable development in the infrastructures, environment, and energy sectors.

92 Cogeneration involves simultaneous production of electricity and heat using a single fuel source such as natural gas. This can result in higher thermal efficiency and can reduce carbon dioxide emissions substantially.

93 Ibid

94 Michael Kaneloss, "GE Looks to Smart Grids for Airports, Railroads in Ecomagination 2.0," www.greentechmedia.com, June 24, 2010.

95 Ibid

CASE 26

CEMEX's Acquisition Strategy—The Acquisition of Rinker Group

"The lessons CEMEX has learned in the crisis means it has a lighter, more flexible, and dynamic operating base that will allow its eventual recovery . . . multiplying its profitability not only in the United States but in the majority of its subsidiaries."[1]

—Carlos Hermosillo, Analyst, Vector Brokerage, in January 2010.

"CEMEX is in a much stronger financial position to regain our financial flexibility and, eventually, our investment-grade capital structure."[2]

—Lorenzo Zambrano, Chief Executive Officer, CEMEX, in August 2009.

Introduction

On January 27, 2010, Mexico-based cement company CEMEX S.A.B de C.V (CEMEX) announced that its net sales for the fourth quarter ended December 31, 2009, had dropped by 17% to US$ 3.42 billion. Moreover, the company reported that its annual net sales in fiscal 2009 had dropped by 28% to US$ 14.5 billion as compared to the net sales reported in fiscal 2008. In 2009, the company reported a fall of 35% in its earnings before interest, depreciation, taxes, and amortization (EBIDTA) to US$ 2.7 billion. CEMEX had been facing problems like lower net sales and high debt since mid-2007 since its acquisition of Australia-based major cement company, the Rinker Group (Rinker).

As of early 2010, CEMEX was the largest cement company in the world in terms of production capacity. It was one of the companies based in an emerging nation like Mexico that had grown to become one of the top multinational companies in the global cement industry. Most of CEMEX's expansion in the domestic market as well as abroad came through acquisitions. Over the decades, it had developed strong expertise in successfully integrating acquired companies and reaping significant benefits. The company also relied on technology to optimize its operational efficiency, which placed it among the most profitable cement companies in the world.

CEMEX, which was known for its post-merger integration skills, also managed its cash flows well and used the free cash flows to amortize and eventually pay off the debt it had incurred for an acquisition. However, in mid-2007, CEMEX completed its largest acquisition ever by paying US$ 14.2 billion for acquiring Rinker. CEMEX financed the Rinker acquisition completely through a debt from a syndicate of banks. It estimated that Rinker's operations would result in strong cash flows and that, along with its own cash flows, it would be able to successfully service the huge debt burden. The company had set ambitious targets of achieving within 24 months leverage ratios similar to the ones that had existed prior to Rinker's acquisition. However, the US, which after acquisition was CEMEX's largest market, faced an economic slowdown due to the subprime crisis[3] that emerged in late 2007.

CEMEX, which derived a major portion of its revenues from the US, had to deal with low demand for its products since late 2007. The huge debt it had incurred for Rinker's acquisition added to the company's woes. The deficit in its anticipated free cash flows forced it to refinance its debts, sell assets, and take several cost-cutting measures like job cuts. The subprime crisis affected many of the financial institutions including commercial banks and investment banks which resulted in cautious lending from banks. CEMEX's debt credit rating was downgraded

*This case was written by **A. Harish**, under the direction of **Vivek Gupta**, IBS Center for Management Research. It was compiled from published sources and is intended to be used as a basis for class discussion rather than to illustrate either effective or ineffective handling of a management situation.*

by several credit rating agencies, which dented its credibility. With low credibility, CEMEX's cost of capital increased as it had to pay higher interest on the debt raised by the company.

By early 2010, analysts were predicting that the US markets would recover from the economic crisis and that the construction activity in the country would pick up. They also said that the stimulus packages announced by the US government in 2008 and 2009 would be used for infrastructure projects which would also add to the demand for building materials. CEMEX Vice president for Finance and Legal, Hector Medina, said, "While we are seeing a bottoming out in some of our markets as evidenced by some leading indicators, we expect first quarter 2010 to continue to be weak and that most of the expected growth in EBITDA will occur in the second half of the year."[4]

Background Note

CEMEX had its roots in a cement company called Cementos Hidalgo which was founded way back to 1906 in Monterrey, Northern Mexico. Cementos Hidalgo had a production capacity of 5,000 metric tons (MT) of cement per annum. In 1920, Lorenzo Zambrano established Cementos Portland Monterrey with a production capacity of 20,000 MT of cement per annum near Monterrey. In 1931, Cementos Hidalgo and Cementos Portland Monterrey merged to form Cementos Mexicanos. By 1959, Cementos Mexicanos had expanded its production capacity to produce over 230,420 MT of gray cement and 14,692 tons of white cement. Till the late 1960s, the company operated as a local company in Monterrey. In the late 1960s, the company started expanding to other parts of the country like Southern and Central Mexico through acquisitions and also by opening new plants.

In 1976, Cementos Mexicanos went public and got its shares listed on the Mexico stock exchange. It also became the largest cement producer in the same year after acquiring three plants of Cementos Guadalajara. By the mid-1980s, Cementos Mexicanos' annual cement production capacity had crossed 15 million MT. The mid-1980s, however, brought a major challenge for Cementos Mexicanos, which had been thriving in Mexico since its inception. Mexico started relaxing its protectionist policies and allowed multinational companies to operate in the country.

In 1985, Lorenzo Zambrano (Zambrano)[5], grandson of Cementos Mexicanos founder Lorenzo

Zambrano, was made the Chairman and CEO of Cementos Mexicanos. With a strong academic background[6] and experience in working with Cementos Mexicanos since 1968, Zambrano embarked on an aggressive expansion plan. He also focused on improving operational efficiency and customer satisfaction. Till the mid-1980s, the practice in the cement industry in Mexico was to provide its customers with an expected delivery time which usually ranged between 3 and 5 hours. Cementos Mexicanos also followed the same practice before Zambrano became Chairman and CEO.

CEMEX did not have an Information Technology (IT) department and scheduling delivery trucks and plant operations was done manually. This was operationally inefficient. Zambrano created an IT department which observed customer interaction and delivery methods implemented at several companies like FedEx, Exxon and City of Houston's 911 emergency system. In 1989, CEMEX implemented a satellite communication system called CEMEXnet which connected all the plants of CEMEX via satellite. A central office was opened to coordinate operational activities at several plants. This helped the plants to have information relating to supply and demand.

In 1988, Cementos Mexicanos was renamed as CEMEX S.A.B de C.V. During the late 1980s, CEMEX acquired several small cement plants in Mexico including Cementos Anahuac[7] in 1987 and Cementos Tolteca[8], its biggest domestic competitor, in 1989. By the year 1990, CEMEX had acquired a 65% market share in Mexico and was one of the ten largest companies in the world. In 1992, CEMEX expanded internationally by acquiring Valenciana and Sanson, Spain's two largest cement companies, for US$ 1.84 billion. CEMEX's investors expressed concerns on the rapid pace at which it was going ahead with its expansion plans and the amount of debt the company had taken for funding these acquisitions. To address these concerns, CEMEX paid off a large portion of its debts by selling the nonstrategic assets of the Spanish companies it had acquired.

In 1994, CEMEX acquired a 60% equity stake in Vencemos, Venezuela's largest cement manufacturer at that time, for US$ 550 million. Its other acquisitions during the year included Cemento Bayano in Panama and Balcones in the US. In 1995, CEMEX acquired Cementos Nacionales, a leading cement company in the Dominican Republic. In 1996, CEMEX emerged as the third largest cement company in the world after acquiring Colombia's

Cementos Diamante[9] and Samper. In 1997, CEMEX started its Asian operations by acquiring Rizal Cement in the Philippines. In 1999, CEMEX's acquisitions included APO Cements in the Philippines, Assiut Cement Company in Egypt, and Dementos del Pacifico of Costa Rica. In 1999, CEMEX's shares were listed on the New York Stock Exchange.

In 2000, CEMEX became North America's largest cement company by acquiring Houston-based Southdown[10], then the second largest cement producer in the US, for US$ 2.63 billion. This was the largest acquisition made by CEMEX till that time. In the same year, CEMEX launched the CEMEX Way, an initiative to identify, incorporate, and execute standardized best practices in different functional areas like logistics, finance, human resources, and planning throughout the organization.

In 2001, CEMEX acquired the Saraburi Cement Company in Thailand. In the same year, it launched an online customer service initiative where customers could place orders, purchase products, and access other services and information electronically. As most of CEMEX's growth came from acquisitions, the company had developed strong post-merger integration (PMI) expertise. After completing an acquisition, it usually deployed a post-merger integration team that analyzed the operations of the acquired company to identify the areas where costs could be cut, reduce headcount, and upgrade technical and management systems to fall in-line with what were being followed at CEMEX. This expertise helped CEMEX in turning around several ailing companies it had acquired by cutting down on costs and improving operational efficiency.

In the early 2000s, CEMEX concentrated on expanding its presence in developing markets like the Philippines, Indonesia, and Thailand. The company's profitability was higher than its major international rivals—Holcim and Lafarge—because of its concentration on developing nations where profit margins were higher. Developing nations also offered CEMEX's businesses a longer term growth potential. In 2003, CEMEX launched a company-wide procurement process and global sourcing office to consolidate its international sourcing operations and realize the benefits of economies of scale.

In 2005, CEMEX acquired the UK-based RMC Group[11] for US$ 5.8 billion. The acquisition made the company a worldwide leader in the ready-mix concrete market and increased its exposure to the European markets significantly. It also doubled the size of

CEMEX's operations, taking its total annual cement production capacity to 97 million MT. CEMEX ended the year 2006 with revenues of US$ 18.2 billion and a net profit of US$ 2.3 billion (Refer to Exhibit I, II and III for Financial Statements of CEMEX).

CEMEX had a three-point acquisition strategy—the acquired company must provide risk adjusted returns in excess of the company's weighted average cost of capital, it must enhance the company's geographical presence, and it must contribute to CEMEX's capital structure[12].

The Acquisition Integration Process

CEMEX had learnt in the course of its business that implementing the technical and management standards it followed in its existing plants was not sufficient to ensure the smooth integration of an acquired company. The company realized that it had to learn the processes already implemented in the acquired company, compare it with the corresponding processes it followed, and retain the better of the two. CEMEX then made efforts to implement the best practices learned from the acquired company across its worldwide operations. This acquisition integration process was later named as the 'CEMEX Way.'

The 'CEMEX Way' was an internal benchmarking process which resulted in a core set of best business practices based on which CEMEX conducted business across the globe. It was driven by five guidelines developed by the company (Refer to Table I for CEMEX Way Guidelines).

After acquiring a target company, CEMEX deployed multinational standardization teams

Table I CEMEX Way Guidelines

Efficiently manage the global knowledge base
Identify and disseminate the best practices
Standardize business processes
Implement key information and Internet-based technologies
Foster innovation

Source: www.cemex.com.

comprising experts from various functional areas like Finance, HR, and IT. The work was overseen by an executive at the Vice-president level. The PMI team studied the processes of the acquired company. Typically, 20% of the processes of an acquired company were retained. The remaining 80% processes were stored in a centralized database, and were compared with internal and external processes. If deemed to be superior to the existing processes, they were then implemented in all other plants. According to industry experts, around 70% of the processes followed in CEMEX operations were actually adopted from the acquired companies.

The teams for each PMI operation were selected on an ad hoc basis. Functional level managers, typically middle level managers, were selected from different plants of CEMEX. These managers were responsible for understanding the existing processes of the acquired company and identifying those processes which were superior to the processes that were being followed at CEMEX. Since these managers had gained expertise of working on a particular process at CEMEX, they taught the managers at the acquired company about the processes at CEMEX. Also, they were experienced in the functional departments of CEMEX,

and so were able to judge better whether the corresponding processes in the acquired company would be able to positively contribute to CEMEX's operations.

Acquisition of Rinker

On October 30, 2006, CEMEX made an offer to buy all issued and outstanding shares of Rinker for US$ 12.8 billion. The offer was at a 27% premium over Rinker's share closing price as on October 27, 2006, and at a 26.2% premium over Rinker's three-month volume weighted average price.[13] CEMEX expected to derive annual cost synergies of US$ 130 million from the second year after completing the acquisition.

Rinker had generated approximately 50% of its revenues from the commercial and civil construction sector in the fiscal 2005. Its product portfolio was diversified and included aggregates, concrete, cement pipes, cement, gypsum wallboard supply, concrete block, and asphalt. The acquisition of Rinker significantly enhanced the position of CEMEX in the ready-mix and aggregates sector though the impact on cement production capacity was not much (Refer to Table II for Global Cement Industry Rankings in 2005).

Table II Global Cement Industry Rankings (2005)

Cement (In million metric tons)		Ready-Mix (In million cubic meters)		Aggregates (In million metric tons)	
Company	Capacity	Company	Sales Volume	Company	Sales Volume
Holcim	183	CEMEX+Rinker	97	CEMEX+Rinker	284
Lafarge	155	CEMEX	76	CRH	253
CEMEX+Rinker	97	Holcim	40	Lafarge	240
CEMEX	94	Lafarge	39	Hanson	240
Heidelberg	86	Heidelberg	28	Vulcan	236
Italcementi	64	Italcementi	21	Martin Marietta	184
Anhui Conch	62	Rinker	21	CEMEX	175
Taiheiyo	46	Hanson	20	Holcim	174
Buzzi	34	CRH	19	Rinker	118
Eurocement	31	Tarmac	8	Colas	101
Rinker	3	Vicat / Cimpor	7	Heidelberg	98
Others	~1,750	Others	~2,900	Others	~18,000

Source: www.cemex.com.

Rinker was the market leader in some of the key markets in the US like Florida, Arizona, and had a wide presence in Australia. It was one of the top three companies in the ready mix business, among the top five in aggregates[14] in the US, and among the top three in building materials in Australia. Rinker had huge reserves of aggregates, around 3.6 billion MT, in the US and Australia which were estimated to last for 30 years of production in the US and 43 years of production in Australia.

Rinker provided CEMEX with an opportunity to diversify geographically and increase its presence in Australia. In the fiscal 2005, CEMEX generated the highest amount of EBIDTA from its Mexican operations followed by the US. Rinker's acquisition brought down CEMEX's significant reliance on the Mexican markets. However, the acquisition increased CEMEX's reliance on the US markets (Refer to Figure I for Geographical Contribution of CEMEX and CEMEX + Rinker EBIDTA in 2005).

CEMEX announced that the markets in the US where Rinker held most of its assets and operations were complementary to its operations in the US and would enhance its position in the country. The company expected that the demand for building materials in the US would be robust in the long term. In addition to geographical diversification, Rinker's acquisition also offered it an opportunity to change the product- wise contribution to the CEMEX's EBIDTA (Refer to Figure II for Product Wise contribution to CEMEX and CEMEX+ Rinker EBIDTA in 2005).

Following the announcement of acquisition by CEMEX, Rinker's share price increased and traded over CEMEX's bid price of A$ 17,[15] implying that CEMEX had to increase its bid in order to get shareholders' approval for the acquisition (**Refer to Exhibit IV for Rinker's Stock Price Chart**). Rinker's board rejected CEMEX's initial bid.

After failing to convince Rinker's board and shareholders to approve the deal, CEMEX increased its offer to A$ 19.41 in April 2007. Rinker's board approved the deal. The upward revision saw the total acquisition bid of CEMEX amounting to US$ 14.2 billion after adjusting for the exchange rate fluctuations between the Australian and the US dollar during the intervening period. (Refer to Exhibits V and VI **for Rinker's Financial Statements**).

In order to convince Rinker's retail shareholders in Australia, CEMEX took the help of Georgeson, one of Australia's leading proxy solicitation and shareholder communications firms. With the help of Georgeson, in April 2007, CEMEX conducted a three-phase canvassing campaign, where it contacted Rinker's shareholders in Australia to deliver key messages and to motivate them by communicating the benefits of accepting its offer within a given time frame (Refer to Table III **for the reasons communicated to Rinker's shareholders to accept the offer**).

On April 05, 2007, CEMEX also got approval from the Department of Justice (DoJ) in the US for Rinker's acquisition after agreeing to sell 39 ready mix concrete, concrete block, and aggregate facilities in the country. The DoJ required CEMEX to

---

Figure I Geographical Contribution of CEMEX and CEMEX + Rinker EBIDTA (2005)

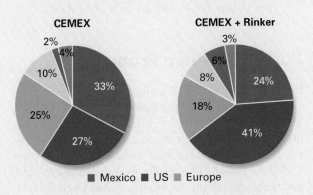

Adapted from data available in www.cemex.com

Figure II Product Wise Contribution to CEMEX and CEMEX + Rinker EBIDT A (2005)

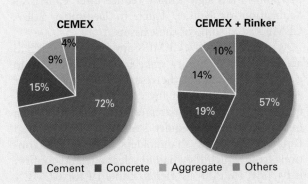

Adapted from data available in www.cemex.com

Table III Reasons Communicated to Rinker's Shareholders to Accept the Offer

1. All Rinker directors recommended that you accept CEMEX's offer and have decided to accept the offer in respect of their own Rinker's shares.

2. Rinker's major shareholder, Perpetual, who held approximately 10% of Rinker has accepted CEMEX's offer.

3. You will receive a 45% premium and full value for your Rinker's shares.

4. You will receive the announced Rinker dividend of A$ 0.25 regardless of when you accept the offer.

5. CEMEX's offer is within the independent expert's valuation range.

6. There is no reason to delay your acceptance, the offer had been declared final and cannot legally be increased.

7. If CEMEX acquired over 50% but less than 100% of Rinker and you do not accept, then you will become a minority shareholder in Rinker. Changes under CEMEX management may include a lowering of Rinker's dividend payout ratio.

8. If the CEMEX Offer does not succeed, Rinker's share price is likely to fall.

Source: www.sec.gov

Table IV CEMEX Payment Options

Option 1: US$ 15.85 for each of their Rinker shares converted into and paid in A$.

Option 2: A$ 19.50 per share for their first 2,000 Rinker shares (or for all of their shares if they held 2,000 Rinker shares or less) and US$ 15.85 for each of their remaining shares (if any) converted into and paid in A$.

Option 3: US$ 15.85 for each of their Rinker shares paid in US$.

Option 4: A$ 19.50 per share for their first 2,000 Rinker shares (or for all of their shares if they held 2,000 Rinker shares or less) and US$ 15.85 for each of their remaining shares (if any) paid in US$.

Source: www.ato.gov.au

According to the company sources, if a shareholder did not elect an option before the deadline, then CEMEX would pay them using Option 1, in case the shareholder's registered address with Rinker was in Australia, and Option 3, if the shareholder's registered address with Rinker was outside Australia.

By the end of December 2007, CEMEX reported that its PMI team had been able to complete the core postmerger integration process at Rinker. The company said it had identified the best practices and would capitalize US$ 400 million resulting from synergies in fiscal 2008 and 2009, US$ 270 million above what it had estimated before completing the acquisition. Typically, CEMEX relied on the free cash flows to pay off the debts it had raised for any acquisition. In the case of Rinker's acquisition, CEMEX expected to generate enough free cash flows right from the first year to pay off its annual debt obligations.

sell some of its plants in Tampa, St. Petersburg, Fort Walton Beach, Panama City, Pensacola, Jacksonville, Orlando, Fort Myers, and Naples where the competition would significantly reduce after CEMEX's acquisition of Rinker. Later, in December 2007, CEMEX sold some of these assets.

On July 10, 2007, CEMEX announced that it had acquired a 90% equity stake in Rinker and would compulsorily acquire the rest of the shares. Under Australian law, a company could compulsorily acquire the remaining shares once it had acquired a minimum of 90% equity stake. CEMEX offered Rinker's remaining shareholders four payment options from which they had to select one and confirm it by July 16, 2007 (Refer to Table IV for CEMEX Payment Options).

Post-Acquisition Problems

In January 2008, CEMEX announced its financial results for the financial year ended December 31, 2007. The company reported net sales of US$ 21.7 billion, 19% higher than the net sales reported in fiscal 2006. Its net profit rose to US$ 2.9 billion from US$ 2.37 billion. The results included Rinker's sales and net profit for the six months ended December 31, 2007. CEMEX ended the fiscal 2007 with a debt of

US$ 19.9 billion[16] as against a debt of US$ 5.81 billion at the end of fiscal 2006. Its net-debt-to-EBIDTA ratio went up to 3.6 by the end of 2007, from 1.4 at the end of fiscal 2006. CEMEX's interest coverage ratio fell to 5.7 at the end of fiscal 2007 from 8.4 at the end of fiscal 2006 mainly due to the additional debt it had raised for financing Rinker's acquisition. CEMEX said that its target was to bring down the net-debt-EBIDTA ratio to 2.7 and to maintain its interest coverage ratio at above 4.5 by mid-2009. However, CEMEX failed to achieve these financial targets due to a significant fall in cement demand in its major markets including the US in fiscal 2008 and 2009 (Refer to Exhibit VII for Note on Cement Industry in US) and the huge debt burden post Rinker's acquisition.

Fall In Cement Demand

In late 2007, the subprime crisis in the US resulted in a significant slowdown in the growth of residential mortgage markets in the US. Prices in the real-estate sector started falling sharply. The demand for housing properties began to decline. The crisis eventually spread to other sectors as a number of financial institutions who reported significant losses, tightened their lending norms. The construction industry which was highly capital-intensive and relied heavily on external funding for executing projects was adversely impacted. The demand for residential and commercial properties plunged deeply in the US beginning late 2007. One of the industries that was adversely affected by the slowdown in the residential and commercial real estate industry was the building materials industry.

CEMEX was one of the major players in the building materials industry in the US which saw its net sales and sales volumes falling sharply in the fiscal 2007 and 2008. The crisis which originated in the US spread to other major world economies and resulted in a global economic slowdown in 2008 (Refer to Table V and Table VI for Country Wise Volume Growth of CEMEX Products in fiscal 2007 and 2008).

Huge Debt Burden

CEMEX had financed Rinker's acquisition by raising short-term and long-term debts from a syndicate of banks including the Royal Bank of Scotland, HSBC, Banco Santander, BNP Paribas, and Citibank. The

Table V Country Wise Volume Growth (%) of CEMEX Products (2007)

Product/Country	Cement	Ready Mix	Aggregates
Mexico	4	8	NA
US	(8)	13	75
Spain	(5)	(4)	N
United Kingdom	12	(2)	2
Germany	(6)	NA	NA
France	NA	5	2
South/Central America and Caribbean	8	NA	NA
Africa and Middle East	8	NA	NA
Asia and Australia	7	NA	NA
Australia	NA	5	7
Philippines	12	NA	NA

Source: CEMEX Annual Report 2007.
*NA- not available in the annual reports.

Table VI   Country Wise Volume Growth (%) of CEMEX Products (2008)

Product/Country	Cement	Ready Mix	Aggregates
Mexico	(4)	(6)	
US	(14)	(13)	(3)
Spain	(30)	(26)	
United Kingdom	(16)	(21)	(11)
Germany	4	NA	
France	NA	0	(5)
South/Central America and Caribbean	(13)	NA	NA
Africa and Middle East	8	NA	NA
Asia and Australia	(1)	NA	NA
Australia	NA	6	5
Philippines	(2)	NA	NA

Source: CEMEX Annual Report 2008.
*NA- not available in the annual report.

Table VII   CEMEX Debt Issuances (2006–2007)

Nominal Amount (In Million)	Issue Date	Repurchase Option	Interest Rate (%)
€ 730	May 2007	Tenth Anniversary	6.3
US$ 730	February 2007	Eighth Anniversary	6.6
US$ 750	December 2006	Fifth Anniversary	6.2
US$ 900	December 2006	Tenth Anniversary	6.7

Source: CEMEX Annual Report, 2007.

debt instruments involved had maturities starting from 2009 till 2011.

In late 2006 and 2007, CEMEX issued several debt instruments the proceeds of which were predominantly targeted at paying off its existing debts as well as the debt it had incurred for acquiring Rinker (**Refer to Table VII for CEMEX's debt issuances in late 2006 and 2007**).

In 2008, CEMEX could not raise new capital from the financial markets as they had witnessed a significant downturn. In February 2008, CEMEX

decided to sell assets worth around US$ 2 billion to reduce some of its debt load. However, analysts opined that CEMEX needed to sell around US$ 2.7 billion worth of assets in order to meet its debt obligations. A Mexico-based analyst said, "CEMEX is likely to need to sell more than they say. The debt issue is a big challenge."[17]

In March 2008, CEMEX sold its 9.5% equity stake in Mexican telecom company Axtel for US$ 257 million. By mid-2008, another of CEMEX's key markets, Spain, started facing an economic slowdown, due to the impact of the recession on American and European countries. Economists also predicted that the slowdown in the US would impact Mexico, its #2 trade partner. In July 2008, CEMEX sold its subsidiaries in Austria and Hungary to Austria-based construction company, Strabag, for around € 310 million (Refer to Exhibit VIII for CEMEX Contractual Obligations for year 2008).

In October 2008, the credit rating agency Standard & Poor's[18] (S&P) lowered its credit rating on the long-term corporate credit and senior unsecured debt ratings of CEMEX to 'BBB-' from BBB and said that its outlook on the company was negative. Juan Pablo Becerra, Analyst at S&P, said, "The rating actions reflect our expectations that CEMEX's financial performance for the rest of 2008 and into 2009 will fall short of our previous expectations, given the weakening of economic growth prospects in its principal markets and around the globe. In addition, CEMEX faces important debt maturities (US$ 5.7 billion) at the end of 2009 (particularly in December when US$ 3.7 billion related to its acquisition of Rinker Group Limited are due), which pose a significant challenge to the company in light of current market conditions. The negative outlook reflects the risk of further deterioration in the company's financial condition due to the weakness in the global economy. In particular, a downgrade is likely if CEMEX fails to improve its FFO-to-total net adjusted debt ratio to a low 20% by 2010 and if it is unable to refinance its 2009 maturities well in advance."[19] Soon after the ratings were lowered, CEMEX decided to cut 6000 jobs worldwide as a cost-cutting measure. In the same month, Fitch Ratings,[20] another credit rating agency, downgraded the credit rating of CEMEX to below investment grade standard.

In November 2008, CEMEX announced that it had sold its operations in Canary Islands to a Spanish Investment holding company, Cimpor Inversiones, for US$ 211 million. On December 11, 2008, CEMEX reported that it had been successful in refinancing US$ 72 million debt mostly due in December 2008 and January 2009. These debt obligations would now be due in September 2011. However, the amount refinanced was just 17% of the total US$ 418 million debt CEMEX had actually planned to refinance. Failure to refinance this debt completely led to CEMEX's stock price falling by 19% on the same day to close at US$ 8.3 (Refer to Exhibit IX for CEMEX Stock Price Chart).

CEMEX reported net sales of US$ 21.7 billion in the fiscal 2008, which was almost flat compared to the corresponding figures of fiscal 2007. CEMEX's cost of sales as a percent of total sales increased from 66.6% to 68.3%. The company reported a 5% drop in EBIDTA at US$ 4.5 billion as compared to 2007. Its interest coverage ratio in fiscal 2008 came down to 4.9 from 5.7 in fiscal 2007. The Mexican peso which depreciated vis-à-vis the US dollar in 2008 resulted in foreign exchange losses of US$ 386 million (Refer to Exhibit X for Mexican Peso VS American Dollar Chart). CEMEX lost US$ 1.35 billion on financial instruments like currency swaps of which most was attributed to the depreciation of the peso against the US dollar. The company reported a free cash flow of US$ 2.6 billion in 2008 (Refer to Exhibit XI for CEMEX Cash Flow Statement of 2008) of which US$ 1.56 billion went into capital expenditure for capacity expansion and the rest for reducing debt. CEMEX had a net debt of US$ 17.91 billion and its net-debt-to-EBDITA rose to 4 in 2008.

In January 2009, CEMEX announced that it would close down the operations of its Davenport plant and lay off 125 employees to align its operations with weakened demand. S&P had downgraded CEMEX's rating to BB+, a notch below investment grade status BBB-. On March 05, 2009, CEMEX announced that it would delay its proposed plan to sell bonds to raise US$ 500 million that was to fund its repayment of the US$ 4.24 billion of debt that was maturing between the second quarter and fourth quarter of fiscal 2009. CEMEX decided to delay the US$ 500 million bond sale as not enough investors showed an interest in subscribing to the issue despite its extensive road shows in London and New York. Following its failure to raise capital, credit rating agencies downgraded the rating on CEMEX again. S&P downgraded CEMEX's rating by 5 notches to B- from BB+.

In April 2009, CEMEX announced very disappointing results for the first quarter of 2009. The company reported a 99.36% drop in its net profits to US$ 3 million as compared to US$ 470 million in the corresponding quarter in 2008. During the same period, its revenues fell by 32% to US$ 3.7 billion. CEMEX's free cash flows, which were important for repaying its debt, fell by 76% in the same period to US$ 118 million. CEMEX's management assured the investors that it was progressing well in the debt restructuring talks with its lenders. It said that the depreciation of the peso against the US dollar and weak sales in its major markets like the US and Spain were the main reasons for its poor financial performance. CEMEX received a large chunk of its revenues in Mexican pesos whereas most of its debt was in US dollars. The peso's depreciation against the US dollar exacerbated its debt obligations. CEMEX said that it had stopped most of its capital-intensive expansion projects to save cash for repaying its debt.

In June 2009, CEMEX announced that it would be selling the Australian operations of Rinker to its rival Holcim for US$ 1.6 billion. According to industry analysts, the price at which CEMEX sold the Australian operations was almost half of what it had paid for acquiring them from Rinker in 2007. They opined that the poor demand for cement in CEMEX's major markets coupled with huge debt liabilities had forced it to exit one of the lucrative markets for cement production.

Future Tense?

In July 2009, CEMEX lowered its free cash flow forecasts for the fiscal year 2009 to US$ 1.6 billion as against the previous forecast of US$ 2.05 billion. This led to worries among the company's shareholders and lenders. In August 2009, CEMEX announced that all its creditors had agreed to support its proposal for refinancing a debt of US$ 15 billion maturing over the next two years. According to the new plan, the debt that was to mature between 2009 and 2011 would have extended maturities till 2014.

However, in spite of refinancing approvals from the lenders, credit rating agencies did not upgrade the rating of CEMEX to investment grade as there were uncertainties in the economic scenario. Also, they were not certain about CEMEX's ability to generate sufficient cash flows in the years through 2014 to repay its debt obligations. Juan Pablo Becerra, Credit Analyst at S&P, said, "For an improvement in the rating, we would have to see a more stable macroeconomic environment, a refinancing not just of 2009 debt but also of that in 2010 and 2011 and a cut in company debt levels."[21]

According to financial experts, the cost of refinancing would add to CEMEX's annual interest burden, estimated to be an additional US$ 2 billion. Moreover, they opined that CEMEX may require additional refinancing in future, given the uncertainty

in demand for its products in its major markets. The fresh refinancing terms limited the company's ability to invest in expansion projects or to go in for new acquisitions.

In its effort to raise capital, in September 2009, CEMEX issued 1.3 billion Ordinary Participatory Notes (OPOs) in the form of American Depository Shares (ADS). Each ADS comprised 10 OPOs. Each ADS was priced at US$ 12.5 and OPOs were priced at MXP 16.64825.[22] Of the issued 1.3 billion, 325 million CPOs were sold in Mexico and the rest in other countries in the form of ADS. CEMEX raised US$ 1.8 billion from this issue.

In December 2009, CEMEX also raised US$ 1.25 billion through the issue of notes maturing in seven years and carried an annual coupon rate of 9.5% and € 350 million in eight year notes carrying an annual coupon rate of 9.625%. Financial analysts expressed concern over CEMEX's strategy to raise capital by issuing fresh bonds to repay a portion of its earlier debts. According to Gonzalo Fernandez of Santander brokerage, "We are still somewhat concerned that CEMEX continues refinancing banking debt with bonds, and that it is not effectively reducing debt."[23]

Industry analysts remained skeptical about CEMEX's ability to significantly improve its financial performance in the near future. They opined that after Rinker's acquisition, CEMEX could not generate enough free cash flows to repay the debt like it had done in the case of earlier acquisitions.

In early 2010, CEMEX's problems continued. On January 26, 2010, the company announced disappointing results for the fiscal year 2009. The company generated revenues of US$ 14.5 billion, about 28% lower as compared to fiscal 2008. During the same period, the company's EBIDTA decreased by 35% to US$ 2.7 billion. The free cash flows after maintenance capital expenditure was also down by 53% to US$ 1.2 billion.

Industry analysts opined that CEMEX needed to expand its operations in major cement consuming markets like China and India. However, until it had repaid a significant part of the debt, the company's creditors would not allow CEMEX to expand its operations in these countries. Moreover, analysts pointed out that after selling several assets globally, CEMEX's reliance on the US markets had further increased Hence, the company's future success relied heavily on the economic recovery in the US.

Exhibit I CEMEX—Income Statements (2004–08) (In US$ millions)

	2004	2005	2006	2007	2008
Net Sales	8,149.36	15,320.96	18,249.36	21,672.99	21,688.53
Cost of Sales	(4,586.35)	(9,271.20)	(11,648.47)	(14,441.03)	(14,822.86)
Gross Profit	3,563.01	6,049.76	6,600.89	7,231.96	6,865.68
Selling, General and Administrative Expenses	(1,711.33)	(3,563.10)	(3,655.06)	(4,260.50)	(4,379.01)
Operating Income	1,851.68	2,486.66	2,945.83	2,971.46	2,486.67
Other Expenses, Net	(513.50)	(316.43)	(49.86)	(300.52)	(1,916.96)
Operating Income After Other Expenses, Net	1,338.18	2,170.23	2,895.97	2,670.94	569.71
Financial Expenses	(372.23)	(526.17)	(493.91)	(806.64)	(911.65)
Financial Income	23.42	39.26	45.71	78.96	51.63
Exchange Gain (Loss), Net	(23.56)	(78.82)	20.30	(22.24)	(385.91)
Monetary Position Gain (Loss)	385.87	418.83	409.44	630.92	37.24
Gain (Loss) on Financial Instruments	119.84	386.20	(13.68)	218.56	(1,353.05)
Total Comprehensive Financing Cost (Income)	133.34	239.31	(32.14)	99.56	(2,561.75)
Net income Before Income Taxes	1,501.15	2,408.48	2,879.51	2,770.50	(1,992.04)
Income Tax	(183.45)	(330.26)	(497.30)	(439.20)	2,101.24
Net income Before Participation of Uncons. Subs	1,288.07	2,079.28	2,366.52	2,331.30	109.20
Participation in Unconsolidated Subsidiaries	40.06	87.35	121.69	136.20	97.90
Consolidated Net Income	1,328.13	2,166.63	2,488.21	2,467.50	207.10
Net Income Attributable to Minority Interest	20.93	55.04	110.28	76.67	3.98
Majority Interest Net Income	1,307.20	2,111.59	2,377.93	2,390.83	203.13
Earnings per ADS (NYSE:CX)	3.93	6.10	3.31	3.22	0.27
EBITDA*	2,538.26	3,557.10	4,137.68	4,586.11	4,343.11
Free Cash Flow*	1,478.00	2,013.00	1,943.00	1,144.00	1,040.00

Source: www.cemex.com.

Exhibit II CEMEX Quarterly Income Statements (2009) (In US$ Millions)

	1Q	2Q	3Q	4Q
Net Sales	3,660.12	4,188.11	4,217.08	3,443.80
Cost of Sales	(2,614.98)	(2,906.51)	(2,897.06)	(2,532.49)

(continued)

Exhibit II (*continued*)

	1Q	2Q	3Q	4Q
Gross Profit	1,045.14	1,281.60	1,320.02	911.31
Selling, General and Administrative Expenses	(719.48)	(870.62)	(909.02)	(813.00)
Operating Income	325.66	410.98	411.01	98.31
Other Expenses, Net	(37.87)	(100.55)	(61.85)	(219.84)
Operating Income After Other Expenses, Net	287.79	310.43	349.16	(121.53)
Financial Expenses	(205.08)	(210.47)	(275.08)	(315.94)
Financial Income	7.14	5.84	10.82	8.69
Exchange Gain (Loss), Net	(138.22)	80.75	15.99	50.18
Monetary Position Gain (Loss)	5.28	7.53	9.98	7.96
Gain (Loss) on Financial Instruments	(138.72)	(5.01)	(23.02)	20.72
Total Comprehensive Financing Cost (Income)	(469.60)	(121.35)	(261.30)	(228.40)
Net income Before Income Taxes	(181.81)	189.08	87.85	(349.93)
Income Tax	189.78	(4.41)	25.56	613.20
Net income Before Participation of Uncons. Subs	7.96	184.67	113.42	263.28
Participation in Unconsolidated Subsidiaries	(2.19)	7.34	20.37	1.78
Consolidated Net Income	5.78	192.01	133.79	(213.15)
Net Income Attributable to Minority Interest	2.98	5.45	12.84	(3.70)
Majority Interest Net Income	2.79	186.56	120.95	(209.45)
Earnings per ADS (2)	0.00	0.24	0.14	(0.22)
EBITDA*	712.22	811.59	805.56	473.69

Source: www.cemex.com.

Exhibit III CEMEX Balance Sheets (2006–08) (In Mexican Pesos millions)

Balance Sheet	2008	2007	2006
Assets			
Current Assets			
Cash and investments	13,604	8,670	18,494
Trade receivables less allowance for doubtful accounts	18,276	20,719	16,525
Other accounts receivable	9,945	9,830	9,206
Inventories,net	22,358	19,631	13,974
Other current assets	4,012	2,394	2,255
Total current assets	68,195	61,244	60,454

Exhibit III (continued)

Balance Sheet	2008	2007	2006
Non-current Assets			
Investment in associates	14,200	10,220	8,712
Other investments and non-current accounts receivable	24,633	11,339	9,966
Property, machinery and equipment, net	281,858	262,189	201,425
Goodwill, intangible assets and deferred charges, net	234,736	197,322	70,526
Total non-current assets	555,427	481,070	290,629
Total assets	623,622	542,314	351,083
Liabilities and stockholders' equity			
Current liabilities			
Short-term debt including current maturities of long-term debt	95,270	36,257	14,657
other financial obligations	3,462		
Trade payables	22,543	23,660	20,110
Other accounts payable and accrued expenses	31,462	23,471	17,203
Total current liabilities	152,737	83,388	51,970
Non-current Liabilities			
Long-term debt	162,824	180,654	73,674
other financial obligations	1,823	0	0
Employee benefits	6,788	7,650	7,484
Deferred income tax liability	38,439	50,307	30,119
other non-current liabilities	23,744	16,162	14,725
Total non-current liabilities	233,618	254,773	126,002
Total liabilities	386,355	338,161	177,972
Shareholder's Equity			
Majority interest:			
Common Stock	4,117	4,115	4,113
Additional Paid-in capital	70,171	63,379	56,982
Other equity reserves	28,730	(104,574)	(91,244)
Retained earnings	85,396	174,140	152,921
Net income	2,278	26,108	27,855
Total majority interest	190,692	163,168	150,627
Minority interest and perpetual debentures	46,575	40,985	22,484
Total stockholders' equity	237,267	204,153	173,111
Total liabilities and stockholder's equity	623,622	542,314	351,083

Source: CEMEX Annual Reports 2007–08.

Exhibit IV   Rinker Stock Price Chart (April 2006—October 2006)

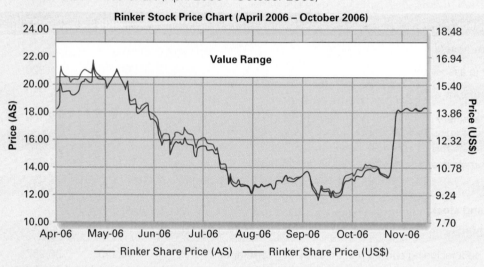

Source: www.sec.gov.

Exhibit V   Income Statements of Rinker (2006–07) (In US$ millions)

Year ended March 31	2007	2006
Trading revenue	5,337.30	5108.40
Cost of sales	(2,744.00)	(2,666.30)
Warehouse and distribution costs	(1,058.60)	(1,015.20)
Selling, general and administrative costs		
-general	(366.30)	(373.80)
-takeover defence costs	(14.50)	
Share of profits from investments accounted for using the equity method	25.30	32.60
Other income	44.50	68.40
Other expenses	(5.80)	(8.50)
Profit before finance and income tax expense	1,217.90	1,145.60
Interest Income	15.90	21.7
Finance Costs	(57.30)	(41.8)
Profit before income tax	1,176.50	1,125.50
Income tax	(390.10)	(381.9)
Net profit	786.40	743.6

Source: Rinker Annual Report 2007.

Exhibit VI Balance Sheets of Rinker (2006–2007)

Year ended March 31	2007	2006
Current Assets		
Cash and cash equivalents	185.9	289.1
Receivables	671.4	672.3
Inventories	373.7	330.9
Other current assets	23.1	20.7
Current Assets	1,254.10	1,313.00
Non-current assets		
Receivables	22.3	45.2
Inventories	9.8	8.6
Investments accounted for using the equity method	148	132.9
Other financial assets	40.3	32.6
Property, plant and equipment	2,233.10	1,963.40
Intangibles, including goodwill	937.1	901.7
Other non-current assets	59.6	59.8
Non-current assets	3,450.20	3,144.20
Total Assets	4,704.30	4,457.20
Current liabilities		
Payables	511.8	542.2
Borrowings	9.4	5.4
Income tax liabilities	49.1	62.4
Provisions	77.4	76.2
Current liabilities	647.7	686.2
Non-current Liabilities		
Payables	88.8	94.1
Borrowings	1,092.30	645.2
Net deferred income tax liabilities	218	205.8
Provisions	144.5	138.6
Non-current Liabilities	1,543.60	1,083.70
Total Liabilities	2,191.30	1,769.90
Net Assets	2,513.00	2,687.30
Equity		
Contributed equity(a)	636	1,138.70
Shares held in trust	−52.3	−44.2
Reserves	286.5	182.4
Retained profits	1,632.70	1,401.30
Equity attributable to members of Rinker Group Limited	2,502.90	2,678.20
Minority interests	10.1	9.1
Total equity	2,513.00	2,687.30

Source: Rinker Annual Report 2007.

Exhibit VII   A Note on Cement Industry in the US (2005–2009)

Cement has been one of the most commonly used construction materials in the world. The construction boom in the US in early 2000s through mid-2006 fueled the demand for cement from both the domestic cement producers as well as imports from foreign cement producers. In response to the increasing demand, several cement companies in the US invested in the latest technology to improve the efficiency of their plants as well as increasing their production capacities significantly. The cement production touched a record high of 99.319 million MT in 2005. The production contracted marginally for the years 2006 and 2007 before contracting by 25% from the peak to reach 75 million MT in 2009. The annual production of 75 million MT was the lowest in the US since the mid-1990s (Refer to Table A for Cement Production, Trade and Consumption in the US between 1995 and 2009).

Table A   Cement Production, Trade, and Consumption in*US (In million MT except year)

Year	Production	Imports	Exports	Aggregate Consumption
1995	76.906	10.969	0.759	86.003
1996	79.266	11.565	0.803	90.355
1997	82.582	14.523	0.791	96.018
1998	83.931	19.878	0.743	103.457
1999	85.952	24.578	0.694	108.862
2000	87.846	24.561	0.738	110.470
2001	88.900	23.694	0.746	112.810
2002	89.732	22.198	0.834	110.020
2003	92.843	21.015	0.837	114.091
2004	97.434	25.396	0.749	121.981
2005	99.319	30.403	0.766	128.276
2006	98.167	32.141	0.723	127.595
2007	95.464	21.496	0.885	116.695
2008	87.700	11.000	0.950	98.610
2009	75.000	10.000	0.900	84.000

Adapted from data available with US Geological Survey, January 2010.

The share of cement imports in the US domestic consumption peaked in 2006 when it hit 25.2%. That share had come down drastically to 11.90% by 2009. In absolute terms, the cement imports in the US fell from the peak of 32.141 million MT in 2006 to 10 million MT in 2009. However, the exports increased from 0.723 million MT per annum in 2006 to 0.9 million MT in 2009 as many global companies including CEMEX diverted their local production to other countries.

Despite a significant reduction in production volumes in 2008 and 2009, the average production volumes remained at around 91.13 million MT per annum over the five-year period ending 2009. The average figure was about the same as compared to the average production volume of 91.35 million MT per annum over the five-year period ending 2004. However, the average annual cement industry revenue was recorded at around US$ 10.2 billion per annum over the five years ending 2009 as compared to US$ 9.2 billion per annum over the five years ending 2004. The higher realization was due to the uptrend in the average prices of cement and related products since the mid-2000s. The cement industry's EBITDA also decreased from 54.5% of revenue in 2006 to 46% of revenue in 2009.

Exhibit VII (*continued*)

Housing starts, which represented new construction activity in the housing sector in the US, reflected the demand for cement from the housing sector. The starts fell to 550,000 in 2009 from a cyclical peak of 2,068,300 in 2005. On an average, around 21 MT of cement was consumed to construct a single family house with an average size of 2,500 square feet. In the year 2009, the cement consumption in the US fell to 84 million MT while the domestic production was at 75 million MT. In the same year, the industry reported revenue of US$ 8.25 billion, a fall of 14.8 percent as compared to 2008 revenues (Refer to Table B for Cement Industry Revenue in US between 1995 and 2009).

Table B   Cement Industry Revenue in the US (1995–2009)

Year	Industry Revenue (In US$ Million)	Growth (%)
1995	7,230.10	8.9
1996	7,727.80	6.9
1997	8,533.40	10.4
1998	9,024.10	5.8
1999	8,955.20	−0.8
2000	8,927.40	−0.3
2001	9,215.40	3.2
2002	9,862.70	7
2003	9,113.50	−7.6
2004	9,930.80	9
2005	10,756.60	8.3
2006	11,522.00	7.1
2007	11,000.00	−4.5
2008	10,000.00	−9.1
2009	8,525.00	−14.8

Adapted from data available with US Geological Survey, January 2010.

Though the new construction activity and prices in the housing sector declined because of the subprime crisis, construction activity in the nonhousing sector helped the cement industry to a certain extent. The nonhousing sector, including industrial buildings, bridges, roads, and other infrastructure projects, was provided financial support by the US administration through various stimulus packages to revive the sagging economy.

Though the years 2008 and 2009 had been tough for the cement industry, analysts expected the future for the industry in the US to be better. They estimated that the cement industry would record a strong cyclical growth in revenues at an average annual growth rate of 4.5% over the next five years till 2014. They expected the average annual production to be around 80.8 million MT during this period. Some analysts expected that domestic companies would resume running their facilities at full capacity to improve their productivity and combat low cost imports from the Asian countries. The cement imports were expected to rebound to 22.5 million MT by 2014.

A significant 77.5% market share in the US cement industry was controlled by the top five players. As of 2009, CEMEX was the leading player with a 25% market share followed by Holcim Inc (17.5%), HeidelbergCement AG (15%), Lafarge North America (15%), and Texas Industries Inc (5%).

Compiled from various sources.

Exhibit VIII   CEMEX–Contractual Obligations as of December 31, 2008 (In US$ Million)

Maturing	Less than 1 year	1–3 years	3–5 years	More than 5 years	2008 Total	2007 Total
Long-term debt	4,161	8,565	1,396	1,876	15,998	18,100
Capital Lease Obligation	14	10	3	—	27	51
Total debt	4,175	8,575	1,393	1,876	16,025	18,151
Operating Leases	214	339	228	179	960	841
Interest Payments on Debt	357	566	213	136	1,272	2,624
Interest rate derivatives	9	53	5	25	92	407
Pension plans and other benefits	164	309	311	825	1,609	1,925
Inactive derivative financial instruments	252	30	95	8	385	—
Total Contractual obligations	71,050	135,641	30,929	41,893	279,513	261,513

Source: CEMEX Annual Report 2008.

Exhibit IX   CEMEX Stock Price Chart

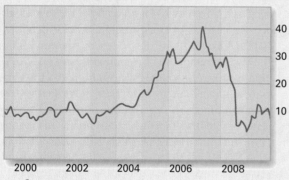

Cemex Stock Price Chart

Source: www.reuters.com.

Exhibit X   Mexican Peso vs US$ Chart

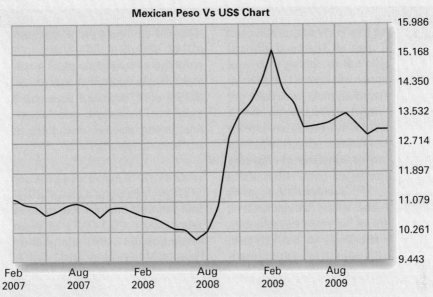

Mexican Peso Vs US$ Chart

Source: www. forexdirectory. net
*X-axis= US$ value in Mexican Pesos
Y-axis= Time Period

Exhibit XI   CEMEX Cash Flow Statement (2008) (In US$ millions)

	2008
Operating Activities	
Consolidated Net income	2,278
Non-Cash Items:	
Depreciation and amortization of assets	20,864
Impairment of assets	21,125
Equity in income of associates	(1,098)
Other expenses, net	(4,727)
Comprehensive financing result	28,725
Income taxes paid in cash	(23,562)
Change in working capital, excluding financial expenses and income taxes	1,243
Net cash flows provided by operating activities before comprehensive financing results and income taxes	44,848
Financial expenses paid in cash	(9,951)
Income taxes paid in cash	(3,625)
Net cash flows provided by operating activities before comprehensive financing results and income taxes	31,272
	(continued)

Exhibit XI (continued)

	2008
Investing activities	
Property, machinery and equipment, net	(21,248)
Disposal of subsidiaries and associates, net	10,845
Investment derivatives	2,856
Intangible assets and other deferred charges	(1,975)
Long-term assets, net	(2,838)
Others, net	586
Net cash flows used in investing activities	(11,774)
Financing Activities	
Issuance of common stock	6,794
Financing Derivatives	(12,765)
Dividends paid	(7,009)
Repayment of debt, net	(3,710)
Issuance of perpetual debentures, net of interest paid	(1,801)
Noncurrent liabilities, net	1,897
Net cash flows used in financing activities	(16,594)
Cash and investments conversion effect	2,030
Increase in cash and investments	4,934
Cash and investments at beginning of the year	8,670
Cash and investments at the end of year	13,604

Source: CEMEX Annual Report 2008.

Suggested Readings and References:

1. CRH Buying CEMEX Cement Assets, www.domain-b.com, 18 September 2007.
2. William Patalon III, Global Cement Giant CEMEX Looks to Cut Costs, Debt After Rinker Buyout, http://moneymorning.com, December 14, 2007.
3. Fitch: CEMEX Results in Line; Expect Further U.S. Slowdown, www.bnamericas.com, January 30, 2008.
4. Robin Emmott, **Mexico's CEMEX Starts Big Asset Sale to Pay Debt**, w.reuters.com, April 01, 2008.
5. Michael Tian, CEMEX Faces an Uncertain Future, http://quicktake.morningstar.com, October 10, 2008.
6. **S&P Cuts CEMEX CCR To 'BBB-', Outlook** Still Negative, http://uk.reuters.com, October 14, 2008.
7. Neil Gerrard, CEMEX To Cut 6,000 Jobs Worldwide; UK Sales Drop 19%, www.contractjournal.com, October 17, 2008.
8. CEMEX Sells Plant In Canary Islands To Reduce Debt From Rinker Acquisition, www.domain-b.com, 11 November 2008.
9. Shanna McCord, CEMEX Will Shut Down For Six Months, Lay Off More Than 100, www.mercurynews.com, January 09, 2009.
10. CEMEX In Trouble, http://concreteconstruction.net, March 06, 2009.
11. Robin Emmott and Andrea Ricci, No CEMEX Upgrade Soon Even After Debt Refinanced- S&P, www.reuters.com, March 11, 2009.
12. David Lee Smith, **CEMEX's Financial Bungee Jumping**, http://www.fool.com, May 01, 2009.
13. CEMEX to sell Australian operations to Holcim Group, www.domain-b.com, June 15, 2009.
14. Robin Emmott, CEMEX Sell Assets Cheap, Tries To Refinance, www.reuters.com, June 15, 2009.
15. Laura Mandaro, CEMEX Could Sell Stock To Relieve Debt Squeeze, www.marketwatch.com, June 18, 2009.
16. Robin Emmott, **CEMEX's 2nd**-qtr Profit Falls On US Housing Impact, www.reuters.com, July 22, 2008.

17. Robin Emmott and Chris Aspin, CEMEX Sees Worsening U.S. Housing Market, www.reuters.com, July 23, 2008.
18. Robin Emmott, CEMEX Creditors Back Debt Plan; Sales View Bleak, www.reuters.com, July 29, 2009.
19. Robin Emmott, Buy Or Sell-**Mexico's** CEMEX Fate Hangs On Debt Talks, www.reuters.com, July 30, 2009.
20. Gabriela Lopez, **Mexico's CEMEX Wins Time On $1.2 Bln Debt**, www.reuters.com, July 31, 2009.
21. Gabriela Lopez, **Mexico's CEMEX Says All Creditors Support Debt Deal**, www.reuters.com, August 10, 2009.
22. Robert Campbell, CEMEX Gains On Debt News, But Questions Remain, www.reuters.com, August 11, 2009.
23. Anthony Harrup, CEMEX Given Rinker Debt Lifeline, www.theaustralian.com.au, August 12, 2009.
24. Thomas Black, CEMEX Extends Payments on $15 Billion in Debt to 2014, www.bloomberg.com, August 14, 2009.
25. Patricia Oey, CEMEX Completes Debt Restructuring, www.morningstar.com, August 14, 2009.
26. Chris Sleight, CEMEX to Launch US $1.8 Billion Share Issue, www.khl.com, September 09, 2009.
27. CEMEX Reports Third Quarter 2009 Results, http://news.moneycentral.msn.com, October 27, 2009.
28. Thomas Black, **CEMEX Should Have Financed 'More Conservatively': Week Ahead**, www.bloomberg.com, November 02, 2009.
29. Kejal Vyas, CEMEX Raises $1.25B, EUR350M In Bond Offer As Buyers Step Up, http://online.wsj.com, December 09, 2009.
30. Robin Emmott, **Mexico's CEMEX Sells Nearly $1.8 bn in Bonds**, www.reuters.com, December 09, 2009.
31. Veronica Navarro Espinosa, CEMEX Prices $500 Million of 2016 Bonds in Re-Opening, www.businessweek.com, January 13, 2010.
32. Gabriela Lopez, CEMEX Juggles Debt But US Still a Worry, ww.forexyard.com, January 19, 2010.
33. Thomas Black, CEMEX Falls as 2010 EBITDA Forecast Trails Estimates, www.bloomberg.com, January 27, 2010.
34. **Mexico's CEMEX Reports $265 Million Profit For 4q,** www.businessweek.com.
35. www.cio.com.
36. www.sec.gov.
37. www.cemex.com.

Endnotes

1 Gabriela Lopez, "CEMEX Juggles Debt But U.S.Still a Worry," ww.forexyard.com, January 19, 2010.
2 Thomas Black, "CEMEX Extends Payments on $15 Billion in Debt to 2014," www.bloomberg.com, August 14, 2009.
3 The sub-prime crisis that emerged in the US in late 2007 led to a crash in the prices of several asset classes. Investments of several financial institutions and individuals incurred deep losses. Several industries eliminated thousands of jobs resulting in an economic slowdown and a global financial crisis.
4 Thomas Black, Cemex Falls as 2010 EBITDA Forecast Trails Estimates, www.bloomberg.com, January 27, 2010.
5 Both the founder and his grandson, who eventually became the CEO of Cementos Mexicano, were given the same name, Lorenzo Zambrano.
6 Lorenzo Zambrano spent his teenage years in Missouri Military Academy in Mexico. He earned an engineering graduate degree from the Institute Tecnologico in Monterrey and an MBA degree from Stanford University.
7 Cementos Anahuac was a cement company in Mexico with two plants and total capacity of 4 million MT per year.
8 Cementos Tolteca was a cement company in Mexico with seven plants and total capacity of 6.8 million MT per year.
9 Founded in 1927, Cementos Diamante was a Colombia-based company engaged in the production, sale, and distribution of cement and ready-made concrete.
10 Founded in 1930, Southdown was a Houston, Texas-based cement and ready-mix concrete manufacturing company.
11 The RMC Group, formerly known as Ready Mix Concrete PLC, was founded in 1930 and was based in Egham.
12 One of the important criteria in CEMEX's acquisition strategy was that the acquisition should contribute to its capital structure. By that, the company meant that it should manage its investment grade rating even after acquiring the target company. 'BBB-' and above rating awarded by Standard & Poor's rating services company are considered as investment grade rating in the US.
13 Volume weighted average price is the ratio of value traded to the total volume over a particular period of time. Value traded is the summation of the product of share volume and traded price of each transaction and volume is the total volume of shares traded during a particular period. VWAP = X (number of shares bought X share price)/Total number of shares.
14 Aggregates are inert granular materials such as sand, gravel, or crushed stone that along with water and cement are an essential ingredient for concrete.
15 On February 22, 2010, US$ 1= A$ 1.10965.
16 The US$ 19.9 billion debt included Rinker's US$ 1.1 billion outstanding debt at the time of acquisition.
17 Robin Emmott, "Mexico's Cemex Starts Big Asset Sale to Pay Debt," www.reuters.com, April 01, 2008.
18 Standard & Poor's is one of the leading credit rating agencies based in the US. It is a division of McGraw Hill and publishes financial research reports on different types of financial securities. It was founded in 1860.
19 "S&P Cuts Cemex CCR to 'BBB-', Outlook Still Negative," http://uk.reuters.com, October 14, 2008.
20 Founded in 1913, Fitch Ratings is one of the leading credit rating agencies dual head quartered at London and New York.
21 Robin Emmott and Andrea Ricci, "No Cemex Upgrade Soon Even After Debt Refinanced- S&P," www.reuters.com, March 11, 2009.
22 On February 22, 2010, US$ 1= MXP 12.8087.
23 Gabriela Lopez, "CEMEX Juggles Debt But US Still a Worry," ww.forexyard.com, January 19, 2010.

CASE 27

3M—The Second Century

Charles W.L. Hill
University of Washington

Established in 1902, 3M was one of the largest technology driven enterprises in the United States with annual sales of $26 billion, (63% of which were outside the United States) by 2010. The company was solidly profitable, earning $4.09 billion in net income in 2010, and generating a return on invested capital of 20.53%. Throughout its history, 3M's researchers had driven much of the company's growth. In 2010, the company sold some 55,000 products, including Post-it Notes, Flexible Circuits, Scotch Tape, abrasives, specialty chemicals, Thinsulate insulation products, Nexcare bandage, optical films, fiber optic connectors, drug delivery systems and much more. Around 7,350 of the company's 80,000 employees were technical employees. 3M's annual R&D budget exceeded $1.4 billion. The company had garnered over 8,000 patents since 1990, with 589 new patents awarded in 2010 alone. 3M was organized into 35 different business units grouped together into 6 main areas; consumer and office products; display and graphics; electronics and telecommunications; health care; industrial and transportation; safety, security and protection services (see Exhibit 1 for details).

The company's 100-year anniversary in 2002 was a time for celebration, but also one for strategic reflection. During the prior decade, 3M had grown profits and sales by 6–7% per annum, a respectable figure, but one that lagged behind the growth rates achieved by some other technology-based enterprises and diversified industrial enterprises like General Electric. In 2001, 3M took a step away from its past when the company hired James McNerney Jr. as CEO, the first outsider to hold this position. McNerney, who joined 3M after heading up GE's fast growing medical equipment business (and losing out in the race to replace legendary GE CEO, Jack Welch), was quick to signal that he wanted 3M to accelerate its growth rate. McNerney set an ambitious target for 3M–to grow sales by 11% per annum

and profits by 12% per annum. Many wondered if McNerney could achieve this without damaging the innovation engine that had propelled 3M to its current stature. The question remained unanswered, as McNerney left to run the Boeing Company in 2005. His successor, however, George Buckley, another outsider, seemed committed to continuing on the course McNerney had set for the company.

The History of 3M: Building Innovative Capabilities

The 3M story begins in 1902 when 5 Minnesota business men established the Minnesota Mining and Manufacturing company to mine a mineral that they thought was corundum, which is ideal for making sandpaper. The mineral, however, turned out to be low-grade anorthosite, nowhere near as suitable for making sandpaper, and the company nearly failed. To try and salvage the business, 3M turned to making the sandpaper using materials purchased from another source.

In 1907, 3M hired a 20-year old business student, William McKnight, as assistant bookkeeper. This turned out to be a pivotal move in the history of the company. The hardworking McKnight soon made his mark. By 1929, he was CEO of the company, and in 1949 he became chairman of 3M's board of directors, a position that he held until 1966.

From Sandpaper to Post-it Notes

It was McKnight, then 3M's president, who hired the company's first scientist, Richard Carlton, in 1921. Around the same time, McKnight's interest had been peaked by an odd request from a Philadelphian printer named Francis Okie for samples of every sandpaper grit size that 3M made. McKnight dispatched

Exhibit 1   Financial Facts—Year-End 2010

3M is one of 30 companies in the Dow Jones Industrial Average and also is a component of the Standard & Poor's 500 Index.

Sales	
Worldwide	$26.66 billion
International	$17.45 billion
65 percent of company's total	
Net Income	
Net Income	$4.085 billion
Percent to sales	15.3 percent
Earnings per share—diluted	$5.63
Taxes	
Income tax expense	$1.592 billion
Dividends	
(Paid every quarter since 1916) Cash dividends per share	$2.10
One original share, if held, is now	3,072 shares
R&D and Related Expenditures	
For 2010	$1.434 billion
Total for last five years	$6.055 billion
Capital Spending	
For 2010	$1.091 billion
Total for last five years	$6.055 billion
Employees	
Worldwide	80,057
United States	32,955
International	47,102
Organization	
• More than 35 business units, organized into six businesses: Consumer and Office; Display and Graphics; Electro and Communications; Health Care; Industrial and Transportation; Safety, Security and Protection Services	
• Operations in more than 65 countries—38 international companies with manufacturing operations, 35 with laboratories	
• In the United States, operations in 28 states	
Patents	
U.S. patents awarded in 2010	589

Source: 3M Website http://phx.corporate-ir.net/phoenix.zhtml?c=80574&p=irol-irhome

3M's East coast sales manager to find out why Okie wanted the samples. The sales manager discovered that Okie had invented a new kind of sandpaper that he had patented. It was waterproof sandpaper that could be used with water or oil to reduce dust and decrease the friction that marred auto finishes. In addition, the lack of dust reduced the poisoning associated with inhaling the dust of paint that had a high lead content. Okie had a problem though; he had no financial backers to commercialize the sandpaper. 3M quickly stepped in to the breach, purchasing the rights to Okie's Wetordry waterproof sandpaper, and hiring the young printer to come and join Richard Carlton in 3M's lab. Wetordry sandpaper revolutionized the sandpaper industry, and was the driver of significant growth at 3M.

Another key player in the company's history, Richard Drew, also joined 3M in 1921. Hired straight out of the University of Minnesota, Drew would round out the trio of scientists, Carlton, Okie and Drew, who under McKnight's leadership would do much to shape 3M's innovative organization.

McKnight charged the newly hired Drew with developing a stronger adhesive to better bind the grit for sandpaper to paper backing. While experimenting with adhesives, Drew accidentally developed a weak adhesive that had an interest quality—if placed on the back of a strip of paper and stuck to a surface, the strip of paper could be peeled off the surface it was adhered to without leaving any adhesive residue on that surface. This discovery gave Drew an epiphany. He had been visiting auto-body paint shops to see how 3M's Wetordry sand paper was used, and he noticed that there was a problem with paint running. His epiphany was to cover the back of a strip of paper with his weak adhesive, and use it as "masking tape" to cover parts of the auto's body that were not to be painted. An excited Drew took his idea to McKnight, and explained how masking tape might create an entirely new business for 3M. McKnight reminded Drew that he had been hired to fix a specific problem, and pointedly suggested that he concentrate only on doing that.

Chastised, Dew went back to his lab, but he could not get the idea out of his mind, so he continued to work on it at night, long after everyone else had gone home. Drew succeeded in perfecting the masking tape product, and then went to visit several auto-body shops to show them his innovation. He quickly received several commitments for orders. Drew then went to see McKnight again. He told him that he had continued to work on the masking tape idea on his own time, had perfected the product, and got several customers interested in purchasing it. This time it was McKnight's turn to be chastised. Realizing that he had almost killed a good business idea, McKnight reversed his original position, and gave Drew the go ahead to pursue the idea.[1]

Introduced into the market in 1925, Drew's invention of masking tape represented the first significant product diversification at 3M. Company legend has it that this incident was also the genesis for 3M's famous 15% rule. Reflecting on Drew's work, both McKnight and Carlton both agreed that technical people could disagree with management, and should be allowed to do some experimentation on their own. The company then established a norm that technical people could spend up to 15% of their own workweek on projects that might benefit the consumer, without having to justify the project to their manager.

Drew himself was not finished. In the late-1920s, he was working with cellophane, a product that had been invented by DuPont, when lightning struck for a second time. Why, Drew wondered, couldn't cellophane be coated with an adhesive and used as a sealing tape? The result was Scotch Cellophane Tape. The first batch was delivered to a customer in September 1930, and Scotch Tape went on to become one of 3M's best selling products. Years later, Drew noted: "Would there have been any masking or cellophane tape if it hadn't been for earlier 3M research on adhesive binders for 3M™ Wetordry™ Abrasive Paper? Probably not!"[2]

Over the years, other scientists followed Drew's footsteps at 3M, creating a wide range of innovative products by leveraging existing technology and applying it to new areas. Two famous examples illustrate how many of these innovations occurred—the invention of Scotch Guard, and the development of the ubiquitous "Post-it Notes."

The genesis of Scotchgard was in 1953, when a 3M scientist named Patsy Sherman was working on a new kind of rubber for jet aircraft fuel lines. Some of the latex mixture splashed onto a pair of canvas tennis shoes. Over time, the spot stayed clean while the rest of the canvas soiled. Sherman enlisted the help of fellow chemist Sam Smith. Together they began to investigate polymers, and it didn't take long for them to realize that they were on to something. They discovered an oil and water repellant substance, based on the fluorocarbon fluid used in air conditioners, which had enormous potential for protecting fabrics from stains. It took several years before the team perfected a way to apply the treatment using water as the carrier, thereby making it economically feasible for use as a finish in textile plants.

Three years after the accidental spill, the first rain and stain repellent for use on wool was announced. Experience and time revealed that one product could not, however, effectively protect all fabrics, so 3M continued working, producing a wide range of Scotchgard products that could be used to protect all kinds of fabrics.[3]

The story of Post-it Notes began with Spencer Silver, a senior scientist studying adhesives.[4] In 1968, Silver had developed an adhesive with properties like no other; it was a pressure sensitive adhesive that would adhere to a surface, but was weak enough to easily peel off the surface and leave no residue. Silver spent several years shopping his adhesive around 3M, to no avail. It was a classic case of a technology is search of a product. Then, one day in 1973, Art Fry, a new product development researcher who had attended one of Silver's seminars, was singing in his church choir. He was frustrated that his bookmarks kept falling out of his hymn book, when he had a "Eureka" moment. Fry realized that Silver's adhesive could be used to make a wonderfully reliable bookmark.

Fry went to work the next day, and using his 15% time, started to develop the bookmark. When he started using the sample to write notes to his boss, Fry suddenly realized that he had stumbled on a much bigger potential use for the product. Before the product could be commercialized, however, Fry had to solve a host of technical and manufacturing problems. With the support of his boss, Fry persisted and after 18 months the product development effort moved from 15% time to a formal development effort funded by 3M's own seed capital.

The first Post-it Notes were test marketed in 1977 in 4 major cities, but customers were lukewarm at best. This did not support the experience within 3M, where people in Fry's division were using samples all the time to write messages to each other. Further research revealed that the test marketing effort, which focused on ads and brochures, didn't resonate well with consumers, who didn't seem to value Post-it Notes until they had the actual product in their hands. In 1978, 3M tried again, this time

descending on Boise, Idaho, where they handed out samples. Follow up research revealed that 90% of consumers who tried the product said they would buy it. Armed with this knowledge, 3M rolled out the national launch of Post-it Notes in 1980. The product subsequently became a best seller.

Institutionalizing Innovation

Early on, McKnight set an ambitious target for 3M–a 10% annual increase in sales and 25% profit target. He also indicated how he thought that should be achieved—with a commitment to plow 5% of sales back into R&D every year. The question, however, was how to ensure that 3M would continue to produce new products?

The answer was not apparent all at once, but rather evolved over the years from experience. A prime example was the 15% rule, which developed after McKnight's experience with Drew. In addition to the 15% rule and the continued commitment to push money back into R&D, a number of other mechanisms evolved at 3M to spur innovation.

Initially, research took place in the business units that made and sold products, but by the 1930s, 3M had already diversified into several different fields, thanks in large part to the efforts of Drew and others. McKnight and Carlton realized that there was a need for a central research function. In 1937 they established a central research laboratory which was charged with supplementing the work of product divisions and undertaking long-term basic research. From the outset, the researchers at the lab were multidisciplinary, with people from different scientific disciplines often working next to each other on research benches.

As the company continued to grow, it became clear that there was a need for some mechanism to knit together the company's increasingly diverse business operations. This led to the establishment of the 3M Technical Forum in 1951. The goal of Technical Forum was to foster idea sharing, discussion, and problem solving between technical employees located in different divisions and the central research laboratory. The Technical Forum sponsored "problem solving sessions" at which businesses would present their most recent technical nightmares in the hope that somebody might be able to suggest a solution—and that often was the case. The forum also established an annual event in which each division put up a booth to show off its latest technologies. Chapters were also created to focus on specific disciplines, such as polymer chemistry or coating processes.

During the 1970s, the Technical Forum cloned itself, establishing forums in Australia and England. By 2001, the forum had grown to 9,500 members in 8 U.S. locations and 19 other countries, becoming an international network of researchers who could share ideas, solve problems, and leverage technology.

According to Marylee Paulson, who coordinated the Technical Forum from 1979 to 1992, the great virtue of the Technical Forum is to cross-pollinate ideas:

> 3M has lots of polymer chemists. They may be in tape; they may be medical or several other divisions. The forum pulls them across 3M to share what they know. It's a simple but amazingly effective way to bring like minds together.[5]

In 1999, 3M created another unit within the company, 3M Innovative Properties (3M, IPC) to leverage technical know-how. 3M IPC is explicitly charged with protecting and leveraging 3M's intellectual property around the world. At 3M there had been a long tradition that while divisions "own" their products, the company has a whole "owns" the underlying technology, or intellectual property. One task of 3M IPC is to find ways in which 3M technology can be applied across business units to produce unique marketable products. Historically, the company has been remarkably successful at leveraging company technology to produce new product ideas (see Exhibit 2 for some examples).

Another key to institutionalizing innovation at 3M has been the principle of "patient money." The basic idea is that producing revolutionary new products requires substantial long-term investments, and often repeated failures, before a major payoff occurs.

Exhibit 2   Examples of Leveraging Technology at 3M[6]

Richard Miller, a corporate scientist in 3M Pharmaceuticals, began experimental development of an antiherpes medicinal cream in 1982. After several years of development, his research team found that the interferon-based materials they were working with could be applied to any skin-based virus. The innovative chemistry they were working with was applied topically and was more effective than other compounds on the market. They found that the cream was particularly effective to inhibiting the growth mechanism of genital warts. Competitive materials on the market at the time were caustic and tended to be painful. Miller's team obtained FDA approval for its Aldara (imiquimod) line of topical patient-applied creams in 1997.

Miller then applied the same Aldara-based chemical mechanism to basal cell carcinomas and found that, here too, it was particularly effective to restricting the growth of the skin cancer. "The patient benefit is quite remarkable," says Miller. New results in efficacy have been presented for treating skin cancers. His team recently completed phase III clinical testing and expects to apply later this year for FDA approval for this disease preventative. This material is already FDA approved for use in the treatment of genital warts. Doctors are free to choose to use it to treat those patients with skin cancers.

Andrew Ouderkirk is a corporate scientist in 3M's Film & Light Management Technology Center. 3M has been working in light management materials applied to polymer-based films since the 1930s, according to Ouderkirk. Every decade since then, 3M has introduced some unique thin-film structure for a specific customer application from high-performance safety reflectors for street signs, to polarized lighting products. Every decade, 3Ms technology base has become more specialized and more sophisticated. Their technology has now reached the point at which they can produce multiple-layer interference films, each to 100-nm thicknesses, and hold the tolerances on each layer to within +/− 3 nm. "Our laminated films are now starting to compete with vacuum-coated films in some applications," says Ouderkirk.

Rick Weiss is technical director of 3M's Microreplication Technology Center, one of 3M's 12 core technology centers. The basic microreplication technology was discovered In the early-1960s, when 3M researchers were developing the fresnel lenses for overhead projectors. 3M scientists have expanded upon this technology to use it on a wide variety of applications including optical reflectors for solar collectors, and adhesive coatings with air bleed ribs that allow large area films to be applied without allowing the characteristic "bubbles" appear. Weiss is currently working on development of dimensionally precise barrier ribs that can be applied to separate the individual "gas" cells on the new high resolution large screen commercial plasma displays. Other applications include fluid management where capillary action can be used in biological testing systems to split a drop of blood into a large number of parts.

The principle can be traced back to 3M's early days. It took the company 12 years before its initial sandpaper business started to show a profit, a fact that drove home the importance of taking the long view. Throughout the company's history, similar examples can be found. Scotchlite reflective sheeting, now widely used on road signs, didn't show much profit for 10 years. The same was true of flurochemicals and duplicating products. Patent money doesn't mean substantial funding for long periods of time, however. Rather, it might imply that a small group of 5 researchers is supported for 10 years while they work on a technology.

More generally, if a researcher creates a new technology or idea, they can begin working on it using 15% of their time. If the idea shows promise, they may request seed capital from their business unit managers to develop it further. If that funding is denied, which can occur, they are free to take the idea to any other 3M business unit. Unlike many other companies, requests for seed capital do not require that researchers draft detailed business plans that are reviewed by top management; that comes later in the process. As one former senior technology manager has noted:

> In the early stages of a new product or technology, it shouldn't be overly managed. If we start asking for business plans too early and insist on tight financial evaluations, we'll kill an idea or surely slow it down.[7]

Explaining the patent money philosophy, Ron Baukol, a former Executive Vice President of 3M's international operations, and a manager who started as a researcher, has noted that:

> You just know that some things are going to be worth working on, and that requires technological patience . . . you don't put too much money into the investigation, but you keep one to five people working on it for twenty years if you have to. You do that because you know that, once you have cracked the code, it's going to be big.[8]

An internal review of 3M's innovation process in the early-1980s concluded that despite the liberal process for funding new product ideas, some promising ideas did not receive funding from business units, or the central research budget. This led to the establishment of Genesis Grants, which provide up to $100,000 in seed capital for projects that do not get funded through 3M's regular channels, in 1985.

About a dozen of these grants will be given every year. One of the recipients of these grants, a project that focused on creating a multilayered reflective film, has subsequently produced a break though reflective technology that may have applications in a wide range of businesses, from better reflective strips on road signs to computer displays and the reflective linings in light fixtures. Company estimates in 2002 suggested that the commercialization of this technology might ultimately generate $1 billion in sales for 3M.

Underlying the patent money philosophy is recognition that innovation is a very risky business. 3M has long acknowledged that failure is an accepted and essential part of the new product development process. As former 3M CEO Lew Lehr once noted:

> We estimate that 60% of our formal new product development programs never make it. When this happens, the important thing is to not punish the people involved.[9]

In an effort to reduce the probability of failure, in the 1960s, 3M started to establish a process for auditing the product development efforts ongoing in the company's business units. The idea has been to provide a peer review, or technical audit, of major development projects taking place in the company. A typical technical audit team is composed of 10–15 business and technical people, including technical directors and senior scientists from other divisions. The audit team will look at the strengths and weaknesses of a development program, and its probability of success, both from a technical standpoint and a business standpoint. The team then will make non-binding recommendations, but are normally taken very seriously by the managers of a project. For example, if an audit team concludes that a project has enormous potential, but is terribly underfunded, managers of the unit would often increase the funding level. Of course, the converse can also happen, and in many instances, the audit team can provide useful feedback and technical ideas that can help a development team to improve their project's chance of success.

By the 1990s, the continuing growth of 3M had produced a company that was simultaneously pursuing a vast array of new product ideas. This was a natural outcome of 3M's decentralized and bottom up approach to innovation, but it was problematic in one crucial respect, the company's R&D resources were being spread too thinly over a wide range of opportunities, resulting in potentially major projects being under funded. To try and channel R&D resources into projects that had blockbuster potential, 3M introduced what was known as the Pacing Plus Program in 1994.

The program asked businesses to select a small number of programs that would receive priority funding, but 3M's senior executives made the final decision on which programs were to be selected for the Pacing Plus Program. An earlier attempt to do this in 1990 had been met with limited success because each sector in 3M submitted as many as 200 programs. The Pacing Plus Program narrowed the list down to 25 key programs that, by 1996, were receiving some 20% of 3M's entire R&D funds (by the early-2000s the number of projects funded under the Pacing Plus Program had grown to 60). The focus was on "leapfrog technologies," revolutionary ideas that might change the basis of competition and lead to entirely new technology platforms that might in typical 3M fashion, spawn an entire range of new products.

To further foster a culture of entrepreneurial innovation and risk taking, 3M established a number of reward and recognition programs to honor employees who make significant contributions to the company. These include the Carton Society Award, which honors employees for outstanding career scientific achievements, and the Circle of Technical Excellence and Innovation Award, which recognizes people who have made exceptional contributions to 3M's technical capabilities, among others.

Another key component of 3M's innovative culture has been an emphasis on dual career tracks. Right for its early days, many of the key players in 3M's history, people like Richard Drew, chose to stay in research, turning down opportunities to go into the management side of the business. Over the years, this became formalized in a dual career path. Today, technical employees can choose to follow a technical career path or a management career path, with equal advancement opportunities. This can allow researchers to develop their technical professional interests, without being financially penalized for not going into management.

Although 3M's innovative culture emphasizes the role of technical employees in producing innovations, the company also has a strong tradition of emphasizing that new product ideas often come from watching customers at work. Richard Drew's original idea for masking tape, for example, came from watching workers use 3M Wetordry sandpaper in auto body shops. As with much else at 3M, the tone was set by McKnight, who insisted that salespeople needed to "get behind the smokestacks" of 3M customers, going onto the factory floor, talking to workers, and finding out what problems they were experiencing. Over the years, this theme had become ingrained in 3M's culture, with salespeople often requesting time to watch customers work, and then brining their insights about customer problems back into their organization.

By the mid-1990s, McKnight's notion of getting behind the smokestacks had evolved into the idea that 3M could learn a tremendous amount from what were termed "lead users," who were customers working in very demanding conditions. Over the years, 3M had observed that in many cases, customers can be innovators, developing new products to solve problems that they face in their workplace. This was most likely to occur for customers working in very demanding conditions. To take advantage of this process, 3M has instituted a lead user process in the company in which cross-functional teams from a business unit observe how customers work in demanding situations.

For example, 3M now has a $100 million business selling surgical drapes, which are drapes backed with adhesives that are used to cover parts of a body during surgery and help prevent infection. As an aid to new product development, 3M's surgical drapes business had formed a cross-functional team that observed surgeons at work in very demanding situations–including on battlefields, in hospitals in developing nations, and in veterinarian's offices. The result was a new set of product ideas, including low-cost surgical drapes that were affordable in developing nations, and devices for coating a patient's skin and surgical instruments with antimicrobial substances that would reduce the chance of infection during surgery.[10]

Driving the entire innovation machine at 3M has been a series of stretch goals set by top managers. The goals date back to 3M's early days and McKnight's ambitious growth targets. In 1977, the company established "Challenge 81," which called for 25% of sales to come from products that had been on the market for less than 5 years by 1981. By the 1990s, the goal had been raised to the requirement that 30% of sales should come from products that had been on the market less than 4 years.

The flip side of these goals was that many products and businesses that had been 3M staples were phased out over the years. More than 20 of the businesses that were 3M mainstays in 1980, for example, had been phased out by 2000. Analysts estimate that sales from mature products at 3M generally fall by 3% to 4% per annum. The company has a long history of inventing businesses, leading the market for long periods of time, and then shutting those businesses down, or selling them off, when they can no longer meet 3M's own demanding growth targets. Notable examples include the duplicating business, a business 3M invented with Thermo-Fax copiers (which were ultimately made obsolete my Xerox's patented technology) and the video and audio magnetic tape business. The former division was sold off in 1985, and the latter in 1995. In both cases, the company exited these areas because they had become low growth commodity businesses, which could not generate the kind of top line growth for which 3M was looking.

Still, 3M was by no means invulnerable in the realm of innovation, and on occasion squandered huge opportunities, such as the document copying business. 3M invented this business in 1951 when it introduced the world's first commercially successful Thermo-Fax copier (which used specially coated 3M paper to copy original typed documents). 3M dominated the world copier business until 1970, when Xerox surpassed the company with its revolutionary xerographic technology that used plane paper to make copies. 3M anticipated Xerox' move, but rather than try and develop their own plain paper copier, the company invested funds in trying to improve its (increasingly obsolete) copying technology. It wasn't until 1975 that 3M introduced its own plain paper copier, and by then it was too late. Strangely, 3M turned down the chance to acquire Xerox' technology 20 years earlier, when the company's founders had approached 3M.

Building the Organization

McKnight, a strong believer in decentralization, organized the company into product divisions in 1948, making 3M one of the early adopters of this organizational form. Each division was set up as an individual profit center that had the power, autonomy and resources to run independently. At the same time, certain functions remained centralized, including significant R&D, human resources, and finance.

McKnight wanted to keep the divisions small enough that people had a chance to be entrepreneurial, and focused on the customer. A key philosophy of McKnight's was "divide and grow." Put simply, when a division became too big, some of its embryonic businesses were developed into a new division. Not only did this new division then typically attain higher growth rates, but the original division had to find new drivers of growth to offset the contribution of the businesses that had gained independence. This drove the search for further innovations.

At 3M, the process of organic diversification by splitting divisions became known as "renewal." The examples of renewal within 3M are legion. A copying machine project for Thermo-Fax copiers grew into the Office Products Division. When Magnetic Recording Materials was developed from the Electrical Products division, it had become its own division, and then in turn spawned a spate of divisions.

However, this organic process was not without its downside. By the early-1990s some of 3M's key customers were frustrated that they had to do business with a large number of different 3M divisions. In some cases, there could be representatives from 10–20 different 3M divisions calling on the same customer. To cope with this problem, 3M started to assign key account representatives to sell 3M products directly to major customers in 1992. These representatives typically worked across divisional lines. Implementing the strategy required many of 3M's general managers to give up some of their autonomy and power, but the solution seemed to work well, particularly for 3M's consumer and office divisions.

Underpinning the organization that McKnight put in place was his own management philosophy. As explained in a 1948 document, his basic management philosophy consisted of the following values:

As our business grows, it becomes increasingly necessary to delegate responsibility and to encourage men and women to exercise their initiative. This requires considerable tolerance. Those men and women to whom we delegate authority and responsibility, if they are good people, are going to want to do their jobs in their own way.

Mistakes will be made. But if a person is essentially right, the mistakes he or she makes are not as serious in the long run as the mistakes management will make if it undertakes to tell those in authority exactly how they must do their jobs.

Management that is destructively critical when mistakes are made kills initiative. And it's essential that we have many people with initiative if we are to continue to grow.[11]

At just 3% per annum, employee turnover rate at 3M has long been among the lowest in corporate America, a fact that is often attributed to the tolerant, empowering and family-like corporate culture that McKnight helped to establish. Reinforcing this culture has been a progressive approach toward employee compensation and retention. In the depths of the Great Depression, 3M was able to avoid laying off employees while many others didn't because the company's innovation engine was able to keep building new businesses even through the most difficult economic times.

In many ways, 3M was ahead of its time in management philosophy and human resource practices. The company introduced its first profit sharing plan in 1916, and McKnight instituted a pension plan in 1930 and an employee stock purchase plan in 1950. McKnight himself was convinced that people would be much more likely to be loyal in a company if they had a stake within it. 3M also developed a policy of promoting from within, and of giving its employees a plethora of career opportunities within the company.

Going International

The first steps abroad occurred in the 1920s. There were some limited sales of Wetordry sandpaper in Europe during the early-1920s. These increased after 1929 when 3M joined the Durex Corporation, a joint venture for international abrasive product sales in which 3M was involved, along with 8 other United States companies. In 1950, however, the Department of Justice alleged that the Durex Corporation was a mechanism for achieving collusion among U.S. abrasive manufacturers, and a judge ordered that the corporation be dissolved. After the Durex Corporation was dissolved in 1951, 3M was left with a sandpaper factory in Britain, a small plant in France, a sales office in Germany, and a tape factory in Brazil. International sales at this point amounted to no more than 5% of 3M's total revenues.

Although 3M opposed the dissolution of the Durex Corporation, in retrospect it turned out to be one of the most important events in the company's history, for it forced the corporation to build its own international operations. By 2010, international sales amounted to 63% of total revenues.

In 1952, Clarence Sampair was put in charge of 3M's international operations and was responsible for launching them. He was given considerable strategic and operational independence. Sampair and his successor, Maynard Patterson, worked hard to protect the international operations from getting caught in the red tape of a major corporation. For example, Patterson recounts how:

I asked Em Monteiro to start a small company in Columbia. I told him to pick a key person he wanted to take with him "Go start a company," I said, "and no one from St Paul is going to visit you unless you ask for them. We'll stay out of your way, and if someone sticks his nose in your business you call me."[12]

The international businesses were grouped into an International Division that Sampair lead. From the beginning, the company insisted that foreign ventures pay their own way. In addition, 3M's international companies were expected to pay a 5% to 10% royalty to the corporate head office. Starved of working capital, 3M's International Division relied heavily upon local borrowing to fund local operations, a fact that forced those operations to quickly pay their own way.

The international growth at 3M typically occurred in stages. The company would start by exporting to a country and working through sales subsidiaries. In that way, it began to understand the country, the local marketplace, and the local business environment. Next, 3M established warehouses in each nation, and stocked those with goods paid for in local currency. The next phase involved converting products to the sizes and packaging forms that the local market conditions, customs and culture dictated. 3M would ship jumbo-sized rolls of products from the United States, which were then broken down and repackaged for each country. The next stage was designing and building plants, buying machinery and making the plants operational. Over the years, R&D functions were often added, and by the 1980s, considerable R&D was being done outside of the United States.

Both Sampair and Patterson set an innovative, entrepreneurial framework that according to the company, still guides 3M's International Operations today. The philosophy can be reduced to several key and simple commitments: (1) Get in early (within the company, the strategy is known as FIDO—"First in Defeats Others"); (2) Hire talented and motivated local people; (3) Become a good corporate citizen of the country; (4) Grow with the local economy; (5) American products are not one-size-fits-all around the world—tailor products to fit local needs; (6) Enforce patents in local countries.

As 3M stepped into the international market vacuum, foreign sales surged from less than 5% in 1951 to 42% by 1979. By the end of the 1970s, 3M was beginning to understand how important it was to integrate the international operations more closely with the U.S. operations, and to build innovative capabilities overseas. It expanded the company's international R&D presence (there are now more than 2,200 technical employees outside the U.S.), built closer ties between the U.S. and foreign research organizations, and started to transfer more managerial and technical employees between businesses in different countries.

In 1978, the company started the Pathfinder Program to encourage the innovation of new products and new business initiatives born outside the United States. By 1983, products developed under the initiative were generating sales of over $150 million a year. For example, 3M Brazil invented a low-cost, hot-melt adhesive from local raw materials, 3M Germany teamed up with Sumitomo 3M of Japan (a joint venture with Sumitomo) to develop electronic connectors with new features for the worldwide electronics industry, and 3M Philippines developed a Scotch-Brite cleaning pad shaped like a foot after learning that Filipinos polished floors with their feet. On the back of such developments, in 1992, international operations exceeded 50% for the first time in the company's history.

By the 1990s, 3M started to shift away from a country-by-country management structure to more regional management. Drivers behind this development included the fall of trade barriers, the rise of trading blocks such as the European Union and NAFTA, and the need to drive down costs in the face of intense global competition. The first European Business Center (EBC) was created in 1991 to manage 3M's chemical business across Europe. The EBC was responsible for product development, manufacturing, and sales and marketing for Europe, but also for paying attention to local country requirements. Other EBCs soon followed, such as EBCs for Disposable Products and Pharmaceuticals.

As the millennium ended, 3M was transforming its company into a transnational organization characterized by an integrated network of businesses that spanned the globe. The goal was to get the right mix of global scale to deal with competitive pressures, while at the same time maintain 3M's traditional focus on local market differences and decentralize R&D capabilities.

The New Era

The DeSimone Years

In 1991, Desi DeSimone had become CEO of 3M. A long time 3M employee, the Canadian born DeSimone was the epitome of a 21st century manager–he had made his name by building 3M's Brazilian business and spoke 5 languages fluently. Unlike most prior 3M CEOs, DeSimone came from the manufacturing side of the business, rather than the technical aide. He soon received praise for managing 3M through the recession of the early-1990s. By the late-1990s, however, his leadership had come under fire from both inside and outside the company.

In 1998 and 1999, the company missed its earnings targets, and the stock price fell as disappointed investors sold. Sales were flat, profit margins fell, and earnings slumped by 50%. The stock had underperformed the widely tracked S&P 500 Stock Index for most of the 1980s and 1990s.

One cause of the earnings slump in the late-1990s was 3M's sluggish response to the 1997 Asian crisis. During the Asian crisis, the value of several Asian currencies fell by as much as 80% against the U.S. dollar in a matter of months. 3M generated 1/4 of its sales from Asia, but it was slow to cut costs there in the face of slumping demand following the collapse of currency values. At the same time, a flood of cheap Asian products cut into 3M's market share in the United States and Europe as lower currency values made Asian products much cheaper.

Another problem was that for all of its vaunted innovative capabilities, 3M had not produced a new blockbuster product since Post-it Notes. Most of the new products produced during the 1990s were just improvements over existing products, not truly new products.

DeSimone was also blamed for not pushing 3M hard enough earlier in the decade to reduce costs. An example was the company's supply chain excellence program. Back in 1995, 3M's inventory was turning over just 3.5 times a year—sub-par for manufacturing. An internal study suggested that every half-point increase in inventory turnover could reduce 3M's working capital needs by $700 million, and boost its return on invested capital. But by 1998, 3M had made no progress on this front.[13]

By 1998, there was also evidence of internal concerns. Anonymous letters from 3M employees were sent to the board of directors, claiming that DeSimone was not as committed to research as he should have been. Some letters complained that DeSimone was not funding important projects for future growth, others that he had not moved boldly enough to cut costs, and still others that the company's dual career track was not being implemented well, and that technical people were underpaid. Critics argued that he was a slow and cautious decision maker in a time that required decisive strategic decisions. For example, in August 1998, DeSimone announced a restructuring plan that included a commitment to cut 4,500 jobs, but reports suggest that other senior managers wanted 10,000 job cuts, and DeSimone had watered down the proposals.[14]

Despite the criticism, 3M's board, which included 4 previous 3M CEOs among its members, stood behind DeSimone until he retired in 2001. However, the board began a search for a new top executive in February 2000 and signaled that it was looking for an outsider. In December 2000, the company announced that it had found the person they wanted, Jim McNerney, a 51-year old General Electric veteran who ran GE's medical equipment businesses, and before that GE's Asian operations. McNerney was one of the front runners in the race to succeed Jack Welsh as CEO of General Electric, but lost out to Jeffrey Immelt. One week after that announcement, 3M hired McNerney.

McNerney's Plan for 3M

In his first public statement days after being appointed, McNerney said that his focus would be upon getting to know 3M's people and culture and its diverse lines of business:

> I think getting to know some of those businesses and bringing some of GE here to overlay on top of 3M's strong culture of innovation will be particularly important.[15]

It soon became apparent that McNerney's game plan was exactly that: to bring the GE play book to 3M and use it to try and boost 3M's results, while simultaneously not destroying the innovative culture that had produced the company's portfolio of 50,000 products.

The first move came in April 2001, when 3M announced that the company would cut 5,000 jobs, or about 7% of the workforce, in a restructuring effort that would zero in on struggling businesses. To cover severance and other costs of restructuring, 3M announced that it would take a $600 million charge against earnings; the job cuts were expected to save $500 million a year. In another effort to save costs, the company streamlined its purchasing processes, for example, by reducing the number of packaging suppliers on a global basis from 50 to 5, saving another $100 million a year in the process.

Next, McNerney introduced the Six Sigma process, a rigorous statistically-based quality control process that was one of the drivers of process improvement and cost savings at General Electric. At heart, Six Sigma is a management philosophy, accompanied by a set of tools, that is rooted in identifying and prioritizing customers and their needs, reducing variation in all business processes, and selecting and grading all projects based upon their impact on financial results. Six Sigma breaks every task (process) in an organization down into increments to be measured against a perfect model.

McNerney called for Six Sigma to be rolled out across 3M's global operations. He also introduced a 3M-like performance evaluation system at 3M, under which managers were asked to rank every single employee who reported to them.

In addition to boosting performance from existing business, McNerney quickly signaled that he wanted to play a more active role in allocating resources between new business opportunities. At any given time, 3M has around 1,500 products in the development pipeline. McNerney stated that was too many, and he indicated that wanted to funnel more cash to the most promising ideas, those with a potential market of $100 million a year or more, while cutting funding to weaker looking development projects.

In the same vein, he signaled that he wanted to play a more active role in resource allocation than had traditionally been the case for a 3M CEO, using cash from mature businesses to fund growth opportunities elsewhere. He scrapped the requirement that each division get 30% of its sales from products introduced in the past 4 years, noting that:

> To make that number, some managers were resorting to some rather dubious innovations, such as pink Post-it Notes. It became a game, what could you do to get a new SKU?[16]

Some long time 3M watchers, however, worried that by changing resource allocation practices McNerney might harm 3M's innovative culture. If the company's history proves anything, they say, it's that it is hard to tell which of today's tiny products will become tomorrow's home runs. No one predicted that Scotchgard or Post-it Notes would earn millions. They began as little experiments that evolved without planning into big hits. McNerney's innovations all sound fine in theory, they say, but there is a risk that he will transform 3M into "3E" and lose what is valuable in 3M in the process.

In general though, securities analysts greeted McNerney's moves favorably. One noted that "McNerney is all about speed," and that there will be "no more Tower of Babel-everyone speaks-one language." This "one company" vision was meant to replace the program under which 3M systematically placed successful new products into new business centers. The problem with this approach, according to the analyst, was that there was no leveraging of best practices across businesses.[17]

McNerney also signaled that he would reform 3M's regional management structure, replacing it with a global business unit structure that will be defined by either products or markets.

At a meeting for investment analysts, held on September 30, 2003, McNerney summarized a number of achievements.[18] At the time, the indications seemed to suggest that McNerney was helping to revitalize 3M. Profitability, measured by ROIC, had risen from 19.4% in 2001, and was projected to hit 25.5% in 2003. 3M's stock price had risen from $42 just before McNerney was hired, to $73 in October 2003 (see Exhibit 5 for details).

Like his former boss, Jack Welsh at GE, McNerney seemed to place significant value on internal executive education programs as a way of shifting to a performance-oriented culture. McNerney noted that some 20,000 employees had been through Six Sigma training by the third quarter of 2003. Almost 400 higher level managers had been through an Advanced Leadership Development Program setup by McNerney, and offered by 3M's own internal executive education institute. Some 40% of participants had been promoted upon graduating. All of the company's top managers had graduated from an Executive Leadership Program offered by 3M.

McNerney also emphasized the value of 5 initiatives that he put in place at 3M; indirect cost control, global sourcing, e-productivity, Six Sigma, and the 3M Acceleration program. With regard to indirect cost control, some $800 million had been taken out of 3M's cost structure since 2001, primarily by reducing employee numbers, introducing more efficient processes that boosted productivity, benchmarking operations internally and leveraging best practices. According to McNerney, internal benchmarking highlighted another $200–$400 million in potential cost savings over the next few years.

On global sourcing, McNerney noted that more than $500 million had been saved since 2000 by consolidating purchasing, reducing the number of suppliers, switching to lower cost suppliers in developing nations, and introducing dual sourcing policies to keep price increases under control.

The e-productivity program at 3M embraced the entire organization, and all functions. It involved the digitalization of a wide range of processes, from customer ordering and payment, through supply chain management and inventory control, to managing employee processes. The central goal was to boost productivity by using information technology to more effectively manage information within the company, and between the company and its customers and suppliers. McNerney cited some $100 million in annual cost savings from this process.

The Six Sigma program overlays the entire organization, and focuses upon improving processes to boost cash flow, lower costs (through productivity enhancements), and boost growth rates. By late-2003, there were some 7,000 Six Sigma projects in process at 3M. By using working capital more efficiently, Six Sigma programs had helped to generate some $800 million in cash, with the total expected to rise to $1.5 billion by the end of 2004. 3M has applied the Six Sigma process to the company's R&D process, enabling researchers to engage customer information in the initial stages of a design discussion, which according to Jay Inlenfeld, the VP of R&D, Six Sigma tools:

> Allow us to be more closely connected to the market and give us a much higher probability of success in our new product designs.[19]

Finally, the 3M's Acceleration Program is aimed at boosting the growth rate from new products through better resource allocation, particularly by shifting resources from slower growing to faster growing markets. As McNerney noted:

> 3M has always had extremely strong competitive positions, but not in markets that are growing fast enough. The issue has been to shift emphasis into markets that are growing faster.[20]

Part of this program is a tool termed 2X/3X, 2X is an objective for 2 times the number of new products that were introduced in the past, and 3X is a business objective for 2 times as many winning products as there were in the past (see Exhibit 3). 2X focuses upon generating more "major" product initiatives, and 3X upon improving the commercialization of those initiatives. Exhibit 3 illustrates 3M's "stage gate" process, and each gate represents a major decision point in the development of a new product, from idea generation to post launch.

Other initiatives aimed at boosting 3M's organization growth rate through innovation include the Six Sigma process, leadership development programs, and technology leadership (see Exhibit 4). The purpose of these initiatives was to help implement the 2X/3X strategy.

As a further step in the Acceleration Program, 3M decided to centralize its corporate R&D effort. Prior to the arrival of McNerney, there were 12 technology centers staffed by 900 scientists that focused on core technology development. The company is now replacing these with one central research lab, staffed by 500 scientists, some 120 of whom will be located outside the United States. The remaining 400 scientists will be relocated to R&D centers in

the business units. The goal of this new corporate research lab is to focus on developing new technology that might fill high growth "white spaces," which are areas where the company currently has no presence, but where the long-term market potential will be great. Research on fuel cells, which is currently a big research project within 3M, provides a good example of this.

Responding to critics' charges that changes such as these might impact 3M's innovative culture, VP of R&D Inlenfeld noted that

> We are not going to change the basic culture of innovation at 3M. There is a lot of culture in 3M, but we are going to introduce more systematic, more productive tools that allow our researchers to be more successful.[23]

For example, Inlenfeld repeatedly emphasized that the company remains committed to basic 3M principles, such as the 15% rule and leveraging technology across businesses.

By late-2003, McNerney noted that some 600 new product ideas were under development and that collectively, they were expected to reach the market and generate some $5 billion in new revenues between 2003 and 2006, up from $3.5 billion

Exhibit 3 The New Product Development Process at 3M[21]

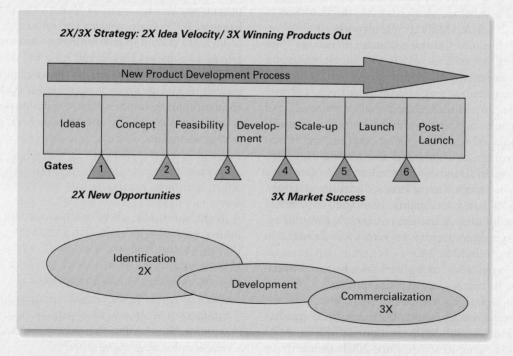

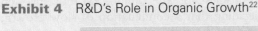

Exhibit 4 R&D's Role in Organic Growth[22]

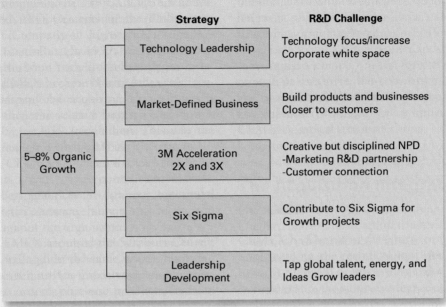

18 months earlier. Some $1 billion of these gains were expected to come in 2003.

George Buckley Takes Over

In mid-2005 McNerney announced that he would leave 3M to become CEO and Chairman of Boeing, a board on which he had served for some time. He was replaced in late-2005 by another outsider, George Buckley, who was Brunswick Industries highly regarded CEO. Buckley, a Brit with a Ph.D. in electrical engineering, described himself as a scientist at heart. Over the next year in several presentations, Buckley outlined his strategy for 3M, and it soon became apparent that he was sticking to the general course laid out by McNerney, albeit with some important corrections.[24]

Buckley did not see 3M as an enterprise that needed radical change. He saw 3M as a company with impressive internal strengths, but one that has been too cautious about pursuing growth opportunities.[25] Buckley's overall strategic vision for 3M included solving customer needs through the provision of innovative and differentiated products that increase the efficiency and competitiveness of customers. Consistent with long-term 3M strategy, he believed this could be achieved by taking 3M's multiple technology platforms, and applying them to different market opportunities.

Controlling costs and boosting productivity through Six Sigma continued to be a major thrust under Buckley. This was hardly a surprise, since Buckley had pushed Six Sigma at Brunswick. By late-2006, some 55,000 3M employees had been trained in Six Sigma methodology, 20,000 projects had been completed, and some 15,000 more were under way. 3M was also adding techniques gleaned from Toyota's lean production methodology to its Six Sigma tool kit. As a result of Six Sigma and other cost control methods, between 2001 and 2005, productivity measured by sales per employee increased from $234 to $311, and some $750 million were taken out of overhead costs.

However, Buckley departed from McNerney's playbook in one significant way, he removed Six Sigma from the labs. The feeling of many at 3M was that Six Sigma's rules choked those working on innovation. As one 3M researcher noted: "It's really tough to schedule innovation."[26] When McNerney left 3M in 2005, the percentage of sales from new products introduced in the last 5 years had fallen to 21%, down from the company's long-term goal of

30%. By 2010, after 5 years of Buckley's leadership, the percentage was back up to 30%. According to many in the company, Buckley had been a champion of researchers at 3M, devoting much of his personal time to empowering researchers, and urging them to restore the luster of 3M.

Buckley had stressed the need for 3M to more aggressively pursue growth opportunities. He wanted the company to use its differentiated brands and technology to continue to develop core businesses and extend those core businesses into adjacent areas. In addition, like McNerney, Buckley wanted the company to focus R&D resources on emerging business opportunities, and he, too, seemed to be prepared to play a more proactive role in this process. Areas of focus included filtration systems, track and trace information technology, energy and mineral extraction, and food safety. 3M has made a number of acquisitions since 2005 to achieve scale and acquire technology and other assets in these areas. In addition, it increased its own investment in technologies related to these growth opportunities, particularly nanotechnology.

Buckley had made selective divestures of businesses not seen as core. Most notably, in November 2006, 3M reached an agreement to sell its pharma-

ceutical business for $2.1 billion. 3M took this step after deciding that a combination of slow growth, and high regulatory and technological risk, made the sector an unattractive one that would dampen the company's growth rate.

Finally, Buckley was committed to continuing internationalization at 3M. 3M doubled its capital investment in the fast growing markets of China, India, Brazil, Russia, and Poland between 2005 and 2010. All of these markets have been expanding 2–3 times as fast as the United States' market.

Judged by the company's financial results, the McNerney and Buckley eras did seem to improve 3M's financial performance. The first decade of the 21st century was a difficult one, marked by sluggish growth in the United States, and in 2008–2009, a steep recession triggered by a global financial crisis. 3M weathered this storm better than most, bouncing out of the recession in 2010 with strong revenue and income growth, helped in large part by its new products and exposure to fast growing international markets. For the decade, revenues expanded from $16 billion in 2001 to $26.66 billion in 2010, earnings per share expanded from $1.79 to $5.63, and ROIC increased from the mid-teens in the 1990s to the mid-20s for most of the decade.

Suggested Readings and References:

1. J. C. Collins and J. I. Porras, *Built to Last* (Harper Business, New York, 1994).
2. M. Conlin, "Too Much Doodle?" *Forbes,* October 19, 1998, 54–56.
3. M. Dickson, "Back to the Future," *Financial Times,* 1994, May 30, 7.
4. J. Hallinan, "3M's Next Chief Plans to Fortify Results with Discipline He Learned at GE Unit," *Wall Street Journal,* December 6, 2000, B17.
5. E. Von Hippel et al., "Creating Breakthroughs at 3M," *Harvard Business Review,* September-October 1999.
6. R. Mullin, "Analysts Rate 3M's New Culture," *Chemical Week,* September 26, 2001, 39–40.
7. 3M. A Century of Innovation, the 3M Story. 3M, 2002. Available at www.3m.com/about3m/century/index.jhtml.
8. 3M Investor Meeting, September 30, 2003, archived at www.corporate-ir.net/ireye/ir_site.zhtml?ticker=MMM&script=2100
9. T. Studt. "3M–Where Innovation Rules," *R&D Magazine,* April 2003, Vol 45, 20–24.
10. De'Ann Weimer, "3M: The Heat is on the Boss," *Business Week,* March 15, 1999, 82–83.
11. J. Useem. "(Tape) + (Light bulb) = ?", *Fortune,* August 12, 2002, 127–131.
12. M. Gunther, M. Adamo, and B. Feldman, "3M's Innovation Revival," *Fortune,* September 27, 2010, 73–76.

Endnotes

1 M. Dickson, "Back to the Future," *Financial Times,* May 30, 1994, 7. www.3m.com/profile/looking/mcknight.jhtml.
2 www.3m.com/about3M/pioneers/drew2.jhtml
3 www.3m.com/about3M/innovation/scotchgard50/index.jhtml
4 3M. A Century of Innovation, the 3M Story. 3M, 2002. Available at http://www.3m.com/about3m/century/index.jhtml

5 3M. A Century of Innovation, the 3M Story. 3M, 2002, page 33. Available at http://www.3m.com/about3m/century/index.jhtml
6 T. Studt, "3M–Where Innovation Rules," *R&D Magazine,* April 2003, Vol 45, 20–24.
7 3M. A Century of Innovation, the 3M Story. 3M, 2002, page 78. Available at http://www.3m.com/about3m/century/index.jhtml

8   3M. A Century of Innovation, the 3M Story. 3M, 2002, page 78. Available at http://www.3m.com/about3m/century/index.jhtml

9   3M. A Century of Innovation, the 3M Story. 3M, 2002, page 42. Available at http://www.3m.com/about3m/century/index.jhtml

10 E. Von Hippel et al., "Creating Breakthroughs at 3M," *Harvard Business Review,* September–October 1999.

11 From 3M Website at www.3m.com/about3M/history/mcknight.jhtml

12 3M. A Century of Innovation, the 3M Story. 3M, 2002,143–144. Available at http://www.3m.com/about3m/century/index.jhtml

13 M. Conlin, "Too Much Doodle?", *Forbes,* October 19, 1998, 54–56.

14 De'Ann Weimer, "3M: The Heat is on the Boss," *Business Week,* March 15, 1999, 82–83.

15 J. Hallinan, "3M's Next Chief Plans to Fortify Results with Discipline He Learned at GE Unit," *Wall Street Journal,* December 6, 2000, B17.

16 J. Useem. "(Tape) + (Light bulb) = ?", *Fortune,* August 12, 2002, 127–131.

17 R. Mullin, "Analysts Rate 3M's New Culture," *Chemical Week,* September 26, 2001, 39–40.

18 3M Investor Meeting, September 30, 2003, archived at http://phx.corporate-ir.net/phoenix.zhtml?c=80574&p=irol-irhome

19 Tim Studt, "3M—Where Innovation Rules," *R&D Magazine,* April 2003, 22.

20 3M Investor Meeting, September 30, 2003, archived at http://phx.corporate-ir.net/phoenix.zhtml?c=80574&p=irol-irhome

21 Adapted from presentation by Jay Inlenfeld, 3M Investor Meeting, September 30, 2003, archived at http://phx.corporate-ir.net/phoenix.zhtml?c=80574&p=irol-irhome

22 Ibid.

23 Tim Studt, "3M—Where Innovation Rules," *R&D Magazine,* April 2003, 21.

24 Material here drawn from George Buckley's presentation to Prudential's investor conference on "Inside our Best Ideas," September 28, 2006. This and other relevant presentations are archived at http://phx.corporate-ir.net/phoenix.zhtml?c=80574&p=irol-irhome

25 J. Sprague, "MMM: Searching for Growth with New CEO Leading," *Citigroup Global Markets,* May 2, 2006.

26 M. Gunther, M. Adamo, and B. Feldman, "3M's Innovation Revival," *Fortune,* September 27, 2010, 74.

CASE 28

The Rise and Fall of Eastman Kodak: Will It Survive Beyond 2012?

Gareth R. Jones
Texas A&M University

In 2011, Antonio Perez, CEO of the Eastman Kodak Co., was reflecting upon his company's current situation. Since he had become CEO in 2005 and launched his strategy to make Kodak a leader in the consumer and business imaging markets, progress had been slow. His efforts to cut costs while heavily investing to develop new digital products had resulted in Kodak losing money in most of the previous years, and Kodak had already cut its profit estimates for 2011.

After spending billions of dollars to create the digital competencies necessary to give Kodak a competitive advantage, and after cutting tens of thousands of jobs, the company's future was still in doubt. Could Kodak survive given the fact its digital rivals were continually introducing new and improved products that made its own look out of date? Was Kodak's new digital business model really working? And, did it have the digital products in place to rebuild its profitability and fulfill its "You press the button, we do the rest" promise? Or, after 10 years of declining sales and profits was the company on the verge of bankruptcy in the face of intense global competition on all product fronts?

Kodak's History

Eastman Kodak Co. was incorporated in New Jersey on October 24, 1901, as successor to the Eastman Dry Plate Co., a business originally established by George Eastman in September 1880. The Dry Plate Co. had been formed to develop a dry photographic plate that was more portable and easier to use than other plates in the rapidly developing photography field. To mass produce the dry plates uniformly, Eastman patented

a plate-coating machine and began to commercially manufacture the plates. Eastman's continuing interest in the infant photographic industry led to his development in 1884 of silver halide paper-based photographic roll film. Eastman capped this invention with his introduction of the first portable camera in 1888. This camera used his own patented film, which was developed using his own proprietary method. Thus, Eastman had gained control of all the stages of the photographic process. His breakthroughs made possible the development of photography as a mass leisure activity. The popularity of the "recorded images" business was immediate, and sales boomed. Eastman's inventions revolutionized the photographic industry, and his company was uniquely placed to lead the world in the development of photographic technology.

From the beginning, Kodak focused on 4 primary objectives to guide the growth of its business: (1) mass production to lower production costs; (2) maintaining the lead in technological developments; (3) extensive product advertising; and (4) the development of a multinational business to exploit the world market. Although common now, those goals were revolutionary at the time. In due course, Kodak's yellow boxes could be found in every country in the world. Preeminent in world markets, Kodak operated research, manufacturing, and distribution networks throughout Europe and the rest of the world. Kodak's leadership in the development of advanced color film for simple, easy-to-use cameras and in quality film processing was maintained by constant research and development in its many research laboratories. Its huge volume of production allowed it to obtain economies of scale. Kodak was also its own supplier of the plastics and chemicals needed to produce film, and it made most of the component parts for its cameras.

Kodak became one of the most profitable American corporations, and its return on shareholders' equity averaged 18% for many years. To maintain its competitive advantage, it continued to heavily invest in research and development in silver halide photography, principally remaining in the photographic business. In this business, as the company used its resources to expand sales and become a global business, the name *Kodak* became a household word signifying unmatched quality. By 1990, approximately 40% of Kodak's revenues came from sales outside the United States.

Starting in the early 1970s, however, and especially in the 1980s, Kodak ran into major problems, reflected in the drop in return on equity. Its preeminence was being increasingly threatened as the photographic industry and industry competition changed. Major innovations were taking place within the photography business, and new methods of recording images and memories beyond silver halide technology, most noticeably digital imaging, were emerging.

Increasing Competition

In the 1970s, Kodak began to face an uncertain environment in all its product markets. First, the color film and paper market from which Kodak made 75% of its profits experienced growing competition from Japanese companies, led by FujiFilm. Fuji invested in huge, low-cost manufacturing plants, using the latest technology to mass-produce film in large volume. Fuji's low production costs and aggressive, competitive price cutting squeezed Kodak's profit margin. Finding no apparent differences in quality, and obtaining more vivid colors with the Japanese product, consumers began to switch to the cheaper Japanese film, and this shift drastically reduced Kodak's market share.

Besides greater industry competition, another liability for Kodak was that it had done little internally to improve productivity to counteract rising costs. Supremacy in the marketplace had made Kodak complacent, and it had been slow to introduce productivity and quality improvements. Furthermore, Kodak (unlike Fuji in Japan) produced film in many different countries in the world rather than in one single country, and this also gave Kodak a cost disadvantage. Thus, the combination of Fuji's efficient production and Kodak's own management style allowed the Japanese to become the cost leaders—to charge lower prices and still maintain profit margins.

Another blow on the camera front came when Kodak lost its patent suit with Polaroid Corp. Kodak had abandoned the instant photography business in the 1940s, when it turned down Edwin Land's offer to develop his instant photography process. Polaroid developed it, and instant photography was wildly successful, capturing a significant share of the photographic market. In response, Kodak set out in the 1960s to develop its own instant camera to compete with Polaroid's. According to testimony in the patent trial, Kodak spent $94 million perfecting its system, only to scrub it when Polaroid introduced the new SX-70 camera in 1972. Kodak then rushed to produce a competing instant camera, hoping to capitalize on the $6.5 billion in sales of instant cameras. However, a federal judge ordered Kodak out of the instant photography business for violating 7 of Polaroid's patents in its rush to produce an instant camera. The cost to Kodak for closing its instant photography operation and exchanging the 16.5 million cameras sold to consumers was over $800 million. By 1985, Kodak reported that it had exited the industry at a cost of $494 million; however, in 1991 Kodak also agreed to pay Polaroid $925 million to settle out of court a suit that Polaroid had brought against Kodak for patent infringement.

On its third product front, photographic processing, Kodak also experienced problems. It faced stiff competition from foreign manufacturers of photographic paper and from new competitors in the film-processing market. Increasingly, film processors were turning to cheaper sources of paper to reduce the costs of film processing. Once again, the Japanese had developed cheaper sources of paper and were eroding Kodak's market share. At the same time, many new independent film-processing companies had emerged and were printing film at far lower rates than Kodak's own official developers. These independent laboratories had opened to serve the needs of drugstores and supermarkets, and many of them offered 24-hour service. They used the less expensive paper to maintain their cost advantage and were willing to accept lower profit margins in return for a higher volume of sales.

As a result, Kodak lost markets for its chemical and paper products—products that had contributed significantly to its revenues and profits. The photographic industry surrounding Kodak had dramatically changed. Competition had increased in all product areas, and Kodak, while still the largest producer, faced increasing threats to its profitability as it was forced to reduce prices to match the competition.

The Emergence of Digital Imaging

Another major problem that Kodak had to confront was not because of increased competition in its *existing* product markets, but because of the emergence of *new* industries that provided alternative means of producing and recording images. The introduction of videotape recorders, and later video cameras, gave consumers an alternative way to use their dollars to produce images, particularly moving images. Video basically destroyed the old, film-based home movie business upon which Kodak had a virtual monopoly. After Sony's introduction of the Betamax machine in 1975 the video industry grew into a multibillion-dollar business. VCRs and first 16mm camera, and the compact 8mm video cameras became increasingly hot-selling items as their prices fell with the growth in demand and the standardization of technology. Then, the later introduction of laser disks, compact disks, and, in the 1990s, DVDs were also significant developments. The vast amount of data that can be recorded on these disks gave them a great advantage in reproducing images through electronic means.

It was increasingly apparent that the entire nature of the imaging and recording process was changing from chemical methods to electronic, digital methods of reproduction. Kodak's managers should have perceived this transformation to digital-based methods as a disruptive technology because its technical preeminence was based on silver halide photography. However, as is always the case with such technologies, the real threat lies in the future. These changes in the competitive environment caused enormous difficulties for Kodak. Between 1972 and 1982, profit margins from sales declined from 16% to 10%. Kodak's glossy image lost its luster. It was in this declining situation that Colby Chandler took over as chairman in July 1983.

Kodak's New Strategy

Chandler saw the need for dramatic changes in Kodak's businesses and quickly pioneered 4 changes in strategy: (1) he strove to increase Kodak's control of its existing chemical-based imaging businesses; (2) he aimed to make Kodak the leader in electronic imaging; (3) he spearheaded attempts by Kodak to diversify into new businesses to increase profitability; and (4) he began on major efforts to reduce costs and improve productivity. To achieve the first 3 objectives, he began a huge program of acquisitions, realizing that Kodak did not have the time to venture new activities internally. Because Kodak was cash rich (it was one of the richest global companies) and had low debt, financing these acquisitions was easy.

For the next 6 years, Chandler acquired businesses in 4 main areas. By 1989, Kodak had been restructured into 4 main operating groups: imaging, information systems, health, and chemicals. At its annual meeting in 1988, Chandler announced that with the recent acquisition of Sterling Drug for $5 billion, the company had achieved its objective: "With a sharp focus on these 4 sectors, we are serving diversified markets from a unified base of science and manufacturing technology. The logical synergy of the Kodak growth strategy means that we are neither diversified as a conglomerate nor a company with a 1-product family."

The way these operating groups developed under Chandler's leadership is described in the following text.

The Imaging Group

Imaging comprised Kodak's original businesses, including consumer products, motion picture and audiovisual products, photo finishing, and consumer electronics. The unit was charged with strengthening Kodak's position in its existing businesses. Kodak's strategy in its photographic imaging business has been to fill gaps in its product line by introducing new products either made by Kodak or bought from Japanese manufacturers and sold under the Kodak name. For example, to maintain market share in the camera business, Kodak introduced a new line of disk cameras to replace the Instamatic lines. Kodak also bought a minority stake and entered into a joint venture with Chinon of Japan to produce a range of 35mm automatic film cameras that would be sold under the Kodak name. This arrangement would capitalize upon Kodak's strong brand image and give Kodak a presence in this market to maintain its camera and film sales. Kodak sold 500,000 cameras and gained 15% of the declining film camera market. In addition, Kodak invested heavily in developing new and advanced film such as a new range of "DX" coded film to match the new 35mm camera market that possesses the vivid color qualities of Fuji's film. Kodak had not developed vivid film color earlier because of its belief that consumers wanted "realistic" color—its managers were still fixated on improving core declining film business.

Kodak also made major moves to solidify its hold on the film-processing market. It attempted to stem the inflow of foreign low-cost photographic paper by gaining control over the processing market. In 1986, it acquired Fox Photo Inc. for $96 million and became the largest national wholesale photograph finisher. In 1987, it acquired the American Photographic Group, and in 1989, it solidified its hold on the photofinishing market by forming a joint venture, Qualex, with the photofinishing operations of Fuqua industries. These acquisitions provided Kodak with a large, captive customer for its chemical and paper products as well as control over the photofinishing market. Also, in 1986 Kodak introduced new improved 1-hour film-processing labs to compete with other photographic developers. To accompany the new labs, Kodak popularized the Kodak "Color Watch" system that requires these labs to use only Kodak paper and chemicals. Kodak's strategy was to stem the flow of business to 1-hour mini-labs and also establish the industry standard for quality processing—it succeeded but the pace of change to the digital world was accelerating and by the end of the 1980s, given the soaring popularity of digital PCs Kodak's managers should have recognized they were on the wrong track.

Kodak's rapidly declining profitability forced it to engage in a massive internal cost-cutting effort to improve the efficiency of the photographic products group. Beginning in 1984, it introduced more and more stringent efficiency targets aimed at reducing waste while increasing productivity. In 1986, it established a baseline for measuring the total cost of waste incurred in the manufacture of film and paper throughout its worldwide operations. By 1987, it had cut that waste by 15%, and by 1989, it announced total cost savings worth $500 million annually. This was peanuts given the rapidly changing

competitive situation—Kodak's managers did not want to shrink their large, bureaucratic company that had become conservative and paternalistic over time. As a result, Kodak's profits dropped dramatically in 1989 as all film makers woke up to the new competitive reality and Polaroid and Fuji also aggressively tried to capture market share by engaging in price cutting and increasing advertising to raise market share. The result was even further major declines in profitability. These rising expenditures offset most of the benefits of Kodak's cost-cutting effort, and there was little prospect of increasing profitability because Kodak's core photographic imaging business was in decline—Kodak already had 80% of the market, it was tied to the fortunes of one industry. In addition, the increasing use and growing applications of digital imaging techniques, led to Chandler's second strategic thrust: an immediate policy of acquisition and diversification into new industries, including the electronic imaging business with the stated goal of being first in film and digital imaging. He thought the two could still co-exist. He could not understand that digital imaging was a disruptive technology.

The Information Systems Group

In 1988, Sony introduced a digital electronic camera that could take still pictures and then transmit them back to a television screen. This was an obvious signal that the threat to Kodak from new digital imaging techniques was going to accelerate. However, at that time, the pictures taken with video film could not match the quality achieved with chemical reproduction. Technology will always advance, and the introduction of CDs was also a sign that new form of digital storage media were on the horizon—the silver halide film media was already out of date as declining sales showed. For Kodak to survive in the imaging business, its managers woke up to the fact that it required expertise in a broad range of new technologies to satisfy customers' recording and imaging needs—they began to see the threat posed by the disruptive technology. Kodak's managers saw in all its film markets different types of digital products were emerging as strong competitors. For example, electronic imaging had become important in the medical sciences and in all business, technical, and research applications driven by introduction of ever more powerful servers and PCs.

However, Kodak's managers did not choose to focus on imaging products and markets close to "photographs"—for example Kodak could have bought Sony or Apple. Instead, they began to target any kind of imaging applications in communications, computer science, and similar applications, that they believed would be important in digital imaging markets of the future. Because Kodak had *no* expertise in digital imaging, its managers decided to acquire companies they perceived did have these skills and then market these companies' products under its own famous brand name. For example, a Kodak electronic publishing system for business documents, and a Kodak imaging record keeping system.

Kodak began its disastrous strategy of acquisitions and joint ventures that wasted much of its huge retained earnings in new imagining technologies that its managers hoped, somehow, would increase its future profitability. In the new information systems group, acquisitions included Atex Inc., Eikonix Corp., and Disconix Inc. Atex made newspaper and magazine electronic publishing and text-editing systems to newspapers and magazines worldwide as well as to government agencies and law firms. Eikonix Corp. was a leader in the design, development, and production of precision digital imaging systems. Further growth within the information systems group came with the development of the Ektaprint line of copier-duplicators that did achieve some success in the competitive high-volume segment of the copier market. In 1988, Kodak announced another major move into the copier service business when it purchased IBM's copier service business and that it would market copiers manufactured by IBM as well as its own Ektaprint copiers. But these copiers were not based on digital imaging—they were still ink-based even though they used digital technology. With these moves, Kodak extended its activities into the electronic areas of artificial intelligence, computer systems, consumer electronics, peripherals, telecommunications, and test and measuring equipment. Kodak was hoping to gain a strong foothold in these new businesses to make up for losses in its traditional business—but it was still not trying to streamline and shrink its core business to reduce its cost structure fast enough, and these acquisitions raised its cost structure.

In addition, top managers now terrified by how far Kodak was behind, decided to purchase imaging companies that made products as diverse as computer workstations and floppy disks! Kodak aggressively acquired any IT companies that might fill in its product lines and obtain technical expertise in digital technology, and help it in its core imaging business. After taking more than a decade to make its first 4 acquisitions, Kodak completed 7 acquisitions in 1985 and more than 10 in 1986. Among the 1985 acquisitions was Verbatim Corp., a major producer of floppy disks. This acquisition made Kodak one of the 3 big producers in the floppy disk industry—an industry in which it had no expertise.

In entering office information systems, Kodak entered new markets where it faced strong competition from established companies such as IBM, Apple, and Sun Microsystems. The Verbatim acquisition brought Kodak into direct competition with 3M. Entering the copier market brought Kodak into direct competition with Japanese firms such as Canon, which was the leader in marketing advanced, new low-cost copiers—and Canon still is today.

In brief, Kodak was entering new businesses where it had little expertise, where it was unfamiliar with the competitive forces, and where there was already strong competition. Soon, Kodak was forced to retreat from many of these markets. In 1990, it announced that it would sell Verbatim to Mitsubishi. (Mitsubishi was immediately criticized by Japanese investors for buying a company with an old, outdated product line!) Kodak was forced to withdraw from many other areas of business simply by selling assets, closing operations, and taking a write-off such as its non-digital videocassette operations. The fast-declining performance of its information systems group, which Kodak attributed to increased competition and delays in bringing out new products, reduced earnings from operations from a profit of $311 million in 1988 to a loss of $360 million in 1989. This was a major wake up call to investors who now realized that Kodak's top managers had no viable business model for the company and were simply wasting its capital.

The Health Group

Kodak's interest in health products emerged from its involvement in the design and production of film for medical and dental X-rays. The growth of digital imaging in medical sciences seemed another opportunity for Kodak to apply its "skills" in new markets, and it began to develop such products as Kodak Ektachem—clinical blood analyzers. It developed other products—Ektascan laser imaging films, printers, and accessories—for improving the display, storage, processing, and retrieval of diagnostic images. This seemed more related to its core business imaging mission.

However, Kodak did not confine its interests in medical and health markets to imaging-based products. In 1984, it established within the health group a life sciences division to develop and commercialize new products deriving from Kodak's distinctive competencies in its still profitable chemical division. Kodak had about 500,000 chemical formulations upon which it could base new products, top managers decided that they could use these resources to enter newly developing biotechnology markets and grow its "life sciences" division that soon engaged in joint ventures with major biotechnology companies such as Amgen and Immunex. However, these advances into biotechnology proved highly expensive, and again Kodak had no expertise in this complex industry! Soon, even its own managers realized this, and in 1988 Kodak quietly exited the industry. What remained of the life sciences division was then folded into the health group in 1988, when Chandler completed Kodak's biggest, and most useless acquisition, the purchase of Sterling Drug, for more than $5 billion.

The Sterling acquisition once again had no relevance to Kodak's business model. Sterling Drug was a global maker of prescription drugs, over-the-counter medicines, and consumer products with familiar brand names such as Bayer Aspirin, Phillips' Milk of Magnesia, and Panadol. Chandler thought this merger would allow Kodak to become a major player in the pharmaceuticals industry. With this acquisition, Kodak's health group became pharmaceutically oriented, and its mission was to develop a full pipeline of major prescription drugs and a world-class portfolio of over-the-counter medicines—something that is an enormously complex, uncertain, and expensive process. Analysts immediately questioned the acquisition because, once again, Chandler was taking Kodak into a new industry where competition was intense and was consolidating because of the massive costs of drug development. Some analysts claimed that the acquisition was aimed at deterring a possible takeover of Kodak—because it was still cash rich and its capital was being wasted! The acquisition of Sterling also resulted in a major decline in profits in 1989; this was growth without profitability.

The Chemical Division

Established almost a hundred years ago to be the high-quality supplier of raw materials for Kodak's film and processing businesses, the Eastman Chemical division was responsible for developing many of the chemicals and plastics that made Kodak the leader in silver-halide filmmaking. The chemical division was also a major supplier of chemicals, fibers, and plastics to thousands of customers worldwide, and Kodak had benefited from the profits from its plastic material and resins unit because of the success of Kodak PET (polyethylene terephthalate), today the major polymer used in soft-drink bottles.

However, in its chemical division, Kodak also ran into the same kinds of problems experienced by its other operating groups. There is intense competition in the plastics industry, not only from U.S. firms like DuPont, but also from large Japanese and European. In specialty plastics and PET, for example, increased competition forced Kodak to reduce prices by 5% and this also led to the plunge in its earnings in 1989. The chemical division, however, had excellent resources and competencies—but not now that they were still controlled by a declining film giant.

Kodak's Failing Business Model Results in Massive Cost Cutting

With the huge profit reversal in 1989 after all the years of acquisition and "internal development," analysts were questioning the existence of the "logical synergy," or economies of scope that Chandler claimed for Kodak's new acquisitions. Certainly, Kodak had new sources of revenue—but was this profitable growth? Was Kodak positioned to compete successfully in the future? What were the synergies that Chandler was talking about? And wasn't any increase in profit due to its attempts to reduce costs?

Indeed, as Chandler made his acquisitions, he also realized the increasing need to change Kodak's management style and organizational structure to reduce costs and allow it to respond more quickly to changes in the competitive environment. Because of its dominance in the industry, in the past, Kodak had not worried about outside competition. As a result, the organizational culture at Kodak emphasized traditional, conservative values rather than entrepreneurial values. Kodak was often described as a conservative, plodding monolith because all decision making had been centralized at the top of the organization among a clique of senior managers. Furthermore, the company had been operating along functional lines. Research, production, and sales and marketing had operated separately in different units at corporate headquarters and dispersed to many different global locations. Kodak's different product groups also operated separately. The result of these factors was a lack of communication and slow, inflexible decision making that led to delays in making new product decisions. When the company attempted to transfer resources between product groups, conflict often resulted, and the separate functional operations also led to poor product group relations, for managers protected their own turf at the expense of corporate goals. Moreover, there was a lack of attention to the bottom line, and management failed to institute measures to control waste.

Another factor encouraging Kodak's conservative orientation was its promotion policy. Seniority and loyalty to "Mother Kodak" counted nearly as much as ability when it came to promotions. Only 12 presidents had led the company since its beginnings in the 1880s. Long after George Eastman's suicide in 1932, the company followed his cautious ways: "If George didn't do it, his successors didn't either."

Kodak's technical orientation also contributed to its problems. Traditionally, its engineers and scientists had dominated decision making, and marketing had been neglected. The engineers and scientists were perfectionists who spent enormous amounts of time developing, analyzing, testing, assessing, and re-testing new products. Little time, however, was spent determining whether the products satisfied consumer needs. As a result of this technical orientation, management passed up the invention of xerography, leaving the new technology to be developed by a small Rochester, New York, firm named Haloid Co.—later Xerox. Similarly, Kodak had passed up the instant camera business.

With its monopoly in the photographic film and paper industry gone, Kodak was in trouble. Chandler had to alter Kodak's management orientation. He began with some radical changes in the company's culture and structure. Forced to cut costs, Chandler began a massive downsizing of the work force to eliminate the fat that had accumulated during Kodak's prosperous past. Kodak's policy of lifetime employment was swept out the door when declining profitability led to continuing employee layoffs and cost reductions. Between 1985 and 1990, Kodak laid off over 100,000 of its former 136,000 employees, less that 10% of its workforce and a tiny percentage that would do nothing to prevent its declining performance. Kodak was now a company that had come unstuck, it could not recognize that it had lost its competitive advantage and that all its new strategies were just accelerating its decline. It was burning money but its top managers did not want to damage the company or its employees, it was obviously a dinosaur.

Every move top managers made failed. Kodak attempted to create a structure and culture to encourage internal venturing. It formed a "venture board" to help underwrite projects imitating 3M and created an "office of submitted ideas" to screen projects. Kodak's attempts at new venturing were unsuccessful, of the 14 ventures that Kodak created 6 were shut down, 3 were sold, and 4 were merged into other divisions. One reason was Kodak's management style, which also affected its new businesses. Kodak's top managers never gave operating executives real authority or abandoned the centralized, conservative approach of the past. Kodak also reorganized its worldwide facilities to increase productivity and lower costs, For example, Kodak streamlined European production by closing duplicate manufacturing facilities and centralizing production and marketing operations, and in doing so thousands more employees were laid off.

George Fisher Tries to Change Kodak

Chandler retired as CEO in 1989, and was replaced by his COO, Kay Whitmore, another Kodak veteran. As Kodak's performance continued to plunge, Whitmore hired new top managers from outside Kodak to help restructure the company. When they proposed selling off Kodak's new acquisitions and laying off tens of thousands more employees to reduce costs Whitmore resisted; he too was entrenched in the old Kodak culture. Kodak's board of directors ousted Whitmore as CEO, and in 1993, George Fisher left his job as CEO of Motorola to become Kodak's new CEO. At Motorola, he had been credited with leading that company into the digital age.

Fisher's strategy was to reverse Chandler's diversification into any industry outside digital imaging and to strengthen its competencies in this industry. Given that Kodak had spent so much money on making useless acquisitions, and the company was now burdened with huge debt from its acquisitions and because of falling profits, Fisher's solution was dramatic. Strategizing about Kodak's 4 business groups Fisher decided that the over-the-counter drugs component of the health products group was reducing Kodak's profitability and he decided to divest it and use the proceeds to pay off debt. Soon, all that was left of this group was the health imaging business. Fisher also decided that the chemicals division, despite its expertise in the invention and manufacture of chemicals, no longer fit with his new digital strategy. Kodak would now buy its chemicals in the open market, and in 1995 he spun the chemicals division off and gave each Kodak shareholder a share in the new company. This was a very profitable move for shareholders who kept their shares in Eastman Chemicals—its price has soared.

The information systems group with its diverse businesses was a more difficult challenge; the new businesses that would promote Kodak's new digital strategy should be kept, and the businesses which would not should be sold off. Fisher decided that Kodak should focus on building its strengths in document imaging and on photocopiers, business imaging, and inkjet printers, and exit all its business that did not fit this theme.

After 2 years, Fisher had reduced Kodak's debt by $7 billion and boosted Kodak's stock price. Fisher still had to confront the problems inside Kodak's core photographic imaging group, and here the solution was neither easy nor quick. Kodak was still plagued by high operating costs that were over 27% of annual revenue, and Fisher knew he needed to reduce these costs by half to compete effectively in the digital world. Kodak's workforce had shrunk by 40,000 to only 95,000 by 1993, and the only means to quickly slash costs was to implement more layoffs and close down its operations. However, Kodak's top managers fought him all the way because they wanted to keep their power, arguing that it was better to find ways to raise revenue than layoff a loyal workforce to reduce costs.

Kodak put off the need to take the hard steps necessary to reduce operating costs by billions. At the same time, top managers were urging Fisher to invest billions of its declining capital in R&D to build competences in digital imaging. Kodak still had no particular competency in making either digital cameras or the software necessary to allow them to operate efficiently. Over the next 5 years, Kodak spent over 4 billion dollars on digital projects, but new digital products were slow to emerge and its competitors were drawing ahead because they had the first-mover advantage. Also, in the 1990s consumers were slow to embrace digital photography because early cameras were expensive, bulky, and complicated to use, and printing digital photographs was also expensive. By 1997, Kodak's digital business was still losing over $100 million a year and Japanese companies were coming out with the first compact easy to use digital cameras. To make things worse, Kodak's share of the film market was falling as a price war broke out to protect market share and it revenues continued to plunge.

To speed product development, Fisher reorganized Kodak's product divisions into 14 autonomous business units based on serving the needs of distinct groups of customers, such as those for its health products or commercial products. The idea was to decentralize decision making and put managers closer to their major customers and so escaping Kodak's suffocating centralized style of decision making. Fisher also changed the top managers in charge of the film and camera units but he did not bring in many outsiders to spearhead the new digital efforts—Kodak's top managers prevented him from doing this. However, the creation of these 14 business units also meant that operating costs soared because each unit had its own complement of functions; thus sales forces and so on were duplicated.

The bottom line was that Fisher was making little progress, was in a weak position, and was pressured by powerful top managers backed by Kodak's directors. The result was that Daniel A. Carp, a Kodak veteran, was named Kodak's president and COO meaning that he was Fisher's heir apparent as Kodak's CEO. Carp had spearheaded the global consolidation of its operations and its entry into major new international markets such as China. He was widely credited with having had a major impact on Kodak's attempts to fight Fuji on a global level and help it to maintain its market share. Henceforth, Kodak's digital and applied imaging, business imaging, and equipment manufacturing—almost all its major operating groups—would now report to Carp.

However, Kodak's revenues and profits continued to decline throughout the 1990s and into the 2000s as it steadily lost market share in its core film business to Fuji and new cheap generic film makers, so prices and profits plunged and so did its market share—down over 25% in the last decade to 66% of the U.S. market meaning the loss of billions in annual revenues. Meanwhile, the quality of the pictures taken by digital cameras was advancing rapidly as as newer models touted higher resolutions (more pixels). The price of basic digital cameras was falling rapidly because of huge economies of scale in global production by companies such as Sony and Canon. Finally, the digital photography market was taking off, but could Kodak meet the challenge?

The answer was no. Kodak had effectively taken control of Japanese camera manufacturer Chinon to make its advanced digital cameras and scanners and Kodak continued to introduce low-priced digital cameras—but it was just one more company in a highly competitive market now dominated by Sony and Canon. Kodak also bought online companies that offered digital processing services over the Internet, and began offering Kodak branded digital picture-maker kiosks in stores where customers could edit and print out their digital images. Although Kodak was making some progress in its digital mission; its digital cameras, digital kiosks, and online photofinishing operations were being increasingly used by customers, it was being left behind by agile competitors. In 1999, Carp replaced Fisher as CEO to head Kodak's fight to develop the digital skills that would lead to innovative new products in all its major businesses. In 1999, its health imaging group announced the fastest digital image management system for echocardiography labs. It also entered the digital radiography market with 3 state-of-the-art digital systems for capturing X-ray images. Its document imaging group announced several new electronic document management systems. It also teamed up with inkjet maker Lexmark to introduce the stand-alone Kodak Personal Picture Maker by Lexmark, which could print color photos from both compact flash cards and smart media. Its commercial and government systems group announced advanced new high-powered digital cameras for uses such as in space and in the military.

With these developments, Kodak's net earnings increased between 1998 and 2000, and its stock price rose. However, one reason for the increase in profits was that the devastating price war with Fuji ended in 1999 as both companies realized it simply reduced both their profits. The main reason was simply the fact that the stock market soared in the late-1990s and Kodak's stock price increased with it—for no good reason. Kodak was still not introducing the new digital imaging products it needed to drive its future profitability. Also, Carp made no major efforts to reduce costs in its film products division, which had powerful managers backing Carp to become CEO to make sure he did nothing threaten their interests. It was the same old story, a rising cost structure and declining revenues and profits.

Kodak in the 2000s

Rapidly advancing digital technology and the emergence of ever more powerful, easy to use digital imaging devices began to increasingly punish Kodak in the 2000s. In the consumer imaging group, for example, Kodak launched a new camera, the EasyShare, in 2001. Over 4 million digital cameras were sold in 2000 and over 6 million in 2001. However, given the huge R&D costs to develop its new products, and intense competition from Japanese companies like Sony and Canon, Kodak could not make any money from its digital cameras because profit margins were razor thin. Moreover, every time it sold a digital camera, it reduced demand for its high-margin film products that really had been the source of its incredible profitability in the past. Kodak was being forced to cannibalize a profitable product (film) for an unprofitable one (digital imaging). Kodak was now a dinosaur in the new digital world and its stock collapsed in 2000 and 2001, falling from $80 to $60 to around $30, as investors now saw the writing on the wall as its profitability plunged.

Carp argued that Kodak would make more money in the future from sales of the highly profitable photographic paper necessary to print these images and from its photofinishing operations. However, consumers were not printing out many of the photographs they took, preferring to save most in digital form and display them on their PCs and then on the rapidly emerging digital photo frames market that made film-based photograph albums obsolete. Revenues would not increase from sales of film or paper. Similarly, the photofinishing market was declining and its own Qualex and Fox photo finishing chains were forced into bankruptcy.

Kodak was also doing poorly in the important health imaging market where its state-of-the-art imaging products were expected to boost its profitability. However, competition increased when health care providers demanded lower prices from imaging suppliers and Kodak was forced to slash its prices to win contracts with other large health care providers. Competition was so intense that in 2001, sales of laser printers and health-related imagining products, which make up Kodak's second biggest business fell 7% and profit fell 30% causing Kodak's stock price to plunge. Also, in 2001 Carp announced another major reorganization of Kodak's businesses to give it a sharper focus on its products and customers, Kodak announced that it would create 4 distinct product groups: the film group, which now contained all its silver halide activities; consumer digital imaging; health imaging, and its commercial imaging group, which continued to develop its business imaging and printing applications. Nevertheless, revenues plunged from $19 billion in 2001 to only $13 billion by 2002 and its profits disappeared.

Analysts wondered if Carp was doing any better than Fisher and if real change was taking place. Now Carp was forced to cut jobs, and by 2003 its workforce was down to 78,000—still far too high a number given its declining performance. Carp was still trying to avoid the massive downsizing that was still needed to take place to make Kodak a viable company because its entrenched, inbred, and unresponsive top managers frustrated real efforts to reduce costs and streamline operations. Despite all the advances it had made in developing its digital skills, Kodak's high operating costs combined with its declining revenues were driving the company further down the road to bankruptcy. Would layoffs or reorganization be enough to turn Kodak's performance around at this point?

2002 proved to be a turning point in the photographic imaging business as sales of digital cameras and other products began to soar at a far faster pace than had been expected. The result for Kodak's film business was disastrous because sales of Kodak film started to fall sharply as did demand for its paper—people printed only a small fraction of the pictures they took. From 2003–2005 this trend accelerated, as it has ever since. Digital cameras became the camera of choice of photographers worldwide and Kodak's

film and paper revenues sunk. Kodak had become unprofitable, which was somewhat ironic given that Kodak's line of EasyShare digital cameras had become one of the best-selling cameras, and Kodak was the number 2 global seller with about 18% of the market. However, profit margins on digital products were razor thin because of intense competition from companies such as Canon, Olympus, and Nikon. Profits earned in digital imaging were not enough to offset the plunging profits in its core film and paper making divisions.

The Decline and Fall of Kodak's Core Film Business

In 2004, Carp announced Kodak's cash-cow film business was in "irreversible decline" and that Kodak would stop investing in its core film business and pour all its resources into developing new digital products, such as new digital cameras and accessories to improve its competitive position and profit margins. It bought the remaining 44% of Chinon, its Japanese division that designed and made its digital cameras to protect its competency in digital imaging. Kodak began a major push to develop new state-of-the-art digital cameras and also to develop new skills in inkjet printing to create digital photo printing systems so its users could directly print from its cameras—and achieve economies of scope. Also, Carp announced Kodak would invest to grow its digital health imaging business that had gained market share and it would launch a new initiative to make advanced digital products for the commercial printing industry.

Analysts and investors reacted badly to this news. Xerox had tried to enter the digital printer business years before with no success against HP, the market leader. Moreover, they wondered how new revenues from digital products could ever make up for the loss of Kodak's film and paper revenues. Carp also announced that to fund this new strategy, Kodak would reduce its hefty dividend by 72% from $1.80 to $0.50 a share that would immediately raise $1.3 billion to invest in digital products. Investors had no faith in Carp's new plan, and Kodak's stock plunged to $22, its lowest price in decades. Kodak's top management came under intense criticism for not reducing its cost structure, and Kodak's stock price continued to fall as it became clear its new strategy would do little to raise its falling revenues—this might be the beginning of Kodak's end.

In 2004, Carp finally announced what the company should have done 10 years before. Kodak would cut its workforce by over 20% by 2007; another 15,000 employees would lose their jobs saving a billion dollars a year in operating costs. Jobs would be lost in film manufacturing at the support and corporate levels and from global downsizing as Kodak reduced its total facilities worldwide by 1/3 and continued to close its out-of-date photofinishing labs that served retailers. This news sent Kodak's share price up by 20% to over $30. But, it was now too late for Kodak to build the competencies that might have offered it a chance to rebuild its presence as a digital imaging company—there were too many agile competitors and digital technology was changing too fast for the company to respond—at least under Carp's leadership.

Antonio Perez Takes Control of Kodak

It had become clear that Carp could and would not radically restructure Kodak's operations and bring it back to profitability. Kodak's board of directors decided to hire Antonio Perez, a former HP printing executive, as its new president and COO, to take charge of the reorganization effort. Perez now made the hard choices about which divisions Kodak would close, and announced the termination of thousands of more managers and employees. Carp resigned and Perez' restructuring efforts were rewarded by his appointment as Kodak's new CEO. He was now in charge of implementing the downsized, streamlined company's new digital imaging strategy. Perez announced a major 3-year restructuring plan in 2004 to try to make Kodak a leader in digital imaging.

With regard to costs, Perez announced that Kodak needed "to install a new, lower-cost business model consistent with the realities of a digital business. The reality of digital businesses is thinner margins—we must continue to move to the business model appropriate for that reality." His main objectives were to reduce operating facilities by 33%, divest redundant operations, and reduce its workforce by another 20%. In 2004, Kodak ended all its traditional camera and film activities except for advanced 35mm film, it allowed Vivitar to make

film cameras using its name, but in 2007 that agreement ended. Kodak also implemented SAP's ERP system to link all segments of its value-chain activities together and to its suppliers to reduce costs after benchmarking its competitors showed it had a much higher cost of goods sold. Using ERP, Kodak's goal was to reduce costs from 19% to 14% by 2007 and, therefore, increase profit margins.

From 2004–2007 Perez laid off 25,000 more employees, shut down and sold operating units, and moved to a more centralized structure. All 4 heads of Kodak's main operating groups report directly to Perez. In 2006, Kodak also signed a deal with Flextronics, a Singapore-based outsourcing company, to make its cameras and inkjet printers that allowed it to close its own manufacturing operations. The costs of this transformation were huge. Kodak lost $900 million in 2004, $1.1 billion in 2005, and $1.6 billion in 2006. Because of its transformation, and the high costs involved in terminating employees while investing in new digital technology its 2006 ROIC was a negative 20% compared to its main digital rival, Canon, that enjoyed a positive 14% ROIC!

Kodak's Increasing Problems, 2007

Kodak's revenues and profits were falling fast, but in its 3 primary digital business groups—consumer imaging, business graphics, and health imaging—Perez continued his push to develop innovative new products. The goals was to reduce costs in its declining film division that still enjoyed much higher profit margins than its digital business groups! Kodak had to increase profit margins in all its digital divisions if it was to survive.

The Medical Imaging Group

By 2006, the costs of research and marketing digital products in its consumer and commercial units was putting intense pressure on the company's resources—and Kodak still had to invest large amounts of capital to develop a lasting competitive advantage in its medical imaging unit. Here, too, in the 2000s, Kodak had made many strategic acquisitions to strengthen its competitive advantage in several areas of medical imaging such as digital mammography and advanced X-rays. It had developed one of the top 5 medical imaging groups in the world. However, in May 2006, Kodak put its medical imaging unit up for sale. It realized that this unit required too much future investment if it was to succeed—and its consumer and commercial groups were not providing the profits necessary to fund this investment. In addition, although the medical unit accounted for nearly 1/5 of Kodak's overall sales in 2005, its operating profit plunged 21% as profit margins fell because of increased competition from major rivals such as GE. In 2007, Kodak announced that it had sold its medical imaging unit to the Onex Corp., Canada's biggest buyout firm, for $2.35 billion. By selling its health imaging unit, Kodak cut another 27,000 jobs, and its global workforce was now under 50,000 from a peak of 145,300 in 1988. Once again Perez said, "We now plan to focus our attention on the significant digital growth opportunities within our businesses in consumer and professional imaging and graphic communications."

Developments in the Consumer Imaging Group

In the consumer group, improving its digital imaging products and services was still the heart of Perez' business model for Kodak; he was determined to make Kodak the leader in digital processing and printing. Perez focused on developing improved digital cameras, inkjet printers, and photofinishing software and services.

Advanced Digital Cameras

Perez pushed designers to continuously innovate new and improved models several times a year to increase profit margins and keep its lead over competitors. It was the market leader in the United States by 2005 in digital camera sales, and total sales and revenues increased sharply. However, by 2006, Kodak's prospects deteriorated as the growth in sales of its digital cameras came to a standstill because of increasing price competition. Now, many new companies like Samsung were making digital cameras that had become a commodity product and profit margins plunged for all digital camera makers. Nevertheless, in 2006, the company brought out new digital cameras products such as its first dual-lens camera, and cameras with Wi-Fi that could connect wirelessly to PCs to download and print photographs, and it used these innovations to once again raise prices. Kodak also entered the growing digital photo-frame market

in 2007 introducing 4 new EasyShare-branded models in sizes from 8″ to 11″, some of which included multiple memory card slots and even Wi-Fi capability to connect with Kodak's cameras.

Since 2007, however, Kodak has been forced to cut the prices of its digital cameras to compete with Canon and Sony, U.S. customers had lost faith that its EasyShare models offered the best value and so Kodak's profits from the sales of its cameras continued to decline. At the same time, increasing digital camera sales led to a major decline in sales of its film products. In 1999, Kodak announced that it was ending production of its consumer film products and its "yellow boxes" disappeared from sight as it sought to cut costs. In sum, its camera business offered little prospect of being able to raise its future profitability.

New Inkjet Printers

A major change in strategy occurred when Perez launched an advertising campaign to promote its new Kodak EasyShare all-in-one inkjet printers. This new line of color digital printers used an advanced Kodak ink that would provide brighter pictures that would keep their clarity for decades. Apparently Perez, who had been in charge of HP's printer business before he left Kodak had all along made the development of digital printers a major part of his turnaround strategy—despite that profit margins were shrinking on these products as well. However, Perez' printer strategy was based upon charging a higher price for the printer than competitors like HP and Lexmark, but a much lower price for the ink cartridge to attract a bigger market share—a razor and razor blades strategy. Black ink cartridges would cost $9.99 and color $14.99, which will average out to about $0.10 per print—far lower than the $0.20–$0.25 per print using a HP printer. Perez believed this would attract the large market segment that still wanted to print out large numbers of photographs, and so would make this product a multibillion revenue generator in the future, Perez announced he expected inkjet printing to result in double digit increases in profit within 3 years.

Kodak's new printers did attract a lot of customers who were alienated by the high costs of ink cartridges, however, as online photo processing and storage solutions became more and more popular, and new mobile devices made it increasingly easy to access photos from the net—on iPods, iPads, and smartphones in general, users had less and less incentive to burden themselves with paper-based photo albums. Nevertheless, its new printers did help increase revenues and profits although they never achieved the gains Perez anticipated. In 2009, it announced its new line of ESP all-in-one digital printers that still used all its EasyShare technology to help users print and share their photographs. Kodak's new printers were popular and helped to increase revenues and profits. For example, in 2010–2011, sales increased by over 40% but this was still not enough to make up for declines in revenues elsewhere in digital imaging.

Digital Photofinishing Another part of Perez' consumer strategy was to invest in developing both on-line, and physical "digital kiosks," channels to allow customers to download, process, print, and store their photographs using its EasyShare software. Kodak's EasyShare Internet service would allow customers to download their images to its online Website, Kodak Gallery, and receive back both printed photographs and the images on a CD.

In a major effort to develop an empire of digital processing kiosks, Kodak began to rapidly install them in stores, pharmacies, and other outlets as fast as possible, especially because they used its inks and paper. It configured these kiosks to give customers total control over which pictures to develop at what quantity, quality, and size. Kodak and Walmart signed an alliance to put 2,000 kiosks into 1,000 Walmart stores, and by 2006, Kodak had over 65,000 kiosks. However, this was an expensive business to operate and profit margins were razor thin as competition increased.

These moves proved popular because it was easy to use and photofinishing revenues increased as it built a base of 30 million customers. But profit margins were slim because competition increased and many other free online programs were being introduced, such as Goggle's Picasa. Between July 2010 and July 2011, profits dropped from $36 million to $2 million and did nothing to help Kodak's bottom line.

Kodak also made major attempts to penetrate the mobile imaging market because of the huge growth in the use of cameras in mobile phones in the 2000s. The Kodak Mobile Imaging Service offered camera phone users several options to view, order, and share prints of all the digital photos on their phones. Users could upload and store pictures from their cameras in their personal Kodak gallery accounts; then after editing using Kodak's free EasyShare software, they could send their favorite photos back to their mobile phones or wirelessly link to its picture Kiosks to arrange to print the best photographs. Kodak also joined up with social media sites like Facebook and Picasa (now linked to Google+), to easily download photos to members of their social community's pages. It has, of course, also developed applications for the Apple iOS, BlackBerry OS and Android OS mobile operating systems to make it easy for users to connect their Kodak EasyShare pictures to the kind of mobile computing device they are using. Kodak benefits from revenues received when mobile customers take advantage of its processing and printing services while they upload and share photographs. For example, any user can request a paper copy, or enlargement of a particular photograph or a series of photos contained in an album. Kodak Kiosks also allows users to upload pictures wirelessly through Bluetooth; customers can beam photos directly to the kiosk from mobile device to get Kodak prints and more. One problem, however, was that increasing sales of powerful cameras in smartphones led to a major decline in the number of customers who intended to upgrade to a more advanced digital camera—smartphones were cannibalizing sales of digital cameras. In addition, this has not proved to be an important source of additional revenues, its greater market share has not translated into higher profits. By 2010, there was intense competition in all areas of the digital imaging and information markets, including PCs, smartphones, MP3 Players and gaming consoles, as more and more people were online and became used to the Web as the place to process and store their documents in different forms—written, graphic, photographic, video, music or movies. Although Kodak had achieved a presence in the consumer digital imaging and storage market segment, it still could not generate the profits needed to offset its losses resulting from the rapid decline of its cash-cow film business—and in its other business areas.

In fact, in July 2011, it announced major decreases in profits and sales across many of its product groups. Sales of cameras were down by 8%; revenues from its photofinishing operations were down 14%; sales of ink and inkjet printers had increased by over 40%, a bright spot, but neverthe-less overall sales had decreased by 10% compared to the previous year and the group had lost $92 million.

The Graphic Communications Group

Although its consumer digital business was its most visible business group, by 2007 Perez, had recog-nized that its graphic communications group that had dealt with business customers also offered an opportunity to grow revenues and profits—if it could develop distinctive competencies. Profit margins are much higher in commercial imaging and packaging because the users of these products are companies with large budgets. The 5 primary customer groups served by this division are commercial printers, in-plant printers, data centers, digital service providers, and packaging companies. For each of these seg-ments, Kodak developed a suite of digital products and services that offered customers a single end-to-end solution to deliver the products and services they needed to compete in their business. Kodak was able to develop this end-to-end solution because of its ac-quisition of specialist digital printing companies such as KPG, CREO, Versamark, and Express. From each acquisition, Kodak gained access to more products and more customers along with more services and solutions to offer them. Perez claimed that no other competitor could offer the same breadth of products and solutions that it could offer. Kodak's product line included image scanners and document manage-ment systems, and the industry's leading portfolio of digital proofing solutions and state-of-the-art color packaging solutions that can be customized to the needs of different customers—whether they need cardboard boxes, or rigid or flexible cardboard or plastic packaging.

Following his decision to make Kodak a major competitor in consumer inkjet printing, because of his HP printing background, Perez also decided to make it a major player in commercial printing as well—bringing into direct competition with HP, Xe-rox, and Canon by 2009. Kodak had developed an award-winning wide-format inkjet printing process including the most robust toner-based platforms for 4-color and monochrome printing. Kodak also claimed to have the leading continuous inkjet tech-nology for high-speed, high-volume printing, as well as imprinting capabilities that could be combined with traditional offset printing for those customers

still in the process of making the transition to digital printing.

At the same time, he decided to invest resources to improve Kodak's packaging solutions to utilize its expertise in color processing and he made pack-ing another avenue to increase revenues and profits. Kodak then announced in July 2011 that second-quarter sales from this group were $685 million, similar to the previous year; however, this group also lost $45 (compared $17 million in the same quarter a year ago) because of the enormous development and marketing costs necessary to support growth in its commercial inkjet operations.

Will Kodak Survive?

In January 2009, Kodak posted a $137 million loss and announced plans to cut 4,500 jobs that de-creased its workforce to about 18,000, and in June 2009, it announced it would retire its Kodachrome film—the main source of its incredible past financial success. In fact, its losses have been increasing in the last 5 years, but the extent of these losses had been disguised because of the way the company had sold many of its assets to reduce its losses and engaged in patent battles. For example, in 2007, it sold its Light Management Film Group to Rohm & Hass, and in 209 it sold its Organic Light-Emitting Diode (OLED) business unit to LG Electronics, both were advanced LED flatscreen technologies that it could no longer afford to invest in—but brought in a few hundred million dollars.

Then, to find new sources of revenue to offset losses, Kodak launched a series of lawsuits against other electronic companies, claiming that they had infringed on the huge library of digital patents that it had generated over the years. In 2008, Kodak se-lected its first targets, Samsung and LEG, which it claimed had used its technology in the cameras in their mobile phones. A U.S. judge decided in 2009 that these companies had infringed on its patents, but they decided not to appeal. Kodak announced it would settle out of court and develop cross-license agreements with these companies and it is estimated that Kodak received over $900 million from these settlements.

Emboldened by its success, Kodak decided to take on Apple and Research In Motion (RIM) in March 2010. The Kodak complaint, filed with the U.S. International Trade Commission (ITC) claimed that Apple's iPhone and RIM's camera-enabled BlackBerrys infringed upon a Kodak patent that covered technology related to a method for previewing images. At the end of March, the ITC ruled in favor of Kodak; it seemed to have won its patent dispute with Apple and RIM, a victory that might provide it with $1 billion in new licensing revenue. Overnight Kodak's stock soared by 25%. Then, Apple filed a countersuit, and in April 2011, Kodak sold it Microfilm Unit to raise the millions needed to fund its lawsuits. In June 2011, the ITC, under a new judge issued a mixed ruling and announced the final decision would not be made until August 2011—and Kodak's stock plunged 25%. Then, in August 2011 Kodak's stock price soared by 25% after it seemed that it would get protection for its patents. However, in late 2011 its stock plunged again as the value of its patent portfolio became unclear and investors once again fled.

Perez continued to claim he would use the proceeds from intellectual property licensing to continue to invest in the company's now core growth businesses—inkjet printing, packaging and software and services—in order to counter falling revenue from camera film. However, since 2007, Kodak's stock had steadily plunged from $24 to around $1.25 in November 2011. It seemed that Perez' strategies have done little or nothing to turnaround Kodak, which had a market value of only around $300 million in November 2011. Some analysts claimed the only reason the company had not been acquired for this low price was that it had $2.6 billion in unfunded pension obligations because of its huge layoffs over the last decade. Given that Kodak announced it would have to incur more debt—unless it could sell its portfolio of patents profitably—by November 2011 many analysts wondered how the company would survive beyond 2012—and what would finally push it into bankruptcy.

Endnotes

www.kodak.com, Annual reports, 1980–2011.
www.kodak.com, 10K reports, 1980–2011.

CASE 29

Boeing Commercial Aircraft in 2011

Charles W.L. Hill
University of Washington

Introduction

The first decade of the 20th century was one of ups and downs for Boeing Commercial Airplane, the commercial aircraft division of the world's largest aerospace company. In the late-1990s and early-2000s, Boeing had struggled with a number of ethics scandals and production problems that had tarnished the reputation of the company and led to sub-par financial performance. To make maters worse, its global rival, Airbus, had been gaining market share. Between 2001 and 2005, the European company regularly garnered more new orders than Boeing.

The tide started to turn Boeing's way in 2003, when it formally launched its next generation jet, the 787. Built largely out of carbon-fiber composites, the wide-bodied 787 was billed as the most fuel-efficient large jetliner in the world. The 787 was forecasted to consume 20% less fuel than Boeing's older wide-bodied jet, the 767. By 2006, the 787 was logging significant orders. This, together with strong interest in Boeing's best-selling narrow bodied jet, the 737, helped the company to recapture the lead in new commercial jet aircraft orders. Moreover, in 2006 Boeing's rival, Airbus, was struggling with significant production problems and weak orders for its new aircraft, the A380 super-jumbo. Airbus was also late to market with a rival for the 787, the wide-bodied Airbus A350, which would also be built largely out of carbon-fiber. While the 787 was scheduled to enter service in 2008, the A350 would not appear until 2012, giving Boeing a significant lead.

Over the next few years, Boeing encountered a number of production problems and technical design issues with the 787 that resulted in the introduction of the 787 being delayed 5 times. The 787 is now scheduled to enter service in late-2011,

more than 3 years later than planned. Despite this, Boeing has a very healthy backlog for the 787, with 827 jets ordered as of mid-2011, compared to 567 for the rival A350. Airbus has also encountered some production problems of its own with the A350, and delivery of that aircraft model has now slipped into 2013.

Looking forward, Boeing now has some important decisions to make regarding its venerable narrow-bodied 737 aircraft family, which accounts for some 60% of Boeing's total aircraft deliveries. The main competitor for the 737 has long been Airbus' A320. In late-2010, Airbus announced that it would build a new version of the A320, designed to use advanced engines from Pratt & Whitney, and estimated to be 10–15% more efficient than existing engines. Know as the A320NEO (NEO stands for "new engine option"), by August 2011, the aircraft had garnered an impressive 1,029 orders. Airbus' success here forced Boeing's hand. Boeing, too, has stated that they will offer a version of the 737 using new engines (this will require some redesign of the 737, driving up Boeing's R&D costs). However, the company still must decide whether to totally redesign the 737, taking advantage of knowledge gained during the process of developing the 787, to build an all-new 737 out of composites that would also be designed with more efficient engines.

To complicate matters, for the first time in a generation there are several new entrants on the horizon. The Canadian regional jet manufacturer, Bombardier, is starting to gain orders for the 110–130 seat narrow bodied CSeries jet, which would place it in direct competition with the smallest of the 737 and A320 families. In addition, the Commercial Aircraft Corporation of China (Comac) has announced that it will build a 170–190 seat narrow-bodied jet.

The Competitive Environment

By the 2000s, the market for large commercial jet aircraft was dominated by just two companies, Boeing and Airbus. A third player in the industry, McDonnell Douglas, had been historically significant, but had lost share during the 1980s and 1990s. In 1997, Boeing acquired McDonnell Douglas, primarily for its strong military business, because in the mid-1990s Airbus has been gaining orders at Boeing's expense. By the mid-2000s, Boeing and Airbus were splitting the market.

Both Boeing and Airbus have a full range of aircraft. Boeing offers 5 aircraft "families" that range in size from 100 to over 500 seats. They are the narrow bodied 737 and the wide bodied 747, 767, 777 and 787 families. Each family comes in various forms. For example, there are currently 4 main variants of the 737 aircraft. They vary in size from 110 to 215 seats, and in range from 2,000 to over 5,000 miles. List prices vary from $47 million for the smallest member of the 737 family, the 737–600, to $282 million for the largest Boeing aircraft, the 747–8. The newest member of the Boeing family, the 787, lists for between $138 million and $188 million depending upon the model.[1]

Similarly, Airbus offers 5 "families," the narrow bodied A320 family, and the wide bodied A300/310, A330/340, A350 and A380 families. These aircraft vary in size from 100 to 550 seats. The range of list prices is similar to Boeing's. The A380 super-jumbo lists for between $282 million to $302 million, while the smaller A320 lists for between $62 million and $66.5 million.[2] Both companies also offer freighter versions of their wide bodied aircraft.

Airbus was a relatively recent entrant into the market. Airbus began its life as a consortium between a French company and Germany company in 1970. Later, a British and Spanish company joined the consortium. Initially, few people gave Airbus much chance for success, but the consortium gained ground by innovating. It was the first aircraft maker to build planes that "flew by wire," made extensive use of composites, had only two flight crew members (most had three), and used a common cockpit layout across models. It also gained sales by being the first company to offer a wide bodied twin-engine jet, the A300, that was positioned between smaller single aisle planes like the 737 and large aircraft such as the Boeing 747.

In 2001, Airbus became a fully integrated company. The European Defense and Space Company (EADS), formed by a merger between French, German and Spanish interests, acquired 80% of the shares in EADS, and BAE Systems, a British company, took a 20% stake.

Development and Production

The economics of development and production in the industry are characterized by a number of facts. First, the R&D and tooling costs associated with developing a new airliner are very high. Boeing spent some $5 billion to develop the 777. Its latest aircraft, the 787, was initially expected to cost $8 billion to develop, but delays have increased that to at least $12 billion. Development costs for Airbus' A380 super-jumbo reportedly exceeded $15 billion.

Second, given the high upfront costs, in order to break even a company must capture a significant share of projected world demand. The breakeven point for the Airbus super-jumbo, for example, is estimated to be between 250 and 270 aircraft. Estimates of the total potential market for this aircraft vary widely. Boeing has suggested that the total world market will be for no more than 320 aircraft over the next 20 years—Airbus believes that there will be demand for some 1,250 aircraft of this size. It may take 5–10 years of production before Airbus breaks even on the A380–on top of years of negative cash flow during development.[3]

Third, there are significant learning effects in aircraft production.[4] On average, unit costs fall by about 20% each time *cumulative* output of a specific model is doubled. The phenomenon occurs because managers and shop floor workers learn over time how to assemble a particular model of plane more efficiently, reducing assembly time, boosting productivity, and lowering the marginal costs of producing subsequent aircraft.

Fourth, the assembly of aircraft is an enormously complex process. Modern planes have over 1 million component parts that have to be designed to fit with each other, and then produced and brought together at the right time in order to assemble the engine. At several times in the history of the industry, problems with the supply of critical components have held up production schedules and resulted in losses. In 1997, Boeing took a charge of $1.6 billion against earnings when it had to halt the production of its 737 and 747 models due to a lack of component parts. In 2008, Boeing had to delay production of the 787 due to a shortage of fasteners.

Historically, airline manufacturers tried to manage the supply process through vertical integration, by making many of the component parts that went into an aircraft (engines were long the exception to this). Over the last two decades, however, there has been a trend to contract out production of components and even entire sub-assemblies to independent suppliers. On the 777, for example, Boeing outsourced about 65% of the aircraft production, by value, excluding the engines.[5] While helping to reduce costs, contracting out has placed enormous onus on airline manufacturers to work closely with its suppliers to coordinate the entire production process.

Finally, all new aircraft are now designed digitally, and assembled virtually before a single component is produced. Boeing was the first to do this with its 777 in the early-1990s, and with its new version of the 737 in the late-1990s.

Customers

Demand for commercial jet aircraft is very volatile and tends to reflect the financial health of the commercial airline industry, which is prone to boom and bust cycles (see Exhibits 1, 2 and 3). The airline industry has long been characterized by excess capacity, intense price competition, and a perception

---

Exhibit 1 Commercial Aircraft Orders 1990–2010

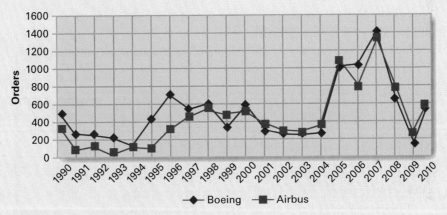

Source: Boeing and Airbus Websites http://www.boeing.com/
http://www.airbus.com/

Exhibit 2 World Airline Industry Revenues

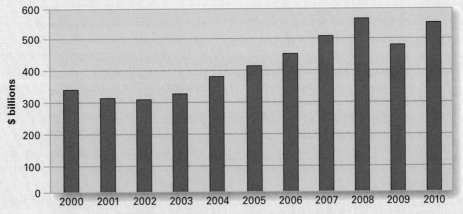

Source: IATA Data.

Exhibit 3   World Airline Industry Net Profit ($ billions) 2001–2010

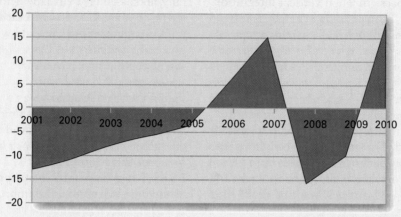

Source: IATA Data.

Exhibit 4   Jet Fuel Prices July 2001–June 2011

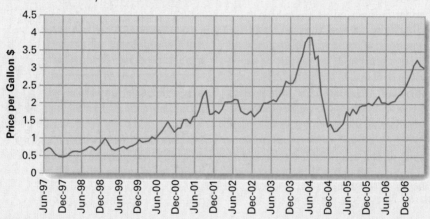

Source: www.iata.org

among the travelling public that airline travel is a commodity. After a moderate boom during the 1990s, the airline industry went through a nasty downturn during 2001–2005. The downturn started in early-2001 due to a slowdown in business travel after the boom of the 1990s. It was compounded by a dramatic slump in airline travel after the terrorist attacks on the United States in September of 2001. Between 2001 and 2005, the entire global airline industry lost some $40 billion, more money than it had made since its inception.[6]

The industry recovered in 2006 and 2007, only to rack up big losses again in 2008 and 2009 due to the recession that was ushered in by the 2008–2009 global financial crisis. High fuel prices during much of the decade made matters worse (prices for jet fuel more than doubled between 2004 and 2006—see Exhibit 4). The bill for jet fuel represented over 25% of the industry's total operating costs in 2006, compared to less than 10% in 2001.[7]

During the 2001–2005 period, losses were particularly severe among the big six airlines in the world's largest market, the United States (American Airlines, United, Delta, Continental, US Airways and Northwest). Three of these airlines (United, Delta and Northwest) were forced to seek Chapter 11 bankruptcy protections. Despite that demand and profits plummeted at the big six airlines, some carriers continued to make profits during 2001–2005, most notably the budget airline Southwest. In addition, other newer budget airlines including AirTran and JetBlue (which was started in 2000), gained market share during this period. Indeed, between 2000 and 2003, the budget airlines in the United States expanded capacity by 44% even as the majors slashed their carrying capacity and parked unused planes in the desert. In 1998, the budget airlines held a 16% share of U.S. market; by mid-2004 their share had risen to 29%.[8]

The key to the success of the budget airlines is a strategy which gives them a 30–50% cost advantage over traditional airlines. The budget airlines all follow the same basic script–they purchase just one type of aircraft (some standardize on Boeing 737s, others on Airbus 320s). They hire nonunion labor and cross-train employees to perform multiple jobs (e.g. to help meet turnaround times, the pilots might help check tickets at the gate). As a result of flexible work rules, Southwest needs only 80 employees to support and fly an aircraft, compared to 115 at the big six airlines. The budget airlines also favor flying "point-to-point," rather than through hubs, and often use cheap secondary airports, rather than major hubs. They focus on large markets with lots of traffic (e.g. up and down the East coast). There are no frills on the flights, no in flight meals . and prices are set low to fill up seats.

In contrast, the operations of major airlines are based on the network or "hub and spoke" system. Under this system, the network airlines route their flights through major hubs. Often, a single airline will dominate a hub (for example, United dominates Chicago's O'Hare airport). This system was developed for good reason—it was a way of efficiently using airline capacity when there wasn't enough demand to fill a plane flying point-to-point. By using a hub and spoke system, the major network airlines have been able to serve some 38,000 city pairs, some of which generate fewer than 50 passengers per day. But by focusing a few hundred city pairs where there is sufficient demand to fill their planes, and flying directly between them (point-to-point) the budget airlines seem to have found a way around this constraint. The network carriers also suffer from a higher cost structure due to their legacy of a unionized workforce. In addition, their costs are higher

by their superior in flight service. In good times, the network carriers can recoup their costs by charging higher prices than the discount airlines, particularly for business travelers, who pay more to book late, and to fly business or first class. In the competitive environment of the 2000s, however, this was no longer the case. Between 2000 and 2010, the price of an average round trip domestic ticket in the U.S. increased from $317 to $338, an increase of 6.7% over the decade, while the consumer price index increased 26.6% (i.e. in real terms prices fell).[9]

Due to the effect of increased competition, the real yield that U.S. airlines got from passengers fell from $0.087 cents per mile in 1980 to 6.37 cents per mile in 1990, $0.0512 cents per mile in 2000, and $0.04 cents per mile in 2005 (these figures are expressed in constant 1978 cents).[10] Real yields are also declining elsewhere. With real yields declining, the only way that airlines can become profitable is to reduce their operating costs.

Outside of the United States, competition has intensified as deregulation has allowed low cost airlines to enter local markets and capture share from long established national airlines that have utilized the hub and spoke model. In Europe, for example, Ryanair and easyJet have adopted the business model of Southwest, and used it to grow aggressively.

By the mid-2000s, large airlines in the U.S. were starting to improve their operating efficiency, helped by growing traffic volumes, higher load factors and reductions in operating costs, particularly labor costs. Load factors refers to the percentage of a plane that is full on average, which hit a record 86% in mid-2006 in the United States, and 81% in international markets. Load factors have remained reasonably high since then, moving between 75% and 85% on a monthly basis between 2006 and 2010.

Demand Projections

Both Boeing and Airbus issue annual projects of likely future demand for commercial jet aircraft. These projections are based upon assumptions about future global economic growth, the resulting growth in demand for air travel, and the financial health of the world's airlines.

In its 2011 report, Boeing assumed that the world economy would grow by 3.3% per annum over the next 20 years, which should generate growth in passenger traffic of 5.1% per annum, and growth in cargo traffic of 5.6% per year. On this basis, Boeing forecast demand for some 33,500 new aircraft valued at more than $4 trillion over the next 20 years. Of this, some 15,370 aircraft will be replacement for aircraft retired from service, and the remaining aircraft will satisfy an expanded market. In 2030, Boeing estimates that the total global fleet of aircraft will be 39,530 up from 17,330 in 2005. Boeing believes that North America will account for 22% of all new orders, Asia Pacific for 34% and Europe for 23%. Passenger traffic is projected to grow at 7% per annum in Asia, versus 2.3% in North America and 4% in Europe.[11]

Regarding the mix of orders, Boeing believes that 70% of all orders by units will be for narrow bodied aircraft such as the 737 and A320, 22% will be for wide-bodied twin aisle jets such as the 787 and 747, and 3% for large aircraft such as the 747 and A380.

The latest Airbus forecast covers 2010–2029. Over that period, Airbus forecasts world passenger traffic to grow by 4.8% per annum, and predicts demand for 25,850 new aircraft worth $3.2 trillion. (Note that Airbus excludes regional jets from its forecast, there are some 2,000 regional jet deliveries included in Boeing's forecasts). Airbus believes that demand for very large aircraft will be robust, amounting to 1,740 large passenger aircraft and freighters in the 747 range and above, or 18% of the total value of aircraft delivered.[12]

The difference in the mix of orders projected by Boeing and Airbus reflect different views of how future demand will evolve. Airbus believes that hubs will continue to play an important role in airline travel, particularly international travel, and that very large jets will be required to transport people between hubs. Airbus bases this assumption partly on an analysis of data over the last 20 years, which shows that traffic between major airline hubs has grown faster than traffic between other city pairs. Airbus also assumes that urban concentrations will continue to grow. Airbus states that demand is simply a function of where people want to go, and most people want to travel between major urban centers. The company notes, for example, that 90% of travelers from the United States to China go to 3 major cities. Fifty other cities make up the remaining 10%, and Airbus believes that very few of these cities will have demand large enough to justify a nonstop service from North America or Europe. Based on this assumption, Airbus sees robust demand for very large aircraft, and particularly its A380 offering.

Boeing has a different view of the future. The company has theorized that hubs will become increasingly congested, and that many travelers will seek to avoid them. Boeing thinks that passengers prefer frequent nonstop service between the cities they wish to visit. Boeing also sees growth in travel between city pairs as being large enough to support an increasing number of direct long-haul flights. The company notes that continued liberalization of regulations governing airline routes around the world will allow for the establishment of more direct flights between city pairs. As in the United States, the company believes that long haul low-cost airlines that focus on serving city pairs and avoid hubs will emerge.

In sum, Boeing believes that airline travelers will demand more frequent nonstop flights, not larger aircraft.[13] To support this, the company has data showing that all of the growth in airline travel since 1995 has been met by the introduction of new nonstop flights between city pairs, and by an increased frequency of flights between city pairs, and not by an increase in airplane size. For example, Boeing notes that following the introduction of the 767, airlines introduced more flights between city pairs in North America and Europe, and more frequent departures. In 1984, 63% of all flights across the North Atlantic were in the 747. By 2004, the figure had declined to 13%, with smaller wide bodied aircraft such as the 767 and 777 dominating traffic. Following the introduction of the 777, which can fly nonstop across the Pacific, and is smaller than the 747, the same process occurred in the North Pacific. In 2006, there were 72 daily flights serving 26 city pairs in North America and Asia.

Boeing's History[14]

William Boeing established the Boeing Company in 1916 in Seattle. In the early-1950s, Boeing took an enormous gamble when it decided to build a large jet aircraft that could be sold both to the military as a tanker, and to commercial airlines as a passenger plane. Known as the "Dash 80," the plane had swept back wings and 4 jet engines. Boeing invested $16 million to develop the Dash 80, 2/3 of the company's entire profits during the post war years. The Dash 80 was the basis for 2 aircraft—the KC-135

Air Force tanker and the Boeing 707. Introduced into service in 1957, the 707 was the world's first commercially successful passenger jet aircraft. Boeing went on to sell some 856 Boeing 707s along with 820 KC-135s. The final 707, a freighter, rolled off the production line in 1994 (production of passenger planes ended in 1978). The closest rival to the 707 was the Douglas DC8, of which some 556 were ultimately sold.

The 707 was followed by a number of other successful jetliners including the 727 (which entered service in 1962), the 737 (which entered service in 1967), and the 747 (which entered service in 1970). The single aisle 737 went on to become the workhorse of many airlines. In the 2000s, a completely redesigned version of the 737 that could seat between 110 and 180 passengers was still selling strong. Cumulative sales of the 737 totaled 6,500 by mid-2006, making it by far the most popular commercial jet aircraft ever sold.

It was the 747 "jumbo jet," however, that probably best defined Boeing. In 1966, when Boeing's board made the decision to develop the 747, they were widely viewed as betting the entire company on the jet. The 747 was born out of the desire of Pan Am, then America's largest airline, for a 400 seat passenger aircraft that could fly 5,000 miles. Pan Am believed that the aircraft would be ideal for the growing volume of trans-continental traffic. However, beyond Pan Am, which committed to purchasing 25 aircraft, demand was very uncertain. Moreover, the estimated $400 million in development and tooling costs placed a heavy burden on Boeing's financial resources. To make a return on its investment, the company estimated it would need to sell close to 400 aircraft. To complicate matters further, Boeing's principal competitors, Lockheed and McDonnell Douglas, were each developing 250 seat jumbo jets.

Boeing's big bet turned out to be auspicious. Pan Am's competitors feared being left behind, and by the end of 1970, almost 200 orders for the aircraft had been placed. Successive models of the 747 extended the range of the aircraft. The 747–400, introduced in 1989, had a range of 8,000 miles and a maximum seating capacity of 550 (although most configurations seated around 400 passengers). By this time, both Douglas and Lockheed had exited the market giving Boeing a lucrative monopoly in the very large commercial jet category. By 2005, the company had

sold nearly 1,430 747s, and was actively selling its latest version of the 747 family, the 747–8 which was scheduled to enter service in 2008.

By the mid-1970s Boeing was beyond the break even point on all of its models (707, 727, 737 and 747). The positive cash flow helped to fund investment in two new aircraft, the narrow bodied 757 and the wide bodied 767. The 757 was designed as a replacement to the aging 727, while the 767 was a response to a similar aircraft from Airbus. These were the first Boeing aircraft to be designed with two person cockpits, rather than three. Indeed, the cockpit layout was identical, allowing crew to shift from one aircraft to the other. The 767 was also the first aircraft for which Boeing subcontracted a significant amount of work to a trio of three Japanese manufacturers—Mitsubishi, Kawasaki, and Fuji—who supplied about 15% of the airframe. Introduced in 1981, both aircraft were successful. Some 1049 757s were sold during the life of the program (which ended in 2003). By 2006, over 950 767s had been sold, and the program was still ongoing.

The next Boeing plane was the 777. A two-engine wide bodied aircraft with seating capacity of up to 400 and a range of almost 8,000 miles, the 777, was initiated in 1990. The 777 was seen as a response to Airbus' successful A330 and A340 wide bodied aircraft. Development costs were estimated at some $5 billion. The 777 was the first wide bodied long-haul jet to have only two engines. It was also the first to be designed entirely on computer. To develop the 777, for the first time Boeing used cross-functional teams composed of engineering and production employees. It also bought major suppliers and customers into the development process. As with the 767, a significant amount of work was outsourced to foreign manufacturers including the Japanese trio of Mitsubishi, Kawasaki, and Fuji who supplied 20% of the 777 airframe. In total, some 60% of parts for the 777 were outsourced. The 777 proved to be another successful venture—by mid-2006, 850 777s had been ordered, far greater than the 200 or so required to break even.

In December 1996, Boeing stunned the aerospace industry by announcing it would merge with long-time rival McDonnell Douglas in a deal estimated to be worth $13.3 billion. The merger was driven by Boeing's desire to strengthen its presence in the defense and space side of the aerospace business, areas in which McDonnell Douglas was traditionally strong. On the commercial side of the aerospace business, Douglas had been losing market share since the 1970s. By 1996, Douglas accounted for less than 10% of production in the large commercial jet aircraft market and only 3% of new orders placed that year. The dearth of new orders meant the long-term outlook for Douglas's commercial business was increasingly murky. With or without the merger, many analysts felt that it was only a matter of time before McDonnell Douglas would be forced to exit from the commercial jet aircraft business. In their view, the merger with Boeing merely accelerated that process.

The merger transformed Boeing into a broad-based aerospace business within which commercial aerospace accounted for 40–60% of total revenue, depending upon the stage of the commercial production cycle. In 2001, for example, the commercial aircraft group accounted for $35 billion in revenues out of a corporate total of $58 billion, or 60%. In 2005, with the delivery cycle at a low point (but the order cycle rebounding), the commercial airplane group accounted for $22.7 billion out of a total of $54.8 billion, or 41%. A wide range of military aircraft, weapons and defense systems, and space systems comprised the balance of their revenue.

In the early-2000s, in a highly symbolic act, Boeing moved its corporate headquarters from Seattle to Chicago. The move was an attempt to put some distance between top corporate officers and the commercial aerospace business, the headquarters of which remained in Seattle. The move was also intended to signal to the investment community that Boeing was far more than its commercial businesses.

To some extent, the move to Chicago may have been driven by a number of production missteps in the late-1990s that occurred at a time when the company should have been enjoying financial success. During the mid-1990s orders had boomed as Boeing cut prices in an aggressive move to gain share from Airbus. However, delivering these aircraft meant that Boeing had to more than double its production schedule between 1996 and 1997. As it attempted to do this, the company ran into some server production bottlenecks.[15] The company scrambled to hire and train some 41,000 workers, recruiting many from suppliers, a move it came to regret when many of the suppliers could not meet Boeing's demands, and shipments of parts were delayed. In the Fall of 1997, things got so bad that Boeing shut down its 747 and 737 production lines so that workers could

catch up with out of sequence work, and wait for backordered parts to arrive. Ultimately, the company had to take a $1.6 billion charge against earnings to account for higher costs and penalties paid to airlines for the late delivery of jets. As a result, Boeing made very little money out of its mid-1990s order boom. The head of Boeing's commercial aerospace business was fired, and the company committed itself to a major acceleration of its attempt to overhaul its production system, elements of which dated back half a century.

Boeing in the 2000s

In the 2000s, 3 things dominated the development of Boeing Commercial Aerospace. First, the company accelerated a decade-long project aimed at improving the company's production methods by adopting the lean production systems initially developed by Toyota and applying them to the manufacture of large jet aircraft. Second, the company considered, and then rejected, the idea of building a successor to the 747. Third, Boeing decided to develop a new wide bodied long haul jetliner, the 787.

Lean Production at Boeing

Boeing's attempt to revolutionize the way planes could be built began in the early-1990s. Beginning in 1990, the company started to send teams of executives to Japan to study the production systems of Japan's leading manufacturers, particularly Toyota. Toyota had pioneered a new way of assembling automobiles, known as lean production (in contrast to conventional mass production).

Toyota's lean production system was developed by one of the company's engineers, Ohno Taiichi.[16] After working at Toyota for 5 years and visiting Ford's U.S. plants, Ohno became convinced that the mass production philosophy for making cars was flawed. He saw numerous problems, including 3 major drawbacks. First, long production runs created massive inventories, which had to be stored in large warehouses. This was expensive because of the cost of warehousing and because inventories tied up capital in unproductive uses. Second, if the initial machine settings were wrong, long production runs resulted in the production of a large number of defects (that is, waste). And third, the mass production system was unable to accommodate consumer preferences for product diversity.

In looking for ways to make shorter production runs economical, Ohno developed a number of techniques designed to reduce setup times for production equipment, a major source of fixed costs. By using a system of levers and pulleys, he was able to reduce the time required to change dies on stamping equipment from a full day in 1950 to 3 minutes by 1971. This advance made small production runs economical, which allowed Toyota to respond better to consumer demands for product diversity. Small production runs also eliminated the need to hold large inventories, thereby reducing warehousing costs. Furthermore, small product runs and the lack of inventory meant that defective parts were produced only in small numbers and entered the assembly process immediately. This reduced waste and made it easier to trace defects to their source and fix the problem. In sum, Ohno's innovations enabled Toyota to produce a more diverse product range at a lower unit cost than was possible with conventional mass production.

Impressed with what Toyota had done, in the mid-1990s, Boeing started to experiment with applying Toyota-like lean production methods to the production of aircraft. Production at Boeing was formerly focused upon producing parts in high volumes, and then storing them in warehouses until they were ready to be used in the assembly process. After visiting Toyota, engineers realized that Boeing was drowning in inventory. A huge amount of space and capital was tied up in things that didn't add value. Moreover, expensive specialized machines often took up a lot of space, and were frequently idle for long stretches of time.

Like Ohno at Toyota, the company engineers started to think about how they could modify equipment and processes at Boeing to reduce waste. Boeing set aside space and time for teams of creative plant employees—design engineers, maintenance technicians, electricians, machinists and operators—to start experimenting with machinery. They called these teams "moonshiners." The term "moonshine" was coined by Japanese executives who visited the United States after World War II. They were impressed by two things in the U.S.—supermarkets, and the stills built by people in the Appalachian hills. They noticed that people built these stills with no money. They would use salvaged parts to make small

stills that produced alcohol that they sold for money. The Japanese took this philosophy back home with them, and applied it to industrial machinery—which is where Boeing executives saw the concept in operation in the 1990s. With the help of Japanese consultants, they decided to apply the moonshine creative philosophy at Boeing—to produce new "right-sized" machines with very little money that could be used to make money.

The moonshine teams were trained in lean production techniques, given a small budget, and then set loose. Initially, many of the moonshine teams focused on redesigning equipment to produce parts. Underlying this choice was a Boeing study, which showed that more than 80% of the parts manufactured for aircraft are less than 12 inches long, and yet the metal working machinery is huge, inflexible, and could only economically produce parts in large lots.[17]

Soon, empowered moonshine teams were designing their own equipment—small-scale machines with wheels on that could be moved around the plant, and that took up little space. One team replaced a large stamping machine that cost 6-figures and was used to produce L-shaped metal parts in batches of 1,000 with a miniature stamping machine powered by a small hydraulic motor that could be wheeled around the plant. With the small machine, that cost a couple of thousand dollars, parts could be produced very quickly in small lots, eliminating the need for inventory. They also made a sanding machine and a parts cleaner of equal size. Now the entire process—from stamping the raw material to the finished part—is completed in minutes (instead of hours or days) just by configuring these machines into a small cell and having them serviced by a single person. The small scale and quick turnaround now made it possible to produce these parts just-in-time, eliminating the need to produce and store inventory.[18]

Another example of a moonshine innovation concerns the process for loading seats onto a plane during assembly. Historically, this was a cumbersome process. After the seats would arrive at Boeing from a supplier, wheels were attached to each seat, and then the seats were delivered to the factory floor in a large container. An overhead crane lifted the container up to the level of the aircraft door. Then, the seats were unloaded and rolled into the aircraft, before being installed. The process was repeated until all of the seats had been loaded. For a single aisle plane this could take 12 hours. For a wide bodied jet, it would take much longer. A moonshine team adapted a hay elevator to perform the same job. It cost a lot less, delivered seats quickly through the passenger door, and took just 2 hours, while eliminating the need for cranes.[19]

Multiply the examples given here, and soon there would be a very significant impact on production costs. A drill machine was built for 5% of the cost of a full scale machine from Ingersoll-Rand; portable routers were built for 0.2% of the cost of a large fixed router; one process that took 2,000 minutes for a 100 part order (20 minutes per part because of setup, machining and transit) now takes 100 minutes (one minute per part); employees building 737 floor beams reduced labor hours by 74%, increased inventory turns from 2 to 18 per year, and reduced manufacturing space by 50%; employees building the 777 tail cut lead time by 70% and reduced space and work in progress by 50%; production of parts for landing gear support used to take 32 moves from machine to machine, and required 10 months—production now takes 3 moves and 25 days.[20]

In general, Boeing found that it was able to produce smaller lots of parts economically, often from machines that it built itself, which were smaller and cost less than the machines available from outside vendors. In turn, these innovations enabled Boeing to switch to just-in-time inventory systems and reduce waste. Boeing was also able to save on space. By eliminating large production machinery at its Auburn facility, replacing much of it with smaller more flexible machines, Boeing was able to free up 1.3 million square feet of space, and sold 7 buildings.[21]

In addition to moonshine teams, Boeing also adopted other process improvement methodologies, using them when deemed appropriate. Six Sigma quality improvement processes are widely used within Boeing. The most wide reaching process change, however, was the decision to switch from a static assembly line to a moving line. In traditional aircraft manufacture, planes are docked in angled stalls. Ramps surround each plane, and workers go in and out to find parts and install them. Moving a plane to the next work station was a complex process. The aircraft had to be lowered from its work station, a powered cart was brought in, the aircraft was towed to the next station, and then it was lifted again. This could take two shifts. A lot of time was wasted bringing parts to a stall, and moving a plane from one stall to the next.

In 2001, Boeing introduced a moving assembly line into its Renton plant near Seattle, which manufactures the 737. With a moving line, each aircraft is attached to a "sled" that rides a magnetic strip embedded in the factory floor, pulling the aircraft at a rate of 2 inches per minute, moving past a series of stations where tools and parts arrive at the moment need, allowing workers to install the proper assemblies. The setup can eliminate wandering for tools and parts, as well as expensive tug pulls or crane lifts (only having tools delivered to workstations, rather than having workers fetch them, was found to save 20–45 minutes on every shift). Preassembly tasks can be performed on feeder lines. For example, inboard and outboard flaps can be assembled on the wing before it will arrive for joining to the fuselage.[22]

Like a Toyota assembly line, the moving line can be stopped if a problem arises. Lights indicate the state of the line. A green light will indicate a normal work flow, the first sign of a stoppage brings a yellow warning light, and if the problem isn't solved within 15 minutes, a purple light will indicate that the line has stopped. Each work area and feeder line has will require its own lights, so there is no doubt where the problem may occur.[23]

The cumulative effects of these process innovations have been significant. By 2005, assembly time for the 737 had been cut from 22 days to just 11 days. In addition, work in process inventory had been reduced by 55% and stored inventory by 59%.[24] By 2006, all of Boeing's production lines, except for the 747, had shifted from static bays to a moving line. The 747 is scheduled to shift to moving line when Boeing starts production of the 747–8.

The Super-Jumbo Decisions

In the early-1990s Boeing and Airbus started to contemplate new aircraft to replace Boeing's aging 747. The success of the 747 had given Boeing a monopoly in the market for very large jet aircraft, making the plane one of the most profitable in the jet age, but the basic design dated back to the 1960s, and some believed there might be sufficient demand for a super-jumbo aircraft with as many as 900 seats.

Initially, the two companies considered establishing a joint venture to share the costs and risks associated with a developing a super-jumbo aircraft, but Boeing withdrew in 1995 citing costs and uncertain demand prospects. Airbus subsequently concluded that Boeing was never serious about the joint venture, and the discussions were nothing more than a ploy to keep Airbus from developing its own plane.[25]

After Boeing withdrew, Airbus started to talk about offering a competitor to the 747 in 1995. The plane, then dubbed the A3XX, was to be a super-jumbo with capacity for over 500 passengers. Indeed, Airbus stated that some versions of the plane might carry as many as 900 passengers. Airbus initially estimated that there would be demand for some 1,400 planes of this size over 20 years, and that development costs would total around $9 billion (estimates ultimately increased to some $15 billion). Boeing's latest 747 offering—the 747–400—could carry around 416 passengers in 3 classes.

Boeing responded by drafting plans to develop new versions of the 747 family. The 747–500X and the 747–600X. The 747–600X was to have a new (larger) wing, a fuselage almost 50 feet longer than the 747–400, would carry 550 passengers in 3 classes and have a range of 7,700 miles. The smaller 747–500X would have carried 460 passengers in 3 classes and had a range of 8,700 miles.

After taking a close look at the market for a super-jumbo replacement to the 747, in early-1997 Boeing announced that it would not proceed with the program. The reasons given for this decision included the limited market and high development costs, which at the time, were estimated to be $7 billion. There were also fears that the wider wing span of the new planes would mean that airports would have to redesign some of their gates to take the aircraft. Boeing, McDonnell Douglas (prior to the merger with Boeing) and the major manufacturers of jet engines all forecast demand for about 500–750 such aircraft over the next 20 years. Airbus alone forecasts demand has high as 1,400 aircraft. Boeing stated that the fragmentation of the market due to the rise of "point-to-point" flights across oceans would limit demand for a super-jumbo. Instead of focusing on the super-jumbo category, Boeing stated that it would develop new versions of the 767 and 777 aircraft that could fly up to 9,000 miles and carry as many as 400 passengers.

Airbus, however, continued to push forward with planes to develop the A3XX. In December 2000, with more than 50 orders in hand, the board of EADS, Airbus' parent company, approved development of the plane, which was now dubbed the A380. Development costs at this point were pegged at $12 billion, and the plane was forecasted to enter service in 2006 with Singapore Airlines. The A380 would have 2 passenger decks, more space per seat and wider aisles. It would carry 555 passengers in great comfort, something that passengers would appreciate on long transoceanic flights. According to Airbus, the plane would carry up to 35% more passengers than the most popular 747–400 configuration, yet cost per seat would be 15–20% lower due to operating efficiencies. Concerns were raised about turnaround time at airport gates for such a large plane, but Airbus stated that dual boarding bridges and wider aisles meant that turnaround times would be no more than those for the 747–400.

Airbus also stated that the A380 was also designed to operate on exiting runways and within existing gates. However, London's Heathrow airport found that it had to spend some $450 million to accommodate the A380, widening taxiways and building a baggage reclaim area for the plane. Similarly, 18 U.S. airports had reportedly spent some $1 billion just to accommodate the A380.[26]

The 787

While Airbus pushed forward with the A380, in March 2001, Boeing announced the development of a radically new aircraft. Dubbed the sonic cruiser, the plane would carry 250 passengers 9,000 miles and fly just below the speed of sound, cutting 1 hour of transatlantic flights and 3 hours of transpacific flights. To keep down operating costs, the sonic cruiser would be built out of low weight carbon-fiber "composites." Although the announcement created considerable interest in the aviation community, in the wake of the recession that hit the airline industry after September 11, 2001, both Boeing and the airlines became considerably less enthusiastic. In March 2002, the program was cancelled. Instead, Boeing said that it would develop a more conventional aircraft using composite technology. The plane was initially known as the 7E7 with the "E" standing for "Efficient" (the plane was renamed the 787 in early-2005).

In April 2004, the 7E7 program was formally launched with an order for 50 aircraft worth $6 billion from All Nippon Airlines of Japan. It was the largest launch order in Boeing's history. The 7E7 was a twin-aisle wide bodied, two-engine plane designed to carry 200–300 passengers up to 8,500 miles, making the 7E7 well suited for long haul point-to-point flights. The range exceeded all but the longest range plane in the 777 family, and the 7E7 could fly 750 miles more than Airbus' closest competitor, the mid-sized A330–200. With a fuselage built entirely out of composites, the aircraft was lighter and would use 20% less fuel than existing aircraft of comparable size.

The plane was also designed with passenger comfort in mind. The seats would be wider, as would the aisles, and the windows would be larger than in existing aircraft. The plane would be pressurized at 6,000 feet altitude, as opposed to 8,000 feet, which is standard industry practice. Airline cabin humidity was typically kept at 10% to avoid moisture buildup and corrosion—but composites don't corrode, so humidity would be closer to 20–30%.[27]

Initial estimates suggested that the jet would cost some $7–8 billion to develop and enter service in 2008. Boeing decided to outsource more work for the 787 than on any other aircraft to date. Boeing would build some 35% of the plane's fuselage and wing structure. The trio of Japanese companies that worked on the 767 and 777, Mitsubishi Heavy Industries, Kawasaki Heavy Industries, and Fuji Heavy Industries, would build another 35%, and some 26% would be built by Italian companies, particularly Alenia.[28] For the first time, Boeing asked its major suppliers to bear some of the development costs for the aircraft.

The plane was to be assembled at Boeing's wide bodied plant in Everett, Washington State. Large subassemblies were to be built by major suppliers, and then shipped to Everett for final assembly. The idea was to "snap together" the parts in Everett in 3 days, cutting down on total assembly time. To speed up transportation, Boeing would adopt air freight as its major transportation method for many components.

Airbus' initial response was to dismiss Boeing's claims of cost savings as inconsequential. They pointed out that even if the 787 used less fuel than the A330, that amount was equivalent to just 4% of total operating costs.[29] However, even by Airbus' calculations, as fuel prices were starting to accelerate, the magnitude of the savings rose. Moreover, Boeing quickly started to snag some significant orders for the 787. In 2004, Boeing booked 56 orders for the 787, and in 2005 some 232 orders. Another 85 orders were booked in the first 9 months of 2006 for a running total of 373—well beyond break even point.

In December 2004, Airbus announced that it would develop a new model, the A350, to compete directly with the 787. The planes were to be long haul twin-aisle jets, seating 200–300 passengers, and constructed of composites. The order flow, however, was slow, with airlines complaining that the A350 did not match the Boeing 787 on operating efficiency, range or passenger comfort. Airbus went back to the drawing board and in mid-2006, it announced a new version of the A350, the A350 XWB for "Extra Wide Body." Airbus estimated that the A350 XWB would cost $10 billion to develop and enter service in 2012, several years behind the 787. The two-engine A350 XWB will carry between 250 and 375 passengers and fly up to 8,500 miles. The largest versions of the A350 XWB will be competing directly with the Boeing 777, not the 787. Like the 787, the A350 XWB it will be built primarily of composite materials. The "Extra Wide Body" is designed to enhance passenger comfort. To finance the A350 XWB, Airbus stated that it would seek launch aid from Germany, France, Spain and the UK, all countries where major parts of Airbus are based.[30]

Trade Tensions

It is impossible to discuss the global aerospace industry without touching on trade issues. Over the last 3 decades, both Boeing and Airbus have charged that their competitor benefited unfairly from government subsidies. Until 2001, Airbus functioned as a consortium of 4 European aircraft manufacturers: one British (20.0% ownership stake), one French (37.9% ownership), one German (37.9% ownership), and one Spanish (4.2% ownership). In the 1980s and early-1990s, Boeing maintained that subsidies from these nations allow Airbus to set unrealistically low prices, to offer concessions and attractive financing terms to airlines, to write off development costs, and to use state-owned airlines to obtain orders. According to a study by the United States Department of Commerce, Airbus received more than $13.5 billion in government subsidies between 1970 and 1990 ($25.9 billion if commercial interest rates are applied). Most of these subsidies were in the form of loans at below-market interest rates and tax breaks.

The subsidies financed research and development and provided attractive financing terms for Airbus's customers. Airbus responded by pointing out that both Boeing had benefited for years from hidden US government subsidies, and particularly Pentagon R&D grants.

In 1992, the 2 sides appeared to reach an agreement that put to rest their long-standing trade dispute. The 1992 pact, which was negotiated by the European Union on behalf of the four member states, limited direct government subsidies to 33% of the total costs of developing a new aircraft and specified that and such subsidies had to be repaid with interest within 17 years. The agreement also limited indirect subsidies, such as government supported military research that has applications to commercial aircraft, to 3% of a country's annual total commercial aerospace revenues, or 4% of commercial aircraft revenues of any single company on that country. Although Airbus officials stated that the controversy had now been resolved, Boeing officials argued that they would still be competing for years against subsidized products.

The trade dispute heated up again in 2004 when Airbus announced the first version of the A350 to compete against Boeing's 787. What raised a red flag for the U.S. government was signs from Airbus that it would apply for $1.7 billion in launch aid to help fund the development of the A350. As far as the United States was concerned, this was too much. In late-2004, U.S. Trade Representative Robert Zoellick issued a statement formally renouncing the 1992 agreement and calling for an end to launch subsidies. According to Zoellick: "since its creation 35 years ago, some Europeans have justified subsidies to Airbus as necessary to support an infant industry. If that rationalization were ever valid, its time has long passed. Airbus now sells more large civil aircraft than Boeing." Zoellick went on to claim that Airbus has received some $3.7 billion in launch aid for the A380 plus another $2.8 billion in indirect subsidies including $1.7 billion in tax payer funded infrastructure improvements for a total of $6.5 billion.

Airbus shot back that Boeing, too, continued to enjoy lavish subsidies, and that the company had received some $12 billion from NASA to development technology, much of which has found its way into commercial jet aircraft. The Europeans also contended that Boeing would receive as much as $3.2 billion in tax breaks from Washington State, where the 787 is to be assembled, and more than $1 billion in loans from the Japanese government to 3 Japanese suppliers, who will build over 1/3 of the 787. Moreover, Airbus was quick to point out that a trade war would not benefit either side, and that Airbus purchased some $6 billion a year in supplies from companies in the United States.

In January 2005, both the U.S. and EU agreed to freeze direct subsidies to the 2 aircraft makers while talks continued. However, in May 2005, news reports suggested (and Airbus confirmed), that the jet maker had applied to 4 EU governments for launch aid for the A350, and that the British government would announce some $700 million in aid at the Paris Air Show in mid-2005. Simultaneously, the EU offered to cut launch aid for the A350 by 30%. Dissatisfied, the U.S. side decided that the talks were going nowhere, and on May 31 the United States formally filed a request with the World Trade Organization (WTO) for the establishment of a dispute resolution panel to resolve the issues. The EU quickly responded by filing a countersuit with the WTO claiming that U.S. aid to Boeing exceeded the terms set out in the 1992 agreement.[31]

In early-2011, the WTO ruled on the complaint by Boeing, and on Airbus's counterclaim. The WTO stated that Airbus had indeed benefitted from some $15 billion in improper launch aid subsidies over the prior 40 years, and that this practice must stop. Boeing, however, had little time to celebrate. In a separate ruling, the WTO stated that Boeing, too, had benefited from improper subsidies, including $5.3 billion from the United States Government to develop the 787 (the WTO stated that most of these subsidies were in the form of payments from NASA to development space technology that subsequently had commercial applications. Both sides in the dispute are engaged in the process of appealing these rulings, which could drag out for years.[32]

The Next Chapter

Huge financial bets have been placed on very different visions of the future of airline travel—Airbus with the A380 and Boeing with the 787. By mid-2011, Airbus had delivered 51 A380s and had a backlog of 236 on order. The rate of new orders had been slow, however; Boeing orders of 827 787s have had a backlog. Airbus also hedged its bets by announcing the A350 XWB, and after a slow start the aircraft has amassed some 567 orders.

Both companies have had substantial production problems and faced significant delays. In mid-2006, Airbus announced that deliveries for the A380 would be delayed by 6 months while the company dealt with "production issues" arising from problems installing the wiring bundles in the A380. Estimates suggest that the delay would cost Airbus some $2.6 billion over 4 years.[33] Within months, Airbus had revised the expected delay to 18 months, and stated that the number of A380s it now needed to sell in order to break even had increased from 250 to 420 aircraft. The company also stated that due to production problems, it would only be able to deliver 84 A380 planes by 2010, compared to an original estimate of 420 (in fact it delivered only half of this amount).[34]

Boeing ran into a number of production and design problems with the 787 that resulted in 5 delay announcements, pushing out the first deliveries more than 3 years. For the 787, Boeing outsourced an unprecedented amount of work to suppliers. This was seen at the time as a risky move, particularly given the amount of new technology incorporated into the 787. As it turns out, several suppliers had problems meeting Boeing's quality specification, supplying substandard parts that had to be reworked or redesigned. The issues included a shortage of fasteners, a misalignment between the cockpit section and the fuselage, and microscopic wrinkles in the fuselage skin. In addition, Boeing found that it had to redesign parts of the section where the wing meets the fuselage. Boeing executives complained that their engineers were often fixing problems "that should not have come to us in the first place."[35]

Some company sources suggest that Boeing erred by not managing its supplier relationships as well as it should have. In particular, there may have been a lack of ongoing communication between Boeing and key suppliers. Boeing tended to throw design specifications "over the wall" to suppliers, and then was surprised when they failed to comply fully with the company's expectations. In addition, Boeing's dependency on single suppliers for key components meant that a problem in any one of those suppliers could create a bottleneck that would hold up production.

In an attempt to fix some of the supply chain issues, in 2009, Boeing purchased a Vought Industries

Aircraft plant for $580 million. Vought had been in a joint venture with the Italian company, Alenia Aeronautical, to make fuselage parts for the 787. Vought had not been able to keep up with the demands of the program and Boeing's acquisition has seen it as a move to exert more control over the production process, and inject capital into Vought.

In another development, Boeing quietly launched the 747–8 program in November 2005. This plane is a completely redesigned version of the 747 and incorporates many of the technological advances developed for the 787, including significant use of composites. It will be offered in both a freighter and intercontinental passenger configuration that will carry 467 passengers in a 3-seat configuration and have a range of 8,000 miles (the 747–400 can carry 416 passengers). The 747–8 will also use the fuel efficient engines developed for the 787, and will have the same cockpit configuration as the 737, 777 and 787. Development costs are estimated to be around $4 billion. By July 2011, Boeing had orders for 78 747–8 freighters and 36 passenger planes. The first deliveries occurred in late-2011.

Looking forward, the primary issue confronting both Airbus and Boeing is what to do about their aging narrow bodies planes, the A320 and the 737 respectively? These aircraft are the workhorses of many airlines comprising some 70% of all units produced by the 2 manufacturers. Strong demand is expected for this category in the future. Boeing estimates that over the next 20 years, airlines will buy 23,000 single aisle jets worth some $1.95 trillion. Ideally, both Boeing and Airbus would probably prefer to wait for a few more years before bearing the R&D costs associated with new product development. The argument often made is that this will give time for new technologies to mature, and make for a better aircraft at the end of the day. However, events have conspired to force their hands.

First, new engine technologies developed by Pratt & Whitney reportedly increases fuel efficiency by 10–15%. Airlines want these new engines on their aircraft, but doing so requires some redesign of the A320 and 737. The wings of the 737 in particular, are too low slung to take the new engines, so Boeing would be required to do some major redesign work.

Second, there are several potential new entrants into the narrow body segment of the market. The Canadian regional jet manufacturer, Bombardier, is developing a 110–150 seat aircraft that makes extensive use of composites to reduce weight. This will reduce operating costs by about 15% compared to the older 737 and A320 models. Known as the CSeries, as of June 2011, Bombardier had 133 firm orders for this aircraft plus options for an additional 129. The first CSeries aircraft are expected to enter service in 2013.

In addition, the Commercial Aircraft Corporation of China (Comac) has announced that it will build a 170–190 seat narrow-bodied jet. Scheduled for introduction in 2016, this will compete with the larger 737 and A320 models. The European low cost airline, Ryanair, has entered into a co-development agreement with Comac and has talked about a 200+ plane order that could be as high as 400. Formerly, Ryanair had been a Boeing customer. Boeing must decide how to confront these growing threats.

Responding to these threats, Airbus in late-2010 announced that it would introduce a redesigned version of the A320 that utilizes the Pratt & Whitney engine. Known as the A320NEO (New Engine Option), the offering has garnered strong interest from airlines, racking up over 1,000 orders by August of 2011.

These developments have presented Boeing with a major strategic dilemma. Should they continue to evaluate what to do with the 737, perhaps waiting a few more years before making the heavy investment associated with redesign. This would allow them to design a high technology successor to the 737 that would incorporate many of the technologies developed for the 787. Alternatively, should they jump into the fray now, and offer a redesigned version of the 737 that can utilize new engine technology?

In a sign of how Boeing's hand may be forced, in July 2011, Boeing announced a large new order from American Airlines for 200 narrow-bodied aircraft. Boeing agreed to fit half of these aircraft with new engine technology, a requirement that will necessitate substantially higher R&D spending. At the same time, American Airlines announced that it would buy 260 A320 aircraft from Airbus, half of which will be A320NEOs. This will be the first order from American Airlines for Airbus since the 1980s.[36]

Endnotes

1 Boeing Website.
2 Airbus Website.
3 J. Palmer, "Big Bird," *Barron's*, December 19, 2005, 25–29; www.yeald.com/Yeald/a/33341/both_a380_and_787_have_bright_futures.html
4 G.J. Steven, "The Learning Curve; From Aircraft to Space Craft," *Management Accounting*, May 1999, 64–66.
5 D. Gates, "Boeing 7E7 Watch: Familiar Suppliers Make Short List," *Seattle Times*.
6 The figures are from the International Airline Travelers Association (IATA).
7 IATA, "2006 Loss Forecast Drops to US$1.7 billion," Press Release, August 31, 2006.
8 "Turbulent Skies: Low Cost Airlines," *The Economist,* July 10, 2004, 68–72; "Silver Linings, Darkening Clouds," *The Economist,* March 27, 2004, 90–92.
9 Air Transport Association, *The Economic Climb Out for U.S. Airlines*, ATA Economics, August 3, 2011 (accessed on ATA Website).
10 Data from the Air Transport Association at www.airlines.org.
11 Boeing, Current Market Outlook, 2011. Archived on Boeing's Website.
12 Airbus' Website. www.airbus.com/en/myairbus/global_market_forcast.html.
13 Presentation by Randy Baseler, Vice President of Boeing Commercial Airplanes, given at the Farnborough Air show, July 2006. Archived at www.boeing.com/nosearch/exec_pres/CMO.pdf.
14 This material is drawn from an earlier version of the Boeing case written by Charles W.L. Hill. See C.W.L. Hill, "The Boeing Corporation: Commercial Aircraft Operations," in C.W.L. Hill and G.R. Jones, *Strategic Management*, third edition (Boston: Houghton Mifflin, 1995). Much of Boeing's history is described in R.J. Sterling, *Legend and Legacy* (St Martin's Press, New York, 1992).
15 S. Browder, "A Fierce Downdraft at Boeing," *Business Week*, January 26, 1988, 34.
16 M.A. Cusumano, *The Japanese Automobile Industry* (Cambridge, Mass.: Harvard University Press, 1989); Ohno Taiichi, *Toyota Production System* (Cambridge, Mass.: Productivity Press, (1990); J. P. Womack, D. T. Jones, and D. Roos, *The Machine That Changed the World* (New York: Rawson Associates, 1990).
17 J. Gillie, "Lean Manufacturing Could Save Boeing's Auburn Washington Plant," *Knight Ridder Tribune Business News*, May 6, 2002, 1.
18 P.V. Arnold, "Boeing Knows Lean," *MRO Today*, February 2002.
19 Boeing, "Converted Farm Machine Improves Production Process," Press Release, July 1, 2003.
20 P.V. Arnold, "Boeing Knows Lean," *MRO Today*, February 2002. Also "Build in Lean: Manufacturing for the Future," on Boeing's Website www.boeing.com/aboutus/environment/create_build.htm.; J.Gillie, "Lean Manufacturing Could Save Boeing's Auburn, Washington Plant," *Knight Ridder Tribune Business News*, May 6, 2002, 1.

21 J. Gillie, "Lean Manufacturing Could Save Boeing's Auburn Washington Plant," *Knight Ridder Tribune Business News*, May 6, 2002, 1.

22 P.V. Arnold, "Boeing Knows Lean," *MRO Today*, February 2002.

23 M. Mecham, "The Lean, Green Line," *Aviation Week*, July 19, 2004, 144–148.

24 Boeing, "Boeing Reduces 737 Airplane's Final Assembly Time by 50 Percent," Press Release, January 27, 2005.

25 *The Economist*, "A Phony War," May 5, 2001, 56–57.

26 J.D. Boyd, "Building Room for Growth," *Traffic World*, August 7, 2006, 1.

27 W. Sweetman, "Boeing, Boeing, Gone," *Popular Science*, June 2004, 97.

28 Anonymous, "Who Will Supply the Parts?", *Seattle Times*, June 15, 2003.

29 W. Sweetman, "Boeing, Boeing, Gone," *Popular Science*, June 2004, 97.

30 D. Michaels and J.L. Lunsford, "Airbus Chief Reveals Plans for New Family of Jetliners," *Wall Street Journal*, July 18, 2006, A3.

31 J. Reppert-Bismarck and W. Echikson, "EU Counter-sues over U.S. Aid to Boeing," *Wall Street Journal*, June 1, 2005, A2; United States Trade Representative Press Release, "United States Takes Next Steps in Airbus WTO Litigation," May 30, 2005.

32 N. Clark, "WTO Rules U.S. Subsidies for Boeing Unfair," *New York Times*, March 31, 2011.

33 Anonymous, "Airbus Agonistes," *Wall Street Journal*, September 6, 2006, A20.

34 Anonymous, "Forecast Dimmer for Profit on Airbus' A380," *Seattle Times*, October 20, 2006, Web Edition.

35 J. Weber, "Boeing to Rein in Dreamliner Outsourcing," *Bloomberg Business Week*, January 16, 2009.

36 Staff Reporter, "American Airlines Orders 200 Boeing 737s, 260 More from Airbus," *Associated Press*, July 19, 2011.

CASE 30

Case Study: Merck, the FDA, and the Vioxx Recall[1]

Anne Lawrence, San Jose State University

In 2006, the pharmaceutical giant Merck faced major challenges. Vioxx, the company's once best-selling prescription painkiller, had been pulled off the market in September 2004 after Merck learned it increased the risk of heart attacks and strokes. When news of the recall broke, the company's stock price had plunged thirty percent to $33 a share, its lowest point in eight years, where it had hovered since. Standard & Poor's had downgraded the company's outlook from "stable" to "negative." In late 2004, the Justice Department had opened a criminal investigation into whether the company had "caused federal health programs to pay for the prescription drug when its use was not warranted."[2] The Securities and Exchange Commission was inquiring into whether Merck had misled investors. By late 2005, more than 6,000 lawsuits had been filed, alleging that Vioxx had caused death or disability. From many quarters, the company faced troubling questions about the development and marketing of Vioxx, new calls for regulatory reform, and concerns about its political influence on Capitol Hill. In the words of Senator Charles Grassley, chairman of a Congressional committee investigating the Vioxx case, "a blockbuster drug [had become] a blockbuster disaster."[3]

Merck, Inc.[4]

Merck, the company in the eye of this storm, was one of the world's leading pharmaceutical firms. As shown in Exhibit 1, in 2005 the company ranked fourth in sales, after Pfizer, Johnson & Johnson, and Glaxo-SmithKline. In assets and market value, it ranked fifth. However, Merck ranked first in profits, earning $7.33 billion on $30.78 billion in sales (24 percent).

Merck had long enjoyed a reputation as one of the most ethical and socially responsible of the major drug companies. For an unprecedented seven consecutive years (1987 to 1993), *Fortune* magazine had named Merck its "most admired" company. In 1987, Merck appeared on the cover of *Time* under the headline, "The Miracle Company." It had consistently appeared on lists of best companies to work for and in the portfolios of social investment funds. The company's philanthropy was legendary. In the 1940s, Merck had given its patent for streptomycin, a powerful antibiotic, to a university foundation. Merck was especially admired for its donation of Mectizan. Merck's scientists had originally developed this drug for veterinary use, but later discovered that it was an effective cure for river blindness, a debilitating parasitic disease afflicting some of the world's poorest people. When the company realized that the victims of river blindness could not afford the drug, it decided to give it away for free, in perpetuity.[5]

In 1950, George W. Merck, the company's long-time CEO, stated in a speech: "We try never to forget that medicine is for the people. It is not for the profits. The profits follow, and if we have remembered that, they never fail to appear. The better we have remembered that, the larger they have been."[6] This statement was often repeated in subsequent years as a touchstone of the company's core values.

Merck was renowned for its research labs, which had a decades-long record of achievement, turning out one innovation after another, including drugs for tuberculosis, cholesterol, hypertension, and AIDS. In the early 2000s, Merck spent around $3 billion annually on research. Some felt that the company's culture had been shaped by its research agenda. Commented the author of a history of Merck, the company was "intense, driven, loyal, scientifically brilliant, collegial, and arrogant."[7] In 2006, although Merck had several medicines in the pipeline—including vaccines for rotavirus and cervical cancer, and drugs for insomnia, lymphoma, and the effects of stroke—some analysts worried that the pace of research had slowed significantly.

Exhibit 1   The World's Top Pharmaceutical Companies, 2005

Company	Sales ($bil)	Profits ($bil)	Assets ($bil)	Market Value ($bil)
Pfizer	40.36	6.20	120.06	285.27
Johnson & Johnson	40.01	6.74	46.66	160.96
Merck	**30.78**	**7.33**	**42.59**	**108.76**
Novartis	26.77	5.40	46.92	116.43
Roche Group	25.18	2.48	45.77	95.38
GlaxoSmithKline	34.16	6.34	29.19	124.79
Aventis	21.66	2.29	31.06	62.98
Bristol-Myers Squibb	19.89	2.90	26.53	56.05
AstraZeneca	20.46	3.29	23.57	83.03
Abbott Labs	18.99	2.44	26.15	69.27

Source: Forbes 2000, available online at www.forbes.com. Listed in order of overall ranking in the Forbes 2000.

Estimating the company's financial liability from the Vioxx lawsuits was difficult. Some 84 million people had taken the drug worldwide over a five-year period from 1999 to 2004. In testimony before Congress, Dr. David Graham, a staff scientist at the Food and Drug Administration (FDA), estimated that as many as 139,000 people in the United States had had heart attacks or strokes as a result of taking Vioxx, and about 55,000 of these had died.[8] Merrill Lynch estimated the company's liability for compensatory damages alone in the range of $4 to $18 billion.[9] However, heart attacks and strokes were common, and they had multiple causes, including genetic predisposition, smoking, obesity, and a sedentary lifestyle. Determining the specific contribution of Vioxx to a particular cardiovascular event would be very difficult. The company vigorously maintained that it had done nothing wrong and vowed to defend every single case in court. By early 2006, only three cases had gone to trial, and the results had been a virtual draw—one decision for the plaintiff, one for Merck, and one hung jury.

Government Regulation of Prescription Drugs

In the United States, prescription medicines—like Vioxx—were regulated by the Food and Drug Administration (FDA).[10] Before a new drug could be sold to the public, its manufacturer had to carry out clinical trials to demonstrate both safety and effectiveness. Advisory panels of outside medical experts reviewed the results of these trials and recommended to the FDA's Office of Drug Safety whether or not to approve a new drug.[11] After a drug was on the market, the agency's Office of New Drugs continued to monitor it for safety, in a process known as post-market surveillance. These two offices both reported to the same boss, the FDA's director of the Center for Drug Evaluation and Research.

Once the FDA had approved a drug, physicians could prescribe it for any purpose, but the manufacturer could market it only for uses for which it had been approved. Therefore, companies had an incentive to continue to study approved drugs to provide data that they were safe and effective for the treatment of other conditions.

In the 1980s, the drug industry and some patient advocates had criticized the FDA for being too slow to approve new medicines. Patients were concerned that they were not getting new medicines fast enough, and drug companies were concerned that they were losing sales revenue. Each month an average drug spent under review represented $41.7 million in lost revenue, according to one study.[12]

In 1992, Congress passed the Prescription Drug User Fee Act (PDUFA). This law, which was supported by the industry, required pharmaceutical companies to pay "user fees" to the FDA to review proposed new medicines. Between 1993 and 2001, the FDA received around $825 million in such fees from drug makers seeking approval. (During this period, it also received $1.3 billion appropriated by Congress). This infusion of new revenue enabled the agency to hire 1,000 new employees and to shorten the approval time for new drugs from 27 months in 1993 to 14 months in 2001.[13]

Despite the benefits of PDUFA, some felt that industry-paid fees were a bad idea.

In an editorial published in December 2004, the *Journal of the American Medical Association (JAMA)* concluded: "It is unreasonable to expect that the same agency that was responsible for approval of drug licensing and labeling would also be committed to actively seek evidence to prove itself wrong (i.e., that the decision to approve the product was subsequently shown to be incorrect)." *JAMA* went on to recommend establishment of a separate agency to monitor drug safety.[14] Dr. David Kessler, a former FDA Commissioner, rejected this idea, responding that "strengthening post-marketing surveillance is certainly in order, but you don't want competing agencies."[15]

Some evidence suggested that the morale of FDA staff charged with evaluating the safety of new medicines had been hurt by relentless pressure to bring drugs to market quickly. In 2002, a survey of agency scientists found that only 13 percent were "completely confident" that the FDA's "final decisions adequately assess the safety of a drug." Thirty-one percent were "somewhat confident" and 5 percent lacked "any confidence." Two-thirds of those surveyed lacked confidence that the agency "adequately monitors the safety of prescription jobs once they are on the market." And nearly one in five said they had "been pressured to approve or recommend approval" for a drug "despite reservations about [its] safety, efficacy or quality."[16]

After the FDA shortened the approval time, the percentage of drugs recalled following approval increased from 1.56% for 1993–1996 to 5.35% for 1997–2001.[17] Vioxx was the ninth drug taken off the market in seven years.

Influence at the Top

The pharmaceutical industry's success in accelerating the approval of new drugs reflected its strong presence in Washington. The major drug companies, their trade association PhRMA (Pharmaceutical Research and Manufacturers of America), and their executives consistently donated large sums of money to both political parties and, through their political action committees, to various candidates. The industry's political contributions are shown in Exhibit 2.

Exhibit 2 Pharmaceutical/Health Products Industry: Political Contributions 1990–2006

Election Cycle	Total Contributions	Contributions from Individuals	Contributions from PACs	Soft Money Contributions	Percentage to Republicans
2006	$5,187,393	$1,753,159	$3,434,234	N/A	70%
2004	$18,181,045	$8,445,485	$9,735,560	N/A	66%
2002	$29,441,951	$3,332,040	$6,957,382	$19,152,529	74%
2000	$26,688,292	$5,660,457	$5,649,913	$15,377,922	69%
1998	$13,169,694	$2,673,845	$4,107,068	$6,388,781	64%
1996	$13,754,796	$3,413,516	$3,584,217	$6,757,063	66%
1994	$7,706,303	$1,935,150	$3,477,146	$2,294,007	56%
1992	$7,924,262	$2,389,370	$3,205,014	$2,329,878	56%
1990	$3,237,592	$771,621	$2,465,971	N/A	54%
Total	$125,291,328	$30,374,643	$42,616,505	$52,300,180	67%

Source: Center for Responsive Politics, online at www.opensecrets.org

Following the Congressional ban on soft money contributions in 2003, the industry shifted much of its contributions to so-called stealth PACs, nonprofit organizations which were permitted by law to take unlimited donations without revealing their source. These organizations could, in turn, make "substantial" political expenditures, providing political activity was not their primary purpose.[18]

In addition, the industry maintained a large corps of lobbyists active in the nation's capital. In 2003, for example, drug companies and their trade association spent $108 million on lobbying and hired 824 individual lobbyists, according to a report by Public Citizen.[19] Merck spent $40.7 million on lobbying between 1998 and 2004.[20] One of the industry's most effective techniques was to hire former elected officials or members of their staffs. For example, Billy Tauzin, formerly a Republican member of Congress from Louisiana and head of the powerful Committee on Energy and Commerce, which oversaw the drug industry, became president of PhRMA at a reported annual salary of $2 million in 2004.[21]

Over the years, the industry's representatives in Washington had established a highly successful record of promoting its political agenda on a range of issues. In addition to faster drug approvals, these had more recently included a Medicare prescription drug benefit, patent protections, and restrictions on drug imports from Canada.

The Blockbuster Model

In the 1990s, 80 percent of growth for the big pharmaceutical firms came from so-called blockbuster drugs.[22] Blockbusters have been defined by *Fortune* magazine as "medicines that serve vast swaths of the population and garner billions of dollars in annual revenue."[23] The ideal blockbuster, from the companies' view, was a medicine that could control chronic but usually nonfatal conditions that afflicted large numbers of people with health insurance. These might include, for example, daily maintenance drugs for high blood pressure or cholesterol, allergies, arthritis pain, or heartburn. Drugs that could actually cure a condition—and thus would not need to be taken for long periods—or were intended to treat diseases, like malaria or tuberculosis, that affected mainly the world's poor, were often less profitable.

Historically, drug companies focused most of their marketing efforts on prescribing physicians.

The industry hired tens of thousands of sales representatives—often, attractive young men and women—to make the rounds of doctors' offices to talk about new products and give out free samples.[24] Drug companies also offered doctors gifts—from free meals to tickets to sporting events—to cultivate their good will. They also routinely sponsored continuing education events for physicians, often featuring reports on their own medicines, and supported doctors financially with opportunities to consult and to conduct clinical trials.[25] In 2003 Merck spent $422 million to market Vioxx to doctors and hospitals.[26]

During the early 2000s, when Vioxx and Pfizer's Celebrex were competing head-to-head, sales representatives for the two firms were hard at work promoting their brand to doctors. Commented one rheumatologist of the competition between Merck and Pfizer at the time: "We were all aware that there was a great deal of marketing. Like a Coke-Pepsi war."[27] An internal Merck training manual for sales representatives, reported in *The Wall Street Journal*, was titled "Dodge Ball Vioxx." It explained how to "dodge" doctors' questions, such as "I am concerned about the cardiovascular effects of Vioxx." Merck later said that this document had been taken out of context and that sales representatives "were not trained to avoid physician's questions."[28]

Direct-to-Consumer Advertising

Although marketing to doctors and hospitals continued to be important, in the late 1990s the focus shifted somewhat. In 1997, the FDA for the first time allowed drug companies to advertise directly to consumers. The industry immediately seized this opportunity, placing numerous ads for drugs—from Viagra to Nexium—on television and in magazines and newspapers. In 2004, the industry spent over $4 billion on such direct-to-consumer, or DTC, advertising. For example, in one ad for Vioxx, Olympic figure skating champion Dorothy Hamill glided gracefully across an outdoor ice rink to the tune of "It's a Beautiful Morning" by the sixties pop group The Rascals, telling viewers that she would "not let arthritis stop me." In all, Merck spent more than $500 million advertising Vioxx.[29]

The industry's media blitz for Vioxx and other drugs was highly effective. According to research by the Harvard School of Public Heath, each dollar spent on DTC advertising yielded $4.25 in sales.

The drug companies defended DTC ads, saying they informed consumers of newly available therapies and encouraged people to seek medical treatment. In the age of the Internet, commented David Jones, an advertising executive whose firm included several major drug companies, "consumers are becoming much more empowered to make their own health care decisions."[30]

However, others criticized DTC advertising, saying that it put pressure on doctors to prescribe drugs that might not be best for the patient. "When a patient comes in and wants something, there is a desire to serve them," said David Wofsy, president of the American College of Rheumatology. "There is a desire on the part of physicians, as there is on anyone else who provides service, to keep the customer happy."[31] Even some industry executives expressed reservations. Said Hank McKinnell, CEO of Pfizer, "I'm beginning to think that direct-to-consumer ads are part of the problem. By having them on television without a very strong message that the doctor needs to determine safety, we've left this impression that all drugs are safe. In fact, no drug is safe."[32]

The Rise of Vioxx

Vioxx, the drug at the center of Merck's legal woes, was a known as "a selective COX-2 inhibitor." Scientists had long understood that an enzyme called cyclo-oxygenase, or COX for short, was associated with pain and inflammation. In the early 1990s, researchers learned that there were really two kinds of COX enzyme. COX-1, it was found, performed several beneficial functions, including protecting the stomach lining. COX-2, on the other hand, contributed to pain and inflammation. Existing anti-inflammatory drugs suppressed both forms of the enzyme, which is why drugs like ibuprofen (Advil) relieved pain, but also caused stomach irritation in some users.

A number of drug companies, including Merck, were intrigued by the possibility of developing a medicine that would block just the COX-2, leaving the stomach-protective COX-1 intact. Such a drug would offer distinctive benefits to some patients, such as arthritis sufferers who were at risk for ulcers (bleeding sores in the intestinal tract).[33] As many as 16,500 people died each year in the United States from this condition.[34]

In May 1999, after several years of research and testing by Merck scientists, the FDA approved Vioxx for the treatment of osteoarthritis, acute pain in adults, and menstrual symptoms. The drug was later approved for rheumatoid arthritis. Although Merck, like other drug companies, never revealed what it spent to develop specific new medicines, estimates of the cost to develop a major new drug ran as high as $800 million.[35]

Vioxx quickly became exactly what Merck had hoped: a blockbuster. At its peak in 2001, Vioxx generated $2.1 billion in sales in the United States alone, contributing almost 10 percent of Merck's total sales revenue worldwide, as shown in Exhibit 3.

Exhibit 3   Vioxx Sales in the United States, 1999–2004

	U.S. Prescriptions Dispensed	U.S. Sales	U.S. Sales of Vioxx as % of Total Merck Sales
1999	4,845,000	$372,697,000	2.2%
2000	20,630,000	$1,526,382,000	7.6%
2001	25,406,000	$2,084,736,000	9.8%
2002	22,044,000	$1,837,680,000	8.6%
2003	19,959,000	$1,813,391,000	8.1%
2004*	13,994,000	$1,342,236,000	5.9%

*Withdrawn from the market in September 2004.

Sources: Columns 1 and 2: IMS Health (www.imshealth.com); Column 3: Merck *Annual Reports* (www.merck.com).

The retail price of Vioxx was around $3.00 per pill, compared with pennies per pill for older anti-inflammatory drugs like aspirin and Advil. Of course, Vioxx was often covered, at least partially, under a user's health insurance, while over-the-counter drugs were not.

Safety Warnings

Even before the drug was approved, some evidence cast doubt on the safety of Vioxx. These clues were later confirmed in other studies.

Merck Research: Internal company e-mails suggested that Merck scientists might have been worried about the cardiovascular risks of Vioxx as early as its development phase. In a 1997 e-mail, reported in *The Wall Street Journal*, Dr. Alise Reicin, a Merck scientist, stated that "the possibility of CV (cardiovascular) events is of great concern." She added, apparently sarcastically, "I just can't wait to be the one to present those results to senior management!" A lawyer representing Merck said this e-mail had been taken out of context.[36]

VIGOR: A study code-named VIGOR, completed in 2000 after the drug was already on the market, compared rheumatoid arthritis patients taking Vioxx with another group taking naproxen (Aleve). Merck financed the research, which was designed to study gastrointestinal side effects. The study found—as the company had expected—that Vioxx was easier on the stomach than naproxen. But it also found that the Vioxx group had nearly five times as many heart attacks (7.3 per thousand person-years) as the naproxen group (1.7 per thousand person-years).[37] Publicly, Merck hypothesized that these findings were due to the heart-protective effect of naproxen, rather than to any defect inherent in Vioxx. Privately, however, the company seemed worried. In an internal e-mail dated March 9, 2000, under the subject line "Vigor," the company's research director, Dr. Edward Scolnick, said that cardiovascular events were "clearly there" and called them "a shame." But, he added, "there is always a hazard."[38] At that time, the company considered reformulating Vioxx by adding an agent to prevent blood clots (and reduce CV risk), but then dropped the project.

The FDA was sufficiently concerned by the VIGOR results that it required Merck to add additional warning language to its label. These changes appeared in April 2002, after lengthy negotiations between the agency and the company over their wording.[39]

Kaiser/Permanente: In August 2004, Dr. David Graham, a scientist at the FDA, reported the results of a study of the records of 1.4 million patients enrolled in the Kaiser health maintenance organization in California. He found that patients on high doses of Vioxx had three times the rate of heart attacks as patients on Celebrex, a competing COX-2 inhibitor made by Pfizer. Merck discounted this finding, saying that studies of patient records were less reliable than double blind clinical studies.[40] Dr. Graham later charged that his superiors at the FDA had "ostracized" him and subjected him to "veiled threats" if he did not qualify his criticism of Vioxx. The FDA called these charges "baloney."[41]

APPROVe: In order to examine the possibility that Vioxx posed a cardiovascular risk, Merck decided to monitor patients enrolled in a clinical trial called APPROVe to see if they those taking Vioxx had more heart attacks and strokes than those who were taking a placebo (sugar pill). This study had been designed to determine if Vioxx reduced the risk of recurrent colon polyps (a precursor to colon cancer); Merck hoped it would lead to FDA approval of the drug for this condition. The APPROVe study was planned before the VIGOR results were known.

Merck Recalls the Drug

On the evening of Thursday, September 23, 2004, Dr. Peter S. Kim, president of Merck Research Labs, received a phone call from scientists monitoring the colon polyp study. Researchers had found, the scientists told him, that after 18 months of continuous use individuals taking Vioxx were more than twice as likely to have a heart attack or stroke than those taking a placebo. The scientists recommended that the study be halted because of "unacceptable" risk.[42]

Dr. Kim later described to a reporter for *The New York Times* the urgent decision-making process that unfolded over the next hours and days as the company responded to this news.

On Friday, I looked at the data with my team. The first thing you do is review the data. We did that. Second is you double-check the data, go through it and make sure that everything is O.K. [At that point] I knew that barring some big mistake in the analysis, we had an issue here. Around noon, I called [CEO] Ray Gilmartin and told him what was up.

He said, 'Figure out what was the best thing for patient safety.' We then spent Friday and the rest of the weekend going over the data and analyzing it in different ways and calling up medical experts to set up meetings where we would discuss the data and their interpretations and what to do.[43]

According to later interviews with some of the doctors consulted that weekend by Merck, the group was of mixed opinion. Some experts argued that Vioxx should stay on the market, with a strong warning label so that doctors and patients could judge the risk for themselves. But others thought the drug should be withdrawn because no one knew why the drug was apparently causing heart attacks. One expert commented that "Merck prides itself on its ethical approach. I couldn't see Merck saying we're going to market a drug with a safety problem."[44]

On Monday, Dr. Kim recommended to Gilmartin that Vioxx be withdrawn from the market. The CEO agreed. The following day, Gilmartin notified the board, and the company contacted the FDA.

On Thursday, September 30, Merck issued a press release, which stated in part:

> Merck & Co., Inc. announced today a voluntary withdrawal of VIOXX®. This decision is based on new data from a 3-year clinical study. In this study, there was an increased risk for cardiovascular (CV) events, such as heart attack and stroke, in patients taking VIOXX 25 mg compared to those taking placebo (sugar pill). While the incidence of CV events was low, there was an increased risk beginning after 18 months of treatment. The cause of the clinical study result is uncertain, but our commitment to our patients is clear . . . Merck is notifying physicians and pharmacists and has informed the Food and Drug Administration of this decision. We are taking this action because we believe it best serves the interests of patients. That is why we undertook this clinical trial to better understand the safety profile of VIOXX. And it's why we instituted this voluntary withdrawal upon learning about these data. Be assured that Merck will continue to do everything we can to maintain the safety of our medicines.

Endnotes

1 By Anne T. Lawrence, San Jose State University. Copyright © 2006 by the author. All rights reserved. An earlier version of this case was presented at the Western Casewriters Association Annual Meeting, Long Beach, California, March 30, 2006. This case was prepared from publicly available materials.

2 "Justice Dept. and SEC Investigating Merck Drug," *New York Times*, November 9, 2004.

3 "Opening Statement of U.S. Senator Chuck Grassley of Iowa," U.S. Senate Committee on Finance, Hearing—FDA, Merck, and Vioxx: Putting Patient Safety First?" November 18, 2004, online at http://finance.senate.gov.

4 A history of Merck may be found in Fran Hawthorne, *The Merck Druggernaut: The Inside Story of a Pharmaceutical Giant* (Hoboken, NJ: John Wiley & Sons, 2003).

5 Merck received the 1991 Business Enterprise Trust Award for this action. See Stephanie Weiss and Kirk O. Hanson, "Merck and Co., Inc.: Addressing Third World Needs" (Business Enterprise Trust, 1991).

6 Hawthorne, op. Cit., pp. 17–18.

7 Hawthorne, op. Cit., p. 38.

8 "FDA Failing in Drug Safety, Official Asserts," *New York Times*, November 19, 2004. The full transcript of the hearing of the U.S. Senate Committee on Finance, "FDA, Merck, and Vioxx: Putting Patient Safety First?" is available online at http://finance.senate.gov.

9 "Despite Warnings, Drug Giant Took Long Path to Vioxx Recall," *New York Times*, November 14, 2004.

10 A history of the FDA and of its relationship to business may be found in Philip J. Hilts, *Protecting America's Health: The FDA, Business, and One Hundred Years of Regulation* (New York: Alfred A. Knopf, 2003).

11 Marcia Angell, *The Trust About the Drug Companies* (New York: Random House, 2004), Ch. 2.

12 Merrill Lynch data reported in "A World of Hurt," *Fortune*, January 10, 2005, p. 18.

13 U.S. General Accounting Office, *Food and Drug Administration: Effect of User Fees on Drug Approval Times, Withdrawals, and Other Agency Activities*, September 2002.

14 "Postmarketing Surveillance—Lack of Vigilance, Lack of Trust," *Journal of the American Medical Association* 92(21), December 1, 2004, p. 2649.

15 "FDA Lax in Drug Safety, Journal Warns," *www.sfgate.com*, November 23, 2004.

16 2002 Survey of 846 FDA scientists conducted by the Office of the Inspector General of the Department of Health and Human Services, online at www.peer.org/FDAscientistsurvey.

17 "Postmarketing Surveillance," op. Cit.

18 "Big PhRMA's Stealth PACs: How the Drug Industry Uses 501(c) Non-Profit Groups to Influence Elections," *Congress Watch*, September 2004.

19 "Drug Industry and HMOs Deployed an Army of Nearly 1,000 Lobbyists to Push Medicare Bill, Report Finds," June 23, 2004, www.citizen.org.

20 Data available online at www.publicintegrity.org.

21 "Rep. Billy Tauzin Demonstrates that Washington's Revolving Door is Spinning Out of Control," *Public Citizen,* December 15, 2004, press release.

22 "The Waning of the Blockbuster," *Business Week,* October 18, 2004.

23 "A World of Hurt," *Fortune,* January 10, 2005, p.20.

24 In 2005, 90,000 sales representatives were employed by the pharmaceutical industry, about one for every eight doctors. The *New York Times* revealed in an investigative article ("Give Me an Rx! Cheerleaders Pep Up Drug Sales," November 28, 2005) that many companies made a point of hiring former college cheerleaders for this role.

25 The influence of the drug industry on the medical professional is documented in Katharine Greider, *The Big Fix: How the Pharmaceutical Industry Rips Off American Consumers* (New York: Public Affairs, 2003).

26 "Drug Pullout," *Modern Healthcare,* October 18, 2004.

27 "Marketing of Vioxx: How Merck Played Game of Catch-Up," *New York Times,* February 11, 2005.

28 "E-Mails Suggest Merck Knew Vioxx's Dangers at Early Stage," *Wall Street Journal,* November 1, 2004.

29 IMS Health estimate reported in: "Will Merck Survive Vioxx?" *Fortune,* November 1, 2004.

30 "With or Without Vioxx, Drug Ads Proliferate," *New York Times,* December 6, 2004.

31 "A 'Smart' Drug Fails the Safety Test," *Washington Post,* October 3, 2004.

32 "A World of Hurt," *Fortune,* January 10, 2005, p. 18.

33 "Medicine Fueled by Marketing Intensified Troubles for Pain Pills," *New York Times,* December 19, 2004.

34 "New Scrutiny of Drugs in Vioxx's Family," *New York Times,* October 4, 2004.

35 This estimate was hotly debated. See, for example, "How Much Does the Pharmaceutical Industry Really Spend on R&D?" Ch. 3 in Marcia Angell, op. Cit., and Merrill Goozner, *The $800 Million Pill: The Truth Behind the Cost of New Drugs* (Berkeley: University of California Press, 2004).

36 "E-Mails Suggest Merck Knew Vioxx's Dangers at Early Stage," *Wall Street Journal,* November 1, 2004.

37 "Comparison of Upper Gastrointestinal Toxicity of Rofecoxib and Naproxen in Patients with Rheumatoid Arthritis," *New England Journal of Medicine,* 2000: 323.

38 "E-Mails Suggest Merck Knew Vioxx's Dangers at Early Stage," *Wall Street Journal,* November 1, 2004.

39 At one of the early Vioxx trials, the plaintiff introduced a Merck internal memo that calculated that the company would make $229 million more in profits if it delayed changes to warning language on the label by four months (*New York Times,* August 20, 2005). The FDA did not have the authority to dictate label language; any changes had to be negotiated with the manufacturer.

40 "Study of Painkiller Suggests Heart Risk," *New York Times,* August 26, 2004.

41 "FDA Official Alleges Pressure to Suppress Vioxx Findings," *Washington Post,* October 8, 2004.

42 "Painful Withdrawal for Makers of Vioxx," *Washington Post,* October 18, 2004. Detailed data reported the following day in *The New York Times* showed that 30 of the 1287 patients taking Vioxx had suffered a heart attack, compared with 11 of 1299 taking a placebo; 15 on Vioxx had had a stroke or transient ischemic attack (minor stroke), compared with 7 taking a placebo.

43 "A Widely Used Arthritis Drug is Withdrawn," *New York Times,* October 1, 2004.

44 "Painful Withdrawal for Makers of Vioxx," *Washington Post,* October 18, 2004.

CASE 31

Nike: Sweatshops and Business Ethics

Charles W.L. Hill, University of Washington

Introduction

Nike is in many ways the quintessential global corporation. Established in 1972 by former University of Oregon track star Phil Knight, Nike is now one of the leading marketers of athletic shoes and apparel on the planet. The company has $10 billion in annual revenues and sells its products in some 140 countries. Nike does not do any manufacturing. Rather, it designs and markets its products, while contracting for their manufacture from a global network of 600 factories scattered around the globe that employ nearly 550,000 people.[1] This huge corporation has made founder Phil Knight one of the richest people in America. Nike's marketing phrase "Just do it!" and "swoosh" logo have become as recognizable in popular culture as the faces of its celebrity sponsors, such as Michael Jordan and Tiger Woods.

For all of its successes, the company has been dogged for more than a decade by repeated and persistent accusations that its products are made in "sweatshops" where workers, many of them children, slave away in hazardous conditions for below-subsistence wages. Nike's wealth, its detractors claim, has been built upon the backs of the world's poor. To many, Nike has become a symbol of the evils of globalization: a rich Western corporation exploiting the world's poor to provide expensive shoes and apparel to the pampered consumers of the developed world. Nike's Niketown stores have become standard targets for anti-globalization protestors. Nike has been the target of repeated criticism and protests from several nongovernmental organizations, such as San Fransisco–based Global Exchange, a human-rights organization dedicated to promoting environmental, political, and social justice around the world.[2] News media have run exposés on working conditions in foreign factories that supply Nike. Students on the campuses of several major U.S. universities with which Nike has lucrative sponsorship deals have protested against the ties, citing Nike's use of sweatshop labor.

For its part, Nike has taken many steps to counter the protests. Yes, it admits, there have been problems in some overseas factories. But the company has signaled a commitment to improving working conditions. It requires that foreign subcontractors meet minimum thresholds for working conditions and pay. It has arranged for factories to be examined by independent auditors and terminated contracts with factories that do not comply with its standards. But for all this effort, the company continues to be a target of protests.

The Case Against Nike

CBS 48 Hours aired a news report on October 17, 1996 depicting a typical exposé against Nike.[3] Reporter Roberta Basin visited a Nike factory in Vietnam. With a shot of the factory, her commentary began:

> The signs are everywhere of an American invasion in search of cheap labor. Millions of people who are literate, disciplined, and desperate for jobs. This is Niketown near what used to be called Saigon, one of 4 factories Nike doesn't own but subcontracts to make a million shoes a month. It takes 25,000 workers, mostly young women, to "Just Do It."
>
> But the workers here don't share in Nike's huge profits. They work 6 days a week for only $40 a month, just $0.20 an hour.

Baskin interviews one of the workers in the factory, a young woman named Lap. Baskin tells the listener:

> Her basic wage, even as a sewing team leader, still doesn't amount to the minimum wage. . . . She's down to 85 lbs. Like most of the young women who make shoes, she has little choice but to accept the low wages and long hours. Nike says that it requires all subcontractors to obey local laws; but Lap has already put in much more overtime than the annual legal limit: 200 hours.

This case is intended to be used as a basis for class discussion rather than as an illustration of either effective or ineffective handling of the situation. Reprinted by permission of Charles W. L. Hill.

Baskin then asks Lap what would happen if she wanted to leave, if she was sick or had to take care of a sick relative: could she leave the factory? Through a translator, Lap replies:

It is not possible if you haven't made enough shoes. You have to meet the quota before you can go home.

The clear implication of the story was that Nike was at fault for allowing such working conditions to persist in the Vietnamese factory (which, incidentally, was owned by a Korean company).

Another example of an attack on Nike's subcontracting practices occurred in June 1996. It was launched by USA, a foundation largely financed by labor unions and domestic-apparel manufacturers that oppose free trade with low-wage countries. According to Joel Joseph, chairman of the foundation, a popular line of high-priced Nike sneakers, the "Air Jordans," were put together by 11-year-olds in Indonesia making $0.14 per hour. A Nike spokeswoman, Donna Gibbs, countered that this was false. According to Gibbs, the average worker made 240,000 *rupiah* ($103) a month working a maximum 54-hour week, or about $0.45 per hour. Moreover, Gibbs noted, Nike had staff members in each factory monitoring conditions to make sure that they obeyed local minimum-wage and child-labor laws.[4]

Another example of the criticism against Nike is the following extracts from a newsletter published by Global Exchange:[5]

During the 1970s, most Nike shoes were made in South Korea and Taiwan. When workers there gained new freedom to organize and wages began to rise, Nike looked for "greener pastures." It found them in Indonesia and China, where Nike started producing in the 1980s, and most recently in Vietnam.

The majority of Nike shoes are made in Indonesia and China, countries with governments that prohibit independent unions and set the minimum wage at rock bottom. The Indonesian government admits that the minimum wage there does not provide enough to supply the basic needs of one person, let alone a family. In early-1997, the entry-level wage was a miserable $2.46 a day. Labor groups estimate that a livable wage in Indonesia is about $4.00 a day.

In Vietnam the pay is even less—$0.20 an hour, or a mere $1.60 a day. But in urban Vietnam, 3 simple meals cost about $2.10 a day, and then of course there is rent, transportation, clothing, health care, and much more. According to Thuyen Nguyen of Vietnam Labor Watch, a living wage in Vietnam is at least $3 a day.

In another attack on Nike's practices, Global Exchange published a report in September 1997 on working conditions in 4 Nike and Reebok subcontractor's factories in southern China.[6] Global Exchange, in conjunction with two Hong Kong human-rights groups, had interviewed workers at the factories in 1995, and again in 1997. According to Global Exchange, in one factory, a Korean-owned subcontractor for Nike, workers as young as 13 earned as little as $0.10 an hour and toiled up to 17 hours daily in enforced silence. Talking during work was not allowed, and violators were fined $1.20 to $3.60, according to the report. The practices were in violation of Chinese labor law, which states that no child under 16 may work in a factory, and the Chinese minimum-wage requirement of $1.90 for an 8-hour day. Nike condemned the study as "erroneous," charging that it incorrectly stated the wages of workers and made irresponsible accusations.

Global Exchange, however, continued to be a major thorn in Nike's side. In November 1997, the organization obtained and then leaked a confidential report by Ernst & Young of an audit that Nike had commissioned of a factory in Vietnam owned by a Nike subcontractor.[7] The factory had 9,200 workers and made 400,000 pairs of shoes per month. The Ernst & Young report painted a dismal picture of thousands of young women, most under age 25, laboring 10 1/2 hours a day, 6 days a week, in excessive heat, noise, and foul air, for slightly more than $10 a week. The report also found that workers with skin or breathing problems had not been transferred to departments free of chemicals, and that more than half the workers who dealt with dangerous chemicals did not wear protective masks or gloves. It claimed workers were exposed to carcinogens that exceeded local legal standards by 177 times in parts of the plant, and that 77% of the employees suffered from respiratory problems.

Put on the defensive yet again, Nike called a news conference and pointed out that it had commissioned the report, and had acted on it.[8] The company stated that it had formulated an action plan to deal with the problems cited in the report, and had slashed overtime, improved safety and ventilation, and reduced the use of toxic chemicals. The company also asserted that the report showed that Nike's internal monitoring system had performed exactly as it should have. According to one spokesman:

"This shows our system of monitoring works. . . . We have uncovered these issues clearly before anyone else, and we have moved fairly expeditiously to correct them."

Nike's Responses

Unaccustomed to playing defense, Nike formulated a number of strategies and tactics over the years to deal with the problems of working conditions and pay in subcontractor facilities. In 1996, Nike hired one-time U.S. ambassador to the United Nations, representative, and former Atlanta mayor Andrew Young to assess working conditions in subcontractors' plants around the world. The following year, after a 2-week tour of 3 countries that included inspections of 15 factories, Young released a mildly critical report. He informed Nike it was doing a good job in its treatment of workers, though it should do better. According to Young, he did not see: "sweatshops, or hostile conditions.... I saw crowded dorms ... but the workers were eating at least 2 meals a day on the job and making what I was told were subsistence wages in those cultures."[9]

Young was widely criticized by human-rights and labor groups for not taking his own translators and for doing slipshod inspections, an assertion he repeatedly denied.

In 1996, Nike joined a presidential task force designed to find a way of banishing sweatshops in the shoe and clothing industries. The task force included industry leaders, representatives from human-rights groups, and labor leaders. In April 1997, they announced an agreement for workers' rights that U.S. companies could agree to when manufacturing abroad. The accord limited the work week to 60 hours, and called for paying at least the local minimum wage in foreign factories. The task force also agreed to establish an independent monitoring association—later named the Fair Labor Association (FLA)—to assess whether companies were abiding by the code.[10]

The FLA now includes among its members the Lawyers Committee for Human Rights, the National Council of Churches, the International Labor Rights Fund, 135 universities (universities have extensive licensing agreements with sports-apparel companies), and companies such as Nike, Reebok, and Levi Strauss.

In early 1997, Nike also began to commission independent organizations such as Ernst & Young to audit the factories of its subcontractors. In September 1997, Nike tried to show its critics that it was involved in more than just a public-relations exercise when it terminated its relationship with 4 Indonesian subcontractors, stating that they had refused to comply with the company's standards for wage levels and working conditions. Nike identified one of the subcontractors, Seyon, which manufactured specialty sports gloves for Nike, saying that Seyon refused to meet a 10.7% increase in the monthly wage, to $70.30, required by the Indonesian government in April 1997.[11]

On May 12, 1998, in a speech given at the National Press Club, Phil Knight spelled out in detail a series of initiatives designed to improve working conditions for the 500,000 people that make products for Nike at subcontractor facilities.[12] Among the initiatives Knight highlighted were the following:

We have effectively changed our minimum age limits from the ILO (International Labor Organization) standards of 15 in most countries and 14 in developing countries to 18 in all footwear manufacturing and 16 in all other types of manufacturing (apparel, accessories and equipment). Existing workers legally employed under the former limits were grandfathered into the new requirements.

During the past 13 months we have moved to a 100 percent factory audit scheme, where every Nike contract factory will receive an annual check by PricewaterhouseCoopers teams who are specially trained on our Code of Conduct Owner's Manual and audit/monitoring procedures. To date they have performed about 300 such monitoring visits. In a few instances in apparel factories they have found workers under our age standards. Those factories have been required to raise their standards to 17 years of age, to require 3 documents certifying age, and to redouble their efforts to ensure workers meet those standards through interviews and records checks.

Our goal was to ensure workers around the globe are protected by requiring factories to have no workers exposed to levels above those mandated by the permissible exposure limits (PELs) for chemicals prescribed in the OSHA indoor air quality standards.[13]

These moves were applauded in the business press, but they were greeted with a skeptical response from Nike's long-term adversaries in the debate over the use of foreign labor. While conceding that Nike's policies were an improvement, one critic writing in the *New York Times* noted that:

Mr. Knight's child labor initiative is . . . a smokescreen. Child labor has not been a big problem with Nike, and Philip Knight knows that better than anyone. But public relations is public relations. So he announces that he's not going to let the factories hire kids, and suddenly that's the headline.

Mr. Knight is like a 3-card monte player. You have to keep a close eye on him at all times.

The biggest problem with Nike is that its overseas workers make wretched, below-subsistence wages. It's not the minimum age that needs raising, it's the minimum wage. Most of the workers in Nike *factories in China and Vietnam make less than $2 a day, well below the subsistence levels in those countries. In Indonesia the pay is less than $1 a day.*

The company's current strategy is to reshape its public image while doing as little as possible for the workers. Does anyone think it was an accident that Nike set up shop in human rights sinkholes, where labor organizing was viewed as a criminal activity and deeply impoverished workers were willing, even eager, to take their places on assembly lines and work for next to nothing?[14]

Other critics question the quality of Nike's auditors, PricewaterhouseCoopers (PwC). Dara O'Rourke, an assistant professor at MIT, followed the PwC auditors around several factories in China, Korea, and Vietnam. He concluded that although the auditors found minor violations of labor laws and codes of conduct, they missed major labor-practice issues, including hazardous working conditions, violations of overtime laws, and violation of wage laws. The problem, according to O'Rourke, was that the auditors had limited training and relied on factory managers for data and for setting up interviews with workers, all of which were performed in the factories. The auditors, in other words, were getting an incomplete and somewhat sanitized view of conditions in the factory.[15]

Continued Controversy

Fueled perhaps by the unforgiving criticisms of Nike that continued after Phil Knight's May 1998 speech, a wave of protests against Nike occurred on many university campuses from 1998 to 2001. The moving force behind the protests was the United Students Against Sweatshops (USAS). The USAS argued that the Fair Labor Association (FLA), which grew out of the presidential task force on sweatshops, was an industry tool, and not a truly independent auditor of foreign factories. The USAS set up an alternative independent auditing organization, the Workers Rights Consortium (WRC), which they charged with auditing factories that produce products under collegiate licensing programs (under which Nike is a high-profile supplier of products). The WRC is backed, and partly funded, by labor unions and refuses to cooperate with companies, arguing that doing so would jeopardize its independence.

By mid-2000, the WRC had persuaded some 48 universities to join, including all 9 campuses of the University of California systems, the University of Michigan, and the University of Oregon, Phil Knight's alma mater. When Knight heard that the University of Oregon would join the WRC, as opposed to the FLA, he withdrew a planned $30 million donation to the university.[16] Despite this, in November 2000 another major northwest university, the University of Washington, announced that it too would join the WRC, although it would also retain its membership in the FLA.[17]

Nike continued to push forward with its own initiatives, updating progress on its Website. In April 2000, in response to accusations that it was still hiding conditions, it announced that it would release the complete reports of all independent audits of its subcontractors' plants. Global Exchange continued to criticize the company, arguing in mid-2001 that the company was not living up to Phil Knight's 1998 promises and that it was intimidating workers from speaking out about abuses.[18]

Endnotes

1   From Nike's corporate Website at www.nikebiz.com.
2   www.globalexchange.org.
3   "Boycott Nike," *CBS News 48 Hours,* October 17, 1996.
4   D. Jones, "Critics Tie Sweatshop Sneakers to 'Air Jordan,'" *USA Today,* June 6, 1996, 1B.
5   Global Exchange Special Report: Nike Just Don't Do It. www.globalexchange.org/education/publications/newsltr6.97p2.html#nike.
6   V. Dobnik, "Chinese Workers Abused Making Nikes, Reeboks," *Seattle Times,* September 21, 1997, A4.
7   S. Greenhouse, "Nike Shoeplant in Vietnam is Called Unsafe for Workers," *New York Times,* November 8, 1997.
8   Ibid.
9   Quoted in: V. Dobnik, "Chinese Workers Abused Making Nikes, Reeboks," *Seattle Times,* September 21, 1997, A4.
10 W. Bounds and H. Stout, "Sweatshop Pact: Good Fit or Threadbare?" *Wall Street Journal,* April 10, 1997, A2.
11 Associated Press Reporter, "Nike Gives Four Factories the Boot," *Los Angeles Times,* September 23, 1997, 20.
12 Archived at www.nikebiz.com/labor/speech_trans.shtml.
13 OSHA is the United States Occupational Safety and Health Agency.
14 B. Herbert, "Nike Blinks," *New York Times,* May 21, 1998.
15 Dara O'Rourke, Monitoring the Monitors: A critique of the Pricewaterhousecoopers (PwC) Labor Monitoring. Department of Urban Studies and Planning, Mit.
16 L. Lee and A. Bernstein, "Who Says Student Protests Don't Matter?" *Business Week,* June 12, 2000, 94–96.
17 R. Dee, "UW to Join Anti-sweatshop Group," *Seattle Post Intelligencer,* November 20, 2000, B2.
18 Anonymous, "Rights Group Says Nike Isn't Fulfilling Promises," *Wall Street Journal,* May 16, 2001.